ENOSH AND HIS GENERATION

SOCIETY OF BIBLICAL LITERATURE
MONOGRAPH SERIES

James L. Crenshaw, Editor

Number 30

ENOSH AND HIS GENERATION

Pre-Israelite Hero and History in Postbiblical Interpretation

by

Steven D. Fraade

Steven D. Fraade

ENOSH AND HIS GENERATION

Pre-Israelite Hero and History in Postbiblical Interpretation

Scholars Press
Chico, California

ENOSH AND HIS GENERATION
Pre-Israelite Hero and History in Postbiblical Interpretation

by

Steven D. Fraade

Library of Congress Cataloging in Publication Data

Fraade, Steven D.
Enosh and his generation.

(Society of Biblical Literature monograph series ; no. 30)
Bibliography: p.
Includes indexes.
1. Bible. O.T. Genesis IV, 26—Criticism, interpretation, etc.—History. 2. Enosh (Biblical figure)
I. Title. II. Series.
BS1235.2.F67 1984 222'.1106'09 83-27137
ISBN 0-89130-724-9
ISBN 0-89130-725-7 (pbk.)

Printed in the United States of America
on acid-free paper

For my parents

אז הוחל לקרא בשם יהוה

οὗτος ἤλπισεν ἐπικαλεῖσθαι τὸ ὄνομα κυρίου τοῦ θεοῦ

הידין שרי למקרא בשמה דמריא

iste coepit invocare nomen Domini

טטא שרא למזדעק בשם יהוה

ביומוי הא בכין שרון בני אינשא למפלוח בפולחנא
נוכריא ולמכנאה יתהון בשום מימרא דייי

בכין ביומוהי חלו בני אנשא מלצלאה בשמא דיוי

It was then that men began to invoke the Lord by name

TABLE OF CONTENTS

Preface ix

Transliteration xi

Abbreviations xii

Introduction 1

Chapter One: Pre-Rabbinic Jewish Interpretations 5
- A. Jewish Greek Scriptures 5
- B. Ben Sira 12
- C. *Jubilees* 16
- D. *2 (Slavonic) Enoch* 18
- E. Philo 19
- F. Josephus 25
- G. Conclusions 27

Chapter Two: Samaritan and Mandaean Interpretations 29
- A. Early Samaritan Traditions 29
- B. Mandaean Traditions 38

Chapter Three: Christian Interpretations 47
- A. Greek and Latin Traditions 48
- B. Syriac Sources 91
- C. Conclusions 104

Chapter Four: Rabbinic Intrepretations 109
- A. Rabbinic Targumim 111
- B. Tannaitic Sources 119
- C. Amoraic Sources 131
- D. Postamoraic Sources 156
- E. *Piyyuṭ* 171
- F. Conclusions 173

Chapter Five: Rabbinic Method and Motivation 179
- A. Rabbinic Methods 179
- B. Rabbinic Motivations 195
- C. Conclusions 226

Chapter Six: Final Conclusions 229

Bibliography 235
Index of Primary Sources 263
General Index 285

PREFACE

My interest in the postbiblical interpretation of the biblical figure Enosh (Adam's grandson) and his times began in 1976, when in two graduate seminars at the University of Pennsylvania—one in the Hebrew text of the Book of Genesis with Professor Jeffrey Tigay, and one in the byzantine Christian chronographers with Professor Robert Kraft—the matter of Gen 4:26 and its interpretation simultaneously arose, occasioning a preliminary study of that simple, yet perplexing phrase. Continued study revealed that the five words with which the Hebrew Bible comments on the birth of Enosh were the subject of extensive commentary among several groups of postbiblical exegetes, each of which brought to the task of interpretation its own distinctive set of concerns. This study quickly became an examination not simply of the biblical exegesis itself, but of the various individuals and communities that could be partially apprehended through the medium of their interpretations of a common scriptural specimen.

Since its inception, many have contributed to the progress and completion of this work, originally a doctoral dissertation at the University of Pennsylvania. My teachers there are the first to be thanked for having exposed me to the tools, methods, and insights of their respective fields: Professors Barry Eichler, Judah Goldin, Robert Kraft, R. E. A. Palmer, Svi Rin, Michael Stone, and Jeffrey Tigay. Professor Goldin's guidance in the art and science of text reading, while never imposing, was ever available. His and Professor Tigay's insightful comments on earlier drafts spurred reflection and correction. As the psalmist (119:99) said (albeit with a different sense): "*mikkol mĕlammĕday hiśkaltî*—from all my teachers I have gained insight."

Several colleagues read this study en route to its present, revised form and offered suggestions, but even more importantly encouragement: Arnold Band, Brevard Childs, James Dittes, Rowan Greer, Wayne Meeks, David Stern, and Emanual Tov.

I had the valuable opportunities to present parts of this study as papers at meetings of the Columbia Seminar on the Hebrew Bible and the Targumic Studies Section of the Society of Biblical Literature. Members of these groups contributed helpful comments and criticisms, some of which have been incorporated in what follows.

Appreciation is due the Memorial Foundation for Jewish Culture and the A. Whitney Griswold Faculty Research Fund at Yale University for help in defraying costs related to this project.

Donald Westblade prepared the indexes with great care, and with support from the Religious Studies Department at Yale.

It has been my pleasure to work with James L. Crenshaw, editor of the SBL Monograph Series, and with the staff of Scholars Press, especially John Crowell and Kim Weir, as they ushered this study into print.

To my wife, Ellen Cohen, who provided unrelenting support and encouragement, especially as completion of this work seemed at times as long in coming as its preparation, I owe an inestimable debt. Her sensitive reading of the manuscript produced many improvements in its style and precision of expression.

Finally, I dedicate this study to my parents, Bert and Dorothy Fraade, whose love of learning and discourse (he) and attention to detail (she) are reflected, I hope to advantage, in what follows.

S. D. F.
New Haven, Connecticut
September, 1984

TRANSLITERATION

The transliteration of Hebrew and Aramaic follows the system of the *Journal of Biblical Literature* (*JBL* 95 [1976] 234): 'bgdhwzḥṭylmns-'pṣqrśšt. Spirants are not indicated. Length of vowels is indicated in citations of primary texts, but not in the titles of books, articles, tractates, etc. In the case of commonly used Hebrew and Aramaic terms or names (e.g., mishnah), however, strict rules of transliteration are not followed.

Mandaic transliteration follows the system of E. S. Drower and R. Macuch (eds.), *A Mandaic Dictionary* (Oxford: Clarendon, 1963), p. xii.

For Greek: th=θ, ph=ϕ, ch=χ, ps=ψ, y=υ (except in dipthongs), ē=η, ō=ω. *Iōta* subscript is not represented; those who know Greek should be able to supply it where needed.

Generally, individual words or short phrases are transliterated, while longer passages are given in their original scripts. For the sake of convenience, and in keeping with common practice, the Samaritan, Syriac, and Mandaic scripts are represented by the equivalent "square" Hebrew characters.

ABBREVIATIONS

The following list contains all nonstandard abbreviations used except those for the names of biblical books (including the Apocrypha). For the latter I have adopted the abbreviations used in the *Journal of Biblical Literature* (*JBL* 95 [1976] 335), which should be easily recognizable.

AB	Anchor Bible
ʿAbod. Zar.	*ʿAboda Zara*
Abr.	Philo, *De Abrahamo*
AgBer.	*ʾAggadat Bereʾšit*
AGJU	Arbeiten zur Geschichte des antiken Judentums und des Urchristentums
ALGHJ	Arbeiten zur Literatur und Geschichte des hellenistischen Judentums
AnBib	Analectica biblica
ANF	*The Ante-Nicene Fathers*
Ant.	Josephus, *Antiquities judaicae*
Ant. Bib.	Pseudo-Philo, *Liber antiquitatum biblicarum*
Ap.	Josephus, *Contra Apionem*
Apoc. Bar.	*Apocalypse of Baruch*
APOT	R. H. Charles (ed.), *Apocrypha and Pseudepigrapha of the Old Testament*
ARN	*ʾAbot deRabbi Nathan* (*ARNA* and *ARNB* refer to rescensions A and B respectively)
b.	Babylonian Talmud, followed by tractate
B. Bat.	*Baba Batra*
BDB	F. Brown, S. R. Driver, and C. A. Briggs, *Hebrew and English Lexicon of the Old Testament*
Ber.	*Berakot*
BHK	R. Kittel, *Biblia hebraica*
BhM	A. Jellinek (ed)., *Bet ha-Midrasch*
Bib.	*Biblica*
BibOr	Biblica et orientalia
B. J.	Josephus, *Bellum judaicum*
BJRL	*Bulletin of the John Rylands Library*
BKAT	Biblischer Kommentar: Altes Testament
B. Meṣ.	*Baba Meṣiʿa*
BO	*Bibliotheca orientalis*

B. Qam.	*Baba Qamma*
BSOAS	*Bulletin of the School of Oriental and African Studies*
CBQMS	Catholic Biblical Quarterly–Monograph Series
CChr. Ser. Lat	Corpus christianorum, Series latina
CD	Cairo Geniza text of the Damascus Document
Conf.	Philo, *De Confusione linguarum*
CSCO	Corpus scriptorum christianorum orientalium
CSEL	Corpus scriptorum ecclesiasticorum latinorum
CSHB	Corpus scriptorum historiae byzantinae
CTg.	Cairo Geniza targum fragments
Dec.	Philo, *De Decalogo*
De. civ. Dei	Augustine, *De civitate Dei*
Dem.	Aphraates, *Demonstrations*
Det.	Philo, *Quod deterius potiori insidiari soleat*
DJD	Discoveries in the Judean Desert
Ep. Arist.	*Epistle of Aristeas*
'Erub.	*'Erubin*
FGrH	F. Jacoby (ed.), *Die Fragmente der griechischen Historiker*
Frg. Tg.	*Fragmentary Targum*
Fug.	Philo, *De Fuga et Inventione*
GCS	Griechischen christlichen Schriftsteller der ersten drei Jahrhunderte
Gig.	Philo, *De Gigantibus*
GKC	*Gesenius' Hebrew Grammar*, ed. E. Kautzsch, trans. E. Cowley
GL	*Left Ginza*
GR	*Right Ginza*
Ḥag.	*Ḥagiga*
HTR	*Harvard Theological Review*
HUCA	*Hebrew Union College Annual*
ICC	International Critical Commentary
IDB	G. A. Buttrick (ed.), *Interpreter's Dictionary of the Bible*
IDBSup.	Supplementary volume to *IDB*
JBL	*Journal of Biblical Literature*
JCS	*Journal of Cuneiform Studies*
JJS	*Journal of Jewish Studies*
JNES	*Journal of Near Eastern Studies*
JPS	Jewish Publication Society
JQR	*Jewish Quarterly Review*
JSJ	*Journal for the Study of Judaism in the Persian, Hellenistic, and Roman Period*
JSS	*Journal of Semitic Studies*

Jub.	*Jubilees*
Ketub.	*Ketubot*
LAB	Ps.-Philo, *Liber Antiquitatem Biblicarum*
LCL	Loeb Classical Library
Leg. All.	Philo, *Legum allegoriae*
Legat.	Philo, *De Legatione ad Gaium*
LSJ	Liddell-Scott-Jones, *Greek–English Lexicon*
LT	*Midraš Leqaḥ Ṭob*
LXX	Septuagint
m.	Mishnah, followed by tractate
MA	*Midraš 'Aggada*
Mak.	*Makkot*
Meg.	*Megilla*
Mek.	*Mekilta deRabbi Ishmael*
MekRS	*Mekilta deRabbi Simeon ben Yoḥai*
MhG	*Midraš haggadol*
Mo'ed Qaṭ	*Mo'ed Qaṭan*
Mos.	Philo, *De Vita Mosis*
MPs.	*Midraš Tehillim* (Psalms)
MT	Masoretic Text
MTan.	*Midraš Tanna'im*
NAB	*New American Bible*
NEB	*New English Bible*
Ned.	*Nedarim*
Nid.	*Nidda*
NJV	New Jewish (Publication Society) Version
NovT	*Novum Testamentum*
NovtSup.	Supplements to *NovT*
OL	Old Latin Version
OLP	Orientalia lovaniensia periodica
OTS	*Oudtestamentische Studiën*
p.	Palestinian (Jerusalem) Talmud, followed by tractate
PAAJR	*Proceedings of the American Academy for Jewish Research*
Pesaḥ	*Pesaḥim*
PG	J. Migne, *Patrologia graeca*
PL	J. Migne, *Patrologia latina*
Post.	Philo, *De Posteritate Caini*
PR	*Pesiqta Rabbati*
Praep. ev.	Eusebius, *Praeparatio evangelica*
Praem.	Philo, *De Praemiis et poenis*
PRE	*Pirqe Rabbi Eliezer*
PRK	*Pesiqta deRab Kahana*

Q	Qumran sigla:
1QapGen	*Genesis Apocryphon* from Qumran Cave 1
1QH	*Hodayot* (Thanksgiving Hymns) from Qumran Cave 1
1QIsa[a]	First copy of Isaiah from Qumran Cave 1
1QpHab	*Pešer on Habakkuk* from Qumran Cave 1
1QS	*Serek haYaḥad* (Manual of Discipline) from Qumran Cave 1
4Q180–181	Texts 180 and 181 in *DJD* 5 from Qumran cave 4
4QEn[f]	Sixth copy of Aramaic fragments of Enoch from Qumran Cave 4
11QJub M3	Hebrew fragment 3 of Jubilees from Qumran Cave 11
4QpsDanA[a] (=4Q*246*)	Pseudo-Daniel fragment from Qumran Cave 4
Qidd.	*Qiddušin*
Qoh	Qohelet (Ecclesiastes)
Qu. in Gen.	Philo, *Quaestiones et solutiones in Genesin*
Quod. Det.	Philo, *Quod deterius potiori insidiari soleat*
R.	Rabbi
Rab.	*Midrash Rabbah*, preceded by name of biblical book, e.g., *Gen. Rab.* = *Genesis Rabbah*
RB	*Revue biblique*
RSV	*Revised Standard Version*
Šabb	*Šabbat*
Sam. Tg.	*Samaritan Targum*
Sanh.	*Sanhedrin*
SBL	Society of Biblical Literature
SBLSCS	SBL Septuagint and Cognate Studies
SC	Sources chrétiennes
Šeb.	*Šebiʿit*
Šebu.	*Šebuʿot*
Sem.	*Semaḥot*
Šeqal	*Šeqalim*
SER	*Seder Eliahu Rabba*
SEZ	*Seder Eliahu Zuṭa*
ShY	*Seper Hayyašar*
Sib. Or.	Sibylline Oracles
SJLA	Studies in Judaism in Late Antiquity
Sob.	Philo, *De Sobrietate*
Sop.	*Soperim*
SOR	*Seder ʿOlam Rabbah*
SPAW	Sitzungsberichte der preussischen Akademie der Wissenschaften
SPB	Studia postbiblica
SPCK	Society for the Promotion of Christian Knowledge

Spec. Leg.	Philo, *De Specialibus Legibus*
Sukk.	*Sukka*
t.	Tosefta, followed by tractate
T.	*Testament*, followed by name of one of Jacob's sons, e.g., *T. Benj.* = *Testament of Benjamin*
Ta'an.	*Ta'anit*
Tanḥ.	*Tanḥuma*
Tanḥ. B.	*Tanḥuma*, ed. S. Buber
TDNT	G. Kittel and G. Friedrich (eds.), *Theological Dictionary of the New Testament*
Tg.	Targum
Tg. Ket.	*Targum of the Writings*
Tg. Neb.	*Targum of the Prophets*
Tg. Neof.	*Targum Neofiti I*
Tg. Neof. m.	*Targum Neofiti* marginal gloss
Tg. Onq.	*Targum Onqelos*
Tg. Ps.-J.	*Targum Pseudo-Jonathan*
TS	Menahem Kasher, *Tora Šelema*
Vg.	Vulgate
VT	*Vestus Testamentum*
VTSup.	Supplements to *VT*
Yebam.	*Yebamot*
YhM	*Yalquṭ Hammakiri*
YR	*Yalquṭ Re'ubeni*
YS	*Yalquṭ Šim'oni*
ZAW	*Zeitschrift für die alttestamentliche Wissenschaft*
Zebaḥ.	*Zebaḥim*
ZNW	*Zeitschrift für die neutestamentliche Wissenschaft*

INTRODUCTION

The present study is an examination of how several classical exegetical traditions interpret one verse of Scripture, Genesis 4:26: "And to Seth [Adam's third son], in turn, a son was born, and he named him Enosh. It was then that men began to invoke the Lord by name."[1] Early in my study of the history of the interpretation of this verse, I was struck by the contrast between the wide range of translations and interpretations advanced by ancient through medieval authorities and the relative unanimity among modern translators and commentators. Can it be that the ancients had more difficulty with the language of the text? Or, were they less concerned with the literalness of Scripture and more prone to interpretative fancy? It is a basic premise of this study that neither of these represents an adequate explanation. Rather, I will begin by assuming that the ancient exegetes need be taken seriously in their attempts to render for their particular audiences the meaning of the biblical text which lay before them.

At the outset I should clarify that it is not my intent to determine the "true" meaning of Gen 4:26 or to demonstrate that any of the exegetical traditions to be examined are "correct" in their understanding of that verse. This task I leave to biblical text-critics and theologians. My interest is with those who tried, in some strikingly different ways, to render this text for their followers. I assume that their work was for them serious and important. Each such exegete or group of exegetes, whether Jewish, Christian, or Samaritan, understood Gen 4:26 to be part of holy, divinely revealed Scripture, whose message was as omnisignificant for their times and communities as it was when first revealed.

This is not to say, of course, that the biblical text of Gen 4:26 will not be of concern. We can only comprehend its history of interpretation if we remain fully attentive to the nuances of its vocabulary, syntax, and literary context—in short, to its potential for being interpreted. Yet, I do not assume that the ancient interpretations are simply the logical extensions or unfoldings (as their creators themselves might claim) of the biblical text. Rather, I assume that one eye must be kept on the historical

[1] This translation is from *The Torah: The Five Books of Moses* (Philadelphia: Jewish Publication Society, 1962) 10. Other modern translations (*RSV*, *NAB*, *NEB*, and AB) differ only slightly in their wording. The Masoretic Text has: ולשת גם־הוא יֻלד־בן ויקרא את שמו אנוש אז הוחל לקרא בשם יהוה

(including cultural) context in which the exegetes and their followers lived, for there too must have arisen stimuli for exegesis, and there too arose literary conventions which gave shape to that exegesis. Biblical text and historical context define two poles of a continuum in which biblical exegesis is born and develops, and from which it is nourished. Presumably, any exegesis, to be rhetorically effective in the community for which it was intended, had to remain rooted in the exigencies of both that text and that context. Determining how this was done, that is, examining the rhetoric of exegesis, is one of the primary tasks of this study.

However, this model needs to be refined. Along with the received biblical text, the ancient exegetes inherited accompanying traditions of interpretation, these traditions themselves often imbued with authority. Thus, each discrete text of exegesis will be examined within a broader history of exegetical tradition. If the biblical text had to remain fixed while historical circumstances were at times precipitously changing, then the exegetical traditions which mediated between the two needed to be both: continuous yet flexible. Determining how this was achieved, that is, how radically new interpretations were grounded in antecedent traditions, is another task of this study.

I will focus not on a single line of exegetical history, but on several: pre-Rabbinic Jewish, Samaritan, Christian, and Rabbinic. Thus, a third task of this study is that of comparison. Since all of these exegetes began with a relatively common sacred text and lived in relative spatial and temporal proximity to each other, a comparison of their exegesis should highlight both the common and distinctive aspects of their work. Such comparison, revealing the exegetical roads not traveled, forces us to ask what motivated the exegetical choices which were made.[2]

This study began as an examination of Rabbinic interpretations of Gen 4:26, the most radical of all. It soon became clear that the Rabbinic traditions could not be fully comprehended in an exegetical vacuum; the motivation for the distinctively Rabbinic interpretation had to be sought through comparison with those of other traditions. And then it became clear that non-Rabbinic exegesis, particularly of the Church Fathers, who were the rabbis' contemporaries and competitors and inheritors of common pre-Rabbinic traditions, was itself of interest. Its particular

[2] Much recent work in comparative biblical exegesis has focused on the *common* elements in the interpretations of the rabbis, early Christians, and pre-Rabbinic Jewish exegetes so as to reveal the influence of one on another, or the existence of a commonly held body of exegetical tradition. This approach is especially demonstrated in the historical method of midrash study proposed by G. Vermes in *Scripture and Tradition in Judaism* (Leiden: E. J. Brill, 1963). The present study, while noting common traditions and traits, is more interested in what can be learned from an examination of how contemporary exegetes *differed* in their approach to a common sacred text.

exegetical problematic and development in history needed to be studied in its own right before responsible comparison could be attempted.

It is the motivational question, the most difficult and speculative one, that allows us to move from the analysis of texts to an understanding of the human beings who created those texts and were significantly affected by them in particular historical contexts. In the end, this study is an examination less of what several groups of ancient exegetes have to say about a particular biblical verse than of what that verse can tell us about its ancient exegetes: What do their interpretations tell us about the methods and concerns with which they approach the biblical text? How do they employ the medium of exegesis in exhorting their followers? To what may their differences in approach to a common biblical text be attributed?

This study begins and is largely preoccupied with the study of texts, since that is the sole medium by which ancient exegesis of Gen 4:26 has reached us. These texts are fully assembled for each tradition in approximate chronological order; no prior selection or synthetic blend has been made.[3] Each testimony is presented in translation, and then critically examined to determine *what* it says and *how* it does so. In cases where a text or its meaning is unclear, discussions of a text-critical or philogical nature are required, but are restricted to footnotes wherever possible. The correct determination of meaning of the individual testimonies will significantly affect our interpretation of the meaning and history of the cumulative tradition.[4]

Although this study is of the exegesis of one small specimen of the Hebrew Bible, its implications are much broader. In order to comprehend the various interpretations of Gen 4:26 it will be necessary to turn

3 Where the examination of a relevant text would add nothing to the analysis it is simply cited in a footnote. Only the Mandaean texts have been treated somewhat synthetically, for reasons given below. See chap. 2, n. 36. In every case references to the text editions used (critical where available) are supplied in the footnotes so the interested reader can consult the original sources. Wherever the language of the source is crucial to its understanding it is given along with its translation. While the focus of this study is biblical exegesis in Greco-Roman times, Christian and Rabbinic traditions of interpretation will be traced into the early Middle Ages, in part so as not to impose arbitrary limits on what appear to be continuous lines of interpretation, and in part so as to view the earlier exegesis in broader historical perspective.

4 A danger of such a study is that exegetical traditions may be lifted from the contexts of the redacted documents which often confer upon them meaning. To reduce this danger, an effort has been made to describe or more fully cite, where appropriate, the textual context in which the testimonies are found, and to consider the relation of a testimony to its context. The study of the *documents* of ancient biblical exegesis, particularly Rabbinic ones, with an eye to how redaction affects exegesis, remains a pressing desideratum. However, it is here asserted that if attentive to these issues the historical and comparative study of the contained exegesis of such documents can proceed, provided that the constitutive traditions are not wrenched from their literary contexts.

as well to postbiblical treatments of that verse's scriptural context: pre-Israelite heroes and history. Recent study of biblical exegesis in the Dead Sea Scrolls, the so-called Pseudepigrapha, and the gnostic texts from Nag Hammadi reveals that many in late antiquity were interested in the persons and the times of earliest human existence.[5] It is hoped that this study of the ancient interpretations of Enosh and his times will enhance our understanding of how ancient exegetes, particularly Rabbinic and patristic, viewed themselves and their followers in relation to the biblical story of humanity's universal beginnings as they recast it.

5 See, for instance, a recent study of traditions relating to Seth, Enosh's father: A. F. J. Klijn, *Seth in Jewish, Christian and Gnostic Literature* (NovTSup 46; Leiden: E. J. Brill, 1977). For treatments of Noah see below, chap. 5, n. 107. For a survey of interpretations of Enoch see S. D. Fraade, "Enoch," *Encyclopedia of Religion* (forthcoming).

Chapter One
PRE-RABBINIC JEWISH INTERPRETATIONS

This investigation begins with pre-Rabbinic Jewish sources that either explicitly or implicitly comment on Gen 4:26b and/or its immediate context. While we cannot be sure of the exegetical sources (whether written or oral) upon which Rabbinic and Christian exegeses actually drew, we may suppose that the extant pre-Rabbinic exegeses are reflective, at least in part, of the exegetical milieu out of which nascent Rabbinic Judaism and Christianity were to emerge.

Although the evidence of these materials is scant when compared to the later sources that will be examined, we can see in them the beginnings of two main lines of interpretation that will gradually emerge so as to distinguish Christian from Jewish exegesis: (a) Enosh viewed as a righteous link in the genealogical ancestry of Israel and mankind, and (b) Enosh's time as one of moral and spiritual degeneration.

A. Jewish Greek Scriptures

Since the Septuagint contains the earliest extant Jewish exegesis of Gen 4:26b (perhaps as early as mid-third century B.C.E.), I shall begin with it: *houtos ēlpisen epikaleisthai to onoma kyriou tou theou* ("He hoped to invoke the name of the Lord God").[1] A careful and detailed analysis of this translation is important for two reasons: (a) This version already contains significant variants from the Hebrew of the MT, which provide the basis, as we shall see, for important interpretations in the writings of Philo and the early Church Fathers. (b) These variants have

1 Although the term *Septuagint* (LXX) should properly only be used for books of the Pentateuch, I will use it for the sake of convenience to refer to the earliest Greek translations of the other books of Jewish Scriptures as well. *Septuaginta Vetus Testamentum Graecum*, vol. 1 (Göttingen: Vandenhoeck and Ruprecht, 1974) 10; *The Old Testament in Greek* (ed. A. Brooke & N. McLean; Cambridge: at the University Press, 1906) 10. The other Greek versions according to *Origenis Hexaplorum* (ed. F. Field; 2 vols.; Oxford: Clarendon, 1875) 1.20 are:

Aquila: *tote ērchthē tou kalein (kaleisthai) en onomati (kyriou)*. "Then was begun the calling in the name (of the Lord)."

Symmachus: *tote archē egeneto* . . . "Then was the beginning . . ."

Hebraios: *houtos ēlpisen epikaleisthai tō onomati kyriou tou theou*. "He hoped to call on the name of the Lord God."

been claimed by some to derive from a Hebrew text antedating that of the MT. Virtually every word of the LXX translation is noteworthy.

(1) *ēlpisen*. The verb *hwḥl*, vocalized in the MT as *hûḥal*, appears to have been understood by the Greek translator(s) as *hôḥil* (*hôḥîl*), the *hiph'il* of *yḥl* ("hope"), the only such confusion of the roots *ḥll* and *yḥl* in the LXX. This should not be surprising since Gen 4:26 contains the only scriptural occurrence of *ḥll* in the *hoph'al*, and since its usage here is awkward and ambiguous. The *hiph'il* of *yḥl*, however, appears thirteen times in the MT, five of which are translated in the LXX with the verb *elpizō*.[2] While the Hebraios translation agrees with the LXX, both Aquila and Symmachus render passively ("then it was begun," "then was the beginning"). Since all of the Greek translations either translate as if the Hebrew verb were *yḥl* or render passively, we should assume that they all translated Hebrew texts which read *hwḥl*.

This is significant since a number of scholars have suggested that the Hebrew *Vorlage* of the LXX was *zeh hēḥēl* ("this one began") and that this represents the "original" text.[3] The fact that the LXX renders *hwḥl* with an active singular verb, however, is not sufficient reason to suggest a Hebrew reading *hēḥēl*. We will see that other ancient witnesses, which we need not assume to be dependent on the LXX, render this passive form "it was begun" actively, sometimes supplying a subject noun or pronoun: *Jubilees* 4:12: "He began"; Samaritan Pentateuch and Targum and Syriac *Peshiṭta*: "Then he/one began"; Rabbinic targumim: "Then they/men began." Only Aquila and Symmachus resist representing the passive *hûḥal* with an active form.

Obviously, the passive construction "then was begun" is ambiguous.

[2] These observations are based on E. Hatch and H. Redpath, *A Concordance to the Septuagint* (two vols. and supp.; Oxford: Clarendon, 1897–1902) and E. C. dos Santos, *An Expanded Hebrew Index for the Hatch-Redpath Concordance to the Septuagint* (Jerusalem: Dugith Publishers, Baptist House, n.d.).

[3] As in Gen 10:8, where MT *hû' hēḥēl* is translated by the LXX as *houtos ērxato*. H. Gunkel, *Genesis* (Göttingen: Vandenhoeck und Ruprecht, 1901) 50; F. Delitzsch, *Neuer Commentar über die Genesis* (Leipzig: Dörffling und Franke, 1887) 134; A. Dillmann, *Genesis Critically and Exegetically Expounded* (trans. W. Stevenson; 2 vols.; Edinburgh: T. & T. Clark, 1897) 1.210; J. Skinner, *A Critical and Exegetical Commentary on Genesis* (N.Y.: Charles Scribner's Sons, 1910) 126; U. Cassuto, *A Commentary on the Book of Genesis, From Adam to Noah* (Jerusalem: Magnes, 1961) 246–47; S. Sandmel, "Genesis 4:26b," *HUCA* 32 (1961) 27; G. Spurrell, *Notes on the Hebrew Text of the Book of Genesis* (Oxford: Clarendon, 1887) 64. This mistake is most recently repeated in A.F.J. Klijn, *Seth in Jewish, Christian and Gnostic Literature* (Leiden: E.J. Brill, 1977) 5. For a well reasoned critique of those who are too quick to "correct" the MT on the basis of the versions, see Moshe Greenberg, "The Use of the Ancient Versions for Interpreting the Hebrew Text: A Sampling from Ezekiel 2:1–3:11," in *Congress Volume, Göttingen, 1977*, International Organization for the Study of the Old Testament (Leiden: E.J. Brill, 1978) 131–48. See too Emanuel Tov, *The Text-Critical Use of the Septuagint in Biblical Research* (Jerusalem Biblical Studies 3; Jerusalem: Simor, 1981).

It can be understood in two ways: (a) Then was begun by him = he began (was the first), referring to the antecedent Enosh (or possibly Seth). (b) It was begun by men = men began, referring to Enosh's contemporaries. The choice between these two possibilities lies at the heart of what distinguishes Rabbinic from non-Rabbinic translations and exegeses: does the Bible speak of Enosh or his contemporaries? The LXX clearly chooses the former possibility. It logically assumes that after announcing Enosh's birth, Scripture wishes to tell us about Enosh.[4]

It should be noted that the choice of an active form to represent a passive verb denoting an indefinite subject is very common in the early translations and reflects a development within late biblical and early postbiblical Hebrew in which the passive is far less frequently used to denote an indefinite subject.[5]

The uniqueness of the LXX translation, then, is not that it renders *hwḥl* with an active verb (which in itself is not unusual) but that it changes the verb entirely. What motivated such a change? Was the translator simply unfamiliar (as he might well have been) with the hapax *hoph'al* of the verb *ḥll* and therefore failed to recognize it, or did he have trouble with the idea of Enosh having instituted divine worship?[6]

4 As in Gen 4:1–2, 17–22, 25; 5:22–24, 29; etc. We will see that several later traditions understand 4:26b as an explanation of Enosh's naming in 4:26a.

5 In biblical Hebrew, an indefinite subject is commonly expressed by the following forms: active third person singular or plural, plural participle, passive. See GKC 144 d, e, f, g, i, k for discussion and examples. In mishnaic Hebrew, however, the passive is no longer used for this purpose. See Moshe Segal, *Diqduq lešon hammišna* (Tel Aviv: Dvir, 1936) 63–66.

This development can be witnessed already in the Bible's own internal "rewriting." For example, 2 Kgs 14:20 *wayyiqqābēr* (*niph'al*, "he was buried") appears in 2 Chr 25:28 as *wayyiqbĕrû 'ōtô* (*qal*, "they buried him"). Cf. Josh 21:9 (indefinite active singular) and 1 Chr 6:50 (indefinite active plural). E. Y. Kutscher (*The Language and Linguistic Background of the Isaiah Scroll* [Jerusalem: Magnes, 1959] 303) has demonstrated the same pattern in the Isaiah Scroll from Qumran (1QIsa[a]). For example, of seven indefinite uses of *yiqqārē'* ("is called") in Isaiah, six appear in the Scroll as *yiqrĕ'û* ("they call"). Note as well that the *hoph'al* (or perhaps "passive qal") form *yuqqaḥ* ("will be taken") in Isa 49:24 is rendered in the Scroll as *yiqqĕḥû* ("they will take"). But even more interesting is the fact that the MT passive third person singular appears in the Scroll as an active third person *singular* form: MT Isa 26:1 *yûšar haššîr* ("the song will be sung") = 1QIsa *yāšîr haššîr* ("[one] will sing the song"). MT Isa 26:10 *yuḥan rāšā'* ("the wicked will be spared") = 1QIsa *yāḥûn rāšā'* ("[one] will spare the wicked"). These last two examples are similarly rendered in the active in the *Targum of the Prophets* and in the LXX.

The rendering of an indefinite passive construction with an active verb is very common in the ancient translations (targumim, *Peshiṭta*, Vulgate, and less commonly in the LXX). See, for example, their renderings of Gen 18:4; Exod 21:30; Lev 11:38; each having a *hoph'al* or "passive *qal*" in the MT. For further discussion see Ch. Rabin, "The Ancient Versions and the Indefinite Subject," *Textus* 2 (1962) 60–76, esp. p. 71 n. 5.

6 If Enosh is denied actually having "called on the name of the Lord," the first to do so would be Abraham (Gen 12:8; 13:4; 21:33; 26:25). In fact, this expression is used with

The first possibility seems to be the most likely. We cannot, however, rule out the possibility that the translator may (also) have had a conscious motivation, for example, to deny Enosh the honor of having been the first true worshiper of God, or, conversely, to stress the hope (enthusiasm) with which he approached and anticipated divine worship. We will see that these latter possibilities, whether intended by the LXX translator or not, are developed by exegetes of the LXX.[7] In any case, the resulting translation is no less (and possibly more) ambiguous and awkward than the Hebrew original. Although the LXX identifies the subject of Gen 4:26b (Enosh, but some will say Seth), it remains unclear whether he only "hoped" to call upon the name of the Lord, *but did not*, or whether he in fact did worship God, having hoped or looked forward to doing so.

A few traditions that quote the LXX insert the word *prōtos* (first). Philo cites Gen 4:26b as: *houtos ēlpise prōton epikaleisthai* . . . ("This man first hoped to call . . . ").[8] George Syncellus quotes our verse as: *Enōs ēlpisen epikaleisthai to onoma kyriou tou theou prōtos* ("Enosh was the first to hope. . . ").[9] These sources clearly reflect a tradition that understands *hwḥl* both in the sense of "hoping" (LXX) and "beginning" (MT).[10] It is unclear whether these derive the insertion of *prōtos* from a variant LXX text, from an intermediary tradition no longer extant, or from a desire to reconcile the LXX reading with a contemporary understanding of the Hebrew text (e.g., Aquila or Symmachus).

(2) *houtos*. How are we to understand the LXX translation of MT *'āz* ("then") with *houtos* ("he")? There appear to be three basic possibilities:

regard to Abraham more than with any other biblical figure.

[7] Elias Bickerman ("The Septuagint as a Translation," in *Studies in Jewish and Christian History*, vol. 1 [Leiden: E. J. Brill, 1976] 191 n. 63) states: "Often the divergence between the 'Seventy' and the Masoretes goes back to the different vocalization of the same consonantal text. . . . Sometimes the 'Seventy' just did not know the meaning of a rare word, and guessed its meaning from the context." On conjectural vocalizations of the LXX translators, see E. Tov, *The Text-Critical Use of the Septuagint*, 160–74. Tov states (p. 169): "It is difficult to specify a certain vocalization as conjectural. However, when the vocalization reflects a more common word than the rare one or *hapax legomenon* indicated by MT, it may be that the translator had difficulty in establishing the meaning of MT."

[8] *Det.* 138–40 (LCL) 2.294–95. Elsewhere (*Abr.* 8–9 [LCL] 6.9–11), Philo refers to Enosh as the "first lover of hope." Eusebius (*Praep. ev.* 7.8 [ed. E. Gifford] 1.389–90) similarly states that because of his hope, Enosh was the "first" to be called a true man.

[9] *Chronographia*, in *Corpus Scriptorum Historiae Byzantinae*, vol. 6 (ed. W. Dindorf; Bonn: E. Weber, 1829) 17. In Rufinus' translation of Origen's commentary to Romans (8.3) we find: "Enos primus speravit invocare nomen Domini." *PG* 41.1165A. *Primus*, assumably, is a translation of *prōtos*.

[10] The Hebrew verb *hēḥēl*, meaning "he began," can also, when followed by an infinitive, mean "first to. . . " See Gen 9:20; 10:8, especially the *NJV* and H. Orlinsky, *Notes on the New Translation of the Torah* (Philadelphia: JPS, 1970) 80–81. The LXX, however, translates these passages with *archomai*. Cf. 1 Sam 14:35 ("it was the first altar").

(a) The LXX is based on a variant Hebrew text containing *zeh*, which is commonly translated in the LXX with *houtos*. The reading *zh hwḥl*, however, would only make sense if the verb were vocalized *hôḥil* (active) and not *hûḥal* (passive), as in the MT.[11] (b) Because of phonetic similarities, *'āz* and *zeh* may have been confused, especially if demanded by the context.[12] (c) The Hebrew text read *'āz*, but once the verb was rendered in the active voice ("he hoped") it would have been unclear who the antecedent subject was, Enosh or Seth. The demonstrative pronoun would have been used to convey the emphatic sense of "this one" or "the latter," namely Enosh.[13] While the last possibility seems the most plausible to me, the others should not be dismissed since the evidence is not substantial enough to permit a conclusive choice.[14] Whatever the origin of the LXX's *houtos*, it clearly suggests that the subject of Gen 4:26b is no longer indefinite, but rather definite. Our phrase now clearly refers to someone in particular, most likely Enosh, although some later interpreters will want it to speak of Seth. As a result, a basic ambiguity in Gen 4:26b has been removed, and the phrase can no longer be taken to refer to mankind in general in Enosh's time. This, of course, will

11 Note, however, *MTan.* ad Deut 32:17 (ed. D. Hoffmann) 195, which paraphrases Gen 4:26b as: *hw' hwḥl lqr' 'bwdh zrh bšm hmqwm*, while *MhG* ad Deut 32:7 (ed. S. Fisch) 414 reads *hw' hḥl*, as does *MhG* ad Gen 4:26 (ed. M. Margulies) 128.

12 Cf. the biblical words *hallāz* and *hallāzeh*, which are synonyms for *zeh* and *hazzeh*, occurring nine times in Scripture. See BDB 229. These are translated with *ekeinos* in the LXX.

13 For such an emphatic use of *houtos* see LSJ 1275–6. Such a usage is evidenced in other namings: Gen 5:29 (Noah) and 10:8 (Nimrod). Ch. Rabin ("The Ancient Versions and the Indefinite Subject," 71 n. 5) suggests that the LXX, like the other versions, once understanding the verb to be active needed to supply a subject. Similarly, P. Schäfer, "Der Götzendienst des Enosch," in *Studien Zur Geschichte und Theologie des Rabbinischen Judenthums* (AGJU 15; Leiden: E. J. Brill, 1978) 136.

14 It is interesting that the words *zeh* and *'āz* may be related not only phonetically but also in meaning. Thus, in *Gesenius' Hebrew Grammar* (GKC 100) *'āz* is cited as an example of a "primitive adverb . . . standing in very close relation to the demonstrative pronoun." I have found two other instances where *'āz* is translated with a form of the demonstrative pronoun *houtos* in the LXX (Jer 11:15; Mal 3:16).

It should also be noted that the word *'āz* can have a nontemporal emphatic meaning: "thus, in this manner, this being the case" (standard Hebrew lexicons). In this regard, it is interesting that two LXX manuscripts to Gen 4:26b read *houtōs* (an adverbial form of *houtos*), meaning "thus, therefore, in this way" (LSJ 1276). While the actual form *houtos* appears nowhere else in LXX as a translation of MT *'āz*, *houtōs* is so used in three instances (Ezek 32:14; Mic 3:4, Job 11:15), while appearing twelve times as a translation of *zeh*. Similarly, we will see that the targumic renderings *bikdên* and *bĕkên* can also mean "thus." Any such nontemporal rendering of *'āz* would suggest an interpretation of Gen 4:26b as an explanation of the naming of Enosh in the first half of the verse. We will see that such an interpretation is evidenced in later exegesis, both of the MT and the LXX.

This evidence suggests a certain fluidity of meaning between *'āz* and *zeh*, and the possibility that *houtos* could represent a translation of either.

greatly determine the exegetical course of Jews and Christians who will later attempt to interpret this verse as it appears in the LXX.

(3) *epikaleisthai*. The Hebrew phrase *qārā' bĕšēm YHWH* occurs frequently in Scripture (about thirty times). In almost every case the LXX uses the middle voice of the verb *epikaleō*. In Gen 4:26b (and in Zeph 3:9) the form of the present infinitive could be either the middle or passive voice, since the two forms are identical. However, in other instances, where the middle and passive voices can be distinguished, the LXX, with only a few exceptions, uses the middle voice.

In all cases where the LXX uses the middle of *epikaleō* to translate *qārā' bĕšēm* the context clearly suggests some type of divine worship. In those instances where the active voice of *epikaleō* or an altogether different verb is used, the context seems to have suggested to the translators a different meaning. Thus, in Exod 33:19; 34:5; Isa 43:1; and 45:3 the subject of the phrase is understood to be God, and it is rendered with the active of *kaleō*.[15] Similarly, in 1 Kgs 18:24, MT *ûqĕrā'tem bĕšēm 'ĕlōhêkem* ("You will call upon the name of your god," directed at the worshippers of Baal) is translated by the LXX with the verb *boaō* ("cry, howl, shout"), while in the same verse, *wa'ănî 'eqrā' bĕšēm YHWH* ("and I will call upon the name of the Lord") is translated, as usual, with the middle of *epikaleō*. Similarly, the *Targum of the Prophets* uses the verb *qry* ("call") with respect to Baal and *ṣly* ("pray") with respect to God. The LXX, therefore, distinguishes the "calling" of divine worship by reserving for it the middle form of *epikaleō*.[16]

[15] This is the common understanding of these verses. However, there are Jewish targumic traditions that regard Moses as the subject of the phrase *wayyiqrā' bĕšēm* YHWH in Exod 34:5: *Tg. Pseudo-Jonathan* (ed. D. Rieder) 134; *Tg. Neofiti* (ed. A. Diez Macho) 2.225. Cf. Ibn Ezra ad Exod 33:19; 34:5 (ed. A. Viser) 2.213, 220.

[16] Isa 41:25 is the only instance where the LXX uses a passive form to translate *qārā' bĕšēm*, using the verb *klēzō* ("name, call"). The Hebrew *yiqrā' bišmî* (*RSV*: "He shall call on My name") is translated by the LXX with *klēthēsontai* (Heb.: *yiqqārē'*) *to onomati mou* ("they will be called by My name"). The Hebrew text before the Greek translator appears to have been still fluid, for we find in 1QIsa[a]: *wyqr' bšmw*, which is difficult to explain. The MT suggests that Cyrus, who is "stirred up" by God to destroy Israel's enemies, "converts" to the worship of YHWH. For modern emendations of the MT see *BHK*, *BHS*, and Claus Westermann, *Isaiah 40–66: A Commentary* (trans. D. Stalker; Philadelphia: Westminster, 1969) 81, 87–88. The *Tg. of the Prophets* reads *'agbĕrînêh bišmî* ("I will strengthen him with My name"). The LXX would seem to suggest that those who come from the North and East will bear God's name, perhaps meaning that they will bear witness to Him. See I. L. Seeligmann, *The Septuagint Version of Isaiah: A Discussion of its Problems* (Leiden: E. J. Brill, 1948) 117. For a similar translation see Symmachus, Ps 80:19, cited below, chap. 3, note 50. Compare the biblical expression *niqrā' šēm YHWH 'al* ("the name of the Lord is called upon someone," about twenty occurrences in Scripture, e.g., Gen 48:16; Deut 28:10; Isa 63:19), which can denote God's "ownership" of people, and is regularly translated by the LXX with the passive of *epikaleō*. According to Rabbinic tradition, when Scripture says that the Lord is Israel's God, this means that

This evidence strongly suggests that the LXX translation *epikaleisthai* in Gen 4:26b is middle in voice, since the passive form of this verb is *nowhere* used in the LXX to translate the phrase "to call upon the name of the Lord." The earliest sources dependent on the LXX all take the verb to be middle and understand it to refer to the invoking of YHWH's name in worship.[17] However, the possibility of interpreting *epikaleisthai* passively remains, and, as we shall see in chapter 3, from the fourth century on .is increasingly adopted by important Christian exegetes who take the verse to mean that Enosh himself (or Seth) *was called* by God's name.

(4) *kyriou tou theou.* The LXX rendering of MT *YHWH* with *kyriou tou theou* ("Lord God") is found in the Hebraios version but not in Aquila and Symmachus.[18] The LXX translator most likely had the expression *YHWH 'ĕlōhîm* in mind (common in Gen 2:4–3:24; cf. 2 Kgs 5:11). A similar insertion appears in the LXX rendering of 1 Kgs 18:24, where *'eqrā' bĕšēm YHWH* is translated *epikalesomai en onomati kyriou tou mou*, having *YHWH 'ĕlōhay* in mind, as we find in the *Peshiṭta*. While the Greek version of Gen 4:26b may be based on a Hebrew variant, it may just as well represent a translator's addition (pseudovariant).[19] As we shall see, some later commentators interpreted this addition to Enosh's credit.

While variants in the LXX have been claimed by some to reflect a Hebrew *Vorlage* differing from, and even superior to, the MT, the above evidence suggests that such departures may just as well have originated at the translation or interpretation level and not with the Hebrew text itself. The LXX seems to take Gen 4:26b to refer positively to Enosh himself (although it was later construed by some to refer to Seth). But how positive a statement is intended by the LXX is unclear, depending on one's understanding of the awkward *ēlpisen*, Enosh's "hoping". As we shall see, later Greek-speaking exegetes wishing to interpret Gen 4:26 as a positive statement concerning Enosh could find in the wording of the LXX several opportunities not present in the MT for grounding their praises.

God's name "rests" upon Israel. See *Sifre Deut* 31 (ed. Finkelstein) 53. For Israel called by God's name see Ben Sira 36:17: *rḥm 'l 'm nqr' bšmk* ("have pity on the people called by thy name"). Cf. Ben Sira 47:18 (Hebrew).

17 See the passages in Philo and Eusebius cited above, n. 8, as well as the Old Latin version to be discussed in chapter 3.

18 F. Field (*Origenis Hexaplorum*, 20 n. 36) cites a marginal gloss in the Syro-Hexapla: **πιπι**, a common rendering of the Hebrew letters of the tetragram into Greek letters. Perhaps, then, the original Greek Text retained the tetragram or its representation.

19 On pseudo-variants see E. Tov, "'On Pseudo-Variants' Reflected in the Septuagint," *JSS* 20 (1975) 165–77.

B. Ben Sira (Ecclesiasticus)

The Book of Ben Sira, thought to have been written ca. 180 B.C.E., contains the first extant inclusion of Enosh in a selective list (chain) of ancient righteous ancestors. We will see that this pattern is well evidenced in subsequent Jewish, but not rabbinic, writings, and in early Samaritan and Christian literatures.

In concluding the "Praise of the Fathers," the Hebrew text of Ben Sira 49:14–16 reads:

מעט נוצר[ו] על הארץ (כחניך) [כחנוך] וגם הוא נלקח פנים
כיוסף אם נולד גבר וגם גויתו נפקדה
ושם ושת ואנוש נפקדו ועל כל חי תפארת אדם.[20]

> Few have ever been created on earth like Enoch, who was taken before the Presence [God].[21]
> Has any man been born like Joseph, whose [dead] body was cared for?[22]
> So too, Shem and Seth and Enosh were honored, but [preeminent] over every living thing is the glory of Adam.[23]

[20] The Hebrew text is from the Cairo Geniza MS. B and can be found in the following editions: *The Book of Ben Sira: Text, Concordance and an Analysis of the Vocabulary*, The Historical Dictionary of the Hebrew Language (Jerusalem: Academy of the Hebrew Language and the Shrine of the Book, 1973) 62; M. H. Segal, ed., *Seper Ben Sira' Haššalem* (2nd ed.; Jerusalem: Bialik Institute, 1972) 337; Solomon Schechter, ed., *The Wisdom of Ben Sira: Portions of the Book of Ecclesiasticus From Hebrew Manuscripts in the Cairo Geniza* (Cambridge: University Press, 1899) 19; Israel Lévi, ed., *L'Ecclésiastique ou La Sagesse de Jésus, Fils de Sira*, pt. 2 (Paris: Bibliothèque de L'école de hautes études, 1901) 204; Rudolf Smend, ed., *Die Weisheit des Jesus Sirach: Hebräisch und Deutsch* (Berlin: Georg Reimer, 1906) 57. The fragments from Masada and Qumran do not include this passage.

[21] The word *pānîm* is problematic. I have taken it to refer to the divine presence, understanding the phrase *nilqaḥ pānîm* to be a paraphrase of Gen 5:24: *kî-lāqaḥ 'ōtô 'ĕlōhîm* ("for God took him"). See Eliezer Ben Yehudah, *A Complete Dictionary of Ancient and Modern Hebrew* (Hebrew), vol. 10 (Jerusalem, 1944) 4996a, which lists as a meaning of *pānîm*, "*nôkĕḥût* ('presence'), a term for God or a king." For further support and other proposed meanings see S. D. Fraade, "Enosh and His Generation: Scriptural Translation and Interpretation in Late Antiquity," (Ph.D. diss., University of Pennsylvania, 1980) 47 n. 2.

[22] The Greek translation reads, *kai ta osta autou epeskepēsan* ("and his bones were looked after"). The reference here is to the care with which the Israelites removed Joseph's bones from Egypt to be given a proper burial in Palestine. See Gen 50:24–25; Exod 13:19. In Rabbinic traditions, the removal of Joseph's bones receives special attention as an indication of his (and Moses') glory: *m. Soṭa* 1:9; *b. Soṭa* 13a-b; *Mek. Bešallaḥ* 1 (ed. Lauterbach) 1.176–82. Cf. *T. Joseph* 20:2.

[23] R. H. Charles incorrectly translates "Shem, Seth, and Enoch" (*APOT* 1.506). None of the ancient versions includes Enoch's name here. Charles, like others before and after him, confuses the names of Enosh and Enoch. Perhaps he still had the latter in mind from v. 14. A. F. J. Klijn (*Seth in Jewish, Christian, and Gnostic Literature* [Leiden: E. J. Brill, 1977] 20 n. 72) repeats Charles's error. Note Lévi (p. 205), who takes *'ādām* to mean not "Adam," but "man, humanity." His argument, based on a supposed parallelism with the

In this version, the author, having chronologically recounted his praises of the biblical fathers through Nehemiah, reverts briefly to some of the earliest biblical figures, of whom only Enoch has previously been praised.[24] Their inclusion now may be intended to correct their earlier omission (especially in the case of Joseph), but this passage may also serve as a conclusion to the praises of the ancient ancestors, returning briefly to the earliest ones, before concluding with Ben Sira's contemporary, the High Priest Simon (ca. 220 B.C.E.). While Enoch has previously (44:16) been praised, the others are mentioned here for the first time.

What is of interest, of course, is Enosh's inclusion in this select list. The prepatriarchal figures listed (Adam, Seth, Enosh, Enoch, and Shem) are precisely those about whom Scripture contains positive statements in addition to mere genealogical mention: Adam was directly created by God in His image (Gen 1:26–27), Seth was "another seed" appointed by God to replace Abel (Gen 4:25), Enosh was the first to invoke God's name in worship (4:26), Enoch escaped death (5:24), and Shem received Noah's blessing (9:26) and was the head of the Semitic line. We may assume that such biblical statements, though not explicitly referred to by Ben Sira, were in the back of his mind and were assumed by him to be familiar to his readers; otherwise, further explication would have been required. Therefore, although we cannot know for certain the Hebrew text of Gen 4:26b, which Ben Sira used, from his inclusion here of Enosh's name we can assume that he interpreted Gen 4:26b to refer positively to Enosh the individual.

The order (Shem, Seth, Enosh) does not follow the biblical chronology.[25] It has been suggested that Shem has been placed at the head of the list because of his importance as the Semite progenitor.[26] It has also been suggested that the order is for the sake of alliteration (*šēm*, *šēt*, *'ĕnôš*), even if such an intent was unconscious.[27] We may add that it

preceding verses, is unconvincing. Martin Hengel (*Judaism and Hellenism* [2 vols.; trans. John Bowden; Philadelphia: Fortress, 1974] 1.188) suggests that this is an apocalyptic term analogous to the Qumran phrase *kwl kbwd 'dm* (1QS 4:23; 1QH 17:15; CD 3:20). Geza Vermes (*The Dead Sea Scrolls in English* [Baltimore: Penguin Books, 1968] 78, 100, 198) translates "all the glory of Adam," while Theodore Gaster (*The Dead Sea Scriptures in English Translation* [Garden City, N. Y.: Anchor/Doubleday, 1976] 51, 70, 204) translates "all mortal glory." In the Scrolls the expression clearly refers to some future reward.

24 Ben Sira 44:16. However, the Hebrew text of Ben Sira from Masada (as well as the Syriac version) begins the "Praise of the Fathers" with Noah (44:17) and not with Enoch, suggesting that Ben Sira originally mentioned Enoch only once, in the context of his praise of the antediluvian heroes at the *conclusion* of his survey. See Y. Yadin, *The Ben Sira Scroll from Masada* (Jerusalem: Israel Exploration Society, 1965) 38.

25 Cf. 1 Chr 1:1–4. The Greek version of Ben Sira has "Shem and Seth" (omitting Enosh), the Syriac and Arabic versions read "Seth, Shem, and Enosh," while the Vulgate has "Seth and Shem."

26 Schechter, 63; Segal, 340.

27 Norbert Peters, *Das Buch Jesus Sirach oder Ecclesiasticus* (Munich: Aschendorffsche

may have been desirable to place Enosh last in the triad so that the parallelism of Enosh/Adam in the two hemistichs of verse 16 would stand out more clearly, perhaps as a pun since both names mean "man."[28]

As we have said, the Hebrew version of Ben Sira clearly counts Enosh among the praiseworthy fathers.[29] What, however, is meant by the Hebrew *nipqĕdû*? Literally it may be translated "were visited," and echoes *nipqĕdâ* in the preceding hemistiche. While with respect to Joseph's bones it has the sense "were cared for," here it seems to mean "were honored," which is the meaning we find in the Greek translation, *edoxasthēsan*. There is no reason to assume, as some have, that the Greek translation reflects a variant Hebrew original (*nikbĕdû*).[30]

We encounter a problem in the fact that the Greek version of Ben Sira does not include Enosh's name. Rather, it reads: "Shem and Seth were distinguished among men (*en anthrōpois edoxasthēsan*), but over every living thing of creation, Adam [holds preeminence]."[31] Here in place of Enosh's name we find "among men." There are two possible explanations for this discrepancy:

(1) The Greek reflects a mistranslation of the Hebrew *'ĕnôš*, which can represent either the proper name Enosh, or the term for "man" (mankind). Indeed, the word *'ĕnôš* is used as a collective noun in the Hebrew version of Ben Sira nineteen times, while appearing as the proper name Enosh only once. Of the nineteen occurrences of *'ĕnôš* as a collective noun, twelve are translated into Greek with a form of *anthrōpos*, four with a form of *anēr*, while in three cases a paraphrase results in a circumlocution. In four instances (other than 49:16), the singular *'ĕnôš*

Verlagsbuchhandlung, 1913) 423–24.

28 There are twelve biblical occurrences of the collective noun *'ĕnôš* parallel to another expression for "man" (usually *'ādām* or *ben-'ādām*, but also *geber*). In ten of these cases the word *'ĕnôš* is in the first clause (e.g., Isa 13:12; Ps 8:5; Job 25:6), while in two (Ps 144:3; Job 36:25) it is in the second. Thus, the Hebrew version of Ben Sira *may* be following biblical style, even if adapting it to *'ĕnôš* and *'ādām* as proper names.

29 Adam's place of preeminence is also noteworthy, particularly in light of the mixed treatment he receives in later Rabbinic traditions and his negative estimation in early Christianity (especially Pauline). See Smend, 476.

30 P. Schäfer ("Der Götzendienst des Enosch," 137–38) translates, "wurde zum Guten gedacht." The Hebrew verb *pqd* is most commonly translated with the Greek verbs *episkeptomai* or *episkopeō* ("look upon, visit, consider," LSJ 656, 657), both in Ben Sira (e.g., 49:15) and the rest of the Greek Bible. But there are several other instances where the usual Greek is inadequate for translating a particular nuance of the Hebrew verb *pqd* and a different Greek verb is chosen. Thus, in Ben Sira 39:30 (31) we find the verb *hetoimaxomai* ("to be prepared"), and in 50:1 we have the verb *hyporraptō* ("to mend, repair"). For similar examples from the rest of the Bible see Num 31:49; 1 Sam 25:7; Ezek 38:8. In all of these examples the Hebrew verb *pqd* is in the *niph'al*. Smend's argument (p. 476) that the Hebrew originally had *nibrĕ'û* ("were created") is not convincing.

31 *Sapientia Jesu Filii Sirach*, *Septuaginta Vetus Testamentum Graecum*, vol. 12, pt. 2 (ed. Joseph Ziegler; Göttingen: Vandenhoeck und Ruprecht, 1965) 357.

is translated with the plural dative form *anthrōpois*.[32] Similarly, in three instances, the rare passive participle *ʾānûš* ("weak") is translated by the LXX with *anthrōpos*: Isa 17:11; Jer 17:9; 17:16. Therefore, the Greek rendering *anthrōpois* in 49:16 could very likely represent a Hebrew original reading *ʾĕnôš*, which was (perhaps automatically) understood to mean "mankind." We would still have to explain the translation of *wĕ-* with the Greek *en* (Hebrew *bĕ-*).

(2) The second possibility, suggested by R. Smend, is that the Hebrew originally read *beʾĕnôš* (and not *weʾĕnôš*, as in our text) and is *correctly* translated by the Greek to mean "among men."[33] The extant Hebrew text would, according to this view, reflect an emendation which, in translating back into Hebrew, added Enosh to the list of prepatriarchal fathers. However, a translator would not normally have rendered *en anthrōpois* (clearly plural) with *weʾĕnôš*. Thus, if we were to adopt Smend's proposal we would have to accept the extant Hebrew text as representing a significant emendation.

Hence, we must choose between two possibilities: did the Greek translator alter (misunderstand) his Hebrew original, or is the extant Hebrew text an emendation of the Greek translation of the original Hebrew? Judging from the Book of Ben Sira as a whole, either is possible. Since the discovery of the Qumran and Massada fragments of Ben Sira, greater reliability has been attributed by scholars to the Geniza texts (especially MS. B) than theretofore. Of the two possibilities which we have presented the first appears to be more likely: the variant can easily be accounted for at the level of translation, without resorting to a supposed *major* textual emendation. We will see below that other early traditions speak of a *triad* of antediluvian righteous.

It is significant that the Syriac version has: *šyt wšym wʾnwš bʾnšʾ* ("Seth and Shem and Enosh among mankind").[34] This probably reflects a

[32] The Syriac consistently follows the Greek in translating the Hebrew word *ʾĕnôš*: When the Greek has *anthrōpos*, the Syriac has *ʾnšh*; when the Greek has a form of *anēr*, the Syriac has *gbrh*; and when the Greek has the plural *anthrōpoi*, the Syriac usually has *bry ʾnšh* (or *brynšh*). These observations are based on *The Book of Ben Sira: Text, Concordance, and an Analysis of the Vocabulary*; R. Smend, *Griechisch-Syrisch-Hebräisches Index zur Weisheit des Jesus Sirach* (Berlin: Georg Reimer, 1907); Michael M. Winter, *A Concordance to the Peshiṭta Version of Ben Sira* (Leiden: E. J. Brill, 1976); Hatch and Redpath, *A Concordance to the Septuagint* (2 vols. and supp.; Oxford: Clarendon, 1897–1902).

[33] R. Smend, *Die Weisheit des Jesus Sirach*, 57, 89, 475–76. Smend cites 45:14 for another example of a confused *wāw* and *bēt*. There, however, the Greek translation of the Hebrew *wkl ywm tmyd pʿmym* ("and every day twice without fail") with *kathʾ hēmeran endelechōs dis* ("[on] every day twice without fail") is simply paraphrastic, using the idiomatic Greek expression *kathʾ hēmeran* ("daily," see LSJ 883a). Segal (p. 340), Peters (pp. 423–24), and Lévi (p. 240) all accept the Hebrew reading *weʾĕnôš*.

[34] For the Syriac, I have consulted the Walton Polyglott: *Biblia Sacra Polyglotta* (ed.

harmonization of the Greek and extant Hebrew versions. Since the Syriac translation is generally thought to have been composed about 300 C.E., we can establish that date as the *terminus ad quem* for the inclusion of Enosh in the Hebrew list (assuming that the Syriac version is not itself corrupt). Whether or not we can with certainty push Enosh's inclusion back to the time of the *original* Hebrew composition (200–175 B.C.E.) remains beyond the limits of our data. We have simply demonstrated a high degree of probability.

C. *Jubilees*

Jubilees 4:12, in the context of paraphrasing Genesis 4–5, reads: "He [Enosh] began to call on the name of the Lord on the Earth."[35] Since *Jubilees* is generally dated in the second century B.C.E., it would represent the earliest attestation of what some have argued to be the "original" Hebrew text: *zeh* (or *hû'*) *hēḥēl*, which credits Enosh with being the first to invoke the Lord by name.[36]

Unfortunately, the Greek and Hebrew fragments of *Jubilees*, which are often helpful in hypothesizing the biblical Hebrew *Vorlage*, do not include *Jub.* 4:12.[37] James VanderKam has noted that *Jub.* 4:12 agrees with the LXX against the MT in reading "he" and not "then." He suggests that *Jubilees* used a Hebrew text which had *zeh* rather than *'āz*, arguing by analogy with the Hebrew fragment of *Jub.* 4:17 (11QJub M3), which reads: *wyqr' 't šmw ḥnwk* (*vacat*) *zh ry'šwn lmd spr* ("And he [Jared] called his name Enoch . . . This one was the first to learn writing").[38] While the analogy is interesting, it is not conclusive. *Jub.* 4:16–17 is a *paraphrastic* expansion of Gen 5:18 ("and [Jared] begot Enoch"). Would we be justified in assuming that this passage also reflects a scriptural variant? *Jub.* 4:12 is similarly expansive, adding "on the

---

Brian Walton; 6 vols.; London: Thomas Roycroft, 1657) 4.124.

35 *APOT* 2.18; R. H. Charles, trans. and ed., *The Book of Jubilees* (London: Adam and Charles Black, 1902) 32. For the Ethiopic text see R. H. Charles, ed., *The Ethiopic Version of the Hebrew Book of Jubilees* (Oxford: Clarendon, 1897) 15, which reads: *w'tū qădăm ṣw'ō smă* . . . ("He first invoked the name . . .").

36 See the commentaries listed above, n. 3. On the dating of *Jubilees* see James C. VanderKam's recent work, which makes use of the Hebrew fragments from Qumran (11QJub): *Textual and Historical Studies in the Book of Jubilees* (Missoula, Mont.: Scholars Press, 1977).

37 For the Greek fragments I have checked *Fragmenta Pseudepigraphum Quae Supersunt Graeca* (ed. Albert-Marie Denis; Leiden: E. J. Brill, 1970) 70–102. For the Hebrew fragments we have A. S. van der Woude, "Fragmente des Buches Jubiläen aus Qumran Höhle XI (11QJub)," in *Tradition und Glaube: Das frühe Christentum in seiner Umwelt* (ed. G. Jeremias et al.; Göttingen: Vandenhoeck & Ruprecht, 1971) 140–46, pl. 8; as well as J. T. Milik, "A propos de 11QJub," *Bib.* 54 (1973) 77–78.

38 VanderKam, *Textual and Historical Studies*, List F, p. 153, pp. 29–30. For the fragment see Milik, "A propos de 11QJub," 78.

Earth." Most likely, the intent of the paraphrase was: "He was the first on earth to. . . "

Thus, while the author of *Jubilees* may have had a Hebrew text which read *zeh hēḥēl*, we must allow for the possibility that he was simply paraphrasing an awkward Hebrew passive expression, which, as we have seen, may also have caused difficulty for the translator of the LXX. In either case, *Jubilees* clearly understands Gen 4:26b to refer specifically to Enosh, and represents our earliest statement explicitly crediting Enosh with being the *first* human to worship God by "calling on His name."

Jubilees 19:23–25 again refers positively to Enosh, and like Ben Sira includes his name in a list of righteous pre-Israelite ancestors. Abraham, in blessing Jacob, says:

> 23. And all the blessings wherewith the Lord hath blessed me and my seed belong to Jacob and his seed always. 24. And in his seed shall my name be blessed, and the name of my fathers, Shem, and Noah, and Enoch, and Mahalalel, and Enos, and Seth, and Adam. 25. And these shall serve to lay the foundations of the heaven, and to strengthen the earth, and to renew all the luminaries which are in the firmament.[39]

The list of righteous ancestors is in reverse chronological order, since it is given from Abraham's perspective. The inclusion of Mahalalel is noteworthy, since nothing significant is said about him in the Bible or in postbiblical sources.[40] It is likely that his name was added to bring the list to seven, but Methuselah's inclusion would have been more to be expected. Once again we have a *selective* list that includes Enosh, without saying anything in particular about him.

Unfortunately, the passage is ambiguous since it does not make clear to whom the word *these* of verse 25 refers. Who are the "foundations" of the universe, Jacob's seed or the seven prepatriarchal ancestors? According to A. Dillmann, it is the former, according to L. Ginzberg, the latter.[41] Ginzberg speaks of the great importance which the *Jubilees*

39 *The Book of Jubilees* (trans. R. H. Charles) 128. For the Ethiopic and Latin texts see R. H. Charles, ed., *The Ethiopic Version of the Hebrew Book of Jubilees*, 58–59. Enosh's name is included in both the Latin and Ethiopic versions. This passage is not extant in the Greek and Hebrew fragments.

40 In *Jub.* 4:15 we are told that he married his niece Berakiel. In *1 Enoch* 83:6–9 Mahalalel wakes Enoch from his dream and helps him to interpret it. His name also appears in *2 Enoch* 33:10 discussed below. In Rabbinic sources the only mention of Mahalalel is in *AgBer.* (ed. Buber) intro. p. 37, where it is said that he repented his sins, praising (*hll*) and extolling God.

41 Dillmann's view is referred to in Hermann Rönsch, *Das Buch der Jubiläen; oder, Die kleine Genesis* (Leipzig: Fues, 1874; repr. Amsterdam: Ropopi, 1970) 116: "*et ipsi* . . . Hierzu bemerkt Dillmann, dieser Satz umschreibe den Gedanken, dass mit Gründung der israelitischen Gemeinde eine neue Schöpfung beginne." For Ginzberg's view, see *Eine*

attributes to these seven figures "für die religiöse Entwicklung der Menschheit." In a note he adds:

> Die eigentlich Tendenz dieser Schrift besteht bekanntlich darin, die mosäischen Institutionen auf die Urzeit zurückzufuhren und mit der Urgeschichte in Zusammenhang zu bringen. Wenn jedoch XIX, 24 gerade sieben Männer als die eigentlichen Träger der Uroffenbarungen erscheinen, so ist dies kein Zufall, sondern es liegt hier wohl die Vorstellung von den "sieben Säulen der Welt" vor. . . , die Instrumente der göttlichen Offenbarung.[42]

If Ginzberg is correct, this list may represent an early version of the tradition of the seven shepherds or pillars, which appears in later Jewish and Christian traditions, to be discussed below.

Enosh appears in one other place in *Jubilees*, in 4:13. There we are told that Enosh "took Noam his sister to be his wife, and she bore him a son. . . , and he called his name Kenan."[43] Whereas the biblical text does not specify who were the wives of Seth, Enosh, Enoch, etc., *Jubilees* makes certain that they do not marry outside the Sethite line, even if this requires incest. The purity of the antediluvian Sethite line is a recurring motif in later Jewish and especially Christian writings, which often attribute the Flood to the intermarrying of the Sethite and Cainite lines.[44]

D. 2 (*Slavonic*) *Enoch*

In *2 Enoch* 33:10–11, in the longer recension, God, after having imparted to Enoch secret teachings and having had him write them down to be given to mankind, appoints guardian angels to protect them from the Flood:

> And I will give thee, Enoch, My messenger, the great captain Michael, for thy writings and for the writings of thy fathers, Adam, Seth, Enos, Kainan, Malaleel (Mahalalel), and Jared, thy father. And I shall not require them till the last age, for I have instructed My two angels, Ariukh and Pariukh, whom I have put upon the earth as their guardians.[45]

---

unbekannte jüdische Sekte, vol. 1 (New York, 1922) 295–97.

[42] Ginzberg, 297 n. 1. On the "seven pillars of the world," see L. Ginzberg, "Clementina or Pseudo-Clementine Literature," *The Jewish Encyclopedia*, 14 (1903) 114b. We will note below (chap. 4, n. 137) that according to one Rabbinic tradition, Enosh is counted as one of the seven messianic shepherds.

[43] *APOT* 2.18. There are no extant Greek or Hebrew fragments of this passage.

[44] See L. Ginzberg, *Legends of the Jews* (7 vols.; Philadelphia: Jewish Publication Society of America, 1913–38) 5.172 n. 14. These traditions will be discussed below. For an interesting interpretation of *Jubilees*'s Sethite genealogy, see P. Schäfer, "Der Götzendienst des Enosch," 143–47, which we will consider in chapter 4 in conjunction with Rabbinic traditions that link the fall of the angels with the Generation of Enosh.

[45] *The Book of the Secrets of Enoch* (trans. W. R. Morfill; Oxford: Clarendon, 1896) 48; *APOT* 2.452. Cf. 35:2. The shorter recension ("B" in Charles's and Morfill's editions)

While other traditions speak of secret writings of Seth and Enoch, this is the only Jewish source to suggest that such wisdom was imparted to, and recorded by, Enosh.[46] The six names represent an inclusive list of Enosh's predecessors. Enosh's name, therefore, is included only by virtue of his position in the biblical genealogy.

In a fragment usually appended to *2 Enoch* we find a story of the birth of the priest Melchizedek. His father prays to God: "and thou shalt honour him with Thy servants the priests, with Seth, and Enoch, and Tharasidam, Maleleil, and Enos, and thy servant, and thus Melchizedek shall be a priest in another generation."[47] Significantly, Melchizedek is the seventh in the chain. A familiar pattern is once again repeated: Enosh is part of a list of early heroes, here described as "priests," who serve as models, or prefigurations, for the subsequent unfolding of religious history.

E. Philo (ca. 25 B.C.E.-ca. 45 C.E.)

In Philo's writings we find the earliest extant attempt to resolve the difficulties of the LXX translation of Gen 4:26b, and the first *discussion* of Enosh as a righteous antediluvian. As we will see in chapter 3, Philo's view of Enosh significantly influences the course of Christian exegesis. Less obvious is how some of what Philo says presages Rabbinic exegesis.

Like other biblical figures, Enosh is viewed by Philo as an exemplar of a particular attribute of faith: hope. For Philo, the pre-Mosaic heroes of the Bible embody in their lives and deeds those virtues later to be expressed in the obligatory statutes received at Sinai. These figures, according to him, should by example inspire the reader to strive for similar attainments. By living lives of piety long before the laws were formally revealed, they demonstrate that the written laws are simply concrete expressions of what can be intuitively recognized as the unwritten laws of nature.[48]

---

mentions only the writings of Adam and Seth. Only the Slavic text of the shorter recension has been published: *Le Livre des Secrets d'Hénoch* (ed. and trans. A. Vaillant; Paris: Institut d'Études Slaves, 1952) 34, 35. *2 Enoch* was probably composed in Greek in the decades preceding the destruction of the Temple in 70 C.E. For a description and bibliography see James H. Charlesworth, *The Pseudepigrapha and Modern Research* (Missoula, Mont.: Scholars Press, 1976) 103–6.

46 For Seth, we learn of the "Stelae of Seth," pillars on which he recorded antediluvian wisdom so it would not perish in the Flood. Our earliest source for this tradition is Josephus' *Antiquities* 1.2.3 §§ 70–71. Cf. *Jeraḥmeel* 24.7; 26.16 (trans. Gaster) 51, 56, where the pillars are associated with Jubal. For other sources, see L. Ginzberg, *Legends*, 5.149 n. 53. For a much later Christian tradition attributing astrological books to Enosh, see *Book of the Bee*, chap. 18, cited in E. A. Wallis Budge, *The Book of the Cave of Treasures* (London: Religious Tract Society, 1927) 78.

47 *The Book of the Secrets of Enoch* (trans. W. R. Morfill & R. H. Charles) 91. In Vaillant's edition (p. 81) the list is somewhat different, but still contains Enosh.

48 *Abr.* 4–5. See H. A. Wolfson, *Philo: Foundations of Religious Philosophy in Judaism*,

Of course, the particular association of Enosh with hope derives from the LXX reading *ēlpise* ("he hoped"). Philo is the earliest writer explicitly to attribute significance to Enosh's name, which he identifies with *anthrōpos*, meaning man or mankind. In *The Worst Attacks the Better* he writes: "For what could be found more in keeping with one who is truly a man than a hope and expectation of obtaining good things from the one bountiful God."[49] Enosh is true man precisely because he hopes. Significantly, Philo interprets Gen 4:26 in light of the following verse, 5:1 ("This is the book of the nativity of mankind"[50]):

> This is, to tell the truth, men's only birth in the strict sense, since those who do not set their hope on God have no part in a rational nature. Accordingly having first said of Enos "this man hoped (and ventured[51]) to call on the name of the Lord God," he adds expressly, "this is the book of the nativity of man." In saying this he utters an important truth, for an entry is hereby made in the book of God to the effect that man only is hopeful. The converse therefore is true, that he that is despondent (*dyselpis*) is not human.[52]

Based on this interpretation, Philo offers a definition of Man as portrayed by Moses (i.e., Scripture): "a soul so constituted as to hope on the God that really is."[53] Finally, Philo contrasts Enosh with men like Cain

---

Christianity, and Islam (2 vols.; Cambridge, Mass.: Harvard Univ. Press, 1968) 1.450–51; 2.182–83. On Philo's allegorical treatment of biblical figures see Wolfson, 1.126. On his notion of "natural law" see Wolfson, 2.165–87; and V. Nikiprowetzky, *Le Commentaire de l'Écriture chez Philon d'Alexandrie* (Leiden: E. J. Brill, 1977) 117–55.

49 *Quod. Det.* 138 (trans. F. H. Colson; LCL) 2.294–95. On Philo's interpretation of biblical names see S. Belkin, "The Interpretation of Names in Philo" (Hebrew), *Ḥoreb* 12 (1956–57) 3–61, esp. pp. 54–56, where Philo's interpretation of Enosh is discussed.

50 MT: *zeh sēper tôlĕdôt 'ādām*, generally translated, "This is the book [record] of the descendants of Adam." The LXX translates: *hautē hē biblos geneseōs anthrōpōn* ("this is the book of the descent [or, as Philo takes it, birth] of mankind"). The LXX differs from the MT in understanding *twldt* in the singular (*tôlĕdat*; cf. chap. 2, n. 16, below). Unlike the Aramaic translations, it understands *'ādām* not as the proper name Adam but as the collective noun "man" (mankind). The Greek noun *genesis* can mean both descent and birth, while the Hebrew *tôlĕdôt* usually refers to descent and not birth. Philo's interpretation clearly derives from the Greek version.

51 The parenthetical "and ventured" is inserted in Colson's translation but does not appear in the Greek texts, neither in the Loeb edition nor in that of L. Cohn, ed., *Philonis Alexandrini Opera Quae Supersunt* (7 vols.; Berlin: George Reimer, 1896–1930) 1.289. As we will see, this insertion is misleading.

52 *Quod. Det.* 138–39. Philo's linking of Gen 4:26 and 5:1 is occasioned by the obvious discontinuity between the two successive verses. His interpretation seeks to connect the otherwise disjointed phrases. As we will see, he is not unique in this respect. Cf. Philo's treatment of Gen 2:4 in *Leg. All.* 1.19, 20, and of Gen 6:9 in *Abr.* 31.

53 A similar definition appears in *Qu. in Gen.* 1.80: "What is man? Man is that which more than other kinds of animals has obtained a very large and extraordinary portion of hope."

who because of their despondent natures are worthless—not worthy of being called by the word *man*.[54]

This basic interpretation of Enosh is given in other works of Philo, where the different contexts elicit some significant variations. Most important for our purposes is his treatment of Enosh in *On Abraham* 7–15.[55] There Philo organizes the early biblical heroes into two triads: Enosh, Enoch, and Noah; Abraham, Isaac, and Jacob. Each figure represents not only an attribute of faith, but a stage in the "possession of blessings" (*metousia agathōn*).[56] Enosh represents the first step in this progression, embodying the attribute of hope:

> Moses called the first lover of hope "Man" (*anthrōpos*), thus bestowing on him as a special favour the name which is common to the race (for the Chaldean name for Man is Enos), on the grounds that he alone is a true man who expects good things and rests firmly on comfortable hopes.[57]

Philo notes that just as Homer is called "the poet," Enosh is called "man," suggesting "*the* man," or man in preeminence.[58] He contrasts this ideal hoper to the despondent person who is "no man, but a beast in human shape."[59]

Once again we find Philo linking Gen 4:26 with 5:1, by stating that Enosh is the founder of a new race of men, "from which all impurity had been strained," understanding Gen 5:1 as: "This is the book [record]

[54] *Quod. Det.* 140.

[55] Philo's other major treatment of Enosh is to be found in *Praem.* 10–14. There Enosh is again praised for his hope, "that most vital form of seed which the Creator sowed in the rich soil of the rational soul . . . the fountainhead of the lives which we lead." *Praem.* 10–11 (LCL) 8.318–19. Wolfson (*Philo*, 2.166–67) understands Philo's discussion of hope to be a "paraphrase" of Aristotle and Plato. Philo goes on to tell us that Enosh's perfect hope rests entirely on God as creator and provider, since Scripture specifies God as the object of his hope. The reward for one who so hopes is to become true, ideal man, as suggested to Philo by Enosh's name. To Philo, Enosh represents not only the means by which the contest of virtue is waged (hope in God), but the reward as well: the full realization of a person as *man*, being a mixture of mortal and immortal.

[56] *Abr.* 7 (trans. F. H. Colson; LCL) 6.6–7. See the introduction in the Loeb edition, 6.x. E. Goodenough's contention (*By Light, Light: The Mystic Gospel of Hellenistic Judaism* [New Haven, Conn.: Yale Univ. Press, 1935] 129–230, 238) that these pre-Mosaic figures represent stages in a mystic ascent is questionable. Goodenough is probably right, however, in finding significance in the numerical arrangement three, three, and Moses as seventh (p. 129). This scheme is repeated in *Praem.* 10–14.

[57] *Abr.* 7–8 (LCL) 6.8–9.

[58] *Abr.* 10 (LCL) 6.8–11.

[59] Cf. *Abr.* 33 (LCL) 6.20–21, where in discussing Noah, the *anthrōpos dikaios* ("just man"), Philo states: "After *man* he adds *just*, implying by the combination that the unjust man is no man, or more properly speaking a beast in human form, and that the follower after righteousness alone is man."

of the coming into being of the *true* man" (*hē biblos geneseōs tou pros alētheian anthrōpou*). Philo explains the disjunction of Gen 4:26 and 5:1 through a play on the name Enosh and the noun *anthrōpos* ("man"): it is with Enosh (Gen 4:26) that the true line of man (Gen 5:1) comes into being, the evil Cainite descendants of Adam (Gen 4:1–24) having been "strained" out. He continues: "The word ['book'] was appropriate because the hoper deserves a memorial written not on pieces of paper which moths shall destroy but in the undying book of nature where good actions are registered."[60]

Enosh has the further distinction of being the fourth generation.[61] The number four, according to Philo, is held in high honor both by the "all-wise Moses" and the "other philosophers." Just as the number four is "holy and praiseworthy" (*hagios esti kai ainetos*), so too is the hopeful man.

Philo concludes his discussion of Enosh in *On Abraham* by noting that the hope of which he speaks is an unwritten law of nature. While some may find hopefulness through "exhortation or command," he who acquires it intuitively is the true hoper. Hope is the first virtue to be acquired, leading in turn to the others. It is "set by nature as a door keeper at the portals of the royal virtues within, to which access cannot be gained unless we have first paid our respects to her."[62]

So far, Philo's treatment of Enosh has been very positive, viewing him as an epitome of man. But we soon see an important modification of this view. After treating Enoch (repentance[63]) and Noah (justice) Philo

60 *Abr*. 9, 11 (LCL) 6.8–11. On Enosh as the founder of a new race of true men see C. Siegfried (*Philo von Alexandria als Ausleger des Alten Testaments* [Jena: Herman Dufft, 1975] 257–58), who rightly compares Philo's treatment of Gen 5:1 with that found in *Gen. Rab*. 24.6 (ed. Theodor-Albeck) 235–36: "These were descendants, while the early ones were not descendants. What were they? Divinities! . . . Another interpretation . . . Demons." This Rabbinic tradition will be discussed in chapter 4. Philo similarly interprets the "book" of Gen 5:1 as a book of nature or natural law in *Qu. in Gen*. 1.80 (LCL) supp. 1.49: "And this is celebrated as if inscribed in nature, for the mind of man naturally hopes."

61 *Abr*. 12–13 (LCL) 6.10–11. Usually Enosh is counted as the third (Adam, Seth, Enosh as in 1 Chr 1:1). Apparently, Philo either counts Abel as the second, with Cain being discredited, or Cain as the second, since Abel dies without progeny. Thus, Seth would be third and Enosh fourth. Were it not for this comment, one might assume that Philo's selection of the triad Enosh, Enoch, and Noah is determined in part by the significance of the numbers three, seven, and ten.

62 *Abr*. 15–16 (LCL) 6.10–13.

63 Philo's interpretation of Enoch is based on the Greek version of Gen 5:24: *metethēken auton ho theos* ("God transferred him"), which is understood to mean that Enoch, having previously been a sinner, had a change of heart and repented with God's help. See *Abr*. 17–18. Cf. the Greek version of Ben Sira 44:16: "Enoch pleased the Lord and was carried off (*methetethē*) to heaven as an example of repentance (*metanoia*) to further generations." See John G. Snaith's note ad loc.: *Ecclesiasticus or the Wisdom of Jesus Son of Sirach* (Cambridge: Cambridge Univ. Press, 1974) 217.

concludes his description of the first triad:

> Now these three mentioned above, whether we think of them as men or types of soul, form a series of regular graduation: the perfect man [Noah] is complete from the first; the transferred [Enoch] stands half-way, since he devoted the earlier part of life to vice but the latter to virtue to which he passed over and migrated; the hoper (*ho elpizōn*, Enosh), as his very name shows, is defective (*ellipēs*) inasmuch as though he always desired the excellent he has not yet been able to attain it, but resembles sailors eager to put into port, who yet remain at sea unable to reach their haven.[64]

This first triad (Enosh, Enoch, and Noah) is to Philo inferior to the second (Abraham, Isaac, and Jacob): "The first we may compare to the studies of children, but the latter to the exercises of athletes who are preparing for games which are really sacred."[65] Enosh, the ideal man, is now portrayed by Philo as being flawed.

Before trying to understand this sudden shift let us be sure we understand Philo's reading of Gen 4:26b. In the passages which we have examined, Philo repeatedly makes several points with regard to Enosh: Enosh represents the virtue of hope—not ordinary hope, but hope in God, a virtue recorded in nature. As such, Enosh both represents and defines the true man. He is the progenitor of the human race. Yet with all Philo's emphasis on the Greek verb *ēlpise* ("he hoped"), he virtually ignores the verb *epikaleisthai* ("to call"). Whenever Philo paraphrases Gen 4:26b, he does so as "Enosh placed his hope in the Lord," and not "Enosh hoped to call on the name of the Lord."

Philo's circumlocution reveals what must have been regarded as an ambiguity in the LXX: did Enosh actually "call on the name of the Lord" or not? What is the meaning of his hoping? Does it reflect an aspiration which he never fulfilled? If so, what would have stopped him? Or, does the word *ēlpise* indicate the *quality* of Enosh's worship? He called on the name of the Lord God *in hope*; that is, Enosh had sufficient faith "to call on the name of the Lord." In most of his discussion, Philo seems to avoid this crucial question.

In our examination of the LXX text we noted that in *Quod. Det.* 138 Philo cites Gen 4:26b as, "This man *first* hoped to call on the name of the Lord God." Similarly, in *Abr.* 7 he refers to Enosh as the "first lover of hope." This may suggest that Philo was familiar with translations or interpretations of Gen 4:26 which, unlike the LXX, attributed the *beginnings* of divine worship to Enosh. It would have made sense, then, for

64 *Abr.* 47 (LCL) 6.26–29.

65 *Abr.* 48 (LCL) 6.28–29. Philo similarly contrasts Enoch and Abraham in *De Mutatione Nominum* 5.39.

Philo to reconcile the Hebrew and Greek versions by interpreting Enosh as the one who first worshipped God in hope, thereby combining two views of Enosh: the first worshipper of God, and the one who hoped to worship God.

But this Philo does not do. Rather, he focuses almost entirely on Enosh the hoper. While this interpretation is occasioned by the ambiguous LXX misvocalization of the unusual Hebrew for *hwḥl*, it is motivated by Philo's broader treatment of early biblical heroes as epitomes of virtue, and by his rather Platonic interest in the virtue of hope.[66]

At first, this focus on Enosh the hoper produces a very positive view of Enosh. To Philo Enosh becomes an allegory for the ideal man and ideal hope. It would seem that Philo, through allegory, has lifted Enosh from his scriptural and "historical" context, focusing entirely on his name ("man") and his attribute ("hope"). But then Philo wishes to view Enosh in relation to a chain of righteous biblical ancestors which reaches its zenith in Moses, that is, within the context of Israel's sacred history. Within this context the pre-Israelite righteous are inferior to their Israelite successors. Thus, Philo's two approaches to Enosh, allegorizing him and viewing him in the context of scriptural history, produce, paradoxically, conflicting results. When viewed alone, when lifted from the scriptural context, Enosh is the embodiment of the highest virtue, hope, exemplifying the highest form of hope: hope which rests in God. As such, Enosh represents *man* par excellence. Yet, when viewed in the broader context of Scripture, as Philo understands it, as part of a progression of righteous ancestors culminating in Moses, Enosh represents an important, but most preliminary stage of spiritual excellence, overshadowed by his successors.[67] No longer is Enosh simply the hoper, but the one who hoping to call on the name of the Lord, never does. Enosh represents an important ideal, unrealized in his own time.

While the Greek Bible facilitates, and perhaps even occasions, Philo's idealization of Enosh, it also facilitates Philo's qualification of his merit. While Enosh's name and hope suggest to Philo his ideal nature, the latter (*elpizō*) is used to indicate his defective nature (*ellipēs*).[68] Had he wanted, Philo could easily have resolved this paradox (as will subsequent Christian exegetes), making Enosh a truly ideal epitome of hope (faith) in God. But he chooses not to, deferring instead to the paramountcy of the Israelite patriarchs. It is certainly significant that in choosing three prepatriarchal figures, Philo includes Enosh, setting him

66 See Wolfson, *Philo*, 2.166–67.

67 Cf. Philo's treatment of Shem as "the foundation, the root, as it were, of noble qualities and from that root sprung up wise Abraham, a tree yielding sweet nutriment, and his fruit was Isaac. . . ." *Sob.* 65 (LCL) 3.476–77.

68 *Abr.* 47.

as the first, while paying only the slightest attention to such figures as Seth, Methuselah, and Shem.[69] Yet, in the larger context it is Noah, Abraham, and especially Moses who are the focus of Philo's attention. Philo's positive and hesitant views of Enosh will echo in later Jewish, Christian, and Samaritan interpretations.

F. Josephus (37–ca. 110 C.E.)

Josephus says nothing about Enosh except to include him in two genealogical lists.[70] However, he includes some traditions about Seth and his descendants that will prove important for understanding Christian interpretations to be discussed in chapter 3, and a view of antediluvian history that will prove relevant to Rabbinic traditions to be discussed in chapter 4.

In *Ant.* 1.2.3 §§ 67–71, after providing a detailed account of the vices of Cain and his descendants based on a negative assessment of their "civilized" achievements (Gen 4:17–24,)[71] Josephus turns to Seth and his progeny, who are distinguished for their righteousness:

> Many other children were born to him [Adam], and among them Seth; it would take me too long to speak of the rest, and I will only endeavor to narrate the story of the progeny of Seth. He, after being brought up and attaining to years of discretion, cultivated virtue, excelled in it himself, and left descendants who imitated his ways. These, being all of virtuous character, inhabited the same country without dissension and in prosperity, meeting with no untoward incident to the day of their death; they also discovered the science of the heavenly bodies and their orderly array.[72]

69 These figures are elsewhere briefly mentioned but do not fit into Philo's overall scheme to the same extent as does Enosh. On Seth see *Qu. in Gen.* 1.81; on Shem, *Sob.* 52–58, 65; on Methuselah, *Post.* 40–41, 44–45, 73–74.

70 *Ant.* 1.3.2 § 79 and 1.3.4 § 83. Interestingly, Josephus does not treat the Sethite genealogy of Genesis 5 in its Scriptural sequence after the descendants of Cain (Genesis 4), but in the context of the Flood story (Genesis 6–8).

71 This negative assessment of the achievements of Cain and his descendants is suggested by Scripture itself in Gen 4:1–24, and is emphasized by Philo, Pseudo-Philo, Rabbinic, and Christian exegetes. See below, chapter 5. See T. W. Franxman, *Genesis and the "Jewish Antiquities" of Flavius Josephus* (BibOr 35; Rome: Biblical Institute, 1979) 65–77; L. Feldman, "Hellenizations in Josephus' Portrayal of Man's Decline," in *Religions in Antiquity: Essays in Memory of Erwin Ramsdel Goodenough* (ed. J. Neusner; Leiden: E. J. Brill, 1968) 336–52.

72 *Ant.* 1.2.3 §§ 68–69 (trans. H. Thackeray; LCL) 4.30–33. The text continues with the legend of how the Sethites, being foretold of a flood of water or fire, erected two pillars, one of brick and one of stone, on which they inscribed their discoveries so that they would not be lost to mankind. This legend reappears in various, often amplified, forms in later Jewish, Christian, and Gnostic literature, some of which will be discussed below. For a comprehensive treatment, see A. F. J. Klijn, *Seth in Jewish, Christian and Gnostic Literature* (Leiden: E. J. Brill, 1977). See also L. Ginzberg, *Legends*, 1.120–22; 5.148–50 (esp.

While the Cainites were pursuing lives of crafty greed, insolence, and violence, the Sethites lived virtuous lives in harmony with one another. Josephus continues:

> For seven generations these people continued to believe in God as Lord of the universe and in everything to take virtue for their guide; then, in the course of time, they abandoned the customs of their fathers for a life of depravity. They no longer rendered to God His due honours, nor took account of justice towards men, but displayed by their actions a zeal for vice twofold greater than they had formerly shown for virtue, and thereby drew upon themselves the enmity of God.[73]

Josephus next tells of the "angels of God" who consort with women, begetting "giants" and bringing on the Flood.

Interestingly, Josephus describes the descendants of Seth in general terms, mentioning their individual names only later in his account of the Flood.[74] Presumably, Enosh, though not mentioned in his own right, is included among the seven generations of righteous Sethites. This failure to comment on Enosh and Gen 4:26b is curious considering Josephus' otherwise detailed elaborations on the protohistory of Genesis.[75] It would appear that Josephus' main interest is in contrasting the evil Cain and the righteous Seth, and their respective genealogical lines. Significantly, Josephus does not appear to describe the corrupting of the Sethites *by* the Cainites, as is common in later sources.[76] Rather, the degeneration of

---

n. 53); and S. Rappaport, *Agada und Exegese bei Flavius Josephus* (Frankfurt a. M.: J. Kauffmann, 1930) 6–9, 87–90. For the development of another tradition about Seth see Esther Cassier Quinn, *The Quest of Seth for the Oil of Life* (Chicago: University of Chicago, 1962). For the Arabic glorification of Seth see Theodore Gluck, "The Arabic Legend of Seth, the Father of Mankind" (Ph.D. diss., Yale University, 1968). See Franxman, *Genesis and the "Jewish Antiquities,"* 77–80. For Christian venerations of Seth, see below, chap. 3, nn. 59, 86, 134.

[73] *Ant.* 1.3.1 § 72 (LCL) 4.32–55. It is unclear where Josephus gets the number seven. The Bible speaks of ten generations before the Flood. Since Seth represents the second generation, Josephus seems to place the beginnings of Sethite decline in the eighth generation. According to Rabbinic traditions, God did not bring the flood until the righteous Methuselah (eighth generation) had died. This interpretation is based on the fact that the biblical genealogy itself places the Flood in the year of Methuselah's death. Cf. the Appendix to *2 Enoch* (trans. W. T. Morfill) 86–87, where it is said that as long as Methuselah lived, the people remained virtuous. See L. Ginzberg, *Legends*, 1.152–54; 5.175 n. 20. In *Recognitions of (Pseudo-) Clement* 1.29 the corruption is explicitly identified with the eighth generation of mankind. *Chronicles of Jerahmeel* 24.11 (trans. T. Gaster) 52 also places the corruption of mankind after the seventh generation of Sethites.

[74] See above, n. 69.

[75] Franxman (*Genesis and the "Jewish Antiquities,"* 21) shows that Gen 1:1–11:32, the shortest of four divisions in the original Book of Genesis (the others being Gen 12:1–25:10; 25:11–36:43; and 37:1–50:26), appears as the second largest in Josephus' retelling in the *Jewish Antiquities*.

[76] See next note and chap. 3, n. 54.

the Sethites seems to occur apart from any Cainite influence. Josephus simply recounts that the Sethites, who at first continue the pious attributes of their namesake, "in the course of time" become religiously and morally corrupt. However, what the relation of this Sethite degeneration is to the intercourse of the "angels of God" with women (Gen 6:2,4), which follows immediately after Josephus' treatment of the Sethites, and to the consequent Flood is not at all clear from his account.[77]

G. Conclusions

From these pre-Rabbinic Jewish sources it is clear that Enosh was viewed as an important antediluvian figure in Jewish circles, at least as far back as the second century B.C.E. In most of these sources, however, his name is only cited as part of a "chain" of such righteous antediluvians. His positive estimation, indicated by his inclusion in such select lists, in all probability derives from a positive understanding of Gen 4:26. However, except for Philo, we find no explicit exegesis of this verse, perhaps suggesting that its meaning was clear and required little explication.[78]

77 The differentiation and contrast of Sethites and Cainites can easily derive from Scripture itself. Genesis 4–5 traces the two genealogical lines side by side, as if to contrast them. With Seth's replacing of Abel in Gen 4:25, a new righteous line of descent is established. It is through this Sethite line and not the Cainite line that Adam's "seed" is carried. Philo (*Post.* 40–48) already comments on the identical or similar names found in the two lists (esp. Enoch, Methuselah, and Lamech). According to Philo, each name has two meanings, one suggesting piety and one suggesting impiety. The former belongs to the Sethite, the latter to the Cainite. A similar view is evidenced in *1 Enoch* 85, perhaps as early as the second century B.C.E. Here in Enoch's dream vision the black (evil) cows represent Cain and his progeny, while the white (righteous) cows represent Seth and his progeny. In *1 Enoch* 86 (now extant in its original Aramaic, 4QEn^{f}), the Flood is brought about by the intercourse of fallen stars (the sons or angels of God of Gen 6:2,4) with the black cows (Cainite women). According to P. Schäfer (see above, n. 43), *Jubilees* 4 reflects a similar view. In Josephus' account it is unclear with whom the angels of God have intercourse. After describing the Sethite degenerations he abruptly states: "For (*gar*) many angels of God now consorted with women and begat sons who were overbearing and disdainful of every virtue. . . . But Noah, indignant at their conduct and viewing their counsels with displeasure, urged them to come to a better frame of mind and amend their ways." Franxman (*Genesis and the "Jewish Antiquities,"* 81 n. 38) argues that the Sethite degeneration is caused both by their intercourse with the Cainites and by the influence of the angel-offspring. However, Josephus attributes the Sethite decline to neither. Josephus simply describes the inherently corrupt nature of the Cainites and the eventual degeneration of the righteous Sethites as preludes to the tradition (perhaps taken from another source) of the intercourse of the angels with the women, which produces the evil Giant offspring. The three need not be connected, except that they all prepare for the Flood. Except for Noah and his family all of mankind is now corrupt, and this is not simply the fault of the "angels of God." This understanding will be important to our later treatment of Rabbinic and Christian treatments of the pre-Flood generations.

78 The charge of "argument from silence" may be made here, but it seems to me that in

Against this background, Philo stands out sharply. While he too treats Enosh as part of a chain of righteous ancestors, he devotes significant attention to the interpretation of the figure of Enosh. As we have repeatedly seen, however, Philo bases his interpretation on the Greek version of the text and not the Hebrew.[79] What catches his attention is Enosh's "hope," which has entered the LXX version most likely as a mistranslation of the Hebrew *hwḥl*.[80]

It is the Greek Bible which enables Philo to transform Enosh into a figure of major importance, and then into one who shrinks in the shadow of his Israelite successors. These two aspects, held together by Philo in paradoxical tension, will be split apart in Christian and Rabbinic interpretations.

As we enter the period of Christian and Rabbinic commentary, the two earliest texts of Gen 4:26b, the Hebrew and the Greek, are already accompanied by traditions of interpretation which seek to resolve difficulties contained within them: whose activity is described by Gen 4:26b, what exactly is that activity, what is its significance, and how does it relate to the larger scriptural context?

Three lines of interpretation have begun to emerge which will be significantly amplified in subsequent commentary: (a) Enosh as an important antediluvian or pre-Israelite link in the chain of righteous ancestors. (b) Enosh as representative of true, ideal man. (c) Enosh as someone whose piety is flawed and who lives in a period of cultural, moral, and spiritual degeneration.

---

this case the silence is quite eloquent. In all of our earliest works of Jewish biblical exegesis there is not, except for Philo, any *explicit* interpretation of Gen 4:26: Josephus is silent, nothing in *Jubilees* except the oblique interpretation that we have cited, nothing in Ps.-Philo's *LAB*, and nothing from Qumran, all of which otherwise show interest in the antediluvian righteous. Whether the LXX reflects an interpretation of Enosh or simply an awkward rendering of the ambiguous passive verb *hwḥl* is hard to say, but the former certainly cannot be assumed.

Regarding "chains" of righteous ancestors, a subject to which we will return in chapter 2, note 1 Macc 2:51–61: "Remember the deeds of our ancestors, which they did in their generations." Eleven biblical ancestors, beginning with Abraham and ending with Daniel, are given as examples of steadfast faith. The author of 1 Maccabees is *not* interested here in pre-Israelite righteous figures, and therefore, makes no mention of Enosh.

79 This does not rule out the possibility that Philo was at some level familiar with the Hebrew text, or with traditions deriving from it. It simply was not the Scripture that he was interpreting.

80 On Philo's reliance on Platonic thought for his preoccupation with Enosh's hope see above, nn. 54, 65.

Chapter Two
SAMARITAN AND MANDAEAN INTERPRETATIONS

A. Early Samaritan Traditions

The Samaritan Pentateuch reads: *'z hḥl lqr' bšm YHWH.*[1] This is identical to the MT except for the verb, which most likely represents the *hiph'il* form *hēḥēl*, given this version's proclivity to full use of *matres lectionis.*[2]

It would seem, then, that the Samaritan Pentateuch, like the LXX and *Jubilees*, renders Gen 4:26b in the active singular, but unlike them retains the word *'āz*. Its variant is less severe, but its meaning is less clear. Assuming a vocalization *hēḥēl*, it could mean either "then he [Enosh] began" or "then one began."[3] In Samaritan exegesis, as we will presently see, Gen 4:26b is always understood to speak of Enosh, suggesting that the Samaritan Pentateuch was read *hēḥēl*. While some have argued that this attests to a variant Hebrew *Vorlage*,[4] it could simply represent an understanding of "then was begun" (*hûḥal*) as "then he began (was the first)" (*hēḥēl*).

There are two versions of the *Samaritan Targum* of Gen 4:26b. One

[1] *Der Hebräische Pentateuch der Samaritaner* (ed. A. Von Gall; Giessen: A. Töpelmann, 1918) 7; as well as the new edition, *Pentateuco Hebreo-Samaritano, Genesis: Edición critica sobre la base de manuscritos inéditos* (ed. Luis-Fernando Giron Blanc; Madrid: Consejo Superior de Investigaciones Cientificas, 1976) 167. Neither shows variants for *hḥl*. Most scholars date the Samaritan version in the second/first century B.C.E. and assume a Palestinian provenance. See R. Pummer, "The Present State of Samaritan Studies I," *JSS* 22 (1977) 43–45; J.D. Purvis, "Samaritan Pentateuch," *IDBSup* 772–75.

[2] However, the Samaritan Pentateuch is not adverse to *yuqqaḥ* (*yqḥ*) in Gen 18:4, *wayyuggad* (*wygd*) in Gen 27:42, or *yuttan* (*ytn*) in Lev 11:38, where in each case it follows the MT. Thus, while *huḥal* (*hḥl*) cannot be ruled out, it would be difficult to explain. The modern Samaritan reading of the Pentateuch supports *hēḥēl*. See Z. Ben-Ḥayyim, *The Literary and Oral Tradition of Hebrew and Aramaic Amongst the Samaritans* (Hebrew), vol. 4 (Jerusalem: The Bialik Institute: 1977) 356, as well as 98.

[3] On the latter possibility, see above, chap. 1, n. 5, for the example of MT Isa 26:1 *yûšar haššîr* = IQIsa *yāšîr haššîr* ("The song will be sung" = "one will sing the song"). I have not been able to find a clear example of this phenomenon in the Samaritan Pentateuch. For an example of the Samaritan Pentateuch supplying a definite subject of a verb which in the MT has an indefinite subject, see Gen 16:14: MT: "Therefore the well was called (*qārā'*) Beer-lahai roi." Samaritan Pentateuch: "Therefore she [Hagar] called (*qār'â*) the well Beer-lahai-roi."

[4] See above, chap. 1, n. 3.

has *'dyn šry lmqry bšm YHWH* ("Then he began to call upon the name of the Lord").[5] The other has *ṭṭ' šr' lmzd'q bšm YHWH* ("Then he began [was the first] *to be called* by the name of the Lord").[6] The first simply renders the Samaritan Pentateuch in Aramaic. The second is more difficult to explain. The form *lmzd'q* is the *'ithpe'el* infinitive of *z'q*, which root, as in the first half of the verse, means "to call." Although the *'ithpe'el* form of this verb is not listed in Aramaic lexicons, its use elsewhere suggests a passive meaning, "was called."[7] A similar usage can be found in *Memar Meqar* 5.3 (ed. J. Macdonald) 1.124, where Moses is addressed: *hslk 'h mn 'zd'q 'lhym* ("O you who were called a god"), apparently a reference to Exod 4:16 and 7:1.[8] Thus, Enosh, like Moses, is said to have been privileged to bear a divine epithet. As we will see, Enosh and Moses are associated elsewhere in early Samaritan literature.

We will see that Christian exegetes also interpreted the verb "to call" passively, in reference either to Seth or to Enosh, based on the ambiguous form *epikaleisthai* in the LXX. It is not necessary, however, to assume any direct relationship between the *Samaritan Targum* and those Christian traditions. Rather, we should consider the possibility that the Samaritan translator understood the unvocalized *lqr'* to be the passive form *liqqārē'*. Although the normal *niph'al* form is *lĕhiqqārē'*, the *hē'* of the *niph'al* infinitive is elided following a preposition in several MT examples, e.g.,

[5] This version is given by A. Tal (*Hattargum haššomroni lattora*, vol. 1 [Tel Aviv: University of Tel Aviv, 1979/80] 14) from MS Bodleian Sam. C2. It also appears in *Memar Marqah* 2.6 (ed. Macdonald) 1.37.

[6] This version is given by A. Tal (*Hattargum haššomroni*, 15) from MS British Museum Or. 5036. I have found the same reading (with *ṭṭ'* instead of *ṭṭ'* [= Greek *tote*, "then"] and *šrh* instead *šr'*) in a microfilm copy of MS British Museum Or. 7562, considered by Tal ("The Samaritan Targum to the Pentateuch: Its Distinctive Characteristics and its Metamorphosis," *JSS* 21 [1976] 26–38) to be the earliest and most reliable version of the Targum. This version is also printed in *Das samaritanische Targum zum Pentateuch* (ed. A. Brüll; Frankfurt a. M.: W. Erras, 1875) 1.5; *Die Samaritanische Pentateuch-Version des Genesis* (ed. M. Heidenheim; Leipzig; O. Schulze, 1884) 5; *Pentateuchus Samaritanus* (ed. H. Petermann and C. Vollers; Berlin: W. Moeser, 1872–91) 8. The *Samaritan Targum* in its present form is believed by scholars to predate *Memar Marqah* (fourth century C.E.), but not by much. See Pummer, "The Present State of Samaritan Studies I," 47.

[7] We sorely need a lexicon of Samaritan Aramaic. J. H. Petermann's *Brevis Linguae Samaritanae* (Paris: H. Reuther, 1873) contains an inadequate glossary, which does not list the *'ithpe'el* of *z'q*. This form, however, does appear three times in *Hammeliṣ*, a tenth-century Samaritan glossary of biblical Hebrew words with their Arabic and Aramaic equivalents, as a translation of *qr'* in the *niph'al*. See Z. Ben-Ḥayyim, *The Literary and Oral Tradition of Hebrew and Aramaic Amongst the Samaritans* (Hebrew), vol. 2 (Jerusalem: The Bialik Institute, 1957) 579.8,17; 589.303. Thus, the *Samaritan Targum* of Gen 48:6 translates MT *yiqqārĕ'û* ("they shall be called") with *yzd'qwn*. On the root *z'q* meaning "to call," see Tal, "The Samaritan Targum to the Pentateuch," 36.

[8] Similarly, in *The Samaritan Liturgy* (ed. A. E. Cowley; 2 vols.; Oxford: Clarendon, 1909) 1.54.28 we find *wmwšh d'zd'q 'lhym* ("and Moses who was called Elohim").

bikkāšĕlô (Prov 24:17), *lērā'ôt* (Isa 1:12, though perhaps originally *lir'ôt*).[9] Similarly, in *Sifre Deut* 49 (ed. L. Finkelstein) 114 the biblical phrase *kōl 'ăšer yiqrā' bĕšem YHWH* (Joel 3:5, "Everyone who invokes the name of the Lord") is interpreted passively (*yiqqārē'*): "But how is it possible for a person to be called by the name of the Lord? Rather, (as) the Lord is called (*niqrā'*) 'compassionate' (Exod 34:6), you also should be compassionate."[10]

Thus, it is likely that a Samaritan Aramaic translator interpreted the Hebrew verb *lqr'* passively, as if it read *liqqārē'*. There certainly are no grounds for assuming that the Samaritan Hebrew version from which he worked was any different from the one we know. Except for this one change the second version of the *Samaritan Targum* mirrors the Samaritan Pentateuch, understanding Gen 4:26b to refer to Enosh. What might have been the translator's motivation for such a change? Since the Hebrew text which he used should not have caused him any difficulty, we may assume that he had some exegetical or homiletical motivation. We will have to wait until we have examined other Samaritan traditions which relate to Gen 4:26 and Enosh before we can suggest an answer.

Our greatest source of early Samaritan traditions regarding Enosh and Gen 4:26b is *Memar Marqah*, which after the *Samaritan Targum* is the most important early work of Samaritan biblical exegesis.[11] Enosh is mentioned nine times in *Memar Marqah*. In seven of these he appears as part of a list or chain (*šlšlt*) of righteous ancestors.[12] In the remaining two instances he is mentioned in conjunction with Moses.[13]

9 GKC 51L, p. 139.

10 Cf. *p. Ber.* 9.1 (13b, top); *YhM* ad Joel 3:5 (ed. A. Greenup) 24–25; *b. B. Bat.* 75b. See also Saul Lieberman, *Hellenism in Jewish Palestine* (New York: Jewish Theological Seminary of America, 1962) 6–7 n. 21. I have previously (chap. 1, n. 16) noted LXX Isa 41:25 and Symmachus ad Ps 80:19, which translate active forms of the verb *qr'* passively in Greek. Cf. chap. 3, n. 66.

11 All citations (both Aramaic and English, except where noted) are from *Memar Marqah: The Teaching of Marqah* (ed. and trans. J. Macdonald; 2 vols.; Berlin: Alfred Töpelmann, 1963). For a review of this edition see Z. Ben-Ḥayyim in *BO* 23 (1966) 185–91. I have also consulted the text, translation, and notes of M. Heidenheim in *Der Commentar Marqah's des Samaritaners*, vol. 3 of *Bibliotheca Samaritana: Texte aus Samaria und Studien zum Samaritanismus* (ed. Heidenheim; 3 vols. in 1; Leipzig, 1884–1896; repr. Amsterdam: Philo Press, 1971). *Memar Marqah* is generally considered to date from the fourth century C.E.

12 *Memar Marqah* 1.2, 9; 2.8, 10; 3.2; 4.9; 6.2. These seven passages are treated individually and more fully in S. D. Fraade, "Enosh and His Generation: Scriptural Translation and Interpretation in Late Antiquity" (Ph.D. diss., University of Pennsylvania, 1980) 73–83. On such chains of righteous ancestors, see J. Macdonald, *The Theology of the Samaritans* (London: SCM Press, 1964) 272, 317, 326, 329, 344; T. H. Gaster, "Samaritans," in *IDB* 4.174; J. Bowman, "The Exegesis of the Pentateuch Among the Samaritans and Among the Rabbis," in *Oudtestamentische Studiën* 8 (ed. P. A. H. DeBoer; Leiden: E. J. Brill, 1950) 225, 238–41.

13 *Memar Marqah* 2.6, 12, to be discussed below.

Let us first consider the seven passages in *Memar Marqah* in which Enosh appears as part of a chain of righteous ancestors. In all but one of these Enosh's merit derives from his having "called on the name of the Lord."[14] In fact, Enosh is sometimes credited simply with having called (the object of his calling being understood), and is referred to as "Enosh the caller."[15] But in listing Enosh among the early righteous Marqah says other things about him as well. Enosh is said to be both the founder of mankind, since his name (meaning "man") becomes that of all men, and the progenitor of a particular line of *righteous* descendants. Marqah, like Philo, finds significance in Enosh's name and in Scripture's juxtaposition of Gen 4:26b and 5:1.[16] The number of individuals in a particular righteous chain is

[14] Only *Memar Marqah* 1.2 (ed. Macdonald) 1.6 fails to mention Enosh's deed. In that passage, God, speaking from the burning bush, tells Moses of righteous ancestors whom He delivered from harm and blessed. Besides Enosh are listed Adam, Noah, Abraham, Isaac, Jacob, and Joseph. Of Enosh we find: "I delivered (*plṭt*) Enosh and made him an object of commemoration (*wʿbdh lh dkrn*) which will never be forgotten as long as the world lasts." The expression *ʿbdh lh dkrn* may refer to Enosh's name, which is memorialized in mankind. For *zkr/dkr* as a synonym for "name" see Exod 3:15. On the possibility that this text originally referred not to Enosh but to Enoch (whose names are easily and frequently confused), see S. D. Fraade, "Enosh and His Generation," 74–75.

[15] *Memar Marqah* 1.9; 2.8; 3.2 (ed. Macdonald) 1.21, 40, 60. In a *piyyuṭ* (liturgical poem) attributed to Amran Darah (fourth century C.E.) we find a list of "the righteous of the world," each with an appropriate epithet: "Adam the first, and Seth the replacement [for Abel], and Enosh the proclaimer (*wʾnwš qrʾh*), and Enoch the one who prays, and Noah the righteous, . . . and Moses the prophet [tenth in the list], . . . " The list, containing sixteen in all, concludes with Caleb "the inheritor." Although other biblical figures are credited by Scripture with having "called on the name of the Lord," only Enosh, having been the first, is credited in Samaritan literature with the epithet "*the* proclaimer." We will recall that Philo refers to Enosh alone as "the hoper." See Z. Ben-Ḥayyim, *The Literary and Oral Tradition*, vol. 3, pt. 2, p. 61.22; and A. E. Cowley, ed., *The Samaritan Liturgy* (2 vols.; Oxford: Clarendon, 1909) 1.42. On Amran Darah, see Ben-Ḥayyim, 12–15.

[16] *Memar Marqah* 1.2; 1.9; 4.9; 6.2 (ed. Macdonald) 1.6, 21, 102, 132. Note especially *Memar Marqah* 1.9 (ed. Macdonald) 1.21. Here Marqah attributes special significance to the first ten days of the first lunar month (Nisan), as it is on the tenth of that month that the Israelites are commanded to acquire the paschal lamb for slaughtering on the fourteenth (Exod 12:3). Each of the first nine days is associated with a particular pre-Mosaic righteous figure, the tenth with Moses. Thus, the first day is for "the creation of Adam and the praise which he rendered," and the second is for the "performance (sacrifice) of Abel." The third day is "for the proclamation of Enosh (*lmqrth dʾnwš*), in whom the generation of man was made known (*dbh ʾtydʿt twldt ʾadm*)." The phrase *twldt ʾdm* (*tôlĕdat ʾādām*, singular, unlike *tôlĕdōt adam*, plural, of the MT) is a clear allusion to Gen 5:1. Thus, with Enosh and his proclamation mankind begins, i.e., is distinguished from the other creatures. Like Philo and Rabbinic traditions that I will examine, Marqah exegetically links Gen 4:26b and 5:1. Perhaps Marqah, like Philo, wishes to connect Enosh's name in Gen 4:26b with *ʾādām* of 5:1, both meaning "man." Heidenheim's text (p. 21) reads *bh ʾtʿbd*, which he translates (p. 31), "mit ihm begann die Toldoth Adam's." Another possibility is that Marqah wishes to read Gen 5:1 not as *zeh seper* ("this is the book"), but as *zeh sippēr* ("this one [Enosh] recounted [made known]"). If so, the passage should be translated, "Enosh, *by* whom the generation of man was made known." Such an understanding of Gen 5:1 would eliminate the apparent

usually limited to a "whole" number: 7, 10, 12, 13.[17] The lists often conclude with Moses, or with Phinehas, or with Joshua and Caleb. Such chains of righteous ancestors are always selective and not simply genealogically inclusive. While Enosh is regularly included in Marqah's lists, other biblical figures such as Seth, Methuselah, Shem, and Melchizedek, often appearing as righteous patriarchs in other traditions, are noticeably absent. In light of these omissions, Enosh's inclusion is all the more noteworthy. Significantly, the early righteous figures in these chains sometimes presage later, more central events or personalities in Israelite sacred history. In particular they prepare the way for Moses, the greatest saint of all. Not only is Enosh, through his name, memorialized in all mankind, but his specific act, that of proclaiming God's name, is said to foreshadow future events.[18]

We turn, finally, to two passages in *Memar Marqah* in which Enosh is mentioned in his own right, rather than as part of a chain of righteous ancestors. In both Enosh stands in important relation to Moses.

Memar Marqah 2.6 (ed. Macdonald) 1.37; 2.56. Here we find the following introduction to the Song of Moses: נביות משה הך הוא משרי למקרי מקרא אנוש דרבה בה בקשטה מטע שרי למקרי בשם יהוה ("Observe the prophetic status of Moses, how he began to proclaim in the words of Enosh, by which he magnified the True One;[19] at that time men began

disjunction between it and Gen 4:26b. Similarly, in *Memar Marqah* 6.2 (ed. Macdonald) 1.132 Enosh is rewarded for calling on God's name by being made *ryš lkl zrʿ ʾdm* ("the head of the whole human race"). Macdonald incorrectly, it seems to me, translates *ryš* as "root." For *ryš* (= *rʾš*) as head, chief, beginning, see Petermann, 74; Ben-Ḥayyim, 2.30.2.

[17] On Marqah's use of such "whole" numbers, especially the number ten in connection with Moses, see S. Lowy, *The Principles of Samaritan Bible Exegesis* (Leiden: E. J. Brill, 1977) 198–99.

[18] In *Memar Marqah* 1.9 (discussed in the previous note) it is clear that the righteous patriarchs who precede Moses also prepare for him. Whereas God reveals Himself to them through an angel, to Moses he reveals Himself directly. Cf. *ARNB* 1 (ed. Schechter) 2. In *Memar Marqah* 2.10 (ed. Macdonald) 1.47 eight of Moses' predecessors, including Enosh, are associated with Mt. Gerizim, the Samaritan holy mountain. Enosh is said to have called upon the name of the Lord on Mt. Gerizim; his worship prefigures that of the Samaritan cult. Most significantly, in *Memar Marqah* 2.8 (ed. Macdonald) 1.40 we are told that the deeds and attributes of Israel's righteous ancestors were manifested anew for the Israelites at the shore of the Sea of Reeds. Seven are thus invoked: Adam, Enosh, Enoch, Abraham, Isaac, Jacob, and Joseph. Of Enosh we are told, "The proclamation of Enosh was repeated (*mtḥddh*, well rehearsed, sharpened) and proclaimed in their mouths." For such a use of the verb *ḥdd* see *Sifre Deut* 34 (ed. Finkelstein) 60, and *b. Qidd.* 30a. What had once been the proclamation of a single person is now the song of the whole people. In *Memar Marqah* 2.6, to be discussed presently, Enosh's proclamation is again associated with Moses' song.

[19] The phrase *drbh bh bqšṭh* is problematic. Macdonald seems to have translated incorrectly. He suggests that Enosh in proclaiming God's name magnified Him (the True One). The Aramaic, however, does not support such a rendering. The verb *rbh* in its present form (assumably *qal*) cannot be causative (the *paʿel* form being *rby*). In the present form it is regularly attested in all dialects of Aramaic as being *intransitive* in meaning: he grew up or became great. See J. H. Petermann, *Brevis Linguae Samaritanae*, glossary, 73, s.v.

to call upon the name of the Lord"). The allusion is to the fact that with regard to both Enosh's proclamation and Moses' song (Exod 15:1) the *Samaritan Targum* uses the word *ṭṭ*ʿ (= Greek *tote*; MT: *ʾāz*, "then"). Next follows a difficult passage which interprets the significance of the word *ṭṭ*ʿ with which, according to Samaritan tradition, Moses began his song.[20] The *ṭṭ*ʿ of Enosh's proclamation, however, does *not* receive particular attention, its significance being simply that it foreshadows Moses' Song at the Sea. The *ṭṭ*ʿ of Gen 4:26b points to that of Exod 15:1. Moses' Song fulfills what was begun by Enosh, while Enosh foreshadows Moses.[21]

Memar Marqah 2.12 (ed. Macdonald) 1.50; 2.81.[22] This last example is perhaps the most interesting, but also the most perplexing. Marqah discusses the revelation of the divine name YHWH ("I am who I am") to Moses:

אהיה אשר אהיה יתה חזיתך מגן יהי לך לא תדחל מן קרב אנכי מגן לך
אמרת לאברהם לא תדחל מן כלום זה שמי לעלם לך נביי חכמת בדיל דאת
אחיד כפוריה ושמי יהוה לא חכמת לון שליח טב קדמיך מגלי אצלחותה

---

rbh: "magnus fuit. auctus est, crevit." I suggest that the word *qšṭh* here refers not to God, but has the meaning "truth" (Petermann, ibid., p. 73, s.v. *qšṭ*: "*qšṭh* veritas"). Thus, *bh bqšṭh* would mean "truly," or "in truth," the *bh* being anticipatory. For the word *bqšṭ*ʾ meaning "truly" in Palestinian Aramaic, see 1QapGen 2:5 and Joseph Fitzmyer's note ad loc. in *The Genesis Apocryphon of Qumran Cave I: A Commentary* (Rome: Pontifical Biblical Institute, 1966) 76. Note as well *Tg. Neof.*, *Tg. Ps.-J.*, and *Frg. Tg.* of Gen 5:24: *wplḥ hnwk bqwšt*ʾ *qdm yy* ("and Enoch worshipped the Lord in truth"). The whole phrase would mean: "the proclamation of Enosh, who was truly great." Other less likely possibilities would be: "by which he became truly great," referring either to Moses or to Enosh, and "who grew up in the Lord," or "who grew up in truth." See Heidenheim (p. 53), who translates, "die Verkündigung Enosch's, der in der Warheit gross war."

20 The *ṭet* of *ṭṭ*ʿ is interpreted in light of the verb *nṭ*ʿ as used in Gen 2:8 and 21:33 (*wayyiṭṭa*ʿ), in both places referring to the planting of a garden or grove. Thus, of Moses we are told: "He composed his Song a garden of praises." After interpreting *ṭṭ*ʿ of the targum, Marqah turns to *ʾāz* of the Samaritan Pentateuch (and MT). This word, we are told, includes an allusion both to Creation (*ʾaleph*) and to Sabbath (*zayin*): "Beginning was created and Sabbath brought into being."

21 Rabbinic sources similarly associated the *ʾāz* of Gen 4:26 with that of Exod 15:1. See *Exod Rab.* 23.4; *Tanh. Bešallaḥ* 12 (ed. Buber) 60. J. Bowman ("The Exegesis of the Pentateuch Among the Samaritans and Among the Rabbis," 256 n. 23) is wrong in stating: "Jewish targum and midrash naturally draw no attention to the initial wording of Gen 4:26 in connection with Exod 15:1." Heidenheim (p. 172 n. 219), citing *Exod Rab.* 23, recognizes the parallel interpretation.

We should note that Marqah frequently draws parallels between Moses and earlier biblical characters. In 2.9 (ed. Macdonald) 1.42 Marqah draws an analogy between the Flood and the crossing of the Red Sea. "This is my God . . . the God of my father" (Exod 15:2) is interpreted: "The God of my father Noah, whom He delivered from the Flood, and who saved us from the waters of the Red Sea." Noah and the Flood foreshadow Moses and the Sea.

22 The translation that follows differs from Macdonald's, which I find misleading at points, as specified in the following notes. Heidenheim's translation (p. 81) is no better.

אז החל לקרא בשם יהוה רבה כתבת לאנוש מגד כתוב ושמי יהוה לא חכמת
לון ספר דאיטבו אתחדד לך וקרא תמן אברהם בשם יהוה . . .

> "I am who I am" (Exod 3:14) I have revealed to you. Let it be a shield to you. Do not be afraid of battle. I am a shield to you (cf. Gen 15:1). I said to Abraham, "Fear not (ibid.) anything." "This is my name forever" (Exod 3:15). To you, my prophet, I have revealed it so you may apprehend the unbelievers. "My name, the Lord (YHWH), I did not make known to them" (Exod 6:3, targum).[23] A good apostle has preceded (or, is before) you who makes known prosperity: "Then he began to call on the great name of the Lord" (Gen 4:26). For Enosh I have inscribed good.[24] It is written, "My name, the Lord, I did not make known to them." A record of goodness was repeated for you.[25] "Abraham there called on the name of the Lord" (Gen 13:4).[26]

In this passage Abraham and Enosh are given as examples of biblical figures who knew and used God's name before it was revealed to Moses. It is implied that God's name can be a shield or protection against unbelievers just as it was for Abraham.[27] Both Enosh and Abraham are

[23] There are two versions of the *Samaritan Targum* of Exod 6:3. The one given in *Memar Marqah* is found in MS Schechem 3 (A. Tal, *Hattargum haššomroni lattora*, 241). The version usually appearing in printed editions (e.g., A. Brüll, ed., *Das samaritanische Targum*, 68) and found in MS British Museum Or. 7562 (A. Tal, *Hattargum*, 240) is *wšmy YHWH l' 't'kmt* (= *'tḥkmt*) *lwn* ("By my name, the Lord, I did not make myself known to them"). See also *Hammeliṣ* (in Ben-Ḥayyim, *The Literary and Oral Tradition*, 2.244.22). The second version, using the passive *'ithpa'al* form, reflects the Hebrew *niph'al* form *nôda'tî* (MT and Samaritan Pentateuch): "I was made known." Similarly, *Tg. Ps.-J.* and a Geniza Fragment (Cambridge B8, fol. 9a) have *'ytyd't*. The Aramaic form in *Memar Marqah* is most likely the *pa'el*, meaning "I made known." Cf. *Tg. Onqelos*: *hôda'ît*; *Tg. Neofiti*: *'wd'yt*; *Peshiṭta*: *ḥwyt*; LXX *edēlōsa*; and Vg.: *indicavi*; all being active. Thus, the versions, like the *Samaritan Targum*(s), are divided as to the sense of *nôda'tî*. On the meaning of Exod 6:3 and its relation to understandings of Gen 4:26b, see below, chap. 5, nn. 67, 68.

[24] Macdonald translates, "Concerning Enosh I have written down information." Note Marqah's insertion of "great" (*rbh*) in his citation of Gen 4:26b. Heidenheim (p. 81) connects this word with what follows: "Eine Auszeichnung wird damit dem Enosch zugeschrieben."

[25] Macdonald translates, "A record of prosperity has been created for you." On the verb *ḥdd* meaning to sharpen, rehearse, etc., see *Memar Marqah* 2.8 (ed. Macdonald) 1.40; above, note 18. In 2.8 Enosh's proclamation was repeated by the Israelites at the Sea. In 2.12 it is repeated, it would appear, by Abraham. Heidenheim (p. 81, and p. 182 n. 363) completely reworks this sentence: "der Glanz seiner Herrlichkeit erglänzte dir."

[26] Macdonald and Heidenheim misidentified the biblical citation, identifying it as Gen 12:8. Marqah is more likely citing the *Samaritan Targum* of Gen 13:4 (ed. Tal, 38), the Hebrew of which reads (MT and Samaritan Pentateuch): *wayyiqrā' šām 'abrām bĕšēm YHWH*.

[27] If, as we have indicated in the previous note, Marqah's citation of Abraham's "calling on the name of the Lord," is from Gen 13:4 and not 12:8, we should note that the preceding verses (12:10–20) tell of Abraham's escape from potential danger at the hands of the Egyptians. The drama of the story and Abraham's subsequent worship is amplified in the

rewarded for their invoking of God's name in worship. Both foreshadow Moses' proclaiming of God's name.

What is indeed strange in this passage is Marqah's use of Exod 6:3 in connection first with Enosh and then with Abraham. This biblical phrase is usually understood to mean that God revealed his name YHWH for the first time to Moses, having been known to the patriarchs, Moses' predecessors, as El Shaddai.[28] This seems the opposite of what Marqah is asserting: that Enosh and Abraham, in proclaiming the name YHWH, foreshadow the revelation to Moses. There appear two possible ways to resolve this difficulty.

(1) The Samaritan tradition, like (as we shall see below) Rabbinic traditions, never denies that God was known to the patriarchs as YHWH. To them Exod 6:3 signifies not the first knowledge of God's name, but rather the first revelation by God *Himself* of his name along with its hidden meaning. The key aspect of Exod 6:3 is not God's revealing of his name, but his revealing of Himself. Thus both the MT and the Samaritan Pentateuch have the *passive* (not causative) form *nwdʿty*. In light of this, we may understand Marqah to say: They (Enosh and Abraham) knew my name and proclaimed it, preparing the way for you (Moses) to whom I now make myself known by personally disclosing my name.[29]

(2) The second possibility is that Marqah in removing Exod 6:3 from its scriptural context has the word "to them" refer not to the patriarchs but to its new antecedent: "unbelievers" (*kpwryh*). God's name as a shield and source of strength was entrusted to Enosh, Abraham, and Moses, but not to the unbelievers of their respective ages.[30] Since, as we know, the divine name YHWH and its various permutations were used by all sorts of groups (Jewish as well as non-Jewish) as a magical prophylactic, we may have here a polemical response: the divine name yields its protective power only to those to whom it has been directly entrusted.

Despite the above suggestions, this passage remains somewhat of an

---

Genesis Apocryphon. In 1QapGen 21:3–4 after a paraphrase of Gen 13:4 we find: "I [Abraham] gave thanks there before God for all the flocks and the good things which he had given me; because he had done good to me; because he had brought me back to this land in safety." Abraham's worship in Gen 13:4 is interpreted as a thanksgiving prayer for God's protection while in Egypt.

28 This understanding of the biblical passage will be questioned below, chap. 5, n. 68.

29 Bowman ("The Exegesis of the Pentateuch," 241) states: "Marqah here is at pains to have God say that Gen 4:26 and Exod 6:3 do not really clash. Moses was the first to whom God revealed that name directly, even Abraham when God spoke to him had not heard God use the name." That Marqah is "at pains" in his interpretation is not so evident. What appears to us as a difficult interpretation may have been quite natural for the ancient exegete.

30 Heidenheim (p. 81) associates the word "to them" with the "unbelievers," but incorrectly understands the Aramaic *ḥkmt* as the *second* person perfect: "damit den Abtrünnigen gegenüber du Zeugniss [reading *hʿyd*] ablegen sollst. Aber meinen Namen Jhvh sollst du ihnen nicht kund thun."

enigma. For our purposes, however, the following is clear: Enosh is cited here as an ancestor who is praised and rewarded for having proclaimed God's name in worship. Enosh, like Moses, had a special relationship with the divine name. Both Enosh and Moses represent new stages in human familiarity with God's name. Enosh's significance, once again, lies in the way he points to Moses' glory, which is, after all, the focus of Marqah's work.

We may now reconsider the version of the *Samaritan Targum* which states that Enosh was the first "to be called by the name of the Lord."[31] We have noted that *Memar Marqah* and the Samaritan liturgy state: "Moses was called Elohim."[32] Both Moses and Enosh are distinguished by a special relationship to God: they are both bearers of His name. They "bear" His name in two ways. (a) They receive, proclaim, and/or transmit it. (b) They are called by it, as a sign of their righteous characters and special relationships to God.[33]

Let us summarize the early Samaritan traditions that we have examined. Enosh appears frequently as one of the earliest links in the Samaritan chain of ancestors, whose righteous deeds and attributes prepare for and foreshadow those of Moses. His merit lies in the fact that he is the one who proclaims God's name, a clear allusion to Gen 4:26. He is sometimes seen as the head of later generations of mankind, perhaps an allusion to his name and/or to the phrasing of Gen 5:1. As we have seen, Enosh is brought into particular association with Moses, his proclamation being compared with Moses' song, and his familiarity with God's name foreshadowing that of Moses. In relation to both the chain of ancestors and Moses, however, Enosh's significance is secondary. He simply provides part of the backdrop to the later unfolding of Samaritan sacred history.

As a postscript to this section, I should note that in later Samaritan traditions Enosh may have become an angelic figure. One of the four ruling angels, according to the Samaritans, has the name Anusa. We know little about these angels other than that they are said to have attended to the ark of the baby Moses. J. Montgomery identifies the angel Anusa with Enosh, while J. E. H. Thompson derives the name from the Egyptian charioteers' cry of fear (Exod 14:23). Macdonald cites

31 Above, n. 6.

32 Above, n. 8.

33 See our earlier discussion of LXX Isa 41:25 (see above, chap. 1, n. 16), where we noted that those who worship God are considered bearers of His name. We will encounter similar interpretations from Christian exegetes. We note again the biblical phrase *niqrāʾ šēm YHWH ʿal*, i.e., God's name is "recalled in" or "proclaimed over" those who worship Him (*NJV* ad Gen 48:16; Deut 28:10; cf. Isa 63:19). A similar phenomenon is attested in Rabbinic tradition where the phrase *ʾĕlōhîm ʾattem* (Ps 82:6) is interpreted to refer to Israel, who when they stood at Sinai were called "gods." See below, chap. 3, n. 82.

both views, but does not seem to indicate a preference.[34] The name of this angel appears in the Samaritan Day of Atonement liturgy as *'nwšh*.[35] I have been unable to find any further information about this angelic figure. Its occurrence is of interest in light of the Mandaean angelic figure Anush (Uthra), which we will now briefly consider.

B. Mandaean Traditions

In Mandaean texts we find a prominent mythical figure named Anush, or Anush Uthra, supposed by most scholars to take his name from the biblical Enosh. Because of the late dates of these Mandaean texts (in their present forms no earlier than the seventh century C.E.), and the uncertain relation of their traditions to the Hebrew Bible and to biblical exegesis, we will here simply summarize the Mandaean traditions about Anush.[36]

[34] J. A. Montgomery, *The Samaritans: The Earliest Jewish Sect, Their History, Theology and Literature* (Philadelphia: John C. Winston, 1907) 219; J. E. H. Thompson, *The Samaritans: Their Testimony to the Religion of Israel* (Edinburgh: Oliver and Boyd, 1919) 189; John Macdonald, *The Theology of the Samaritans*, 399.

[35] See A. E. Cowley, ed., *The Samaritan Liturgy*, 2.626, where in an acrostic hymn attributed to Abraham ben Jacob (eighteenth century) Anusa is said to descend from heaven to earth. Also in M. Heidenheim, ed., *Bibliotheca Samaritana*, 2.29. Other biblical names appear in Samaritan traditions with the addition of a final *hē'*. See for instance *nmrdh* for Nimrod in *Memar Marqah* 2.4 (ed. Macdonald) 1.6.

[36] For a more complete discussion of the Mandaean traditions concerning Anush, see S. D. Fraade, "Enosh and His Generation," 94–114. On the current state of Mandaean studies, see E. M. Yamauchi, "The Present State of Mandaean Studies," *JNES* 25 (1966) 88–96. See also the comments of W. Meeks in *The Prophet-King: Moses Traditions and the Johannine Christology* (NovTSup 14; Leiden: E. J. Brill, 1967) 258–63. Standard works on Mandaean religion, mythology, and history are: K. Rudolph, *Die Mandäer* (2 vols.; Göttingen: Vandenhoeck & Ruprecht, 1960–61); E. S. Drower, *The Secret Adam: A Study of Naṣoraean Gnosis* (Oxford: Clarendon, 1960); E. S. Drower, *The Mandaeans of Iraq and Iran: Their Cults, Customs, Legends, and Folklore* (Oxford: Clarendon, 1937); S. A. Pallis, *Mandaean Studies* (trans. E. H. Pallis; London: Oxford University, 1926); W. Brandt, *Die mandäische Religion: ihre Entwicklung und geschichtliche Bedeutung* (Leipzig: J. C. Hinrichs, 1889).

It is generally agreed that the Mandaean sect, or at least its precursor, had its origins on Palestinian soil, perhaps as early as the first century C.E. To what extent this early group was Jewish or influenced by Jewish elements in its environment, however, is unclear. At some point, the sect appears to have emigrated to Mesopotamia, where its religious life and beliefs took the forms in which we know them. In Mesopotamia, Syrian Christian, Iranian, and Babylonian elements were absorbed into whatever foundations were brought from Palestine. Thus, the Mandaean figure of Anush Uthra, like the Mandaean mythology in general, has incorporated many disparate elements over a long period of time. Since the Anush traditions are not entirely consistent, it would be a serious oversimplification to give the impression that the Mandaean Anush has a uniform identity.

While it would seem that some biblical figures and events are alluded to in Mandaean sources, there is no indication that they derive from Mandaean interpretation of the Bible. Such allusions may have their roots in some "proto-Mandaean" (perhaps Jewish) stage in the development of Mandaean tradition, or they may have been later

The figure Anush (or Anosh)[37] is often called Anush Uthra (Anush the Beneficent) and is one of three such Uthras, the other two being the Hibil and Shitil.[38] The three often appear as a triad, in the order Hibil, Shitil, Anush. Most scholars agree that these three derive their names from the biblical figures Abel, Seth, and Enosh. In three passages in the *Right Ginza* we find: "the great Anush (*anus rba*), the son of the great Shitil, the son of the great Adam, the son of the great King of Light."[39] This clearly echoes the biblical genealogy. Yet elsewhere in the same work we find: "Hibil [the son of Adam] begat a son, whose name was Shitil, and Shitil begat a son whose name was Anush."[40] Here the triad Hibil, Shitil, and Anush has been taken to be a genealogical progression, with Hibil replacing Adam as Seth's father, rather than his brother as in Genesis. In still other passages, Hibil, Shitil, and Anush appear as brothers; the three sons of Adakas (also known as Adam Qadmaia or Adam Kasia, the metaphysical primal man), or of Adam Pagria (human

---

absorbed along with other influences from Jewish, Christian, or Muslim groups who did interpret the Bible and with whom the Mandaeans came into contact. Although Moslem writers refer to the Mandaeans (calling them Sabaeans [*as-ṣabia*], or Baptists) along with Jews and Christians as a "people of the Book," there is little indication that biblical exegesis played a major role in Mandaean accounts of their history, religious beliefs, or practices. Therefore, while the Mandaean figure Anush may be associated with the biblical Enosh, he cannot be said to be an interpretation of him. Cf. Yamauchi, 89; Pallis, 127–33. Since the Mandaean sources never cite or even allude to Gen 4:26, the Anush traditions, while of interest to us, are of secondary significance in our study of the exegesis of this verse in antiquity.

37 *'nws*, but in some passages *'nws*. We follow Lady Drower's system of vocalization, as employed in *A Mandaic Dictionary* (ed. E. S. Drower and R. Macuch; Oxford: Clarendon, 1963). Some earlier treatments confuse the Mandaean Anush with the biblical Enoch.

38 The following numbers indicate the frequency with which Anush's name is mentioned in each of the most important Mandaean sources: *Ginza*, 49; *Book of John*, 25; *Qulasta* (Prayer Book), 19; *Haran Gawaita*, 15. Surprisingly, neither Anush nor the other Uthras are mentioned in the Mandaic incantation inscriptions which have been published. See Edwin M. Yamauchi, *Mandaic Incantation Texts* (New Haven: American Oriental Society, 1967) 37–38.

39 The *Right Ginza*, thought to have been compiled in the seventh or early eighth century, is probably the earliest Mandaean work. Citations are from the German translation of Mark Lidzbarski, *Ginzā: der Schatz oder das grosse Buch der Mandäer* (Göttingen: Vandenhoeck & Ruprecht, 1925). We use the abbreviations *GR* (*Right Ginza*) and *GL* (*Left Ginza*): *GR* 11, p. 251.12; *GR* 12:1, p. 269.9, p. 270.8. The edition of H. Petermann (*Thesaurus Liber Magnus vulgo "Liber Adami" appellatus, opus Mandaeorum summi ponderis* [2 vols.; Leipzig: Weigil, 1867]) was not available to me. The eleventh book of the *Right Ginza* is called *raza usidra d-anuš rba* ("The Mystery and the Book of the Great Anush"), since Anush is the speaker, revealing the mysteries of the world which he has learned from Manda-d-Haiye. In chapter 1 I pointed out a Jewish tradition attributing secret "writings" to Enosh and mentioned a similar reference in a later Christian source. See above, chap. 1, nn. 44, 45.

40 *GR* 10, p. 243.30.

Adam).[41] There certainly seems to be no single view of Anush's relationship to the others. The three Uthras take their names from the Bible, and all appear as primal figures, but otherwise they bear no relation to the biblical antediluvians.

Anush, like Hibil and Shitil, is often called *'utra*, a term that means "wealth" and is used by the Mandaeans to refer to heavenly spirits, spirits of life and light. These Uthras are semidivine beings with functions very similar to those of angels. They serve as representatives and helpers (*adiauria*) of Manda-d-Haiye ("knowledge of life"), the supreme spirit, as well as guardians (*naṭria*) and instructors of the Mandaeans. These savior spirits assist the soul, a captive in the physical world, in its journey through life and after death to reunion with the "world of light" from which it originated. The Uthras are generally said to have come into being before the physical world was created, but they are also portrayed as having been transformed from physical into ethereal beings.[42] The three Uthras Hibil, Shitil, and Anush come to man's assistance at various stages in life, especially in connection with such religious experiences as baptism and prayer. Hibil is assigned to the redemption of the imprisoned souls of the underworld, perhaps an interpretation of his name, which in Mandaic means "destructive death."[43] Shitil is the guardian of the human soul, being a spiritual guide, but he is the least frequently mentioned of the three.[44] Anush is the patron saint of the Mandaeans, the promoter of their secret wisdom (*naṣiruta*). He is said to represent the divine soul within man.[45]

In many passages the three Uthras are mentioned together as a triad, without any distinction made between them. This is especially obvious in the liturgy where they are frequently invoked for assistance or blessings: "Through the strength of Hibil, Sitil, and Anuš, secure seal and guard these souls who go down to the Jordan and will be baptized."[46]

41 Drower, *The Secret Adam*, 35–38.

42 See *A Mandaic Dictionary*, s.v. *'utra*, 347; M. Lidzbarski, "Uthra and Malakha," *Orientalische Studien, Theodor Nöldeke zum siebzigsten Geburtstag gewidmet* (Giessen: A. Töpelmann, 1906) 1.537–47; Drower, *The Secret Adam*, 56–65.

43 *A Mandaic Dictionary*, 129.

44 We will encounter Christian exegetes who also understand Seth to represent man's spiritual aspect. There are apparent plays in the Mandaean sources on Shitil's name as meaning "plant" or "transplant" (*štl*). We will note Christian sources which interpret his name to mean "resurrection." Shitil is clearly the least important of the Uthras, usually appearing only as part of the triad. On Shitil, see Drower, *The Secret Adam*, 36–37.

45 Drower, *The Secret Adam*, 34–38.

46 E. S. Drower, trans., *The Canonical Prayerbook of the Mandaeans* (Leiden: E. J. Brill, 1959) 10. I will refer to the Prayerbook as *Qulasta*. "Jordan" need not necessarily refer to the Jordan River, since in Mandaic it comes to mean "river" in general. See *A Mandaic Dictionary*, s.v. *iardna*, 187. The *Qulasta* is generally regarded as one of our oldest Mandaean sources. For other liturgical references to the triad Hibil, Shitil, and

Of the three figures, Anush seems to emerge as the most significant Uthra. He is often mentioned apart from the triad; that is, he has an important identity independent of the others. Anush is referred to as *anuš 'utra sagia*: the great Anush Uthra, or the great Uthra Anush.[47] He is also called *anuš 'utra šliḥa*: Anush Uthra the Apostle.[48] We also find "king (*malka*) Anush Uthra."[49] Anush is frequently mentioned for his healing powers.[50] He appears to have a particular function as the one who facilitates and delivers prayers: "Anuš lifteth up (*ramia*) my hymns."[51] While Anush's association with prayer may derive ultimately from Gen 4:26b, it is more likely that Anush is simply associated with prayer as the chief guardian of Naṣorean faith, prayer being considered one of the most important means of spiritual perfection and enlightenment.

It appears that Anush's significance as the chief Uthra may derive in part from his name, which suggests that he is the personification of the human race.[52] This would be similar to what we witnessed in Philo and *Memar Marqah*. For instance, in the liturgy we find: "(Praised are) our father Hibil, Sitil, and Anuš the name and head of the whole race."[53] Since, as we have seen (nn. 43, 44), Hibil's and Shitil's names may have been interpreted, it would not be surprising to find Anush's name interpreted. Since in Mandaic *anaša* means "human being," Anush could very

Anush, see *Qulasta*, 87, 104, 260, 296.

47 *Qulasta*, 91, 172. The latter reads: "The radiance of Hibil is beauteous, the light of Sitil is bright, and this is the effulgence (*tuqna*) of the great Uthra Anus, which is great and boundless." Clearly, Anush is the most highly praised.

48 *GR* 13, p. 286.19. Cf. *Memar Marqah* 2.12 (ed. Macdonald) 1.50 where Enosh is referred to as a "good apostle" (*slyḥ ṭb*).

49 *Qulasta*, 104.

50 E.g., *GR* 15.11, p. 341.20–27, where Anush heals Miriai, perhaps modeled after Mary Magdalene (cf. Luke 8:2).

51 *Qualasta*, 108. Similarly, ibid., 155.

52 See E. S. Drower, trans., *The Thousand and Twelve Questions* (Berlin: Akademie-Verlag, 1960) 293.

53 *Qulasta*, 58. The text in Drower's edition is on p. 85. Lady Drower translates "our fathers," but the form *abun* would have to be singular ("our father"). The plural form would be *abahatan* (*'bhtn*). See Rudolf Macuch, *Handbook of Classical and Modern Mandaic* (Berlin: Walter de Gruyter, 1965) 159. Similarly, in *Qulasta*, 22 (text, 35) we find: "Praised be our father (*abun*) Hibil, Sitil, and Anush the head of the whole race." Here, where *abun* again appears, Lady Drower has translated "our father." M. Lidzbarski, in his edition of the liturgy (*Mandäische Liturgen* [Berlin: Weidmansche Buchhandlung, 1920] 41), suggests that this passage originally read: "Praised is our father Hibil, the chief of the whole race." According to him, only subsequently were the names Shitil and Anush added and the participle changed to plural. This requires too many unnecessary changes. Since this passage is clearly parallel to the first, Lidzbarski would have to explain how Hibil is the "name" of the race. It is more likely that Hibil, sometimes portrayed as the first son or light emanation of Adam Kasia or Manda-d-Haiye, is alone considered the "father" of the race, while Anush alone is "the name and head of the whole race" or just the "head of the whole race." The nouns "name" and "head" are clearly singular, referring most likely to Anush.

easily have been interpreted as the "name and head of the whole human race."[54] Elsewhere we find Anush referred to as the "Head of the Age." Apparently, being the last Uthra, he is associated with the final (present) historical epoch.[55]

Finally, brief mention should be made of passages in which Anush Uthra appears to be associated with the New Testament figures of John the Baptist and Jesus.[56]

In the *Haran Gawaita*[57] Anush Uthra appears in conjuncton with Yahia-Yuhana, presumably John the Baptist. At the command of the "Great Father of Glory" Anush Uthra raises John from birth and instructs him in the secret religion (*naṣiruta*). Anush then brings him to Jerusalem where John performs miracles of healing, teaches disciples, and is called the "envoy of the High King of Light." After John's death the Jews persecute the Naṣoreans (Mandaeans). In response, Anush Uthra destroys the Jewish temple and humiliates the Jews. He then travels to Babylonia where he destroys the Jewish rulers, establishing in their place seven Naṣorean leaders and the Naṣorean people (presumably John's followers). Anush Uthra continues as the guide and protector of the Naṣorean sect throughout their subsequent history.[58] This account, having a clearly anti-Jewish thrust, traces the origins of the Naṣorean (Mandaean) sect to Jerusalem at the time of John the Baptist. Leaving aside questions of historicity, the view of Anush Uthra given here is consistent with the briefer mentions of him in the *Qulasta* and *Ginza*: he is a redeemer figure who is the "patron saint" of the Mandaean people, transmitting to them *naṣiruta*, and intervening and performing miracles on their behalf. In this particular story, Anush acts initially through a human intermediary (John) who assumes some of Anush's functions

[54] *A Mandaic Dictionary*, 24. This interpretation is very similar to ones which we have encountered in Philo and *Memar Marqah*, and which we will also see in Christian sources. No dependence, however, need necessarily be assumed. Cf. especially *Memar Marqah* 6.2 (ed. Macdonald) 1.132, where Enosh is called *ryš lkl zr' 'dm* ("the head of the whole human race"). See above, n. 16.

[55] *Haran Gawaita* (ed. and trans. E. S. Drower; Vatican: Bibiotheca Apostolica Vaticana, 1953) 8. Carl Kraeling (*Anthropos and Son of Man*: *A Study in the Religious Syncretism of the Hellenistic Orient* [New York: Columbia University, 1927] 64–66) argues that the Mandaeans divided history into four ages and assigned one of the divine messengers (Manda-d-Haiye, Hibil, Shitil, and Anush) to each. Anush is thus the fourth and is associated with the fourth or final age. The Samaritans, apparently, also divide history into four ages, as does the Book of Daniel. See R. J. Coggins, *Samaritans and Jews* (Atlanta: John Knox, 1975) 147. We will recall that Philo (*Abr.* 12–13) honors Enosh as the fourth. See above, chap. 1, n. 60.

[56] For a fuller discussion of these passages, see S. D. Fraade, "Enosh and His Generation," 105–11.

[57] Ed. and trans. E. S. Drower, 5–10.

[58] Ibid., 21.

(healing and instruction).[59]

A similar tradition of Anush Uthra's appearance in Jerusalem is related in the *Right Ginza*.[60] There we are told that Anush appears amongst men in the days of Paltus (Pilate) as a "bodily semblance," performing miraculous healings, teaching and converting Jews in the name of the "high King of Light," and appointing sixty prophets who emigrated from Jerusalem. Anush Uthra then ascends to heaven, Jerusalem is destroyed, and the Jews go into exile. In this passage Anush acts without a human intermediary.[61]

Since the description of Anush's healing and teaching activities in Jerusalem at the time of Pilate are transparently suggestive of descriptions of Jesus in the synoptic Gospels (e.g., Matt 11:5; Luke 7:22), some scholars have suggested that we have articulated in this tradition of Anush Uthra a common Hellenistic myth which also, although less clearly, underlies the Gospels' account of Jesus: Primal (or primeval) man (*anthropos* = Anush = Enosh) dies only to return to life as a divine messenger and redeemer of that aspect of fallen man (the soul) trapped in each person and longing to be led back to its source in the "light world." Anush, according to this view, represents the "Mandaean Jesus."[62]

This theory has been devastatingly refuted in recent years.[63] Most

59 Rudolph (*Die Mandäer*, 1.69–75) argues that the figure of John in Mandaean sources is secondary and late. As I have stated, John is simply an intermediary figure through whom the ethereal Anush is able to appear among men. As Rudolf states (1.73): "Johannes ist für die mandäische Religion überhaupt nicht konstitutiv." This is a clear rejection of Rudolf Bultmann's theory that the Mandaeans were originally followers of John the Baptist, to whom can be traced major components of their mythology. Bultmann's thesis is most clearly presented in "Die Bedeutung der neuerschlossenen mandäischen und manichäischen Quellen fur das Verständnis des Johannesevangeliums," *ZNW* 24 (1925) 100–46.

60 *GR* 1, pp. 29.32–30.14. For a translation, see Drower, *Secret Adam*, 39.

61 The same tradition appears in slightly different form in *GR* 2.1, pp. 47.40–48.14. This passage, after saying that Anush Uthra "gained believers amongst the Jews," states: "He led out everyone who was zealous and steadfast in belief in the One, the master of all worlds." This probably refers to Anush's leading of the Mandaeans to Mesopotamia. In still another passage (*GR* 15.11, p. 341.28–33), we are told that 365 "prophets" left Jerusalem.

62 See R. Reitzenstein, *Das mandäische Buch des Herrn der Grösse und die Evangelienüberlieferung* (Heidelberg: Carl Winter, 1919), especially pp. 22–25, 36–38, 44–47; idem, *Hellenistic Mystery-Religions: Their Basic Ideas and Significance* (trans. J. E. Steely; Pittsburgh: Pickwick Press, 1978) 15; W. Bousset, *Kyrios Christos* (trans. J. E. Steely; Nashville: Abingdon, 1970) 45, 75–76, 194–97; R. Bultmann, *ZNW* 24 (1925) 110–45 (see above, n. 59); C. H. Kraeling, *Anthropos and Son of Man: A Study in the Religious Syncretism of the Hellenistic Orient*, especially pp. 64–70; F. C. Burkitt, *Church and Gnosis* (Cambridge: University Press, 1932) 112; W. Brandt, "Mandaeans," *Encyclopedia of Religion and Ethics* 8 (1916) 384b. See also M. Lidzbarski, *Ginzā*, intro., p. xii.

63 For a clear statement of the Reitzenstein-Bultmann theory and the subsequent refutations, see Wayne Meeks, *The Prophet King*, 6–17. For a discussion of this issue as it pertains to the figure of Anush, see S. D. Fraade, "Enosh and His Generation," 109–11.

scholars now see the depiction of Anush Uthra in these two passages as representing not a mythic *Vorlage* of the NT portrayal of Jesus, but a polemical response to the Christian depictions of the claims for Jesus: Anush Uthra and not the "false messiah" Jesus was the one who appeared in Jerusalem at the time of Pilate, worked miraculous healings, attracted throngs of followers, caused the downfall of the Jewish powers, and founded a new sect. Anush Uthra, already associated with healing and revealed teaching, and known as the patron Uthra of the Naṣoreans would have been the logical candidate for this role in the anti-Christian polemic.[64]

Let us summarize our findings concerning the Mandaean figure Anush. He is one of three Uthras, or redeeming spirits, sent by the Supreme spirit, Manda-d-Haiye, to guide men's souls to reunion with the "light world" from which they originated. These three, sometimes thought of as sons or descendants of Adam (either Kasia or Pagria), take their names from the first three biblical fathers after Adam (according to the Sethite genealogy): Abel, Seth, and Enosh. As in other circles, Anush's name may be interpreted to symbolize "mankind," understood by the Mandaeans as Naṣorean mankind. Being the last Uthra, he is also the one associated with the final (present) historical epoch and, therefore, serves a somewhat apocalyptic function. Anush is particularly known for his powers of healing, and for his facilitating and fulfilling of prayer.

If the Mandaean sources show no familiarity with Gen 4:26, from where did they derive their elevated perception of Anush? This is a question which cannot be answered with any certainty. We have seen that in early non-Rabbinic Jewish and Samaritan sources Enosh frequently appears in select lists of righteous ancients. These figures are credited with piety, with having received and revealed to mankind divine wisdom, and with being sources of blessing to future generations of humanity. In some circles these figures even achieve semidivine status, being taken up to heaven (e.g., Enoch/Metatron). Furthermore, as we shall see, the biblical antediluvians were also venerated by Christians. Thus, the Mandaeans may have been sufficiently impressed with the veneration lavished by their neighbors on these biblical figures as to adopt the names of Adam and his three "sons" into their own mythology. Perhaps the fact that the names of Abel, Seth, and Enosh were suitable for interpretation made them especially attractive. There also seems to have been a certain attractiveness to working with a triad of righteous figures.[65]

64 E. S. Drower argues that the Mandaean polemic against Christianity probably developed only after the Mandaeans were well settled in Mesopotamia, being a response to the Nestorian Church, and not the early Christian Church. Thus, Anush's function as "Mandaean Jesus" is a late and not constitutive element. See her article "Mandaean Polemic," *BSOAS* 25 (1962) 338-48.

65 We have seen that Ben Sira speaks of the triad Shem, Seth, and Enosh. Philo associates

It would seem that Enosh was originally adopted not for any *individual* merits, but simply as one of three figures adopted as a group, and that it was only later that he assumed his somewhat distinctive identity within Mandaean traditions, being to some extent reshaped in response to Christian claims for Jesus. In the traditions as we now have them, Anush is not simply Enosh with a slightly different name. Rather, he is a *new* figure linked to the biblical Enosh by an almost identical name.[66] However, except for their names, the two have nothing specifically in common. If Anush were not called Anush, we would never recognize him as deriving from the biblical Enosh. The Mandaeans may simply have appropriated the first three names of one of the chains of righteous ancestors that circulated amongst their neighbors. As we have seen, these lists often circulated without anything distinctive being said about the *individual* names. Once appropriated these names began to take on distinctively Mandaean identities.[67] Thus, the divine figure that we observe in Anush Uthra is a product of Mandaean mythology and not of biblical exegesis. However, the very fact that we find his name in the Mandaean literature attests to the veneration which was accorded to Enosh by one or more of the groups with whom the Mandaeans came into contact.[68]

Enosh, Enoch, and Noah, as does *Memar Marqah* 4.9 (ed. Macdonald) 1.102.

66 The two names are identical (*'nwš*) except for vocalization.

67 Pallis' suggestion (*Mandaean Studies*, 127) that the biblical names were given to the three Uthra figures only after they had achieved their identities seems to me less convincing, since the three regularly appear as a triad in the earliest Mandaean writings.

68 While it has been argued that the Mandaeans may have drawn on Jewish and Christian traditions for their depiction of Anush, no one has suggested, to my knowledge, any possible dependence on Samaritan traditions. We have seen several parallels between the Samaritan and Mandaean traditions. See above, nn. 34, 35, 48, 54, 55. For a Samaritan inclusion of Abel in a list of righteous ancestors, see *Memar Marqah* 1.9 (ed. Macdonald) 1.21. The possibility of a relationship between Samaritan and Mandaean traditions requires further attention. See the comments of M. Gaster in his edition of *The Asatir: The Samaritan Book of the "Secrets of Moses"* (London: Royal Asiatic Society, 1927) 125–34. If there were any Samaritan influence it would have occurred while the group was still in Palestine, a period about which we know next to nothing. There is no reason to assume, as is generally done, that the Mandaeans originated near the Jordan River. They may have originally have been more dispersed in Palestine, raising the possibility of contact with other groups, e.g., Samaritans and Essenes. However, at this point in Mandaean studies such possibilities remain hypothetical. We should note that while the figure of Enosh plays no role whatsoever in the "gnostic" writings from Nag Hammadi, he appears in one Manichaean text, where he is included in a list of ancient prophets. See W. Henning, "Ein manichäisches Henochbuch," *SPAW* (1934) 28. Similarly, the Cologne Mani Codex includes Enosh in a list of ancient figures to whom apocalypses are attributed. See A. Henrichs and L. Koenen, "Ein griechischer Mani-Codex," *Zeitschrift für Papyrologie und Epigraphik* 19 (1975) 57.

Chapter Three
CHRISTIAN INTERPRETATIONS

Much of early Christian exegesis simply continues two lines of interpretation already encountered in pre-Rabbinic Jewish (as well as Samaritan) tradition: (a) Enosh represents ideal man (Enosh = man), who places his faith (or hope) in God through worship of Him.[1] (b) Enosh is an important link in a chain of ancient righteous heroes whose deeds and attributes foreshadow those of later patriarchs, priests, and prophets.[2] However, as Christian exegesis develops it builds on these two themes in radically new ways so as to constitute a particularly Christian view of Enosh's righteousness.

The Christian traditions of exegesis are of three types: (a) Enosh is included in a select chain of righteous ancestors but nothing specific is said about him. As we have argued for similar non-Christian lists, the mere inclusion of Enosh in such select lists implies a positive interpretation of Gen 4:26b. (b) Enosh is included in a select chain of righteous ancestors and his particular merits are discussed, usually revealing understandings of his name and/or Gen 4:26b. These two types of chains may be further divided along three lines: (i) those which contain nothing inherently Christian, (ii) those which contain nothing inherently Christian save that they conclude with Jesus (as Jewish and Samaritan chains often conclude with Moses),[3] and (iii) those in which the description of the chain of righteous ancestors is inherently Christian in that each member is said to prefigure, foreshadow, or bear witness to Jesus or the Christian Church. (c) Enosh is treated not as part of a chain but as a figure who in his own right is of particular significance to Christian sacred history and faith.[4]

1 This line of interpretation is particularly reminiscent of Philo, who significantly influenced several of the Church Fathers to be discussed below.

2 Although this chain motif was particularly prevalent in the Samaritan traditions which we have surveyed, it was also evident to varying degrees in Ben Sira, *Jubilees*, *2 Enoch*, and Philo.

3 When such lists are found in early Christian collections, it is tempting to suggest that an originally non-Christian list was adapted by Christians simply by adding Jesus' name. See below, n. 20.

4 The one major Christian writer who does not fit into one of these three categories is Jerome (ca. 342–420), who neither treats Enosh within a chain of righteous ancestors nor attributes to him special Christian significance. This may be, in part, because Jerome is more interested in explicating the meaning of the received Hebrew text of Scripture than

The first two categories are of interest for the way in which a familiar pattern of treating Enosh as part of a chain of righteous ancestors is first adopted and then adapted to a Christian context. The third type of exegesis, which, as may be expected, becomes increasingly prevalent as time progresses, represents a distinctively Christian approach to Enosh that owes little (but not nothing) to Jewish antecedents. We will discuss some selected examples of each type, but will deal in greater depth with the third type, the distinctively Christian exegesis of Enosh and Gen 4:26b. Within each category of exegesis the selected examples will be treated in roughly chronological order.[5] The exegeses of the Syriac sources will be treated as a group after the Greek and Latin sources since they represent a somewhat separate tradition deriving from a different version of Scripture.

A. Greek and Latin Traditions

The Greek and Latin Christian sources depend on the LXX version of Gen 4:26b, which as we have seen in chapter one, contains its own ambiguities demanding of explication. The Old Latin version most likely represents a simple translation of the LXX into Latin: *hic speravit invocare nomen domini dei* ("He hoped to invoke the name of the Lord God").[6]

---

in the larger theological issues that his contemporary Christian exegetes were addressing. Jerome's interpretations of Enosh and Gen 4:26 are referred to below in nn. 34, 46, and 47, and chap. 4, n. 15. The closest Jerome comes to a particularly Christian interpretation of Enosh is in his *Commentary to Galatians* 1.3 ad Gal 3:8–9 (*PL* 26.380), where he, like Paul, gives Abraham as a model of one who achieves righteousness through faith rather than by works, and then adds the example of Enosh, who "in consideration of preeminent faith in God is said to have hoped to call upon the Lord God."

[5] This ordering is based upon commonly accepted datings of the authors or, where known, the individual works. It should be stressed, however, that since the authors often overlap and the individual works cannot always be dated, the chronological ordering is only approximate. When two writers are contemporaries, and no further information is available, I have arranged them according to the years of their deaths. Except where otherwise indicated, I have obtained information on the authors and their works from the following reference works: *The Oxford Dictionary of the Christian Church* (ed. F. L. Cross and E. A. Livingstone; second ed.; London: Oxford University, 1974); *A Dictionary of Christian Biography, Literature, Sects and Doctrines* (ed. W. Smith and H. Wace; 4 vols.; London: John Murray, 1877–87); B. Altaner, *Patrology* (trans. H. C. Graef; New York: Herder and Herder, 1960); J. Quasten, *Patrology* (3 vols.; Utrecht–Antwerp: Spectrum Publishers, 1964–66).

For a more complete treatment of all the Christian sources see S. D. Fraade, "Enosh and His Generation: Scriptural Translation and Interpretation in Late Antiquity" (Ph.D. diss., University of Pennsylvania, 1980) 115–220.

[6] *Vetus Latina: Die Reste der altlateinischen Bibel*, vol. 2: Genesis (ed. B. Fischer; Frieburg: Herder, 1951) 92–93. Also in *Biblorum Sacrorum Latinae Versiones Antiquae*, vol. 1 (ed. D. P. Sabatier; repr. Munich, 1976) 24. The OL reading is not attested prior to the fourth century C.E. It is cited by Jerome (348–420 C.E.) in *Quaestiones Hebraicae in Genesim* ad Gen 4:26, 10.1 (in CChr Ser. Lat. 72 [Turnhout, 1959] 8); *Commentary on Galatians* 1 (*PL* 26.354B); Augustine (354–430 C.E.), *De civ. Dei* 15.18, 21; Ambrose (339–97), *De Isaac* 1 (*PL* 14.528); *De Paradiso* 19 (PL 14.299).

Note that the word *hic*, like the Greek *houtos*, has the force of "this one, the latter," referring most likely to Enosh.[7] Note too that the OL understands the LXX's *epikaleisthai* to be middle and accordingly translates it actively.

The Vulgate, presumably the work of Jerome, has: *iste coepit invocare nomen Domini* ("He [this man] began to invoke the name of the Lord").[8] This version reflects the LXX and OL in its use of the demonstrative pronoun (*iste*), but reflects the MT in its use of the verb "begin." Its rendering is equivalent to that of *Jub.* 4:12.[9] Elsewhere, in his *Quaestiones Hebraicae in Genesim* ad Gen 4:26, Jerome displays a familiarity (either direct or indirect) with the Hebrew passive "was begun."[10] It would appear, then, that Jerome combined the LXX's understanding of Enosh as the subject of Gen 4:26b with the recognition (derived either from the received Hebrew text or from Aquila or Symmachus) that the verb of Gen 4:26b was to be understood as "was begun" and not "hoped."[11]

Before turning to our earliest examples of Christian treatments of Enosh, we need note that except for the genealogical list in Luke 3 (v. 38), which traces Jesus' ancestry back to Adam through David, Abraham, and the Sethite line, the New Testament does not contain any mention of or allusion to Enosh.[12]

1. Chains of righteous ancestors that include Enosh but say nothing about him in particular.

a. Methodius of Olympus (d. 311)

Convivium decem Virginum 7.5.[13] Here Methodius speaks of those righteous men who lived between Adam and Noah (the antediluvians), and who because of their proximity to creation and paradise were not in

[7] C. T. Lewis and C. Short, *A New Latin Dictionary* (Oxford: Clarendon, 1884) 852; *Oxford Latin Dictionary*, fas. 4 (Oxford: Clarendon, 1973) 794–95.

[8] *Biblia Sacra* (ed. R. Weber; 2 vols.; Stuttgart: Wurttembergische Bibelanstalt, 1975) 1.9. The Vulgate is generally assumed to be the work of Jerome (ca. 400).

[9] See above, chap. 1, n. 34.

[10] See below, n. 47.

[11] It is generally agreed that Jerome worked with both the received Hebrew text and the Hexapla. See J. Gribomont, "Latin Versions," *IDBSup* 530–31; H. F. D. Sparks, "Jerome as Biblical Scholar," *Cambridge History of the Bible* (ed. P. R. Ackroyd & C. F. Evans; 3 vols.; Cambridge: Cambridge University, 1970) 1.517–26.

[12] Note Enosh's absence in Heb 11:1–31, where we find a catalog of righteous ancients who maintain faith (*pistis*) despite adversity: Abel, Enoch, Noah, Abraham, Isaac, Jacob, Joseph, Moses, the people of Israel, and Rahab; ten in all. Not unlike the lists that we have examined in Jewish and Samaritan sources, three antediluvians are included, but Enosh is not among them. The fact that Enosh is not included in this list does not necessarily imply a negative evaluation of him, but simply that for the author of this passage he was not as important as those listed. There seems to be nothing distinctively Christian about this list.

[13] For the Greek text see GCS 27 (ed. G. N. Bonwetsch, 1917) 76–77. For an English translation, *ANF* 6.333.

need of precepts and laws for their salvation. They were "the offspring of the first age."

> For these had great honour, being associated with the angels, and often seeing God manifested visible, and not in a dream. For consider what confidence Seth had towards God, and Abel, and Enosh, and Enoch, and Methuselah, and Noah, the first lovers of righteousness, and the first of the first-born children who are written in heaven (cf. Heb 12:23), being thought worthy of the kingdom, as a kind of first-fruits of the plants for salvation, coming out as early fruit to God.

We have here the same select list of antediluvian righteous as we have seen in non-Christian sources. Despite Adam's sin, the antediluvian righteous *still* enjoy a paradisiacal existence, close to God and not needful of laws to obtain salvation.[14]

b. The Apostolic Constitutions (ca. 380)

In six passages in this collection we find selective chains of righteous ancestors which include Enosh: 2.55.1; 6.12.13; 7.38.2; 7.39.3; 8.5.3; 8.12.4.[15] Three of the six chains conclude with Jesus (2.55; 7.38; 8.5). Enosh is usually preceded by Abel and Seth and followed by Enoch and Noah. These righteous ancestors are referred to as prophets (2.55), saints (7.39), righteous (2.55; 8.12), and priests (8.5).

In three passages Enosh stands in relationship to his antediluvian contemporaries. In 2.55 we find an enumeration of instances of divine providence: in every age since Creation God has chosen righteous men through whom to call the world and Israel to repentance.

> For God, being a God of mercy from the beginning, called every generation (*genea*) to repentance by righteous men and prophets. He instructed those before the flood by Abel, and Sem and Seth, also by Enos,[16] and by Enoch that was translated; those at the flood by Noah; the inhabitants of Sodom by hospitable Lot; those after the flood by Melchizedek, and the patriarchs, and Job beloved of God; . . .

This "history" continues through Moses, Joshua, Caleb, Phineas, John, Jesus, the twelve apostles, and Paul.

[14] This is similar to Philo's view of the pre-Mosaic righteous. See above, chap. 1, n. 47. We will encounter a similar view of the earliest righteous in *Apostolic Constitutions* 6.12.

[15] The Greek text consulted is that of F. X. Funk, ed., *Didascalia et Constitutiones Apostolorum* (2 vols.; Paderborn, 1905) 1.155, 333, 438, 440, 474, 502. English translations are from *ANF* 7.420, 455, 475, 476, 482, 488. For more complete treatments of these passages, see S. D. Fraade, "Enosh and His Generation," 116–19.

[16] The order Shem, Seth, Enosh is the same as in Ben Sira 49:16. See chap. 1, nn. 25–27.

Similarly in 7.38 we find the following "prayer for the assistance of the righteous":

> We give thee thanks for all things, O Lord that Thou hast not taken away Thy mercies and Thy compassions from us; but in every succeeding generation Thou dost save, and deliver, and assist, and protect: for Thou didst assist in the days of Enosh and Enoch, in the days of Moses and Joshua, in the days of the Judges, in the days of Samuel and of Elijah, and of the prophets, in the days of David and of the Kings, in the days of Esther and Mordecai, in the days of Judith, in the days of Judas Maccabeus and his brethren, and in our own days hast Thou assisted us by Thy great High Priest, Jesus Christ Thy Son.

Note that the first age, the antediluvian age, is associated with Enosh and Enoch alone, that the patriarchal period is skipped entirely, and that the "history" ends with the tenth epoch, that of Jesus.[17]

In 7.39, in what seem to be instructions for the indoctrination of converts, the neophytes are to be taught "how God punished the wicked with water and fire, and did glorify the saints in every generation": Seth, Enosh, Enoch, Noah, Abraham "and his posterity," Melchizedek, Job, Moses, Joshua, Caleb, Phineas, "and those that were holy in every generation." There is nothing distinctively Christian about this list.

The above examples are variations on a common theme which we have witnessed in non-Christian sources as well: every generation has its saints who are rewarded and who serve as prophets, priests, and teachers for their respective ages. Here, as elsewhere, Enosh is regularly included as such a saint.

Finally, we take note of 6.12, which in discussing Christian judaizers states that Gentile converts are only required to

> abstain from the pollutions of the Gentiles, and from what is sacrifice to idols, and from blood, and from things strangled, and from fornication; which laws were given to the ancients who lived before the law, under the law of nature: Enos, Enoch, Noah, Melchizedek, Job, and if there be any other of the same sort.

We have here a paraphrase of Acts 15:19–21, which concludes, "for from early generations (*ek geneōn archaiōn*) Moses has had in every city those who preach him, for he is read every Sabbath in the synagogues." For the author of our passage of the *Constitutions*, the earliest preachers were the pre-Israelite (universal) righteous who lived naturally under the moral law before it was formally revealed through Moses.[18]

[17] Given the omission of the biblical patriarchs, the inclusion of such later popular heroes as Esther, Mordecai, Judith, and Judas Maccabeus is significant.

[18] We have witnessed similar treatments of the pre-Israelite righteous in Philo and Methodius of Olympus. See above, n. 14.

It is difficult to determine the provenance of these passages. While parts of the *Apostolic Constitutions* are thought to derive from the earlier nonextant *Apostolic Tradition* of Hippolytus of Rome (ca. 215), there is no clear indication that the passages which mention Enosh stem from this earlier work.[19] While some of these traditions of chains of righteous ancestors may have originated in Jewish liturgy or tradition and only later have been adapted to Christian needs, such cannot be determined with any certainty.[20] The basic contents of these lists of righteous ancestors who are praised for their steadfast faith, who were rewarded by God, and who served as luminaries to their contemporaries, could, with only the slightest adaptation, have been equally at home in the teachings of Jewish, Samaritan, and Christian groups. What we seem to have are traditions which draw upon a common stock of lore concerning the chain of ancient righteous ancestors. All we can say with certainty is that Enosh was a regular part of this common stock, judging from the frequency with which his name is included in these selective lists.

2. Chains of righteous ancestors in which Enosh has special significance.

Under this heading we will look at discussions of Enosh in the writings of Origen, Eusebius, and Ambrose, all of whom place him in the context of a succession of righteous ancestors, but attribute special significance to him in relation to Christian sacred history and faith.[21]

a. Origen (ca. 185–ca. 254)

In the extant writings of Origen, certainly one of the most prolific exegetes of the early Church, we find only three references to Enosh, all of which come down to us via second or third hands.[22] Origen's treatments of

[19] Enosh does not appear in the so-called *Epitome* of the Eighth Book of the *Constitutions*, usually thought to make direct use of the *Apostolic Tradition*. See G. Dix, ed., *The Treatise on the Apostolic Tradition of St. Hippolytus of Rome* (London: SPCK, 1937; cor. ed., 1968) lxxiv–lxxvi; J. Quasten, *Patrology*, 2.180–5. For the Greek text of the *Epitome* I have consulted Funk, 2.72–96.

[20] For the view that such passages derive from an originally Jewish liturgy, see E. Goodenough, *By Light, Light* (New Haven: Yale University, 1935; repr. Amsterdam: Philo Press, 1969) 313–14, 322–23, 326, 330–31. See also W. Bousset, "Eine jüdische Gebetssammlung im siebenten Buch der apostolischen Konstitutionen," in *Nachrichten von der königlichen Gesellschaft der Wissenschaften zu Göttingen, Philologisch-historische Klasse*, 1915 (Berlin, 1916) 435–89, esp. 446–47, 472–73.

[21] For another Christian treatment of Enosh of this sort see Gregory of Nazianzus (329-389), *The Theological Orations* 2.18 (*PG* 36.49).

[22] Two of these are preserved by Rufinus (ca. 345–410) in his Latin translation of Origen's commentary to Romans, and a third (see next note) is attributed to Origen by Pamphilus of Caesarea in the latter's *Apology for Origen* (written ca. 308), for which we

Enosh are of particular interest because of their seeming inconsistency: in one passage Gen 4:26b is cited to Enosh's discredit, in another to his credit.[23]

Commentary to Romans, Book 5.1.[24] In this passage Origen comments on Rom 5:12–14, which we may first cite (*RSV*):

> Therefore as sin came into the world through one man and death through sin, and so death spread to all men because all men sinned—sin indeed was in the world before the law was given, but sin is not counted where there is no law. Yet death reigned from Adam to Moses, even over those whose sins were not like the transgression of Adam, who was a type of the one who was to come.

After referring to Rom 3:23 ("since all have sinned and fall short of the glory of God"), Origen demonstrates that all of the early biblical heroes were imperfect in their righteousness, thereby providing support for Paul's statement that all men "from Adam to Moses" sinned and, therefore, died.[25] Thus, Origen notes that Abel delayed in bringing his sacrifice, since as Scripture says (Gen 4:3–4), he did not offer it immediately, but only "after a while" (*post dies*), following Cain. Next, Origen says of Enosh:

> And even if you say Enosh [was just], he "hoped to call on the name of the Lord" (*speravit invocare nomen domini*). Why did he hope and not at once call, but feigned and delayed? (*cur speravit et cur non statim invocat, sed dissimulat et moratur*).

In the same manner Origen treats Enoch, Methuselah, Noah, and Abraham, finding for each some indication in Scripture that they were imperfect.

Origen finds fault with precisely those ancestors who elsewhere in Jewish, Samaritan, and Christian traditions are selected for inclusion in the chain of the righteous. It would appear that he is simply using a

---

are again dependent on Rufinus' translation. Although Rufinus often took liberties in his translations, these usually revolve around doctrinal issues (e.g. Origen's treatment of the trinity), none of which are present in the passages dealing with Enosh. Thus, we have little reason to suspect the reliability of Rufinus' translations of the passages that we will discuss.

23 Origen mentions Enosh in a third passage, as quoted in Pamphilus' *Apologia pro Origene*, extant in Rufinus' Latin translation (*PG* 14.1306; 17.592). Here Origen lists Enosh as part of a list of ten "saints" (beginning with Adam and ending with Jesus, the tenth), "who Scripture testifies were just and the chosen of God." The faithful must believe that the biblical saints were in fact saints, "that Enosh truly 'hoped to call on the name of the Lord God' " (*quod Enos vere speravit invocare nomen Domini Dei*). For further discussion of this passage see S. D. Fraade, "Enosh and His Generation," 127–29.

24 For the Latin text see *PG* 14.1011–12.

25 Similarly, in Rabbinic sources we are told that although Adam was the first to die for his sins, each man's death comes as punishment for his own sins: *Tanḥ. B. Bere'šit* 29 (p. 21); *Ḥuqqat* 39 (p. 124). See L. Ginzberg, *Legends of the Jews* (7 vols.; Philadelphia: Jewish Publication Society, 1913–38) 5.128–31 n. 142.

stock list of righteous biblical ancestors and adopting it to his exegetical needs. Thus, Enosh is included in Origen's list because of his customary inclusion in such lists. Otherwise, there would have been no need to prove that Paul's statements in Rom 3:23 and 5:12 hold true *even* for Enosh. Origen simply uses Gen 4:26b as a prooftext for Rom 5:12-14. He finds a suggestion of Enosh's shortcoming in the word "hoped" (*speravit, elpise*): Enosh hoped to call on the name of the Lord but never did, or if he did, it was only after some delay. We have examined a similar interpretation in Philo: yes, Enosh was righteous, but in an imperfect way.[26]

Commentary to Romans, Book 8.3.[27] Origen comments on Rom 10:12, which we may first cite (*RSV*): "For there is no distinction between Jew and Greek; the same Lord is Lord of all and bestows his riches upon all who call upon him. For, 'every one who calls upon the Lord will be saved' (Joel 2:32 [3:5])." Origen, like Paul, understands Joel 2:32 as a prophecy referring to Jesus: whoever (whether Jew or gentile) calls upon Jesus (i.e., puts his faith in him) will be saved.[28] Origen states:

> It seems to me that a great thing is meant in the divine Scriptures by this word "invocation." For it is not written about any sort of men, but about mighty and outstanding ones (*de ingentibus et praecipuis*), such as "Enosh [who] first hoped to call upon the name of the Lord," and in Psalms (98[99]:6), "Moses and Aaron

26 Since Philo is the *only* other ancient exegete to treat Enosh in this way, it is possible that Origen has been influenced by him. In the same passage Origen interprets Methuselah's name to mean "emission of death" (*emissio mortis*), an interpretation that we find identically in Philo, *Post.* 40: *exapastolē thanatou*, undoubtedly based on a Hebrew pun: *mwt* + *šlḥ*. Cf. *YS* Ezek. 367 (Salonika) 114d, where Methuselah is included among the thirteen who did not "taste" death. Origen's treatment of the antediluvian heroes is also reminiscent of Rabbinic attempts to qualify their praise: Enoch was *not* translated (*Gen. Rab.* 25.1), and Noah was a *ṣaddîq* ("righteous man") only relative to his own generation (*Gen. Rab.* 30.9). While there is, in general, substantial evidence for Origen's reliance on both Philo and Palestinian Sages for exegetical traditions, it is difficult to determine direct dependence in a specific instance such as this. See N. R. M. DeLange, *Origen and the Jews: Studies in Jewish-Christian Relations in Third Century Palestine* (Cambridge University Press, 1976) 15–28.

27 *PG* 14.1165.

28 Rom 10:12–14 is only one of several NT passages that applies the biblical expression *epikaleisthai to onoma kyriou* to Jesus. See as well: Acts 9:14, 21; 22:16; 1 Cor 1:2; 2 Tim 2:22. I have already referred to Rabbinic traditions that interpret Joel 3:5 passively (chap. 2, n. 10). On the NT use of *Kyrios* see W. Foerster, s.v. *kyrios*, *TDNT* 3 (1965) 1086–95; J. A. Fitzmyer, "The Semitic Background of the New Testament Kyrios Title," in *A Wandering Aramean: Collected Aramaic Essays* (SBL Monograph Series no. 25; Missoula: Scholars Press, 1979) 115–42; F. Hahn, *The Titles of Jesus in Christology: Their History in Early Christianity* (trans. H. Knight and G. Ogg; New York: World Publishing Co., 1969) 68–135. For a similar statement from a Reformation writer see Luther (1483–1546), *Lectures on Genesis* (ed. J. Pelikan) 1.328, who says that "name of the Lord" is a reference to Jesus, and that Adam, Seth, and Enosh in calling on "the name of the Lord" awaited redemption through Jesus.

> were among His priests, and Samuel among those who called on His name. They called to the Lord and He answered them. In a pillar of cloud He spoke to them."

We get here a very different treatment of Gen 4:26 than earlier in Book 5.1. Now Enosh is one of the "mighty and outstanding" men of the past who called on the name of the Lord. Origen says nothing here about Enosh's having feigned or delayed in his worship! Interestingly, Abraham, to whom Scripture most frequently (four times) ascribes the "calling on God's name," is not mentioned by Origen in this context.

Further along in the same discussion Origen states that when Paul refers to "calling on the name of the Lord," he means calling on Jesus, as in Joel's prophecy. Therefore, when Paul says (Rom 10:14), "But how are men to call upon him in whom they have not believed?" he is referring to the Jews, says Origen, who did not believe in Jesus and, consequently, could not call on him. Origen states that in 1 Cor 1:2 Paul refers to the Church members as "those who in every place call on the name of the Lord Jesus Christ" (*hoi epikaloumenoi to onoma tou kyriou . . .*). Returning to Enosh, Moses, Aaron, and Samuel, Origen continues:

> If, therefore, Enosh, Moses, Aaron, and Samuel all "called upon the Lord and He heard them" (Ps. 98 [99]:6), without doubt they called upon Jesus Christ the Lord. And if to call upon the name of the Lord and to pray to the Lord are one and the same, as God is called upon, necessarily Christ is called upon, and as God is prayed to, so Christ is necessarily prayed to.[29]

Thus, Origen holds that Enosh, along with Moses, Aaron, and Samuel, called on the name of the Lord (Jesus) *and was heard*. It is tempting to suggest that Origen derives his interpretation either by giving the verb *ēlpise* a prophetic sense; that is, Enosh had the faith (hope) to call upon one who had not yet come into the world; or by taking the LXX rendering "name of the Lord God" to refer to the Lord Jesus and God. Yet, in the cases of Moses, Aaron, and Samuel, concerning whom we find the same interpretation, there is no such Scriptural warrant. Therefore, we must assume that for Origen the Jesus upon whom Enosh, Moses, Aaron, and Samuel call is not the historical Jesus, but the *eternal* Word of God. Origen finds in these "Old Testament" figures foreshadowings of the kind of faith demanded by Paul in the New Testament. The connecting link between the "Old" and the "New" lies in the identical language used by the LXX and Paul: *epikaleisthai to onoma kyriou*. While *we* might say that the New Testament simply adapts the language of the LXX, Origen understands the language of the Old Testament to foreshadow that of the New, and, therefore, these biblical figures in their "calling on the name of the Lord" typologically foreshadow the Church, and bear

[29] *PG* 14.1165–66.

witness to the eternal Jesus. In this interpretation Enosh's "hope" is ignored.

What do we make of Origen's seemingly inconsistent treatment of Enosh as (a) one who *only* hoped to call on the name of the Lord, and (b) one whose calling on the name of the Lord (Jesus) earns him the epithets "mighty" and "outstanding"? There is no reason to suspect either passage of being corrupt, nor of being incorrectly attributed. The simplest solution is to see here something characteristic of Origen's exegesis: what Origen says in one exegetical context sometimes contradicts what he says in another. His statements must be evaluated in terms of the contexts in which they appear.[30] In the passages which we have examined Origen is principally interpreting the New Testament and not the Book of Genesis. Therefore, his interpretations of Gen 4:26 must be viewed in terms of what he wants to say regarding the NT traditions on which he is commenting. Origen's reliance on Jewish exegetical traditions should not be confused with his primary vocation as a Christian exegete. To Origen, Enosh as a biblical saint is to be venerated. His hope to call on the name of the Lord, like that of other biblical figures, is understood to refer to faith in and witness to both God and Jesus. But since Enosh lives in the shadow of Adam's sin, and since he himself is only a shadow of better things to come, his piety is of necessity blemished.[31]

These passages taken together suggest a qualified praise of Enosh which is strikingly similar to that of Philo. While Origen's dependence on Philo is generally acknowledged, it should be noted that each had his own exegetical motivation for reservations. Philo's interpretation is informed, in part, by his view of the antediluvian non-Israelite heroes as being inferior to their Israelite successors. Origen, as a Christian, views all "Old Testament" figures as imperfect, since they live between Adam and Jesus. Both Philo and Origen view Enosh allegorically as ideal, and historically as flawed. Both Philo and Origen take their cue from the problematic LXX expression "hoped to call," turning a potential difficulty to their respective exegetical advantages.

b. Eusebius Pamphili of Caesarea (ca. 263–340)

Eusebius is the first Church Father to discuss Enosh at length. He is also, it seems, the Church Father most dependent on Philo for his interpretation of Enosh, while adapting significantly Philo's exegesis to a Christian perspective.

[30] See DeLange, *Origen and the Jews*, 6.

[31] On the tension between allegory and typology in Origen's exegesis of the two "Testaments," see R. A. Greer, *The Captain of Our Salvation: A Study in the Patristic Exegesis of Hebrews* (BGBE 15; Tübingen: J. C. B. Mohr, 1973) 8–18.

Praeparatio Evangelica 7.8.[32] Here Eusebius proposes to recount the history of the Hebrews from before the Flood until Moses, as recorded in "their own writings." He begins by discussing the antediluvian generations, in which were "a certain number of righteous men beloved of God (*theophileis*), one of whom 'hoped to call upon the name of the Lord God' ":

> Now this shows that to none but the creator of all things he [Enosh] gave the title both of Lord (*despotēs*) and God (*theos*) of the universe: for he was persuaded that not only by creative power had He well and orderly disposed the whole, but also, like the Lord as it were of a great city, was the ruler of the whole, and dispenser and master of the house, being at once Lord (*kyrios*), and king (*basileus*), and God (*theos*). The first to lay to heart the idea and the name of this Being as Lord and God was the godly man (*ho dēloumenos theophilēs*) of whom I speak, and who in place of all substance, and title, and abundance or rather in place of all good "hoped to call upon the name of the Lord God," having procured him for a treasure to himself of blessings both of soul and body. In consequence of this it is recorded that he was the first to be called among the Hebrews a true man (*alēthēs anthrōpos*).[33] At all events he is named Enos, which is "true man" by a well applied appellation. For it is said that we ought to consider and to call no other a "true man" than him who attains to the knowledge of God and to piety, who is at the same time full of knowledge (*gnōstikon*) and reverence (*eusebēs*).

Eusebius continues by distinguishing such a "true man" both from the irrational animals and from "man of the common multitude," who is designated by the name Adam, meaning "earthborn" (gēgenēs).[34] Thus,

[32] For the Greek text and English translation I have used Eusebii Pamphili, *Praeparatio Evangelica* (ed. and trans. E. H. Gifford; 4 vols. in 5; Oxford: E Typographeo Academico, 1903) 1.388–91; 3.329–31. I have also examined Eusèbe de Césarée, *La Preparation Evangelique, Book 7* (ed. Eduard Des Places, with introduction, translation, and notes by Guy Schroeder; SC 215; Paris, Les Editions du Cerf, 1975) 174–81. The Greek text is also available in GCS 42.1 (ed. Karl Mras, 1954) 370–78; and in *PG* 21.520–29.

[33] It is tempting to read this as a pun on Gen 4:26b: he was the first to call/he was the first to be called. We have already witnessed in the Samaritan Targum a passive interpretation of *liqrō'*, and will soon encounter several passive interpretations of *epikaleisthai* by Christian exegetes. At least one modern commentator has suggested emending the Hebrew text of the Bible so as to read: Then men began to be called by this name [Enosh], or: This one was the first to be called by this name. N. H. Tur-Sinai (Torczyner), *Pešuṭo šel miqra'*, vol. 1 (Jerusalem: Kiryat Sefer, 1962) 21–22. Apparently, Tur-Sinai wants to amend *yhwh* to *hzh*.

[34] Eusebius similarly treats the names Adam and Enosh in *Praep. ev.* 11.6 (ed. Gifford) 2.74–75; 3.553–54. There, however, he adduces other meanings as well. Adam besides meaning "earthborn" means "red, . . . the natural color of the body, . . . the man of body and flesh." This is undoubtedly based on the Hebrew pun *'ādām/'ădāmâ/'ādōm* (Adam/earth/red). Similarly, Enosh besides meaning "the rational man within us," also means "forgetful" (*epilēsmōn*). Gifford suggests an "etymology" either from the Greek *anous*

says Eusebius, the Hebrews accorded to Enosh the honor of being "the first of the beloved of God" (*prōtos theophilōn*) since he "first hoped to call upon the name of the Lord God" (*prōtos ēlpise* . . .). Enosh represents man's rational soul which is capable of both knowing God and recognizing the piety required for divine worship. He first knows God and then "hopes in the God whom he knew." Eusebius continues:

> For not to neglect nor put in a secondary place the true knowledge of God, but ever and through all to "hope to call upon the name of the Lord God," partly as Lord of the household (*oiketōn despotos*), and partly as a gracious and good father (*hileōs kai agathos patēr*).

In concluding, Eusebius admonishes his audience to imitate Enosh so that "equalling the example of the man of whom I speak, we would call upon the name of the Creator and Lord of all with a steadfast and good hope." After treating Enosh, Eusebius passes to the antediluvians Enoch and Noah, and the postdiluvians Melchizedek, Abraham, Isaac, Jacob, Job, Joseph, and Moses; ten in all.

We are immediately struck by the similarities between Eusebius' treatment of Enosh and that of Philo.[35] Like Philo, Eusebius treats three antediluvian figures: Enosh, Enoch, and Noah. Similarly, for both the chain of

("foolish, without understanding") or from the Hebrew/Aramaic root *nš'/nšy*, meaning "to forget." Max Grünbaum (*Neue Beiträge zur semitischen Sagenkunde* [Leiden: E. J. Brill, 1893] 24–25) favors the latter derivation, citing *b. Sanh.* 25a for a (doubtful) play on the collective noun *'ĕnāš* (Aramaic for *'ĕnôš*) and the verb *nšy*. Cf. *MPs.* 9.16 (ed. Buber) 91, which states that the collective noun *'ĕnôš* refers to the "foolish man" (*šôṭeh*). Note, however, that while Rabbinic sources interpret Enosh's name negatively (meaning "weak or sick," see below), they never connect his name with the verb *nš'/nšy*. It seems more likely, therefore, that Eusebius' interpretation is based on the Greek *anous*. Eusebius' negative interpretation of Enosh's name in Book 11 does not, however, figure in his treatment of Enosh in Book 7.

Eusebius' twofold explication of Enosh's name is similar to what we find in the writings of Jerome. In *Questiones Hebraicae in Genesim* ad Gen 4:26 (CChr Ser. Lat. 72) 8, Jerome contrasts "Adam" meaning "man" (*homo*) with "Enosh" meaning "man or he-man" (*homo vel vir*). Lewis and Short (*A Latin Dictionary*, 1884) define *vir* as, "the man of courage, principle, honor; the one who deserves the name of a man." Jerome continues, "and very nicely (*pulchre*), for since he had this distinction it is written about him: Then was the beginning of calling upon the name of the Lord." Jerome assumes a connection between Enosh's name and Gen 4:26b but does not state what it is. Elsewhere, in his *Liber Interpretationis Hebraicorum* (CCHr Ser. Lat. 72) 65, Jerome gives the following as an interpretation of Enosh's name: homo sive desperatus vel violtentus ("man, or desperate, or violent"). It is not clear what the source of Jerome's interpretation of Enosh's name might have been. Perhaps he was familiar with Rabbinic interpretations of Enosh's name as deriving from the Hebrew root *'nš* meaning "weak" (see below, chap. 5). In any case, Jerome's negative interpretation of Enosh's name here contrasts sharply and is not easily reconciled with his positive interpretation of it in his exegesis of Gen 4:26.

35 See Schroeder's introduction, 60–63.

biblical righteous men culminates with Moses.[36] For Eusebius as for Philo these ancients are paradigms of virtue to be emulated (cf. *Praep. ev.* 7.7). Both stress that Enosh places his hope in God and not in earthly gain. Eusebius like Philo interprets Enosh's name to mean "true man," and distinguishes him from the animals as well as from baser sorts of men. They both consider him to represent rational man. Finally, Eusebius like Philo speaks of Enosh as the *first* to call on the name of the Lord.[37]

However, there are also some significant differences, ways in which Eusebius either differs from Philo or provides us with new information concerning Enosh. First, unlike Philo, Eusebius resolves the paradox of Enosh's "hoping" and "calling" positively. Enosh did in fact call on God, doing so with hope, or faith. Enosh called on God in a manner *superior* to that of his predecessors. Thus, Eusebius admonishes his audience to follow Enosh's example by calling on God's name "with a steadfast and good hope" (*meta bebaias kai agathēs elpidos*). For Eusebius, Enosh's "calling" is a sign of his knowledge (*gnōstikos*), while his "hoping" is a sign of his piety (*eusebeia*). Enosh attained not only knowledge of God, but also the proper quality with which to worship Him: hope.

Secondly, Eusebius places great stress on Enosh's calling on the name of the *Lord God*. Enosh was the first to call God by two names, each representing a set of attributes. The name *kyrios* refers to God the ruler and master, while that of *theos* refers to God the creator and "gracious and good father." While a similar interpretation of the divine names is found in Philo, it is not applied by Philo to Gen 4:26.[38]

Finally, Eusebius places much greater emphasis than does Philo on Enosh's priority. Enosh is the first to be called a true man, the first to

[36] In Philo's list Moses is seventh, in Eusebius' he is tenth. Eusebius has added Melchizedek, Job, and Joseph. See Schroeder, 61.

[37] It is difficult to know whether Eusebius is here dependent on Philo or whether he knows of this meaning from elsewhere, e.g., Aquila's version. It should be stressed that Eusebius nowhere refers to Philo by name in this section.

[38] See Philo, *Sob.* 55. Conversely, the rabbis take *YHWH* (=*kyrios*) to refer to God's attribute of mercy, and *'ĕlōhîm* (=*theos*) to God as strict judge. There is reason to believe, however, that among the rabbis this distinction was not fixed until late, and that originally they exercised greater flexibility in interpreting God's names, for instance, taking *YHWH* to refer to the punishing God and *'ĕlōhîm* to the Creator. See A. Marmorstein, *The Old Rabbinic Doctrine of God*, vol. 1 (London: Oxford University, 1927) 41–53; N. A. Dahl and A. P. Segal, "Philo and the Rabbis on the Names of God," *JSJ* 9 (1978) 1–28; V. Nikiprowetzky, *Le Commentaire de l'écriture chez Philo d'Alexandrie* (Leiden: E. J. Brill, 1977) 58–62. We will see a similar interpretation of the two divine names in LXX Gen 4:26b in the commentary of Didymus the Blind of Alexandria. See below, n. 65.

Since in Greek as in Hebrew the verb "to call" can mean to invoke as well as to name, Gen 4:26b could be understood to refer to Enosh's calling on (praying to) God by name, as well as his calling Him by the name "Lord." We will observe the same "double translation" in other Christian exegetes (see below, n. 163), and in Rabbinic targum and midrash.

call God *kyrios* and *theos*, the first of the "beloved of God," and the first to hope "to call on the name of the Lord God." Eusebius discusses Enosh at greater length than any of the other nine righteous figures.

In part, Eusebius' favorable treatment of Enosh is a result of his having resolved the problem of Enosh's "hope": Enosh was the first to call on (worship) God with hope (i.e., faith or trust). However, we may also recognize in this difference between Eusebius and Philo a fundamental difference in their exegetical concerns. Philo clearly states that the antediluvian heroes are inferior in their virtue to those who follow them. The first triad (Enosh, Enoch, and Noah) prepares for the second (Abraham, Isaac, and Jacob), while the whole chain culminates with Moses, whom Philo treats at greater length than any of Moses' predecessors. However, even within the first triad Philo notes a progression of increasing piety. Thus, Enosh standing at the head of the chain is only of preliminary significance. This tendency is typically Jewish and, as we shall see, is even more pronounced in Rabbinic sources; the antediluvian, non-Israelite heroes are not allowed to overshadow the Israelite patriarchs, with whom, from a Jewish perspective, the history of the chosen people truly begins.[39]

Such an approach is not at all evidenced in Eusebius. There is nothing in Eusebius to suggest that Enosh's role is preparatory, no indication that he is superseded by those who follow. For Eusebius, the Hebrew Bible as a whole prepares for the Gospel, and, therefore, within the Hebrew Bible itself Enosh is no less important than Abraham or Moses. In fact, the very non-Israelite identity of a figure like Enosh and his proximity to the beginnings of human history may have made him even more attractive as a model for Christian faith. Eusebius, unlike Origen and later Christian writers who increasingly stress Enosh's importance, does not explicitly link Enosh with Jesus or the Church. In this sense, Eusebius stays closer to Philo in describing Enosh's more universal religious significance. Yet, Eusebius, unlike Philo, does not view Enosh and the other antediluvian heroes in the shadow of the succeeding Israelite patriarchs, and thereby reveals his inherently Christian perspective. Enosh, being for Eusebius the earliest noteworthy righteous antediluvian, is the most important.[40] Eusebius' praise of Enosh as ideal man is unqualified, his allegorization, unlike Philo's, is complete.

[39] As we have seen, Samaritan traditions also attribute to Enosh and the other antediluvians a preparatory function. For the Samaritans, however, it is the centrality of Moses which is the determining factor.

[40] Significantly, Eusebius, like Philo, ignores Seth. It is difficult to determine whether Seth's absence reflects Eusebius' own attitude, or his dependence on Philo, at least for the outlines of his discussion.

c. Ambrose of Milan (ca. 339–97)

Ambrose, like others before him, focuses on Enosh's spiritual excellence, and, like Eusebius, expresses unqualified praise of him.

De Paradiso 1.3.19–23.[41] In this passage Ambrose, in describing the four ages of the world, lists the righteous men of the first (antediluvian) age: Abel, Enosh, Enoch, and Noah. Of Enosh he says: Enos, hoc est homo ad imaginem Dei factus, qui speravit invocare nomen Domini Dei ("Enosh is man made in the image of God, who hoped to call upon the name of the Lord God"). Ambrose, like so many others, interprets Enosh's name to mean "man"—not man in general, but that ideal man who is in the image of God. This implies that after Adam's "fall" not all men were born "in the image of God." The divine image was transmitted only through a chain of select few.[42] For the second half of Gen 4:26 Ambrose simply gives the Old Latin version without commenting. Thus, Enosh's significance lies both in his name and in his having hoped "to call upon the name of the Lord." These two attributes merit his inclusion in the select list of antediluvian righteous.

Further along in the same passage Ambrose mentions Enosh once again, in discussing the four rivers of Paradise (Gen 2:11–14). The first river corresponds to the first of the four ages. The three stones which are found in the land encompassed by this river each represent one of the antediluvian figures: Enosh, Enoch, and Noah. Of Enosh he says:

> For it seems to us that Enosh was good gold (*aurum bonum*) who prudently desired to know the name of the Lord (*qui prudenter Dei nomen scire desideravit*).[43]

Here Ambrose singles out the same three antediluvians as did Philo and Eusebius.[44] Enosh, being the first, is associated with the first stone, gold, of Gen 2.11. Ambrose's paraphrase of the Greek or Latin version avoids the verb *spero* ("hope") and uses instead *desidero* ("wish, long for"). While this variation may be slight, the nuance of Ambrose's choice is more positive: Enosh was eager to know God's name. Like Eusebius, Ambrose avoids what for Philo and Origen was an indication of Enosh's failure.

De Isaac et Anima 1.2.[45] Here Ambrose speaks of the value of withdrawing oneself from the "pleasures of flesh," of raising one's soul away

41 *PL* 14.299.

42 Thus, Gen 5:3 is often understood to mean that Seth inherited the "divine image" from Adam, but since no such statement is made with regard to Cain (and his progeny), they did not. This interpretation arises from the ambiguity of the Hebrew *'ādām* in Gen 1:26, 27. Is man in general created in the divine image or only Adam? In chapter 4 I will treat Rabbinic traditions that similarly speak of the progressive decline of the "divine image" in the generations after Enosh.

43 *PL* 14.300.

44 See above, chap. 2, n. 65.

45 *PL* 14.528.

from its body. To do so is to be truly a man, "which in the speech of the Chaldaeans is Enosh, in Latin *homo*." Next we find the common confusion of Enosh and Enoch:

> Moreover, Enosh who began and hoped to call upon God (*qui assumpsit et speravit invocare Deum*) is also believed to have been translated. Thus, one does not seem to be a man unless one hopes in God. Whoever, moreover, hopes in God is shown by a manifest interpretation of truth not to dwell on earth, but to cling, as if translated, to God.[46]

Once again, Ambrose tries to eliminate the problematic ambiguity in the LXX/Old Latin version: Enosh began *and* hoped. In other words, he was the first to place his hope in God. Once again, two interpretations of the verb *hûḥal* are conflated. Ambrose echoes Eusebius: Enosh is true man, who by placing his hope in God removes himself from earthly and bodily concerns.[47] Ambrose, himself having ascetic leanings, finds the same in Enosh.[48]

[46] For a similar confusion, see the Pseudo-Clementine *Recognitions* 4.12.1 (GCS 51 [ed. B. Rehm, 1965] 152; *ANF* 8.137): "He translated to immortality (*ad immortales Transtulit*) a certain one of the first race of men, because He saw that he was not unmindful of His grace and because 'he hoped to call on the name of the Lord'; while the rest . . . were condemned to a terrible death [the Flood]."

Similarly, Jerome in *Adversus Jovianum* 1.17 confuses (we might say, merges) Enosh and Enoch, saying that Enoch was "translated" because he was the "first to call upon God and to believe in the Creator" (*primus invocaverit Deum, et crediderit in Creatorem*). As we have seen, Enosh and Enoch often appear successively in the selective chains of righteous ancestors. While their names may be confused in Hebrew (*'nwš* and *ḥnwk*), they are even more susceptible to confusion in Greek (*Enōs* and *Enōch*). For similar confusions of Enosh and Enoch, see above, chap. 1, n. 23; chap. 2, n. 14; below, n. 159.

[47] Whether Ambrose is directly dependent on Eusebius is difficult to determine. His paraphrase "began and hoped" may be derived from Eusebius or from Philo (perhaps via Origen), or from other witnesses to the Hebrew Bible (e.g., Aquila). A similar combination of the meanings "hope" and "begin" can be found in the writings of Jerome. In the Vulgate Jerome uses "begin" (*coepit*, see above, nn. 8–11). Similarly, in *Adversus Jovianum* 1.17 (*PL* 23.237; *ANF* 6.360) he says that Enosh was the "first to call upon God" (*primus invocaverit Deum*). In *Quaestiones Hebraicae in Genesim* ad Gen 4:26 (CChr Ser. Lat. 72.8) he comes closer to the Hebrew passive: "then was the beginning" (*tunc initium fuit*), similar to Symmachus' *tote archē egeneto*. However, in his *Commentary to Galatians* 1.3 ad Gal 3:8–9 (*PL* 26.380), in praising Enosh's faith, Jerome tells us that Enosh "is said to have hoped to call upon the Lord God" (*sperasse scribitur invocare Dominum Deum*. It would appear that in the first three cases Jerome depends on the received Hebrew text (or a Greek equivalent), while in the last example he depends on the tradition of the LXX (or the OL).

See above, n. 31, and chap. 1, nn. 8–10, for similar conflations of the verbs "hope" (from the Greek) and "begin" (from the Hebrew). On this phenomenon in the interpretation of the LXX, see Henry Swete, *An Introduction to the Old Testament in Greek* (Cambridge: University Press, 1900) 374–75.

[48] The ascetic view of Enosh is also expressed by Clement of Alexandria in *Excerpta ex Theodoto* 54.3 (SC 23 [ed. F. Sagnard, 1948] 170–71): "And because Seth was spiritual he

3. Enosh as a figure of particular significance to Christian sacred history and faith.

Beginning in the fourth century, Enosh is interpreted not simply as one of several links in a chain of righteous ancients, but as a figure who as the first godlike man both stands at the head of a righteous genealogy that leads to Jesus and the Church and prefigures or foreshadows them as "son of God."

a. Eusebius of Emesa (ca. 300–360)

Eusebius of Emesa is our first extant witness to an interpretation of Gen 4:26b that as it develops attributes increasing Christian significance to Enosh.

Commentary on Genesis. In a Greek fragment of a commentary on Genesis attributed to Eusebius of Emesa we find the following comment on the LXX translation of Gen 4:26b:

> In the Hebraios [version] it does not say thus, but, "this one hoped to be called by the name of the Lord God" (*houtos ēlpisen epikaleisthai tō onomati kyriou tou theou*), that is, to be called (*legesthai*) the "Son of God" and "God." For the descendants of Seth were righteous (*dikaioi*). Therefore, Scripture, being consistent with itself, says after this (Gen 6:2): "And the sons of God beheld the daughters of men." This refers to the righteous ones. For there had not yet been intermingling (*epimixia*) between the descendants of Seth and those of Cain.[49]

It appears that Eusebius of Emesa draws attention to the fact that the Hebraios version uses the dative form *tō onomati*, rather than the accusative form *to onoma* of the LXX. Since, as we have indicated, the infinitive

---

neither tends flocks nor tills the soil, but produces a child as spiritual things do (*hōs ta pneumatika*). And him [Enosh] who 'hoped to call upon the name of the Lord,' who looked upward and whose 'citizenship is in heaven' [Phil 3:20], him the world does not contain (*touton ho kosmos ou chōrei*)." Enosh in directing his attention "upward" (i.e., to God) becomes a "citizen of heaven," that is, one whose mind is not "set on earthly things" (Phil 3:19).

[49] Cited in *Origenis Hexaplorum* (ed. F. Field; 2 vols.; Oxford: Clarendon, 1875) 1.20 n. 28. Also in *PG* 86.556. The same passage is found in Procopius of Gaza (ca. 475–ca. 538), *Commentary to Genesis* (*PG* 87.261). This raises the question whether the passage was original with Eusebius of Emesa and later adopted by Procopius, or original with Procopius and later falsely ascribed to Eusebius of Emesa. Since there is neither internal nor external evidence which contradicts the attribution to Eusebius of Emesa, I will assume it to be correct. Further along in his commentary (*PG* 87.265–8), Procopius gives the same interpretation of Gen 6:2–4 in his own words: "The elect race, the descendants of Seth and Enosh, it calls 'angels' and 'sons of God,' on account of their piety (*hosiotēs*)." Eusebius of Emesa should be distinguished from the more famous Eusebius Pamphili of Caesarea, who was the former's teacher. H. Gelzer (*Sextus Julius Africanus und die byzantinische Chronographie* [2 vols.; Leipzig, 1885–98; repr. New York: Burt Franklin, n.d.] 1.62) mistakenly attributes the present passage to Eusebius of Caesaria.

epikaleisthai could be middle or passive, Eusebius takes the dative form as an indication of the passive voice, "was called *by* [or with] the name of the Lord God."[50]

According to Eusebius of Emesa, Enosh (though not specified by name) hoped to be called "Son of God" and "God." His descendants are the "sons of God" who consort with the "daughters of men" in Gen 6:2. But how does Eusebius derive the expression "Son of God" from Gen 4:26b? It may be that he interprets *kyrios* as a synonym for "Son of God," since both are used as epithets for Jesus in the New Testament.[51] It is more likely, however, that Eusebius simply considers "God" and "Son of God" to be synonyms when used as epithets for righteous humans. They are both understood to mean "godlike." Accordingly, "to be called by the name of the Lord God" does not simply mean to be called "Lord" or "God," but to be called by an epithet which employs the names "Lord" or "God," e.g., "Son of God."[52] The epithet "Son of

[50] The nature and origin of what is referred to as *ho hebraios* is uncertain. See DeLange, *Origen and the Jews*, 25–26; and *Origenis Hexaplorum* (ed. F. Field) 1.lxxi–lxxvii. Aquila, although translating *hwḥl* differently ("was begun"), also uses the dative, but following the preposition *en* (see chap. 1, n. 1). Aquila's version is the basis of a similar interpretation by Theodoret of Cyrus, cited below, n. 104. An examination of Greek translation of the phrase "to call on the name of the Lord" is instructive: In a clear majority of cases, the LXX uses a middle form of *epikaleō* with the accusative *to onoma*. In a few instances the dative *onomati* is used, but always following the preposition *en* or *epi*, e.g., Gen 12:8: *kai epekalesato epi tō onomati kyriou* ("and he called *upon* the name of the Lord"). However, in Isa 41:25, where *yiqrā' bišmî* is translated passively, we find the passive plus dative: *klēthēsontai tō onomati mou* ("they shall be called *by* [with] my name"). Similarly, in Symmachus' passive translation of Ps 80:19 (*ûbĕšimkā niqrā'*) we find: *kai tō onomati sou klēthēsmetha* ("and we will be called *by* your name"). Therefore, the dative form *tō onomati* might very well have been taken to mean "by the name," suggesting a passive understanding of *epikaleisthai*. While *legesthai* is similarly ambiguous, it is not generally used in the middle voice to mean naming or calling. See LSJ 1033–34.

[51] On *kyrios* in the NT see above, n. 28. On "Son of God" as an epithet of Jesus in the NT, see E. Schweizer, s.v. *huios*, *TDNT* 8 (1972) 363–92; F. Hahn, *The Titles of Jesus*, 279–333. On the Jewish background to the "Son of God" epithet, see J. Fitzmyer, *A Wandering Aramean: Collected Aramaic Essays* (SBL Monograph Series 25; Missoula: Scholars Press, 1979) 87–96, 102–7, 115–42; B. Byrne, *"Sons of God"–"Seed of Abraham": A Study of the Idea of the Sonship of God of All Christians in Paul Against the Jewish Background* (AnBib 83; Rome: Biblical Institute, 1979), especially pp. 9–78 for Rabbinic and pre-Rabbinic Jewish sources that speak of Israel as "sons" of God. Of course, the literature concerning these NT epithets is vast. The above cited references will direct the reader to other treatments.

[52] See above, chap. 1, n. 16; chap. 2, n. 10; below, nn. 105, 106. We now have an Aramaic text from Qumran which implies the very same thing: to be called "son of God" is to be called by God's name. The fragment is 4QpsDanA[a] (=4Q*246*), published by J. Fitzmyer, in "The Contribution of Qumran Aramaic to the Study of the New Testament," *NTS* 20 (1974) 391–94 (republished in *A Wandering Aramean*, 90–94; with an Addendum, pp. 101–7). According to Fitzmyer's reconstruction and translation: "[. . . He shall be called the son of] the [G]reat [God], and by his name shall he be named (*wbšmh ytknh*).

God" is included in his paraphrase of Gen 4:26b because of its presence in Gen 6:2. The underlying motivation for this exegesis, therefore, would seem to lie less in Gen 4:26b than in Gen 6:2, where Christian exegetes had been troubled for some time by the identity of the "sons of God."

The earliest Christian exegetes inherited the view that these "sons of God" were the "fallen angels," frequently referred to in Jewish sources of Second Temple times (especially *1 Enoch* 6–11). As legend had it, these angels descended to earth, where they either seduced or were seduced by the women and gave birth to the "giants" of Gen 6:4. To these angels and giants were traced the origins of much evil in the world.[53] Beginning in the third century, however, Christian exegetes became uncomfortable with this interpretation since it attributed evil, carnal behavior to incorporeal beings. Therefore, a trend emerged of "naturalizing" Gen 6:2ff., that is, understanding the "sons of God" not as supernatural beings, but as humans. This was most commonly done by taking the old, originally Jewish tradition of the "descendants of Seth" and the "descendants of Cain" and applying it to Gen 6:2. The "sons of God" are now understood to be the "descendants of Seth," while the "daughters of man" are taken to be the "descendants of Cain."[54]

He shall be hailed (as) the Son of God, and they shall call him Son of the Most High." The consensus is that this apocalyptic text refers to a *human* king, although his identity is not clear.

A less certain example of this phenomenon is 4QDibHam ("Les paroles des luminaires") 3:4–6 as rendered by B. Byrne ("Sons of God," 27): "We only have been called by thy name (*rq bšmkh [nz]krnw*) and for thy glory hast thou created us (*wlkbwdkh brtnw*) and to (the rank) of sons hast thou established us to thyself (*wbnym śmtnw lkh*) before the eyes of all the nations. For thou hast called Israel 'My son, my first born' (Exod 4:22) and thou hast schooled us (*wtysrnw*) as a man schools his own son . . ." M. Baillet (*RB* 68 [1961] 202) reconstructs the text as *rq bšmkh [hz]krnw*), and translates (p. 203), "Nous n'avons inv[oqué] que Ton nom." G. Vermes (*The Dead Sea Scrolls in English* [Baltimore: Penguin, 1968] 203) follows Baillet and translates, "We have called on Thy Name alone." I think, however, that Byrne has a good case in arguing for the *niph'al* perfect *nzkrnw*, given the fact that the context speaks of Israel as the recipient of divine favor. While Baillet states (p. 218) that "for thy glory hast thou created us" is taken from Isa 43:7 (*wlkbwdy br'tyw*), he fails to note the preceding words in Isaiah: "Everyone who is called by my name" (*kl hnqr' bšmy*). If Byrne is correct, then we have here another example from Qumran of being called by God's name associated with being considered God's son.

53 Some LXX versions have "Sons of God," while others have "angels of God." See below, n. 55. See B. J. Bamberger, *Fallen Angels* (Philadelphia: The Jewish Publication Society, 1952) 15–49 for the Jewish apocryphal traditions, and pp. 61–86 for New Testament and Patristic traditions; L. Ginzberg, *Legends*, 1.147–51; 5.169–72. This legend is now evidenced in the Dead Sea Scrolls: 4Q*180–81* in *DJD* 5 (ed. John M. Allegro, 1968) 77–79, pls. 27, 18; and probably in 1QapGen 2, and other fragments. See Devorah Dimant, " 'The Fallen Angels' in the Dead Sea Scrolls and in the Apocryphal and Pseudepigraphic Books Related to Them" (Ph.D. diss., Hebrew University, 1974).

54 See Bamberger, *Fallen Angels* 78–81. Cf. *Recognitions of (Pseudo-) Clement* 1.29 which speaks of the "sons of God" as "righteous men who had lived the life of angels." However, cf. *Recognitions* 4.26, and *Homilies* 4.12–13, where the story of the fallen

Eusebius of Emesa was not the first to adopt this line of interpretation. Our earliest extant source for this view is found in a fragment from the *Chronicles* of Julius Africanus (ca. 160–ca. 240), in which Africanus comments on Gen 6:2–4:

> When men became numerous on the earth, the angels of heaven came together (*synēlthon*) with the daughters of men. In some versions I have found "the sons of God" (*hoi huioi tou theou*).[55] What is meant, in my opinion, is that the descendants of Seth are called by the Spirit "sons of God" since the genealogies of the righteous and the patriarchs up until the Savior [Jesus] are traced from him [Seth]. But the descendants of Cain it calls "the seed of man," having nothing divine on account of the wickedness of their race and the dissimilarity of their natures, so that when they intermixed they caused God vexation.[56] But if we conclude that this [phrase "sons of God"] refers to angels, we must assume that they are the ones who transmitted knowledge about magic and sorcery, as well as about mathematics and the movements of celestial bodies to women, and by whose power the giants were

---

angels is retained. While Philo generally speaks of the "sons of God" as being incorporeal spirits or demons, he also states that Moses gives that name to "good and excellent men." *Qu. in Gen.* 1.92. Cf. *Gig.* 6–15. Early Rabbinic traditions similarly "demythologize" the "sons of God" of Gen 6:2, understanding them to be sons of judges or nobles. Cf. Symmachus' translation, *hoi huioi tōn dynasteuontōn* ("sons of the mighty"); the targumim ad loc.; and *Gen. Rab.* 26.5 (ed. Theodor-Albeck) 247–48, with Theodor's notes; P. S. Alexander, "The Targumim and Early Exegesis of 'Sons of God' in Gen 6," *JJS* 23 (1972) 60–71; Bamberger, *Fallen Angels*, 90–92. Rabbinic sources, however, do *not* know of the identification of the "sons of God" with the descendants of Seth. This appears to have been a distinctively Christian interpretation. Only in later, medieval Jewish sources is this view evidenced: *Jeraḥmeel* 24.10 (trans. M. Gaster) 51–52; Ibn Ezra ad Gen 6:2; RaMBaN ad Gen 6:4; Jehuda Halevi, *Kuzari* 1.95; 2.14. See also S. D. Luzzatto's *Commentary to the Pentateuch* (Hebrew) (ed. P. Schlesinger; Tel-Aviv: Dvir, 1965) 36. Cf. *AgBer.* (ed. Buber) intro. xxxviii-xxxix and *Zohar* 1.37a, where the "sons of God" are identified with the descendants of *Cain*. The tradition of the righteous Sethites and evil Cainites, already evidenced in very early non-Rabbinic sources (see chap. 1, n. 76), does not appear in Rabbinic sources until *Pirqe Rabbi Eliezer* (eighth century), where in chap. 22 (Warsaw) 50b–51a the "daughters of men" of Gen 6:2 are identified with the daughters of Cain, but the "sons of God" are still the fallen angels. See D. Luria's n. 16 ad loc. Similarly, see *Zohar* 1.55a. For further discussion, see Bamberger, *Fallen Angels*, 150–55. On the biblical expression *bĕnê 'ĕlōhîm* itself, see *'Enṣiqlopedya miqra'it* 2.172–74.

55 These two views are reflected in the various witnesses to the LXX text of Gen 6:2, 4, some having "sons of God," and others having "angels of God." See *Septuaginta Vetus Testamentum Graecum*, vol. 1 (ed. J. W. Wevers; Göttingen: Vandenhoeck and Ruprecht, 1974) 108–9.

56 *Kai dia to tēs physeōs anomoion, epimichthentōn autōn, tēn aganaktēsin poiēsasthai ton theon.* It is unclear whether Africanus means the intermingling of the Cainites among themselves, or with the Sethites. I have taken *to tēs physeōs anomoion* to refer to the Cainites' own dissimilar (impure) nature, and *epimichthentōn* to refer to their mixing with the Sethites. Philo (*Abr.* 9) distinguishes the pure race of Enosh from the "mixed race" (*michtos genos*) which preceded him. In *1 Enoch* 86 we are told that the black cows (Cainites) intermingled, changing pastures and stalls, so as to live with one another.

> conceived.[57] Because of them, wickedness came into being and God decided to obliterate the whole faithless race of living beings in the deluge.[58]

Africanus presents two possible interpretations. He seems to favor the first: since the Sethites are the righteous line from which descend not only the biblical patriarchs but Jesus the messiah himself, they are referred to as "sons of God" on account of their piety.[59]

Returning to Eusebius of Emesa, we see that he differs from Africanus in two significant ways. First, he recognizes only one interpretation of "sons of God" in Gen 6:2. Second, he links this interpretation with an interpretation of Gen 4:26. Taking the verb *epikaleisthai* passively, Eusebius finds in Gen 4:26b the origin of the term "sons of God" as an epithet for righteous humans. Enosh, by virtue of his righteousness, hoped to be called by a divine epithet, e.g., "God" (*theos*) or "son of God." It would seem that to Eusebius these are synonymous terms, at least when used for righteous humans. It is not clear from this passage whether, according to Eusebius, Enosh himself was ever called "God" or "son of God"; the ambiguity of the verb "hope" is simply let stand. In any case, Enosh's descendants, the whole Sethite line, are referred to as "sons of God," presumably because of their righteousness. Enosh's hope for himself, as expressed in Gen 4:26b, is fulfilled in his descendants, according to Gen 6:2.

While the distinction between the righteous descendants of Seth and the wicked descendants of Cain is very old, going back to our earliest

57 The Greek syntax is difficult here and may be variously translated, but the sense for our purposes is clear enough: These are the fallen angels who by teaching the "civilized" arts to manking induced their downfall. Cf. *1 Enoch* 9. Africanus' expressions "by whose power" and (above) "came together" appear to be euphemisms, avoiding the statement that the angels had intercourse with women. See Bamberger, *Fallen Angels*, 273 n. 23.

58 The passage is quoted by George Syncellus in his *Chronographia* (ed. W. Dindorf; CSHB; Bonn: Weber, 1829) 34–35. It can also be found in M. Routh, ed., *Reliquiae Sacrae* (5 vols.; 2nd ed., Oxford: E Typographeo Academico, 1846) 2.238; and *PG* 10.65.

59 Thus Seth is the progenitor of the righteous and the Messiah, who trace their ancestry back to Adam through him. Cf. Luke 3:23–38. A similar interpretation of the biblical genealogies is already found in Philo, *Post.* 42, 172–74. Rabbinic sources also state that Seth is the ancestor of the righteous and the Messiah, sometimes interpreting "another seed" of Gen 4:25 messianically: *Gen. Rab.* 23.5; *PRE* 22. See Ginzberg, *Legends*, 5.149 n. 52. So-called gnostic groups are also reported to have venerated Seth as the ancestor of the Messiah, and to have identified the two. See Epiphanius, *Panarion* (*Haereses*) 39.3–5 (GCS 31 [ed. Karl Holl, 1922] 668–72). Much of this is now confirmed in the newly discovered "gnostic" texts themselves, which emphasize Seth's role as the bearer of the messianic "seed." See A. F. J. Klijn, *Seth in Jewish, Christian and Gnostic Literature* (Leiden: E. J. Brill, 1977) 81–117; G. Stroumsa, "Another Seed: Studies in Sethian Gnosticism" (Ph.D. diss., Harvard, 1978). In Arabic sources Seth is the bearer of divine light, passed from generation to generation until the "messenger of God." See T. Gluck, "The Arabic Legend of Seth, the Father of Mankind" (Ph.D. diss., Yale Univ., 1968) 85ff.

Jewish sources and perhaps to the Hebrew Bible itself, Africanus is the first we know of to combine this tradition with a desire to "demythologize" Gen 6:2–4. Eusebius of Emesa, in turn, is the first to link this interpretation of Gen 6:2 to a passive interpretation of *epikaleisthai* in Gen 4:26b.[60] However, his interpretation results in an ambiguity: the righteous descendants of Seth earn the title "sons of God" in recognition of their piety, but it is Enosh, Seth's son, who is the first to be called (or to hope to be called) by this name. Later Christian exegetes will try to iron out this wrinkle.

b. Didymus the Blind of Alexandria (ca. 313–398)

Didymus, a contemporary of Eusebius of Emesa, presents a very similar, although distinctive, interpretation of Enosh as having hoped to *be called* by God's name. Since there is no reason to assume that the two had any influence on one another, it may be that they arrived at similar understandings of Gen 4:26 concurrently, yet independently.

On Genesis.[61] This recently discovered and published commentary contains an interesting and somewhat unique interpretation of Gen 4:26. Didymus begins by stating that when a saint gives birth to a saint the offspring inherits both the physical and the spiritual characteristics of the parent:

> Seth, therefore, who was begotten in place of a just one [Abel], gave birth to Enosh; a just to a just. And this one [Enosh] instead of having a proper name is called "man" (*anthrōpos kaleitai*), which name bears witness to the virtue of his soul, preserving the "in the image" and the state of being truly man (*sōzousēs to kat' eikona kai tēn tou ontōs ontos anthrōpou katastasin*). For Enosh according to the Hebrews is "man." Truly, it [Scripture] confers upon him that which is distinctive of man. "He," it says, "hoped to be called (*epikaleisthai*) by the name of the Lord," that action

60 Since we do not have Africanus' *History* in its entirety, we cannot know whether he too may have elsewhere drawn a connection between Gen 6:2 and 4:26b. Certainly, in the extant fragments he makes no such association. Heinrich Gelzer (*Sextus Julius Africanus*, 61–62), however, takes another reference to Africanus by George Syncellus as proof that Africanus already interpreted Gen 4:26b to mean that Enosh *was called* "God." However, there are not sufficient grounds for this assumption, as we shall see when we examine the passage in question in our discussion of Syncellus. See below, n. 128.

61 Didymus' complete commentary on Genesis was found in sixth/seventh century papyrus codices discovered near Tour, south of Cairo, in 1941. I have used the published edition: Didyme L'Aveugle, *Sur la Genèse* (ed. and trans. P. Nautin; 2 vols.; SC 233, 244; Paris: Les Editions du Cerf, 1976–78) 1.330–33. Didymus mentions Enosh once again ad Gen 7:1 (ed. Nautin, 2.90), but only to say that he, like Abel, was righteous. Previously only a few fragments from this commentary were known (see *PG* 39.1112–14), but our passage was not among them. Didymus was an ascetic theologian in Alexandria, and is said to have taught Jerome and Rufinus. He defended Origen, who seems to have had significant influence on him. See Quasten, *Patrology*, 3.85–86.

> which is fitting for the righteous man. For the true hope is to resemble God as much as possible (*elpis de hē tō onti hautē estin to homoiōthevai to theo kata to dynaton*).[62] "To hope to be called by the name of the Lord God" also denotes one who has subjected himself to the authority (*exousia*) and instruction (*didaskalia*) of God.

At first, Didymus seems to follow Philo: Enosh, meaning "man," represents true man (or man in his "being"). But Didymus adds a notion that we have also witnessed in Ambrose: Enosh means man in the image of God, that is, man who is godlike.[63] Next, Didymus interprets the second half of Gen 4:26, taking *epikaleisthai* to be passive: Enosh hoped to be called by God's name; that is, he aspired to being like God, subjecting himself to God's authority and instruction.[64] This last comment suggests that Didymus, like Eusebius of Caesarea, understood the divine names *kyrios* and *theos* to reflect two different divine attributes: God the master, and God the benefactor.[65] While Eusebius states that Enosh recognized and had faith in these two divine attributes, Didymus stresses that Enosh subjected himself to these two aspects of God.

Didymus' interpretation is significant in two respects. First, he interprets Gen 4:26b as an explanation of the name Enosh in 4:26a. If Enosh is man in God's image, it is fitting that Scripture attributes to such a man the hope to resemble God (to be called by God's name), that is, truly to realize the potential of that image.[66] Didymus sounds very much like

62 "Likeness to God so far as possible" is a tag from Plato, *Theaetus* 176B, perhaps via Philo (*Fug.* 63; cf. *Spec. Leg.* 4.188). For its influence on the Platonic tradition, see J. Dillon, *The Middle Platonists: A Study of Platonism 80 BC-AD 220* (London: Duckworth, 1977) 9, 44, 123, 145, 299. On *Imitatio Dei* in early Jewish tradition, see H. A. Wolfson, *Philo: Foundations of Religious Philosophy in Judaism, Christianity, and Islam* (2 vols.; Cambridge: Harvard University, 1968) 2.194–96; G. F. Moore, *Judaism in the First Centuries of the Christian Era* (3 vols.; Cambridge: Harvard, 1927–40) 1.441; 2.110–11, 172–73; S. Schechter, *Aspects of Rabbinic Theology* (New York: Macmillan, 1909) 199–218; E. E. Urbach, *The Sages: Their Concepts and Beliefs* (trans. I. Abrahams; 2 vols.; Jerusalem: Magnes, 1975) 1.383; 2.852 nn. 48–49; A. Marmorstein, "The Imitation of God (Imitatio Dei) in the Haggadah," in *Studies in Jewish Theology* (ed. J. Rabbinowitz and M. S. Lew; London, 1950) 106–21; M. Smith, "The Image of God," *BJRL* 40 (1958) 473–512. See below, n. 66.

63 The implication is that Enosh inherited the "divine image" from Seth. In chapter 4 I will discuss Rabbinic traditions that similarly affirm that Enosh was in God's image, like Seth and Adam before him, but unlike his successors.

64 Didymus cites the standard LXX version. It is the context of his interpretation which suggests a passive understanding of *epikaleisthai*. Nautin translates, "être appelé du nom."

65 In a note to his edition of our text Nautin states (p. 333): "Il semble que Didyme rapporte la puissance au titre de 'Seigneur' et l'enseignement au titre de 'Dieu,' sous l'influence de Philon, *Sob.* 55. Chez Philon, le second titre évoquait en réalité le bienfaiteur, amis pour Didyme, comme pour Origène, le bienfait par excellence c'est l'enseignement." On Philo's interpretation of the divine names, see above, n. 38.

66 Didymus' interpretation is strikingly similar to what we find in *Sifre Deut.* 49 (ed.

Philo, who stated that Enosh was "that living being whose nature is a mixture of mortal and immortal," who strives to be man par excellence. While Philo creates an elaborate picture of this ideal man, we have seen that he is unable satisfactorily to root his interpretation in the biblical verse itself, in part because the LXX has Enosh only hope to call on God's name. Thus, Philo can interpret Enosh the hoper positively only by disregarding the words "to call on the name of the Lord." Didymus, however, by interpreting the verb *epikaleisthai* passively, roots his positive interpretation of Enosh in these very words. Enosh's hope is now entirely positive: he hopes (aspires) to resemble God. To Didymus Gen 4:26 as a whole means: Seth called his son Enosh, meaning ideal man, or man in God's image, *for* this one hoped to be called by God's name, i.e., to resemble God.

The second significant aspect of Didymus' interpretation is that it interprets the verb *epikaleisthai* passively without any allusion to Gen 6:2. Before this commentary was known it could be said that those Christian exegetes who understood *epikaleisthai* to be passive were motivated by the need to explain the "sons of God" as referring to the once righteous descendants of Seth or Enosh. Didymus' interpretation may suggest that the motivation for such a passive understanding of *epikaleisthai* could also derive from Gen 4:26 itself. Those Christian exegetes who interpret Gen 4:26 in relation to the "sons of God" of Gen 6:2 suggest a particularly Christian typology: Enosh as the first "son of God" corresponds to (foreshadows) the New Testament "son of God." This suggestion is missing from Didymus' exegesis, which focuses entirely on Enosh in his own right as representing man par excellence, i.e., godlike man. Didymus' passive reading of *epikaleisthai* carries the exegesis of Philo and Eusebius of Caesarea one step forward: Enosh as true man aspires to be godlike.

c. John Chrysostom (ca. 347–407)

Chrysostom's exegesis is of particular interest, and therefore will be considered in some detail, since it mirrors the changing Christian interpretation of Gen 4:26: Enosh as a righteous paradigm develops into Enosh the first human to be called by God's name.

Homilies in Genesis 20.4.[67] In this passage Chrysostom takes Gen 4:26 as an example of how men demonstrate prudence (*eugnōmosynē*) in naming their offspring:

Finkelstein) 114, where Joel 3:5 (*kōl 'ăšer-yiqrā' běšem YHWH*) is interpreted passively (*yiqqārē'*) in the sense of *Imitatio Dei*. See above, chap. 2, n. 10.

[67] *PG* 53.172. Chrysostom's *Homilies in Genesis* are thought to have been delivered in Antioch around the year 388. See Quasten, *Patrology*, 3.434.

> For this one, Seth, it says, giving birth to a son, named him Enosh. Then, the divine Scripture, wishing to interpret for us the naming, says: "He hoped to call upon the name of the Lord God."

Chrysostom, like Didymus, takes Gen 4:26b as an explanation of the naming of Enosh. However, unlike Didymus, he does not state the connection. There is nothing in the context of Chrysostom's comments to suggest a passive understanding of the verb *epikaleisthai*, nor is there any hint of a pun on the meaning of Enosh. We can only guess at his intent.[68]

Chrysostom next explains how the "blessed prophet" wished to begin the human genealogy anew with Seth, and to abandon the genealogy of Cain's line with Lamech, since Cain had lost his natural privilege of primogeniture due to his evil character (*hē kakia tēs proaireseōs*). Seth, however, because of his prudent disposition (*hē tēs proaireseōs eugnomōsynē*), now receives the rights of primogeniture and his descendants are deemed worthy of inclusion in the geneaology.[69] Returning to Enosh, Chrysostom says:

> Just as Enosh was named (*eklēthē*) because of [his] calling on the name of the Lord, so too those who descend from him are honored with the same name. With this the blessed prophet stops the narrative and begins again from the start.[70]

Both Seth and Enosh are praised: Seth is praised for his prudence in naming Enosh, and is rewarded by being granted the privilege of primogeniture, which by nature belongs to Cain. Enosh is praised for his faithfulness and is rewarded by being given the name "man," which also becomes the collective name of his descendants. Since, according to Chrysostom, it is Seth's prudence and Enosh's piety which earn them their roles as progenitors of mankind, the biblical narrative breaks off with Gen 4:26 and begins the genealogy anew, this time excluding the Cainites, and tracing the lineage of mankind (*genesis anthrōpōn*, Gen

[68] We can certainly come up with a number of explanations that *may* lie behind Chrysostom's statement: (a) Enosh is the true *man*, and as such places his hope in God (Philo and Eusebius). (b) Enosh is man in his weakness or frailty (Hebrew *'nš*), who must turn to God for support, etc. Chrysostom *himself*, however, does not indicate what he has in mind. We have noted (above, n. 34) that Jerome too assumes a connection between the two halves of the verse, but does not indicate what that connection might be.

[69] The same word, *eugnōmosynē*, was used previously by Chrysostom in reference to men's "prudence" in naming their children. It would appear, therefore, that Seth is praised for the sagacity with which he names Enosh.

[70] We have seen in Philo and Marqah similar attempts to explain the sudden break between Gen 4:26b and 5:1 by interpreting one in light of the other. See above, chap. 1, n. 49; chap. 2, n. 16. We will witness similar interpretations in Augustine and in Rabbinic commentaries.

5:1) through Seth and Enosh. Thus, Gen 4:26 is interpreted by Chrysostom to both Seth's and Enosh's credit.

Homilies in Genesis 22.2–3.[71] In this passage Chrysostom quite polemically rejects the "blasphemous" interpretation of Gen 6:2 that identifies the "sons of God" with the fallen angels. He argues that the term "sons" or "sons of God" is nowhere else in the Bible applied to angels: *anthrōpoi men gar eklēthēsan huioi theou, aggeloi de oudamōs* ("while men are called 'sons of God,' angels never"). Chrysostom gives several scriptural examples in which, he claims, men are referred to as "gods" or "sons of God": Ps 81(82):6; Isa 1:2; Exod 4:22.[72] Furthermore, argues Chrysostom, it is preposterous to imagine incorporeal beings having intercourse with women. In support, he cites Jesus' "own" words (Matt 22:30; cf. Mark 12:25; Luke 20:35): "For in the resurrection they neither marry nor are given in marriage, but are like angels of God."[73]

Having refuted the view that "sons of God" are angels, Chrystostom continues:

> We previously demonstrated to you that Scripture habitually (*ethos*) calls men "sons of God." Since, therefore, these [sons of God] are the ones who trace their descent from Seth and from his son Enosh; for this one, it says, hoped to call upon the name of the Lord God; his descendants were called "sons of God" in the Holy Scripture because of imitating the virtue (*aretē*) of their forefathers as far back as he. And it names "sons of man" those who were born before Seth, the sons of Cain, and those who are descended from him [Cain].

Chrysostom concludes by offering a paraphrase of Gen 6:2 in which he identifies the "sons of God" as "the descendants of Seth and Enosh" (*hoi apo tou Sēth kai tou Enōs*).

In this passage Chrysostom, like Eusebius of Emesa before him, turns to Gen 4:26 in order to elucidate Gen 6:2: If "sons of God" refers to righteous humans, and since Genesis 4–5 distinguishes the righteous descendants of Seth from the evil ones of Cain, the "sons of God" must refer to

[71] *PG* 53.187–89.

[72] It should be noted that Chrysostom's examples either refer to Israel as God's "son (child)" or "sons" (Exod 4:22; Isa 1:2), or to men as "gods" (Ps 81 [82]:6). None of his examples refers explicitly to humans as "son(s) of God." It is surprising, therefore, that he does not cite Hos 2:1, where the Israelites are referred to as "children of the living God." Cf. Wis 18:13, where Israel is referred to as *theou huion* ("son of God"); Dan 3:25, where the fourth man in the furnace is *dmh lbr 'lhyn* ("like a son of the gods"). Chrysostom also fails to cite Job 1:6; 2:1; 38:7, where the term "sons of God" is clearly used as a name for angelic beings (the LXX has *aggeloi*).

[73] The standard Greek text of Matt 22:30 and Mark 12:25 has *hos aggeloi en tō ouranō* ("like angels in heaven"), but a number of testimonies witness a variant *aggeloi theou*. See the critical apparatus of Nestle-Aland, *Novum Testamentum Graece* (Stuttgart: Deutsche Bibelstiftung, 1979) 63, 131.

the former. These human "sons of God" derive their special status not only from their genealogical descent, but also from their imitating their ancestors Seth and Enosh.[74] Gen 4:26b is cited here *parenthetically* in order to identify Enosh with that virtue of his which, by implication, was imitated. While Seth, standing opposite Cain, is the head of the Sethite line genealogically speaking, it is Enosh whose virtuous act (or intention) is specifically referred to as the object of imitation. Thus, for Chrysostom, Gen 4:26 is not cited in order to prove the identification of the term "sons of God" with humans; for that purpose he uses other scriptural verses. Rather, Gen 4:26 is cited in order to show *why* the descendants of Seth were so honored. In this passage, as in the previous one, Chrysostom comes very close to interpreting the verb *epikaleisthai* passively, but, it seems, never does.

Expositio in Psalmum 49:1.[75] Chrysostom's commentary on Psalms is generally thought to have been written about twelve years after his commentary on Genesis.[76] For the first time he explicitly interprets Gen 4:26 to mean that Enosh *was called* by God's name.

Chrysostom is troubled by the phrase *theos theōn* ("God of gods") in Ps 49(50):1, since it might be taken to suggest that the Lord God is only one of several gods, and that the Bible in calling those other gods by the name of God affirms their divinity.[77] Chrysostom cites other scriptural cases in which the word *theos* (or *theoi*) seems to refer to something or someone other than God: Ps 81(82):6 ("I have said, you are gods"); 1 Cor 8:5 ("there are many called 'gods' and 'lords' "); Exod 22:27 ("you shall not revile gods"); Gen 6:2 ("the sons of God beheld the daughters of men"); Lev 24:15–16 ("whoever curses [a] god shall bear his sin"); and Jer 10:11 ("gods who have created neither heaven nor earth").[78] Chrysostom then asks:

74 This is similar to Didymus' statement that the righteous inherit from their parents not just a physical resemblance, but a spiritual one as well. Thus, the Sethites acquire their special status not only by virtue of their descent, but also as a reward for their imitating the spiritual attributes of their ancestors. The genealogy, thus, is twofold: biological and spiritual.

75 *PG* 55.240–42.

76 See Quasten, *Patrology*, 3.435.

77 This passage was problematic for the rabbis as well. See *MPs*. 50.1 (ed. Buber) 278–79, where *mînîm* (sectarians) come to R. Simlai (fl. 279–320), inquiring about Ps 50:1. He responds: " 'they spoke and called' is not written here, but 'he spoke and called.' " Thus, the *mînîm* must have figured that the Psalmist speaks of a plurality of gods. R. Simlai's students are not satisfied with their teacher's flimsy explanation, and to them he replies: "The three [names, *'ēl, 'ĕlōhîm, YHWH]* are one name. And why is God's name mentioned three times here? In accord with the three good attributes with which the world was created: wisdom, understanding, and knowledge." Cf. *p. Ber*. 9.1 (12a). *Tg. Ket*. Ps 50:1 has: *tqyp' 'lh' yhwh* ("The Mighty One, God, YHWH"). See below, n. 82.

78 In Ps 81:6; Exod 22:27; and Jer 10:4, the LXX uses the plural *theoi* ("gods") in translating *'ĕlōhîm*, whereas it usually uses the singular *theos*. In Lev 24:15, however, it uses the singular *theos*, suggesting that it takes *'ĕlōhîm* here to refer to God. Chrysostom seems

> Therefore, what is meant by this term in these various testimonies? And which gods are referred to? Rulers (*hoi archontes*)![79] Thus, it says, "you shall not revile gods (*theoi*) nor curse the rulers of your people (*archōn tou laou sou*)" (Exod 22:28). It refers to those who descend from ancestors of distinction. For since Enosh showed himself to be greatly righteous, he was called by the name of God (*eklēthē tō onomati tou theou*).[80] All of that one's descendants and those of his brother mingled with one another.[81] Those descending from the one of distinction Scripture calls "sons of God," for they began [were the first], it says, to be called by the name of God (*ērxanto . . . epikaleisthai tō onomati tou theou*). And so too it says that the people of the Jews were honored with this name in the statement, "I have said, you are gods and sons of the most high,"[82] for He calls the people thus on account of [His] fitting benevolence (*di' oikeian philanthrōpian*).

So, according to Chrysostom, *theos* is often used in the Bible to refer to righteous humans who are honored with the title "gods."[83] Many problematic verses can be explained once we understand that "god" or "gods" can refer to humans. This approach is itself not new for Chrysostom, for he already applied it in explicating Gen 6:2 in his *Homilies*. What is new is Chrysostom's explicit reference to Enosh as the *first* human to be called by God's name as a sign of honor. In this passage the verb *epikaleisthai* is clearly understood to be passive, an apparent shift

---

to interpret this last verse as referring to humans, probably by analogy with Exod 22:27. Except for Lev 24:15, these verses are similarly interpreted to refer to humans in other versions as well: Targum (Ps 82:6; Exod 22:27; Gen 6:2,4; Jer 10:11), Samaritan Tg. (Gen 6:2,4); *Peshiṭta* (Exod 22:27). The Vulgate consistently follows the LXX in distinguishing *'ĕlōhîm* as "gods" from "God."

79 Cf. the targumic translation of *bĕnê 'ĕlōhim* with *bĕnê rabrĕbayā';* Samaritan Tg., *bry šlṭnyh;* Symmachus, *hoioi tōn dynasteuontōn;* all meaning "sons of the great, mighty, or rulers."

80 Note that here and below, where Chrysostom clearly understands *epikaleisthai* passively, he uses the dative *tō onomati*, while earlier in *Homilies in Genesis*, where he seems to have understood the same verb to be active, he used the accusative *to onoma*. See above, n. 50.

81 There seems to be some confusion of Enosh and Seth here, for "his brother" must refer to Cain, who is Seth's and not Enosh's brother.

82 The Greek text of Chrysostom reads *huioi Israel* misquoting Ps 81:6, *huioi hypsistou*. Likewise, in Rabbinic traditions, Ps 82:6 is interpreted to refer to the Israelites, who when standing at Mt. Sinai were like "gods": *b. 'Abod. Zar.* 5a; *Exod. Rab.* 32.1, 7; *Sifre Deut.* 306; *Lev. Rab.* 4.1; 11.3; 18.3; and parallels.

83 Chrysostom continues by explaining that the term *theos* is also used in the Bible to refer to non-gods who are *falsely* called "gods" by the pagans. According to him, the biblical intent is not to honor such non-gods, but to demonstrate the error in their so being called. He cites 1 Cor 8:5, where Paul refers to the "so-called gods" (*legomenoi theoi*). Hence, in Ps 49(50):1 Scripture calls these non-gods "gods" only in order to deny their worth, by stating that God is the master even of these so-called gods. The problem of the Bible's calling of false gods "gods" is similarly dealt with in *Mek. Baḥodeš* 6, to be treated in chapter 4.

since his writing of the *Homilies*. However, according to Chrysostom, Enosh's descendants earned the very same distinction; they too began (*ērxanto*) to be called by the name of God. This paraphrase cannot be based on the LXX *houtos ēlpisen epikaleisthai* ("he hoped to call"), but probably derives from Aquila's passive translation *tote ērchthē* ("then was begun"), which can be interpreted to refer both to Enosh and to his descendants.[84]

In this last passage a number of exegetical traditions converge, all of which but the last were already evidenced in Chrysostom's earlier writings: (a) The word *theos* (or *theoi*) in several scriptural passages refers to humans of distinction. (b) The expression "sons of God" in Gen 6:2 cannot refer to incorporeal beings, so it must likewise refer to such humans. (c) These "sons of God" are the descendants of the righteous Seth (and Enosh), who in mingling with the Cainites increased evil in the world to a point necessitating the Flood. (d) These Sethites are called "sons of God" not only because of their own righteousness but also because they are descendants (and imitators) of Enosh, who was the *first to be called* by God's name on account of his virtue. The passive interpretation of *epikaleisthai*, avoided by Chrysostom in his *Homilies*, now provides the final cement which holds together a masterful argument. The passive interpretation of *epikaleisthai* is now not only unmistakable, but is clearly linked to an interpretation of scriptural godlike humans who are called "sons of God" and "gods" originating with the antediluvian Sethites and with Enosh in particular. We might say that Chrysostom broadens Eusebius of Emesa's interpretation of Gen 4:26 so as to deal not simply with the problematic "sons of God" of Gen 6:2, but more generally with the recurring phenomenon of godlike humans who are called by God's name in Scripture. The implications for an understanding of the New Testament "Son" and "sons of God" are left implicit.

d. Augustine (354–430)

Augustine, like other Christian Church Fathers of the fourth century, attributes great significance to Enosh as an ancient righteous figure who foreshadows Christian faith in Jesus. However, Augustine, writing in Latin, worked from the Old Latin version of the Bible, which unlike the LXX did not permit a passive understanding of the verb "to call" in Gen 4:26b. Therefore, Augustine's interpretation of Enosh's importance rests not on an interpretation of Enosh as one who hoped to be called by God's name, but

[84] Chrysostom is the first Christian exegete to paraphrase "was begun" in the active plural. His paraphrase is very similar to that of the rabbis, which we will first witness in the targumim: then was begun by men, or men began. While the targumim understand the phrase to refer negatively to Enosh's contemporaries, Chrysostom takes it to refer positively to Enosh's descendants.

on an interpretation of the *prophetic* character of his hope.

In *De Civitate Dei* 15.17–18[85] Augustine attributes great significance to the two biblical genealogies given in Genesis 4–5, that of the descendants of Seth and that of the descendants of Cain. The former represents the "City of God" (*civitas Dei*), while the latter the "Earthly City" (*civitas terrena*). The characteristics of each city, says Augustine, are reflected in what Scripture tells us concerning the sons of Seth and the sons of Cain.

Augustine interprets Seth's name to mean "resurrection."[86] Enosh's name means "man," but unlike that of Adam refers to incorporeal or asexual man:

> Enosh, on the other hand, means man in a sense which, according to scholars of the Hebrew language, does not allow it to be applied to woman; it stands for son of resurrection (*tamquam filius resurrectionis*), where people "will neither be given in marriage nor marry" (Luke 20:35). For there will be no generation at the resurrection, when they have arrived there through regeneration.[87]

Thus, if Seth means "resurrection," Enosh is the "son of resurrection," which term suggests the "sons of resurrection" (*tes anastaseos huioi*) or "sons of God" of Luke 20:35–36, who neither marry nor are subject to death. Augustine notes that this celibate state is reflected in the Sethite geneaology, in which no women are mentioned by name, whereas in the Cainite genealogy women (Adah, Zillah) *are* named.

Augustine continues his interpretation of Enosh by citing Gen 4:26 (Old Latin) and commenting:

> It is in hope, then, that man, son of resurrection, lives, in hope that the City of God, which springs from a belief in the resurrection of Christ, lives so long as it sojourns on earth. For since

85 CSEL 40.2 (ed. Emanuel Hoffmann, 1900) 95–99. The English translation is from Saint Augustine, *The City of God Against the Pagans* (trans. P. Levine; LCL, vol. 4; Cambridge: Harvard University, 1966) 510–21.

86 The name Seth (*šēt*) is variously interpreted in other sources (Philo, Mandaean, Rabbinic) to mean "foundation" (from the root *šyt*), "watering" (from *šth*), or "planting" (from *štl*). While any of these may have messianic overtones, Augustine may derive his interpretation from "another seed" (Gen 4:25). Seth, being Abel's replacement, can be viewed as a life resurrected. Seth is also interpreted as resurrection (*exanastasis*) in Anastasius Sinaita (d. ca. 700), *Viae Dux* (*PG* 89.236–37), which explains that the divine likeness and countenance was renewed in Seth. Cf. Jerome, *Liber interpretationis Hebraicorum Nominum* (CChr. 72.71). On Seth representing the "seed" of the Messiah, see above, n. 59.

87 LCL 4.512–13. Philo (*Leg. All.* 1.31–42) draws a similar distinction between "heavenly man" (*ouranios anthrōpos*) and "earthly man" (*gēïnos anthrōpos*). The former is in the "image of God" and "is altogether without part or lot in corruptible and terrestrial substance" (LCL 1.167). Ambrose similarly interprets Enosh as being (a) ideal man, (b) man in the image of God, (c) man who withdraws from the "pleasures of flesh." See above, n. 48.

> Abel's name means mourning and his brother Seth's means resurrection, the death of Christ and his coming to life from among the dead are foreshadowed in these two men. And belief in this gives rise here on earth to the City of God, that is, to a man who "hoped to call upon the name of the Lord God."[88]

While Seth represents Jesus' resurrection, Enosh represents that man who believes in Jesus' resurrection, and hopes to call on his name.[89] Since it is belief in that resurrection which sustains the City of God on earth, Enosh symbolizes that City through his faith (hope) in the Lord Jesus. Augustine, citing Rom 8:24–25 ("hope that is seen is not hope"), says that true hope cannot be in what one sees, but only in what one does not see, but must await. Thus, Enosh's hope is a *prophetic* one:

> Why, therefore, should that be said of Enos in particular which is known to be true of all godly men equally? The reason is this: he is mentioned as the first offspring of the father of the generations that have been reserved for a better portion, that is, are to participate in the city above; and it is therefore fitting that we should have foreshadowed in him the man, that is, the society of men, that lives not according to man in the actuality of earthly happiness, but according to God in the hope of eternal happiness. Now it is not said: "He hoped in the Lord God," or: "He called upon the name of the Lord God." Rather Scripture states: "He hoped to call upon the name of the Lord God." The words "he hoped to call" can only mean, prophetically, that a people would arise which, chosen by grace,[90] would call upon the name of the Lord God. . . . For the words: "And he called his name Enos," which means man, and those that follow: "He hoped to call upon the name of the Lord God," make it sufficiently plain that man should not place his hope in himself. As we read elsewhere, "Cursed is everyone who places his hope in man" (Jer 17:5); and thus no one should place his hope in himself if he is to be a citizen of that other city, which is not dedicated, after the manner of Cain's son,[91] in this present time, that is, in the transcience of this mortal age, but in the immortality of everlasting bliss.[92]

Augustine suggests that what is original with Enosh is not his calling on the

88 LCL 4.516–17.

89 Cf. Origen's treatment of Enosh in his *Commentary to Romans* 8.3 (above, n. 27). While Origen similarly understands Jesus to be the object of Enosh's calling, he does not base this interpretation on the verb "hope" (which he elsewhere views negatively), and does not suggest that Enosh's activity was prophetic.

90 The people "chosen by grace" (*electionem gratiae*) would appear to be the Christian elect. Cf. Romans 11:5. Augustine cites Joel 2:32 (3:5) for another prophecy of people who will "call upon the name of the Lord," interpreted by Paul (Rom 10:13) to refer to the Church. Cf. Origen on this same passage, above, n. 28.

91 The allusion here is to Gen 4:17, where Cain builds a city and names it after his son. This city is understood by Augustine to represent the Earthly City.

92 LCL 4.518–21.

name (worshipping) of God, but the prophetic faith in the expectation of the otherworldly City of God, embodied in Jesus' resurrection. Thus, Enosh to Augustine is a prophet who both foreshadows the Church (as "son of the resurrection") and faithfully awaits it. He represents the City of God on earth and hopes for its final fulfillment. He lives on earth, but puts his hope in heaven.

In *De Civitate Dei* 15.21[93] Augustine more sharply delineates the contrast between the Cainite and Sethite genealogies of Genesis 4–5 as representing respectively the Earthly City and the City of God. While the Cainite genealogy proceeds without interruption until the Flood (ending with Lamech), the Sethite line is interrupted following Enosh, and after the phrase "this is the book of the descent of man" (Gen 5:1) begins again with Adam. According to Augustine, this peculiarity lends particular significance to Enosh. It is he, and not Seth, who both heads and typifies the whole Sethite line, i.e., the City of God on earth.

> It must be that this was the right way to present the two cities, the one by citing a slayer at its beginning and end (for Lamech too confesses to his two wives that he had committed a murder [Gen 4:23]), the other by citing the man who hoped to call upon the name of the Lord God. For while the City of God sojourns as an alien in the present world, this calling upon the Lord is its whole and supreme occupation in this mortal life of ours, and it was to be represented in the person of one man who was son certainly of a resurrection of a man who was slain. This one person exemplifies the unity of the entire heavenly city, which, though not yet fulfilled, is destined to be fulfilled, according to that prophetic foreshadowing which preceded it.[94]

Augustine next contrasts Seth's son with Cain's son (Enoch of Gen 4:17). The latter, being "the son of earthly possession," has a "name in the earthly city since it was established in his name."[95] Enosh, however, does not place his confidence in earthly possessions but in God: "He foreshadows the society of men that says, 'Like a fruitful olive tree in the house of God, I have put my hope in the mercy of God' (Ps 52:8)." Such a man does not "seek the hollow renown of a celebrated name on earth, for 'blessed is the man whose hope is in the name of the Lord, and who has no regard for vanities and lying follies' (Ps 40:4)."[96] Augustine seems to find significance

93 CSEL 40.2.105–7; LCL 4.536–43.

94 Cf. Hebrews 11:8–16, especially vs. 10, in which Paul says of Abraham, "for he looked forward to the city which has foundations, whose builder and maker is God."

95 Cain's name (*qayin*) is taken to mean "possession" (from *qnh*, as in Gen 4:1). Cain's naming of a city (Gen 4:17) after his son is likewise understood as a sign of his greed for material possessions and fame. Cf. Philo, *Post.* 49–51; Josephus, *Ant.* 1.2.1 §§52–3. Similar Rabbinic interpretations of Cain and his descendants will be treated below in chapter 5.

96 The Latin version of Ps 40:4 undoubtedly rests on the LXX (39:5): *makarios anēr, hou estin to onoma kyriou elpis autou.* Similarly, the *Peshiṭta* has: *ṭwbwhy lbrnš' d'l šmh*

in Enosh's name: Enosh lacks a proper name of his own, being called simply "man." Thus, Augustine links the two halves of Gen 4:26: Enosh, who lacks a name, places his hope in calling upon the Lord's name. Cain, by contrast, has a proper name which suggests earthly possession and greed, and names a city after his son. This interpretation of Enosh's name is very different from that of previous interpreters (especially Philo and Eusebius) who stress that Enosh's name is one of distinction. Augustine concludes, "Thus we have the two cities set before us, one existing in the actuality of this world and the other in hope placed in God."

In the above passages, Augustine has woven together a number of motifs which we have seen elsewhere: (a) The descendants of Seth are the righteous line, to which the Messiah belongs. (b) Enosh means asexual man, or "son of the resurrection," a term which in the NT is associated with "son of God" as a term for the Christian believer. (c) Enosh's hope is a prophetic one, which foreshadows both Jesus, and the Church which would similarly "call on the name of the Lord." (d) Enosh, being otherworldly, places his hope not in himself or in the material, earthly realm, but in the heavenly one.

Augustine integrates these motifs into his theology of the two cities. But he is also able to "solve" a number of exegetical problems in ways that are consistent with his broader purposes: (a) the relation of the name Enosh to Gen 4:26b, (b) the problem of Enosh's *hoping* to call on the name of the Lord, (c) the significance of the two genealogies in Genesis 4–5, (d) the abrupt break after Gen 4:26 and the recapitulation of the Sethite genealogy in Genesis 5. Augustine does so by offering interpretations of Enosh's name, of his hope, and of his calling on the name of the Lord which are wholly positive and consistent with one another, as with Augustine's broader theology. Like others before him going back to Philo, he takes advantage of the LXX/Old Latin reading "hoped." He stresses the prophetic, otherworldly, acorporeal, and asexual qualities of Enosh's name and hope, thereby arriving at a view of Enosh as a prophetic symbol and foreshadowing of the City of God.[97] Unlike his contemporary Greek Church Fathers, Augustine displays no tendency to interpret the verb "to call" passively, since the Latin version from which he worked did not contain the ambiguity which permits such an interpretation.[98] However, Augustine is

dmry' tkyl. The MT (40:5), however, has: *'ašrê haggeber 'ăšer śām YHWH mibṭaḥô*. ("Happy is the man who *makes* the Lord his trust"). The Greek and Latin versions (reading *śām* as *šēm*) permit Augustine to connect this verse with Enosh because of the words "hope" and "name of the Lord."

97 Augustine's interpretation may be said to be both allegorical and typological.

98 In *De civ. Dei* 15.22–23 Augustine advocates a "naturalistic" interpretation of Gen 6:2ff., understanding the "sons of God" to be the inhabitants of the City of God, the descendants of Seth, who are led astray by the beauty of the women of the Earthly City. According to Augustine, the Sethites could equally be called "sons of God" and "gods," both being names acquired through righteousness. For Augustine, however, this interpretation is *independent*

able to arrive at much the same view of Enosh as foreshadowing the New Testament "sons of God" through his exegesis of the Old Latin version, focusing more entirely on Enosh's name and hope in relation to their problematic scriptural context.[99]

e. Cyril of Alexandria (d. 444)

Cyril of Alexandria stresses the righteous qualities of Enosh which caused him to be called "God" by his contemporaries, and to become an "adopted son of God" (*huiothesia*). The latter expression has, as Cyril makes clear, important Christological connotations.[100] Cyril bases his interpretation of Enosh and Gen 4:26b on a passive understanding of the verb *epikaleisthai*, linking it to his interpretation of the "sons of God" in Gen 6:2–4 in a novel way which greatly accentuates Enosh's importance.

Glaphyra, Book 2.[101] Here Cyril speaks of the "divine Enosh" (*ho thespesios Enōs*), of whom Scripture says: *houtos ēlpisen epikaleisthai tō onomati kyriou tou theou autou*. The use of the dative *tō onomati* probably suggests, as we have witnessed elsewhere, a passive interpretation of *epikaleisthai*.[102] Cyril confirms our suspicion when further along he paraphrases Gen 4:26b: "Thus, Enosh hoped to be called (*klēthēsesthai*) by others by the name (*ep' onomati*) of the Lord his God; that is, 'God' (*theos*)." Cyril explains that Enosh's contemporaries called him God (*theon ōnomazon auton*) in recognition of his "excelling in the glories of piety" (*tois tēs hosiotētos hemrepōn auchēmasi*).[103] The verb "hope," which caused some previous exegetes trouble and which enabled others to stress Enosh's otherworldly, prophetic faith, is not commented upon by Cyril. Enosh hopes to be called "God" and *is*. Cyril repeatedly states that it was Enosh's *contemporaries* who called him "God."[104]

---

of his exegesis of Gen. 4:26. Similarly, Jerome rejects the "angelic" interpretation of Gen 6:2–4, but never connects that rejection with his interpretation of Gen 4:26. See *Homilies* 45 ad Ps 132 (CChr. 78.281); *Quaestiones Hebraicae in Genesim* ad Gen 6:2 (CChr. 72.9).

99 We will witness a similar tendency in the Syriac sources to be examined below, especially in the commentary of Isho'dad of Merv.

100 Whether these connotations bear any relation to the Christological debates between the theologians of Alexandria and Antioch, in which Cyril was an active and important participant, is very difficult to determine. See below, n. 113.

101 *PG* 69.48. This work was probably composed around 420. See Quasten, *Patrology*, 3.121.

102 See above, nn. 50, 80.

103 Cyril makes similar statements further along, *PG* 69.52. These passages are repeated virtually verbatim by Anastasius Sinaita (d. ca. 700) in *Quaestiones* 25 (*PG* 89.552). Since Anastasius simply restates Cyril's words, his testimony will not be examined separately. However, in another context (*PG* 89.236–37) Anastasius explicitly states that it is *Seth* who was called "God" by his contemporaries. We will note below in our examination of the Christian chronographers a similar tendency to substitute Seth for Enosh as the subject of Gen 4:26b.

104 This interpretation is also found in Theodoret of Cyrus (near Antioch, ca. 393–ca. 466), *Quaestiones in Genesim*, Quaes. 47 (*PG* 80.147), thought to have been written

In the same passage, Cyril sets this interpretation in a Christological framework. He says that the honor of being called by God's name is bestowed upon man as an "adopted son (*huiothesia*) of the Lord of all," in fraternity with Jesus, through whom such superhuman glory is acquired. Cyril, like Eusebius of Emesa before him, seems to equate being called "God" with being a "son of God."[105] But Cyril adds something new, or at least something which had not previously been explicitly stated. "Son of God" is no longer simply an epithet for a righteous, godlike human, but now suggests a relationship of a human to God which has *Christological* implications: it is through identification with Jesus, *the* Son of God, that pious men acquire, through divine grace, the title "son of God." Implicitly, Enosh is the first such son of God in fraternity with Jesus.[106]

---

shortly after 453. According to Theodoret it was Enosh's kinsmen who first called the godlike Enosh "God" (*ōnomasthē theos*) and "godlike" (*houtos prōtos tēs theias prosēgorias tetychēke*) in recognition of his piety (*eusebeia*). Theodoret is unique in citing Aquila's translation as the basis for his interpretation: "then was begun the being called by the name of the Lord (*kaleisthai tō onomati kyriou*)." Aquila's translation is a significant choice for three reasons: it eliminates the problematic verb "hope," it contains the dative *tō onomati* suggesting "was called" (see above, nn. 50, 80, 102), and implies (at least to Theodoret) that Enosh was the *first* to be called by God's name. Like Eusebius of Emesa, Chrysostom, and Cyril, Theodoret's interpretation of Gen 4:26 is occasioned by his desire to interpret the "sons of God" of Gen 6:2–4 as being humans. Some have wrongly, I think, understood Theodoret to refer Gen 4:26b to Seth. See J. A. Fabricius, *Codex Pseudepigraphus Veteris Testamenti* (2 vols.; Hamburg: T. C. Felginer, 1722) 1.144, under the heading "Sethus Deus"; W. Bousset, *Hauptprobleme der Gnosis* (Göttingen: Vandenhoeck and Ruprecht, 1907) 382 n. 2; L. Ginzberg, *Legends of the Jews*, 5.151. For more on Theodoret's interpretation, see below, nn. 112, 113.

105 Cyril cites Ps 81(82):6 as a prooftext: "I have said: You are gods (*theoi*) and all sons of the Most High." We have seen that this verse is frequently cited as a biblical proof for the honoring of humans with the epithet "God" (cf. John 10:34). See above, nn. 72, 78, 82, as well as Augustine, *De civ. Dei* 15.22–23. For Cyril, this verse is particularly fitting since it identifies such human "gods" as "sons of God." On the identification of being called by God's name with being called a "son of God," in *Jewish* sources, see above, n. 52.

106 While "son of God" may simply be a term of honor for righteous humans, implicitly, for both Jews and Christians, it is also a term for Israel's relationship to God as "sons." See above, n. 51. For Jewish exegetes "son of God" could apply generally to all the members of the *covenantal* community, as well as more specifically to those select members who through righteousness earn a relationship of intimacy with God. See *Sifre Deut*. 94. Christian exegetes would tend to understand the term as referring to all Christians. Just as Jewish writers would have been unable to apply this term to non-Jews or non-Israelites, Christian writers would have had trouble applying it to non-Christians, once the term had become associated with Jesus and the Christian faithful. Logically, Christian exegetes understood those Old Testament Israelites to whom the term was applied as Christian prefigurations. For the NT faithful as "sons of God," see Matt 5:9, 45; Luke 6:35; 20:36; John 1:12; Rom 8:14, 16; Gal 3:26. On Jesus and the righteous of the Church being "brethren," i.e., sons of the same Father, see Heb 2:11–13. On the faithful being "adopted sons," see Rom 8:15, 23; Gal 4:5. See below, n. 145.

A little further on in the *Glaphyra*[107] Cyril relates his exegesis of Gen 4:26 to that of Gen 6:2. He supports the reading "sons of God" (rather than "angels of God") by citing the translations of Aquila, *huioi tōn theōn* ("sons of gods"), and of Symmachus, *huioi tōn dynasteuontōn* ("sons of the powerful"). He comments: "They called the descendants of Seth and of Enosh 'sons of gods' and 'sons of the powerful' because of the piety and love of God which was in them." Cyril takes the translations of Aquila and Symmachus to preclude any reference to angels. How these translations are to be understood in relation to the Sethites, however, is not so clear. The phrase "because of the piety and love of God which was in them" is ambiguous. Does it refer to Seth and Enosh or to their descendants? Are the sons of Seth and Enosh "sons of gods" and "sons of the powerful" because Seth and Enosh were gods and powerful (Aquila and Symmachus take literally the plural form *'ĕlōhîm*), or are these terms simply understood by Cyril as epithets of extreme honor? In other words, is the word "sons" meant to denote descent or association? Cyril does not explicitly clarify this question. Considering his earlier remarks, we may suppose that he intends the latter explanation: "sons of gods" are the godlike, and "sons of the powerful" are humans of exceptional (moral) strength.[108] However, the former explanation, evidenced as we shall see in his later writings, cannot be ruled out. At best, Cyril vacillates between the two interpretations.[109] Note that Seth and Enosh occupy here *equal* places of importance.

Contra Julianum, Book 9.[110] In this work, written some fifteen years after the *Glaphyra*, Cyril clearly understands the "sons of God" of Gen 6:2 to refer to the descendants of Enosh, who was called "God."[111]

107 *PG* 69.53.

108 Such a usage of "son" or "sons" is not unusual in the LXX, but probably reflects biblical influence: 2 Sam 7:10, *huioi adikias* ("the wicked"); 2 Kgs 14:14, *huioi tōn symmixeōn* ("hostages"). Similarly, in the NT in Luke 10:6 we have *huios eirēnēs* ("a peaceful person"). See LSJ 1847, s.v. *huios*, 4.

109 It may simply be that the distinction between "son" by descent and "son" by association is not clearly drawn here. Augustine (*De civ. Dei* 15.22–23) similarly equates the expressions "sons of gods" with "sons of God." He says, essentially, that since being called a "god" and a "son of God" are synonymous, the righteous Sethites could be called both "sons of God" (i.e., godlike) and "sons of (those called) gods." A sharp distinction is not made.

110 *PG* 76.956. This work was probably composed around 433–41. See Quasten, *Patrology*, 3.129–30.

111 Julian had argued that Gen 6:2–4 speaks of supernatural angels who were degraded through sexual union with mortal women and whose offspring were the semi-divine "giants." Cyril, in response, claims that the reading "angels of God" is a corrupt interpolation into the text of the LXX. In support he cites Symmachus' version ("sons of the mighty"), which he claims must refer to humans. For Julian's view see Julian, *Against the Galileans*, trans. W. C. Wright, in *The Works of Emperor Julian* (LCL; 3 vols.; London: W. Heinemann, 1923) 3.400–401. Clearly, the old Jewish tradition of "sons of God" being

As in the *Glaphyra*, Cyril interprets Gen 4:26b to mean that Enosh was "honored with the name of God (*tē tou theou klēsei tetimētai*) by his contemporaries, for he was called 'God' (*theos gar ōnomastai*), being a guardian of righteousness and every virtue." The descendants of Enosh, he says, were known as "[posterity] of God" (*tou epiklēsin theou*), since they followed the righteous ways of their ancestors, and kept apart from the unsavory race of Cain. In Noah's time they were called "sons of God," "that is, those of Enosh's blood" (*tout' estin hoi ex haimatos tou Enōs*). For the first time a Christian exegete clearly understands the "sons of God" of Gen 6:2 to be the descendants of the godlike Enosh, understanding the word "sons" as a term not simply of association, but of descent. Thus, the term "sons of God" in Gen 6:2 is particularized. No longer does it denote "adopted sons of God" in the New Testament sense, applying to both Enosh and his descendants, and foreshadowing their successors, but simply to the antediluvian descendants of the godlike Enosh in contrast to their Cainite contemporaries. The term, in the context of Gen 6:2–4, is no longer a divine epithet for righteous humans.[112]

Either an inconsistency or an exegetical shift is reflected in these writings of Cyril. Cyril began with a line of interpretation already evidenced in Chrysostom and having its roots as far back as Eusebius of

---

fallen angels had not died, perhaps having gained renewed circulation with Julian's revitalization of "paganism." It certainly continued to be embellished in some Jewish, Christian, and Gnostic circles. Such a "mythological" interpretation would have been unacceptable to a rationalist such as Cyril. A. Kerrigan (*St. Cyril of Alexandria: Interpreter of the Old Testament* [Rome: Pontifical Biblical Institute, 1952] 281–90) discusses Cyril's interpretation of Gen 6:2–4 under the heading "St. Cyril's Antimythical Leanings." But there must have also been particularly Christian motivations for naturalizing the "sons of God" of Gen 6:2–4. Since the New Testament refers to both Jesus and his followers as "sons of God," the term had to be rid of any negative and embarrassing Old Testament associations.

112 Cyril's interpretation here resembles that of Aquila, Symmachus, and Rabbinic literature: "sons of God" of Gen 6:2–4 are the children of judges or nobles. See above, n. 54.

The same interpretation is given in Cyril's *Responsiones ad Tiberium diaconom Sociosque* (in *Sancti patris nostri Cyrilli archiepiscopi Alexandrini in d. Joannis evangelium* (ed. P. E. Pusey; 3 vols.; Oxford, 1892, repr. Brussells, 1965) 3.600–602. Once again we find Enosh called "God" by his contemporaries because of his "very great righteousness," and Enosh's descendants being "the sons of him who is called 'God,' that is, Enosh" (*hoi huioi tou epiklēthentos theou, toutesti, tou Enōs*). Theodoret (see above, n. 104) similarly states that the descendants of Enosh, who was called "God," bear the name "sons of God," "just as we [who are] descendants from the Lord Christ are called 'Christians.' "

We recall our earlier comments (n. 72) that while Chrysostom asserts that humans are frequently referred to in Scripture as "sons of God," he is unable to provide the necessary evidence. All he can show is that the righteous are referred to as "gods" and "sons." Thus, his argument is flawed. Cyril, by adopting a genealogical interpretation of "sons of God," avoids this pitfall. Unlike Chrysostom, he does not claim that "sons of God" in Gen 6:2–4 is an epithet for godlike men, but only that Enosh is called "God" and the "sons of God" are his descendants.

Emesa and Africanus: righteous humans are sometimes called "gods" (or "sons of God/gods") in Scripture, and Gen 4:26b (in the Greek versions) can be understood to mean that Enosh hoped/was the first to be so called. While earlier exegetes were somewhat ambiguous as to their passive understanding of the verb *epikaleisthai*, Cyril is entirely unambiguous. Like others before him, Cyril identifies the terms "God" and "son of God" when used as epithets for righteous humans, but unlike his predecessors he initially suggests Christological significance to these terms *in the context of* his exegesis of Gen 4:26. Enosh is called "God" as an "adopted son of God." He not only foreshadows the New Testament "sons of God" but is himself one. Presumably, the "sons of God" of Gen 6:2–4 earn the same title since they imitate and continue the ways of their righteous ancestors Enosh *and* Seth. But then Cyril shifts and comes to view the "sons of God" of Gen 6:2–4 as descendants of the "God" Enosh. Seth is no longer mentioned and it is Enosh alone who stands at the head of the righteous antediluvian line. Cyril even goes so far as to contrast the descendants of Enosh with those of Cain, although he surely recognizes that genealogically it is Seth who stands at the head of the line. It is Enosh's righteousness that is preserved by this line, just as Cain's ways are imitated by the Cainites. However, now the Sethites receive their name "sons of God" not on account of their righteous ways but on account of Enosh. Now it is only Enosh and not his descendants who is said by Scripture to have been called "God." The Sethites are called "sons of God" only by virtue of their descent from Enosh. It is Enosh alone who is now the object of Cyril's praise; he alone amongst the antediluvians is accorded the honor of a divine epithet.

It is difficult to explain Cyril's genealogical interpretation of the "sons of God" of Gen 6:2–4, and his particular emphasis on Enosh's piety, divine name, and prominence as the head of the Sethite line. It has been suggested that Cyril's exegesis needs to be viewed in the context of the debate over the "person of Christ" that not only raged in Cyril's time, but in which he was a principal participant.[113] However, two considerations mitigate against such interpretations: (a) The interpretation of the "sons of God" of

[113] For bibliography on these debates, see Quasten, *Patrology*, 3.116–19, 136–42, 514–15. For a summary of the various positions, see J. Pelikan, *The Christian Tradition: A History of the Development of Doctrine*, vol. 1 (Chicago: University of Chicago, 1971) 226–77. L. R. Wickham ("The Sons of God and the Daughters of Man," in *Language and Meaning: Studies in Hebrew Language and Biblical Exegesis* [*OTS* 19; Leiden: E. J. Brill, 1974] 135–47) argues that Cyril and other Christian theologians of the Alexandrian school used Gen 6:2 to prove the existence of biblical "sons of God" by grace in biblical times, and hence "the reality of the Lord's true sonship prior to the Incarnation." Wickham, however, ignores the fact that Cyril shifts his interpretation from "sons of God" by grace or adoption to "sons of God" by descent or nature. In "Enosh and His Generation" (176–80) I suggest another explanation of Cyril's exegesis of Gen 4:26 and 6:2–4 in terms of the fifth century Christological debates, but I am no longer satisfied with it.

Gen 6:2–4 never appears as an issue in the Christological debates, even when they concern Jesus' divine sonship. (b) Theodoret of Cyrus, who expresses almost the identical exegesis of Gen 4:26 and 6:2–4,[114] is a proponent of the Nestorian school, opposing Cyril in the theological debates. It is simpler, it seems to me, to explain Cyril's exegesis as developing earlier, similar traditions of interpretation (e.g., Eusebius of Emesa and Chrysostom) in such a way as to obviate some of their internal difficulties.[115] The process of naturalizing the "sons of God" of Gen 6:2–4 is carried one step further; not only are they not angels, but at the time of their corruption they are not even godlike humans. Rather, they are only the descendants of the godlike Enosh, who alone remains a righteous antediluvian paradigm for the New Testament "adopted" sons of God (and perhaps even Son of God).

f. Byzantine Chronicles

We complete our survey of Greek and Latin Christian interpretation of Gen 4:26 with the Byzantine chronicles of the seventh through twelfth centuries. These continue some of the lines of interpretation that we have witnessed in the Greek Church fathers, but give them some interesting new twists. In particular, the increasing emphasis on Enosh's importance, which we have noted, is reversed, and Seth again emerges as the most important of the antediluvian righteous, even to the point of being considered the subject of Gen 4:26b. We shall consider possible reasons for this shift of emphasis after examining a few of the chronicles.

The earliest Byzantine chronicle to deal with Gen 4:26b is the anonymous *Paschal Chronicle* (ca. 630). As is by now familiar, Gen 4:26 is discussed in conjunction with exegesis of Gen 6:2–4:

> Some interpreters correctly explain that the select race of Seth were called "angels of God" by Moses. For Genesis teaches that while the women of the tribe of Cain excelled in vengeful murder, brother-hatred, and apostasy, the foremost descendants of Seth began (*ērxanto*) to call on the name of the Lord, that is, an angelic hymn (*aggelikos hymnos*). For Genesis says: "To Seth was born a son. He called his name Enosh. This one began (*ērxato*) to call on the name of the Lord God." . . . For the descendants of Seth were like angels (*aggelois homoiōthentes*), singing an angelic hymn, while the descendants of Cain were joined with the damned, and God was provoked to anger.[116]

114 See above, nn. 104, 112.

115 See above, nn. 72, 112, and my discussion of Eusebius of Emesa's interpretation. For examples where Cyril's scriptural exegesis *is* reflective of his theological positions, see R. A. Greer, *The Captain of Our Salvation*, 307–55.

116 *Chronicon Paschale* (ed. L. Dindorf; CSHB 1; Bonn: Weber, 1832) 38. Also, *PG* 92.108.

Here the reading "angels of God," rejected in the other sources which we have examined, is adopted.[117] However, "angels of God" refers now not to real angels but to the Sethites who are *like* angels in that they sing an angelic hymn, referred to in Gen 4:26b.[118] Thus, Gen 6:2 is once again demythologized, taken to refer to the intercourse of Sethites and Cainites, and once again with the help of Gen 4:26b, but now without interpreting the ambiguous verb *epikaleisthai* passively. The author seems to use a version similar to Aquila's (*ērchthē*, "was begun"), eliminating the problematic verb "hope." Although he understands Gen 4:26b to refer to an individual (Enosh or Seth) who began (*ērxato*) to call upon the name of the Lord God, he also takes it to refer to the Sethites in general ("they began," *ērxanto*).[119] Enosh's name is never mentioned, and it may even be Seth, the father of the Sethites, who is understood to be the subject of Gen 4:26b. However, whichever one is intended only began an activity which is said to typify the righteous Sethite line as a whole. Nothing is said concerning the virtues of Enosh or Seth in particular. Gen 4:26b is now more important for what it says about the Sethites than for what it says about Enosh or Seth.[120]

George Syncellus (fl. ca. 800), upon whom several later chronographers are dependent, evidences both early Jewish traditions which venerate Seth and his descendants and Christian interpretations of Gen 4:26b. In his *Chronographia*[121] he identifies the "descendants of Seth" not only with the "sons of God," but also with the "Watchers": "Seth's offspring [were] called 'sons of God' and 'Watchers'." We are told that Seth was "snatched up by angels" in order to be told about the impending transgression of the Watchers, the cataclysm, and the coming of the Savior. Seth reveals this knowledge to his descendants, who, like him, were righteous, beautiful, and lived "like angels."[122] Syncellus recounts

117 See above, n. 55.

118 Note that in *Memar Marqah* 2.6–7, 8, Enosh's "invocation" is identified with Moses' *song* at the Sea of Reeds. See above, chap. 2, nn. 18–21.

119 Cf. John Chrysostom, *Expositio in Psalmum* 49.1, discussed above, n. 84.

120 This is the opposite tendency from what we saw in Cyril of Alexandria, for whom Gen 4:26b was mainly significant for the merit it attributed to Enosh.

121 *Chronographia* (ed. W. Dindorf; CSHB; Bonn: Weber, 1829) 16–28, 34–35. I have benefited from the detailed notes by W. Adler, "Notes to the Text of George Syncellus and Pseudo-Malalas," distributed with "Materials Relating to Seth in an Anonymous Chronographer (Pseudo-Malalas) and in the Chronography of George Syncellus," at the Joint Pseudepigrapha/Nag Hammadi Special Session of the Society of Biblical Literature, San Francisco, Dec. 1977.

122 Pp. 16–17. Such traditions about Seth, the revelation to him and his progeny, and the angelic lives which they lived derive ultimately from Josephus, *Ant.* 1.2.3. §§69–71. On Seth's godlike physical beauty, see Anastasius Sinaita, *Viae Dux* (*PG* 90.236–7), and George Cedrenus (early twelfth century) *Historiarum Compendium* (ed. Bekker; CSHB 1; Bonn: Weber, 1838) 16–17. The angel-like existence of the Sethites prior to their mingling with the Cainites is also stressed in the Syriac commentaries and chronicles to be discussed below.

in some detail how these Watchers (descendants of Seth) went astray with the "daughters of man," fathering the giants, spreading evil, and causing the Flood. He draws upon a number of sources, both Jewish (Josephus, *1 Enoch*) and non-Jewish (Berossus, Zosimus, Africanus, Ephraem). Then of Enosh he says:

> From Adam until the birth of Enosh was 435 years, Scripture revealing that Enosh was the first to be called by [or, to call upon] the name of the Lord God, that is, to be addressed by the name of God [or, to address God by name].[123] Enosh is interpreted as "man" according to the Hebrew meaning. Thus, also the Savior is the son of the real man (*huios tou ontos anthrōpou*) according to Africanus' Natural History.[124]

There are a few problems with this passage. First, does Syncellus understand the infinitive *epikaleisthai* to be middle or passive? By paraphrasing this verb with another equally ambiguous one, *prosagoreuesthai*, he does not help us much. Yet, the following factors seem to me to tip the balance in favor of a passive understanding:[125] (a) The verb *prosagoreō* does not appear in the lexicons with a deponent middle voice.[126] (b) If this verb were intended here with an active meaning, we would expect the noun *theos* to be the direct object in the accusative case. (c) The dative *onomati*, as we have seen, is often used with verbs of naming to mean "by the name of."[127]

123 *epikaleisthai to onoma kyriou tou theou prōtos, tout' esti prosagoreuesthai onomati theou*. I have taken both infinitives to be passive rather than middle. On Syncellus' use of *prōtos* ("first"), see above, chap. 1, n. 9.

124 *Chronographia*, (ed. W. Dindorf) 17–18. This passage is repeated almost verbatim in Cedrenus (ed. Bekker) 17.

125 This ambiguous paraphrase is also given by Cedrenus (ed. Bekker) 17, but there the context suggests a passive meaning. Note that Cedrenus says of Seth: "He was *also* called 'God' because of the radiance of his face" (*ōnomasthē de kai theos dia tēn lampsin tou prosōpou autou*). Another Byzantine chronographer, Michael Glycas (*Annalium* [ed. Bekker; CSHB; Bonn: Weber, 1836] 228), states that not only was Seth called "God," but Enosh "also because of his righteousness was considered a god" (*theon kai auton dia tēn aretēn autou nomizomenon*). John Zonoras (12th century) also echoes Syncellus' paraphrase, but clearly interprets *epikaleisthai* to be active (*Annalium* 1.4 [ed. Pindar; CSHB 1; Bonn: Weber, 1846] 25): *ton te theon prosagoreusai ton kyrion* ("and to address God as the Lord"). Similarly, Leo Grammaticus, *Chronographia* (ed. Bekker; CSHB: [Bonn: Weber, 1942] 9: *toutesti en theou onomati prosagoreuein ton theon* ("that is, to address God by the name of God"). Note that in the last two examples the infinitive is clearly active, and the noun *theos* is supplied as the direct object in the accusative case.

126 See LSJ 1499–1500.

127 See Eusebius of Emesa's use of the Hebraios version and Theodoret of Cyrus' use of Aquila, both interpreting the dative *onomati* to suggest a passive infinitive. See above, nn. 50, 104. H. Gelzer (*Sextus Julius Africanus und die byzantinische Chronographie*, 62) also understands Syncellus to say that Enosh was called "God.": "Synkellos' Ausdruck *prosagoreuesthai onomati theou* und die Parallele mit dem Gottmenschen lassen keinen Zweifel, dass Africanus annahm, Enos sei Gott genannt worden, und in ihm einen der

The interpretation of Enosh as "real" (or "true" or "ideal") man should by now be very familiar. What, however, is the relation of Enosh to the Savior as the "son of the true man"? What is meant by the attribution to Africanus? Beginning with the last question, it appears that Syncellus does not attribute the interpretation of Gen 4:26 and Enosh to Africanus, but only the statement concerning the Savior. Africanus in his "Natural History," which is probably identical with his "Chronicles," known to us only in fragments, must have interpreted Jesus' title "son of man" to mean "son of the true man." Whether or not Africanus said this in relation to Enosh is hard to tell. We know that elsewhere, in a fragment cited by Syncellus and discussed by us above (n. 59), he traces Jesus' ancestry back to Seth. Whether this is what is also intended here is not clear.[128] It appears safest to say that Syncellus is simply associating his interpretation of Enosh with Africanus' interpretation of Jesus as "son of man." Enosh as the "real" man simply prefigures Jesus as the "son (descendant) of (the real) man."

Thus, Syncellus juxtaposes several interpretations of Enosh: he was the first to be called by the name of God, he is "true man," and he prefigures Jesus as "son of man." However, Syncellus does *not* relate these interpretations to his interpretations of the "sons of God" as the descendants of Seth; Gen 6:2–4 is explicated *without* resort to Gen 4:26b. The "sons of God" earn their name, presumably, by virtue of their righteous, angelic, and physically beautiful qualities, which they derive from *Seth*, the progenitor of their line.

Finally, in the *Chronographia* of John Malalas we find two interpretations of Gen 4:26 in a passage which is probably from the writings of a later chronographer.[129] The author first applies our verse to Enosh and then to Seth, but is clearly more interested in the latter. Of Enosh he says: "When Seth was 205 years old, he fathered the other Enosh (*egennēse ton Enōs heteron*), who 'hoped to call on (*epikaleisthai*) the name of the Lord.' " That is all he says about Enosh. What he means by

---

alttestamentlichen Typen des Menschensohns erkannte." I do not, however, agree with Gelzer's attribution of this interpretation to Africanus.

128 Gelzer (61–62) understands the whole passage to derive from Africanus, but this, it seems to me, cannot be established.

129 John Malalas, a Byzantine chronographer, wrote his *Chronographia* some time in the late sixth century. See *The Oxford Dictionary of the Christian Church* (1974) 750. However, the only existing manuscript (twelfth century, Oxford MS Bodleian Baroccianus 182) lacks the first chapter, from which the passage which we are considering comes. This chapter, apparently, was supplied in later editions from another anonymous chronography so as to complete the history from the Creation. Some have identified this anonymous chronographer as George Harmartolus (mid-ninth century). See L. Dindorf's introduction to his edition, *Joannis Malalae Chronographia* (CSHB; Bonn: Weber, 1831) v; and W. Adler, et. al., "Materials Relating to Seth in an Anonymous Chronographer (Pseudo-Malalas) and in the Chronography of George Syncellus" (above, n. 121) iii-iv.

"other" Enosh is not at all clear.[130] There is no indication whether the author understands the verb *epikaleisthai* to be passive or active. Since he does not elaborate, we have assumed he intends the latter, but the former remains a possibility, particularly in light of his second interpretation of this verse.

Next the author discusses at some length the various discoveries attributed to Seth (Hebrew letters, astronomical and astrological phenomena), and how his descendants recorded their knowledge of the impending cataclysm on stone and clay tablets (cf. Josephus, *Ant.* 1.2.3.). After this, he returns to Seth and says:

> Concerning him it is said: The sons of God went into the daughters of men (that is, the daughters descended from Cain), for the people of that time called Seth "God," because he discovered the Jewish letters and the names of the stars. In addition, they marveled at his great piety, so that he was the first to be called and invoked as "God" (*prōton epikaleisthai theon kai onomazesthai*), just as the Lord also said to Moses: "I have appointed you 'god' to Pharaoh" (Exod 7:1). Concerning the virtuous and spiritual ones and the judges, He said: "Do not curse gods, nor revile rulers of your people" (Exod 22:27). Appropriately, let the children of Seth and of Enosh and of Enoch be considered "sons of God" (and "sons of gods" according to Symmachus [sic]), that is, those, who overcome by lust, went into the daughters of Cain, from whom the giants were born from unlawful union. Through the righteous Seth they were strong and mighty; through the unrighteous and polluted Cain they were evil and most wicked.[131]

It would appear that Gen 4:26b, with *epikaleisthai* now being understood as passive, is the basis for the statement that *Seth* was the first human to be called "God." As we have remarked several times, the Greek *houtos*, while logically referring to Enosh, is ambiguous enough to permit its being applied to Seth.[132] The author, like Cyril of Alexandria, seems to understand "sons of God" (or "sons of gods") to mean *descendants* of the godlike. But unlike Cyril, he understands them to derive their divine name principally from Seth. It is from him that they also derive their moral and physical excellence. Enosh is now simply one link in the chain of righteous Sethites.[133]

[130] Since there is only one Enosh in Scripture, the author may be contrasting Enosh with Enoch, their names being frequently confused. See above, n. 46.

[131] *Joannis Malalae Chronographia* (ed. L. Dindorf) 5–7. Also, *PG* 97.69–72. On the adducing of scriptural verses which show that certain humans are called "gods" as a sign of honor, see above, nn. 72, 78, 82, 83, 105.

[132] See above, chap. 1, n. 13; above, n. 104; and below, n. 134.

[133] Note that besides Seth, Enosh and Enoch are singled out. It may be implied here that Enosh and Enoch were also called "God," and that the Sethites receive their name from them as well, especially if we take seriously the reference to Aquila's "sons of gods." In any case, it is now Seth who is the first and foremost human to have been called "God."

Whether by intent or not, the author of this chronology has resolved a difficulty inherent in the previous interpretations of "sons of God" in light of Gen 4:26b, going back to Eusebius of Emesa: the Sethites are the descendants of *Seth* genealogically, but they derive their excellence and divine name as descendants of *Enosh*. Our anonymous author, having apparently received ancient traditions that venerated Seth for his discoveries, prophetic and worldly wisdom, beauty, piety, and perhaps even messianic significance, has no difficulty understanding Gen 4:26b to refer to him.[134] Enosh has been replaced by Seth as the spiritual progenitor of the righteous "sons of God," and, in a sense, we have come full circle back to, of all people, Josephus, who, as we have noted, venerates Seth and ignores Enosh in explaining that the Flood was caused by the degeneration of the descendants of the righteous and wise Seth.[135]

134 Such veneration of Seth in conjunction with his being called "God" is found in other Christian writings of this period. For instance, Anastasius Sinaita (d. ca. 700) in his *Viae Dux* (PG 89.236–37) says that when Seth's contemporaries saw his face, shining with the "grace and brilliance of the Holy Spirit," they called him "God," for which reason Scripture calls his descendants "sons of God," that is, sons of (a) god by descent. However, Anastasius does not use Gen 4:26 to prove his point. Similarly, Michael Glycas (*Annalium* [ed. Bekker] 228) says that because of Seth's righteousness and discoveries, he was "considered to be God" (*theos einai . . . nomizomenos*), but adds that Enosh too was considered a "god." Similarly, see George Cedrenus, *Historiarum Compendium* (ed. Bekker) 17. The identification of *Seth* as the subject of Gen 4:26b is also evidenced in *Suidae Lexicon* (ed. Ada Adler; pt. 4; Leipzig: B. G. Teubner, 1935) 348, s.v. *Seth*. In this late tenth-century literary and historical encyclopedia, Seth is said to have been called "God" by men, for his invention of the Hebrew letters and the names of the planets, and for his piety. Perhaps quoting Pseudo-Malalas, it says: *prōtos epikaleisthai theos kai onomazesthai*. It also cites Exod 7:1 and 22:27 for other Scriptural examples of humans called "gods." The "sons of God," it says, were the descendants of Seth, Enosh, and Enoch.

While we have noted that the veneration of Seth and his descendants for their piety, wisdom, and discoveries goes back at least to Josephus, it is not clear whether the Christian chronographers draw directly on Josephus or on some other, possibly intermediary, sources, whether Jewish, Christian (possibly gnostic), or Arabic. See above, chap. 1, n. 71; chap. 3, nn. 59, 86. Clearly, the above mentioned traditions about Seth go beyond what is said by Josephus. In general, the Byzantine chronicles are thought to preserve relics of pre- (or extra-) Rabbinic legends to the Bible. Besides H. Gelzer's study mentioned above (n. 49), see D. Flusser, "Palea Historica: An Unknown Source of Biblical Legends," *Scripta Hierosolymitana* 22 (1971) 48–79; R. Fishman-Duker, "The Second Temple Period in Byzantine Chronicles," *Byzantion* 47 (1977) 126–56; idem, "Remembering the Elephants: 3 Macc. 5–6 in Byzantine Chronicles," *Byzantion* 48 (1978) 51–63.

The association of Seth's inventions and innovations with his being called "God," however, is unique to these later Christian sources. This may reflect the influence of the sort of euhemeristic heurematography found in Philo of Biblos, to be discussed in chapter 5.

135 See above, chap. 1, n. 74. Of course, the above account goes beyond Josephus in at least two key respects: (a) The "sons (angels) of God" of Gen 6:2–4 are the descendants of Seth, since Gen 4:26b speaks of Seth/Enosh, the patriarch of the line, as having been called "God." (b) The sons of Seth degenerated through intercourse with the daughters of Cain. While the first interpretation in its earliest form is Christian (see above, n. 54), the second has ancient

B. Syriac Sources

Although the Syriac sources that we will examine contain traditions similar to, and perhaps in some cases even dependent upon, those found in the Greek Fathers, they are treated here separately, since they exhibit certain distinct traits, and since they are to a significant extent interpretations of a different scriptural version, the *Peshiṭta*.

As we shall see, the Syriac sources are generally less interested in Gen 4:26b for what it says about Enosh, than for what it says about the righteous antediluvian Sethites as a group, as distinguished from the wicked Cainites. In this way, the Syriac sources continue a line of interpretation that we have traced back to pre-Rabbinic Jewish sources, especially Josephus: the Flood was preceded and precipitated by the degeneration of the righteous, pious, and wise Sethites. Like the Church Fathers whom we have examined, these writers differ in the degree to which they focus on Enosh in particular, and in the ways they employ Gen 4:26b as a prooftext.[136]

1. The *Peshiṭta*

The *Peshiṭta* translation of Gen 4:26b is virtually identical to the Samaritan Pentateuch's version/paraphrase, which we have treated above.[137] Since there is no reason to assume any direct relationship between the two (i.e., that the former is a translation of the latter into Aramaic), they may simply represent identical understandings of a commonly received Hebrew text:

Samaritan Pentateuch: *'z hḥl lqr' bšm yhwh*
Peshiṭta: *hydyn šry lmqr' bšm' dmry'*.[138]
("Then [he/one] began to call upon the name of the Lord")

Like the Samaritan Pentateuch, the *Peshiṭta* retains the word "then" (unlike the LXX) and renders the passive *hûḥal* with what would be an

Jewish roots (see chap. 1, n. 76). Our anonymous chronicler, unlike many of his Christian predecessors, describes the achievements of Seth and his descendants and their subsequent degeneration without suggesting the kinds of particularly Christian interpretations of Seth and Enosh and their descendants which we have come to expect.

136 In addition to the reference works cited above in n. 5, I have consulted A. Baumstark, *Geschichte der syrischen Literatur* (Bonn: A. Marcus and E. Weber, 1922); and W. Wright, *A Short History of Syriac Literature* (London: Adam and Charles Black, 1894). The earliest Syriac Father, Aphraates (fl. ca. 340), says nothing significant about Enosh or Gen 4:26. He mentions Enosh only in a genealogical context of tracing Jesus' descent back to Adam (*Demonstrations* 13.6; 23.21–24, 31). In *Dem.* 13.5 and 18.9 Aphraates speaks of the mixing of the Sethites and the accursed Cainites prior to the Flood, but does not identify this with Gen 6:2–4, nor with 4:26.

137 Chap. 2, nn. 1–3.

138 *Pentateuchus Syriace* (ed. G. Barnes; London: Apud Societem Bibiophilorum Britannicam et Externam, 1914) 8. The newest edition, *The Old Testament in Syriac*, pt. 1, fasc. 1 (Leiden: E. J. Brill, 1977) 8, contains the same reading.

active form: the perfect, third person masculine singular, *pa'el*, *šarî* ("began"), having as its understood subject "he" (Enosh, but possibly Seth). However, as we cautioned with respect to the Samaritan Pentateuch, this could also be understood in an indefinite sense, "then one began," or "people began."[139] While this interpretation is not evidenced in Samaritan exegeses of the Samaritan Pentateuch and *Targum*, which consistently take Enosh as the subject of Gen 4:26b, it *is* evidenced, as we shall presently see, in some Syriac interpretations of the *Peshiṭta*.

2. Ephraem Syrus (ca. 306–373)

At roughly the same time that Eusebius of Emesa in Syria and Didymus in Egypt were interpreting the LXX to mean that Enosh had "hoped to be called by the name of the Lord," Ephraem in Mesopotamia was proposing a similar interpretation.

Commentary to Genesis ad 4:26:

> When Seth begat Enosh, it is written, "Then [he] began to call on the name of the Lord" (*Peshiṭta*). For since Seth had separated (*prš*) himself from the house of Cain, they [his descendants] were called by the name of the Lord (*'tqryw lhwn bšm mryh*), that is, the righteous people of the Lord (*'m' zdyq' dmry'*).[140]

Clearly, Ephraem interprets the verb "to call" of Gen 4:26b passively: Because Seth and his descendants separated themselves from the Cainites, they were called by (with) God's name, since they were known as "the righteous people of the Lord." It is difficult to see how the *Peshiṭta* version quoted by Ephraem could have suggested such an interpretation. The infinitive form *lmqr'* is *pe'al* (active), which can hardly be confused with the *ethpe'el* (passive) form *lmtqryw* ("to be called"). Ephraem may have derived his interpretation either from a passive understanding of the Hebrew verb *lqr'* (*liqqārē'*),[141] or from traditions that understood the LXX *epikaleisthai* passively, of which we have seen several. The latter possibility is certainly the more probable, but it should be stressed that while such a dependence may be inferred, it cannot be demonstrated with certainty. Unfortunately, Ephraem himself does not show how he

139 Chap. 2, nn. 3–4. Although it is possible, as some have claimed, that both the Samaritan Pentateuch and the *Peshiṭta* attest a variant consonantal *Vorlage* (*hḥl*), it is not necessary to assume this.

140 *Sancti Ephraem Syri in Genesim et in Exodum Commentarii* (ed. R.-M. Tonneau; CSCO 152; Louvain: L. Durbecq, 1955) 54–55. For a Latin translation, see CSCO 153.43. For an excellent treatment of Ephraem's interpretation of the antediluvians, see T. Kronholm, *Motifs from Genesis 1–11 in the Genuine Hymns of Ephrem the Syrian, With Particular Reference to the Influence of Jewish Exegetical Tradition* (Lund: CWK Gleerup, 1978) 150–71.

141 Cf. the *Samaritan Targum*, above, chap. 2, nn. 9–10.

connects the active version with the passive interpretation.

Ephraem takes Gen 4:26b to refer not simply to Enosh, but to Seth's descendants in general. In fact, except for the introductory words, Enosh's name is not mentioned here. Greek Fathers whom we have examined generally say that *Enosh*, on account of his piety, was the first to be called "by God's name," and then add that Enosh's descendants were also so honored, either because they imitated his righteous ways, or because of genealogical descent. Ephraem, on the other hand, connects Gen 4:26b *directly* with the Sethites as a whole.[142] This characteristic may reveal the influence of the *Peshiṭta* version. Since this version does not supply a subject for the verb *šry*, it could be interpreted either as "he (Seth or Enosh) began" or "one began." The latter permits an indefinite subject: "Then (with or after Enosh's birth) they (the Sethites) began . . ." The LXX translation, in contrast, supplies a demonstrative pronoun as the subject: *houtos ēlpise* ("this one hoped"). While this is usually taken to refer to Enosh, we have seen that it could be construed to refer to Seth. The LXX could *not*, however, be the basis of an indefinite interpretation ("*they* were called"), as we find in Ephraem. If we are correct, it would appear that Ephraem may have been dependent on both the LXX (for the passive understanding of the verb "to call") and the *Peshiṭta* (for the indefinite subject of the phrase).[143]

142 We witnessed a similar tendency in Chrysostom and the *Paschal Chronicle*. See next note.

143 We also find "they began" in the Rabbinic targumim, except there the "they" refers to Enosh's contemporaries. These will be treated in chapter 4. Similarly, in Chrysostom, *Expositio in Psalmum* 49.1 and in the *Paschal Chronicle* we have observed the paraphrase *erxanto* ("they began"), in both cases referring to Seth's descendants, perhaps under the influence of Aquila's version, "it was begun." There appears to be no evidence, however, for Ephraem's having been influenced by Aquila's translation. We should note that it is possible in Aramaic for an active infinitive to have a passive meaning, especially when preceded by an indefinite subject. For examples and discussion see W. F. Stinespring, "The Active Infinitive with Passive Meaning in Biblical Aramaic," *JBL* 81 (1962) 391–94. Thus, it is conceivable that the *Peshiṭta* could be understood, "then [mankind] began to call [itself = be called] with the name of the Lord." It seems unlikely, however, that such an interpretation would have been initially suggested by the *Peshiṭta* itself. Rather, the interpretation seems to derive more naturally from the LXX. The *Peshiṭta* would have been ambiguous enough, however, to accommodate such an interpretation once already well established.

Similar interpretations appear elsewhere in Ephraem's writings. In his *Commentary to Genesis* ad 6:2 (CSCO 152.55–56) he states that the "sons of gods" (*bny 'lh'*, as in Aquila) are the "sons of Seth," "since the sons of Seth were called 'the righteous people of God' (*zdyq' 'm' d'lh' mtknyn hww*)." Although Gen 4:26b is not mentioned in this context, the epithet "righteous people of God" is virtually identical with "righteous people of the Lord" used in his interpretation of Gen 4:26b. "Lord" suits Gen 4:26b while "God" suits Gen 6:2. Ephraem simply associates the terms "sons of God/gods" and "people of God/the Lord" as if they were synonymous, both being titles of honor bestowed upon the righteous Sethites. Elsewhere, in *Contra Haeresis* 19.1 (CSCO 169.67), Ephraem says that

De Nativitate 1.48.[144] In this passage Ephraem attributes specifically Christian significance to the tradition of Seth *and* Enosh having been called "sons of gods":

> Seth and Enosh and Kenan were called "sons of gods" (*bny 'lh' 'tknyw*). They waited for (*skyw*) the Son of God (*br' d'lh'*), that they may be his brethren through mercy (*d'ḥ' brḥm' nhwwn lh*).

Once again we have an antediluvian triad: Seth, Enosh, Kenan. Since Kenan (Enosh's son) seems to have no importance in his own right, he has probably been added to make a genealogical threesome. These three (and assumably the other Sethites) await the New Testament Son of God, and are themselves called "sons of gods" in anticipation of the redemption they will experience with his incarnation. Since the Sethites and Jesus are all called "sons of God," the Sethites can hope to be his "brethren," i.e., sons of the same father.[145] Ephraem continues with Methuselah, Enoch, Lamech, and Noah (seven in all), who similarly await Jesus' arrival as an intercessor on their behalf.[146] Thus, the Sethites, in bearing the same name as Jesus as adopted "sons of God," foreshadow

---

the interpretation of "sons of God" as angels is held by heretics (*ṭ'y'*). A similar interpretation of the descendants of Seth as "sons of God" is found in *De Paradiso* 1.11 (CSCO 174.3), where the separation and subsequent mingling of the Sethites and Cainites is more fully and poetically described; and in *De Ieiunio* 2.2 (CSCO 246.4–5), where it is made clear that the Sethites lost their "great name" (*šmhwn rb'*), presumably either "sons of God/gods" or "righteous people of God/the Lord," which they acquired in Enosh's days, as soon as they came off their mountain to mingle with the degenerate Cainites.

R. Murray (*Symbols of Church and Kingdom: A Study of Early Syriac Tradition* [Cambridge University Press, 1975] 221) states that Ephraem in identifying the "sons of God" with the descendants of Seth is "following a Jewish tradition." However, as we have stated above (n. 54), the identification of the "sons of God" with the Sethites is not found in Jewish sources until medieval times (e.g., *Jeraḥmeel* 24.10–12), while it first appears in Christian sources in the fragment of Julius Africanus (d. ca. 240) which we have examined. For more on Ephraem's interpretation of "sons of God/gods" in Gen 6:2–4, see S. D. Fraade, "Enosh and His Generation," 194–97, esp. n. 136.

144 *Des Heiligen Ephraem des Syrers Hymnen de Nativitate* (ed. Edmund Beck; CSCO 186; Louvain: L. Durbecq, 1959) 7. German translation, CSCO 187.6.

145 The idea of Enosh's prophetic awaiting of Jesus' incarnation is most forthrightly articulated by Augustine, *De civ. Dei* 15.17–18, 21, discussed above. Ephraem rests this interpretation on Gen 6:2–4, which assigns the epithet "sons of God/gods" to the Sethites as a group, and simply singles out the first three Sethites for special mention. The christological interpretation of the "sons of God" of Gen 6:2 was also evidenced in Cyril of Alexandria, *Glaphyra* 2. The notion that Jesus' incarnation enables human beings to become "sons of God" is commonplace in Patristic Christological reflections, building on NT expressions of this motif: Heb 2:11–13; Rom 8:14–17; Gal 4:4–7. See above, n. 106; Byrne, "*Sons of God*," 97–103, 174–86, 213–16, and literature cited there.

146 Cf. Rom 8:22–23: "We know that the whole creation has been groaning in travail together until now; and not only the creation, but we ourselves, who have the first fruits of the Spirit, groan inwardly as we wait for adoption as sons, the redemption of our bodies."

Jesus as they await his eventual coming. In their hope to be his "brethren" they also foreshadow the Church. The Sethite line, as T. Kronholm states, "representing divine activity in the midst of a godless human race on its way towards the catastrophe forms a series of vital links between Adam and Christ."[147]

In these passages that we have examined, Ephraem displays only minimal interest in Enosh as an individual figure, applying to the Sethite antediluvians as a group traditions which we have previously seen applied to Enosh in particular. Enosh is significant simply as one of the earliest links in the Sethite righteous chain. Unlike Greek and Latin exegetes, Ephraem has nothing to say about Enosh's name, or about his particular righteous attributes. Gen 4:26b is important for Ephraem since it establishes that the Sethites were called "sons of God" on account of their having been called by God's name, being the "righteous people of God the Lord." The Sethites as "sons of God" foreshadow the NT "Son of God" and "sons of God." Ephraem's limited interest in Enosh may, as we have suggested, be due to the ambiguous form of the *Peshiṭta*, which does not explicitly identify Enosh as the subject of Gen 4:26b. But probably just as significant is the prominent role which Seth plays as the progenitor of the Sethite line, which Ephraem wishes to contrast with the wicked Cainites.[148] Thus for Ephraem Gen 4:26b is more important for what it says about the Sethites than about Enosh. This is similar to what we observed in the exegesis of the byzantine chronographers.

3. *The Cave of Treasures*

This work in its present form is thought to date from the sixth century C.E., while its original is probably from the fourth century, written

[147] *Motifs from Genesis 1–11*, 163. Kronholm states (p. 164) concerning this passage: "This treatment of Gen 5, under obvious influence from Heb 11:4–7 (where however only Abel, Enoch and Noah are mentioned by name), represents a comprehension of the figures of Seth (Gen 4:25–5:8), Enos (Gen 5:6–11), and Cainan (Gen 5:9–14), Enoch (Gen 5:18–24), Methuselah (Gen 5:21–27), and Lamech (Gen 5:25–30) as being holy and righteous in generations of progressive decline and bearers of divine revelation." There seems, however, to be no reason to assume that Ephraem is modeling his list after Heb 11:4–7, since such traditions of a chain of righteous ancestors are widely evidenced in many sources.

[148] This is similar to what we witnessed in the byzantine chronographers, especially Ps.-Malalas. According to Ephraem, *Seth* is the one in whom God reimplanted His image after it had been blemished as a consequence of Adam's "fall" and Abel's murder. Thus, Seth replaces not only Abel (as in Gen 4:25), but Adam as well, as the vessel of the divine image and messianic seed. Seth is said to be a symbol (*r'z'*) of Jesus (*Contra Haereses* 5.12). See Kronholm, 150–54. For other traditions venerating Seth, see above, n. 134. Enoch is also significant for Ephraem and receives substantial attention, since in overcoming death and in regaining Paradise he is an "antipode of fallen Adam/man." See Kronholm, 154–63.

near Edessa in Syriac.[149] It is, thus, roughly contemporaneous with Ephraem.

The section with which we are concerned discusses the succession of Adam's progeny, who dwell on the mountain of the Cave of Treasures, close to Paradise, while Cain and his descendants dwell in the plain below. Adam at his death commands Seth to rule his people in righteousness and to keep them separate from Cain's offspring. Of the people who dwelt on the mountain we are told: "Because of their purity (*dkywthwn*) they received the name which is the best of all names and were called the 'sons of God' (*mtqryn bny 'lh'*)."[150] At his deathbed, Seth appoints Enosh to rule the people, repeating the instructions which Adam had commanded him, and having the people swear not to mix with the Cainites. Of Enosh we are told:

> And he became governor (*mdbrn'*) of the children of his people, and he kept all the commandments which his father Seth had commanded him, and he urged them to be constant in prayer (*mḥpṭ lhwn dnhwwn 'mynyn bṣlwt'*).[151]

The account continues to describe Lamech's murder of Cain, which is said to have occurred in Enosh's days. Before his death, Enosh gathers his progeny, blesses them, and has them promise not to go down the mountain to mingle with the Cainites. The narrative continues in similar

149 See J. H. Charlesworth, *The Pseudepigrapha and Modern Research* (Missoula, Mo.: Scholars Press, 1976) 91–92. For the Syriac text and a German translation, see C. Bezold, ed. and trans., *Die Schatzhöhle* (2 vols. in 1; Leipzig: J. C. Hinrichs'sche Buchhandlung, 1883). The English translation quoted below is from E. A. W. Budge, trans., *The Cave of Treasures* (London: The Religious Tract Society, 1927), which also contains a lengthy introduction. Relevant to our discussion is the so-called *Book of Adam and Eve*, which contains similar traditions to the *Cave of Treasures*: A. Dillmann, trans., *Das christliche Adambuch des Morgenlandes* (Göttingen: Dieterichsche Buchhandlung, 1853); S. C. Malan, trans., *The Book of Adam and Eve* (London: Williams and Norgate, 1882).

150 Bezold, 42; Budge, 74; Malan, 118; Dillmann, 82–83. In the *Book of Adam and Eve* (Malan, 137), we are told that when the Sethites disobeyed the command to remain separate from the Cainites they were no longer called "children of God," but "children of the devil." We find the same interpretation in Augustine and Ephraem: the name "sons of God" is an *acquired* name, and thus can be lost when no longer deserved. This tradition appears in several subsequent Syriac chronicles. For instance, in the *Chronicle* of Michael the Syrian (1166–99) (ed. J. B. Chabot; 4 vols; Paris, 1899–1924; reprint Brussels: Culture et Civilisation, 1963) 4.2, we find: "They [the Sethites] wished to please God in purity (*bdkywt'*) and ascended Mt. Hermon. They lived there a holy life (*dwbr' qdyš'*), abstaining from marriage. Because of this they were called 'Sons of God' (*mtkryn bny 'lwhym*) and 'Watchers.' " Similarly in *Chronicon Anonymum ad Annum Christi 1234* (CSCO 81) 32–34.

151 Bezold, 48; Budge, 77. Cf. Malan, 121; Dillmann, 84. Cf. *Chronicum Anonymum*, 35: "He [Enosh] increasingly urged (*mḥpṭ*) the sons of God to pursue a holy life (*dwbr' qdyš'*)." Before this the chronicle says: "Enosh called on the name of the Lord more than any one else of his time (*ytyr mn kl dbzbnh*)."

fashion to describe the rules of Kenan, Mahalalel, and Jared. In Jared's days, however, the Sethites break their oath and descend (*yrd*) the mountain to mingle with the Cainites. Yet, the text makes clear that Enoch, Methuselah, Lamech, and Noah remained on the mountain.[152]

It would appear that Enosh's significance as a "governor" derives simply from his inclusion in the genealogy of Genesis 5. Little is said about Enosh that is not said about Seth before him or about the others who succeed him. Gen 4:26 is never cited explicitly, the identification of the human "sons of God" with the Sethites being simply asserted without need for a prooftext. However, the statement that Enosh "urged them to be constant in prayer (*ṣlwt'*)," which is said *only* of Enosh, may be an allusion to the verb "to call" in Gen 4:26b, which verb in Rabbinic sources is regularly interpreted to refer to prayer.[153] Thus, Enosh simply follows Seth in leading the Sethites in their pursuit of piety apart from the evil Cainites. While what little is said of Enosh in particular may derive from Gen 4:26b, this verse does not play a prominent role in the exegesis.

4. Isho'dad of Merv (fl. 850)

After Ephraem there is a large gap in the extant Syriac interpretations of Gen 4:26b and Enosh. Several Nestorian commentaries of the late eighth and ninth centuries treat our subjects, apparently drawing upon earlier traditions of interpretation whose origins are for the most part unknown to us. The most extensive of these, upon which some of the others seem to draw, is that of Isho'dad of Merv, Bishop of Hedatta and candidate for the patriarchal throne in 852.[154]

152 The story of the seduction of the Sethites by the Cainites is related in greater detail in the *Book of Adam and Eve* (trans. Malan) 125–38; Dillman, 92–95.

153 The Aramaic verb *ṣly* is regularly used in the Rabbinic targumim to translate the biblical Hebrew verb *qr'* when denoting worship. See below, chap. 4, nn. 14, 21.

154 An anonymous Syriac commentary on Genesis has been published on the basis of MS Mingana 553 by A. Levene under the title, *The Early Syrian Fathers on Genesis* (London: Taylor's Foreign Press, 1951). Levene claims that this is a compilation of teachings from various Church Fathers, but deriving mainly from Theodore of Mopsuestia (ca. 350–428). Others have ascribed this anonymous commentary to Sabrisho bar Paulus (fl. ca. 1190). See A. Scher, in *Revue des Bibliotheques* 17 (1907) 227–29; Baumstark, *Geschichte*, 290. Evidence for either of these ascriptions is lacking, however. All we can say is that this compilation, like that of Isho'dad, derives its traditions from several sources, including traditions going back to Ephraem and Theodore of Mopsuestia (whose interpretation of Gen 4:26 is not preserved) as well as to Greek Fathers of the Antiochene school. See especially T. Jansma, "Investigations into the Early Syrian Fathers on Genesis: An Approach to the Exegesis of the Nestorian Church and to the Comparison of Nestorian and Jewish Exegesis," *OTS* 12 (1958) 69–181. More recently, L. Van Rompay ("A Hitherto Unknown Nestorian Commentary on Genesis and Exodus 1–9, 32 in the Syriac Manuscript [Olim] Diharbekr 32," *OLP* 5 [1974] 53–78) has argued that Mingana 553 is based on an unpublished commentary from the eighth/ninth century, but also makes use of Isho'dad's commentary or a common source. Unfortunately, the text of this commentary, which presumably

Commentary on Genesis ad 4:26. In his commentary, Isho'dad first speaks about the names Seth and Enosh:

> Seth [means] foundation (*št'št'*), that is, after Adam. For Adam sinned and Abel was killed. Cain was rejected and in the end all of his seed was destroyed in the flood. He [Seth] is the foundation of the human species. Enosh [means] sweetness, or "by [in] the name of the Lord," or "immortal" (*ḥlywt' 'w bšm mry' 'w l' mywtwt'*).[155]

Seth is the head of the human species since Adam and Cain were disqualified on account of their sins and Abel was killed.[156] Isho'dad's interpretation of Enosh's name is more problematic. It in effect contains three interpretations, perhaps representing originally separate traditions which are here combined:

(a) Enosh means "sweetness." This can best be explained as a play on the Hebrew verb *hûḥal*, as if it derived from the root *ḥly*, which in Aramaic (including Syriac) can mean "to sweeten."[157] This interpretation,

---

interprets Gen 4:26, is not yet available. On folio 6a–b of MS Mingana 553 (ed. Levine, pp. 57–58, 80–81) we find traditions almost identical to those that will be discussed from Isho'dad of Merv. I will assume that the version in MS Mingana is dependent (whether directly or indirectly) on Isho'dad, or that the two draw upon a third source which cannot be identified. Variants to Isho'dad's interpretation which appear in MS Mingana 553 will be cited in the notes which follow.

Other Nestorian commentaries which share traditions with that of Isho'dad are those of Theodorus bar Koni (end of eighth century) and Isho bar Nun (d. 828). Also relevant is the commentary of the Christian Arab Ibn aṭ-Ṭaiyib (d. 1043). These will be cited below where pertinent.

155 *Commentaire D'Išo'dad de Merv sur L'Ancien Testament, I. Genese* (ed. J.-M. Voste and C. Van Den Eynde; CSCO 126; Louvain: L. Durbecq, 1950) 107–8. For a French translation, see CSCO 156.114–15. The text as found in MS Mingana 553, fol. 6a (ed. Levene, p. 58) has a somewhat different version: "Seth [means] foundation. It says, 'Then [he] began to call upon the name of the Lord'; that is, he dedicated himself to God that he might be called his servant [intimate] (*prš npšh l'lh' dbytyh ntqr'*), and he had nothing to do with Cain. Enosh [means] sweetness, or by [in] the name of the Lord." It appears that Gen 4:26b is cited here in reference to Seth and not Enosh.

156 This interpretation is based on a pun on Seth's name, deriving it from the roon *šyt*, meaning "set, fix, establish," a play already expressed by the Bible itself (Gen 4:25). A virtually identical interpretation appears in *Num. Rab.* 14.12: "He named him Seth. For from him the world was established (*hŵstt*), since Abel and Cain were banished from the world." See Levene's note, p. 170; and T. Jansma, "Investigations," 176–77. For other interpretations of Seth's name, see above, n. 86.

157 Of course, the correct biblical Hebrew form would then have to be *hwḥlh*, but such is not of primary concern to punsters. In biblical Hebrew the root *ḥlh* means "be sick or weak" (BDB 317–18). In Aramaic (including Syriac), however, one sense of being "weak" is being "sweet": M. Jastrow, *A Dictionary of the Talmud Babli and Jerushalmi, and the Midrashic Literature* (2 vols.; New York: Choreb, 1926) 1.467–68; *A Compendious Syriac Dictionary* (ed. J. Payne Smith; Oxford: Clarendon, 1903) 143. Similar plays on the roots *ḥll* and *ḥly* will be discussed in chapter 5. Levene (p. 170) suggests that the interpretation "sweetness" derives from Enosh's name itself, which means "man in his frailty." The specific sense of

then, is ultimately dependent on the *Hebrew* text of the Bible and is most likely the product of someone familiar with Hebrew or Aramaic, whether a Jew or Christian. If we are correct, this interpretation views Gen 4:26b as an explanation of the name Enosh in 4:26a.

(b) Enosh denotes "by (in) the name of the Lord." This interpretation most likely derives from a passive understanding of the verb "to call" in Gen 4:26b: Enosh began (or hoped) to be called "by the name of the Lord." We have seen this interpretation in several Greek Christian sources as well as in Ephraem (*'tqryw lhwn bšm mry'*), and we will encounter it again later in Isho'dad's commentary. Thus, if Enosh is said to have been called "by the name of the Lord," then this latter expression may have been taken as his cognomen. As we have argued in the case of Ephraem, such an interpretation most likely derives ultimately from the Septuagint. Isho'dad probably adopted this interpretation from an intermediary source such as Ephraem. Once again, Gen 4:26b is understood to contain an explanation of the name Enosh.[158]

(c) Enosh means "immortal." This interpretation is best explained as a mistaking of Enosh and Enoch, since, as we have seen, the two figures are often confused, and the latter is generally reputed to have escaped death.[159]

After commenting on Gen 5:3,[160] Isho'dad *returns* to Gen 4:26 and offers three interpretations of the second half of this verse:

(a) First, Gen 4:26b is quoted according to the *Peshiṭta* followed by a Syriac translation of the LXX: "The Greek [has] 'this one hoped' (*ywnyt. hn' sbr*). That is, Enosh formed this name of the Lord (*gblh lšmh hn' dmry') with the divine* power which operated in him, reckoning that all creatures are His works."[161] The emphasis here is not on Enosh's *invoking*

"sweetness," however, is better explained from the play *ḥll/ḥly*, especially since the noun *ḥlywt'* has as its root *ḥly*.

158 Levene (p. 170) calls this "etymology" "fanciful." His suggestion that *Seth* in naming Enosh "called upon the name of the Lord" fails to explain this as an interpretation of Enosh's name.

159 In MS Mingana 553 this third etymology is absent (see above, n. 155), as it is in the parallel in Theodorus bar Koni (fl. ca. 890), *Liber Scholiorum*, vol. 1 (ed. A. Scher; CSCO 55; Louvain, 1954) 184. Isho'dad devotes a discussion to Enoch's immortality shortly after our passage in commenting on Gen 5:22–24 (CSCO 126.108–9). Even though here, as elsewhere (see above, n. 46), we have explained traditions of Enosh's immortality or "translation" as a confusion with Enoch, we must admit to the possibility that an extra-biblical interpretation of Enosh as immortal also circulated, despite the fact that Gen 5:11 speaks of his death.

160 In commenting on Gen 5:3 ("He [Adam] begot a son after his likeness in his image"), Isho'dad stresses that despite Adam's fall, the divine image was not lost but was reimplanted in Seth, who transmitted it through his descendants to Jesus, in whom it again became full (cf. 2 Cor 4:4; Col 1:15). We find the same tradition in MS Mingana 553, fol. 6a (ed. Levene, pp. 25, 80).

161 This tradition also appears in the work of a contemporary of Isho'dad, Isho bar Nun

of the Lord by name, but on his *calling* God "Lord," that is, his uttering (literally, shaping) of God's name. This interpretation could derive from the Greek verb *epikaleisthai* as well as from the Hebrew/Aramaic *qr'/qry*, since they both can be used in the sense either of invoking or of naming.[162] The Syriac verb *sbr* is clearly a translation of the LXX *ēlpise* and may suggest that the interpretation derives ultimately from an interpretation of the LXX as: This one [Enosh] hoped to call God by the name "Lord." The Syriac *sbr* has the meaning "hope" in a positive sense: he trusted, had the confidence. Thus, Enosh in being the first to call God "Lord," exhibits faith and conviction.[163] This is reminiscent of Greek Fathers (e.g., Eusebius, Ambrose, Didymus, and Augustine) who similarly sought to interpret the verb "hope" positively, to Enosh's credit.[164]

(b) Next, Isho'dad gives what seems to be a mixture of the *Peshiṭta* and a Syriac translation of the LXX: *šry lmsbrw bšmh dmry'* ("[He] began to trust [hope] in the name of the Lord"):

> That is, he [Enosh] separated himself, as his father had done, from the "tribe" of Cain the murderer and dedicated himself to God (*w'ktb npšh l'lh'*), so that he and his sons were called "of God" and were pleasing to Him (*dhw 'm bnwhy d'lh' ntqrwn wlh nšprwn*), and for that reason were called "sons of God," that is, intimates of God (*bny 'lwhym 'tqryw hnw bytyy l'lh'*).

The meaning of this interpretation is clear, and is very similar to that found in Ephraem's commentary. The righteous Sethites are rewarded for their avoidance of the Cainites by being called "sons of God." Isho'dad takes "sons" not as a genealogical term, but as an associational one: they were "godlike," or "intimates of God."[165] What is harder to determine is the

---

(d. 828): *The Selected Questions of Ishō Bar Nun on the Pentateuch* (MS Cambridge Add. 2017; ed. E. G. Clarke; Leiden; E. J. Brill, 1962) fol. 9v. 9–13; translation, p. 27. Clarke in discussing the various parallels to this passage suggests (p. 112) that the text of Isho'dad "represents the text of the common source." The reading *hw sbr* is also found in the *Chronography of Bar Hebraeus* (d. 1286) (ed. and trans. E. A. W. Budge; 2 vols.; Oxford University Press, 1932) 2.2a–b; translation, 1.3; and in the *Chronicle* of Michael the Syrian (ed. J. B. Chabot) 4.2.

162 Thus, we find three interpretations of this verb in Syriac as in Greek Christian exegesis: invoking God's name, calling God by His name, being called by God's name. Similarly, see Ibn aṭ-Ṭaiyib *Commentaire sur la Genèse* (ed. and trans., J. C. J. Sanders; CSCO 274, 275; Louvain, 1967) 2.43 n. 5. See above, nn. 38, 65.

163 On the Syriac verb *sbr* having such meanings, see J. Payne Smith, *A Compendious Syriac Dictionary*, 359. We first witnessed this positive interpretation of Enosh's hope in Eusebius of Caesarea, and subsequently in others. Philo, we recall, placed great emphasis on Enosh's "hoping," but ultimately interpreted it as a sign of imperfection.

164 Clarke (p. 111) argues that this interpretation was originally based on the LXX, and that the *Peshiṭta* version was later added to introduce it.

165 On the Syriac word *byty*, meaning an "associate, intimate, friend," see J. Payne Smith, *Compendious Syriac Dictionary*, 45. This usage is analogous to the Rabbinic use of *ben bayit* to mean "servant, attendant," also with a sense of intimacy. See Jastrow, *Dictionary*,

relation of the interpretation to the "version" cited, which seems to be a hybrid of the LXX and *Peshiṭta*. I would suggest that originally the LXX was the basis of the present interpretation, derived most likely from a passive understanding of the verb *epikaleisthai*.[166] When this tradition was adopted by a Syrian author, the LXX was rendered into Syriac, and that in turn was "corrupted" under the influence of the *Peshiṭta* ("he began to trust"). As we have noted, the LXX version can be interpreted to refer to Enosh or Seth, while the *Peshiṭta* is even more ambiguous and can be understood to refer to either, or to an indefinite subject, such as the Sethites in general. The present passage takes Gen 4:26b to refer first to Enosh in particular and then to his descendants in general, all of whom were called "sons of God" in recognition of their piety.[167]

(c) Finally, our phrase is cited as: *hw šry lmqr' bšmh dmry'* ("He began to call on the name of the Lord"). This is the *Peshiṭta* version, except that *hydyn* ("then") is replaced by *hw* ("he"), perhaps under the influence of the LXX (*houtos*):

> That is, in every deed which he performed he turned to the Lord for help and called [on Him]. The word "to call" indicates that he would continually call for everything, and not that he called [once]. "I do," he said, "this thing in the name of the Lord."

This interpretation is ostensibly based on the infinitive (rather than finite) form of the verb "to call." That Enosh "began to call" suggests that thereafter this was an ongoing activity of his. Once again, the interpretation is more suitable to the LXX than to the *Peshiṭta*, since the former omits the word "then."[168] Gen 4:26b is understood to mean that Enosh dedicated all of his activity to God's name, perhaps, as before, in recognition of the Lord as master of all.[169]

168; E. Z. Melamed in *Leshonenu* 20 (1956) 110–11. The exact same tradition appears in Ibn aṭ-Ṭaiyib, *Commentaire* (CSCO 274.45). In Theodorus bar Koni *Liber Scholiorum* (CSCO 55.98) *Seth* is given as the subject of Gen 4:26b, but the phrase is interpreted to refer to his descendants in general: "Seth hoped to call on the name of the Lord, for they separated themselves from intercourse with daughters of Cain. Therefore, they were called 'sons of God', that is, intimates of God." The expression "intimate of God" is also used in MS Mingana 553, fol. 6a (ed. Levene, p. 17), where the tradition appears to be applied to Seth alone, and not to Enosh. See above, n. 155. Cf. Isho'dad's interpretation of Gen 6:2, below, n. 175.

166 Clarke (p. 114) suggests tracing this passive interpretation back to Eusebius of Emesa. Similarly, Van den Eynde, CSCO 156.115, n. 3.

167 We first witnessed this tendency explicitly in John Chrysostom (see above, n. 84), but implicitly already in Eusebius of Emesa.

168 If this interpretation was originally based on the LXX, perhaps it was responding to the present rather than aorist infinitive *epikaleisthai*, denoting continuous activity.

169 Similarly in Ibn aṭ-Ṭaiyib (trans. Sanders, 43): "Selon d'autres l'Écriture veut dire qu'Énoš commença à invoquer le nom du Seigneur, c.-à- d. en toute action il louait le nom du Seigneur."

Each of these three interpretations of Gen 4:26b begins with a version of the verse which in some way combines the translation of the LXX with that of the *Peshiṭta*: the first simply cites the *Peshiṭta* followed by the Septuagint in Syriac ("this one hoped"), the second has "[he] began to trust [hope]," while the third has "this one began." In all three cases, however, we have shown that the interpretation seems to derive in some significant way from the LXX. We have here the work either of a Syriac exegete who is familiar with and influenced by the LXX, or of a Syriac compiler, who is adapting Greek Christian exegesis to a Syriac audience. The latter appears to me to be the more likely.[170]

Commentary on Genesis ad 6:2.[171] For Isho'dad as for so many others, the interpretation of Gen 4:26b is tied to that of Gen 6:2. He refutes the view that the "sons of God" of Gen 6:2 were supernatural angels, citing what appears to be an Aramaic version of Symmachus' Greek translation: *bny dšlyṭn'* (=*huioi tōn dynasteuontōn*, "sons of rulers"), and giving other scriptural examples where humans are referred to as "gods" or "sons of God."[172] He states:

> Furthermore, they called themselves (*qrw npšhwn*) "sons of God" since as it says, "[one] began to call on [to be called by] the name of the Lord," and they vowed to serve Him etc., like sons [serve] their father.

Once again, basing himself on the *Peshiṭta* version, Isho'dad takes the subject of Gen 4:26b to be indefinite: one began, or they began, referring to the Sethites in general, rather than to Enosh in particular. Yet the interpretation seems to derive ultimately from a passive interpretation of the verb "to call" in the LXX.[173]

170 See Clarke, *The Selected Questions of Isho Bar Nun*, 111. Such a process, however, involves more than a simple translation from Greek into Syriac. As we have seen, in adapting the exegesis of the LXX to the Syriac language and the *Peshiṭta* version, subtle but significant changes are affected: (a) Whereas the interpretation of the LXX usually refers to Enosh in particular (*houtos*), once adapted to the *Peshiṭta* understanding ("then [one] began") it could refer just as easily to Seth or to his descendants in general. (b) The sense of the Syriac verb *sbr* is more positive than that of the Greek (*ēlpise*), and thus to Enosh is now attributed "trust" or "confidence" in God or His name.

171 CSCO 126.111–12; French translation, CSCO 156.118–20.

172 His arguments and prooftexts are virtually identical to those of John Chrysostom in *Expositio in Psalmum* 49.1, discussed above, strongly suggesting direct or indirect dependence. Isho'dad also "demythologizes" the giants of Gen 6:4, understanding them to be humans of unusual size and strength, similar to Seth and Enosh, men "known for their mighty strength (*gnbrwt'*)." CSCO 126.112.12–13. Cf. Augustine, *De civ. Dei* 15.23.

173 One might argue that Isho'dad (like the Rabbinic targumim) is simply supplying a direct object for the verb "to call": (one) began to call (oneself) by the name of the Lord. However, in light of the frequency with which Isho'dad elsewhere renders the verb "to call" passively, an interpretation based originally on a passive understanding of the LXX *epikaleisthai* seems more likely. See above, n. 143.

The term "sons of God" is explained in two ways: (a) It refers to the Sethites who according to Gen 4:26b are called by God's name. (b) Taken metaphorically, it refers to those who, in serving God, subject themselves to Him as one does to a father. Thus, they serve Him *as if* they were his "sons." These two interpretations may both derive from the verb "to call" of Gen 4:26b. The first understands the verb passively (they were called by God's name) while the second takes it actively in the sense of worship (they worshipped or served God by name).[174] Here as elsewhere in Isho'dad the two interpretations are essentially connected. For the Sethites to have been called "sons of God" or "by the name of the Lord," does not mean for Isho'dad that they were actually divine. Rather, it means that they enjoyed a special relationship with God, as his intimates and servants, in return for having devoted themselves to Him (calling on *His* name) rather than to the ways of the Cainites.

It appears that Isho'dad of Merv compiled an anthology of interpretations of Enosh and Gen 4:26. Since they may originate from different sources it would be a mistake to attempt a uniform synthesis. Yet some common threads run through the traditions which he preserves. Like those of Ephraem, these interpretations seem to derive originally from the LXX translation, being very similar to what we have witnessed in several Greek Church Fathers: the Sethites were called "sons of God" since Scripture says that Enosh was "called by the name of the Lord." However, once this interpretation was attached to the Syriac version of the Bible a problem arose since this version could not support a passive interpretation of the verb "to call." Rather than abandon this interpretation of the "sons of God" as the righteous Sethites, the *Peshiṭta* was itself interpreted to support this understanding. Enosh in proclaiming God's name "Lord" declared Him to be master of all. Enosh dedicated himself to God's ways rather than to those of the Cainites, and in so doing was called a "servant" of God the master. As such, he and his descendants were also called "sons of God," now understood to mean servants or intimates of God. Although the original, passive understanding of the verb "to call" is retained, it is now supplemented with an active interpretation which leads to the same

[174] On a few occasions the targumim use the verb *plḥ* to translate the Hebrew *qr'* in the phrase "to call on the name of the Lord." Thus, to call on God is to worship Him is to serve Him. See *Tg. Neof.* ad Gen 12:8; 21:33; 22:14; *Tg. Onq.* ad Gen 22:14; 33:20. A similar interpretation is given by Isho'dad for Abraham's calling on God's name (Gen 12:8): "And the words 'he called upon the name of the Lord' [mean that] he dedicated himself to Him, recognizing Him as God, declaring Him alone to be Lord, so that he was called His servant and intimate (*'bdh wbytyh ntqr'*). And this is similar to what is said concerning Enosh: 'This one,' it says, 'began to call on the name of the Lord' " (CSCO 126.144). Both Enosh and Abraham in calling on the name of the Lord affirm His mastery over all and their subservience to Him as intimate servants, or "sons."

conclusion.[175] For Isho'dad, or for the authors of the interpretations he collects, Enosh is more important than he was for Ephraem, for it is through Enosh's faith as expressed in Gen 4:26b that the Sethites first obtain the epithet "sons of God."[176]

C. Conclusions

We have surveyed a wide range of Christian exegesis relating to Enosh and Gen 4:26. The similarities as well as the differences between these interpretations need now to be considered. Are there any patterns which emerge? Is there an overriding Christian exegesis to be discerned? If so, how is it to be explained?

Three exegetical approaches, each evidenced in pre-Rabbinic Jewish explications of our subject, have been adopted and adapted by Christian interpreters.

The first approach, also well evidenced in the early Samaritan traditions that we examined, views Enosh primarily as an early link in the chain of righteous Israelite ancestors.[177] In this context Enosh is generally not discussed much in his own right. He, like the other links in the chain, provides a model of piety and a proof of God's regard for those who despite temptation and adversity maintain complete faith in Him. For Enosh in particular, this faith is suggested by the "hope" he places in God and the worship of God. Thus, the LXX/Old Latin (mis)translation "he hoped" continues to be important in distinguishing Enosh's piety, even if it is not explicitly interpreted. This approach, which displays only slight variations from its Jewish (and perhaps Samaritan) antecedents, is most evident in the earliest Christian sources which we examined, where particularly Christian exegesis is implicit at best.[178]

The second approach, reflective of Philo's exegesis and perhaps even dependent (whether directly or indirectly) on it, pays greater attention to Enosh in his own right as representing "true man." In this category I include Eusebius of Caesarea, Ambrose, Didymus, and Augustine.[179] Like

175 We have described a similar phenomenon in Augustine's exegesis of Gen 4:26. See above, n. 99.

176 Because of the ambiguity of the *Peshiṭta* text, the connection of this interpretation with Enosh is somewhat weak. Therefore, later versions of this tradition, such as that found in Theodorus bar Koni (see n. 166), transfer it to Seth, making him both the genealogical and spiritual progenitor of the righteous line. This is precisely the shift which we observed in the Byzantine chronographers, especially Pseudo-Malalas.

177 For examples, see our treatment of Methodius of Olympus and the Apostolic Constitutions at the beginning of this chapter.

178 For instance, Jesus may conclude the chain of righteous (e.g. *Apostolic Constitutions* 2.55; 7.38; 8.5), or a New Testament phrase may be used to praise or describe the ancient righteous (e.g., Methodius' allusion to Heb 12.23).

179 While Origen and Jerome view Enosh positively, their praise of him is somewhat

Philo they stress the significance of Enosh's name, meaning "man," understanding it allegorically to suggest man par excellence. Also like Philo they stress Enosh's virtue of hope, but go even further than Philo in viewing Enosh's exemplary hope wholly positively.[180] This is achieved by variously interpreting Enosh's "calling on the name of the Lord God" so as to mean more than simple divine worship: (a) Eusebius: Enosh places his hope not in earthly substance but in God, whom he calls both "Lord" and "God" in recognition of His powers of mastery and creation. (b) Ambrose: Enosh is man in God's image, who desires to know God's name, and who clings to God rather than to earthly concerns. (c) Didymus: Enosh is man in the divine image, who hopes to be called by God's name, that is, to resemble God and submit to his authority and instruction. (d) Augustine: Enosh represents spiritual, asexual man, who lives in prophetic expectation (hope) of the fulfillment of the City of God in the resurrection of Jesus and in the community of Christian elect who will similarly call on His name.[181] In all of these, Enosh's name in the first half of Gen 4:26 is understood to be explained by the second half of the verse.[182]

The third approach, reminiscent of Josephus' retelling of Gen 4–5, treats Enosh in the context of describing the corruption of the Sethite "sons of God" prior to the Flood.[183] This approach to Gen 4:26 is not evidenced in Christian writings until the mid-fourth century. I include here Eusebius of Emesa, John Chrysostom, Cyril, the Byzantine chronographers, Ephraem, and Isho'dad of Merv.[184] These exegetes understand Gen 4:26b to mean that Enosh, because of his piety and righteousness, hoped/was the first to *be called* (understanding the LXX *epikaleisthai* as passive) by God's name, that is, to be called "God" or "son of God," causing his progeny to be called "sons of God" in Gen 6:2–4.[185]

---

muted, if not contradicted by negative interpretations found elsewhere. On Origen, see above, nn. 22–31. On Jerome, see above, nn. 4, 34. George Syncellus also adduces the interpretation of "Enosh" as "true man," but how he uses this interpretation is unclear.

180 As we have seen, the only Christian exegete to express a negative view of Enosh's hope is Origen, in his *Commentary to Romans*, Book 5.1.

181 Origen, in his *Commentary to Romans*, Book 8.3, is the first Christian we know of who understands Enosh to have called on Jesus. However, it is not clear what exactly he has in mind.

182 We have observed this tendency in pre-Rabbinic Jewish exegesis, especially Philo, and will see it again in Rabbinic interpretations of Gen 4:26. It reflects a natural expectation, considering how frequently the Bible, especially in the early chapters of Genesis, explains through a wordplay the naming of a newborn. See chap. 1, n. 4.

183 For the Jewish antecedents to this interpretation, see chap. 1, n. 76, and above, n. 54.

184 While Isho'dad includes interpretations of this type, he also includes interpretations similar to those of the second approach, e.g., Enosh placed his hope in God, and called Him "Lord."

185 Didymus similarly interprets Enosh as having hoped to *be called* by God's name, in the sense of *imitatio dei*, but he does not apply this interpretation to the Sethites in general or to the "sons of God" in Gen 6:2–4. It should be stressed that these sources contain no suggestion

As we have noted, there are some significant differences between the interpretations of this group of commentators: (a) the extent to which Enosh receives particular praise, (b) the specific virtues which earn Enosh and his descendants the titles "God" or "son of God," (c) whether the "sons of God" are so named in recognition of their own righteousness, or because they are descendants of the godlike Enosh. Despite such differences, all of these Christian exegetes present essentially the same picture of antediluvian history: Adam's descendants were divided into two families, the faithful, godlike ("sons of God") Sethites and the wicked Cainites. The eventual intermarriage of these two lines corrupted the former and threatened the preservation of the divine image and messianic seed, causing God to bring the Flood. Implicit in all of these, and made explicit in some (especially Cyril and Ephraem), is the idea that the antediluvian "sons of God" (Seth, Enosh, and their descendants) foreshadow and prefigure the New Testament "sons of God" (Jesus and his "brethren," the Christian elect). For the most part (the notable exception being Cyril), Enosh's particular significance is less central in this approach than in the previous one (Enosh as true man). Here the concern is more tied to "demythologizing" the angelic "sons of God" of Gen 6:2–4 and to portraying the "fall" of the Sethites in general, and less tied to depicting what Enosh as true man represents.

While this third approach may be said to be the most particularly Christian in its implications and the most radical in its exegesis of Gen 4:26b, it contains within itself difficulties which eventually get resolved at the expense of the veneration of Enosh: (a) It is Seth who stands at the head of the righteous antediluvians, yet it is from Enosh that they derive their name "sons of God." (b) While Enosh is said to have been called "God" or "son of God," the LXX only says that he *hoped* to be so called.[186] These difficulties get resolved in two ways: (a) taking Gen 4:26b to refer to Seth and not Enosh, facilitated by the ambiguous *houtos*,[187] (b) accommodating

of actual deification of Enosh or his descendants. They do not claim that Enosh was or became a god, but only that because of his godlike behavior and character he was referred to, by Scripture or his contemporaries, with a divine epithet. I have intentionally tried to stay clear of the question of a Hellenistic divine-man (*theios anēr*) typology in early Christianity. That such a "type" existed, especially in so-called Hellenistic Judaism, has been called into serious doubt. See most recently Carl Holladay, *Theoios Anēr in Hellenistic Judaism* (SBL Dissertation Series 40; Missoula, Mo.: Scholars Press, 1977), especially chapter 1, which contains a survey of the literature. That charismatic miracle workers, lawgivers, rulers, and wise men in the Greco-Roman world were called or considered "gods" is well established. That such figures can be considered a cohesive "type" is another matter altogether.

186 Note how Theodoret of Cyrus eliminates this problem by basing his interpretation on Aquila's translation. See above, n. 104. Other Christian commentators are unwilling, however, to substitute Aquila's translation for that of the LXX.

187 This transfer is evident in the Byzantine chronographers, especially Pseudo-Malalas (see above, n. 132), and in the later Syriac commentators, especially Theodorus bar Koni (see above, n. 166). While this interpretation is facilitated by the ambiguous subject of Gen 4:26b,

this interpretation to an *active* understanding of the verb "to call" in such a way as to produce a positive view of Enosh's hope. This latter shift, particularly evident in Augustine and the Syriac commentators, brings us back to the second approach described above, ultimately traceable to Philo, but now with a more explicitly Christian thrust: Enosh, as true man, fervently hopes/prophetically expects to call on the name of God/Jesus, that is, to place all hope and faith in Him alone as master. By so doing, Enosh merits being considered a servant or son of God. Thus, the identification of the "sons of God" with the descendants of Seth and Enosh is retained, but is no longer necessarily dependent on a *passive* understanding of the verb "to call" in Gen 4:26b.[188] The second and third approaches are combined: Gen 4:26b now serves both to describe Enosh as true man and to identify Enosh and his progeny as "sons of God," a term of great significance to Christian theology and Christology.[189]

Each of the three approaches which we have described—Enosh's significance as a link in the chain of righteous ancestors, Enosh's significance as representing true man who places his hope in God, and Enosh's significance in the context of the corruption of the Sethite "sons of God"—can be traced back (not necessarily genetically) to pre-Rabbinic Jewish exegesis. Yet each has been adapted, in some cases more radically than in others, to Christian self-definition through the medium of scriptural exegesis. What emerges is what may be said to be a distinctively Christian view of antediluvian heroes and history. The descendants of Seth, and Enosh as true man in particular, are seen (in contrast to the violent, perverse, and materialistic Cainites) as primeval, *universal* models of faith and piety, who in placing their hope in heaven earn the epithet "sons of God," thereby prefiguring the Christian elect who at the other end of history and the messianic chain similarly call on the name of the Lord (Jesus) and bear the name "sons of God."[190] Gen 4:26 is interpreted allegorically to define true man, and typologically to identify that true man with the Christian believer.

---

it also reflects Jewish, Christian, and perhaps Arabic traditions which highly venerated Seth. See above, nn. 59, 86, 122, 125, 134, 156.

188 We saw this particularly in the commentaries of Ephraem and Isho'dad where interpretations based originally on a passive understanding of the verb "to call" in the LXX are retained but accommodated to a scriptural version (the *Peshiṭta*) which does not permit such a passive understanding. The same may be true for exegetes, such as Augustine, who depend on the Latin version.

189 Joseph Fitzmyer (*A Wandering Aramean*, 102) rightly states: "The designation of Jesus in the NT as the 'Son of God' is widespread, and no other title of his can claim as much significance for later theological development than it. If the title *ho huios tou anthrōpou* [son of man] outstrips it in enigma, it certainly does not in implication."

190 The veneration of Seth, Enoch, Noah, and Melchizedek in several extra-Rabbinic Jewish writings (particularly in the Pseudepigrapha and the Dead Sea Scrolls) may reflect a similarly "apocalyptic" perspective on earliest human history.

Chapter Four
RABBINIC INTERPRETATIONS

In the preceding chapter we saw how Christian exegetes both continued lines of interpretation found in pre-Rabbinic Jewish writings and redirected those inherited lines of interpretation in new directions. We observed that such Christian reshapings of tradition had to be understood *both* in terms of the tensions contained *within* the inherited biblical and postbiblical traditions themselves, and in terms of a developing *Christian* reading of those traditions. Despite the variety of Christian interpretations, we were able to discern some common threads which characterize early Christian exegesis of Enosh and his time and to interpret them as reflections of broader issues of Christian thought and self-definition.

Since Rabbinic interpretations of Enosh and his times parallel in time those of the Church Fathers, and presumably draw upon, at least initially, common biblical and postbiblical traditions, it will be interesting to compare the Rabbinic treatment of our subject and to view it against the backdrop of antecedent and contemporary non-Rabbinic approaches. To what extent are the rabbis confronting similar questions arising from Gen 4:26 and its accompanying traditions, and to what extent do the rabbis pose new questions that similarly need to be interpreted as reflections of broader issues of Rabbinic thought and self-definition?

While the rabbinic interpretation is variegated in form and content, it is possible to preview its main traits, which place it in sharp contrast to Christian and pre-Rabbinic Jewish exegesis: (a) The Rabbinic traditions, with only a few exceptions, understand Gen 4:26 to refer not to Enosh in particular, or to his decendants, but to his contemporaries, the Generation of Enosh (*dôr 'ĕnôš*). The notion of the "Generation of Enosh" is unattested not only in Scripture but in *all* non-Rabbinic traditions of interpretation as well. For the rabbis, Gen 4:26 describes one of the earliest *ages* of human history. (b) Gen 4:26 is understood to describe the origins of "strange worship" (*'ăbôdâ zārâ*), or idolatry, in Enosh's time.[1]

[1] As we shall see, the word idolatry does not adequately translate the Hebrew expression *'ăbôdâ zārâ* and its parallels (*'ăbôdat 'elîlîm* and *'ăbôdat kôkābîm*). The Hebrew expression has the general sense of unprescribed worship, and is not limited to the worship of idols, that is, physical objects and images. Thus, the worship of celestial phenomena, angels, and humans is equally "idolatrous." In the traditions that I will examine, the object of idolatry is often not indicated, and the term *'ăbôdâ zārâ* is used as a general term for

According to this interpretation of Gen 4:26, the Generation of Enosh *ceased* to worship God and *began* to apply God's name to the worship of false gods. Thus, Gen 4:26, so often interpreted in non-Rabbinic sources (Jewish, Samaritan, and Christian) as a positive statement about Enosh, is *consistently* interpreted by the rabbis as a negative statement about his contemporaries (eventually including him) as the originators of idolatry. In fact, *not once* in all of Rabbinic literature is this verse cited to refer positively to the beginnings of divine worship.[2]

While Christian exegesis is at times radical in its reading of Gen 4:26, especially when it interprets this verse to mean not that Enosh called upon God's name but that Enosh *was called* by God's name, such exegesis could be reconciled with an interpretation of Enosh as the innovator of divine worship. Both interpretations coexist in Christian exegesis since both view Enosh positively. The rabbis, however, in *conversely* interpreting Gen 4:26 to refer to the beginnings of idolatry, seem to reject irreconcilably the view of Enosh as the originator of divine worship. We will certainly want to ask, *why* such a radically different line of interpretation, so different from what we have seen in other traditions of interpretation, both Jewish and non-Jewish, and so at odds with what would *seem* to be the simple meaning of Gen 4:26? What does this interpretation suggest concerning the Rabbinic reading of Gen 4:26 and its scriptural context, and concerning Rabbinic attitudes to pre-Rabbinic Jewish and contemporary Christian understandings of Enosh? What does this interpretation tell us about the rabbis themselves? As intriguing as such questions of Rabbinic exegetical method and motivation are, we will not directly address them until the next chapter. For now, we will focus on the traditions themselves. What do they say and how do they say it? When does the tradition of the Generation of Enosh emerge and how does it evolve as it is transmitted from generation to generation of sages?

Thus, our present task is to trace the history of Rabbinic interpretation. In order to do so we will have to present the traditions in some chronological order, recognizing all the while the inherent difficulties in dating Rabbinic traditions, and realizing that, in truth, we can only trace the history of interpretation in its extant *literary* forms.[3] Thus, our chronological scheme

---

the worship of "other gods," or for the improper worship of Israel's God. For further discussion of Rabbinic polemics against idolatry see Saul Lieberman, *Hellenism in Jewish Palestine* (New York: Jewish Theological Seminary of America, 1962) 115–38; E. E. Urbach, "The Laws of Idolatry in the Light of Historical and Archaeological Facts in the Third Century," *Eretz-Israel* 5 (1958) 189–205 (Heb. Section). For a broader discussion see Jose Faur and L. I. Rabinowitz, "Idolatry," *Encyclopedia Judaica* (16 vols.; Jerusalem: Keter, 1972) 8.1227–37.

2 See below, n. 58. Not until the medieval Jewish commentators do we find the positive interpretation of Gen 4:26b.

3 In most cases, the oral and even literary prehistory of a tradition found in one of our

is relative at best. First, we will examine the Rabbinic Aramaic translations (*targumim*) of Gen 4:26. Then, we will treat relevant traditions found in the so-called tannaitic corpora, generally thought to have been compiled during the first half of the third century C.E., but comprising traditions thought to derive from the first two centuries C.E. (if not earlier).[4] Next, we will view interpretations found in the amoraic collections, compiled between the fourth and sixth centuries. Finally, we will consider post-amoraic and early medieval traditions of interpretation.[5]

A. Rabbinic Targumim

We treat first the Rabbinic Aramaic translations of Gen 4:26b not because in their present forms they chronologically precede the interpretations of the midrashim, but because they *may* reflect ways of reading

---

sources is beyond our grasp. Similarly, other traditions probably circulated which are no longer extant. Thus, a true "history of interpretation" is an impossibility.

[4] In reality, the so-called tannaitic midrashim as we have them are most likely the products of amoraic editors, who may either have simply *collected* tannaitic traditions or have significantly *reworked* those traditions in shaping them to fit their present literary contexts. If the latter, then the constituent traditions cannot automatically be assumed to be "tannaitic." For more detailed discussion of this point see S. D. Fraade, "Sifre Deuteronomy 26 (ad Deut. 3:23): How Conscious the Composition?" *HUCA* 54 (1983) 245–301.

[5] The dating of a compilation, in most cases only roughly agreed upon by scholars, will be assumed to provide the *terminus ad quem* for the traditions contained therein. Of course, compilations, by their very nature, may contain traditions of earlier vintage. However, unless there is clear evidence pointing to an earlier dating, the date of the compilation will be adopted as the chief criterion for locating its constituent traditions within the chronological framework. Where a particular tradition appears in several collections, it will be examined as it appears in the earliest source, indicating and evaluating in the notes significant later variants. Only if such a tradition has undergone major revision in a later source will it be treated again in its later form at a subsequent stage in our chronology. It is possible that a tradition bears meanings determined by its present literary context that it may not have borne prior to its inclusion in that context. At times I will suggest dating a tradition earlier than the source in which it first appears, if it is attributed to a named sage in such a way as not to cast doubt on the attribution. In such cases it will be assumed that the tradition circulated at the time when the sage flourished, but not that its extant form represents his *ipsissima verba*. In determining the floruit of a sage, I have consulted H. L. Strack, *Introduction to the Talmud and Midrash* (Philadelphia: Jewish Publication Society of America, 1931) 105–34; A. Hyman, *Toledot tanna'im we'amora'im* (3 vols.; Jerusalem, 1964); I. H. Weiss, *Dor dor wedorešayw*, vols. 1–3 (Wilna: Zawadski, 1911). For a fuller discussion of the problems of datings and attributions see J. Neusner, *The Rabbinic Traditions About the Pharisees Before 70*, vol. 3 (Leiden: E. J. Brill, 1971) 3, 180–238. For the dating of the midrashic compilations, I have consulted L. Zunz, *Hadderašot beyiśra'el* (ed. and rev. Ch. Albeck; Jerusalem: Bialik Institute, 1974); E. Schürer, *The History of the Jewish People in the Age of Jesus Christ*, vol. 1 (ed. and rev. G. Vermes and F. Millar; Edinburgh: T. & T. Clark, 1973) 68–117; H. L. Strack, *Introduction to the Talmud and Midrash*, 201–34; and entries in the new *Encyclopaedia Judaica*.

Gen 4:26 that are assumed by the midrashim, and even more importantly because they provide a shorthand expression of Rabbinic exegesis that will serve as an introduction to the more complex traditions of the midrashim.[6]

1. Palestinian Targumim

There are four extant versions of the so-called Palestinian Jewish Aramaic translations of Gen 4:26b.[7] While they all state that Enosh's contemporaries began (were the first) to apply God's name to the worship of idols or false gods, they evidence subtle yet significant differences in how they say this.

Fragment Targum: ביומוי הא בכין שרון בני אינשא למפלוח בפולחנא נוכריא ולמכנא יתהון בשום מימרא דיי׳ ("In his days, then, men began worshipping foreign cults and calling them by the name of the Memra of the Lord").[8]

Targum Neofiti I: בכדין שרו בני אנשא למהוי עבדין להון טעון ומכניין יתהון בש[ם] ממרה דייי ("Then, men began to make idols for themselves, calling them by the name of the Memra of the Lord"). A marginal gloss provides a reading similar to that of the *Fragment Targum*: הא בכדין שרון למפלח בפולחנא נוכראה [ולמכניה] יתיה בשם ממ[רה דייי].[9]

Targum Pseudo-Jonathan: הוא דרא דביומוהי שריאו למטעי ועבדו להון טעוון ומכנין לטעוותהון בשום מימרא דה׳ ("That was the generation in whose days they began to go astray, making idols for themselves, and calling their idols by the name of the Memra of the Lord").[10]

These targumim all understand the Hebrew word *'āz* of Gen 4:26 to

[6] Despite extensive scholarly debate, there is still no consensus on the provenance and dating of the extant targumim, nor on the nature of their relationships to one another or to other sources of translation and exegetical tradition. For summary and bibliographic statements see M. P. Miller, "Targum, Midrash, and the Use of the Old Testament in the New Testament," *JSJ* 2 (1971) 29–82; Y. Komlosh, *The Bible in the Light of the Aramaic Translations* (Hebrew) (Tel Aviv: Dvir, 1973) 38–56; R. Le Deaut, "The Current State of Targumic Studies," *Biblical Theology Bulletin* 4 (1974) 3–32; M. McNamara, "Targums," *IDBSup* (1976) 856–61.

[7] By using the commonly applied term Palestinian with respect to these translations, I do not necessarily assume for them a common content, provenance, or dating, nor that *Targum Onqelos* is *wholly* "Babylonian." Cairo Geniza targum fragments are not extant for Gen 4:26.

[8] M. L. Klein, *The Fragment Targums of the Pentateuch According to their Extant Sources* (2 vols.; AnBib 76; Rome: Biblical Institute, 1980) 1.48 (text); 2.9 (trans.); from MS Paris, Bibliothèque nationale Hebr. 110. Klein's text differs only slightly from the earlier edition of M. Ginsburger: *Das Fragmententhargum* (*Thargum jeruschalmi zum Pentateuch*) (Berlin, 1897/8; reprint Jerusalem, 1968/9).

[9] *Neofiti I* (ed. A. Diez Macho; 6 vols.; Madrid and Barcelona: Consejo Superior de Investigaciones Cientificas, 1968–79) 1.27; and the facsimile edition: *The Palestinian Targum to the Pentateuch—Codex Vatican* (2 vols.; Jerusalem: Makor, 1970) 1.10.

[10] *Pseudo-Jonathan*: *Targum Jonathan ben Uziel on the Pentateuch* (ed. D. Rieder; Jerusalem, 1974) 7.

refer not only to the time of Enosh's birth, but more generally to the time in which he is thought to have lived. The *Fragment Targum*, *Targum Neofiti*, and *Neofiti Margin* use *bikden* or *beken* to translate *'āz*, as is customary elsewhere in these translations. These terms can mean either "then" or "thus, therefore," as can the Hebrew *'āz*.[11] Here, the temporal sense is probably intended, but the meaning "therefore" should not be ignored, since the second half of the verse may, as we have seen, be understood as an explanation of Enosh's naming in the first half. This is especially possible in the *Fragment Targum*, where the word *bĕyômôhî* ("in his days," i.e., in Enosh's days) has already provided the temporal sense.

It is interesting that *Targum Pseudo-Jonathan* alone paraphrases, "that was the *generation* in whose days." While this difference may be insignificant, it *may* indicate a later version of the translation tradition. We will see that the tannaitic sources consistently refer to "the days of Enosh," while only in amoraic and later compilations do we encounter the fixed expression "the Generation of Enosh" (*dôr 'ĕnôš*, or *dôrô šel 'ĕnôš*), often associated with the Generation of the Flood and the Generation of the Separation (the Tower of Babel generation).

The passive *hoph'al* form *hûḥal* ("was begun"), appearing nowhere else in Scripture, is translated by all of these targumim with the *pe'al* active plural of the verb *šry*, which verb is almost always used in the Aramaic translations to render the Hebrew verb *hēḥēl* when meaning "to begin." Thus, the ambiguous expression "then was begun" (begun by whom?) is understood to refer not to Enosh (or Seth), as in the LXX and its dependent traditions, but to an indefinite collective subject: then was begun by men, or men (humanity) began. These targumim are the *only* ancient versions to so translate.[12] The *Fragment Targum* and *Targum Neofiti* express this interpretation most explicitly by adding the collective expression *bĕnê 'ĕnāšā'* ("humanity"), which would appear to be redundant.[13] Thus, Gen 4:26b is understood to refer not to a particular

[11] The Aramaic *bikdên* (*Tg. Neofiti* and *Neofiti m*) usually means "thus, therefore, in this manner": M. Jastrow, *A Dictionary of the Targumim, the Talmud Babli and Yerushalmi, and the Midrashic Literature* (New York: Choreb, 1926) 315a; G. Dalman, *Aramäisch-Neuhebräisches Handwörterbuch* (Frankfurt: J. Kauffmann, 1922) 96b, 193a; J. Levy, *Chaldäisches Wörterbuch über die Targumim* (2 vols.; Leipzig: Baumgartner's Buchhandlung, 1867) 1.182a. A survey of its usage in *Tg. Neofiti* reveals, however, that this word appears regularly as a translation of MT *'āz* both in its meaning "thus" and "then." It should be recalled that the LXX translation *houtos* ("this one") was understood by some as *houtōs* ("thus"). See above, chap. 1, n. 14.

[12] We saw, however, in our examination of Christian interpretations, that the *Peshiṭta* ("then he/one began") and Aquila ("then was begun") could be interpreted to suggest an indefinite subject, but that such an indefinite subject was interpreted by Christians to refer not to mankind in general but to the Sethites. See above, chap. 3, nn. 84, 119, 143.

[13] For other targumic uses of this expression, see, for example, Gen 3:20 ("she was the mother of all the living"), which is translated by *Tgs. Onqelos* and *Ps. Jonathan* as "she

individual or group of people, but to humanity in general.

What is truly unusual is the manner in which these targumim translate the phrase "to call on the name of the Lord," taking it to refer not to divine worship, but to the worship of false gods. However, this phrase should not in its own right have presented a problem for the Aramaic translators. It appears some thirty times in Scripture, seven of these in the Pentateuch, and the targumim consistently translate it so as to refer to prayer, using the verb *ṣly*.[14]

The targumim take as the object of worship not God, but false gods. They achieve this by recognizing an ellipsis in the biblical phrase: "Then was begun the calling/worship (of false gods) by/with the name of the Lord." When we examine these targumim more closely we see that they provide a *double* translation of the verb "to call," indicating a two-fold interpretation of the sin of Enosh's contemporaries: (a) They *worshipped* (or made) false gods. (b) They *called* those false gods by God's name.[15] This is most evident in the *Fragment Targum* and *Targum Neofiti Margin*, where the verb *liqrō'* is rendered both with the Aramaic verb *plḥ* ("to worship"), as well as with *kny* ("to name"). While the latter verb, *kny*, is easily recognized as a rendering of the Hebrew verb *liqrō'*, the verb *plḥ* has not been recognized by commentators as such. Yet, there

---

was the mother of all humanity." The same term appears in the targumim of Gen 6:1 (for *'ādām*, "man") and of Gen 11:5 (for *běně 'ādām*, "humanity"). For further examples and discussion see G. Vermes, "The Use of Bar Nash/Bar Nasha in Jewish Aramaic," in *Post-Biblical Jewish Studies* (Leiden: E. J. Brill, 1975) 147–65; and C. Colpe, "*ho huios tou anthrōpou*," in *TDNT* 8 (1972) 401–4.

[14] This phrase (as well as others, e.g., the verb *ṣ'q)* is generally interpreted in the targumim and other Rabbinic sources to refer to divine prayer: *Gen. Rab.* 39.16 (ed. Theodor-Albeck) 381 and Theodor's note ad loc.; *Tanḥ. Bešallaḥ* 9; *Mek. Bešallaḥ* 3 (ed. J. Lauterbach) 1.206; *MekRS* ad Exod 14:10 (ed. Epstein-Melamed) 53; *b. Soṭa* 10a; *LT* ad Gen 12:8 (ed. S. Buber) 30a, where Buber's note 48 cites MS Florence: "'And he called upon the name of the Lord': 'Calling' can only mean prayer." See also L. Ginzberg, *Genizah Studies*, vol. 1 (New York: Jewish Theological Seminary, 1928) 15, for a Genizah midrash fragment attributed to Saadia Gaon that associates the beginnings of divine *prayer* with Abraham, based on Gen 12:8.

By contrast, the *Genesis Apocryphon* (1QapGen) 19:7 and 21:2, in its paraphrase of Abraham's travels, translates the phrase *qārā' běšēm YHWH* quite easily into Aramaic: *wqryt bšm 'lh'/mrh* (Gen 12:8; 13:4; 21:33; cf. *Jub.* 13:16).

[15] This twofold understanding of Gen 4:26b was known to Jerome (346–420 C.E.) in his *Hebraicae Quastiones Genesis* (see above, chap. 3, n. 47): "Licet plerique Hebraeorum aliud arbitrentur quod: Tunc primum in nomine domini et in similitudine eius fabricata sint idola." We saw that some Christian exegetes interpreted *epikaleisthai* to mean "to invoke," while others understood it to mean "to name." See chap. 3, nn. 38 and 162. A comprehensive study of the phenomenon of double translation in the biblical versions is a desideratum. See A. Shinan, "The Form and Content of the Aggadah in the 'Palestinian' Targumim on the Pentateuch and its Place Within Rabbinic Literature," (Hebrew) (Ph.D. diss., Hebrew University, 1977) 202–19 (English Summary, x). While Shinan cites the targumim of Gen 4:26 to exemplify this phenomenon, he misidentifies, it seems to me, the double translation as "began" and "profaned."

are at least ten other instances in Genesis alone where a targum translates the Hebrew verb *qr'* with *plḥ*, three of these in the expression "to call on the name of the Lord."[16]

Targum Pseudo-Jonathan and *Targum Neofiti*, however, use the verb *'bd* to describe the sin of Enosh's contemporaries. While this verb can have the same meaning as *plḥ* ("to serve or worship") in Hebrew, it is *never* used by the targumim to translate the Hebrew verb *qr'*, being consistently used in the targumim to translate the verb *'śh* ("to do or make"), which is its common meaning in Aramaic and seems to be its meaning here. Thus, we have two slightly different descriptions of the two-fold sin of Enosh's contemporaries: (a) According to *Fragmentary Targum* and *Targum Neofiti Margin*, they *worshipped* false gods, calling them by God's name. (b) According to *Targum Neofiti* and *Targum Pseudo-Jonathan*, they *made* for themselves idols, calling them by God's name. Although the two amount to the same thing, it is likely that the latter represents a secondary stage of translation tradition, being one step removed from the well attested translation of *qr'* with *plḥ*, as found in the *Fragment Targum* and *Targum Neofiti Margin*.[17]

Targum Pseudo-Jonathan in adding a third verb, *t'y* ("to go astray"), represents an even later stage of development, since this verb is clearly a play on the noun *ta'ăwwan* ("idol") which follows. Since this noun is also present in *Targum Neofiti*, it would appear that *Targum Pseudo-Jonathan* is dependent on a tradition similar to that found in *Targum Neofiti*, again suggesting that its version of the translation tradition is later than the others.

None of the words of Gen 4:26b should have caused the translators any difficulties. The one word which may have caused them trouble, the passive form *hûḥal*, is simply transposed to the active plural and translated "they began," a common and straightforward procedure.[18] For some reason, the Hebrew verse as it stands did not make sense to the translators as announcing the beginnings of divine worship in Enosh's time. Why, then, not finding difficulty with the words or syntax of Gen

[16] See Gen 12:8; 13:4; and 21:33, where *Targum Neofiti*, *Neofiti Margin*, and the *Fragment Targum* render *qārā' bĕšēm* with the Aramaic double translation *plḥ wṣly* ("he worshipped and he prayed"). See also *Tg. Neof. m.* Gen 26:25; *Tg. Onq.*, *Tg. Neof.*, and *Frg. Tg.* Gen 22:14; *Tg. Onq.* and *Tg. Neof. m.* Gen 33:20, for translations of the Hebrew *qr'* with the Aramaic *plḥ*. Cf. chap. 3, n. 174.

[17] Alternatively, one could argue that both types of translation go back to a common tradition of interpretation, with only the *Fragment Targum* and *Targum Neofiti* displaying the desire to link the two-fold sin to a two-fold translation of the verb *qr'*. Whether the tradition of a two-fold sin itself represents a combining of two originally distinct traditions is impossible to determine. We will see that the same two interpretations are evidenced in the earliest Rabbinic midrashic traditions. It is possible, though not likely, that this targumic use of the Aramaic verb *'bd* reflects a Hebraism, meaning "worship."

[18] See above chap. 1, n. 5.

4:26 did they depart so radically from what, even for them, would seem to be the "plain" sense of this verse? Before attempting to answer this question we will have to examine *Targum Onqelos*, as well as the larger context of Rabbinic interpretation of Gen 4:26.

2. *Targum Onqelos*

The best attested text of *Targum Onqelos* of Gen 4:26b is: בכין ביומוהי חַלּוּ בני אנשא מלצלאה בשמא דיוי. This is usually translated: "Then, in his days, men refrained from praying in the name of the Lord."[19] *Targum Onqelos* is similar to the Palestinian targumim in rendering the Hebrew *'āz* with *běkên*, in rendering the indefinite passive *hûḥal* in the active plural, and in supplying the expressions *běyômôhî* ("in his days") and *běnê 'ěnāšā'* ("humanity"), all of which, strictly speaking, are not required.[20] Thus, like the other targumim, *Targum Onqelos* stresses that Gen 4:26b refers not to Enosh the individual but to his contemporaries in general.

Unlike the Palestinian targumim, however, *Targum Onqelos* renders the Hebrew verb *qr'* ("to call") with the Aramaic verb *ṣly* ("to pray"), as it and the Palestinian targumim do consistently elsewhere.[21] Thus, this targum understands our verse to refer not to idolatry, but to divine prayer. Problematic in *Targum Onqelos* is its use of the verb *ḥlw*, which is found vocalized in two ways: *ḥallû*, from the root *ḥll*, and *ḥālû* from the root *ḥwl* (but not *ḥly* as some have supposed). A. Sperber's choice of the former appears correct, in which case the verb would represent the third person

[19] A. Sperber, ed., *The Bible in Aramaic*, vol. 1 (Leiden: E. J. Brill, 1959) 7. The edition of A. Berliner (*Targum Onkelos* [2 vols.; Berlin: Gorzelanczyk, 1884] 1.5) reads *ḥālû*, which in Sperber's critical apparatus is cited for British Museum MS Or. 2228.

A second version of *Tg. Onqelos* is cited by David Qimḥi (RaDaQ, ca. 1200) in his commentary on Genesis (*Peruš RaDaQ ʿal Hattora, Seper Bere'šit* [ed. A. Ginzburg; Pressburg, 1842] 21a): בכן ביומוהי שריאו בני אנשא לצלאה בשמה דה׳ ("Then in his days men began to pray in the name of the Lord"). This variant is noted by Sperber in his critical apparatus from *Biblica Hebraica* (Lisbon, 1941) and *Biblica Sacra Complutensis* (1616/17), but is not evidenced in any of the manuscripts. This version of *Tg. Onqelos* would be the *only* Rabbinic tradition that understands Gen 4:26b to refer to the beginnings of divine worship. Since the common reading is the more difficult, it is likely that the variant is a later gloss, attempting to reconcile *Tg. Onqelos* with what was eventually (by medieval times) accepted as the "literal" meaning of the phrase.

[20] On the addition of these words see the commentaries Ben Zion Judah Berkowitz, *Leḥem Wešimla* (Wilna: Romm, 1850) 8a; and Baruch Schefftel, *Be'ure 'Onqelos* (Munich: Th. Ackermann, 1888) 13. These expressions *may* reflect the influence of Palestinian targumim. On the phrase *běnê 'ěnāšā'*, see above, n. 13.

[21] Elsewhere in the Torah, the expression *qārā' běšēm YHWH* is always translated by *Tg. Onqelos* with *ṣly*, except in Exod 33:19 and 34:5, where *qr'* is used. These two verses, it may be recalled, were also exceptions in the LXX, where they are understood as God proclaiming His name. See above, chap. 1, n. 15.

plural perfect *pe'al* of the geminate *ḥll*, the same verb generally understood to be the root of MT *hûḥal*.[22] The *pe'al* of *ḥll* is nowhere else evidenced in *Targum Onqelos*.[23]

Numerous suggestions have been made for the meaning of the form *ḥallû*. While several scholars and commentators have suggested that it means "they profaned" or "were profaned," the syntax, especially the use of the preposition *mēm* before the infinitive *lĕṣalā'ā* ("*from* praying"), does not favor this.[24] Furthermore, throughout the Pentateuch, whenever *Targum Onqelos* means "profane," it consistently uses the *'aph'el* of *ḥll* and

[22] G. Dalman, *Grammatik des jüdisch-palästinischen Aramäisch* (Leipzig: J. C. Hinrichs, 1905) 404–5. While G. Dalman (*Aramäisch-Neuhebräisches Handwörterbuch*, 149) lists *Tg. Onq.* Gen 4:26 under *ḥll*, meaning "profan sein," M. Jastrow (*Dictionary*, 432) and J. Levy (*Chaldäisches Wörterbuch*, 1.243) list it under *ḥwl*, meaning "men became lax in worshipping," and "die Menschen hörten auf (erschlafften) im Namen Gottes zu beten," respectively. Similarly, M. Aberbach and B. Grossfeld (*Targum Onkelos to Genesis: A Critical Analysis Together with an English Translation of the Text* [New York: Ktav, 1982] 46–47) translate "were lax" and derive from the root *ḥwl*. However, the preferred vocalization *ḥallû* (Sperber) cannot reflect the root *ḥwl*, but only *ḥll*.

[23] Only the feminine passive participle *ḥălîlā'* is used in translating the Hebrew *ḥălālâ* of Lev 21:14. These observations are based on Chaim Kasowski, *Concordance to Targum Onqelos* (5 vols. in 1; Jerusalem: Rav Kook Institute, 1933–1945).

I was able to find only one other targumic use of the *pe'al* of *ḥll* in all of Scripture. In Ezek 22:26 the MT *wā'ēḥal bĕtôkām* ("I have been profaned among them") is translated by *Tg. of the Prophets* with *wĕḥallat rĕ'ûtî bênêhôn*. See A. Sperber, *The Bible in Aramaic*, vol. 3 (1962) 315. I have argued elsewhere ("Enosh and his Generation," 36–38) that the targum means not "my favor *was profaned* among them" (since the *'ittaph'al* and not the *pe'al* of *ḥll* is elsewhere used in the targum to denote this sense), but "my favor diminished (ceased) among them." The targumist feeling uncomfortable with the uncommon notion of God himself (not his name, Sabbath, or sanctuary, as elsewhere) being profaned, used a clever word play to suggest that God's presence was not destroyed with the Temple.

[24] Those who interpret *ḥlw* in this targum to mean "profaned" or "were profaned" include: G. Spurrell, *Notes on the Hebrew Text of Genesis* (Oxford: Clarendon, 1887) 64; J. Skinner, *A Critical and Exegetical Commentary on Genesis* (ICC; New York: Scribner's, 1910) 127; S. Samdmel, "Genesis 4:26b" *HUCA* 32 (1961) 19; A. Dillmann, *Genesis Critically and Exegetically Expounded* (trans. W. Stevenson; 2 vols.; Edinburgh: T. & T. Clark, 1897) 1.210; Y. Komlosh, *The Bible in the Light of the Aramaic Translations*, 149–50; A. Klijn, *Seth in Jewish, Christian, and Gnostic Literature* (NovTSup. 46; Leiden: E. J. Brill, 1977) 5; A. Shinan, "The Form and Content of the Aggadah," 208–10; as well as such commentaries as Nathan Adler, *Netina Lagger* (in *Seder ḥamišša ḥumeše tora, 'orim gedolim* [Vilna, 1912]); and M. Lowenstein, *Nepeš hagger* (Pietrokov, 1906) 42. This interpretation understands *Tg. Onqelos* (and Rabbinic exegesis in general) to reflect a play on the root *ḥll*, which can mean both "begin" and "profane." To what extent such a play underlies Rabbinic exegesis will be discussed in chapter 5.

Note that the *mēm* prefix is consistently used by *Tg. Onqelos* in translating Hebrew verbs meaning "cease" with an equivalent Aramaic verb (*mn'*, *psq*) when followed by an infinitive. Cf. Gen 11:8; 18:11; 41:49; Num 9:13; Deut 23:23. See my discussion of Hos 8:10, in "Enosh and His Generation," 353–54.

not *pe'al*.[25] I have elsewhere demonstrated on linguistic and lexical grounds that the root *ḥll* in Hebrew and Aramaic can bear the sense "to refrain or desist from" some activity, deriving from its basic meaning of "break, open, loosen, unbind."[26] Therefore, *Targum Onqelos* means that Enosh's contemporaries *refrained* from prayer to God, and not, as other have claimed, that they profaned the worship of God, or themselves became profane with respect to their worship.[27] Implied in this interpretation of *Targum Onqelos* is the notion that mankind from the beginning

[25] This was first noted in an anonymous medieval commentary to *Tg. Onqelos* called by S. D. Luzzatto *Ya'ar* (for the date of the manuscript: 5211=1451 CE) and published by Nathan Adler under the name *Patšegen*. On this commentary see S. D. Luzzatto, *'Oheb ger* (*Philoxenos*) (Cracow: Y. Fischeer, 1895) 25; Y. Komlosh; *The Bible in the Light of the Aramaic Translations*, 37. Komlosh thinks that the writer was a contemporary of the RaMBaN (Naḥmanides, 1194–1270). I have consulted the printing in *Seder ḥamišša ḥummeše tora, 'orim gedolim* (Vilna, 1912) 488–99, with an introduction by Adler. This commentary, the most extensive on *Tg. Onq.* Gen 4:26, understands Onqelos to mean "they refrained" (*nimnĕ'û*) but admits being unable to provide a suitable Aramaic etymology. E. Melamed (*Millon 'arammi 'ivri letargum 'onqelos* [Jerusalem: *Yešibat ša'are raḥamim*, 1971] 54) cites the *Ya'ar* for the correct translation of *ḥlw* in our verse.

Of twenty-four instances in the Torah of *ḥll* meaning "profane," twenty-one are translated by *Tg. Onqelos* with the *'aph'el* of *ḥll*, two with the *'ittaph'al* (the passive of the *'aph'el*) of *ḥll*, and one with the *pe'al* of *bṭl* (Num 30:3, to be discussed in the next note).

[26] See S. D. Fraade, "Enosh and His Generation," 34–36, 347–56. Critical to this understanding is the use of the Hebrew verb *hēḥēl* to refer to breaking, abolishing, or annulling a vow, oath, or covenant, and by extension to ceasing an activity. My analysis showed that the meaning "profane" is secondary to that of "loosen, undo, open." The most common example cited is Num 30:3: *lō' yaḥēl dĕbārô* (*NJV*: "He shall not break his pledge"), which is translated by *Tg. Onqelos*: *lā' yĕbaṭṭēl pitgamêh* ("He shall not annul his word"). In this common usage *hēḥēl* has the same meaning as *hēpēr*, also rendered with the verb *baṭṭēl* in the targumim. The verb *bṭl*, in Aramaic and Mishnaic Hebrew, frequently means "cease." Such an understanding of *hēḥēl* is well evidenced in Rabbinic tradition, where it frequently figures in plays on the verb *ḥll*: *b. Ber.* 32a; *Exod. Rab.* 32.4; *PRK* 17.2; *Lam. Rab.* 1.2; *Sifre Deut.* 27; *Sifre Num.* 134; *MhG* ad Deut 3:24; *Deut. Rab.* 2.8; *YS Wa'etḥannan* 815. Especially relevant is *b. Soṭa* 9b–10a: "Abimelech's oath had become null (*hwḥlh* = *hûḥallâ*, in Munich MS)," meaning that it had come to an end. See Rashi and Zvi Chajes ad loc.; and S. D. Fraade, "Enosh and His Generation," 351–53. Note also Hos 8:10, where *wayyāḥēllû mĕ'āt mimmaśśā' melek śārîm* is usually translated (following the LXX), "they shall *cease* for a little while from anointing king and chiefs."

[27] As we shall see, it is only in medieval interpretations that this play on *hûḥal* is evidenced. For others who translate or interpret *Tg. Onqelos* to mean that men refrained from divine worship see: Ben-Zion Berkowitz, *'Abne ṣiyyon* (Wilna: Romm, 1877) 6a; J. Etheridge, *The Targums on Onkelos and Jonathan ben Uzziel on the Pentateuch* (London, 1862; reprint N.Y.: Ktav, 1968) 44; J. Bowker, *The Targums and Rabbinic Literature* (Cambridge: University Press, 1969) 134; Y. Komlosh, *The Bible in the Light of the Aramaic Translations*, 149–50, 215–16. B. Schefftel (*Be'ure 'onqelos* [Munich, 1888] 13) translates, "They weakened in their worship of the Lord," taking the targum to be an expression of "weakness and feebleness" (*hûlšâ wĕripyôn*), being a play on the name Enosh ('ānûš, meaning "weak"). He apparently derives this interpretation from the root *ḥwl*. Cf. above, n. 22.

knew and worshipped God and was familiar with His name, but subsequently ceased to pray to Him.

If this understanding is correct, we may note that *Targum Onqelos* offers, like the other targumim but even more so, a *converse* translation of Gen 4:26b.[28] To the ancients the idea of man's ceasing to worship God is equivalent to that of his turning to the worship of "false" gods.[29] So the two translations are essentially the same in their basic interpretation, but express that interpretation in relation to the biblical verse in very different ways. The Palestinian targumim are expansive. They translate the verb *hûḥal* fairly literally, but perceiving an ellipsis supply new direct objects to the verb "to call." *Targum Onqelos* adds only minimal words and stays closer to the biblical text, both linguistically and syntactically. It is in this sense that it is more "literal," in method if not in meaning. This targum leaves "the name of the Lord" as the direct object of the verb "to call," understanding it to refer to prayer, and focuses instead on the verb *ḥll*, which it retains, but now with a new, in fact *opposite* meaning. This seems to be characteristic of *Targum Onqelos*: it strives to embody accepted Rabbinic tradition while still remaining as close as it can to the biblical text.[30]

B. Tannaitic Sources

Already in the tannaitic midrashim we find a developed tradition associating idolatrous behavior with Enosh's contemporaries. This tradition first appears in the *Mekilta of R. Ishmael* and in *Sifre Deuteronomy*. Establishing its correct text and interpretation will be important to understanding the Rabbinic exegesis of Gen 4:26 in its earliest extant form and in its subsequent development. We will present the text as it appears in the *Mekilta*, citing variants from the *Sifre* as well as from later parallels.

[28] Such apparent reversals of scriptural meaning are not uncommon in the targumim. See M. Klein, "Converse Translation: A Targumic Technique," *Bib.* 57 (1976) 515–37.

[29] For example, *Sifre Deut.* 43 (ed. Finkelstein) 96 states: "When one separates himself from the words of Torah, he goes and cleaves to idolatry." Similarly, *Sifre Deut.* 54 and 87 and parallels.

[30] This characterization of *Tg. Onqelos* is best stated by M. Ohana ("Agneau Pascal et Circoncision," *VT* 23 [1973] 392): "S'il [*Tg. Onqelos* = O] n'est pas aussi explicite que TjI [*Tg. Ps.-Jonathan*], c'est parce que telle est sa methode: Il a tendance à ne se détacher ouvertement du texte que si une traduction littérale condredisait clairement l'interprétation reçus . . . . O fidèlement reflète, sur de très nombreux points, les traditions halakhiques et exégétiques que nous trouvons dans la littérature rabbinique, parfois clairement, parfois de manière très subtile, mais toujours avec le maximum de concision. Ainsi, même si O reste dans l'ensemble aussi près du texte que possible, il cherche assez souvent, grâce au choix des mots, à faire en sorte que son targum puisse avoir le même potentiel midrashique que le texte hébreu lui meme." We have noted that *Tg. Onqelos* usually uses the verbs *mnʿ* or *psq* to express "cease" or "refrain." Since the *peʿal* of *ḥll* is nowhere else used in this targum, it is reasonable to assume that it was here chosen so as to remain as close as possible to the scriptural verb *hûḥal*.

Mekilta Baḥodeš 6.[31] This passage contains seven interpretations of the expression *'ĕlōhîm 'ăḥērîm* ("other gods") in the second commandment of the Decalogue (Exod 20:3; Deut 5:7): "You shall have no other gods besides Me." The mere fact that we find seven interpretations of the words "other gods" (not to mention another two of the commandment as a whole) is a signal that this must have been a problematic phrase. The other interpretations are: the gods of others, backward gods, gods who turn their worshippers into "others" (most likely, heretics), gods that are strangers to their worshippers, new gods, and finally, gods who came into the world later than he who worships them (man).[32] The main problem which all of these interpretations face is stated in the opening of the passage: "Other gods. but are they [in fact] gods (*'ĕlôhôt*)? Has it not been said: 'And have cast their gods into the fire; for they are not gods (*lō' 'ĕlōhîm*)' (Isa 37:19)?" In other words, does the fact that Scripture calls them "gods," using the same word as it does for God, mean that these "other gods" are regarded as divine beings? Each of the above mentioned interpretations looks to the adjective "other" for an explanation which will deny divinity to these "gods." These gods are no-gods, mere creations of mortal men, powerless gods.[33]

With the context clear, let us look at the fifth interpretation, which cites Gen 4:26b. We will present it as it appears in the two oldest complete *Mekilta* manuscripts, Munich and Oxford.[34] The passage has been divided

[31] For critical editions of the text see *Mekilta deRabbi Ishmael* (ed. and trans. J. Lauterbach; 3 vols.; Philadelphia: Jewish Publication Society, 1933–5) 2.239–40; *Mechilta D'Rabbi Ismael* (ed. H. Horovitz and I. Rabin; Frankfurt am Main: J. Kauffmann, 1928) 223. The same passage appears in *Sifre Deut.* 43 (ed. Finkelstein) 96–97; and in somewhat different form in *MTan.* ad Deut 5:7; 32:17 (ed. Hoffmann) 20, 195. For other parallels see *Gen. Rab.* 23.7 (ed. Theodor-Albeck) 228; *Tanḥ. B. Noaḥ* 24 (p. 52); *Tanḥ. Noaḥ* 18; *Tanḥ. Yitro* 16; *MPs.* 88.2 (ed. Buber) 380; *MhG* ad Gen 4:26 (ed. Margulies) 128; *YS Bere'šit* 39 (ed. Salonika) 14a; *YS Yitro* 286 (ed. Salonika) 42d; *YS 'Eqeb* 866 (ed. Salonika) 309a; *YhM* ad Amos 5:8 (ed. Greenut) 46–47. See as well L. Ginzberg, *Legends of the Jews* (7 vols.; Philadelphia: Jewish Publication Society, 1913–38) 5.151–52.

[32] The various interpretations are attributed to second, third, and fourth generation tannaim, spanning over a century (ca. 80–200). The last interpretation is that of Rabbi Judah the Patriarch. The larger passage, therefore, appears to be an editorial composite.

[33] We have encountered this very same polemic in John Chrysostom's *Expositio in Psalmum 49.1* (*PG* 55.241): The gods of the pagans are called "gods" (*theoi* = *'ĕlōhîm*), not in order to honor them, but to indicate the mistake of those who so name them. Why does the Psalmist say "God of gods"? Not to show that they exist, but to reveal the people's error in imagining that they exist (*ouch hōs ontōn, all' hōs para pois peplanēmenois hypopteuomenōn*) for God is the master (*despotes*) even of these so-called gods. See above, chap. 3, n. 83. Cf. 1 Cor 8:5.

[34] Oxford MS 151 (MS Marshall Or. 24) pt. 2, 125r, which I was able to examine on microfilm at the Jewish Theological Seminary Library; Bavarian State Library, Munich Cod. Hebr. 117, 73r. The latter has recently been published in facsimile: *The Munich Mekilta* (Early Hebrew Manuscripts in Facsimile, vol. 7; ed. with intro. by J. Goldin; Copenhagen: Rosenkilde and Bagger, 1980). These two manuscripts offer the best witnesses to the *Mekilta* text.

into three sections (A, B, C) to facilitate analysis:

1 A ר׳ יוסי אומר אלהים אחרים למה נאמר שלא ליתן פתחון פה
2 לאומות העולם לומר אלו נקראו בשמו כבר היה בהם צורך
3 והרי נקראו בשמו ואין בהם צורך.
4 B אימתי נקראו בשמו בימי אנוש בן שת שנאמר אז הוחל לקרוא
5 בשם ה׳
6 C באותה שעה עלה אוקינוס והציף שלישו של עולם אמר להם
7 המקום אתם עשיתם מעשה חדש וקראתם עצמכם אף אני אעשה
8 מעשה חדש ואקרא עצמי וכן הוא אומר הקורא למי הים וגו׳
9 [וישפכם על פני הארץ ה׳ שמו].[35]

[A] R. Jose [ben Ḥalafta, ca. 140 C.E.] says: 'Other Gods.' Why is this said? In order not to give the nations of the world an excuse for saying: 'If they had been called by His name, they would have had some worth.' But behold, they have been called by His name and they [still] have no worth. [B] When were they called by His name? In the days of Enosh the son of Seth, as it is said, 'Then was begun [men began] to call [false gods] by the name of the Lord.' [C] At that time the ocean rose and flooded a third of the world. God said to them: 'You have done something new by calling *'aṣmĕkem*.[36] I too will do something new and will call *'aṣmî*. And thus it says, 'Who calls [summons] the waters of the sea [and pours them out upon the earth—His name is the Lord] (Amos 5:8; 9:6).

The Hebrew syntax of Part A is difficult. If we understand the word *'lw* to be the particle *'illû*, we must assume that it introduces a contrary to fact (unfulfilled) condition.[37] Thus, if Scripture had not called these false deities "gods," the "nations of the world" would still have argued for their

See L. Finkelstein, "The Mekilta and Its Text," *PAAJR* 5 (1933–4) 17–21.

[35] The Munich and Oxford manuscripts differ only in the slightest detail: In line 2 the Oxford MS omits the words *kbr*. In line 4 the Munich MS has *bymy dwr 'nwš* and *'z hwḥl lqrw' wgwmr*. In line 7 the Oxford MS has *'ṣmykm* and in line 8 it concludes *hqwr' lmy hym*. Both the Horovitz-Rabin and Lauterbach editions depart from these two manuscripts (and the earliest printed edition) by changing the text as follows: In line 7, Horovitz-Rabin has *wqr'tm 'ṣmkm bšmy* while Lauterbach has *wqr'tm 'ṣmkm 'lwhwt*. Similarly, in line 8, Horovitz-Rabin has *w'qr' 'ṣmy bšmy* while Lauterbach has *w'qr' 'ṣmy yy*. Horovitz-Rabin has adopted the reading found in *Tanḥ. Yitro* 16, while Lauterbach has adopted that of *YS Yitro* 286. The parallel in *Sifre Deut.* 43 has *wqr'tm l'ṣmkm* and *w'qr' l'ṣmy* as the best attested readings, as does *MTan.* ad Deut 32:17, and *MhG* ad. Gen 4:26. Thus, the reading presented here is better attested, although more difficult, than those adopted by Lauterbach and Horwitz-Rabin.

[36] The words *'aṣmĕkem* and *'aṣmî* are left untranslated since their meaning here is unclear. They will be discussed below.

[37] On the use of *'illû* in contrary to fact conditions, see M. H. Segal, *A Grammar of Mishnaic Hebrew* (Oxford: Clarendon 1927) 230. In some later versions of our tradition we find this sense explicitly stated: "In order not to give the nations of the world an excuse for saying: 'They have *not* been called *'ĕlōhîm*. For if they had been called by His name, they would have had some worth.' But behold they have been called by His name and they have no worth." *MTan.* ad Deut 5:7; *Tanḥ. Yitro* 16.

divinity, since Scripture would have been silent on the question: "If only they were called *'ĕlōhîm* they [would be shown to have] worth." According to R. Jose, God in the decalogue intentionally refers to these heathen deities as "gods," only to add the adjective *'ăḥērîm* ("strange, alien") thereby denying any worth which one might think they had on account of the epithet *'ĕlōhîm*. Thus, the expression is understood to mean not "gods other than Me," but "strange false-gods," or so-called gods of no worth.

Another possibility is to understand the condition as a fulfilled one, taking *'lw* as the demonstrative pronoun *'ēllû*. The "nations of the world" argue that since these phenomena are frequently referred to in the Bible by the divine epithet *'ĕlōhîm*, they must be regarded as divine.[38] Once again, R. Jose responds that the decalogue, in calling them *'ăḥērîm*, explicitly denies that they have any worth. Such, it appears, is how the *Mekilta of R. Shim'on* understands this interpretation: "*'ĕlōhîm*. Perhaps since they are called *'ĕlōhîm* [you might think that] they have some worth before me. Therefore it says *'ăḥērîm*."[39]

[38] For scriptural examples of false gods or gods of the nations called *'ĕlōhîm* see Exod 18:11; 22:19; 1 Kgs 18:24; Jer 10:11; Ps 86:8. For other examples see BDB 43b. The ancient translations try to distinguish between *'ĕlōhîm* when meaning God and when meaning "gods." The LXX does this simply by using the singular *theos* for the former and the plural *theoi* for the latter. The targumim are not as consistent. They usually avoid using *'elāh* (*'elāhā'*) for false gods. In some cases they substitute the word "deity" (*daḥălā'*, never used for God, e.g., Exod 32:1, 23), while in others we find "idol" (*ta'ăwā'*, e.g., Exod 22:19). In other instances a circumlocution is used, as in Exod 18:11, where "the Lord is greater than all gods (*'ĕlōhîm*)" is translated by *Tg. Onqelos*: "The Lord is great and there is no god (*'ĕlāh*) besides Him." One further example is particularly relevant to our discussion. In Jer 10:11 we find in *Aramaic*: "Let the gods (*'ĕlāhayyā'*) who did not make heaven and earth perish. . . " The targum renders "gods" with "idols without worth" (*ta'ăwān dĕlêt bĕhôn ṣĕrôk*). The Aramaic *ṣĕrôk* is identical in meaning to the Hebrew *ṣôrek* of the *Mekilta* passage. In both cases, the word indicates that the so-called gods are worthless, i.e., lacking in efficacy. For other examples of this use of *ṣĕrôk* or *ṣôrek* see *Tg. Onqelos* Deut 32:17; *Sifre Deut.* 318 (ed. Finkelstein) 364; *MTan.* ad Deut 32:17 (ed. Hoffmann) 195; *Mek. Baḥodeš* 6 (ed. Lauterbach) 2.245–46.

For another midrashic effort at denying divinity to false gods called *'ĕlōhîm* in Scripture see *Sifra Qedošim* ad Lev 19:4 (ed. Weiss) 87a, where "do not turn to idols (*hā'ĕlîlîm*) or make molten gods (*wĕ'lōhê massēkâ*)" is explained: "At first they are only idols (*'ĕlîlîm*), but once you turn after them you make of them 'gods' (*'ĕlôhôt*)." Their only divinity is that which is conferred upon them by their worshippers. Cf. Rashi ad Lev 19:4.

[39] *Mekilta D'Rabbi Šim'on b. Jochai* (ed. J. N. Epstein and E. Z. Melamed; Jerusalem: Mekize Nirdamim, 1955) 146, lines 25–26. For a similar interpretation of this passage in the *Mekilta* see the commentary *Merkebet hammišneh* (Lvov, 1895) fol. 89b, which paraphrases the Second Commandment in light of our midrash: "Even those who are called by the name *'ĕlōhîm*, that is, the angels who minister before me, 'thou shalt not have.'" In other words, even though they are called "gods," you should not worship them, for they are only My servants. For the same interpretation see M. Kasher, *Ḥumaš tora šelema*, vol. 16 (New York: American Biblical Encyclopedia Society, 1954) 232–33. Note Ibn Ezra ad Exod 20:3: "It says *'ĕlōhîm* corresponding to (*kĕneged*) the thinking of their worshipers."

This interpretation of *'ĕlōhîm 'ăḥērîm* as false gods which are *mistakenly* called "gods" leads to the matter of Enosh's contemporaries in Part B. This section asks, And when were such no-gods first called "gods," that is, when were they first given God's name? The Mekilta answers, "In the days of Enosh," and gives Gen 4:26b as the prooftext.

What is truly remarkable is the way in which our biblical phrase is cited. As it is usually understood, announcing the beginnings of divine worship, it would make no sense here. The context clearly suggests an interpretation similar to that found in the "Palestinian" targumim: Then mankind began to call false gods by the name of the Lord.[40] The midrash *assumes* that this is how its audience, whoever they may be, understands Gen 4:26b. Interestingly, *Tg. Onqelos*' rendering of Gen. 4:26b would *not* fit the context of the midrash, while that of the other Rabbinic targumim clearly would. Thus, the earliest extant Rabbinic midrash concerning Enosh's contemporaries appears in a source whose main interest is the elucidation of *'ĕlōhîm 'ăḥērîm* in Exod 20:3 (or Deut 5:7), and which parenthetically refers to what would seem to have been a well established interpretation of Gen 4:26. It would appear that at the time this midrash circulated the commonly accepted Rabbinic interpretation of Gen 4:26 was similar to that which *underlies* the Palestinian targumim.[41] The verse only had to be cited for this interpretation to come to mind. The tradition lying behind *Tg. Onqelos*, however, was either not known, or at least not favored.[42] Note that this midrash as a whole makes no distinction between the name *'ĕlōhîm* (in Part A) and the tetragram *YHWH* (in Parts B and C). To call false gods *'ĕlōhîm* appears to be synonymous with calling them "by the name of the Lord."[43] We found the same phenomenon in the Christian

[40] In *MTan.* ad Deut 32:17 (ed. Hoffmann) 195 we find this explicitly stated: "In the days of Enosh they called them 'gods' (*'ĕlôhôt*), as it says, 'Then was begun to call on the name of the Lord,' that is, 'was begun to call *'ăbôdâ zārâ* by the name of the Lord.'" Cf. *MhG* ad Deut 32:17 (ed. S. Fisch) 414; *MhG* ad Gen 4:26 (ed. Margulies) 128.

[41] We should not assume that the whole passage (Parts A, B, and C) is attributed to R. Jose. Part A, R. Jose's interpretation of *'ĕlōhîm 'ăḥērîm*, could easily have once stood alone. In fact, *MekRS* has an equivalent (perhaps abbreviated form) of Part A without Parts B and C, and without the attribution to R. Jose. Part B may have originally been an explanatory gloss, with Part C, perhaps originating as an interpretation of Amos 5:8 and 9:6, providing another tradition that bears on the sin and punishment of Enosh's contemporaries. Thus, the passage as we have it may be a composite, and it cannot be assumed that the interpretation of Gen 4:26 is R. Jose's, or even that he would have been familiar with it. For a *terminus ad quem* for Part C, see below, n. 49.

[42] This may suggest that *Tg. Onqelos*' translation is later than both this midrash and the Palestinian targumim. However, given the fact of *Tg. Onqelos*' distinctive "literal" method in general (see above, n. 30), which here expresses a similar interpretation of Gen 4:26, we should be wary of jumping to such a conclusion.

[43] For *'ĕlōhîm* as one of God's names, see *Mek. Kaspa'* 4 (ed. Lauterbach) 3.181; *ARNA* 34 (ed. Schechter) 99; *ARNB* 38 (ed. Schechter) 100; *p. Meg.* 1.9 (71d); *b. Šebu.* 35a–b; *Sop.* 4.1. Note as well *MPs.* 50.1, cited above, chap. 3, n. 77. Cf. CD 15.1.

sources, both Greek and Syriac, which use Gen 4:26b to explain the expression *bĕnê ʾĕlōhîm* ("sons of God") in Gen 6:2.

Part C of this midrash is even more interesting, but also more difficult. Continuing on the matter of Enosh's contemporaries, it says that as a punishment for their misconduct God called the sea to drown them. But the text here is quite problematic: "You have done something new by calling on [or invoking] *ʿaṣmĕkem*. I also will do something new and will call on *ʿaṣmî*." A prooftext is provided from Amos 5:8: "Who *calls* [summons] the waters of the sea [and pours them out upon the earth—His name is the Lord]." The *Mekilta* passage in its very parallel structure exemplifies the Rabbinic principle of "measure for measure" (*middâ kĕneged middâ*): You did something new, I will do something new; you called, I will call. Yet what meanings do *ʿaṣmĕkem* and *ʿaṣmî* have here? It is no wonder that later versions and commentators "corrected" the text in numerous ways so as to make sense of it.[44] Before adopting any of these later variants (as do the Horovitz-Rabin and Lauterbach editions), we should examine our text more closely.

There is no reason to assume that the people's sin in Part B is significantly different from that in Part C. In Part B this sin is clear: Enosh's contemporaries called false deities by God's name, that is, they called them "gods" (these being the *ʾĕlōhîm ʾăḥērîm* of the Decalogue). The proof is Gen 4:26b, as understood by the Palestinian targumim. Part C, it seems, comes not to offer a different interpretation of that sin, but to demonstrate that the punishment received fits the crime, measure for measure. The parallelism of the "measure for measure" principle lies mainly in the notion of two "callings," that of the people and that of God. But now the verb "to call" is understood not in the sense of naming, but in the sense of invoking or summoning. This is most clearly expressed in the two prooftexts which are cited. Gen 4:26b uses the verb *liqrōʾ* to describe the people's activity, calling on (worshipping) false gods, while Amos 5:8 uses the same verb to describe God's response, calling on (summoning) the sea. The false gods are useless against the might of the sea.

The crux of our difficulty lies in our understanding of the words *ʿaṣmĕkem* and *ʿaṣmî*. The ideal solution would allow us to retain three things: (a) the text as preserved in our best manuscripts and earliest printings (of both the *Mekilta* and the *Sifre*), (b) the obvious parallelism

[44] Many of these later variants are listed in the critical apparatuses of the Horovitz-Rabin and Lauterbach editions. Horovitz in his notes to the *Mekilta* passage responds to M. Friedmann's remark that "there is no need for all these corrections, for the passage is intelligible in itself": "But for me the opposite is the case; the passage is unintelligible (*sātûm wĕḥātûm*) even with all the emendations and interpretations." As we noted above, n. 35, both Lauterbach and Horovitz-Rabin adopt texts which suggest that the people called themselves by God's name.

within Part C, (c) an understanding of Part C which is in consonance with its context, that is, Parts A and B, without undue harmonization. This can be facilitated in three ways:

(1) The words *ʿaṣmĕkem* and *ʿaṣmî* refer to the objects of the two callings in the prooftexts: *ʿaṣmĕkem* refers to the people's idolatry, while *ʿaṣmî* refers to the sea. There are two ways to accomplish this interpretation. First, the noun *ʿeṣem* has an attested meaning of "substance" or "possessions." Thus, our passage would mean: You called on your possessions, now I will call on mine.[45] Second, the words *ʿṣmkm* and *ʿṣmy* may be understood as inflected forms of *ʿōṣem* ("strength, power"): *ʿōṣmĕkem* (or *ʿōṣmêkem*) and *ʿōṣmî*. If so, the passage would mean: You called on your forces, I will call on mine.[46] In an unvocalized text the inflected forms of *ʿeṣem* and *ʿōṣem* would be identical. In either case the sense is: You called on yours, now I will call on mine.[47]

45 See Jastrow, *Dictionary* 1103, where *Gen. Rab.* 64.7 ad Gen 26:16 (ed. Theodor-Albeck) 707 is cited as an example: "(Abimelech) said to (Isaac), 'All the possessions which you have acquired (*kl ʿṣmwt šʿṣmt*), are they not from us?'" Note that the Oxford *Mekilta* Manuscript, the Oxford MS of *YS Yitro* 286 (*Yalquṭ šimʿoni ʿal hattora* [Jerusalem: Rav Kook Institute, 1973] 447), and the Oxford MS of *Gen. Rab* 23.7 (see the critical apparatus of Theodor-Albeck, p. 228) all have the plural inflected form *ʿṣmykm* while *YS ʿEqeb* 866 (ed. Salonika) 309a has *lʿṣmykm*. Such spellings *may* reflect an understanding of this word not as a reflexive pronoun, but as the inflected plural of the noun *ʿeṣem*.

46 Note that *Gen. Rab* 64.7 (cited by Jastrow for *ʿeṣem* meaning "possessions") is given by R. Nathan b. Yeḥiel in *Aruch Completum* (ed. A. Kohut; 8 vols.; Vienna, 1878–92; reprint Jerusalem, 1970) 6.241b as an example of *ʿeṣem* meaning "strength" (*tôqep wĕkōaḥ*). In the commentary of David Qimḥi (RaDaQ, ca. 1160–ca. 1235) ad Gen. 4:26b (ed. A. Ginzburg) 21a we find the following: "Then men began to call upon the stars and constellations by the name of the Lord; that is, they worshipped and prayed to them. For they thought them to be intermediaries between God and the rest of His creation and they saw fit to worship them for their greatness and might (*ligdûlatām ûlĕʿoṣmām*)." According to RaDaQ, the people called these celestial bodies "gods," thinking they had power. Certainly, RaDaQ's use of *ʿōṣem* may be coincidental, but it may also reflect his understanding of this midrashic tradition. For similar views of the sin of Enosh's contemporaries see below, n. 53.

47 M. Kasher (*TS* 2.341 n. 158) paraphrases our midrash: "They called their own work (*maʿăśeh ʿaṣmām*) by the name of the Lord." Adopting his understanding of *ʿaṣmĕkem* and *ʿaṣmî*, we might paraphrase: You called on your works (to aid you), I will call on mine. This is what we find in the London MS of *Sifre Deut.* 43: "You called on your works (*lĕmaʿăśêkem*)." The reading found in *Sifre Deut.* 43 and *MTan.* ad Deut 32:17, *lʿṣmkm* and *lʿšmy*, may support the sense of "summoning," since the verb *qārāʾ* followed by the preposition *lĕ-* often has this meaning, rather than the sense of "naming." See E. Ben Yehudah, *Thesaurus*, 6126. This line of interpretation is suggested by L. Finkelstein in his notes to the *Sifre* passage (p. 97): "That is to say, you called upon 'idolatry' to save you." For later versions of our text that supply "idolatry" as the object of the people's "calling" and the sea as the object of God's "calling" see: *Tanḥ. Noaḥ* 18; *Tanḥ B. Noaḥ* 24; *MPs.* 88.2; and the *piyyuṭim* to be discussed later in this chapter. The *ʿEphat ṣedeq* edition of the *Mekilta* (Vilna, 1884) suggests *ḥammānîm* ("sun pillars," or idols) for *ʿaṣmĕkem* and *lĕmê hayyām* ("the waters of the sea") for *ʿaṣmî*.

(2) The words *'aṣmĕkem* and *'aṣmî* are simply intended for emphasis: You yourselves called, now I myself will call. The objects of the respective callings are known from the prooftexts.[48]

(3) The final possibility is to follow the reading found in the *Sifre*, understanding *lĕ'aṣmĕkem* as "for yourselves" and *lĕ'aṣmî* as "for myself." In support of this we may note that two of the targumim (*Ps.-Jonathan* and *Neofiti*) translate Gen 4:26b with "they made [worshipped] idols for themselves (*lhwn*)." Perhaps the addition of "for themselves," not found in the *Fragment Tg.* or in *Tg. Neofiti Margin*, is insignificant. However, in *Sifra Qedošim* ad Lev 19:4 (ed. Weiss) 872 we find: "From this verse it is said that whoever makes an idol [performs idolatry] for himself (*lĕ'aṣmô*) transgresses two warnings: 'do not make' and 'not for yourselves' (*lō' lākem*)." Therefore, the making (and perhaps the worship) of idols is all the more grievous when done for one's own sake, i.e., benefit. This passage in the *Sifra* clearly interprets *lākem* of Lev 19:4 to mean *lĕ'aṣmĕkem*, "for yourselves." May the word *lĕkā* in the Decalogue have been similarly construed? It is difficult to know. In any case, our tradition as it appears in the *Sifre* may be taken to mean: "You called [on false gods] for yourselves, now I will call [on the sea] for myself."[49]

[48] The Gaon of Wilna (1720–97) in his emendation to the *Mekilta* text (*Mekhilta d'Rabbi Ishmael with Amendations* [sic] *of the Gaon of Vilno and the Commentary of Birkath Haneziv* [Jerusalem, 1970] 193) suggests omitting the words *'aṣmĕkem* and *'aṣmî* entirely and reading: "You have done something new by calling; I too will do something new and will call [summon] the waters of the sea." The parallelism now clearly centers on the verb "to call." While there is no textual warrant for removing the words *'aṣmĕkem* and *'aṣmî*, this interpretation suggests that they are not crucial to our understanding of the passage.

[49] In what appears to be a later version of our text, we find in *Gen. Rab* 23.7 (ed. Theodor-Albeck) 228, following MS London: אמר ר׳ אחא אתם עשיתם עבודה זרה וקראתם לשמכם אף אני אקרא למי הים לשמי ואכלה אותן הרשעים מן העולם. The Hebrew syntax here is very difficult (the printed editions are even worse) but in light of our discussion I would translate as follows: "R. Aḥa [ca. 330] said: You have made idols [performed idolatry] and called [upon them] for yourselves. I too will call upon the waters of the sea for myself and will remove you wicked ones from the world." The traditional commentators (following the printed version) take this statement to mean that the people performed idolatry by calling themselves by God's name, either calling one another "gods" or adopting theophoric names. See the commentary *Mattenot Kehunna* (by Issachar Berman b. Naphtali, sixteenth century) and that of the MaHaRZU (R. Ze'eb Wolf ben Israel Issar Einhorn, d. 1862) in *Midraš Rabba* (Vilna, 1884–87) 54a; Rashi ad Gen 4:26; and Kasher, *TS* 2.341, n. 158. However, such an interpretation cannot be supported from the oldest manuscripts (including now Vatican 60). It seems best to understand *lĕšimkem* and *lišmî* as paraphrases of the original *lĕ'aṣmĕkem* and *lĕ'aṣmî*, and to retain the original parallelism by taking the object of the people's "calling" to be their idolatry, and that of God's to be the sea, as in Gen 4:26b (as understood by the rabbis) and Amos 5:8. If we are correct, it would appear that the *Mekilta* and *Sifre* texts represent two slightly different recensions of the same tradition, with R. Aḥa's statement in *Genesis Rabba* being dependent on the latter (*lĕ'aṣmĕkem* becoming *lĕšimkem*). Thus, it may be that R. Aḥa provides a *terminus ad quem* (330 C.E.)

Any one of these possibilities would permit us to understand the midrash without amending the manuscript readings. Whichever we choose, the basic sense of the passage remains the same. The people of Enosh's time sin by invoking or worshipping false gods. They *call upon* these false deities for succor. God responds by *calling upon* or summoning the sea to punish. The action by which the people sin is the same by which they are punished.

Furthermore, both the sin and the punishment represent something new (*maʿăśeh ḥādāš*). Idolatrous worship is new and it is unprecedented. The implication is that the very first men knew and worshipped the Lord, *ʿăbôdâ zārâ* being a later perversion. This same view is expressed in R. Judah the Patriarch's interpretation of *ʾĕlōhîm ʾăḥērîm*: "Gods that are later than he who was last in the order of creation. And who is it that was last in the order of the things created? The one who calls them 'gods'".[50] The sense that Enosh's contemporaries did something new most likely derives from the MT *hûḥal*: they began, or were the first. Similarly, God's response is something new. The waters which had been held back at creation are now summoned to overflow their bounds for the *first* time.[51]

---

for the tradition found in the *Mekilta* and *Sifre*. Furthermore, it may be that under the influence of a misunderstanding of this passage in *Genesis Rabba*, the *Mekilta* and *Sifre* texts were in turn misunderstood and emended to refer to Enosh's contemporaries' having called themselves by God's name.

This misunderstanding of the *Mekilta* is basic to P. Schäfer's analysis of the Rabbinic tradition of the "Generation of Enosh." Schäfer argues that underlying the Rabbinic tradition of the *Mekilta* is an ancient "myth" (traceable to *Jubilees*) of the intercourse of women with angels (Gen 6:2–4) *in Enosh's time*, and the consequent beginnings of theophoric names. See his "Der Götzendienst des Enosch: zur Bildung und Entwicklung aggadischen Traditionen im nachbiblischen Judentum," in *Studien zur Geschichte und Theologie des Rabbinischen Judenthums* (AGJU 15; Leiden: E. J. Brill, 1978) 134–52.

50 Ed. Lauterbach, 2.241. It is unclear whether Rabbi refers to "gods" who were created after man; i.e., they are men's creations; or to phenomena which may have been created before man, e.g., celestial bodies, but were only considered "gods" once man was created. Note that in *MTan.* ad Deut 32:7 the tradition of the flood in Enosh's time is given as an interpretation of "new ones who came but lately": "Are they of late? [Rather] in the day's of Enosh they were called 'gods' as it says. . . " The same interpretation can be found in *ARNB* 38 (ed. Schechter) 101.

51 See *Sifre Deut.* 47 (ed. Finkelstein) 107, where in the name of R. Joshua b. Karḥa (ca. 330 C.E.) it is similarly stated that when man changes his behavior, God changes the order of creation: "Because they altered their deeds, the Omnipresent altered the (natural) order of the world." In *SOR* 4 the same statement is found in reference to the Flood Generation. Cf. *Qoh. Rab.* 1.4.

We shall see that the tradition of a flood in Enosh's time is more fully developed in later sources. Note that the flood in Enosh's time covers only a third of the world. We will have more to say on the partial nature of this flood in the next section. The idea of God's having established at Creation fixed boundaries (*ḥōq, gĕbûl*) beyond which the waters of the sea were not to extend is well evidenced in Scripture: Jer 5:22; Ps 104:9; 148:6; Job 26:10; 28:36; 38:10–11.

Like the Palestinian targumim, this midrash presents two interpretations of the verb "to call" in Gen 4:26. In Part B the verb is clearly understood to mean "to name." The people of Enosh's time sinned by applying God's name to false gods. However, in Part C the same verb is interpreted to mean "to call upon, to worship, or to summon," in describing the actions of the people and God.[52] These two understandings of the verb "to call," both in the targumim (especially *Fragment Tg.* and *Neofiti Margin*) and the *Mekilta* and *Sifre*, need not be viewed as contradictory. Rather, they complement one another, denoting two aspects of idolatrous worship: the worshipper *calls* to the supposed deity for help (i.e., worships it), and he *calls* that deity "God." This twofold view of idolatry agrees with biblical and Rabbinic statements found elsewhere. In Exod 32:4 (cf. 1 Kgs 12:28) the Israelites not only form the golden calf but consecrate it by saying: "This is thy God O Israel." In *m. Sanh.* 7:6 (cf. *t. Sanh.* 10.23) we are told that the idolater is not only he who worships the idol, but also he who accepts it as his god by saying: "Thou art my god" (*'ēlî 'āttâ*). This mishnah echoes Isa 44:17, which scorns the man who takes some wood, and after using part of it for cooking and heat, carves an idol from the rest. He forms it, bows down to it, prays to it, and then utters the clincher: "Save me, for you are my god!" It may be that our midrash not only announces when "strange worship" began, but describes (whether or not by intent) its constitutive elements as well.[53]

It is clear that the *Mekilta* passage that we have examined does not represent the beginnings of Rabbinic exegesis of Gen 4:26. Its exegesis already makes two important assumptions: (a) that Gen 4:26b refers to the calling of false gods by God's name, (b) that there was a flood in Enosh's time, prior to the biblical Flood.[54] The main point of the midrash is to show

[52] The ambiguity of the verb "to call" in Gen 4:26b has been noted above, n. 15; chap. 3, n. 162.

[53] See J. Faur, "The Biblical Idea of Idolatry," *JQR* 69 (1978) 1–15. Faur argues that what differentiates "idolatry" from "iconolatry" is the assertion that the venerated object is (or contains) God, and is consequently worshipped as such. This understanding of idolatry as the confusing of the Creator with his creations, or of God as master with His servants is evidenced early in Jewish literature. See Wisdom of Solomon (first century B.C.E.) 13:1–9 and Philo. *Dec.* 61. *T. Judah* 19:1 (ed. De Jonge) 72 defines idolatry as the naming as gods those that are not gods (*tous mē ontas theous onomazousin*). Similarly, medieval Jewish commentators understand idolatry to have begun with the Generation of Enosh as the at first innocent worship of God's heavenly servants as a means to honoring the Master. See Maimonides, *Hilkot 'abodat kokabim* 1.1; 2.1; R. Levi b. Gerson (RaLBaG, d. 1343), *Peruš 'al hattora derek be'ur* (Venice, 1547) 17d; R. Nissim b. Reuben Gerondi (RaN, d. 1380), *Commentary on the Bible* (ed. L. A. Feldman; Jerusalem: Shalem Institute, 1968) 70; and RaDaQ ad Gen 4:26 (see above, n. 46). Maimonides shares the view that the crucial step in idolatry is the calling of the idolatrous object by God's name. In *Hilkot 'abodat kokabim* 3.4 he states that once the worshipper says "you are my God," he cannot retract his words.

[54] It appears from the midrash that the tradition of this flood is assumed to be common knowledge, since there is no effort made to describe it (which third of the world did it

that the flood was God's way of punishing the people for their idolatrous behavior, and especially that this punishment fit their sin "measure for measure." The tradition is carefully constructed so that each element of the people's action is mirrored in God's response. The midrash is similar to the targumim in describing the people's sin, but goes beyond them in describing the nature of God's response and how it justly corresponds to the sin.[55]

Our earliest Rabbinic tradition, however, tells us nothing concerning the specifics of this earliest "idolatry." What exactly was worshipped and how was it worshipped? Concerning these questions nothing is said. Thus, we do not seem to have here a polemic against a particular form of idolatry. The midrashic tradition is primarily interested in explaining some problematic scriptural passages, and in so doing draws some moral lessons: (a) "Strange worship" is very old, going back to antediluvian times, yet it is a human innovation, a perversion of the originally established order.[56] (b) "Strange worship" involves the calling of and calling upon false gods by God's name. (c) God responds justly, with a punishment which fits the crime.[57] Finally, we should note what will soon become evident as a recurring phenomenon: the Rabbinic exegesis of Gen 4:26 is not interested in the individual Enosh. He is not mentioned in the earliest exegesis of Gen 4:26, which is understood to refer rather to his contemporaries. In light of the veneration of Enosh that we repeatedly saw in non-Rabbinic sources we are led to ask, Is Enosh implicated in the idolatry of his contemporaries?

cover?) or to reconcile it with the biblical account which locates the first flood in Noah's time. What the ultimate origins of this tradition are, however, is impossible to determine, since the *Mekilta* text is the earliest source to mention it. The tradition of this flood is significantly amplified in amoraic sources that we will discuss. In chapter 5 we will return to possible motivations for the development of such a tradition.

55 It seems that at some point in the transmission of this tradition it was noticed that the "measure for measure" parallels could be extended one step further, since both Gen 4:26b and Amos 5:8 contained God's name. Thus in *Tanḥ. Yitro* 16 we find: וקראתם עצמכם בשמי and ואקרא עצמי בשמי. The word *bišmî* (in or by my name) has been added to the two halves. Since, as we have indicated, there are a few ways to translate *'aṣmĕkem* and *'aṣmî*, this may be variously understood. But essentially it means: You called upon your works in My name, I will call upon my works in My name. However, it must be stressed that this is a later version of the original tradition, being evidenced only in significantly later sources. This new version was subsequently misunderstood (perhaps under the influence of *Gen. Rab.* 23.7; see above, n. 49) to mean that the people's sin consisted of calling themselves by God's name. This new understanding, however, destroyed the original parallelism and resulted, in turn, in further modifications. Cf. *Tanḥ. Noaḥ* 18; *MPs.* 88.2.

56 Cf. *Sifra Beḥuqqotay* ad Lev 26:14 (ed. Weiss) 111b, which states that one can only rebel against his master if he has known him. Thus, idolatry, frequently referred to by the rabbis as a form of rebellion, could not precede monotheistic divine worship, but must represent a secondary development, a degeneration.

57 These exegetical and moral concerns expressed in our passage are typical of Rabbinic treatments of idolatry. For a fuller discussion, see Saul Lieberman, *Hellenism in Jewish Palestine*, 115–27.

The amoraic sources will provide a mixed response.

Although we have no further statements about Enosh and his contemporaries in the tannaitic sources,[58] we should note that in a number of tannaitic passages the absence of any mention of the Generation of Enosh is surprising. Most significant is *m. Sanh.* 10:3 (cf. *t. Sanh.* 13.6–12), where we find a catalog of the wicked generations who "have no portion in the world to come." The list begins with the Generation of the Flood, and continues with the Generation of the Separation (the Tower of Babel), the people of Sodom, the Spies, the Generation of the Wilderness, the Company of Korah, and the Ten Tribes (seven in all). Neither in the printed versions nor in the manuscripts do we find any mention of the Generation of Enosh.[59] Similarly, in *Mek. Širta'* 2 (ed. Lauterbach) 2.13–19 we find Exod 15:1 ("for He is highly exalted") interpreted to mean that the nations of the world who have acted haughtily before God are brought to no account. The principle is exemplified with the Generation of the Flood, the people of the Tower, the people of Sodom, the Egyptians, and others. Once again, there is no mention of the Generation of Enosh as one of the rebellious generations.[60] In contrast, we will see that in the amoraic sources the Generation of Enosh is frequently mentioned as one of the early generations of evildoers. Realizing that we cannot construct too firm a conclusion from such tannaitic silences, we

[58] Gen 4:26b is cited in one other tannaitic passage, but nothing is said there about Enosh or his contemporaries. In *Mek. Širta'* 1 (ed. Lauterbach) 2.1, in commenting on the word *'āz* of Exod 15:1 ("Then Moses and the Israelites sang. . . "), our verse is cited with six others as an example of *'āz* referring to the past. Otherwise, nothing is said indicating an interpretation of Gen 4:26b. The same tradition appears in *MekRS* (ed. Epstein-Melamed) 70–71, but with only five examples, including Gen 4:26b. See also *Tanḥ. Bešallaḥ* 10. J. Goldin (*The Song at the Sea* [New Haven, Conn.: Yale Univ. Press, 1971] 65–66) suggests that the midrash may be citing Gen 4:26b in a positive sense, since the other prooftexts "strike a festive or joyful note." It seems to me that Gen 4:26b is cited here with neither positive nor negative connotations. We also saw the initial words of Gen 4:26b and Exod 15:1 associated in *Memar Marqah* 2.6. In *Tanḥ. B. Bešallaḥ* 12 (p. 60) and *Exod. Rab.* 23.4 the *'āz* of Exod 15:1 is also associated with that of Gen 4:26b, but there, as we shall see, the interpretation of Gen 4:26b is unmistakably negative.

[59] The Mishnah manuscripts differ significantly from the printed editions, including that of Bomberg. The Kaufmann Codex, MS Parma (De Rossi 138), MS Paris 328–29, and the Cambridge MS (Add. 470.1) all omit the Generations of the Separation and of the Spies from the list, leaving only five "generations." The full list of seven appears, however, in the text of the *Tosefta* (ed. Zuckermandel, 434–35), for which I have not been able to examine manuscripts. It would appear that the mishnaic list originally contained five, with two more subsequently added to bring the total to seven. In light of this, it is all the more remarkable that the Generation of Enosh appears in none of the versions of this tradition. Cf. *ARNA* 36 (ed. Schechter) 106–7, where we again find five groups listed.

[60] Cf. *MekRS* (ed. Epstein-Melamed) 74; *Num. Rab.* 9.24; *Tanḥ. Bešallaḥ* 12. For other tannaitic sources that mention a chain of rebellious generations but omit the Generation of Enosh see *Sifre Deut.* 43, 310, 311, 318, 324 (ed. Finkelstein) 93–94, 350, 351, 361, 375; *t. Soṭa* 3.6–12. Cf. *m. B. Meṣ* 4:2.

may surmise that in tannaitic times there was already a notion of a chain of rebellious generations, but that Enosh's contemporaries, known for their idolatrous activity, were not yet considered to be one of those wicked generations, perhaps because they are not referred to as such in Scripture. In this regard, it may be significant that the tannaitic passages which we have examined begin by saying "in the days of Enosh, the son of Seth" and not "in the Generation of Enosh."[61] Gen 4:26 does not yet represent a period of history as it does, as we shall see, in the amoraic collections.

C. Amoraic Sources

We turn now to the amoraic sources, namely those talmudic and midrashic collections that are thought to preserve the teachings of the amoraim (200–500 C.E.), but were compiled between the fourth and sixth centuries. We will begin with *Genesis Rabba*, since it is probably the earliest collection of amoraic midrashim, thought to have been compiled in the late fourth or early fifth century. Of all our Rabbinic sources it contains the largest number of references to Enosh and his generation. In this collection, as in the other amoraic sources to be discussed, the tradition of the Generation of Enosh is significantly more developed than what we found in the tannaitic sources. Still, the focus continues to be more on the nature of the divine punishments received by this generation, now more fully described and with more profound consequences, than on the nature of their sin. The Generation of Enosh takes its place as an important link in a chain of early rebellious generations.

Genesis Rabba 23.6:[62]

[61] The Munich MS alone reads "in the Generation of Enosh." We have noted that only *Tg. Ps.-Jonathan* has "that was the generation (*dārā'*) in whose days," the other targumim having, "in his days." The notion of there having been ten rebellious generations (*dôrôt*) from Adam until Noah is already expressed in *m. 'Abot* 5:2, but the ten generations are not enumerated by name. Cf. *ARNA* 32 (ed. Schechter) 92; *ARNB* 36 (ed. Schechter) 92; *SER* 29 (31) (ed. Friedmann) 162.

[62] The text is from *Midrash Bereshit Rabba* (ed. J. Theodor and Ch. Albeck: 3 vols.; Berlin, 1912–27; 2nd corrected printing, Jerusalem: Wahrmann Books, 1965) 227. The Theodor-Albeck text faithfully follows the London MS (British Museum, Add. 27169). This text differs in some significant details from the standard printed text. I have also consulted the facsimile edition of MS Vatican 60, an important manuscript not recorded in Theodor's critical apparatus, and have found it to be essentially identical with the Theodor-Albeck text, but with a few variants that will be cited in the following notes. The translation that follows is my own, but it closely follows that of H. Freedman in *Midrash Rabbah: Genesis* (2 vols.; London: Soncino, 1939) 1.196–97. The same tradition appears in *Gen. Rab.* 24.6 (ed. Theodor-Albeck) 235; *Bere'šit Rabbati* (ed. Ch. Albeck) 50; *YS Bere'šit* 39 (ed. Salonika) 14a; *YS Dibre Hayyamim* 1072 (ed. Salonika) 187b. Several elements of this tradition are common to *YS Bere'šit* 47 (ed. Salonika) 16a, whose source is not given (except in the Oxford MS where it is identified as the *49 Middot*).

A ולשת גם הוא יולד בן ויקרא את שמו אנוש. בעון קומי אבא כהן ברדלא אדם שת אנוש ושתק אמר להם עד כאן בדמות וצלם מכאן ואילך קינטורין.

B ארבעה דברים נשתנו בימי אנוש ההרים נעשו טרשים התחיל המת מרחיש ונעשו פניהם כקופות ונעשו חולין [חולים] למזיקים.

C אמר ר׳ יצחק הן הן שגרמו לעצמן ליעשות חולין למזיקים מה בין דגחין לצלמה לדגחין לבר נש אז הוחל לקרא בשם ה׳

[A] "And to Seth, in turn, a son was born, and he named him Enosh." Abba Kohen Bardela [Palestine, ca. 203][63] was asked: "[Why does Scripture enumerate] Adam, Seth, Enosh, and is then silent?"[64] He replied: "Thus far [until Enosh] in the [Divine] likeness and image, henceforth centaurs."[65] [B] Four things changed in the days of Enosh: The mountains became barren rocks, the dead began to beget worms, [men's] faces became ape-like, and they became vulnerable to menacing creatures.[66] [C] R. Isaac [b. Pinḥas, Palestine, ca. 300] said: "It is they themselves who were responsible for becoming prey to menacing creatures [for they argued]: 'What is the difference whether one bows down before an image or bows down before a man?'" [Hence,] "Then men began to worship [images] in the name of the Lord."[67]

63 Abba Kohen is counted either as one of the last Tannaim, or first Amoraim. He seemingly was a contemporary of R. Yannai, perhaps in Sepphoris. See A. Hyman, *Toledot tanna'im we'amora'im*, 1.56–57; and *Sifre Deut.* 2 (ed. Finkelstein) 9.6, with Finkelstein's note ad loc.

64 After Gen 4:26 the Sethite genealogy abruptly stops and then begins anew with Adam in Genesis 5. For a similar use of the verb *štq* see *Gen. Rab.* 25.1 (ed. Theodor-Albeck) 239.

65 Greek: *kentauros*, "half-man and half-horse." In *Odyssey* 21.303 the term is used opposite *andres* (men). See LSJ 939a. "For the Greeks Centaurs are representative of wild life, animal desires, and barbarism." *The Oxford Classical Dictionary* (ed. N. G. L. Hammond and H. H. Scullard; 2nd ed.; Oxford: Clarendon, 1970) s. v. "Centaurs," 220b. See also *Aruch Completum* (ed. A. Kohut) s.v. *qînṭôrîn*, 7.134: *min 'ănāšîm bĕlî tarbût* ("uncivilized men"). In some manuscripts we find *qynn qynṭwryn* (Kenan, Centaurs). See Paris MS 149; Vatican MS 60; *YS Dibre Hayyamim* 1072; *YS Bere'šit* 39; and RaMBaN ad Gen 6:4. This variant clearly suggests a play on the same Kenan, Enosh's son (Gen 5:9–14): beginning with Kenan, men were born like Centaurs. It may be that this play is to be recognized in our text, even without these variants.

66 The British Museum MS, Vatican MS 60, and the Venice printing read *ḥwlym*. The text could be pointed either *ḥûllîn/ḥûllîm* ("profane") or *ḥôlîm/ḥôlîn* ("sick, weak"). The former is generally preferred. The presence of a *mēm* or *nûn* cannot be a determining factor, given the interchangeability of these letters as plural endings in Rabbinic Hebrew. All four vocalized forms are attested in other tannaitic and amoraic passages. On *ḥûllîm* as a well evidenced form see J. N. Epstein, *Mabo' lenusaḥ hammišna* (2 vols.; Jerusalem, 1948) 2.1230. The word *mazzîqîm* is usually translated in this passage as "demons." I have chosen a more general and literal translation, "menacing creatures," for reasons that will become clear below.

67 In the Theodor-Albeck edition, Gen 4:26b is cited as the conclusion of this passage, presumably serving as the prooftext for R. Isaac's statement. However, it could just as

The question posed in Part A derives from the obvious discontinuity between Gen 4:26 and 5:1. The Sethite genealogy ends abruptly with Enosh, only to be recapitulated from Adam and continued through Noah. As we have seen, this disruption in the biblical narrative provoked comments from other exegetes as well, both Jewish and non-Jewish, the earliest known to us being Philo.[68]

Abba Kohen's response, however, is startling, being significantly different from the other comments we have witnessed. He suggests that the first three generations were born in the divine likeness and image, but subsequently a radical change occurred.[69] After Enosh, men were no longer godlike, but like centaurs, that is, beastly. This change is not explained. Were men now entirely devoid of the divine image, or had that image simply diminished? Was the change affected in all men or only in some? Was it a temporary or permanent change? Was the change one of physique, character, or both? While these questions cannot be answered with certainty from our text, it would appear from the midrashic and scriptural contexts the Abba Kohen is speaking of a general and widespread change in man's nature.[70]

The implication of this interpretation is that the first three men, Adam, Seth, and Enosh, were in some way semi-divine, but that their

---

easily be intended to introduce the next passage (23:7), being the basis for the comments contained therein. But cf. *Gen. Rab.* 24.6 (ed., Theodor-Albeck) 235, and Theodor's notes.

[68] See above, chap. 1, n. 49 (Philo); chap. 2, n. 16 (Marqah); chap. 3, n. 70 (Chrysostom), n. 93 (Augustine).

[69] That Seth shared in the divine image is derived, no doubt, from Gen 5:3, "And [Adam] begot a son in his likeness after his image," since Adam himself was created in God's likeness and image (Gen 1:26, 27; 5:1). This statement is not made for any of the other descendants of Adam in Genesis 5. Why Enosh should be considered to have been born in the divine image is not so clear. Some later commentators point to the phrase (Gen 4:26a), "And to Seth, to him too (*gām hū'*), was born a son," in which the words "to him too" would appear redundant, perhaps meaning that just as Seth was born to Adam in the divine image, so too Enosh to Seth. See RaDaQ ad Gen 4:26 (ed. Ginzburg) 21a; the MaHaRZU ad *Gen. Rab.* 23.6 (*Midraš Rabba* [Vilna] 53b). On Cain not having been born in Adam's likeness and image, see *PRE* 22 (ed. Warsaw) 50a. See also Halevi, *Kuzari* 1.95.

[70] The metaphor is probably not to be taken too literally. There is no suggestion in Rabbinic literature that the divine image disappears entirely from man. The sense is probably that while the earliest men were more godlike than beastlike, in their descendants the proportions were reversed. Much of Rabbinic ethics takes as its basis the assumption that human life is sacred because man was/is created in the divine image. See for example, *m. 'Abot* 3:14: "[R. Akiba] used to say: 'Beloved is man in that he was/is created in the image [of God].'" The Bible itself (Gen 9:6) makes clear that the immorality of bloodshed is based on man's having been made in God's image. On man having been created out of an even mixture of godlike and beastlike elements, see *Sifre Deut.* 306 (ed. Finkelstein) 340–41; *Gen. Rab.* 14.3 (ed. Theodor-Albeck) 128; *Lev. Rab.* 9.9 (ed. Margulies) 193; *ARNA* 37 (ed. Schechter) 109. For further examples and discussion see M. Smith, "The Image of God," *BJRL* 40 (1958) 473–512; idem, "On the Shape of God and the Humanity of Gentiles," in *Religions in Antiquity: Essays in Memory of E. R. Goodenough* (ed. J. Neusner; Leiden: E. J. Brill, 1968) 315–26.

descendants (including those listed in Genesis 5) were more fully mortal or human in a negative sense. Contrast this with Philo's interpretation that with Enosh true man (humanity in a positive sense) began.[71] We have seen that non-Rabbinic sources often state that the divine seed or image was transmitted through an unbroken chain of righteous ancestors beginning with Adam and continuing through the Sethite genealogy of Genesis 5.[72] Thus, the Sethite line represents the godlike side of man, while the Cainite line represents the godless side. Abba Kohen's statement contrasts not two concurrent genealogical lines of mankind, but the first three generations with subsequent mankind.[73] After Enosh, mankind *as a whole* undergoes a moral as well as physical decline. It appears, however, that Enosh the individual is considered part of the old, uncorrupted order.

Part B of our midrash supplements Part A by providing a list of four other changes which occur in the "days of Enosh." It is unclear whether this is still part of Abba Kohen's response, or is added by the compiler. I take the latter to be more probable. While no specific mention is made yet of the sin of Enosh's contemporaries, it can be assumed that these

[71] Both views get expressed in *Gen. Rab.* 24.6 (ed. Theodor-Albeck) 235–36, which comments on Gen 5:1, "This is the record of the descendants (*tôlĕdôt*) of Adam." The midrash asks: "These are *tôlĕdôt*, but the former ones were not *tôlĕdôt*. What were they?" The first answer is, "gods" (*'ĕlôhôt*). *Gen. Rab.* 23.6 (our present passage) is repeated as evidence. The sense clearly is that Adam, Seth, and Enosh having been created in the divine likeness and image were *'ĕlôhôt*, while their descendants beginning with Kenan were human descendants (*tôlĕdôt 'ādām*). On the word *tôlĕdôt*, meaning "mortals," see *Gen. Rab.* 12.7 (ed. Theodor-Albeck) 106. The second response (from *Gen. Rab.* 20.11; cf. *b. 'Erub* 18b) is that the former were "spirits" (*rûḥôt*), referring to a tradition that for one hundred and thirty years after Abel's death Adam and Eve separated themselves from one another and begat spirits (demons). See Ginzberg, *Legends*, 5.148, n. 47; and Theodor's note ad loc. The third response is that the earlier ones were not *tôlĕdôt*, since they were destroyed by the flood waters. This is clearly a reference to the Cainites who were totally wiped out in the Flood, leaving no further progeny. It is not clear whether the flood waters referred to here are those of Enosh's time or of Noah's time. See Theodor and Ps.-Rashi ad loc. Thus, one interpretation takes *tôlĕdôt 'ādām* negatively, while two understand it positively.

[72] See for instance above, chap. 3, nn. 59, 160. Christian and Samaritan sources stress that no matter how corrupt mankind became, the pure genealogical chain remained intact.

[73] What is not clear in his statement is how the Cainites of Gen 4:17–24 fit into this scheme. While they may be (and in fact in some Rabbinic sources are) considered part of the Generation of Enosh, Cain himself, the first murderer, precedes both Enosh and Seth. Does Abba Kohen suggest that all men until Enosh were in the divine image (Adam had other sons and daughters, Gen 5:4), or that only these three were so distinguished? It would appear that Abba Kohen is drawing a distinction only within the Sethite line recorded in Gen 4:25–26 and Genesis 5. P. Schäfer (see above, n. 49) argues that our midrash is reflective of *Jub.* 4:11ff., which depicts the human "intermarriage" with angels as beginning with Kenan.

radical changes do not arbitrarily occur in their time, but are the consequences of their idolatrous behavior.

The first two changes, affecting the mountains and the dead, appear as part of a list of punishments meted out to Adam (man), Eve (woman), the snake, and the earth in *ARNB* 42 (ed. Schechter) 116–17, a list that amplifies the biblical curses of Gen 3:14–19.[74] While Adam's physical appearance is elsewhere reported to have changed as a consequence of his sin (e.g., his height was reduced[75]), the curse of apelike appearance is most commonly associated with the generation that built the Tower of Babel.[76] This change most likely represents the same type of transformation as that from divine likeness to centaurs. Since man is understood by the rabbis as having been created with both angelic and animal qualities, a diminishing of his divine likeness could conversely be described as an increase in his animal likeness.[77]

Much more problematic is the fourth change, man's becoming vulnerable to menacing creatures (*ḥwlym lmzyqyn*). Since an understanding of this ambiguous expression is crucial for the interpretation of this midrashic passage and its implied exegesis of Gen 4:26b, we will have to examine it in some detail. An examination of the Rabbinic concordances and indexes did not reveal a single other occurrence of the phrase *ḥwlym lmzyqyn* (except in traditions directly dependent on the *Genesis Rabbah* passage). However, in two midrashic passages we find *ḥwlym* used in ways similar to its use here.

The *Sifra* ad Lev 19:12 comments on the verse, "You shall not swear falsely by my name, profaning the name of your God: I am the Lord," as follows:[78]

74 For an English translation and notes, see *The Fathers According to Rabbi Nathan, Version B* (trans. Anthony J. Saldarini; Leiden: E. J. Brill, 1975) 250–54. Cf. *Pereq 'adam hari'šon* in *Ozar Midrashim* (ed. J. D. Eisenstein; 2 vols.; New York, 1915) 1.9–11; *PRE* 14 (ed. Warsaw) 34b; *Num. Rab.* 5.4.

75 *b. Ḥag.* 12a; *b. Sanh.* 38b; *Gen. Rab.* 12.6; 19.8 (ed. Theodor-Albeck) 102, 178; *Num. Rab.* 13.2: *PRK* 1.1; 5.3 (ed. Mandelbaum) 2, 83; *PR* 15 (ed. Friedmann) 68b; *Tanḥ. Bere'šit* 6; *Tanḥ. B. Bere'šit* 18 (p. 13; intro. p. 156); *MhG* ad Exod 40:34 (ed. Margulies) 792; *YS Bere'šit* 27 (ed. Salonika) 10b. *YS Bere'šit* 47 (source unknown) is the only tradition to include this punishment in those meted out to the Generation of Enosh. This passage will be treated below.

76 See Ginzberg, *Legends*, 1.180; 5.201 n. 88; *b. Sanh.* 109a; *Tanḥ. Noaḥ* 18; *MA* ad Gen 11:8 (ed. Buber) 30; *MPs.* 1.13 (ed. Buber) 12; *ShY* (ed. Goldschmidt) 31; *Jeraḥmeel* 30.5 (trans. Gaster) 64. Cf. Ps.-Philo, *Ant. Bib.* 7.5 (ed. Kisch) 132; *3 Apoc. Bar.* 2:3, 7; 3:3; *1 Enoch* 19:2. Similarly, both Rabbinic and Moslem traditions speak of Sabbath violators being transformed into apes. See Ginzberg, *Legends*, 6.85 n. 452.

77 See above, n. 70. While modern evolutionists interpret man's apelike appearance as a sign of his humble origins, the midrash takes it as a sign of his somewhat later degeneration. This view is necessitated by biblical statements that man was originally created in the divine image and likeness.

78 Ed. Weiss, 88c. I have also consulted *Torath Cohanim (Sifra) Codex Vatican 31*

> "Profaning (*wĕḥillaltā*) the name of the Lord [*sic*] your God": This teaches that a vain oath is a profanation of the [divine] name. Another interpretation of *wĕḥillaltā*: You will become vulnerable to beasts and animals (*ḥwlym lḥyh wlbhmh*[79]). And so Scripture says (Isa 24:6): "That is why a curse consumes (*'ākĕlâ*) the earth,/ And its inhabitants pay the penalty;/ That is why earth's dwellers have dwindled (*ḥārû*[80]),/ And but few men are left."

We seem to have here a play on the verb *ḥll*.[81] According to the *Sifra* passage, those who profane God's name (through a vain oath) are punished (cursed) by becoming prey (or profane, common food) to animals. Once again we have an example of the principle "measure for measure." In his commentary to the *Sifra* text the Byzantine Rabbenu Hillel states:

> "Vulnerable to beasts and animals": That is to say, even though it says (Gen 9:2), "The fear and dread of you shall be upon all the beasts of the earth," when you swear falsely by my name you become vulnerable to beasts. For your fear shall not be upon them, but rather they will eat you.[82]

Thus, man's primeval domination of the animal world is diminished as a consequence of his sin. Once again, man's sinful behavior causes a change in the natural order and man's relation to it. The animals, like the sea, become God's punishing agents.[83]

(Jerusalem: Makor, 1972). *Codex Vatican 66* (ed. L. Finkelstein) is not extant here. For parallels, see *MhG* ad Lev 19:12 (ed. Steinzaltz) 544; *YS Qedošim* 605 (ed. Salonika) 169c; *LT* ad Lev 19:12 (ed. Buber) 106.

79 Weiss's edition and *Codex Vatican* 31 read *ḥwlym*, while *MhG*, *YS*, and *LT* read *ḥwlyn*. A similar expression appears elsewhere, where it is less relevant to our discussion. In *b. Pesaḥ.* 21a Rabbah b. Ulla (ca. 350) interprets *m. Pesaḥ.* 2:1 to mean: "The whole time that it is permitted to a priest to eat *tĕrûmâ* ('Heave-offering'), a [lay] Israelite may feed *ḥûllîn* ('unconsecrated food') to animals, beasts and fowl (*ḥwlyn lbhmh lḥyh wl'wpwt*)." On the eve of Passover, laymen could eat leaven only until the fifth hour (see *m. Pesaḥ.* 1:5), but could feed unconsecrated leaven to their animals (i.e., could derive benefit from it) for another hour. *Ḥûllîn*, no longer suitable for human consumption, could be "thrown to the dogs," while *tĕrûmâ* had to be properly disposed of. Cf. *b. Qidd.* 57b–58a.

80 *YS* has *ḥālû* (perhaps, "have become weak"). This may have suggested another play on the verb *ḥll* of *wĕḥillaltā*. It has been suggested that the biblical text was originally *ḥādĕlû* ("have ceased to be"): G. Gray, *The Book of Isaiah* (ICC; 2 vols.; New York: Charles Scribner's Sons, 1912) 1.412, 414. The targum reads *sāpû* ("ceased"). The LXX has *ptōchoi esontai* ("they will become beggarly"), perhaps reflecting *dallû*, while 1QIsa[a] has *ḥwrw* (*ḥāwĕrû*, "have become pale").

81 However, we cannot rule out the possibility that we have a play on the roots *ḥll* and *ḥlh* (*ḥly*). Such an interpretation would be based on understanding *ḥwlym* as *ḥôlîm*: "you will become weak (prey) with respect to beasts and animals." The basic meaning remains the same. This interpretation would be strengthened if the verb *ḥārû* in the Isa 24:6 prooftext could be shown to mean "became weak." See preceding note.

82 *Sipra' 'im peruš rabbenu hillel* (ed. S. Koleditzky; 2 vols.; Jerusalem, 1960–61) 2.82.

83 The motif of wild animals as punishing agents of God for man's sinful behavior is common in the Bible, and is employed in post-biblical interpretation. See: Lev 26:22; 2 Kgs

Sifre Deut 319 (ed. Finkelstein) 365 cites four interpretations of Deut 32:18, "You forgot the God who brought you forth (*mĕḥōlĕlekā*, *polel* of *ḥwl*)," each punning in a different way on the verb *mĕḥōlĕlekā*. The third interpretation is attributed to R. Nehemiah (ca. 150): "God who makes you vulnerable to all the inhabitants of the world" (*ḥwlym ʻl kl bʼy hʻwlm*). The sense is that when Israel does God's will, they are "holy" (*qōdeš*) to God (Jer 2:3), and protected from the nations as from other menaces. But when they do not obey God's will, He removes His protection and they become vulnerable (*ḥûllîm*, free game) to such menaces.[84]

In light of these two parallel usages, let us reexamine the phrase *ḥwlym lmzqym* in *Gen. Rab.* 23.6. While *ḥwlym* could mean "weak" (*ḥôlîm*, from *ḥly*),[85] it seems more likely, given the above parallels, that it means "unconsecrated" (*ḥûllîm*, from *ḥll*), in the sense of vulnerability.[86] Either way, this change clearly reflects a play on the verb *hûḥal* of Gen 4:26b.

While *mazzîqîm* here is usually translated "demons," the close resemblance to the exegesis of *Sifra* ad Lev 19:12 makes it advisable to consider whether *mazzîqîm* could refer to animals. The best support for such a meaning is found in *Sifra* ad Lev 26:6 (ed. Weiss) 111a:

> "I will give the land respite from vicious beasts (*hayyâ rāʻâ*)": R. Judah [b. El'ai, ca. 130–160] said: "[God] will remove them from the world." R. Simeon [b. Yoḥai, ca. 130–160] said: "He will remove them by [causing them] to injure no more (*šĕlōʼ yazzîqû*)." R. Simeon said: "When is the Lord's praise [greater], when there are no

---

17:24–26; Ezek 14:15, 21; 29:5; 32:4; 33:27; Josephus, *Ant.* 1.2.1 § 59; Philo, *Qu. in Gen.* 1.74; *Gen. Rab.* 22.11 (the last three on Cain's becoming vulnerable to wild beasts); *ARNA* 29; *Sem.* 8:15 (ed. Higger) 164–65. For vain oaths and profaning God's name as punishable by wild beasts, see *m. ʼAbot* 5:9; *b. Šabb.* 33a. For idolatry as punishable by wild animals ("measure for measure"), see Wis 11:15–18. For the converse, the righteous man's immunity to animal harm, see below, n. 88.

84 See the commentary *Zeraʻ ʼabraham* as cited by M. Friedmann, ed., *Sipre debe rab* (Vienna, 1864) 137a n. 6. Friedmann's n. 7 to this interpretation is incorrectly cited by Finkelstein (p. 365) in his note on the previous interpretation.

85 We will see below that some later texts associate the beginnings of sickness or weakness with Enosh's generation, playing on *hûḥal*, as if from *ḥly*, and Enosh's name, from *ʼnš*, meaning weak.

86 This is the sense preferred by most of the commentaries. See especially *Mattenot Kehunna* and Ps.-Rashi ad loc. These commentaries use the expression *hepqēr* ("public property," that is, "free game"). See Theodor's note ad loc., where he cites an interpretation, "*mûpqārîn*, abandoned." If *qōdeš* can mean "untouchable" (as in Jer 2:3), *ḥûllîm*, its opposite, may mean "touchable." It should be cautioned, however, that except for the above examples this usage is not generally found, *ḥûllîm* (*ḥûllîn*) being used to refer to unconsecrated food in the context of sacrifice and purity. When A. F. J. Klijn (*Seth in Jewish, Christian and Gnostic Literature*, 7) paraphrases, "at the time of Enosh, people would be influenced by demons," the expression *ḥûllîm* has been stretched beyond recognition.

> beasts (*mazzîqîm*) or when there are beasts which do not injure (*mazzîqîm*)? Certainly when there are beasts which do not injure."

The midrash emphasizes the miraculous nature of the promise. Beasts, whose very nature is to injure (as indicated by the word *mazzîqîm*), will be transformed, not destroyed, so that they will no longer be injurious to man. Clearly, the word *mazzîqîm* here is a synonym for the biblical *ḥayyâ rā'â*. The enmity between man and animal, and more specifically man's vulnerability to animal attack, is a feature of the present order. It was neither original to Creation, nor, as this *Sifra* passage indicates, will it extend into the world to come. Perhaps the *Genesis Rabbah* passage which we are examining tells when the present condition began, while the *Sifra* passage predicts when it will end. Both passages depict a radical transformation.

The punishment of becoming prey to animals appears frequently in Rabbinic sources, in association with both Adam's "fall" and the rebellious generations. In some traditions it is seen as a radical change in the original harmonious relationship between man and animal, only to be rectified in the future world.[87] Often in Rabbinic traditions, however, it is viewed as the punishment only of the wicked, the righteous still being largely immune to harm by animals.[88] A number of such traditions are of particular relevance to our text because of the striking similarity of motifs expressed.

The amplified list of punishments meted out to Adam (man), to which we have already referred (*ARNB* 42), has as the eighth punishment: "He is given over to a wild beast to be killed by it." Thus, it may

[87] See Ginzberg, *Legends*, 5.119 n. 113. Cf. Philo, *Praem.* 15.85–90; *Sib. Or.* 3.793. However, according to *Gen. Rab.* 25.2 (ed. Theodor-Albeck) 239–40, in the name of R. Yoḥanan (ca. 250), when Adam sinned the ox no longer obeyed the plowman. But when Noah arrived the oxen were reconciled (*ninnôḥû*) to the plowmen. According to *Gen. Rab.* 34.12 (ed. Theodor-Albeck) 323–24, man's true dominion over the animals was reinstated with Solomon's reign.

[88] See *Sifre Deut.* 50 (ed. Finkelstein) 115, in which R. Eleazar b. Azaria (ca. 100) states: "If they [Israel] are righteous, they need not fear beasts." Similarly, in *AgBer.* 15 (ed. Buber) 32 we find: "When Israel fears the Lord, the beasts fear Israel." Note especially, *ARNB* 14 (ed. Schechter) 33: "When one and . . . one's household are humble, even his dogs do not harm (*mazzîqîm*). But when he is haughty, everything harms." Conversely, righteous individuals may instill fear in the animals. According to *MA* ad Gen. 9:2 (ed. Buber) 27–28, the Flood Generation was subject to (literally, ruled by) the beasts, but Noah and his sons because of their righteousness still instilled fear in the animals. Note that in *Apocalypsis Mosis* 10–12 (*APOT* 2.143) and *Vita Adae et Evae* 37–39 (*APOT* 2.143–44) we are told of Seth's immunity to attack by a wild beast. The idea that demons and beasts do not bother the righteous is also found in *T. Levi* 18:12; *T. Iss.* 7:7; *T. Naph.* 8:4; *T. Benj.* 5:2. See also Ginzberg, *Legends*, 5.119–20. Jewish and Christian folklores are replete with stories of righteous men unharmed by dangerous animals, as in Dan 6. In Rabbinic lore the best example is that of Ḥanina ben Dosa, who is unharmed by a deadly viper: *b. Ber.* 33a; *t. Ber.* 5.1 (9a).

be that three of the four punishments associated with the Generation of Enosh in *Gen. Rab.* 23.6 are associated with Adam in *ARNB* 42.

A few sources link the righteous man's immunity to beasts to his "divine image." As long as man remains in God's image he has dominion over the animals, but once that image (or likeness) diminishes (as a consequence of his sin), he is subject to their domination. Note how in the following passage man's charge to rule the fish, fowl, and animals (Gen 1:26, 28) is made conditional:

> R. Jacob of Kefar Ḥanan [ca. 280?] said: Concerning him who is "in our image" and "in our likeness" [it says] "have dominion" (*ûrĕdû*, 1:28). But concerning him who is not "in our image" and "in our likeness" [it says], "they shall go down [amongst the animals]" (*yērĕdû*; MT *wĕyirdû*, 1:26).[89]

This midrash notes that in Scripture God first says "let us make man in our image, after our likeness," and then says "they shall rule. . . " The implication drawn is that man merits domination over the animal world by virtue of the divine image in which he was created. It may be recalled that according to *Gen. Rab.* 23.6 the basic change that occurs after Enosh's birth is that men cease to be in the divine image. Man's becoming "vulnerable to menacing creatures" is most likely viewed as one consequence of that underlying change.

We also find Rabbinic traditions that state that man becomes prey to beasts when he resembles them. Once his behavior and/or appearance is no longer distinguishable from theirs, he loses his dominion over them. For instance, in *b. Šabb.* 151b we find: "Rami bar Abba [ca. 300] said: 'A wild beast does not rule over man until he resembles an animal.'"[90] Once again, this fits the context of *Gen. Rab.* 23.6, where humanity is described as becoming centaurs (beastlike) and resembling apes.

Thus, all of the motifs commonly associated with the punishment of vulnerability to animals are present in our passage: punishment for rebellious behavior (especially profanation or misappropriation of God's

[89] *Gen. Rab.* 8.12 (ed. Theodor-Albeck) 65. Also in *MhG* ad Gen 1:26 (ed. Margulies) 56. The midrash is sensitive to the repetition of man's "rule" in Gen 1:26 and 28. The seeming redundancy is eliminated by giving to each a different meaning. The verb in 1:26 is punned upon: *rdh* ("rule")/*yrd* ("descend"). However, we could also vocalize *yērādû*: "they shall be ruled by the animals." See Theodor's note ad loc., the commentaries of Ps.-Rashi and the MaHaRZU (in *Midraš Rabba* [ed. Vilna) 23b], Freedman's translation and note (*Midrash Rabbah: Genesis*, 1.62), and M. Smith, "On the Shape of God and the Humanity of Gentiles," 325. In the tale of Seth and the beast (see previous note) it is the "image of God" that dissuades the beast from attacking.

[90] Also in *b. Sanh.* 38b; *MhG* ad Gen 1:26 (ed. Margulies) 56; *MA* ad Gen 9:2 (ed. Buber) 28. Cf. *MhG* ad Gen 6:4 (ed. Margulies) 136. One of Adam's curses is that he resembles the animals in his diet: *ARNA* 1 (ed. Schechter) 7; *PRE* 14 (ed. Warsaw) 34b; *MhG* ad Gen 3:17 (ed. Margulies) 106.

name), diminished divine image, and resemblance to animals in appearance and/or conduct. Man, by turning from God to false gods, from worship of the Creator to the created, is himself transformed. He is no longer fully in the divine image, but becomes fully mortal; that is, he becomes more like and vulnerable to the animals. While I have demonstrated the serious possibility of *mazzîkîm* here meaning "animals," the more common understanding as "demons" cannot be absolutely refuted. It is also possible that *mazzîqîm* simply denotes menaces in general, as it does in the following early tradition: "The children of the Torah (Israel)," when they fulfill God's will, "will not be touched by any of the menaces (*mazzîqîm*) in the world."[91]

The four changes that are said to have occurred in Enosh's time represent radical transformations in human character, physique, and living conditions. All are seen as changes for the worse, presumably as punishments. They are not viewed as the human condition as created by God, but as consequences of man's subsequent degeneration. As we have shown, except for the change of apelike appearance, all the others appear elsewhere as elaborations of the curses in Gen 3:9–24, when Adam and Eve are expelled from Eden. Our midrash seems to paint a different picture of the beginnings of human sorrow. Following the expulsion from Eden, some humans continued to live carefree lives as demigods. Only after three generations did certain curses of human existence begin. It is to the story of the Generation of Enosh that the origins of these human troubles and weaknesses are traced, and not, as elsewhere, to the story of man's expulsion from Paradise.[92] The underlying transformation that occurs, according to the opening words of our passage, is that men ceased to be godlike, and became increasingly beastlike.[93]

[91] *MekRS* ad Exod 20:22 (ed. Epstein-Melamed) 157; *t. B. Qam.* 7.6. The parallel in *Mek. Baḥodeš* 11 (ed. Lauterbach) 2.290; and *Sifra Qedošim pereq* 10.8 (ed. Weiss) 92d have instead of *mazzîqîm*, *pûrʿānût* ("punishment, visitation"). For *mazzîqîm* as destructive creatures, see *Sem.* 8:15 (ed. Higger) 164–65.

[92] This transfer of curses from Gen 3:9–24 to 4:26 is surprising and demanding of explanation. I will return to this question in the next chapter when I take up the subject of Rabbinic motivation. In the meantime, note the comments of the MaHaRZU: "These changes have their source in the curse of Adam and his sin. But since Adam was God's handiwork, produced in His image and likeness, and since Seth and Enosh were also created in the Divine image and likeness, the curse did not take its full effect on them. But the children of Enosh degenerated completely and the curse took full effect on them."

[93] Our sources never claim that the earliest men were immortals. Despite their godlike qualities they died. Apparently, it was thought that the bodies of these first three men did not decompose after death. See the MaHaRZU, who comments that even their bodies were created in the divine image and hence were miraculously preserved, as the Psalmist says, "So too my body rests secure" (Ps 16:9). So, he says, has been the case with other righteous men who have "guarded their image and not sinned." On the dead bodies of the righteous not being affected by worms see *b. B. Bat.* 17a and *Derek 'Ereṣ Zuṭa'* 1 (end).

Finally, let us look at R. Isaac's statement (Part C), which concludes this passage and which appears to be a later comment on what has preceded.[94] It is intended to explain what precipitated the change of becoming "vulnerable to menacing creatures." We should remember that the present passage has made no mention yet of the sin of Enosh's contemporaries. R. Isaac suggests that these people reasoned, perhaps innocently, as follows: "If it is acceptable, and even proper, to bow before men of honor, why not do so with regard to images."[95] Yet, when the Generation of Enosh began to bow to images, this was considered idolatrous. What kind of images are intended? Although the word *ṣelem* is used of idols in general, the form of the argument seems to suggest human images: if it is correct to bow before an important person, why not bow to his image? Whether anything more specific is intended by R. Isaac is harder to tell.[96] It seems clear, however, that R. Isaac's complaint is not against the custom of bowing before persons of superior authority, but of bowing to human (and perhaps other) images. He identifies the origins of this practice with Enosh's contemporaries.

What the relation of this sin is to the punishment of becoming "vulnerable to menacing creatures" is not made clear. Perhaps the sense is that in *lowering* themselves to images, the people are now *placed under* the power and dominion of the menacing creatures. However, R. Isaac may simply view menacing creatures as an appropriate punishment for the sin of "strange worship" (cf. 2 Kgs 17:24–26; and other examples above, n. 83). We should also ask whether the use of the word *ṣelem* is intended to recall the divine image with which our passage began. One commentator thought so: "The Holy One Blessed be He said: 'If the image of God is no longer venerated by you, then let the image pass from you, leaving room (*māqôm*) for demons (*mazzîqîm*) to rule you.'"[97] This interpretation

[94] R. Isaac flourished a century after Abba Kohen. Note that his final words like the opening words of our passage are in Aramaic, while the rest of the passage is in Hebrew.

[95] We should note that the verb *gḥn* ("bow") is generally not used in the context of worship, neither divine nor idolatrous. Rather, it is used in the sense of bowing one's head in respect before an important person, such as a rabbi, as in *b. Yoma* 57a and *b. Ketub.* 59b. Apparently, this sort of bowing is not considered as severe as prostrating oneself before another human, as Mordecai refuses to do in Esth 3:2. See E. Bickerman, *Four Strange Books of the Bible* (New York: Schocken, 1967) 220–21.

[96] Were these images flat reliefs or statues? Note that in *Jeraḥmeel* 23.7 (trans. Gaster) 50 the *ṣelem* to which people bow is a *gōlem* (humanoid) created by Enosh.

[97] *Mattenot Kehunna*. Here, *mazzîqîm* seem to be demons, since they are envisaged as entering man to take the place of the "image of God," apparently thought, metaphorically at least, to be carried within man. See *Sifre Deut.* 318 (ed. Finkelstein) 364: "What is the manner of a demon (*šēd*)? It enters a man and turns him topsy-turvy." Demons possess men by entering them. Also note that in *Jeraḥmeel* 23.7, after Enosh's creation of an image is described we are told, "On this account Enosh is mentioned in Scripture immediately before the word 'his image' (Gen 5:3)."

suggests that men in turning to human images neglected the divine image, being left unprotected against domination by other powers. While this interpretation does justice to our passage as a whole, it is not certain that this is what R. Isaac intends. Significantly, R. Isaac gives us a somewhat different interpretation of the sin of Enosh's contemporaries than that found in the tannaitic sources. The only way to identify the two interpretations would be to suggest that the same persons whose images were being bowed to, were also being called "gods."[98]

Genesis Rabbah 23.7 (ed. Theodor-Albeck) 227–29:

> R. Simon [ben Pazzi, ca. 280] said: "In three places this expression [the verb *hēḥēl*] is used in the sense of rebellion (*lĕšôn mered*): 'Then men rebelled (*hûḥal*) by calling [false gods] by the name of the Lord'; 'and it came to pass when man rebelled (*hēḥēl*)' (Gen 6:1); 'he [Nimrod] rebelled (*hēḥēl*) by being a man of might' (Gen 10:8)." An objection was raised: "But it is written, 'this is how they have rebelliously (*haḥillām*) acted' (Gen 11:6)." He said to them: "[God] smote Nimrod's head, exclaiming, 'This is the one who incited them to revolt (*zeh himrîdām*).'"[99]

This passage, which also appears as an interpretation of Gen 6:1, notes that the verb *hēḥēl* ("began") is used in three places to describe rebellious activity. In Gen 4:26 it is used to describe the rebellion of Enosh's contemporaries, in Gen 6:1 that of the Flood Generation (or that of the "sons of God"), and in Gen 10:8 to introduce the rebellious Nimrod, whose very name is an expression of rebellion (*mrd*).[100] In each case, the

[98] Perhaps we have here an allusion to the imperial cult, polemicized against elsewhere in Rabbinic literature. Not only were the emperors referred to with divine epithets (e.g., *kyrios*, *theos*, *dominus*, *divus*), but their images were religiously venerated, whether as statues or on military standards. For examples of strong Jewish protests against the display of such imperial images in Jerusalem, see Josephus, *Ant.* 18.3.1 §§ 55–59 (including L. Feldman's notes and bibliography in LCL 9.42–7, 569–70); *B. J.* 2.9.2–3 §§ 169–74; *Megillat Ta'anit* for 3 Kislev; 1QpHab 6:3–5; *Tg. Neb.* Hab 1:16; Josephus, *Ant.* 18.8.2–9 §§ 261–309; *B. J.* 2.10.1–4 §§ 184–98; Philo, *Legat.* 188, 207–8; Tacitus, *Hist.* 5.9. On Jewish encounters with and polemics against emperor worship more generally see Wis 14:16–21; Josephus, *Ap.* 2.6 §§ 66–78; Philo, *Legat.* 134, 138, 148, 346; *Mek. Širta* 8 (ed. Lauterbach) 2.61; *MekRS* ad Exod 15:11 (ed. Melamed-Epstein) 91–92; *Lam. Rab.* 1 (ed. Buber) 84–85; E. M. Smallwood, *The Jews Under Roman Rule From Pompey to Diocletian* (Leiden: E. J. Brill, 1976) 278–84; M. Smith, "The Image of God," *BJRL* 40 (1958) 480–81; E. Urbach, "The Laws of Idolatry," 199; idem, *The Sages: Their Concepts and Beliefs* (trans. I. Abrahams; 2 vols.; Jerusalem: Magnes, 1975) 1.87–92.

[99] This passage also appears in *Gen. Rab.* 26.4 (ed. Theodor-Albeck) 246; in *YS Bere'šit* 40 (ed. Salonika) 14a and in abbreviated form in *LT* ad Gen 4:26 (ed. Buber) 31.

[100] Philo also presents a negative interpretation of Nimrod's name: *Gig.* 65–66. On Nimrod's wickedness, see Ginzberg, *Legends*, 1.177–9; 5.198–204, esp. n. 77. On the expression *lĕšôn mered* cf. *Gen. Rab.* 23.2; 24.6; 26.7 (ed. Theodor-Albeck) 222, 236, 255, where the names Irad, Mehujael, Methusael, and Lamech (Gen 4:18) are interpreted as *lĕšôn mardût* ("expressions of rebellion [*mrd*] or punishment [*rdh*]"). See Kasher, *TS* 2.33, n. 130. On sin as rebellion see S. Schechter, *Aspects of Rabbinic Theology* (New York: Macmillan, 1909) 219–41.

scriptural verse is cited without any explanation of what rebellion is intended. Thus, Gen 4:26b is simply cited as an example of rebellion without any need for explanation. Once again, the intended interpretation of Gen 4:26b (men began to call false gods by the name of God) is assumed to be familiar to the audience, even though it would seem to be the very opposite of the verse's "plain" meaning.[101]

But an objection is raised: is there not a fourth instance (Gen 11:6) where the verb *hēḥēl* is used to describe rebellion, since the story of the building of the Tower of Babel begins with this verb? No, replies R. Simon, this is not a new case, for the rebellion of the people at Babel was instigated by Nimrod.[102] Thus, R. Simon's statement stands. The verb *hēḥēl* is used to describe three rebellions of three generations: the Generation of Enosh, the Generation of the Flood, and the Generation of the Separation.[103]

It is impossible to know which of these three (or four) prooftexts originally occasioned this interpretation. It may be that the unusual form *hûḥal* was taken as an indication that this verb had special significance, having a second, less obvious meaning that could be found by examining its other nearby occurrences (*gĕzērâ šāwâ*). However, it would be difficult to argue that this exegesis is the basis for the Rabbinic converse interpretation of Gen 4:26b. Like the other Rabbinic passages we have examined, this one assumes a negative interpretation to begin with, and simply provides a new way to root that interpretation in Scripture.

Gen. Rab. 23.7 continues as follows:

> [A] R. Aḥa said: "You have made idols [performed idolatry] and

101 See Theodor's note to the passage.

102 The infinitive construct with a possessive suffix *haḥillām* ("their beginning") is understood as the finite *hiph'il* with an object suffix *hĕḥillām*, taken to mean "he caused them to rebel," with *zeh* being understood to refer to Nimrod. The biblical syntax is difficult to translate. All of the ancient versions render the infinitive construct with a finite verb: "this is what they began to do," or "this is what they considered doing." On Nimrod's role in instigating the building of the Tower see especially Josephus, *Ant.* 1.4.2 §§ 113–14; *b. Pesaḥ.* 94b (and parallels: b. *'Erub.* 53a; b. *Ḥag.* 13a; all in the name of R. Joḥanan b. Zakkai, ca. 80 C.E.); as well as other references in Ginzberg, *Legends*, 5.201 n. 88.

103 We may note that there is in fact one more example of the verb *hēḥēl* appearing in the early chapters of Genesis with a negative association. In Gen 9:20 we find: "Noah, the tiller of the soil, was the first (*wayyāḥēl*) to plant a vineyard." Since Noah proceeds to get drunk because of his vineyard and then to uncover himself, this verse could easily have been included as a fourth (or fifth) example of the verb *hēḥēl* suggesting "rebellion." For instance, in *Gen Rab.* 36.6 (ed. Theodor-Albeck) 337 we find the verb *hēḥēl* in this verse interpreted: "He [Noah] was profaned and became *ḥûllîn*" (but note the variants). See also *Tanḥ. B. Noaḥ* 20 (p. 46); *Tanḥ. Noaḥ* 13; *LT* and Rashi ad Gen 9:20. While the rabbis could tolerate a negative interpretation of Noah's drunkenness, they would probably not have been comfortable putting him in the same class with the three rebellious generations. His improper conduct would not necessarily be viewed as rebellion, as would be idolatry. These are the *only* uses of the verb *ḥll* in Genesis until 44:12.

called [upon them] for your own sakes. I too will call upon the waters of the sea for my own sake and will remove you wicked ones from the world." [B] R. Abbahu [ca. 300] taught: "The Ocean (*'ôqyānôs*) is higher (*gābôah*) than the whole world." R. Eleazar B. Menaḥem [ca. 300] said to him: "Is there not a verse fully to this effect: 'Who calls the waters of the sea and pours them out upon the earth,' etc. (Amos 5:8; 9:6)? This obviously means, like one who pours from above to below." [C] "Who calls the waters of the sea" is written twice, corresponding to the two times that the sea rose and inundated the world. How far did it rise the first time, and how far did it rise the second time? R. Yudan [ca. 350], R. Abbahu, and R. Eleazar [b. Pedath, ca. 300] in the name of R. Ḥanina [ca. 250] said: "The first time it rose as far as Acco and Jaffa, while the second time it rose as far as the Barbary Coast." R. Ḥuna [ca. 350] and R. Aḥa [ca. 350] in the name of R. Ḥanina said: "The first time as far as the Barbary Coast and the second as far as Acco and Yaffa, as it is written, 'And said: Thus far (*'ad pōh*) you shall come, but no further,' etc. (Job 38:11). 'Thus far (*'ad pōh*) you shall come,' means as far as Acco; 'and here shall your proud waves be stayed (*ûpō' yāšît*),' means as far as Jaffa (*yāpâ*)." R. Eleazar said: "The first time as far as Calabria, the second as far as the Barbary Coast."[104]

R. Aḥa's statement [A], which we have discussed above (n. 49), is essentially a reworking of the tradition in *Mek. Baḥodeš* 6 (but as preserved in *Sifre Deut.* 43). R. Abbahu's statement and R. Eleazar b. Menaḥem's reply [B] may have originally circulated independently of any interpretation of Gen 4:26b, but since Amos 5:8 became associated with the flood in Enosh's time, it was included in this section of *Genesis Rabbah*.

The word *'ôqyānôs* most likely refers here to the mythological Oceanus (Greek: *ōkeanos*), which was thought by both rabbis and Greeks to encircle the world and to be the source of the other waters of the world. Early navigational explorers identified this with the Atlantic Ocean.[105] R. Abbahu perceives this Oceanus to be higher than the dry

[104] Parallels to all or part of this passage can be found in *YS Bere'šit* 40 (ed. Salonika) 14a; *YS* Amos 543 (ed. Salonika) 125d; *YS* Job 924 (ed. Salonika) 178c; *p. Šeqal.* 6.3 (50a); *PR* supp. chap. 1 (ed. Friedmann) 193a–b; *MPs.* 88.2 (ed. Buber) 380; *YhM* ad Amos 5.8 (ed. Greenup) 46.

[105] We have several other references that suggest Rabbinic notions of Oceanus were similar to those found in Greco-Roman sources. In *b. 'Erub.* 22b we find: "Oceanus surrounds the whole world." Cf. *Midraš 'aśeret haddibrot* (Jellinek, *BhM* 1.63), which states: "The Great Sea encompasses the whole world." Here "Great Sea" (usually the Mediterranean) and Oceanus appear to be identical. The notion of Oceanus surrounding the world is common among Greek writers. See for instance Herodotus 2.21; 4.36. According to some Rabbinic authorities, the ocean is the ultimate source of the moisture that sustains the earth. See *Gen. Rab.* 13.10 (ed. Theodor-Albeck) 119–20; *b. Ta'an.* 9b and other parallels cited by Theodor: "R. Eliezer says: 'The whole world drinks from the waters of the ocean [Oceanus].'" Note how this tradition is combined with that of our passage in *Gen. Rab.* 5.3

land and smaller bodies of water which it encompasses. The cosmology envisioned here is that of a concave bowl, with the Oceanus forming the upper sides, prevented from flooding the world below by the boundary of the seashores, which break the downward flow of the waves.[106] Similarly, we find in *YS* Amos 543 (ed. Salonika) 125c:

> "Who calls the waters of the sea and pours them": Normally when a person makes a fence around his garden the fence is higher (*gābôah*) than the garden, but here the sand is low and the ocean (*'ôqyānôs*) is high.[107]

R. Eleazar b. Menaḥem finds in Amos 5:8 and 9:6 scriptural proof for this view of the Oceanus being higher than the rest of the world, since the verb *špk* ("spill") suggests flow from above to below.[108]

Part C is difficult to understand, in part because the names of both the sages and the places vary in the different manuscripts and parallel passages. What seems to be described here is the formation of the Mediterranean (the Great Sea) by two primeval floodings of the Oceanus. These *two* floodings are suggested by the repetition of Amos 5:8 and 9:5.

---

according to the printed editions: "R. Abbahu taught: The ocean [Oceanus] is higher than the whole world since the whole world drinks of its waters." Cf. Hesiod, *Theogony* 786, where it is said that all the rivers draw their waters from Oceanus via subterranean channels. Note as well *Gen. Rab.* 32.11 (ed. Theodor-Albeck) 298, which states that the fish alone of all that had the "spirit of life" did not perish in the flood, since they fled to Oceanus. From where did they flee? While some interpreters suggest that Noah had taken them aboard the Ark but they returned to the ocean, others suggest that they fled the flooded seas for the undisturbed higher Oceanus. See the MaHaRZU and Theodor ad loc. Cf. *b. Zebaḥ.* 113b; *b. Sanh.* 108a; *b. Qidd.* 13a; Ginzberg, *Legends*, 5.183 n. 43. On Oceanus, see O. Naverre, "Oceanus," in Daremberg and Saglio, *Dictionnaire des Antiquites Greques et Romaines*, 4.1.143–44. See also below, chap. 5, n. 119.

106 Cf. *PRE* 3 (ed. Warsaw) 8a, where we find: "The hooks of heaven [the heavenly canopy] are fastened to the waters of Oceanus, for the waters of Oceanus lie between the ends of the earth and the ends of heaven, and the ends of heaven are spread over the waters of Oceanus." See David Luria's notes 56 and 57 ad loc. Cf. *PRE* 6 (ed. Warsaw) 15a. Similarly, we find in *The Book of Adam and Eve* 1.1 (trans. Malan) 1 that east of Paradise, "one finds nothing but water, that encompasses the whole world and reaches unto the borders of heaven." The notion of the Oceanus extending to the edge of heaven probably derives from Gen 1:7 where the "firmament" divides the upper and lower waters. Cf. *T. Levi* 2:7; *Jub.* 2:4. On God's having set boundaries for the primeval waters, see above, n. 51.

107 The Vilna edition gives the source as "Yelammedenu." I have not found this tradition elsewhere. It appears to confirm our taking R. Abbahu's statement literally to mean that Oceanus is higher than the rest of the world. Other Rabbinic traditions, however, seem to identify Oceanus with the subterranean *tĕhôm*. On these waters of the deep wishing to flood the world in David's time, see J. Heinemann, *Aggadah and its Development* (Hebrew) (Jerusalem: Keter, 1974) chap. 2; L. Ginzberg, *Legends*, 4.96; 6.258 n. 70. Of course, the two bodies of water may be connected, and thus represent a single body of water. See *Gen. Rab.* 5.3 (ed. Theodor-Albeck) 34.

108 For a different interpretation of the verb *špk* in Amos 5:8, see Ibn Ezra ad Gen 1:6 and Amos 5:8. The attribution to R. Eleazar b. Menaḥem is not shared by all the parallels.

In a parallel passage in *p. Šeqal.* 6.3 (50a) we find the expression "sea of foul waters" (*hammûṣā'îm*) of Ezek 47:8 interpreted:

> This is the Great Sea. And why is it called *mûṣā'îm*? In correspondence to the two times that it went forth (*yāṣā'*), once in the Generation of Enosh and once in the Generation of the Separation.[109]

Thus, the ocean first flooded the Mediterranean region in Enosh's time and again in the time of the Tower of Babel, in both instances as punishment for man's rebellious activities.

What is surprising is that the flood of Noah's time (the *only* biblical flood) is not mentioned in this context. It appears that the midrash distinguishes between two types of floods. The one in Noah's time is caused by unrelenting rains that eventually fill the seas and inundate the dry land. When the rains end, the waters subside and the dry land reappears. However, the floods referred to in our passage make no mention of rain. Rather, these are floods caused by the flooding of the ocean.[110] The ocean's "downward" flow, checked by God at creation through the establishment of boundaries, is now unleashed as a form of punishment. It is again checked once it has accomplished its purpose. But these flood waters do not revert or subside.[111]

Since the places mentioned in this passage are on the north, south, and east shores of the Mediterranean, the dispute is over how far the waters of the ocean came in each of the two floodings of the Mediterranean, that is, the order in which the final shores were established. Both floodings were naturally thought to have progressed from west to east, since the Oceanus (Atlantic) lies to the west of the Mediterranean.[112] According to the first view, the first flood filled the sea to its length (to Acco and Yaffa on the Palestinian coast) while the second flood filled it

109 The two floods are also identified with these two generations in *YS* Amos 543; *YS* Job 924; *PR* supp. chap. 1. Note as well *Gen. Rab.* 25.2 (ed. Theodor-Albeck) 240 and parallels, where Amos 5:8 and 9:6 are interpreted to refer to the two times *daily* that the waters *rose* to flood men's graves, until Noah brought rest to the dead. Ps.-Rashi ad loc. states that this flooding began in the Generation of Enosh. For the tradition of a flood of water in the Generation of the Separation, note the Rabbinic interpretation of Gen 11:8 in *Gen. Rab.* 38.10 (ed. Theodor-Albeck) 360; *PR* supp. chap. 1 (ed. Friedmann) 193a–b.

110 J. G. Frazer (*Folklore of the Old Testament*, vol. 1 [London, 1919] 346ff.) gives examples from the folklore of other peoples of floods caused by the rising of the ocean. According to *Zohar* 2.113b, the ocean was about to flood the world again at the time of the Golden Calf incident.

111 See the MaHaRZU ad loc.

112 A similar tradition may lie behind the story of the flooding of Atlantis, said to have been located near the entry to the Mediterranean at Gibraltar. See Plato, *Timaeus*, 24e–25d.

to its width (the Barbary Coast, that is, the African Coast).[113] The second group of rabbis holds the opposite: first the width was established and only finally the length.[114] This group cites Job 38:11 in support, since that verse is interpreted to mean that the final limit was set at Acco and Jaffa, by a pun on the repetitious *'ad pōh* and *ûpō'*.[115] The final view, in the name of R. Eleazar,[116] seems to be that the first flood established the northern shoreline (Calabria being the heel of the Italian peninsula) while the second flood established the southern shoreline, both times the waters reaching eastward as far as Palestine.

The details of this difficult passage need not detain us further. What is clear is that this discussion of the formation of the Mediterranean is associated with the flood in Enosh's time. Unlike the flood in Noah's time this one is a partial one, inundating only those regions which lie beneath the Mediterranean.[117] This flood is caused not by excessive rain, but by God's summoning the ocean (Oceanus) to overflow its boundaries. To repeat: In calling the waters to overflow their boundaries, God radically alters Creation, in response to the innovation of the Generation of Enosh who were the first to call upon false gods.

The remaining references to Enosh and his generation in amoraic collections add little new in their interpretation of Gen 4:26. However, they are significant in two regards: (a) They consistently *assume* an association of the Generation of Enosh with rebellious false worship, without

113 Otherwise it would be difficult to understand how the waters reached the most easterly point first. Some have dismissed this view as being inconceivable. See, for instance, W. Bacher, *Die Agada der palästinensischen Amoräer* (3 vols.; Strassburg, 1892–99) 1.23 n. 4. Bacher states that this interpretation is "by all means incorrect." See Theodor's note ad loc. Because this first interpretation is problematic, it is omitted or curtailed in most of the parallels. But this does not warrant removing it from our text. For a similar understanding of this text, see the MaHaRZU ad loc.

114 If it weren't for the first interpretation, we might assume that the first flood reached lengthwise as far as the Barbary Coast, while the second continued as far as Acco and Jaffa.

115 Perhaps *'ad pōh* is understood as *'ad kōh*.

116 The attribution here is highly uncertain. In *p. Šeqal* 6.3 this is the first interpretation cited and is attributed to R. Eleazar in the name of R. Ḥanina. Elsewhere it is attributed to R. Eleazar in the name of R. Jose b. Ḥanina, or to R. Eleazar b. Jose.

117 What the relation of this tradition is to that which says one-third of the world was flooded in Enosh's time is not clear. Note that in *YR* ad Lev 2:13 (Warsaw, 1884) 16 an anonymous midrash is cited that states that the world (*'ôlām*) is one third sea, one third desert, and one third inhabited land. Is this the same third that was flooded by the sea (or Oceanus) in Enosh's time, or was it a third of the *inhabited* land that was flooded in Enosh's time, this being conceived of as the area of the Mediterranean? Perhaps the expression "one third of the world" is a cliche that should not be taken too literally. Cf. *b. B. Meṣ.* 59b, which states that as a result of R. Eliezer's excommunication, "the world was then smitten: a third of the olive crop, a third of the wheat, and a third of the barley crop."

having to cite Gen 4:26 as a prooftext, or citing it without having to explain. (b) They place the Generation of Enosh within the context of a *chain* of pre-Israelite rebellious generations, and in some cases in relation to God's creation of the world.

According to *Gen. Rab.* 2.3, R. Judah b. R. Simon (ca. 350) interpreted the parts of Gen 1:2 to refer to the early generations (*dôrôt*):

> "The earth was unformed" refers to Adam, who was reduced to nothing and naught. "And void" refers to Cain, who sought to turn back the world to *tohu bohu* [chaos]. "And darkness" refers to the Generation of Enosh, [as it says,] "Their works are in the dark" (Isa 29:15). "Over the surface of the deep" refers to the Generation of the Flood, [as it says,] "In that day all the fountains of the deep burst apart" (Gen 7:11) . . . The Holy One Blessed be He said: "How long will the world conduct itself in darkness? Let the light come." "And God said let there be light" (Gen 1:3) refers to Abraham, as it says, "Who has raised up one from the east" (Isa 41:2).[118] "And God called the light day" refers to Jacob . . .[119]

Thus, the creation of order out of disorder and of light out of darkness on the natural plain is thought to signify a similar development on the historical plain: the pre-Israelite era is seen as one of darkness and confusion, in contrast to the brightness of the Israelite patriarchs. The pre-Israelite period is described as a *succession* of sinful individuals and generations, in contrast to the succession of righteous Israelite patriarchs.[120]

A similar view of pre-Israelite times is expressed in different terms in *Gen. Rab.* 19.7, in the name of R. Abba b. Kahana (ca. 300):

> Originally the Shekinah [divine indwelling] dwelt among the terrestrial beings (*taḥtônîm*). When Adam sinned it removed itself to the first heaven, when Cain sinned it rose to the second heaven, when the Generation of Enosh sinned it rose to the third . . .[121]

118 MT *hēʿîr* ("stirred up") is understood as *hēʾîr* ("caused to shine"). See the printed edition: "Do not read 'stirred up' but 'caused to shine.'" Cf. *Gen. Rab.* 42.3 (ed. Theodor-Albeck) 418; *Exod. Rab.* 15.26.

119 Ed. Theodor-Albeck, 15–16; *YS Bereʾšit* 4 (ed. Salonika) 2c.

120 A similar type of exegesis is found in *Gen. Rab.* 26.1 (ed. Theodor-Albeck) 243–44, where Ps 1:1 is said to have been interpreted by R. Judah (ca. 150) so as to suggest a contrast between Noah ("happy is the man") and three rebellious generations: the Generation of Enosh ("the counsel of the wicked"), the Generation of the Flood ("the way of sinners"), and the Generation of the Separation ("the seat of the scornful"). Cf. *MPs.* 1.12 (ed. Buber) 11; *YS* Ps. 614 (ed. Salonika) 2c. Similarly, some versions of *Gen. Rab.* 27.2 (ed. Theodor-Albeck) 256–57 (e.g., *YS* Qoh. 968 [ed Salonika] 225d) have: "'For all his days are pain' (Qoh 2:23) refers to the Generation of Enosh and the Generation of the Flood." Likewise, *Qoh. Rab.* 2.21–23; *Qoh. Zuṭa'* 2.8 (ed. Buber) 117. For other such interpretations, see *Tanḥ. B. Wayyera'* 24 (p. 99); *MhG* ad Gen 6:5 (ed. Margulies) 141.

121 Ed. Theodor-Albeck, 176. For parallels, see *YS Bereʾšit* 27 (ed. Salonika) 10b; *YS* Ps. 732 (ed. Salonika) 23d; *PR* 5 (ed. Friedmann) 18b; *Tanḥ. B. Naśo'* 24 (p. 38); *Tanḥ.*

The progression (degression) continues with the Generation of the Flood, the Generation of the Separation, the Sodomites, and the Egyptians (seven in all). Then along come seven patriarchs (Abraham, Isaac, Jacob, Levi, Kohath, Amram, and Moses), each of whom causes the Shekinah to come back down a level until with Moses it is restored on earth. Once again, the Generation of Enosh is placed within a chain of *biblical* sinful generations. Presumably, it was their idolatrous activities which caused the removal of the Shekinah one more level. While the specific activity of this generation is not discussed, the tradition of their wrongdoing, being assumed, is employed to supply one more stage in the gradual spiritual alienation of God from man.[122]

This contrast between pre-Israelite and Israelite history is expressed in still another way in *Lev. Rab.* 23.3:

> The whole world was created for the sake of none other than Torah. For twenty-six generations the Holy One Blessed be He gazed upon his world and found it full of thorns and thistles, such as the Generation of Enosh, the Generation of the Flood, and the Sodomites, and he desired to renounce and destroy it, as it says, "The Lord sat enthroned at the Flood" (Ps 29:10).[123] But he found a single rose lily, this being Israel, who would in the future stand before Mt. Sinai. Israel's worth was sufficient to save the whole world.[124]

The worthless character of the pre-Israelite generations (twenty-six from

---

Pequde 6; *Num. Rab.* 13.2; *PRK* 1.1 (ed. Mandelbaum) 2. Cf. *MhG* ad Exod 40:34 (ed. Margulies) 792. Note that *Cant. Rab.* 5.1 (ed. Vilna) 29d has "Enosh sinned," rather than "the Generation of Enosh sinned." The same reading appears in the first printing of *Midraš ḥameš megillot* (1519; facs. reprod., Berlin, 1926). On negative statements about Enosh himself see below, n. 137.

122 On the motif of the removal of the Shekinah (*histallĕqût haššĕkînâ*) in Rabbinic literature, see A. Goldberg, *Untersuchungen über die Vorstellung von der Schekhinah in der frühen rabbinischen Literatur* (Berlin: Walter de Gruyter, 1969) 13–20; J. Abelson, *The Immanence of God in Rabbinical Literature* (London: Macmillan, 1912) 101, 117–39; S. Hacohen, "*ʿEśer massaʿot naseʿa šekina*," *Sinai* 88 (1981) 104–19. According to *Mek. Baḥodeš* 9 (ed. Lauterbach) 2.273–74, "Just as idolatry defiles the land and causes the Shekina to depart, so too whoever is haughty causes the defilement of the land and the removal of the Shekinah." Cf. *Sifre Deut.* 148 (ed. Finkelstein) 203; *Tq. Onq.* Deut 31.18.

In *3 Enosh* 5.3–6 (*Seper Hekalot*), to be discussed below, the removal of the Shekinah is described as having taken place with one move, occurring in the time of Enosh in response to the idolatry of his contemporaries. A similar tradition identifying the removal of the Shekinah with the Generation of Enosh appears in *YR* ad Gen 4:26 (ed. Warsaw, 1884) 105.

123 This verse is elsewhere interpreted as a reference to God's judgment of the wicked. See *MPs.* 29.2 (ed. Buber) 232, and *Tg. Ket.* ad loc. On the tetragram being interpreted in terms of God's "attribute of punishment" see chap. 3, nn. 38, 65.

124 Ed. Margulies, 529–30. Cf. *Cant. Rab.* 2.2. Some variants add the Generation of the Separation, but all have the Generation of Enosh. See Margulies's critical apparatus. On God's suspending punishment for the sake of the righteous see *ARNA* 32 (ed. Schechter) 92–93.

Adam until the giving of the Torah) is contrasted to Israel's value.[125] Interestingly, only three such generations, known for their rebellious wrongdoings, epitomize this whole period of world history. The Generation of Enosh is the earliest such generation mentioned.

One variation of this motif is the notion that these rebellious generations, despite being punished by God, were unable or unwilling to mend their ways, and were unable to learn from the punishments of their predecessors. Thus, in *Gen. Rab.* 26.7 we find Gen 6:4 ("and even afterwards") interpreted by R. Judah in the name of Rabbi (ca. 200):

> The later ones did not learn from the earlier ones: the Generation of the Flood from the Generation of Enosh, the Generation of the Separation from the Generation of the Flood.[126]

This same idea is expressed more graphically in a later version of this tradition:

> "Though you might pound a fool with a pestle [his foolishness will not depart from him]" (Prov 27:22): R. Nehemiah the son of R. Samuel b. Naḥman [ca. 300] said: To what may the matter be compared? To a jar full of locusts. The first one rises and falls, the second one rises and falls, and the second learns not from the first. Thus, the Generation of Enosh arose and worshipped false gods, as it says, "Then men began to call [false gods] by the name of the Lord." What did [God] do? He called the sea to drown them, as it says, "Who calls the waters of the sea . . . " (Amos 5:8). The Generation of the Flood arose and provoked God as it says, "They say to God: 'Depart from us [for we desire not the knowledge of your ways]'" (Job 21:14). And they were destroyed from the world, for they did not learn from the Generation of Enosh.[127]

This hopeless state of pre-Israelite affairs is expressed in still another way in *Gen. Rab.* 38.5 in an interpretation of Jer 51:9 attributed to R. Azariah (ca. 400):

> "We tried to cure Babylon but she was incurable": "We tried to cure Babylon" during the Generation of Enosh. "But she was incurable" in the Generation of the Flood. "Let us leave her and go, each to his own land" (ibid.) [refers to the Generation of the Separation of whom it is said,] "all the land had the same language," etc. (Gen 11:1).[128]

[125] Cf. *m. 'Abot* 5:2, which speaks of twenty unworthy generations from Adam until Abraham.

[126] Ed. Theodor-Albeck, 254. The same tradition appears in *Gen. Rab.* 38.4 (ed. Theodor-Albeck) 353; *YS Bere'šit* 47 (ed. Salonika) 15c; *MPs.* 2.2 (ed. Buber) 24–25; *LT* ad Gen 6:4 (ed. Buber) 34. Rashi also interprets the words "and even afterwards" of Gen 6:4 to refer back to the Generation of Enosh. See below, n. 168.

[127] *Tanḥ B. Noaḥ* 24 (p. 52). Cf. *Tanḥ. Noaḥ* 18; *Gen. Rab.* 38.2, (ed. Theodor-Albeck) 352, 358–59; *YhM* ad Amos 5:8 (ed. Greenup) 46–47.

[128] Ed. Theodor-Albeck, 353. Also in *Gen. Rab.* 39.5 (ed. Theodor-Albeck) 367–68; *YS* Jer 335 (ed. Salonika) 107d.

Once again, a scriptural verse is divided so as to apply to a series of rebellious generations. The commentators interpret the application of "we tried to cure Babylon" to the Generation of Enosh to mean that at that time only one-third of the world was flooded; at first the dosage was light in the hope that the patient would soon recover.[129] Not only is the pre-Israelite period described as a succession of rebellious generations, but each is seen as being worse than its predecessor.

A few passages in *Genesis Rabba* explicitly associate the flood in Enosh's time with the primeval waters contained by God at Creation. For instance, *Gen. Rab.* 4:6 asks: Why after the second day of Creation (the dividing of the waters) did God not say "it is good," as on the other days?

> R. Simon [ca. 300] in the name of R. Joshua b. Levi [ca. 200]: This can be compared to a king who had an intractable legion. The king said, "Since this legion is intractable, I will not have my name inscribed over it." Similarly, the Holy One Blessed be He said, "Since these waters will smite the Generation of Enosh, the Generation of the Flood, and the Generation of the Separation, let there not be written concerning them 'it is good.'"[130]

Similarly, *Gen. Rab.* 5.1 interprets "let the waters be gathered (*yiqqāwû*)" of Gen 1:9 as "let the waters wait (*yĕqawwû*)":

> R. Abba b. Kahana [ca. 300] in the name of R. Levi [ca. 300]: "Let the waters await what I will do with them in the future" . . . The Generation of Enosh arose and rebelled against Him, the Generation of the Flood [arose] and rebelled against Him, and the Generation of the Separation [arose] and rebelled against Him. The Holy One Blessed be He said, "Let those very same waters turn, arise, and advance."[131]

Thus, already at Creation, even before the creation of man, God foresees the rebellious generations to come, and anticipates, with regret, the need to punish them with the ocean. The first flooding is that of the

129 See Ps.-Rashi and *Mattenot Kehunna*. The MaHaRZU tries to show that the Generation of Enosh lived in Babylonia. On God's having been lenient with the Generation of Enosh see *The Mishnah of R. Eliezer* (ed. Enelow) 1.78 and *Menorat Ha-Maor* (ed. Enelow) 4.299. Cf. *AgBer.* 8 (ed. Buber) 21, which has God say: "I have never struck a nation and had to do so again," referring to the Generation of Enosh, the Generation of the Flood, the Generation of the Separation, the Sodomites, the Egyptians, and Sisera. The trouble lies not with God's ability to punish forcefully but with man's inability to learn from the experiences of his predecessors.

130 Ed. Theodor-Albeck, 30. The printed edition reverses the order of the first two generations.

131 Ed. Theodor-Albeck, 32. The same tradition is repeated in *Gen. Rab.* 28.2 (ed. Theodor-Albeck) 260; *Lam. Rab.* 1.16 (ed. Buber) 78–79. Other parallels are listed by Theodor. Note, however, that *YS Bere'šit* 7 (ed. Salonika) 3c and *YS* Ps. 848 (ed. Salonika) 50d omit mention of the Generation of the Separation.

Generation of Enosh, whose sinful behavior is once again assumed rather than proven.[132]

Just as the primeval waters are said to have been set aside by God in expectation of the rebellious generations, so too, according to *Lev. Rab.* 11.7, the primeval light:

> R. Judah bar R. Simon [ca. 350] said: By means of the light which the Holy One Blessed be He created on the first day, Adam could see from one end of the world to the other. But when the Holy One Blessed be He beheld the Generation of Enosh and the Generation of the Flood, that they were corrupted (*mĕqûlqālîn*), he hid it from them, as it says, "But from the wicked their light is withheld" (Job 38:15). Where did he hide it? In the Garden of Eden, [as it says,] "Light is sown for the righteous, and gladness for the upright of heart." (Ps 97:11).[133]

Parallel sources state that this light was set aside for the righteous in the hereafter. Some versions of this tradition state that Adam and Eve enjoyed this light for thirty-six hours, and with the departure of the first Sabbath it was hidden upon their expulsion from Eden. Our text, however, connects God's concealing of this light not with Adam's sin, but with the sins of the rebellious generations.[134]

In the above passages, when God at Creation anticipates man's rebellion, it is not the sins of Adam or Cain that he foresees but those of the rebellious generations, *beginning* with the Generation of Enosh.

132 In *Gen. Rab.* 5.6 (ed. Theodor-Albeck) 35–36, Ps 33:7–8 is interpreted: "He heaps up the ocean waters like a mound" in order that "all the earth fear the Lord." These are the same waters as in "who calls the waters of the sea" (Amos 5:8; 9:6), referring to the two floodings of the Generation of Enosh and the Generation of the Separation. When God commands the waters to be gathered, and the dry land to appear (*tērā'eh*, Gen 1:9), this is so that man will fear (*yārē'*) God. Cf. *Deut. Rab.* 10.2; *Qoh. Rab.* 3.14. On the sea as God's agent (*šālûaḥ*), see *AgBer.* 8 (ed. Buber) 20.

133 Ed. Margulies, 234–35. This tradition appears in *Gen. Rab.* 11.2 and 12.6 according to the printed edition and some manuscripts (including Vatican 60), but not in the London Manuscript upon which Theodor's edition is based. See Theodor's critical apparatus, pp. 88–89, 103. The tradition is better attested in *Gen. Rab.* 42.3 (ed. Theodor-Albeck) 405, but there, according to Theodor's text, the names of the generations are omitted and we find, "when God beheld the wicked." But in MS Vatican 60 the generations, including that of Enosh, are mentioned. See other variants in Theodor's critical apparatus. For other parallels, see *b. Ḥag.* 12a (where the Generation of Enosh is not mentioned, neither in the printed edition nor in the manuscripts); *Exod. Rab.* 35.1; *Num. Rab.* 13.5; *Ruth Rab.* Proem 7; *Esth. Rab.* Proem 11; *Tanḥ. Šemini* 9; *PR* 23 (ed. Friedmann) 118a; *YS* Job 924 (ed. Salonika) 178d. Some parallels add the Generation of the Separation and some omit the Generation of Enosh. See Margulies's critical apparatus.

134 On the hiding of the primal light see *Gen. Rab.* 3.6 (ed. Theodor-Albeck) 21; *MPs.* 27.1 (ed. Buber) 104; *PR* 5, 46 (ed. Friedmann) 19b–20a, 186b; *Tanḥ. Noaḥ* 3; *SEZ* 21 (ed. Friedmann) 33. Note as well *3 Enosh* 5.3–6 (*Seper Hekalot*), to be discussed below, where man continues to bask in the light of the Shekinah until the Generation of Enosh. See Ginzberg, *Legends*, 5.112–24 nn. 104–5.

Only two amoraic traditions refer to the Generation of Enosh apart from the other rebellious generations. Both involve a play on the proper name Enosh and the common noun *'ĕnôš* ("man"), and both presuppose the common Rabbinic understanding of Gen 4:26.

According to *b. Šabb.* 118b:

> R. Ḥiyya bar Abba [ca. 300] said in the name of R. Yoḥanan [ca. 250]: Whoever observes the Sabbath as prescribed, even a worshipper of false gods like (the Generation of) Enosh, is pardoned [for his sins], as it says, "Happy is the man (*'ĕnôš*) who does this, [who keeps the Sabbath] from profaning it" (Isa 56:2). Do not read "from profaning it" (*mēḥallĕlô*), but "he is pardoned" (*māḥûl lô*)."[135]

While the printed edition of the Talmud has "the Generation of Enosh," the Munich MS and other witnesses have just "Enosh."[136] Thus, the better attested reading suggests that R. Joḥanan refers to Enosh the *individual* as an idolater. This is the only clear instance of such an interpretation in tannaitic and amoraic sources, and, therefore, the printed version may represent a harmonization with the prevalent view that distinguishes Enosh from his contemporaries.[137] However, with time we increasingly see

135 The MaHaRŠa' (Samuel Edels, 1555–1631) in his commentary *Ḥidduše 'aggadot* (found in the Vilna Talmud) suggests that the pun derives from the fact that Sabbath is feminine, while *mēḥallĕlô* has a masculine pronominal suffix (cf. Exod 31:14). Therefore, the ending *lô* refers not to the Sabbath but to the "man." Cf. *Sifre Deut.* 319 (ed. Finkelstein) 366: "'God who brought you forth (*mĕḥôlĕlekâ*)': God who forgives you (*môḥēl lĕkâ*)."

136 I have consulted the facsimile edition of the Munich MS (Jerusalem, 1971). See also R. Rabbinovicz, *Diqduqe soperim* (Munich, 1867–97; reprint 16 vols. in 2; New York: M. P. Press, 1976) 2.54, which notes that the earliest printings agree with the Munich MS. Rashi's commentary, however, assumes the text to read, "like the Generation of Enosh." *YS* Isa. 485 (ed. Salonika) 86b and *YhM* ad Isa. 56:2 (ed. J. Spira) 212 both have "like Enosh."

137 All other negative statements about Enosh occur in later sources. See *MhG* ad Gen 4:26, to be discussed below. In *SER* 16 (ed. Friedmann) 80–81 we are told that the first ten generations of mankind enjoyed long lives in order that they could be tested. Enosh like those who succeeded him is said to have been willing to provide for his father but not his grandfather. According to *Zohar* 1.56a and *Jeraḥmeel* 23.6–7 (trans. Gaster) 49–50, Enosh played a significant role in the first idolatry and magic. In *Zohar* 2.192b Enosh is referred to as "Enosh the wicked (*ḥayyāybā'*)," interpreting the collective noun *'ĕnôš* of Isa 8:1 to refer to Enosh the idol-maker. Maimonides (*Hilkot 'abodat kokabim* 1.1,3) clearly states that Enosh himself "was among those who went astray." L. Ginzberg (*Legends*, 5.151) says that Maimonides' view is "very likely on the basis of older sources." Note as well the variant tradition in *Cant. Rab.* 5.1 (see above, n. 121), according to which Enosh himself sinned, causing the Shekinah to remove itself to the third heaven. Cf. *Bere'šit Rabbati* (ed. Albeck) 31–32, which states that Enosh, Kenan, and Mahalalel are recorded in Genesis 5 only for the sake of Enoch, Methusalah, and Noah who descended from them. See below, n. 141.

We witnessed a positive view of Enosh in *Gen. Rab.* 23.6, where Enosh along with Adam and Seth is said to have been in the divine image. See above, n. 69. Note that in the *Feast of Leviathan* (in A. Jellinek, *BhM* 6.150) Enosh is listed as one of seven "shepherds"

Enosh identified with the deeds of the generation that bears his name.[138] R. Joḥanan is clearly punning in two ways on Isa 56:2, taking "man" to suggest "Enosh," and "from profaning it" to suggest "he is pardoned": Happy is the man, even one like Enosh, who keeps the Sabbath, for by so doing he is pardoned for his sins, even idolatry (one of the cardinal sins). Thus, Enosh is *assumed* to epitomize this most radical form of sin.

A somewhat similar tradition is found in *Lam. Rab.* Proem 24:

> "Man (*'ĕnôš*) is regarded as naught (Isa 33:8). The ministering angels said to the Holy One Blessed be He, Not even like the Generation of Enosh, who were the first (*rō'š*) of the idolaters, have you regarded Israel."[139]

The devastation that is described in Isa 33:8 ("Highways are desolate, wayfarers have ceased, a covenant has been renounced, cities rejected, man regarded as naught") is interpreted to refer to the destruction of Jerusalem. The ministering angels complain to God that He has treated Israel more harshly than even the Generation of Enosh. What precisely the midrash has in mind is not clear. Perhaps what is suggested is that the Generation of Enosh, only partially punished, was shown some consideration, while Israel was completely devastated.[140] In any case, the word *'ĕnôš* of Isa 33:8 is identified with the Generation of Enosh, which in turn is identified with the origins of false worship.[141]

---

of Israel who sit at God's side during the messianic banquet. However, other versions of this tradition do *not* include Enosh among the elect seven. See RaDaQ ad Micah 5:4, where Enoch takes Enosh's place; and *b. Sukk.* 52b (= *YS* Micah 522 [ed. Salonika] 129b), where Adam is included instead of Enosh. Note as well the inclusion of Enosh in the list of thirteen universal ancestors from Adam through Noah and his sons, preserved in a mosaic floor in the 'En Gedi Synagogue (sixth-seventh century). It has been suggested that these earliest biblical heroes, along with zodiac signs, months, and later biblical figures, bear witness to the community oath that follows. L. I. Levine (*Ancient Synagogues Revealed* [Jerusalem: Israel Exploration Society, 1982] 143) states, "Given the obvious importance of this oath to the community at large, involving any and all figures and forces respected and feared by the people might not be unlikely." Does this suggest a positive view, if only latent and implicit, of Enosh? Most Rabbinic texts that comment on Gen 4:26b treat Enosh neither positively nor negatively, understanding the verse to speak of his contemporaries.

138 Note the saying: "The leader of a generation is like unto the whole generation": *Tanḥ. B. Ḥuqqat* 53 (p. 129); *Tanḥ. Ḥuqqat* 23; *Num. Rab.* 19.29.

139 Ed. Buber, 13b.

140 The commentary *Yapeh 'anap* (by Samuel Jaffe Ashkenazi, sixteenth century) says that the Generation of Enosh was drowned in the sea, but at least no one laid hands on them. Israel, on the contrary, has been smitten by human hands, with several kinds of punishment. A more likely explanation is that in Enosh's time only a third of the world was destroyed.

141 Is it possible that this tradition, like that of *b. Šabb.* 118b, once referred to Enosh the individual, since the text has *rō'š* in the singular? This is certainly possible, but the comparison seems more likely to be with a *group* of past sinners than with an individual. While Buber's text has *šhyw r'š*, the first printed edition (1519) has *šhyh r'š*, which could

Unlike the non-Rabbinic sources we have examined, no tannaitic or amoraic source uses the fact of Enosh's name meaning "man" to interpret Gen 4:26. The above two traditions, rather, use the association of Enosh and his generation with idolatry to particularize the common noun *ʾĕnoš* elsewhere in Scripture.

Let me briefly summarize the amoraic traditions we have examined. They are generally attributed to Palestinian amoraim of the third and fourth centuries. These sources, like the tannaitic ones previously examined, *assume* a negative interpretation of Gen 4:26b, taking it to refer, it would seem, to the misappropriation of God's name for the worship of false deities. Very little effort is made to explain how this interpretation is derived from the biblical verse itself. None of our amoraic sources describes the specific nature of the sin of Enosh's contemporaries. If we try to picture what it actually was that they are reputed to have done, we are assisted hardly at all by our sources. Rather, the central interest of the amoraic traditions seems to be: (a) describing, in greater detail than the tannaitic antecedants, the consequences of the sin, (b) showing again that these consequences were justified, and (c) placing the sin and punishment of the Generation of Enosh in historiographic context.

The sin of the Generation of Enosh is said to have resulted in radical changes in human character and physiology, as well as in the natural (and even supernatural) world. As we have seen, most of these changes are elsewhere connected with Adam and Eve's expulsion from the Garden of Eden. Our present sources seem to extend the idyllic life of earliest man until the time of Enosh and to identify the beginnings of human degeneration with his contemporaries, and in one source with Enosh himself. The sins of Adam and Cain are individual sins, those of the Generation of Enosh and the succeeding generations implicate humanity as a whole (with some isolated exceptions). It is on the latter that the etiological interests of these amoraic traditions focus. The tradition of a partial flood in Enosh's time, while already alluded to in tannaitic sources, is described in greater detail in the amoraic traditions. It is now linked to the formation of the Ocean at Creation, and to subsequent floodings. Thus, the amoraic sources amplify in detail and in implication traditions found in the tannaitic corpora, without in any significant way contradicting them.

In the amoraic sources the term "Generation of Enosh" appears most

---

have as its subject either "Generation" or "Enosh." In *3 Enoch* 5.10 (= *Seper Hekalot*, see below) we find this phrase clearly applied to Enosh the individual. The same is found in *YR* ad Gen 4:26 (ed. Warsaw) 105. In these passages the word *rōʾš* is clearly used to refer to Enosh either as the first or chief idolater, even though it is the idolatry of his contemporaries which is described. Interestingly, the very same word (*ryš*) is used of Enosh in a positive sense in Samaritan and Mandaean traditions discussed above (chap. 2, nn. 16, 54).

frequently alongside the other rebellious generations, most of whose activities are already known from the Bible. So too the sinful character of the Generation of Enosh is assumed to be familiar, since it is usually alluded to without being specified or proved. This is a change from the tannaitic sources, where we saw that the Generation of Enosh does not appear in conjunction with the other rebellious generations known from the Bible. In the amoraic sources the Generation of Enosh often appears as a part of a chain of evildoers, most frequently being followed by the Generation of the Flood and the Generation of the Separation, and often being the first link in the chain. This is remarkably similar to early Jewish, Christian, and Samaritan traditions which also mention the figure Enosh within the context of an historical chain, the chain of righteous ancestors. In both cases, the specific characters of the constitutive links are of secondary importance to the continuity of the chain itself. If in certain extra-Rabbinic traditions Enosh is the first link in the chain, it is because of his paramount virtues of piety. If for certain Rabbinic traditions the Generation of Enosh is the first link in the chain, it is because of their paramount sin of rebellion.

D. Postamoraic Sources

Finally, I will examine those midrashic traditions, found in postamoraic sources, that have not been evidenced in earlier tannaitic or amoraic collections. Initially, these sources simply echo and combine motifs appearing in the earlier amoraic collections. However, as we move into midrashic collections of early medieval times, the tone and focus of the interpretations change in three significant ways: (a) The sin of the Generation of Enosh is viewed as being more actively and provocatively rebellious. (b) The specifics of their idolatry are more explicitly described. (c) The inherited interpretation of Gen 4:26 is finally linked to the actual words of that verse, especially through interpretation of Enosh's name and the verb *hûḥal*.

In two passages, the tradition of God's foreknowledge at Creation of the rebellious generations is given a new twist: God is almost convinced not to create the world, but His foreknowledge of the Israelite patriarchs convinces him to proceed with Creation, despite the evil that will ensue.

In *Pesiqta Rabbati* 40 the following tradition is attributed to R. Ḥanina (ca. 250):[142]

[142] This dating assumes that R. Ḥanina b. Ḥama is intended. Although this tradition is not found in any of the earlier compilations, there is nothing within it that would rule out an amoraic dating. The translation is based on the edition of M. Friedmann, 166b–167a. This source is based on homilies for the festivals and special Sabbaths, and its order is determined by the calendar. The collection has been dated as early as the sixth century, but a ninth century dating is more common. The present passage appears with only slight

> When the Holy One blessed be He determined to create His world, he looked upon the deeds of the [future] wicked and decided not to create the world: the Generation of Enosh, the Generation of the Flood, the Generation of the Separation, and the Sodomites. But then the Holy One blessed be He observed the deeds of the righteous: of Abraham, Isaac, and Jacob. Once more He looked [at the wicked] and said: "Because of the wicked I will not create the world." [But he changed His mind again and said,] "Behold, I will create the world, and whoever sins, it will not be difficult to rule over him." Therefore, when He intended to create the world with [the attribute of] justice he was unable to do so because of the deeds of the righteous, and when he intended to create it with the [attribute of] mercy he was unable because of the deeds of the wicked. What did He do? He combined the two, the attribute of justice and the attribute of mercy, and created the world, as it says, "On the day when the Lord God made earth and heaven" (Gen 2:4).[143]

God concludes to go ahead with Creation, exercising both stern judgment (in the case of the wicked) and mercy (in the case of the righteous).

In *Tanḥ. Wayyera'* 18 the same conflict is portrayed, but now with God's ministering angels arguing against the creation of man:[144]

> When the Holy One blessed be He determined to create the world, the ministering angels said to Him: "What is man (*'ĕnôš*) that You are mindful of him?" (Ps 8:5). The Holy One blessed be He responded to them: "You say 'what is man that You are mindful of him' since you have foreseen the Generation of Enosh. Rather, let me show you the honor of Abraham [of whom it may be rightly said,] 'that You are *mindful* of him,' as it says, 'and God was *mindful* of Abraham' (Gen 19:29). You say 'and mortal man that You have *taken note* of him' (Ps 8:5), [which refers to Sarah,] as it says, 'the Lord *took note* of Sarah' (Gen 21:1)."

Once again, the common noun *'ĕnôš* is understood to refer to the Generation of Enosh. Psalm 8:5 is understood to represent the angels' complaint: why create man seeing that the Generation of Enosh will come from him? God responds that He has another man in mind, that He is

---

variations in *Bere'šit Rabbati* (ed. Albeck) 37. A very similar tradition is found in *Gen. Rab.* 8.4, but there neither the Generation of Enosh nor any other generation is mentioned.

143 The prooftext is taken to mean that God as both *'ĕlōhîm* (justice) and YHWH (mercy) created the world. On God having exercised strict justice in his destruction of the generations of Enosh, the Flood, and the Separation, see *Tanḥ. B. Wayyera'* 10 (p. 91). In that passage it is Abraham who finally convinces God to improve His reputation by exercising his attribute of mercy in not destroying the innocent of Sodom along with the guilty. Cf. *Tanḥ. Ki Tiśśa'* 17; and Ps.-Rashi ad *Gen. Rab.* 49.9.

144 This compilation, like the previous one, is dated anywhere from the sixth to the ninth century. It is named for R. Tanḥuma, who lived ca. 400, and who may have laid its foundation.

being mindful not of the Generation of Enosh but of Abraham and Sarah.[145]

The contrast between the pre-Israelite generations and the Israelite patriarchs is expressed in *Exod. Rab.* 15.7 in still another way:[146]

> We find that in the beginning the Lord sought to establish the world, but did not find [a suitable foundation] until the patriarchs arose. This is likened to a king who desired to establish a state. He ordered that a suitable site be found on which to build the state. He was about to establish it [at one site] when the waters rose up from the depths and did not permit him to lay the foundation. Once again he was about to lay the foundation at another site, but the waters overturned it. Finally he came to a place where he found a large rock. He said, "Here I will establish the state on these rocks."[147] Similarly, in the beginning the world consisted only of water, and God desired to establish His world, but the wicked did not permit [Him to do so]. What is written of the Generation of Enosh? "Then men began to call [false gods] by the name of the Lord." The waters rose up and drowned them, as it says, "who maketh the Bear, Orion, and the Pleiades" etc. (Job 9:9).[148] And so too the Generation of the Flood was wicked. What is written of them? "Who say unto God 'depart from us'" (Job 22:17). And the waters rose up and did not permit Him to establish upon them a foundation, as it says, "whose foundation was poured as a stream" (Job 22:16). And it says, "On that day all the fountains of the great deep burst apart" (Gen 7:11). When the patriarchs came they were found worthy. The Holy One blessed be He said, "On these I will establish the world."

The identification of the early rebellious generations with floods is now given a new twist. These floods represent not so much God's punishing rod as the forces of primeval chaos that *continue* to obstruct His building plans. The early generations of universal mankind, because of their sinful behavior, cannot provide a foundation for the world in the midst

145 For other Rabbinic interpretations of the common noun *'ĕnôš* as referring to Enosh or his generation, see *b. Šabb.* 118b and *Lam. Rab.* Proem 24, treated above, and n. 193 below. While Ps 8:5 is frequently interpreted to refer to the angels' opposition to the creation of man, only here in *3 Enosh* 5.10 is it taken to refer to the Generation of Enosh. On the general motif of the angelic opposition to man see P. Schäfer, *Rivaltät zwischen Engeln und Menschen: Untersuchungen zur rabbinischen Engelvorstellung* (Studia Judaica 8; Berlin: Walter de Gruyter, 1975).

146 This collection has been dated as early as the seventh century and as late as the eleventh century.

147 Cf. Matt 16:18: "On this rock I will build my church, and the powers of death (literally, the gates of Hades) shall not prevail against it."

148 The prooftext makes no sense here. It is likely that originally Amos 5:8 was cited, "who made Pleiades and Orion," since this verse continues, "who summons the waters of the sea and pours them out upon the earth." This is what we find in the parallel in *YhM* ad Amos 5:8 (ed. Greenup) 47–48. David Luria (RaDaL, 1798–1855) and the MaHaRZU (in the Vilna edition) similarly correct our passage.

of the raging waters. Only the Israelite patriarchs provide such a foundation. Thus, contrary to the biblical account of Creation, it is not the creation of the dry land by divine fiat which provides the foundation for the establishment of the world, but the selection of Israel after a series of rebellious generations.

Finally, the association of the Generation of Enosh with the sea is drawn in one other way, now not with the waters of Creation but with the Reed Sea. According to *Tanḥ. B. Bešallaḥ* 12 (p. 60):

> "Then (*'āz*) sang Moses" etc. (Exod 15:1). What is meant by the word *'āz*? With *'āz* the Holy One blessed be He in the time of the Generation of Enosh made the dry land sea, as it says, "When men began to call [false gods] by the name of the Lord." And for us He made the sea dry land. [Therefore,] we sing his praises with *'āz*.

The word *'āz*, found in Gen 4:26 and Exod 15:1 links two corresponding events: the flooding of the sea in the days of Enosh and the parting of the sea during the Exodus from Egypt. The first is God's response to mankind's degeneration, the second Israel's response to God's beneficence.[149]

The postamoraic sources increasingly stress the rebellious, provocative nature of the idolatry of Enosh's contemporaries. In these accounts, the Generation of Enosh did not simply become lax in its worship, or innocently misdirect their veneration of God's name, but consciously transgressed a divine command. Thus, in *Pesiqta Rabbati* 42 we find:[150]

> "The Lord took note of (*pāqad*) Sarah" (Gen 21:1). There are many uses of the verb *pāqad*: There are those who are commanded (*nitpaqqēd*) but do not comply and there are those who are commanded and comply. I commanded Adam but he did not comply, [as it says,] "and from the tree of knowledge . . . you must not eat" (Gen 2:17), but he ate, [as it says,] "and you ate from the tree which I commanded you: 'you shall not eat of it'" (Gen 3:17). I commanded the angel of death [to punish Adam with death] and he complied. . . . I commanded the Generation of Enosh but they did not comply. Rather, they provoked my anger (*hik'îsûnî*), [as it says,] "then men began to call [false gods] by the name of the Lord." And I commanded the ocean and it complied, [as it says,] "who calls the waters of the sea to drown them" (Amos 5:8; 9:6).

149 The same tradition, in slightly different form, is found in *Exod. Rab.* 23.4 and *YhM* ad Amos 5:8 (ed. Greenup) 47–48. Cf. *Memar Marqah* 2.6, 7, 8 (above, chap. 2, nn. 18, 21), where the song at the Sea is similarly linked to Enosh's proclamation. It is striking that in our present passage (as in *Memar Marqah*) the word *'āz* is understood as part of what is actually said by God at the time of Enosh and by Israel at the Reed Sea. For a later mystical interpretation of the word *'āz* in Exod 15:1, see G. Scholem, *Jewish Gnosticism, Merkabah Mysticism, and Talmudic Tradition* (2nd. ed.; New York: Jewish Theological Seminary, 1965) 64 n. 20.

150 Ed. Friedmann, 178b.

This passage continues in like manner to describe the rebellions of the Generation of the Flood, the Generation of the Tower, and the Sodomites. In each case we find the refrain, "they were commanded but did not comply." The passage concludes with Abraham, who was commanded and *did* comply.

Once again, we find the Generation of Enosh as part of a chain of unrighteous, rebellious generations, which are contrasted with Abraham. The Generation of Enosh by its obstinacy provokes God's anger. What is not clear is in what regard the Generation of Enosh is commanded.[151] Since their failure to comply has to do with their idolatrous worship, we must assume that the midrash takes for granted that God had commanded them to worship only Him, or to worship Him in a prescribed manner.[152] Whereas rebellious man fails to comply with God's demands, the natural world readily complies. Thus, the familiar tradition of the rebellious Generation of Enosh and the punishing sea are easily made to fit the exegetical context of the present midrash.

The same interpretation of the sin of the Generation of Enosh as being a provocative transgression of God's decree is found in *Pesiqta Rabbati* supp. 1, now combined with some other familiar motifs:[153]

> [In the beginning] the waters of creation filled the whole world. What did the Holy One blessed be He do? He overcame them, as it were, and gathered them into the ocean. When the Generation of Enosh arose and provoked (*hikʿîsû*) Him with images (*ṣĕlāmîm*), [as it says,] "then men began to call [images] by the name of the Lord," the Holy One blessed be He said: "Let the very waters which I commanded and which fulfilled my decree come and punish the generation which neglected my decree (*šĕbbiṭṭēl gĕzērātî*)," [as it says,] "who calls the waters of the sea and spills them upon the face of the earth" (Amos 5:8; 9:6). At that moment the waters came as far as Acco and Jaffa. Similarly, the Generation of the Separation arose and provoked God's anger, and the Holy One blessed be He punished them with water, [as it says,] "the Lord scattered them from there" (Gen 11:9). "And he scattered (*wayyāpeṣ*) them" [means] that He flooded them (*hēṣîpām*) with water.[154] For it is

[151] While Adam is clearly commanded by God in Scripture, Enosh is not. Nor for that matter are the other rebellious generations, of whom our passage also says "they were commanded but did not comply." Perhaps we have here a literary device that should not be taken too literally. However, see the following note. The verb *pqd* was also problematic as used by Ben Sira in reference to Enosh. See above, chap. 1, n. 30. On Enosh's generation having been commanded, see below, n. 172.

[152] Is it perhaps implied that they transgressed the second commandment of the Decalogue? Some Rabbinic traditions include the prohibition against idolatry (worship of "other gods") in the moral commands for which pre-Noahite man was responsible. See Ginzberg, *Legends*, 5.92–93 n. 55.

[153] Ed. Friedmann, 193a–b.

[154] The interpretation is achieved by reversing the letters *ṣ* and *p*. The same interpretation is found in *Gen. Rab.* 38.10 (ed. Theodor-Albeck) 360, where Theodor's note should be consulted.

> written twice, "who calls upon the waters of the sea and spills them," once in the Generation of the Flood and once in the Generation of the Separation. And the people in amazement said: "Is such a thing possible, for the waters of the ocean to come as far as Acco and Jaffa?" And the Holy One blessed be He responded: "Fools! How can you be amazed concerning the Generation of the Separation, for did not the same fate befall the Generation of Enosh? What has been has been, and what will be has already been."[155]

Traditions attested separately in either collections are here combined with the more negative view of the sin of Enosh's generation as a rejection of God's decree, an act of insubordination: (a) The flood waters are the same as those gathered by God at Creation. Since they obeyed His will, they are fitting instruments for the punishment of the rebellious generations that did not. (b) The flood in the days of Enosh is the first of two such floods, the second being in the Generation of the Separation.[156] (c) The people of the Generation of Separation had forgotten what had happened to the Generation of Enosh; they failed to learn from their predecessors. (d) The idolatry of the Generation of Enosh involved images.[157]

In *Yalquṭ Šim'oni Bere'šit* 47[158] we find an unusual passage that incorporates several of the motifs we have already seen, but combining them in new ways, and that connects the rebellious activities of Enosh's

155 The passage continues with God stating that in the future He will once again make the sea dry, so that the returning exiles can pass through it, just as He did at the Sea of Reeds.

156 Here again, only two floods are mentioned, the flood in Noah's time being skipped, presumably since the latter is not considered a flood caused by the overflowing of the ocean. On the identification of the two floodings of Amos 5:8 and 9:5 with the Generation of Enosh and the Generation of the Separation, see above, nn. 108, 132. Other Rabbinic traditions that we have examined, however, fail to make this distinction, treating all three floods alike. According to the present passage, the waters reached as far as Jaffa and Acco during the first flood in Enosh's time as well as during the second flood in the time of the Generation of the Separation. Is it implied here that the waters subsided in between? If so, this would represent a departure from earlier traditions (*Gen. Rab.* 23.7 and parallels), according to which the waters reached Acco and Jaffa either during the first flood or the second.

157 The only previous tradition that specified images as the object of idolatrous worship was *Gen. Rab.* 23.6, in the statement attributed to R. Isaac. We noted in our treatment of that passage that the context might suggest images connected with the imperial cult. See above, n. 98. The present context does not permit a judgment as to what kinds of images are meant.

158 Ed. Salonika, 16a, where no source is given. The Oxford MS, however, gives the source as *49 Middot*, a work no longer extant, and of unknown date. Ps.-Rashi ad *Gen. Rab.* 23.3 cites this passage and gives its source as *Barayeta' deR. Yose 32 Middot*, but Theodor (p. 223) states there here too we should read *49 Middot*. On 49 *Middot*, see Eisenstein, *Ozar Midrashim*, 293. This passage appears out of the normal scriptural order as a supplement to the *Bere'šit* section. As a collection, *Yalquṭ Šim'oni* is dated to the early thirteenth century.

generation with those of the descendants of Cain. The latter appear to be included among Enosh's contemporaries.

> Enosh the son of Seth. In his days mankind began to provoke their creator through false worship. It was the third generation and they provoked Him with three transgressions, as it says, "He [Jabal] was the father of those who dwell in tents and [amidst] herds (*miqneh*)" (Gen 4:20): at first they provoked (*mĕqanneh*) Him in secret [in tents].[159] [A] They proceeded to provoke (*lĕhakʿîs*) Him publicly, raising their voices, as it says, "the father of all who play the lyre and the pipe" (Gen 4:21). [B] They proceeded to make images and called them by the name of their creator, as it says, "Then men began to call [images] by the name of the Lord." [C] They proceeded to defile themselves (*mittabbĕlîn*) with every kind of provocation (*kaʿas*), as it says, "Tubal-cain . . . and the sister of Tubal-cain," for they proceeded to defile themselves through prostitution, as it says, "They have committed an abomination (*tebel*)" (Lev 20:12). Three decrees were ordered against them in consequence of their provocations. One was that the ocean was split (*niqraʿ*) and flooded a third of the dry land.[160] One was that the whole world had been level and prairie (*ʿărābâ*)[161] but became mountains and barren rocks and [full of] holes, and in the future will revert to level, as it says, "The whole country shall become like the Arabah" (Zech 14:10), just as it had once been. One was that man's stature was reduced, as it says, "The lofty shall be made low" (Isa 10:33).

Once again, the provocative nature of the sins of Enosh's contemporaries is stressed. Now, however, the sins of the Generation of Enosh include not only the making of images and the calling of those images by God's name (cf. *Tgs. Neofiti* and *Ps.-Jonathan*) but boisterous and licentious behavior as well. The latter two are derived not from Gen 4:26 but from Gen 4:17–24, which describe the activities of Cain's progeny. This makes clear what has elsewhere been implied: the Generation of Enosh is a historical age rather than a genealogical line. Even though the activities of Cain's descendants are described in the Bible prior to the

159 Clearly, we have a play (revocalization) on the word *miqneh*. The word *miqneh* is syntactically problematic within the biblical text: "who dwell in tents and herds." Most translators, both modern and ancient, have had to provide another word to make sense of it. The ancient versions add such words as "who own, keep, or raise." The Rabbinic pun also appears in *Gen. Rab.* 23.3. See Theodor's note ad loc. See also Rashi ad Gen 4:21. David Luria (ad *Gen. Rab.* 23.6) provides a similar interpretation of *qinṭôrîn* (centaurs) and Kenan: "They provoked (*mĕqannîn*) God through their idolatry."

160 The expression "split" with respect to this flood is unusual. It is more commonly used to describe the splitting of the Reed Sea so as to create a path of dry land. We saw the splitting of the Reed Sea associated with the flood in Enosh's time in *Tanḥ. B. Bešallaḥ* 12. See above, n. 149.

161 *ʿărābâ* would usually be translated "desert," but here the association is clearly positive, especially in light of what follows. The term applies not only to the arid desert, but to the fertile regions of the Jordan valley as well. See BDB 787a–b.

announcement of Enosh's birth, chronologically they are seen to fall in the time period of Enosh's contemporaries.

The emphasis on the number three with respect to the Generation of Enosh is unique to this passage: third generation, three sins, three punishments. Perhaps this implies that there was nothing arbitrary in what happened. In earlier passages, the fact that the Generation of Enosh committed one sin and received four punishments may have appeared unfair. Our present passage, by expanding the list of sins of the Generation of Enosh, may wish to redress such an imbalance. Of the three punishments, two have appeared already in *Gen. Rab.* 23.6, while the third, the shortening of man's stature, is usually associated with Adam's expulsion from Eden, but is here delayed until Enosh's time.[162] The picture that emerges, then, is one of widespread and public human depravity, punished with radical, physical changes in man and earth.

The next two passages are unusual in that they actually describe the idolatrous activity of the Generation of Enosh.

In *3 Enoch* (*Seper Hekalot*) 5.3–13[163] it is related that even after Adam and Eve were expelled from Paradise, they were able to sit by the gate of the Garden to bask in the radiant splendor of the Shekinah ("divine indwelling"):

162 See above, n. 75.

163 For the preferred text, see *BhM* 5.172–73. For another, slightly expansive version of the text, see *3 Enoch or the Hebrew Book of Enoch* (ed. and trans. H. Odeberg; Cambridge, 1928; reprint with prolegomenon by J. C. Greenfield, New York: Ktav, 1973) 8–11 (Hebrew), 14–18 (English). The numbering used here follows Odeberg's edition. According to G. Scholem (*Jewish Gnosticism, Merkabah Mysticism, and Talmudic Tradition* [2nd ed.; New York: Jewish Theological Seminary, 1965] 7 n. 19), Jellinek's edition is better than Odeberg's, since the latter relied on a "particularly bad manuscript." There is as yet no consensus concerning the dating of this work. While Odeberg claims third century authorship, Scholem argues for the fifth or sixth century. Everyone agrees that there is old (pre-200) material incorporated in the present work, but no systematic attempt has been made to isolate such traditions. See Scholem, *Jewish Gnosticism*, 7 n. 9; idem, *Major Trends in Jewish Mysticism* (New York: Schocken, 1954) 45, 357–58; J. Charlesworth, *The Pseudepigrapha and Modern Research* (Missoula, Mont.: Scholars Press, 1976) 106–7 (with bibliography); P. S. Alexander, "The Historical Setting of the Hebrew Book of Enoch," *JJS* 28 (1977) 156–80 (arguing for a *terminus ad quem* of 850 for chaps. 3–15 and a Babylonian provenance); I. Gruenwald, *Apocalyptic and Merkavah Mysticism* (AGJU 14; Leiden: E. J. Brill, 1980) 191–208 (suggesting a sixth-century date). The extent of interdependence between the Hekhalot and midrashic writings is also not clear. See I. Gruenwald, "Yannai and Hekhaloth Literature" (Hebrew), *Tarbiz* 36 (1967) 257–77; E. Urbach, "The Traditions about Merkabah Mysticism in the Tannaitic Period" (Hebrew), in *Studies in Mysticism and Religion Presented to G. Scholem* (Jerusalem: Magnes, 1967) 11 n. 41; G. Scholem, *Kabbalah* (New York: Quadrangle, 1974) 14–22. The same tradition is found in *YR* ad Gen 4:26 (ed. Warsaw) 105, from the Kabbalistic commentary *Seper ṣiyyoni* by Menaḥem Ziyyoni b. Meir (fifteenth century).

[A] For whoever beheld the radiance of the Shekinah flies and gnats did not alight upon him, and he did not become ill (*ḥôleh*), nor were any manner of *mazzîqîm* able to injure (*lĕhazzîq*) him. Furthermore, angels (*mal'ākîm*) did not have power over him . . . And everyone beheld the radiant appearance of His Shekinah and did not suffer injury (*'ēnân nizzôqîn*), until the people of the Generation of Enosh came along.

[B] They went from one end of the world to the other, and each one brought silver, gold, precious stones, and pearls, mountainlike heaps of them. And they made idols out of them throughout the world. The size of each idol was one thousand parasangs. And they brought down the sun, the moon, planets, and constellations, and placed them before the idols on their right hand and on their left, to attend them even as they used to attend the Holy One blessed be He, as it is written, "And all the host of heaven was standing by Him, on His right hand and on His left" (1 Kgs 22:19). But how did they have the power with which to bring them down and to make use of them? Uzza and Azza'el taught them sorceries, whereby they brought them down and made use of them, for had it not been so, they would have been unable to bring them down.

[C] At that time the ministering angels brought charges before the Holy One blessed be He saying: "Master of the universe, what do you see in man? 'What is man (*'ĕnôš*) that you are mindful of him?'" (Ps 8:5) 'What is *'ādām*' is not written here, but 'what is *'ĕnôš*,' for he is the head (*rō'š*) of the idol worshippers. Why have you left the highest of the high heavens . . . and come to dwell among mankind who worship idols and equate you to the idols? [Thereupon,] the Holy One blessed be He removed his Shekinah from their midst.

Section A, like *Gen. Rab.* 23.6, associates major changes in the human condition with Enosh's time. No longer does man bask in the protective divine light, no longer is he invulnerable to insects, sickness, malevolent angels, or other menaces (*mazzîqîm*).[164] The tracing of the origin of illness to Enosh's generation is unique to this passage, and could reflect a play on *hûḥal* as if from the root *ḥly* ("to be weak or sick"), or on Enosh's name, meaning "weak."[165] As in earlier passages, such curses

164 Are the *mazzîqîm* here natural pests (with flies and gnats) or supernatural agents (with angels)? Or a third possibility, wild animals? It seems most likely that since the verb *nzq* is used here to refer to injury in general, *mazzîqîm* refer to menacing beings in general, whether natural or supernatural. Regarding flies and gnats (*zĕbûbîn wĕyattûšîn*), the Islamic historial 'al-Ṭabari (839–923), in his *Annales* (ed. de Goeje) 1.1123, preserves the following tradition in the name of Hishām b. Muhammed al-Kalbī (737–821): "The Arabs used to say: Flies have scratched (*ḫdš 'l-ḫdwš*) only since the birth of our father Anush [Enosh]." For *ḫdwš* as a biting or lacerating fly, see *Lisān 'al-'Arab* (Bulaq, 1863–91) 8.181. For the *yattûš* as one of God's punishing agents, see the story of Titus' death in *Lev. Rab.* 22.3 (ed. Margulies) 499–502; *ARNB* 7 (ed. Schechter) 21; and parallels.

165 We noted above, n. 66, that in *Gen. Rab.* 23.6 the phrase *ḥwlym lmzyqym* could be vocalized as *ḥôlîm lĕmazzîqîm* ("sick or weak with respect to menacing creatures"). It is

are connected not with Adam's expulsion from Eden, as might be expected, but with the Generation of Enosh.[166]

In section B the sin of Enosh's contemporaries (and perhaps of Enosh himself[167]) is clearly described as the making and worship of material idols, placed in God's stead. Unique to this passage is the tradition that the fallen angels Uzza and Azza'el taught the Generation of Enosh the magical skills with which to bring down the heavenly bodies so as to serve their idols.[168] The idolatry of the Generation of Enosh is now viewed not as the

---

unclear whether our present passage views sickness as the product of flies or *mazzîqîm*, or as a separate pestilence. Jewish traditions vary regarding the beginnings of illness. *Vita Adae et Evae* 30–31 (*APOT* 2.141) and *Apocalypsis Mosis* 5 (*APOT* 2.141–42) describe Adam as experiencing sickness for the first time before his death. Similarly, *2 Bar.* 56.6 says that diseases began with Adam's sin. In Rabbinic traditions, however, sickness is not mentioned as one of the punishments suffered by the earliest generations. According to L. Ginzberg (*Legends*, 5.118–19), sickness was not considered to be a punishment distinct from death. Interestingly, Rabbinic tradition reports Jacob to have been the first to suffer illness, but in his case he *requests* it as a warning of death and his request is granted as a *reward*. See *Gen. Rab.* 65.9 (ed. Theodor-Albeck) 717–18; Ginzberg, *Legends*, 2.131; 5.364 n. 357. Note that according to *3 Enoch* 3.5 the Shekinah's splendor protects from illness.

166 Although Adam and Eve are cast out of the Garden of Eden they continue to enjoy some of its benefits. A very similar treatment is found in some Christian sources, especially Syriac ones. These describe the Sethites as having lived in close proximity to Paradise, or as Ephraem puts it (*Commentary to Genesis* [CSCO 152.57.14–15]), "in the land beside the fence of Paradise." For a most blissful account of life in Paradise's "suburb," see *The Book of Adam and Eve* 2.11 (trans. Malan) 118–19; *The Cave of Treasures* (trans. Budge) 74–75. In these accounts the first generations of Sethites moved from the top of the paradisaical mountain to its side, but still remained far above the Cainites in the plain below. They are depicted as having had neither to work nor to worry, a very different picture than one would expect from Gen 3:17–19.

167 Note that this source speaks of Enosh as the "head" of the idolaters. See above, n. 141.

168 The names of these angels vary somewhat. Uzza is probably the same as Azza, while Azza'el is the same as Azzi'el and Azazel. Ginzberg, *Legends*, 5.152–53. The association of the fall of these angels with the Generation of Enosh is also found in *YS Bere'šit* 44 (perhaps from *Midrash Abkir*) according to the Oxford MS, but not according to the Salonika printing, where we find instead the Generation of the Flood. In *Jeraḥmeel* 25.1 (trans. Gaster) 52, the angels Shemḥazay and Azza'el came to earth "when the Generation of Enosh arose and worshipped idols, and when the Generation of the Flood arose and went astray." Similarly, *PRE* 7 (ed. Warsaw) 16b states that the angels fell in "the days of the Generation of Enosh." See David Luria's note 32 ad loc., where he suggests that the association of the fallen angels with the Generation of Enosh derives from Gen 6:4: "The Nephilim were on earth in those days, and also after that when the sons of God cohabited with the daughters of men." Thus, "in those days" could be understood to refer to an earlier time when the Nephilim had already been on earth. This is precisely now Rashi interprets these words: "'In those days.' In the days of the Generation of Enosh." Rashi's view is also cited by the RaMBaN ad Gen 6:4. Rashi likewise identifies the fallen angels with the "days of the Generation of Enosh" in his comments to Num 13:33 and *b. Nid.* 61a. Note, however, that according to C. M. Horowitz's posthumously published draft of a critical edition of *PRE* (Jerusalem: Makor, 1972), the words "in the days of Enosh" are omitted in MS Parma De Rossi 563. Thus, apart from our present text, it is impossible

perhaps innocent application of God's name and honors to his creations, but as a deliberate and complete rejection of God.[169]

Section C is similar to the tradition of angelic protest that we saw in *Tanḥ. Wayyera'* 18. There the protest is against the creation of man, here it is against the continued dwelling of God's presence among idolatrous mankind in the time of Enosh. The removal of the Shekinah from man's midst is now identified solely with the Generation of Enosh.[170] Thus, the radical nature of man's abandonment of God corresponds to a similarly radical abandonment of man by God in Enosh's days.

---

convincingly to date the association of the fall of the angels with the Generation of Enosh any earlier than Rashi (1040–1105). The fall of these angels must have originally been associated with the Generation of the Flood, as it is in *1 Enoch* 6–11, and *Jub.* 5:1–9, since this tradition ultimately derives from the "sons of God" and "Nephilim" of Gen 6:1–4. Cf. 4Q*180–181*. The identification with the Generation of Enosh would appear to be secondary. Note that in the midrash on Shemḥazay and Azza'el the angels request to go down to earth in order to test man. They remind God that they warned Him of man's worthlessness at the time of Creation, saying, "what is man (*'ĕnôš*) that You are mindful of him?" It may be that this word *'ĕnôš* enabled later transmitters of the story to associate it with the times of the Generation of Enosh. See above, n. 145. For the Shemḥazay Midrash see *Bere'šit Rabbati* (ed. Albeck) 29–31, especially as cited in Raymundi Martini, *Pugio fidei adversus Mauros et Judaeos* (Leipzig, 1687) 937–38; *AgBer.* (ed. Buber intro.) 38–39; *YS Bere'šit* 44; *Jeraḥmeel* 25 (trans. Gaster) 52–54; Jellinek, *BhM*, 4.127–28; as well as other sources cited by Ginzberg, *Legends*, 5.152–53 n. 56; 169–71 n. 10; and H. Schwarzbaum in his prolegomenon to the reissue of Gaster's translation of *Jeraḥmeel* (New York: Ktav, 1971) 37–38. See as well J. T. Milik, *The Books of Enoch: Aramaic Fragments of Qumran Cave 4* (Oxford: Clarendon, 1976) 321–39, where the various versions of the story are presented and discussed, especially in relation to the so-called "Book of Giants." P. Schäfer ("Die Götzendienst des Enosch," 142–47) argues that the tradition of the fall of the angels in Enosh's time is pre-Rabbinic, and is reflected already in *Mek. Baḥodeš* 6 (understood as tracing the beginnings of theophoric names to Enosh's time). Since I have shown the latter to be a doubtful interpretation (see above, n. 49), the former would also seem to be unlikely, especially considering the otherwise late collections in which such an association is made.

The fallen angels similarly bring down the sun and moon for magical purposes in *MhG* ad Gen 6:5 (ed. Margulies) 141; and in *Tanḥ. Bere'šit* 12. On idolaters being able to control celestial bodies see *Sifre Deut.* 84 (ed. Finkelstein) 148, with S. Lieberman's review in *Kiryat Sefer* 14 (1937–38) 328–29.

169 Thus, in *Gen. Rab.* 23.6, discussed above, the bowing to images appears as an understandable error. See above, n. 95, as well as n. 53. Similarly, in *Jeraḥmeel* 23.6–7 (trans. Gaster) 49–50, Enosh's making of a "golem" and the people's worship of it is described as an innocent mistake. See H. Schwarzbaum's prolegomenon to *Jeraḥmeel*, pp. 35–36; and G. Scholem, *On the Kabbalah and its Symbolism* (trans. R. Manheim; New York: Schocken, 1965) 181 for another version of this story.

170 We saw that in *Gen. Rab.* 19.7 and parallels the Shekinah departs in stages, the third one being in Enosh's time. See above, nn. 121–22. Odeberg, in his notes to our text (p. 13), suggests that this account of the Shekinah's removal is intended to provide the occasion for Enoch's translation to heaven. *Tanḥ. B. Bemidbar* 32 (p. 24) states that God saved Enoch from the fate of the Generation of Enosh. Cf. *Bere'šit Rabbati* (ed. Albeck) 27.7–10, where it is unclear during which wicked generation God's presence and Enoch departed. *Seper Hekhalot* (*3 Enoch*) 4.3 places Enoch's removal during the Generation of the Flood.

A similar protest against God's dwelling among Enosh's contemporaries, now not from the angels, but from God's own attribute of justice, is found in *Bere'šit Rabbati*, but with some significant variations:[171]

> At the time when the Generation of Enosh sinned, the attribute of justice arose and said: "Master of the World, of what benefit is it to you that you have come down from your first palace in which you used to reside to dwell amongst mankind? For You have commanded him a command which is easy to fulfill (*miṣwâ qallâ*) and yet he transgressed it.[172] And, as if that were not enough, they have abandoned You to worship other gods (*'elōhîm 'ăḥērîm*)." What did the people of that generation do? They arose and collected all the silver and gold and pearls and precious stones which were in the world and made a larger tower[173] and erected idols on it and bowed and offered incense to it. And they used insolent and strong language toward heaven, as it says, "They said to God, 'Depart from us'" (Job 21:14).[174] When He saw their deeds and heard their words, he said to the Throne of Glory: "Carry me to the uppermost, most secret chambers, and I will ascend and dwell there. And I will not look upon the deeds of my sons who have abandoned me by bowing before the works of their hands." And so He spoke until the ministering angels arose and brought to His attention the love of Abraham, Isaac, and Jacob, and His mind was set at ease.

A number of motifs are familiar here, but they are combined in a new way. God regrets not so much having created mankind, but having come to dwell among them.[175] This is similar to what we observed in

[171] *Midraš bere'šit rabbati* (ed. Ch. Albeck; Jerusalem: Mekize Nirdamim, 1940) 41. This source appears to contain extracts from a larger work by R. Moses Haddaršan (first half eleventh century). See Albeck's introduction to his edition. The specific tradition cited here appears nowhere else.

[172] It is unclear whether "he" refers to Adam, Enosh, or man in general. The "light" command that was transgressed most likely refers to God's command of Adam not to eat from the Tree of Knowledge. The sin of the Generation of Enosh is additional and perhaps viewed as more serious. See above, n. 151.

[173] *'rgṭwrn*. Albeck's note to line 27 says that this is a "large tower of silver." He derives the word from Greek, understanding *'rg* as "silver" (*argos, argyros*) and *ṭwrn* as tower (*tyrsis*). I have been unable to find any other examples of this word in Rabbinic literature. It is not listed in the Hebrew lexicons, including S. Krauss, *Griechische und lateinische Lehnwörter im Talmud, Midrasch und Targum* (2 vols.; Berlin: Calvary, 1898–99). If Albeck's explanation is correct, it would appear that according to this source, the Generation of Enosh was involved in a collective idolatrous project, like that of the Generation of the Separation. Contrast *ShY* (ed. Goldschmidt) 7, where we find: "And in those days men made images of copper and iron, wood and stone, and they bowed down to them and worshipped them. And each man made his *own* god and bowed down to it."

[174] The use of Job 21:14 is somewhat unusual, since that verse, as we have seen, is usually applied to the Generation of the Flood.

[175] On God's having considered destroying the world because of the deeds of the rebellious generations, including that of Enosh, see *Lev. Rab.* 23.3, treated above. On the

our previous text, in which the Shekinah (not God himself) leaves earth and returns to heaven in response to the idolatry of the Generation of Enosh. Again, we have a rare *description* of the idolatry of the Generation of Enosh, as an intentional and complete rejection of God.[176] But these motifs are combined now with an earlier one: the contrast of the sins of the Generation of Enosh (like those of the other rebellious generations) with the virtues of the Israelite patriarchs.[177] It is in view of the patriarchs that God decides *not* to abandon His creation in response to the infidelity of the Generation of Enosh. Curiously, it is now the ministering angels who convince God not to withdraw from mankind's midst. Presumably, had it not been for the Israelite patriarchs, God would have abandoned his Creation in Enosh's time.

Finally, we turn to three passages, found in early medieval collections, that attempt to derive the tradition of the idolatry of the Generation of Enosh from the words of Gen 4:26.

In *Bere'šit Rabbati* we find:[178]

> "And he begot Enosh" (Gen 5:6). Concerning that which Scripture says, "Come and see what the Lord has done, how he has wrought desolation (*šammôt*) on the earth" (Ps 46:9), do not read "desolation" (*šammôt*), but "names" (*šēmôt*), for by means of their names we can learn of their deeds.[179] Therefore, Enosh because of what befell him (*mě'ôrā'ô*) was called Enosh, since Enosh can only be an expression of calamity (*šeber*). And thus it says, "My wound is incurable (*'ănûšâ*)" (Jer 15:18).

For the rabbis, as for ancient exegetes in general as well as for the Bible itself, proper names invite "etymologies." Psalm 46:9 is interpreted to mean that personal names, at least in the Bible, are Godgiven, having revelatory (or oracular) significance. Here the name Enosh is given as an example of the Rabbinic principle that people's names reflect their deeds or characters. It is remarkable, however, that Enosh's name, so frequently interpreted in extra-Rabbinic Jewish as well as non-Jewish sources, going back as far as Philo and perhaps even to Ben Sira,[180] is not interpreted in Rabbinic sources until the present one, deriving from an eleventh-century collection. And here the sense is unclear: does Enosh's name, interpreted negatively, refer to his deeds or to the events of his time, thereby referring to the deeds of his contemporaries?[181] The word *šeber*, literally meaning

---

attribute of justice in relation to the rebellious generations, see *PR* 40; *Tahṇ. B. Wayyera'* 10; above, n. 143.

176 Cf. above, n. 169.

177 Cf. *Gen. Rab.* 2.3; 19.7; *Exod. Rab.* 15.7; *PR* 40; *Tanḥ. Wayyera'* 18; all treated above.

178 Ed. Albeck, 31 and 56.

179 Cf. *b. Ber.* 7b.

180 See above, chap. 1, n. 28.

181 While names are usually interpreted to reveal something about the person named,

"break or fracture," probably has the sense here of "destruction or calamity,"[182] referring either to the idolatrous activity of Enosh and/or his generation, or more likely to their consequent punishment by flooding.

In *Midraš haggadol* ad Gen 4:26 a negative interpretation of Enosh's name is linked to an interpretation of the verb *hûḥal*:[183]

> "And to Seth, in turn, a son was born, and he called him Enosh." For he was weak-minded (*da'ătô 'ănûšâ*) and his counsel was ill-advised (*nik'ârâ*) as was that of his contemporaries. For they introduced idolatry into the world, as it says, "Then men began to call [false gods] by the name of the Lord." The calling (*qĕrî'â*) on the name of the Lord was profaned (*nitḥallĕlâ*) for the sake of idolatry.

Thus, the common Rabbinic interpretation of Gen 4:26 is derived from the scriptural words in two ways: (a) The name Enosh is related to the verb *'nš*, meaning "to be weak." The implication is that Enosh *and* his generation succumbed to false worship out of weakness.[184] (b) The verb *hûḥal* is interpreted as if it meant "was profaned." The divine worship (calling on the name of the Lord) was profaned once God's name was applied to false gods.[185]

---

they can also refer to events in the life of the parent or in the lifetime of the child. See, for example, Gen 10:25: "The name of the first was Peleg, for in his days the earth was divided (*niplĕgâ*)," referring to the punishment of the generation of the Tower of Babel. Additional examples of this phenomenon will be given in chapter five. Thus, the word *mĕ'ôrā'ô* could refer to Enosh's own deeds (*ma'ăśîm* of the preceding sentence in the text), or to an event in his lifetime. On this word and its use in conjunction with naming, see Jastrow, *Dictionary*, 722; Levy, *Wörterbuch*, 3.8; Ben Yehudah, *Thesaurus*, 2758–59; *Sifre Deut.* 1 (ed. Finkelstein) 7; *Gen. Rab.* 37.7; 94.8 (ed. Theodor-Albeck) 347, 1179; *Exod. Rab.* 1.33.

182 See Jastrow, *Dictionary*, 1517–18; and note Jer 30:12.

183 Ed. Margulies, 128. This Yemenite compilation, drawing on several lost midrashim, dates most likely from the early fourteenth century, although it contains some significantly earlier extracts. Since this collection does not indicate its sources, passages like the present one that lack extant parallels are difficult to date.

184 See also *YR* ad Gen 4:26: "From Enosh on laxity (*ripyôn*) and weakness (*ḥallāš*) entered the world." Similarly the RaMBaN in his commentary to Gen 6:4 (ed. Chavel, 49) states: "Weakness (*ḥûlšâ*) and laxity (*ripyôn*) began to come upon men."

185 See also the Arabic translation of Saadia Gaon (882–942): "Then the calling on the name of the Lord was profaned (*tbdlt*)," in *Version arabe du Pentateuque de R. Saadia ben Iosef al-Fayyoumi* (ed. J. Derenbourg; Paris: E. Leroux, 1893) 8; and *Peruše Rabbenu Sa'adya Ga'on 'al hattora* (ed. J. Kafiḥ; Jerusalem: Mossad Harav Kook, 1963) 18. The verb *bdl* in the fifth form can mean "was neglected" or "put to common use." See E. Lane, *An Arabic-English Lexicon* (8 vols.; London, 1863–93) 1.174; Ibn Manzur, *Lisān al-'Arab* (20 vols. in 10; Bulaq, 1883–91) 13.53. Thus, Saadia's translation may interpret the verb *hûḥal* as "was profaned" or "was neglected." The latter would be similar to *Tg. Onqelos*. Kafiḥ (ibid., 18 n. 13) cites an interpretation of *uncertain* attribution to Saadia: "For they profaned (*ḥillĕlû*) the prayer in the Lord's name and ceased to pray; for *hûḥal* is an expression of *ḥôl* and *ḥûllîn* ('profaning')." The interpretation of *hûḥal* as "was profaned" is cited in RaDaQ (1160–1236) and refuted by Ibn Ezra (1089–1164) in their commentaries to Gen 4:26. See below, chap. 5, nn. 15–16.

Similarly, in *Midraš ʾaggada* ad Gen 4:26 we find the name Enosh and the verb *hûḥal* interpreted, the latter in two ways:[186]

> Enosh. Having the sense, "My wound is incurable (*ʾănûšâ*)" (Jer 15:18). For in his days the name of the Lord was profaned (*naʿăśeh mĕḥullāl*). For they performed idolatry and desisted (*mānĕʿû*) from calling on the name of the Lord. Another interpretation of *hûḥal*: it was nullified (*hitbaṭṭēl*), as in, "He shall not break (*yaḥēl*) his pledge" (Num 30:3), whose targum is, "He shall not annul (*yĕbaṭṭêl*)."

The association of the name Enosh with Jer 15:18 suggests that it is understood to derive from the verb *ʾnš*, meaning "to be sick": Enosh and/or his Generation were sickly.[187] And what was sickly about their behavior? They profaned God's name through alien worship.[188] Thus, as in our previous passage, both halves of Gen 4:26 are interpreted by means of puns in such a way that the second half provides an explanation of the first. What follows appears to be a paraphrase of *Tg. Onqelos* back into Hebrew: "They desisted from calling on the name of the Lord."[189] This is simply another way of saying that they turned to the worship of false gods. Finally, the verb *hûḥal* is interpreted in light of the verb *ḥll* as used in Num 30:3. If the *hiphʿil* of *ḥll*, as rendered by *Tg. Onqelos*, means "annul," then the *hophʿal* can mean "was annulled." This is almost identical to what we found in *PR* supp. chap. 1, treated above: "the generation which annulled (or neglected, *biṭṭēl*) My decree." Thus, we find in this passage two interpretations of the verb *hûḥal*: was profaned and was annulled (made void). In either case the sin of the Generation of Enosh remains the same, but one can choose different ways of deriving it from Scripture.

[186] Ed. Buber, 22. This commentary, which covers the Pentateuch, could not date earlier than the twelfth century since it is based on the work of Moses Haddaršan, and draws upon Rashi and *Midraš leqaḥ ṭob*.

[187] Cf. *AgBer*. Oxford MS (ed. Buber) intro., 37: "And why was he called Enosh? Because he was born in a sick generation (*dôr ʾānûš*)." The name Enosh and the adjective *ʾānûš* are identical when unvocalized. Thus, "Generation of Enosh" could be understood as "sick generation." We earlier (*Gen. Rab.* 38.5) saw the Generation of Enosh associated with incurability in interpretation of Jer 51:9. But in that context there did not seem to have been expressed a pun on Enosh's name.

[188] Cf. *MA*'s interpretation of the verb *hēḥēl* of Gen 6:1 (p. 23): *naʿăśeh ḥûllîn* ("became profane").

[189] In general, *MA* frequently cites *Tg. Onqelos*. See Buber's introduction, p. 5. Note the citation of *Tg. Onqelos* that follows. In the interpretation attributed to Saadia Gaon (see above, n. 185), we find: "They profaned the prayer in the Lord's name and ceased to pray (*ḥādĕlû millĕhitpallēl*)."

E. *Piyyuṭ*

As this survey of Rabbinic interpretations of Enosh and his generation began with the concise statements of the targumim, it will now conclude with two brief examples from the literature of *piyyuṭ* (liturgical poetry), which similarly summarize midrashic tradition and preserve that tradition in the life of the synagogue.

The passages are from introductions to the Avodah Service of Yom Kippur Musaf. While the Avodah Service describes in detail the atonement ritual formerly performed by the High Priest in the Holy of Holies on the Day of Atonement, the introductions provide historical synopses of the background to the day's ritual, beginning with Creation, continuing with the early rebellious generations, the Flood, God's choosing of Israel through the righteous patriarchs, and the appointment of the tribe of Levi to minister in the sanctuary.[190]

The *piyyuṭ 'Attâ kônantâ 'ôlām bĕrōb ḥesed* ("You established the world with mercy"), attributed to Jose ben Jose, contains one of the earliest and most influential versions of the introduction to the Avodah Service, and is the first to include mention of the Generation of Enosh and its punishment. It is preserved in the Piedmont and Yemenite rites.[191] On our subject it says:

להכעיסך, אל החל דור אנוש להמיר כבודך ולקרוא בשם אליל
לים חול שמת חק לא יעבור קראתו לעבדם תמור קראו בשם

> To provoke Your anger, God, the Generation of Enosh began to exchange your honor [for that of other "gods"], to invoke by [Your] name a false god.[192]

190 On the Avodah Service and its introductions see *Maḥzor layyamim hannora'im* (ed. D. Goldschmidt; 2 vols.; Jerusalem: Koren, 1970) 2.18–25; *Piyyute Yose ben Yose* (ed. A. Mirsky; Jerusalem: Bialik Institute, 1977) 23–29; J. Elbogen, *Studien zur Geschichte des jüdischen Gottesdienstes* (Berlin: Mayer and Müller, 1907) 49–190. Elbogen lists some thirty different versions, to which a few more can now be added. On the function of the introductions to the Avodah Service see Mirsky 26–27, and below.

191 *Piyyute Yose ben Yose* (ed. A. Mirsky) 178.145–46; *Maḥzor* (ed. Goldschmidt) 2.468; Elbogen, *Studien*, 81; I. Davidson, *Thesaurus of Medieval Hebrew Poetry* (4 vols.; New York, 1924–33; reprint New York: KTAV, 1970) 1.399 no. 8815. Jose ben Jose is generally dated in the fifth-sixth centuries, although some place him later and others as early as the fourth century. See Mirsky, 11–13. Two other versions of the Avodah introduction are attributed to Jose ben Jose and both contain similar mentions of the Generation of Enosh, its sin, and its punishment: (a) *'Azkîr gĕbûrôt*, in Mirsky, 135–36; Elbogen, *Studien*, 78–79; Davidson, *Thesaurus*, 1.105 no. 2230; and *Siddur R. Saadja Gaon* (ed. I. Davidson, S. Assaf, & B. I. Joel; Jerusalem: *Meqiṣe nirdamim*, 1963) 267. (b) *'Ăsappēr gĕdôlôt*, in Mirsky, 201; Elbogen, *Studien*, 81, 118; Davidson, *Thesaurus*, 1.316 no. 6965.

192 Or, "to invoke the name of a false god." *'Azkir geburot* has, להמיר בשם אליל שם אל (var: אתר) עולם ("to exchange the name of a false god with the name of the [eternal] God of the universe"). *'Asapper gedolot* has, זרע דור שלישי לצלם הוחל לקרוא בשם ("The seed of the third generation began to invoke an image by [God's] name").

> You [at first] established the sand for the sea as a boundary not to be crossed, [but now] you called it [the sea] to destroy them, in return for their having called [false gods] with the name [of God].[193]

The first half of this couplet states the sin of the Generation of Enosh, while the second tells of their punishment, concluding that this punishment was appropriate to their sin. Much of the language is reminiscent of the midrashim. The sin of the Generation of Enosh is an act of rebellion, provoking God to anger.[194] The passive verb *hûḥal* is transposed to the active, with the Generation of Enosh as its subject. Their sin is one of transferring what is due to God to false gods. The phrase לקרוא בשם אליל could either mean that they invoked false gods by name, i.e., worshiped them, or called false gods by God's name.[195] The sea is God's instrument of punishment, overflowing the boundaries set by Him at Creation. This passage ends with the familiar motif of "measure for measure": God *calls* upon the sea to punish those who *called* upon false gods. Thus, the midrashic elements are all familiar, being adapted slightly to poetic form.

A second version of the introduction to the Avodah Service begins *'Ammîṣ kōaḥ* ("You are strong in power"), is attributed to R. Meshullam b. Kolonymus of the tenth century, and is preserved in the Ashkenazi rite. Of the Generation of Enosh, although not by name, it says:

חלו שלישים קרוא בשמך לסמל
חיל נוזלים קראת ושטפום ואבדו

> When the third generation began to call upon idols by Your name,
> You called forth the mighty flowing waters to inundate them so they perished.[196]

193 Or, "in return for their having invoked the name [of a false god]." That God *called* on the mighty waters to burst through their boundaries is also found in *'Azkir geburot* and *'Asapper gedolot*. *'Azkir geburot* adds that the "memorial of human hope" (*zēker tiqwat 'ĕnôš*, Job 14:19, but here taken to allude to Enosh) is destroyed. Cf. *Tanḥ. Noaḥ* 18.

194 We saw the verb *hik'is* used with respect to the Generation of Enosh's rebellion in several postamoraic sources, which unlike the tannaitic sources place greater emphasis on intentional provocativeness of their idolatry. *'Azkir geburot* uses the verb *zmm* ("to conspire") to describe their activity and refers to them as the "generation of perverseness" (*dôr 'ăqalqallôt*).

195 We found both interpretations in the Palestinian targumim and in *Mek. Baḥodeš* 6. See above, nn. 15, 52. The final phrase *qr'w bšm* is similarly ambiguous.

196 *Maḥzor layyamim hannora'im* (ed. Goldschmidt) 2.437; Elbogen, *Studien*, 85–86; Davidson, *Thesaurus*, 1.260 no. 5703. Another version, also ascribed to Meshullam, is found in the Avodah Service beginning *'Ăśôḥēaḥ niplĕ'ôtekā*, in *Maḥzor* (ed. Goldschmidt) 450; Elbogen, *Studien*, 86–87, 126–31; Davidson, *Thesaurus*, 1.355–56 no. 7844. It states, "The scoundrels (*pārîṣê*) of the third [generation] began to act faithlessly, giving rule to idols and casting off the [divine] yoke." On R. Meshullam b. Kolonymus, see I. Elbogen, *Hattepilla beyiśra'el behitpatteḥutah hahisṭorit* (Tel-Aviv: Dvir, 1972) 246.

The word *šālîšîm* is generally understood here to refer to the third generation (of Enosh), whose sin was to *call* graven images by God's name. God in response *called* on the waters to destroy them.

What is interesting in both of these examples is the relative extent to which the rebelliousness of the pre-Israelite generations is stressed in presenting the pre-Levitic history, and the inclusion in both cases of the Generation of Enosh. The rejection of God by these early generations sets the stage for God's establishing of a covenant with Abraham, the maintenance of which is the work of Aaron's descendents, the chosen among the chosen, whose greatest moment is the atonement rite of Yom Kippur, performed by the High Priest in the Holy of Holies.

Contrast this with Ben Sira's praise of the ancient righteous ancestors, including the pre-Israelite ones such as Enosh, which culminates in a paean to the High Priest Simon. For Ben Sira, the High Priest stands at the end of a long chain of righteous ancestors going back to Shem, Enosh, Seth, and Adam (49:16). For the rabbis, the High Priest is viewed within the context of *Israelite* history, which is portrayed in sharp *contrast* to the progressive degeneration that preceded it.[197]

F. Conclusions

Having surveyed some one thousand years of midrashic tradition, what conclusions can be drawn? Three points stand out most clearly:

(1) Unlike the non-Rabbinic sources, both Jewish and non-Jewish, the Rabbinic sources exhibit very little interest in the figure of Enosh the individual. From those very few Rabbinic passages that speak of or allude to Enosh no consistent picture emerges. Some view him as one of the earliest righteous, even godlike antediluvians, while others associate him with the idolatrous behavior of his contemporaries. Certainly, Enosh himself is not the chief concern in the Rabbinic interpretation of Gen 4:26.[198]

(2) The Rabbinic sources consistently understand Gen 4:26 to refer to Enosh's contemporaries. In amoraic and postamoraic sources they are called the Generation of Enosh, and take their place alongside the other early rebellious generations known from the Bible, forming what might be called a "chain" of rebellious generations. The Generation of Enosh is usually the first link in the chain. Each generation introduces some new

[197] The similarities between Ben Sira's "Praise of the Fathers" and of the High Priest Simon and the Avodah Service have been noted by others, most notably, C. Roth, "Ecclesiastes in the Synagogue Service," *JBL* 71 (1952) 171–78. See also Mirsky, 27–29. However, these fail to draw attention to the *contrast* between Ben Sira's treatment of pre-Israelite times and those of the various introductions to the Avodah Service.

[198] We noted a similar phenomenon in our discussion of certain Christian exegetes (particularly the Byzantine chronographers and Syriac Fathers): Enosh is de-emphasized and Gen 4:26 is employed to describe, rather, his descendants. Nowhere, however, do Christian exegetes apply this verse to Enosh's contemporaries ("his generation") as a whole.

form of rebelliousness into the world, continuing in the footsteps of its predecessors, yet failing to learn from their misfortunes, understood as punishments from God. These traditions reveal a motif that may be referred to as *qilqûl haddôrôt*, or the "degeneration of the generations." Interestingly, this chain begins usually not with Adam and Eve and their sin, nor with Cain, but with the Generation of Enosh.

(3) Gen 4:26 is consistently understood to refer not to the origins of divine worship, as it is in the non-Rabbinic sources, but to the origins of "idolatry," that is, the worship of false gods. From the earliest tannaitic sources this sin is viewed as the worship of and reliance on non-deities, which are called "gods," that is, the confusion of the Creator with His created. This interpretation is expressed by the so-called Palestinian targumim and remains consistent throughout most of the Rabbinic period.[199] Very little else is said in the way of describing the specific behavior of Enosh's contemporaries; this would seem not to be a major concern. Our sources, therefore, do not seem to contain a polemic against a particular kind of idolatrous practice.[200] Only in significantly later sources is the idolatry of Enosh's contemporaries actually described, but there the description is in unreal terms.

It is interesting that for the rabbis as for several Christian exegetes Gen 4:26 is understood to refer to non-gods who are called by God's name. For the Christian exegetes, this is intended positively, in connection with righteous humans who merit being called "gods" or "sons of God." For the rabbis, the worship and calling of non-gods by God's name is viewed as a misappropriation of God's name, as definitive of "false worship," and as rebellion against God.[201]

Not only do our Rabbinic sources tell us very little concerning the specific nature of the idolatry of the Generation of Enosh, but they do not seem particularly concerned with showing how their interpretation of Gen 4:26 is derived from the scriptural words themselves. We have

199 Much less frequently, and only in later sources, do we find the interpretation expressed by *Tg. Onqelos*: that Enosh's contemporaries desisted from or neglected the worship of God. This interpretation does not contradict the predominant one, but is its corollary. As we noted above (n. 15), the two-fold interpretation of the Palestinian targumim is attested to by Jerome (346–420 C.E.), who provides a definite *terminus ad quem* for this Rabbinic understanding, already presumed in a tradition attributed to R. Aḥa (330 C.E.) in *Gen. Rab.* 23.7 (see above, n. 49).

200 However, see above, n. 98, where a polemic against emperor worship is suggested.

201 Note that while Christians speak of humans who are called "gods," the Rabbinic focus is broader, being concerned with the calling of any non-god by the name of God, including idols (images), persons, and heavenly phenomena. It should be noted that the rabbis too held that righteous humans could properly be called "gods" (*'ĕlōhîm*) by Scripture in recognition of their outstanding qualities (*imitatio dei*) as long as they were not worshipped as such. For examples, see *Sifre Deut.* 49; *b. Meg.* 18a and *Gen. Rab.* 79.8 (both on Gen 33:20). Cf. *b. B. Bat.* 75b. See above, chap. 2, n. 10; chap. 3, nn. 62, 66.

inferred that the earliest sources understand Gen 4:26 as an ellipsis, supplying "false gods" or "idols" as the direct object of the verb "to call." Only in significantly later, postamoraic collections do we find the Rabbinic interpretation "derived" by interpreting the name "Enosh" or the verb *hûḥal*.[202] This lack of concern for actual exegesis is surprising, especially since the Rabbinic interpretation is essentially the opposite of what one might think to be the "plain" meaning of Gen 4:26.[203] Since we have no reason to believe that the rabbis misunderstood the scriptural words or syntax, their failure to show the relation between Scripture and its interpretation indicates that their understanding of Gen 4:26 was well established and accepted, at least within their own circles, and that their motivation was strong enough so as not to leave room for a more "literal" alternative.

While the Rabbinic sources tell us vey little about the sin of the Generation of Enosh, they tell us a good deal about the punishment of that generation. In fact, this may be said to be their chief concern. Our earliest (tannaitic) sources already presuppose a flood in Enosh's time, but tell us only that it involved the ocean's flooding of a third of the world. In the amoraic sources this tradition is further explained, it now being stated that this flood, the first of three floods, was responsible for the formation of the Mediterranean Sea. The primeval waters (chaos) contained at Creation were then unleashed. However, we are also told in amoraic sources of other consequences of the sin of the Generation of Enosh: important changes for the worse occurred at this time in man's appearance, character, and general condition. This was also a time when, according to one tradition, the Shekinah departed from humanity's midst. In each case, the Rabbinic sources stress that the punishment fit the sin. Just as the sin is understood to represent a radical break from and repudiation of God (even if committed with some innocence), so too the punishments represent radical transformations in man and his environment. As we have seen, several of these changes are elsewhere associated with Adam's expulsion from Eden. Since

202 As we have seen, *Gen. Rab.* 23.6 contains a play on the verb *hûḥal* (*ḥûllîm/hôlîm lĕmazzîqîm*). However, this pun does not appear to lie at the heart of the broader interpretation of Gen 4:26 found in that source. It is only in gaonic and medieval sources (tenth–twelfth centuries) that the Rabbinic interpretation of Gen 4:26 is first explicitly derived from the words of that verse. I will discuss this further in the next chapter.

203 While the early rabbis may not have distinguished "plain" exegesis (*pĕšāṭ*) from freer exegesis (*dĕrāš*) in the same way as did later authorities, they certainly must have been aware that the scriptural words of Gen 4:26 did not *explicitly* say what they understood them to say. As we saw in our examination of the targumim, neither the individual words nor the syntax of the verse should have caused them difficulty. On the question of *pĕšāt* and *dĕrāš* in Rabbinic sources see R. Loewe, "The 'Plain' Meaning of Scripture in Early Jewish Exegesis," *Papers of the Institute of Jewish Studies, London*, vol. 1 (ed. J. G. Weiss; Jerusalem: Magnes, 1964) 140–85; as well as J. Lauterbach, "Peshaṭ," *Jewish Encyclopedia*, 9.653.

our sources usually view the Generation of Enosh as the first generation of sinners, the radical transformations are said to begin with them. It is with this generation that mankind's downward plunge begins, or at least gets fully under way.

What is most startling in the Rabbinic handling of Gen 4:26 is not the ambivalent interpretation of Enosh, nor the description of the Generation of Enosh's sinfulness, but the way in which a radically converse interpretation of this verse is taken for granted and employed in the broader retelling of pre-Israelite history. This retelling is particularly remarkable when contrasted with extra-Rabbinic exegeses, particularly those of the rabbis' contemporaries, the Church Fathers.

The non-Rabbinic sources speak of two families of earliest man, one righteous (the descendants of Seth) and one wicked (the descendants of Cain). The two continue as distinct groups at least until the Flood, and in some traditions throughout history. The righteous group struggles to remain separate from the wicked, and the Flood results, in part, from the mixing of the two "families." Gen 4:26 is employed to describe the pious and godlike qualities of one link (Enosh) in the chain of Sethite righteous ancestors. Christian exegetes come to use this verse to describe Enosh's descendants as being similarly godlike, viewing their own community, the Church, as the typological and even genealogical continuation and fulfillment of that ancient, pre-Israelite, righteous chain. Such a picture is virtually absent from early Rabbinic sources.[204]

Rabbinic traditions, by contrast, view earliest man as being righteous and godlike until the process of degeneration begins with the Generation of Enosh. Then, mankind *as a whole* begins its decline.[205] Only a few righteous individuals remain apart from the general trend, and even their significance is somewhat muted. Gen 4:26 is again used to supply an important chain link, but now the chain is one of rebellious generations.

204 An exception to this pattern is *PRE* 22, which identifies Seth as the progenitor of the righteous and Cain as the progenitor of the wicked. It is unclear whether this passage draws on non-Rabbinic or unknown earlier Rabbinic sources.

205 This picture, while being fairly consistent for the sources which we have examined, is not necessarily so for all Rabbinic literature. We have already raised the problem that Cain and his descendants do not fit this pattern, the first murder already having occurred before Enosh was born. The later Rabbinic sources seem to absorb the descendants of Cain into the Generation of Enosh. The figure of Adam is ambiguously treated in Rabbinic sources. Sometimes he appears as one of the righteous antediluvians and elsewhere as the first sinner. Certainly his "fall" does not play as significant a role in Rabbinic tradition as it does in Christian, especially Pauline, theology. The relative absence of Adam and his sin in the traditions we have examined is remarkable, especially considering the prominence accorded to Adam and his sin in the Bible. That the rabbis could think of beginning an account of humanity's decline with the Generation of Enosh rather than with Adam, transferring to them punishments elsewhere associated with him, certainly represents a radical interpretation of Scripture.

The rebellion of the Generation of Enosh is radical, as are its consequences. Both are seen as serious ruptures in the originally harmonious relations between God, man, and nature. Both are placed within a larger pattern of rebellion and punishment. The degeneration of the generations continues unabated, with increasingly catastrophic consequences, until the first of the new Israelite patriarchs, Abraham, appears. With him a new, chosen chain begins, which averts God's destruction of the world.

It should be stressed that the *origins* of the tradition of Enosh's contemporaries as the first worshippers of false gods cannot be determined. This interpretation of Gen 4:26 is already *assumed* in our earliest midrashic collections (*Mekilta* and *Sifre Deuteronomy*).[206] We have seen how this tradition develops in amoraic and postamoraic sources: (a) The Generation of Enosh takes its place among the other early rebellious generations. (b) The consequences of their sin are described in greater detail, and as representing more radical changes in man and nature. (c) Their idolatry comes to be described in greater and more imaginative detail. (d) The tradition of the Generation of Enosh is finally *derived* from the actual words of Scripture. Yet, it should be remembered that the core of the tradition is not only evidenced but assumed in our earliest sources: Enosh's contemporaries called upon and called non-gods by God's name, and were punished by a partial flooding of the ocean (summoned by God). Neither of these is evidenced in pre-Rabbinic Jewish sources, nor in extra-Rabbinic traditions that may draw on Jewish antecedents. This would seem to rule out the possibility that the Rabbinic interpretation derives from pre-Rabbinic tradition. For instance, if the tradition of a flood in Enosh's time, already well attested in tannaitic sources, was a product of ancient Near Eastern, biblical, or Jewish folklore, we would expect to hear of it in some other than Rabbinic sources. Yet these sources, many of which discuss the antediluvian period at some length, make no mention of or allusion to such a flood.[207] Thus, it would appear that the Rabbinic treatment of Gen 4:26 is distinctively Rabbinic, having no clear parallels elsewhere.[208] The fact that the core of the Rabbinic interpretation seems to have emerged at an early date in such

[206] Dating these documents and their contained traditions is no easy matter. See above, n. 4. With the help of Jerome and *Genesis Rabbah* we established a *terminus ad quem* of ca. 330 C.E. for the tradition contained in the *Mekilta* and *Sifre Deuteronomy*. See above, nn. 15, 41, 49, 199. How much earlier than this the Rabbinic tradition of Enosh's generation circulated is impossible to say.

[207] In the next chapter we will see that only Greek and Roman historians and philosophers speak of a series of ancient floods. The Mesopotamian traditions also speak only of one flood, although the Atraḥasis Epic speaks of preceding plagues. See chap. 5, nn. 118–21.

[208] Only Josephus, in describing the degeneration of the Sethites in the seventh generation (but making no mention of Enosh or his generation in particular), suggests a similar view of antediluvian history. See above, chap 1, n. 77.

sharp contrast to the exegesis of everyone else forces us to assume that the rabbis did not inherit it from their predecessors, but rather had their own distinctive motivations for producing a new understanding of Enosh's contemporaries, their sin and punishment, and their place within the universal prologue to the sacred history of Israel.[209]

[209] This is not to suggest that the Rabbinic traditions were created *ex nihilo*. As we will see in the next chapter, several motifs that seem to have influenced the Rabbinic exegesis are present in pre-Rabbinic and extra-Rabbinic sources. The rabbis undoubtedly built upon a foundation laid by earlier Jewish interpreters of the Bible. All we claim is that the *distinguishing* elements of the Rabbinic interpretation of Gen 4:26 are not to be found elsewhere.

Chapter Five
RABBINIC METHOD AND MOTIVATION

Having examined in some detail Rabbinic interpretations of Enosh and his generation, and having noted how radically these differ from the interpretations of all other exegetes, both Jewish and non-Jewish, I turn now to two critical questions: (a) how did the rabbis link their interpretation to the words of Scripture? and (b) what factors caused them to adopt such a radical interpretation? These two questions lead to considerations of, respectively, method and motivation. While these two concerns are related, it is important to address them separately, being careful not to confuse them. By understanding *how* an interpretation is connected with Scripture, we do not necessarily know *why* the interpretation emerged as it did.

A. Rabbinic Methods

In analyzing the relevant Rabbinic passages, we saw that the Rabbinic exegesis of the words of Gen 4:26b is more often assumed than furnished. Considering the fact that this assumed interpretation is the opposite of what would most likely be understood as the verse's "plain" meaning, it is surprising that the rabbis do not make more of an effort to convince their audience of their interpretation by demonstrating how it is derived from Scripture. We have concluded from this that the Rabbinic interpretation must have been well established, at least in the circles in which it circulated, already in the third century. Despite this relative silence, in a number of passages Rabbinic methods of exegesis are either explicitly stated or at least implicitly suggested.

1. Scriptural Ellipsis

I have argued that in the earliest midrashic sources (*Mekilta*, *Sifre*) the Rabbinic interpretation is effected by correcting an assumed ellipsis in Gen 4:26b, providing "false gods" or "idols" as the direct object of the verb "to call."[1] This method is employed as well in the "Palestinian" targumim,

[1] In *Mekilta Baḥodeš* 6 and in *Sifre Deut.* 43 the supplied direct object of the verb *liqrō'* would appear to be the *'ĕlōhîm 'ăḥērîm* of Exod 20:3 and Deut 5:7, respectively, even though this is not explicitly stated. In *MTan.* ad Deut 32:17, *'ăbôdâ zārâ* is explicitly provided as the direct object. See above, chap. 4, nn. 40, 47. This method continues to be

which contain the same exegesis as the tannaitic sources, both in content and form. Unlike the earliest midrashim, these targumim *explicitly* supply the object of the people's calling or worship. In both cases a two-fold interpretation results: Enosh's contemporaries called upon (worshipped) false gods, and called those false gods by the name of the Lord.[2]

This method of recognizing an ellipsis in Scripture and then inserting the words necessary to achieve the desired interpretation is facilitated by the fact that the expression *liqrōʾ bĕšēm YHWH* does not include a direct object. While the phrase would normally be understood as "to call upon the name of the Lord," that is, to invoke God's name in worship, it could easily accommodate the insertion of a direct object: "to call (someone or something) with/by the name of the Lord." Since this phrase, which occurs so frequently in Scripture, nowhere else causes the rabbis difficulty, regularly being interpreted as denoting prayer, we must assume that these words themselves did not motivate the Rabbinic interpretation, but simply provided the means by which the interpretation could be fit to the verse.

Such fleshing-out of a biblical phrase or passage does not, from the Rabbinic perspective, compromise a belief in Scripture's divine authorship. To the rabbis, part of what makes divine speech different from human is its terse quality, its economy of expression that leaves as much unstated as stated.[3] Thus, Torah by its very divine nature is to be considered elliptical, and part of the job of the Rabbinic exegete is to supply the words that are thought to have been intended, but not revealed in writing. Midrash thereby renders Scripture's meaning more comprehensible (and acceptable) in the contexts in which it is read and studied.[4] Such fleshing-out is particularly resorted to when a biblical passage appears to contradict its own scriptural context, as understood by the rabbis.

---

evidenced throughout later Rabbinic passages, including the medieval commentators, especially Rashi. See below, nn. 15, 16, 18, 43.

[2] See above, chap. 4, n. 15.

[3] This view of Scripture ("written Torah") is implied in the statement found in *Tanḥ. Noaḥ* 3: "The written Torah contains general principles, while the oral Torah, specifics. The oral Torah contains much, while the written Torah, little."

[4] This method is expressed in the ninth of the thirty-two rules of Eliezer ben Jose Hagelili: *derek qĕṣārâ* ("abbreviated or elliptical phraseology"). See H. L. Strack, *Introduction to the Talmud and Midrash* (Philadelphia: Jewish Publication Society of America, 1931) 96, 290–91 n. 13. For the text, see the introduction to *MhG Gen.* (ed. Margulies) 28, and for other sources, Margulies's note on p. 22.

This is to some extent analogous to the amoraic explication of mishnah in the Talmud, often restating a mishnaic saying with the insertion of additional words in order to eliminate a perceived contradiction or inconsistency. See, for example, *m. Pesaḥ* 2:1 as reformulated in *b. Pesaḥ* 21a; and *m. Pesaḥ* 9:5 as restated in *b. Pesaḥ*. 96b.

2. Argument by Analogy (*gĕzērâ šāwâ*)

In *Gen. Rab.* 23.7, we saw the verb *hûḥal* interpreted as an "expression of rebellion," by analogy with uses of the verb *hēḥēl* in Gen 6:1 and 10:8. In our discussion of this passage, we noted that such an interpretation already *assumes* a negative interpretation of Gen 4:26 and could not have been a principal means by which the Rabbinic understanding of this verse was derived from Scripture. All we are told is that the verb *hûḥal* denotes rebellion, the actual form of that rebellion being assumed rather than specified. The statement simply notes that Scripture describes the activities of the first three rebellious generations (of Enosh, the Flood, and the Tower of Babel) in similar terms. To the rabbis this scriptural use of a common verb is not accidental, but can be taken to suggest that these three generations had something in common: rebelliousness. The interpretation, however, does not deny the meaning of these verbs as "to begin." It simply provides added support for the Rabbinic contention that where this verb is used, rebellion is described, providing a lexical basis for the frequent association of these generations in Rabbinic literature.[5]

3. Plays on the Verb *hûḥal*

It has frequently been stated by both traditional commentators and modern scholars that the Rabbinic association of the Generation of Enosh with idolatry is *based* on an interpretation of the verb *hûḥal*, usually understanding the verb to mean "was profaned."[6] While this is often stated quite categorically, a more critical examination of the primary sources reveals that the matter is not so simple. Such a line of interpretation is barely present in the early sources, and only in medieval sources does it appear with any regularity, and then as only one of several explanations.

As we have seen, in the earliest midrashic sources and the "Palestinian" targumim the verb *hûḥal* is regularly understood to mean "it was begun," or more commonly, "they (Enosh's contemporaries) began." The "Palestinian" targumim all translate *hûḥal* in customary fashion with the Aramaic verb *šry* ("began"). The tannaitic sources in stating "you have done something new" most likely reflect the same understanding, as do the amoraic sources that link radical changes in human behavior and conditions to this verse.

The *only* premedieval Rabbinic midrashic source that contains a

[5] For a similar *gĕzērâ šāwâ* applied to rebellious generations, see *Gen. Rab.* 27.3 (ed. Theodor-Albeck) 257. On the subject of *gĕzērâ šāwâ* in the aggadah see I. Heinemann, *Darke ha'aggada* (third ed.; Jerusalem: Magnes, 1970) 122–23. Heinemann cautions against taking such interpretations too literally.

[6] See above, chap. 4, n. 24.

play on the verb *hûḥal* is *Gen. Rab.* 23.6, where one of the changes undergone by Enosh's contemporaries is that they become *ḥûllîm/ ḥôlîm lĕmazzîqîm*. While this most likely represents a play on the verb *hûḥal*, it is given as one of several changes associated with the Generation of Enosh and does not appear to lie at the heart of the exegesis. This change could be omitted without the essential thrust of the interpretation being altered.[7] Nowhere in the tannaitic and amoraic sources is Gen 4:26b rendered as: "then men were profaned through the calling on the name of the Lord," or "then [the calling on the] name of the Lord was profaned."[8] The fact that *Gen. Rab.* 23.6 reveals an awareness of the possibility of punning on the verb *hûḥal* makes all the more remarkable the absence of such puns elsewhere in the tannaitic and amoraic sources. It is only in significantly later sources that such puns become more frequent, explicit, and central to the exegesis. It is crucial that we not make the mistake made by others of reading these later traditions back into the earlier targumic and midrashic sources where they are not evidenced.

Before proceeding to review those *later* traditions that contain explicit interpretations of the verb *hûḥal* in Gen 4:26, it is important to note that the Hebrew verb *ḥll* is frequently the subject of wordplays in early Rabbinic sources.[9] These plays involve either two or more of the many meanings of the verb *ḥll* (undo, nullify a vow, open, begin, profane, pierce, slay) or meanings derived from other verbs with the root consonants *ḥ* and *l*, such as *ḥlh*, *ḥwl*, and *mḥl*, verbs whose wide range of

[7] Note that in *YS Bere'šit* 47 (ed. Salonika) 16a three punishments are listed, but that of becoming vulnerable to menacing creatures is omitted. The basic thrust of *Gen. Rab.* 23.6 is that after Enosh men ceased to be in the divine image, becoming beastlike. One consequence of this change was that men became vulnerable to the creatures (or to demons). In its present form, however, the midrash is responding primarily to the unusual genealogical break after Gen 4:26, and not to the unusual form *hûḥal*. One might argue that ceasing to be in the divine image is equivalent to becoming profane (i.e., unprotected), but this is not a point drawn by this midrashic passage itself. Thus, while it does pun on the verb *hûḥal*, that pun is secondary rather than basic to its interpretation.

[8] Cf. *Gen. Rab.* 36.3 (ed. Theodor-Albeck) 337, where a pun on the verb *hēḥēl* is *central* to the exegesis: "'Noah the tiller of the soil was the first (*wayyāḥel*) to plant a vineyard' (Gen 9:20): He was degraded and became profane (*nitḥallēl wĕna'ăśeh ḥûllîn*)." Note Ibn Ezra's rejection of such an interpretation of *hûḥal* in his Commentary ad loc. See below, n. 15.

[9] For examples see: *b. Ber.* 30b, 32a (note significant variants in *Diqduqe Soperim*); *Exod. Rab.* 43.1–5; *YS Ki Tiśśa'* 392 (ed. Salonika) 81c; *b. Šabb.* 118b; *b. Ḥag* 10a; *b. Soṭa* 9b–10a; *b. 'Abod. Zar.* 4a; *Sifra* ad Lev 26:6 (ed. Weiss) 111a; *Sifre Deut.* 27, 319 (ed. Finkelstein) 41, 365 (the latter discussed above, chap. 4, n. 84); *Sifre Num.* 134 (ed. Horovitz) 180; *MTan.* Deut 3:24 (ed. Hoffman) 15–16; *Deut. Rab.* 2.8 (ed. Lieberman) 47; *Tanḥ B. Wa'etḥannan* (p. 14, supplement); *YS Wa'etḥannan* 815 (ed. Salonika) 296b, from *Yelammedenu*; *PRK* 17.2 (ed. Mandelbaum) 283 and parallels; *Tanḥ. B. Yitro* 1 (p. 69). The biblical verses that are most commonly the subject of such plays on the verb *ḥll* (or *ḥlh*) are Exod 32:11; Num 30:3; Deut 3:24; Judg 13:5; and Ps 77:11.

meanings often overlap. An examination of many such wordplays reveals a number of common features. (a) The wordplays are often not explicit and in some cases it is uncertain which play is intended.[10] (b) The biblical word which is being interpreted is sometimes itself of unusual form and/or uncertain meaning.[11] (c) One source may contain numerous wordplays on a single biblical word or phrase, either overlapping or being entirely independent of one another. Once again, the frequency with which the verb *ḥll* is played upon in Rabbinic texts makes remarkable the near absence of such plays on *hûḥal* of Gen 4:26 in tannaitic and amoraic collections.

(a) *hûḥal* as "was profaned." As I have stressed, the interpretation of the verb *hûḥal* as meaning "was profaned" or "became profane" (taking the subject to be the name of the Lord or the worship of the Lord) does not appear in tannaitic or amoraic midrashic sources.[12] The only midrashic compilations in which it appears are *Midrash Haggadol* and *Midrash Aggadah*, both of which are dated sometime between the twelfth and fourteenth centuries. The former states that "the calling on the name of the Lord was profaned (*nitḥallĕlâ*)," while the latter states that "the name of the Holy One blessed be He was profaned (*naʿăśeh mĕḥûllāl*)."[13] In both cases, the interpretations are unattributed and have no earlier extant parallels. While it is possible that they preserve earlier traditions that for some reason are not preserved in our earlier sources, such a possibility cannot be substantiated. Given the fact that Gen 4:26 and the Generation of Enosh are so frequently referred to in earlier midrashic sources with only an indirect allusion to this interpretation, we can safely say that the interpretation of *hûḥal* as "was profaned" plays at best an insignificant role in early Rabbinic interpretation. It only comes to the fore in postamoraic times. As I

[10] Thus, in *b. Ber.* 32a, while the printed editions read *myḥl* (*mêḥēl*, "break a vow") from the root *ḥll*, the Munich MS has *mwḥl* (*môḥēl*, "remit, forego") from the root *mḥl*. Similarly, in *PRK* 17.2 the Oxford MS reads *ntḥlh* ("became weak," from the root *ḥlh*) as an explanation of *ḥallôtî* (Ps 77:11), while two later manuscripts have *ntḥllh* ("was profaned," from the root *ḥll*). "Became weak" appears to be better supported from the context of the midrash, but cf. *Lam. Rab.* 1.2 (ed. Buber) 30a; *MPs.* 77.3 (ed. Buber) 344; and *YS* Ps. 816 (ed. Salonika) 40d–41a. See W. Braude's note in *Pĕsiḳta dĕ-Rab Kahăna* (Philadelphia: Jewish Publication Society, 1975) 306 n. 12. For a less explicit play, see *Exod. Rab.* 43.1: "'But Moses implored (*wayĕḥal*) the Lord his God': For he stood with irreverence (*qallût rōʾš*) before the Lord." This may reflect a play on *wayĕḥal* (*piʿel* of *ḥlh*) as if it derived from *ḥll* (*wayyāḥēl*), thus interpreting: Moses implored God in an irreverent (or profane) manner.

[11] Thus, *ḥallôtî* (Ps 77:11) is variously interpreted by modern scholars as well as by ancient translators and interpreters as deriving from *ḥlh* ("my sickness or weakness"), *ḥwl* ("my anguish or pain"), or *ḥll* ("my wounding," or as in the LXX, "I have begun.").

[12] I have argued that the interpretation of *ḥûllim lĕmazzîqîm* in *Gen. Rab.* 23.6 is related but not the same.

[13] See above, chap. 4, nn. 183, 186. Cf. *MA* ad Gen 6:1 (ed. Buber) 23, where the verb *hēḥēl* ("began") is interpreted as *naʿăśeh ḥûllîn* ("became profane").

indicated above, the earliest source that *may* explicitly state this interpretation is the Arabic translation of Saadia Gaon (882–942), but even here the meaning of the translation is not certain.[14]

Only with the Jewish medieval biblical commentators do we find relatively datable evidence for the explicit interpretation of *hûḥal* as "was profaned." Abraham Ibn Ezra (1089–1164) in his commentary asserts that *hûḥal* derives from the geminate *ḥll*, meaning "to begin" and gives as the sense of the phrase, "they began to pray," thus being the *first* rabbi to express what is usually thought to be the "plain" sense of this phrase. He explicitly rejects the interpretation that *hûḥal* stems from the meaning "to profane," noting that were this the case, the verb would be immediately followed by "the name of the Lord" without the interceding "to call."[15] Whatever the merits of Ibn Ezra's argument, it is clear that the interpretation of *hûḥal* as "was profaned" was known to him and, presumably, to his audience. Just how well established this interpretation was in Ibn Ezra's time and for how long it had been in circulation is more difficult to determine.

David Qimḥi (RaDaQ, 1160–1236) states that some explain *hûḥal* as an expression of "profaning," while others explain it as an expression of "beginning." While he develops both lines of interpretation, he does not appear to reveal a preference.[16]

14 See above, chap. 4, n. 185, where a similar interpretation *ascribed* to Saadia is also cited.

15 Ibn Ezra, *Peruše hattora* (ed. A. Vizer; 3 vols.; Jerusalem: Mossad Harav Kook, 1976) 1.34. The same argument is advanced by modern scholars: A. Dillmann, *Genesis Critically and Exegetically Expounded* (trans. W. Stevenson; 2 vols.; Edinburgh: T. & T. Clark, 1897) 1.210; J. Skinner, *A Critical and Exegetical Commentary on Genesis* (ICC; New York: Charles Scribner's Sons, 1910) 127; F. Delitzsch, *Neuer Commentar über die Genesis* (Leipzig: Dorffling und Franke, 1887) 134. Elijah Mizraḥi (1452–1525), in his commentary to Rashi ad Gen 4:26 (in *'Oṣar mepareše hattora* [Warsaw, 1862] 20d–21a), refutes Ibn Ezra, claiming that Scripture out of respect (*derek kābôd*) for the divine name did not place it directly after the verb *hûḥal*, which he interprets to mean "was profaned." R. Levi b. Gerson (RaLBag, 1288–1344) also rejects Ibn Ezra's interpretation, while Abravanel (1437–1508) adopts Ibn Ezra's understanding as representing the "plain" (*pěšaṭ*) meaning. In response to Ibn Ezra's argument, it can be said that Gen 4:26b is understood by some to mean that it was the prayer (or calling) in God's name that was profaned and not the divine name itself. See *MhG* and RaDaQ ad loc.

16 *Peruš RaDaQ 'al hattora, seper bere'šit* (ed. A. Ginzburg; Pressburg, 1842) 21a. RaDaQ derives from *hûḥal* meaning "was begun" *two* interpretations: (a) men began to pray, and (b) men began to call stars and constellations by the name of the Lord. He notes that the second interpretation is held not only by the Sages, but by "most men" as well. Note, however, that in another commentary RaDaQ clearly adopts this second interpretation as his own, making no mention of either the "plain" interpretation, or the interpretation of *hûḥal* as "was profaned": "The interpretation of *'āz hûḥal* derives from the sense of 'beginning,' for they began to occupy themselves with natural phenomena and false-gods, and this is the meaning of 'was begun to call on the name of the Lord.'" *Kimḥi's Allegorical Commentary on Genesis*, Appendix I in *The Commentary of David Kimḥi on Isaiah* (ed. Louis Finkelstein; New York: Columbia University, 1926) lxxiv.

We should note that Rashi (R. Solomon Yiṣḥaqi, 1040–1105) understands Gen 4:26b to be elliptical, as did the earlier rabbis, and most likely understands *hûḥal* to mean "was begun." The printed editions of Rashi's commentary have after *'āz hûḥal* the words *lĕšôn ḥûllîn* ("an expression of profaning"). However, an examination of early manuscripts and commentaries makes clear that these words represent a later gloss, perhaps by one of Rashi's students or a later copyist.[17] According to the earliest manuscripts, Rashi states: "*'āz hûḥal* (then was begun/men began): to call the names of man and the names of forms [idols] by the name of the Holy One Blessed be He, to make idols and to call them gods." Thus, according to Rashi, Enosh's contemporaries sinned by calling non-gods by God's name. Rashi, like the rabbis, supplies the object(s) of the verb *liqrō'*, but in no way suggests an interpretation of *hûḥal* as "was profaned."[18]

Thus, it would appear that the interpretation of *hûḥal* as "was profaned" circulated in the twelfth century alongside the traditional Rabbinic interpretation (e.g., Rashi) at a time when a more literal understanding of the verse was for the first time finding Rabbinic exponents (e.g., Ibn Ezra). The earliest such interpretation of *hûḥal* as "was profaned" can be dated is

17 The first to call attention to this fact was S. D. Luzzatto (1800–1865), who argues that Rashi understood *hûḥal* as an "expression of beginning" (*lĕšôn hatḥālâ*): *S. D. Luzzatto's Commentary to the Pentateuch* (ed. P. Schlesinger; Tel Aviv: Dvir, 1965) 36. A. Berliner, in his edition of Rashi's commentary (*Rashi 'al hattora* [second ed.; Frankfurt a. Main: Y. Kaufmann, 1905] 11 n. 14) concurs with Luzzatto. I have examined the following manuscripts at the library of the Jewish Theological Seminary: Bible No. 746 (fifteenth century, Oriental), Bible No. 747 (fourteenth century, Italian), Bible No. 748 (fourteenth century, Persian). I have also examined the following British Museum manuscripts on microfilm: Add. 26917 (sixteenth century, French), Harley 1861 (thirteenth-fourteenth century, German writing), Harley 5709 (thirteenth-fourteenth century, German writing). In *none* of these do the words *lĕšôn ḥûllin* appear. According to Moshe Charaz (*Lešon Ḥayyim* [Jerusalem, 1970] 48–49), the first printing at Reggio in 1475 and that at Venice in 1548 similarly omit *lĕšôn ḥûllîn*. Charaz has a lengthy and worthwhile note on Rashi's interpretation. Furthermore, Elijah Mizraḥi, in his commentary on Rashi (*'Oṣar mepareše hattora*, 20c), cites Rashi's interpretation without the words *lĕšôn ḥûllîn* and states: "Rashi does not at all explicate whether they [the words *'āz hûḥal*] derive from the sense 'beginning'. . . or from the sense 'profaning.'" Mizraḥi continues by proving that Rashi must have understood *hûḥal* as an expression of "beginning" by analogy with Rashi's treatment of Gen 11:6 (*haḥillām*), even though Mizraḥi himself favors the play "was profaned."

18 Note that Rashi specifies two forms of "idolatry": the worship of forms/images and that of humans, in both cases involving the application of God's name to the objects of worship. As previously noted, earliest Rabbinic exegesis does not usually specify the objects of the false worship of the Generation of Enosh; only in later collections is greater specificity to be found. On the application of God's name to the worship of humans, see above, chap. 4, nn. 49, 98, 201. Note that in *Jeraḥmeel* 24.9 the sin of the Generation of Enosh is that "men began to be designated by the names of princes and judges, to be made gods, applying to them the name of the Lord" (הוחל לקרא את שמות האדם השרים דיינים לעשות אלהות בשם יי). The English translation is from Gaster's edition (p. 51), the Hebrew from a photostat of the only existing manuscript, at the Bodleian Library. *Yeraḥmeel* appears to be dependent on Rashi, since it follows so closely Rashi's wording.

the early tenth century with Saadia Gaon, but whether this is indeed Saadia's interpretation is not certain. The fact that after centuries of relative silence, the interpretation of *hûḥal* as "was profaned" first emerges both in midrashic compilations and in the works of biblical commentators at roughly the same time would most likely suggest that these interpretations do not antedate by much the compilations in which they are found, being reflective of contemporary exegesis rather than transmitted tradition. Thus, we have shown that the *explicit* association of the targumic-midrashic interpretation of Gen 4:26 with the interpretation of *hûḥal* as "was profaned" is medieval and not early Rabbinic, even though, as we have also shown, the earlier rabbis must have known of the possibility of interpreting this verb through such a wordplay.[19] I will discuss the possible motivations for such a development after considering other interpretations of *hûḥal*, as well as of the name Enosh.

(b) *huḥal* as "became weak/sick." A second, although less frequent, interpretation of *hûḥal* may also be discerned. A few traditions suggest an interpretation of Gen 4:26 based on the notion that men became weak in their worship, that their worship became weak or sickly, or that they themselves became weak or sick as a consequence of their behavior. We have seen that *3 Enoch* 5.3–6 (*Seper Hekalot*) relates that in Enosh's time men first became ill (*ḥôleh*) and became vulnerable to malevolent creatures.[20] Although Ibn Ezra takes Gen 4:26 to be an announcement of the beginnings of divine worship, in his commentary *Šiṭa 'aḥeret* he gives another possible interpretation of *hûḥal*: "to be weak (*lihĕyôt 'ānûš*)."[21] This interpretation clearly views *hûḥal* as a subtle play on the name Enosh, which can similarly be understood to mean "weak." It has even been suggested (I believe wrongly) that *Tg. Onqelos* be understood to mean that men weakened, or became lax in their worship, understanding *ḥālû* (rather than *ḥallû*) as the perfect third person plural of *ḥwl* or *ḥly*.[22]

19 We need stress again that the expression *ḥwlym lmzyqym* in *Gen. Rab.* 23.6, while most likely representing a play on the verb *hûḥal*, does not appear to lie at the heart of the exegesis there. See above, nn. 7, 8.

20 See above, chap. 4, n. 165. Whether a play on *hûḥal* is here intended is uncertain, and the relation of this passage to *Gen. Rab.* 23.6 (*ḥwlym lmzyqym*) is not clear.

21 Ibn Ezra, *Peruše hattora* (ed. A. Vizer) 1.173, and Vizer's nn. 28, 29. Note as well the interpretation of R. Moses b. Naḥman (RaMBaN, 1194–1270): "Then men began to worship idols and weakness and feebleness first came upon men" (ואז הוחל לעבוד עבודה זרה והוחל לבא באנשים חולשה ורפיון). *Peruše hattora* ad Gen 6:4 (ed. Ch. Chavel; two vols.; Jerusalem: Mossad Harav Kook, 1959–60) 1.49. It is unclear whether RaMBaN intends his remark as an interpretation of the verb *hûḥal* or the name Enosh (meaning "weak"). The same expressions are used in *Seper ṣiyyoni*, cited in *YR* ad Gen 4:26, but there the play seems more clearly to be on the name Enosh. Note also the comments of Ḥayyim Rabbinowitz (1875–1941) in his commentary *Da'at soperim* (New York: Feldheim, 1953), "The recognition of the Lord was weakened (*nehlĕšâ*) amongst mankind."

22 The Aramaic, however, could not derive from the root *ḥly* since the correct form would

Such interpretations do two things: (a) they suggest a wordplay on the verbs *ḥll* and *ḥlh*. While the form *hûḥal* cannot grammatically derive from the root *ḥlh*, for the sake of a pun it is sufficient that there be apparent phonetic resemblance.[23] (b) They link (whether implicitly or explicitly) this play to an understanding of Enosh's name (meaning "weak") in the first half of this verse.[24] While the rabbis must have been aware of both of these possibilities, they pursue neither until medieval times. Only then do puns on *hûḥal* suggesting "became weak or sick" emerge as *explicit* means of linking the traditional Rabbinic view of the Generation of Enosh with the words of Gen 4:26.

(c) *hûḥal* as "was interrupted or neglected." The possibility that *hûḥal* may have been taken to mean "was interrupted" or "men refrained from" is suggested by *Targum Onqelos*, which I examined in chapter four in some detail. Such an understanding of Gen 4:26 as announcing a refraining from or neglect of divine worship, while differing from the predominant Rabbinic tradition that associates this verse with the origins of idolatry, does not contradict it. The sins of ceasing to worship God and turning to the worship of other powers (false gods) would be, to the Rabbinic mind, two sides of the same coin.[25] Thus, as we have argued, *Targum Onqelos* does not present a new or different interpretation of Gen 4:26, but rather a new way of linking the commonly held Rabbinic interpretation to the actual words of the verse. Unlike the early midrashic passages, this targum achieves its intention not by adding words to

---

be *ḥălô*, unless this were a Hebraism. While the form *ḥālû*, found in the printed editions, could be the *peʿal* of either *ḥll* or *ḥwl*, the form *ḥallû*, given by Sperber in his critical edition of the targum, could only be the *peʿal* of *ḥll*. We have noted that both Jastrow and Levy take the targum to mean "they became lax," deriving the verb from the root *ḥwl*. See above, chap. 4, n. 22. Similarly, B. Schefftel understands this targum as a play on the name Enosh. See above, chap. 4, n. 27. Ben Zion Berkowitz in his commentary on *Tg. Onqelos* (*Leḥem weśimla* [Wilna, 1850] 15) states, "It is possible to interpret *ḥālû* as the *qal*, taking it as an expression of weakness (*ripyôn*) similar to *ʾānûš*," a play on the name Enosh.

23 In some instances the forms of the two verbs are so close as to make it difficult to determine which verb is involved. For instance, ancients and moderns have debated the root of the form of *ḥallôtî* (Ps 77:11). See above, n. 11. For a similar example from Rabbinic literature see *b. Ber.* 31a, where *hwḥlh* is interpreted as *hûḥallâ* (from *ḥll*: "[prayer] was begun") and as *hûḥlâ* (from *ḥlh*: "[Daniel] became weak or lax"). See S. Lieberman, *Tosefta Ki-Fshutah, Order Zeraʿim*, Part 1, ad *t. Ber.* 3.6(8) (New York: Jewish Theological Seminary, 1955) 29. For a Rabbinic passage containing several puns on the verbs *ḥll* and *ḥlh* (as well as *ḥwl*), see *b. Ber.* 32a, commenting on Exod 32:11 (*wayĕḥal*). For discussion see S. D. Fraade, "Enosh and His Generation: Scriptural Translation and Interpretation in Late Antiquity" (Ph.D. diss., University of Pennsylvania, 1980) 346. For other such plays see the sources listed above, n. 9, especially *Exod. Rab.* 43.1ff; *Lam. Rab.* 1.2; *MPs.* 77.3.

24 We have witnessed such a linking of Enosh's name to exegesis of Gen 4:26b in Christian, Samaritan, and pre-Rabbinic Jewish interpretations, where both Enosh's name and Gen 4:26b are interpreted *positively*. All of these understand Gen 4:26b as an explanation of Enosh's naming in 26a. See below, nn. 37–39.

25 See above, chap. 4, n. 29.

Scripture, but by reinterpreting one that already exists: the verb *hûḥal*. I have argued that it does so by rendering *hûḥal* not with "men began," but with "men abstained from [praying]".[26]

We have seen that in only one late midrashic source, *Midrash Aggadah*, is the sense of "refraining" from prayer or divine worship expressed. We have noted that this midrashic source may be dependent on *Targum Onqelos* in rendering, "they refrained (*mānĕʿû ʿaṣmām*) from calling on the name of the Lord."[27] This source gives another interpretation of *hûḥal* that is very similar: "it was interrupted (or nullified, *hitbaṭṭēl*)," citing *Targum Onqelos*' translation of Num 30:3.[28]

Thus, with *Midrash Aggadah* appearing to be dependent on *Targum Onqelos*, the latter (generally dated third-fourth centuries C.E.[29]) would represent the earliest (by centuries) extant source in which the Rabbinic tradition of the Generation of Enosh is "derived" from Gen 4:26 through a play on *hûḥal*. We have argued that this unusual method of interpretation is adopted by this targum so as to remain as close as possible to the "letter" (if not the plain sense) of the biblical text.[30] Rabbinic midrash is not so compelled until considerably later, and even then this particular interpretation is only slightly evidenced.

4. Plays on the Name Enosh

In examining non-Rabbinic traditions, we found several sources that wove into their interpretations explanations of the name Enosh, most of them treating his name positively (e.g., the true man, or the progenitor of mankind). By contrast, the explication of Enosh's name is entirely absent in tannaitic and amoraic Rabbinic sources, being found only in significantly later medieval compilations and commentaries. We examined four amoraic exegetical traditions in which the collective noun *ʾĕnôš* ("man") is interpreted to refer negatively to Enosh the person, but

26 Ibid., n. 30.

27 See above, chap. 4, n. 189. *MA* associates abstaining from worshipping God with profaning His name. Similarly, in an interpretation attributed to Saadia Gaon (above, chap. 4, n. 185) we find, "for they profaned (*ḥillĕlû*) the prayer in the Lord's name and ceased to pray (*ḥādĕlû millĕhitpallēl*)." These sources, therefore, may reflect a double pun on the verb *hûḥal*.

28 See above, chap. 4, n. 26. The *Ya'ar* commentary to *Tg. Onqelos* (above, chap. 4, n. 25) similarly cites this translation of Num 30:3 in support of its contention that the targum means, "they refrained" (*nimnĕʿû*). On the correspondence between the verbs *hēḥēl* and *biṭṭēl* (Aramaic, *baṭṭēl*), see above, chap. 4, n. 26; S. D. Fraade, "Enosh and His Generation," 350 nn. 35, 36; 355 nn. 47, 48. Note that in *PR* supp. chap. 1 (ed. Friedmann) 193a–b we saw the verb *biṭṭēl* used to describe the activity of the Generation of Enosh, "the generation which nullified [or neglected] my decree." See above, chap. 4, n. 153.

29 For a summary of the discussion on the dating of *Tg. Onqelos* see Y. Komlosh, *The Bible in the Light of the Aramaic Translations* (Hebrew) (Tel-Aviv: Dvir, 1973) 26–29.

30 See above, chap. 4, n. 30.

these do not represent interpretations of the proper name itself.[31] Given the frequency with which non-Rabbinic exegetes interpret Enosh's name, as well as the rabbis' own proclivity toward name interpretations and puns, this silence in the early Rabbinic sources is remarkable, especially with so transparent a name as Enosh.[32] Perhaps this can be explained by the fact that, in general, the Rabbinic sources show only the slightest interest in Enosh himself, choosing to focus rather on his contemporaries.

Those Rabbinic sources in which we do find interpretations of the name Enosh are all late, medieval midrashic compilations or bible commentaries. All of these derive the name Enosh from the root *'nš*, meaning to be weak or sick.[33] Although in some cases the interpretation suggests that it is Enosh himself who was weak or sickly in his behavior, in the majority it is his contemporaries who are implicated by his name.[34] Thus, even when such sources do interpret the name Enosh, they are still primarily interested in his contemporaries. This is most clearly expressed in the statement, "And why was he called Enosh? Since he was born in a sick [or weak] generation (*dôr 'ānûš*)."[35] What is remarkable is that the Rabbinic

[31] *B. Šabb.* 118b; *Lam. Rab.* Proem 24; *Tanḥ. Wayyera'* 18; *3 Enoch* 5.10. See above, chap. 4, nn. 145, 193. A similar play occurs in *Zohar* 2.192b (interpreting Isa 8:1).

[32] For a discussion of name interpretation in the aggadah see I. Heinemann, *Darke ha'aggada*, 110–12.

[33] Jer 15:18; 17:9; and Mic 1:9 are cited in the sources as examples of the verb *'nš* meaning "weakness." In all three places the verb appears in the passive participle form (*'ānûš*), which is only a slightly different vocalization from the name Enosh (*'ĕnôš*):*'nwš*. For the verb *'nš* meaning "be weak, sick," with other examples, see BDB 60. I have been unable to find post-biblical examples of the root *'nš* used in this way, other than in these plays on the name Enosh. Note that in CD 3:17 we find the expression *pš' 'nwš*, usually understood as *peša' 'ĕnôš* ("human sin"). L. Ginzberg (*Eine unbekannte jüdische Sekte*, vol. 1 [New York, 1922] 17–18), however, argues for translating this expression as "unheilbare Sünde" (*peša' 'ānûš*). In light of a parallel in 1QH 11:10, it seems best not to accept Ginzberg's suggestion. Rather, the expression is analogous to *tiqwat 'ĕnôš* ("human hope") in Job 14:19; Sir 7:17 and *m. 'Abot* 4:4. The Rabbinic sources in which Enosh's name is interpreted are: *Bere'šit Rabbati* (ed. Albeck) 31; *MhG* ad Gen 4:26 (ed. Margulies) 128; *MA* ad Gen 4:26 (ed. Buber) 22; *AgBer.* Oxford MS (ed. Buber) intro. 37. See also above, n. 21, where other medieval sources are given in which it is not clear whether a play is intended on the name Enosh, the verb *hûḥal* (as if from *ḥlh*), or both.

[34] In only *one* of our sources does the negative interpretation of the name Enosh refer specifically to Enosh himself: *MhG* ad Gen 4:26 ("he was weak-minded [*da'tô 'ănûšâ*] and his counsel was ill-advised as was that of his contemporaries"). In one other source (*Bere'šit Rabbati* [ed. Albeck] 31) it is unclear whether the negative interpretation refers to Enosh, his contemporaries, or both: "Enosh because of what befell him (*mĕ'ôrā'ô*) was called Enosh, since Enosh can only be an expression of calamity (*šeber*)." See above, chap. 4, nn. 178–82. In all other instances, the reference is to mankind in general, it not being clear whether Enosh is included.

[35] *AgBer.* Oxford MS (ed. Buber) intro. 37. This source continues by interpreting the names of Enosh's descendants. Each name is interpreted with reference to the *individual's* character or deeds, except for Jared (*yered*), whose name is interpreted, "For in

sources seem aware only of a negative interpretation of the name Enosh, while the non-Rabbinic sources consistently interpret it positively.[36]

As we have noted, several late Rabbinic interpretations of the name Enosh seem to suggest that Gen 4:26b, understood to announce the beginnings of idolatry, is itself an explanation of the name of Enosh in Gen 4:26a. Such a biblical play on the name Enosh might have been a natural expectation since Scripture so often provides such puns, whether explicit or implicit, especially in these early chapters of Genesis (Gen 2:23; 3:20; 4:1, 25; 5:29; all of which, including Gen 4:26, are generally identified with the J source). In such a context where name "etymologies" are usually provided, the absence of an explanation of a name as transparent as Enosh would certainly elicit comment.[37] If the Bible itself were thought to provide an explanation of the name Enosh, then an interpretation of Enosh meaning "weak or sick" would go hand in hand with an understanding of the verb *hûḥal* as "became weak, lax, or sick."[38] Thus, taking the word *'āz* as a conjunction, the verse as a whole could be understood, "And to Seth, in turn, a son was born and he

---

his days his generation sank (*yārĕdû*) to the lowest level."

36 This statement needs slight qualification. Although the Christian sources consistently interpret the name Enosh positively, two Christian exegetes cite negative interpretations of Enosh's name, but do *not* apply such interpretations to Gen 4:26 itself: Eusebius, *Praep. ev.* 11.6, where "Enosh" refers to the forgetful man; and Jerome *Liber interpretationis hebraicorum nominum*, where Enosh is interpreted to mean desperate or violent man. See above, chap. 3, n. 34. While the rabbis recognize a connection between the proper name Enosh and the collective noun *'ĕnôš* ("man"), they interpret the latter negatively, as in *MPs.* 9.16 (ed. Buber) 91, where the collective *'ĕnôš* is said to refer to the "foolish man" (*šôṭeh*). Although, as we have seen, Samaritan tradition views Enosh and his name positively, note that in the Samaritan *Asatir* 2.2 (ed. Gaster) Heb. 5, Eng. 196, Seth builds a city and names it Pilonah, after the name of Enosh. Z. Ben Ḥayyim (*Tarbiz* 14 [1943] 12, 26) argues that the name Pilonah can be understood as a play on the name Enosh, meaning weakness.

37 Such name puns are typical of the J source, but not of E or P. The genealogy of Genesis 5 (P) is devoid of such puns, except for 5:29, generally assigned to J. Thus, the Rabbinic expectation of a play on the name Enosh is a reasonable one. Compare Gen 30:21, where Dinah alone is named without an explanation. E. Speiser, in his commentary (*Genesis* [AB; New York: Doubleday, 1964] 231) takes this omission to be significant and states, "The notice about the birth of one daughter, Dinah, is given at the end, and it is the only instance in which no explanation is linked with the name; the notation may be a later gloss. On the whole, the naming of a child was never a casual matter." Rabbinic traditions respond by providing an explanation of her name: *Gen. Rab.* 72.6 (ed. Theodor-Albeck) 845; *MhG* ad Gen 30:21 (ed. Margulies) 532.

38 This would hold most true if *hûḥal* were interpreted from the root *ḥlh* to mean "became weak or sick." However, the other plays—"became lax" (*ḥwl*), "became profane or vulnerable" (*ḥll*), "abstained from" (*ḥll*)—could similarly be offered in conjunction with an interpretation of Enosh's name as "sickly" or "weak." Note how another tradition describes the origins of degenerate worship: "These were their notions of worship corresponding to their own weakness and timidity of soul." Philo of Byblos' *Phoenician History*, in Eusebius, *Praep. ev.* 1.10.6 (ed. Gifford) 1.45–46; 3.38–39; cf. 1.9.5.

named him Enosh, for it was then that men became weak in their calling on the name [i.e., worship] of the Lord."[39]

It may be argued, however, that a biblical name "etymology" usually reveals something concerning the child himself and not his contemporaries. This objection can be laid to rest since several biblical and postbiblical examples can be found where a naming is said to characterize the newborn's contemporaries. The best such biblical example is Gen 10:25, which states, "The name of the first was Peleg, for in his days the earth was divided (*niplĕgâ*)," referring to the punishment of the generation of the Tower of Babel. The biblical expression "in his days" (*bĕyāmāyw*) is identical to the Aramaic *bĕyômôhî* used by the targumim to translate *'āz* ("then") in Gen 4:26. For another scriptural case see 1 Sam 4:21: "Then she named the child Ichabod [literally, No-Glory], saying, 'Glory has departed from Israel,' because the ark of God has been captured." For examples from postbiblical Jewish literature, see *Jub.* 4:15, "And he called his name Jared (*yered*), for in his days the angels of the Lord descended [*yrd*] on the earth"; and *Jub.* 10:18, "And he [Peleg] called his name Reu (*rĕʿû*) for he said, 'Behold the children have become evil [*rʿh*] through the wicked purpose of building for themselves a city and a tower in the land of Shinar.'"[40] Finally, for the best Rabbinic

[39] We saw that non-Rabbinic traditions also viewed Gen 4:26b as an explanation of Enosh's name in 4:26a, interpreting both positively: Philo. *Abr.* 7–8; *Quod. Det.* 138; Eusebius, *Praep. ev.* 7.8; Ambrose, *De Paradiso* 1.3.19–23; Didymus, *On Genesis* ad Gen 4:26; John Chrysostom, *Homilies in Gen.* 20.4; Jerome, *Qu. Heb. in Gen.* ad Gen 4:26; Augustine, *De civ. Dei* 15.17–18; Isho'dad of Merv, *Commentary on Genesis* ad Gen 4:26; all of which are discussed at length above (chaps. 1 and 3). Note that modern commentators have also sought to relate the two halves of Gen 4:26. They suggest that the name Enosh denotes man in his frail condition (e.g., Ps 8:5; 103:15), and argue that only a man able to accept his own mortality in humility can truly worship God. U. Cassuto, *A Commentary on the Book of Genesis, From Adam to Noah* (trans. I. Abrahams; Jerusalem: Magnes, 1961) 246; F. Delitzsch, *Neuer Commentar über die Genesis*, 133–34; C. F. Keel and F. Delitzsch, *Biblical Commentary on the Old Testament*, (trans. J. Martin; Edinburgh: T. & T. Clark, 1878) 19. J. Skinner (*A Critical and Exegetical Commentary on Genesis*, 127) rejects such allegorical treatment of the name Enosh on the part of scholars, stating, "The idea that it is connected with a growing sense of the distinction between the human and the divine is a baseless fancy."

[40] For this interpretation of the name Jared, see also *1 Enoch* 6:6, now available in Aramaic (*The Books of Enoch: The Aramaic Fragments of Qumran Cave 4* [ed. J. Milik; Oxford: Clarendon, 1976] 152): *nḥtw bywmy yrd*. The same tradition is found in *MA* ad Gen 5:18 (ed. Buber) 23; and *AgBer.* Oxford MS (ed. Buber) intro. 37. Note that in *The Cave of Treasures* (ed. Budge) 84 Yared himself is said to have been perfect and virtuous, yet "in the days of Yared . . . the children of Seth broke the oaths which their fathers had made them to swear. And they began to go down from that holy mountain to the encampment of iniquity of the children of Cain, the murderer, and in this way the fall of the children of Seth took place." Cf. *The Book of Adam and Eve* 2.17, where Jared himself is tricked into leaving the mountain.

examples of such name interpretations, see the interpretation of Jeremiah's name (*yrmyh*) in *PRK* 13.11, 12:

> In ten [*y*] stages the Presence [*yh*] journeyed [up and away from Jerusalem] [*rm*] . . . Another interpretation of the name Jeremiah: For in his days the Temple became a desolation (*'êrîmôn*, from Greek *erēmos*). Another interpretation of the name Jeremiah: For in his days the measure of justice rose to its full height (*nitromĕmâ*).[41]

In none of the above examples does the negative interpretation of the name necessarily imply a negative estimation of the person. From these examples it is clear that while the name Enosh might be interpreted with respect to Enosh the individual, it could just as easily be interpreted in relation to his contemporaries. Being more interested in the Generation of Enosh than in Enosh, the rabbis chose to employ exegesis of his name primarily to discredit his contemporaries. Seth in naming Enosh is thought either to have prophesied or to have described the behavior of mankind, as revealed by Scripture in Gen 4:26b.[42]

While such interpretations of the name Enosh are well within the limits of acceptability of Rabbinic hermeneutics, they do not occur in Rabbinic sources until medieval times, appearing first in the very same compilations in which we witnessed plays on the verb *hûḥal*. Once again, such interpretations seem to reflect late attempts at linking the old, well-established Rabbinic interpretations of Gen 4:26 to the specific words of Scripture; it would appear that the tannaitic and amoraic expositors could have employed exegesis of Enosh's name, but chose not to do so.

5. Conclusions

We have seen that through amoraic times the method by which the Rabbinic interpretation of Gen 4:26 is derived from or linked to Scripture is scarcely articulated. Where it is evidenced, it appears simply as the fleshing-out of what is perceived as an elliptical phrase: Then men began to call (false gods) by the name of the Lord. Only in significantly later sources is the Rabbinic interpretation explicitly linked to Scripture through the explication of specific scriptural words (the verb *hûḥal* and/or the name Enosh.)[43] There is nothing to indicate, however, why these

[41] Ed. Mandelbaum, 234, 236; trans. Braude, 261, 262.

[42] Compare the Rabbinic interpretation of Gen 10:25, in which Eber is said to have acted prophetically, acting under holy inspiration, in naming Peleg: *Gen. Rab.* 37.7 (ed. Theodor-Albeck) 349; *SOR* 1.

[43] We should stress, however, that these methods never replace the old method of elliptical interpretation. The latter is clearly evidenced in Rashi's interpretation, as we have seen (above, nn. 17–18), as well as in RaDaQ (above, n. 16), RaLBaG (*Peruš 'al hattora*

later "literal" methods of explication should not have been employed by earlier generations of Rabbinic exegetes, especially since these early rabbis employ the very same methods in their interpretation of other scriptural passages. Surely, the early rabbis were as aware of the possibilities for such puns as were their successors. These facts raise for us two questions: (a) Why did the tannaim and amoraim not explicitly link their interpretation to the verb *hûḥal* and/or the name Enosh, as we might expect them to have done? (b) Why did later medieval Rabbinic exegetes suddenly begin to use such methods?

In answer to the first question, it would seem that the Rabbinic interpretation of Gen 4:26b was well enough accepted, at least in Rabbinic circles, so as not to require explanation. As we have noted, the tannaitic and amoraic sources are unanimous in their negative interpretation of this verse, even though they seem to have no trouble understanding the apparent "plain" meaning of its individual words. We must assume that the sum of the meanings of the individual words, however, resulted in a sense that was an impossibility (for reasons to be discussed) to these Rabbinic exegetes. As we have noted, the early rabbis were not concerned with deriving the sin of the Generation of Enosh from Scripture, but with describing and justifying its consequences; the fact and nature of this sin in Enosh's time was simply assumed by them. Since they were not primarily interested in discussing Enosh himself, they have left us no comments on his name. Thus, these rabbis simply felt no need to explicate the verb *hûḥal* or the name Enosh, their concerns with Gen 4:26b being altogether different.

The second question we have posed is more difficult. The first Rabbinic source that tries to link the Rabbinic interpretation of Gen 4:26 to the actual words of Scripture is *Targum Onqelos*, which we have argued interprets the verb *hûḥal* to mean "men ceased or refrained from [prayer]." This is in consonance with this targum's general character as a "literal" translation, i.e., an Aramaic paraphrase that stays as close as possible to the letter of the Hebrew text, while still expressing the authoritative Rabbinic interpretation.[44]

Rabbinic midrashic sources, however, do not evidence such "literal" methods of exegesis of Gen 4:26 until many centuries later. I hypothesize (but cannot absolutely prove) that these late midrashic sources are for the first time confronting a "plain" interpretation of this verse that contradicts the received traditional interpretation. Such a "plain" interpretation is first attested in Rabbinic sources in the comments of Ibn Ezra and

---

derek be'ur [Venice, 1547] 17d) and RaN (R. Nissim b. Reuben Gerondi, *Commentary on the Bible* [ed. Leon Feldman; Jerusalem: Shalem Institute, 1968] 70).

44 Of course, the adjective "literal" should not be misunderstood as "correct." I use it here only in a relative sense, having also indicated some of the expansive elements of *Tg. Onq.* Gen 4:26. For a fuller description of this characteristic, see above, chap. 4, n. 30.

RaDaQ: In Enosh's time men first began to pray to God.[45] Other medieval commentators either reject this interpretation as being impossible,[46] or try to reconcile it with the received tradition.[47] But in either case, they must now come to terms with this "plain" interpretation and must justify the traditional interpretation by showing how it is in fact suggested by the words of Scripture itself, something that the tannaim and amoraim were, it would seem, not forced to do. In an age in which Hebrew grammar and lexicography were for the first time studied in their own right, and more rationalistic approaches to the study of Scripture were being promoted (e.g., by Moslem and Karaite exegetes), the traditional, converse interpretations of Gen 4:26b could no longer simply be accepted on good faith but had to be shown to have at least some grounding in the letter of the text.

The "literal" methods of *Targum Onqelos* and the medieval commentators, although similar, had somewhat different motivations. The former was guided by the need for a close authoritative translation of Scripture, while the latter were driven by the need to defend the traditional understanding of Gen 4:26 against possible charges of unfaithfulness to the text of Scripture. Those who in the end could deny neither the "plain" meaning nor the transmitted Rabbinic interpretation were forced to recognize in Gen 4:26b *both* meanings. This was most commonly achieved by suggesting that the verb *hûḥal* had both the meaning "was begun" and "was profaned" (double entendre).[48] Some claimed that while most of Enosh's contemporaries were engaged in idolatrous worship, a select few turned for the first time to the proper worship of God by name.[49] It is within such a *medieval* context that midrashic attempts to derive the received interpretation of Gen 4:26 from the verb *hûḥal* and the name Enosh must be viewed, rather than reading such interpretations back into much earlier sources where they do not play a significant part, at least not in the extant documents available to us.

[45] See above, nn. 15, 16.

[46] E.g., RaLBaG, RaN (above, n. 43), and Mizrahi (above, n. 15).

[47] Thus, Ibn Ezra, in his *Šiṭa 'aḥeret*, after interpreting the verb *hûḥal* to mean "to be weak," says, "Therefore it was necessary to pray," presumably for healing. See above, n. 21. Similarly, R. Samuel b. Meir (RaŠBaM, 1080–1184) interprets our verse, "An expression of beginning, for they began to pray because of their renewed troubles." *Peruš hattora* (ed. D. Rosen; Breslau, 1881) 10.

[48] E.g., Judah Löw ben Bezalel (1517–1609) in *Seper gur 'aryeh* ad Rashi Gen 4:26 (Prague, 1578; reprint Bene Berak, 1972) 45a; *Da'at soperim* ad loc. These take the verb *hûḥal* to mean both "beginning" and "profaning": it was the profaning of God's name which was begun.

[49] E.g., Sforno (in *Miqra'ot gedolot* ad loc), who states, "Then the righteous of the generation began to invoke the name of the Lord in public, . . . for they needed to refute (*listôr*) the notions of the idol worshippers, which had at that time begun, according to the words of the Sages." The same harmonization appears in Luzzatto's commentary (see above, n. 17).

While our examination of Rabbinic exegetical method has shed some light on the motivations of medieval exegetes who sought to ground the inherited traditions of exegesis concerning the Generation of Enosh in the words of Gen 4:26, it has left unanswered the question of why the earliest exponents of these traditions followed an exegetical path so different from those tread by their Jewish predecessors and non-Jewish contemporaries. To this most difficult question I now turn.

B. Rabbinic Motivations

If the Rabbinic texts that we have surveyed so infrequently tell us *how* they connect their interpretation of Gen 4:26 to the actual words of that verse, they give us even fewer clues with regard to *why* they interpret it as they do. They generally cite Gen 4:26 with its Rabbinic meaning *assumed*, without explaining why such a radical interpretation should even be considered. Before proceeding, two related notes of self-caution are in order:

(a) In asking what motivated Rabbinic exegetes we should not expect to arrive at certain answers, but at well-educated guesses. We can never know with certainty what conscious or unconscious motivations, and there could have been several intertwined, were responsible. All we can ask is, which of the available explanations makes the best sense of our data?

(b) We are not interested in ascertaining the *true* meaning of Gen 4:26, and therefore our interest in the question of motivation is not for the sake of determining the reasonableness or unreasonableness of Rabbinic interpretation of that verse. We presume that the Rabbinic exegetes were neither capricious nor mantic in their exegesis, and that they were motivated by real concerns, whether deriving from the text as they read it, from the context in which they read it, or from some confluence of the two.

What might those concerns have been? How are they met through the medium of exegesis of Gen 4:26? What do our responses to these questions suggest concerning the broader activity of Rabbinic thought and self-definition of which the subject of this case study is only a small part?

We can already say two things, both negative: (a) The early rabbis were not particularly troubled by any of the individual words of Gen 4:26, which they understood as did others. (b) There is nothing to suggest that their interpretation was inherited from pre-Rabbinic or extra-Rabbinic lore. Therefore, our question restated is: what so bothered the rabbis about Gen 4:26b as it was *commonly* understood in their days that they could not accept such an interpretation, but rather shaped their own distinctive understanding of this verse's meaning?

Since, as we have seen, it would be a gross oversimplification to speak of a single Rabbinic interpretation of Gen 4:26, our sources reflecting a long and highly variegated (although fairly consistent) history of tradition transmission, we will not search for a *single* Rabbinic motivation. Just as we are unable to determine when and how the Rabbinic tradition interpretation of Gen 4:26 began, so too we cannot be sure whether the motivations of the first Rabbinic exegetes were the same as those of subsequent generations of rabbis, who both transmitted and adapted this interpretation. Thus, we will assume that a number of motivating factors were involved, either concurrently or at different stages, many of which undoubtedly overlapped. Since the suggested motivations are speculative and cannot always be identified with a particular authority or source, they cannot be presented chronologically as were the traditions themselves in chapter four. We will test each proposed motivation against the exegetical traditions themselves, and hope that by so doing we can at least correlate them with the approximate tradition history that we have traced.

1. Etiology of Evil

One exegetical concern that the rabbis often express is the desire to trace the origins of customs, practices, and institutions, whether worthy or unworthy, back to biblical times.[50] Thus, since Rabbinic literature contains frequent polemics against "strange worship," considering it to be not only one of the cardinal human sins, but the sin that is the root of all others,[51] it would be logical to assume that they would have been interested in determining when such behavior first began: is it endemic to human nature, having begun with the very first humans, or did it arise at some subsequent point in human history? While Scripture tells of the first murder (Gen 4:8) and of the first acts of sexual promiscuity (Gen 6:2), it says nothing specifically about the origins of idolatry.[52] Thus, it would be natural for the rabbis to have been interested in not only when idolatry began, but how it began, and what its consequences were.

[50] See I. Heinemann, *Darke ha'aggada*, 99.

[51] See, for example, *Sifre Deut*. 54 (ed. Finkelstein) 122; and *Sifre Num*. 111 (ed. Horovitz) 116. For a similar view see Wis 14:12, 24.

[52] This fact has been noted by Y. Kaufmann (*The Religion of Israel* [trans. and abr. M. Greenberg; Chicago: University of Chicago, 1960] 294), who comments, "No story is dedicated to the origin of idolatry. . . . The absence of a story about the origin of idolatry seems to reflect the feeling that, although an abomination, idolatry is the fruit of sin, a punishment, rather than a primary sin itself." However, it may be argued that for the Bible, the first "idolatry" occurs at Mt. Sinai with the making of the golden calf (Exod 32:4), a violation of the terms of God's covenant with Israel. Only in later biblical books does idolatry become a *universal moral* sin. Thus, the rabbis (and Kaufmann) read this later view of idolatry back into the earlier chapters of Genesis.

While this point sets the background for our discussion of the motivation for the Rabbinic interpretation of Gen 4:26, it hardly provides an adequate explanation. Supposing the rabbis wanted to trace the origins of idolatry, why did they choose to trace it to this verse, which would appear to have as its intention the tracing of another etiology, that of divine worship? Certainly, it would have made much more sense for the rabbis to attribute the origins of idolatry to one of the evil individuals or generations already described by Scripture. The likeliest candidate would have been the builders of the Tower of Babel, whose activity could easily have been redescribed as idolatrous worship.[53]

While the rabbis alone trace the origins of idolatry to the Generation of Enosh, they are not alone in wishing to determine when and how unacceptable forms of divine worship originated in humanity's earliest days. For instance, Eusebius of Caesarea, wishing to demonstrate the unreasonableness of pagan worship, cites several euhemeristic accounts of man's earliest worship (*Praep. ev.* 1.9–10).[54] These relate that at first people looked to the heavens, and thinking that the sun, moon, and stars were gods gave them names and worshipped them. Only subsequently did they degenerate with the worship and mythologizing of terrestrial

53 Thus, Kaufmann infers that "with the confusion of tongues there comes an end to the monotheistic period of history." *The Religion of Israel*, 294; as well as in his essay, "The Biblical Age," in *Great Ages and Ideas of the Jewish People* (ed. Leo Schwarz; New York: Random House, 1956) 14, 42. Rabbinic sources interpret the building of the Tower of Babel as an act of idolatry, but not as the first such act. See *Mek. Kaspa'* 4 (ed. Lauterbach) 3.180–81; *Gen. Rab.* 38.8 (ed. Theodor-Albeck) 358; *b. Sanh.* 109a; where "let us make a name for ourselves" (Gen 11:4) is interpreted to refer to "strange worship."

54 Eusebius quotes most extensively from the *Phoenician History* of Philo of Byblos (first-second centuries C.E.), who claims to present a translation of the ancient history of one Phoenician Sanchuniathon. Most recent scholarship views Philo of Byblos' account to be more reflective of Hellenistic attitudes than of ancient Phoenician tradition (which may still be a distant source). See the introductions to H. W. Attridge and R. A. Oden, Jr., *Philo of Byblos, the Phoenician History: Introduction, Critical Text, Translation, Notes* (CBQMS 9; Washington, D.C.: Catholic Biblical Association of America, 1981); A. I. Baumgarten, *The Phoenician History of Philo of Byblos: A Commentary* (Études préliminaires aux religions orientales dans l'empire Romain 89; Leiden: E. J. Brill, 1981); both of which cite earlier scholarship. For the critical text see F. Jacoby, *FGrH* Nr. 790 (vol. 3C, pp. 802–24). Note particularly Philo's introduction to Sanchuniathon in *Praep. ev.* 1.9.5, repeated in 1.10.6–7 (ed. Gifford) 1.39, 45–46; 3.31, 38–39. Other authors cited by Eusebius are Diodorus of Sicily, Porphyry, and Plato. Such views go back at least to Euhemerus (ca. 290 C.E.) and Hecataeus of Abdera (ca. 300 C.E.), preserved mainly by Diodorus (ca. 60–30 C.E.) in his *Bibliotheka* (especially 6.1 and 1.11–13); also in *Praep. ev.* 2.2. For texts, see *FGrH* Nr. 63 (vol. 1), Nr. 264 (vol. 3A). On euhemerism see the sources cited in Attridge and Oden, 74 n. 20; and M. P. Nilsson, *Geschichte des griechischen Religion* (2nd. ed.; 2 vols.; Munich: Beck, 1961) 2.283–89.

On the early worship of celestial bodies, Eusebius quotes Plato (*Cratylas* 397C), who says that the first Greeks called them "gods" (*theoi*) because of their running (*thein*) nature, and only later was that name applied to other gods.

beings (especially culture heroes), to the erecting of statues and temples, and to the worship of demons and spirits. Of these later developments Eusebius comments:

> These then were men's inventions and representations of our mortal nature, or rather new devices of base and licentious dispositions, according to our divine oracle which says, "The devising of idols was the beginning of fornication" (Wis 14:12).[55]

Against all of this Eusebius sets Israelite worship:

> This is what our holy Scriptures also teach, in which it is contained (Deut 4:19), that in the beginning the worship of the visible luminaries had been assigned to all the nations, and that to the Hebrew race alone had been entrusted the full initiation into the knowledge of God the Maker and Artificer of the universe, and of true piety towards Him.[56]

It is not clear whether Eusebius understands the pagan worship of heavenly bodies to have preceded or developed alongside the true worship of the single God.[57]

In a polemic against idolatry, the author of the Wisdom of Solomon expresses a similar view (13:1–9): idolatry began when men observing the heavenly bodies and natural elements held them "to be the gods who govern the world." The sin of these early men is understandable if not excusable, for in their eagerness to find God they confused Him with His works. The *cult* of idolatry is a *subsequent* outgrowth of this misunderstanding. However, the author of Wisdom clearly understands monotheism to have *preceded* idolatry, stating (14:13–14) "They [the idols] did not exist at the beginning, they will not exist forever; through human vanity they came into the world and hence a sudden end has been designated for them." Thus, idolatry is viewed as a human innovation, a *perversion* of divine worship.[58]

We have seen that Josephus speaks of the first generations of Sethites

[55] *Praep. ev.* 1.9.18 (ed. Gifford) 1.40; 3.34. See above, n. 51.

[56] *Praep. ev.* 1.9.15 (ed. Gifford) 1.40; 3.34.

[57] The euhemeristic philosopher-historians cited by Eusebius locate the origins of celestial worship at the very beginnings of human history. Does Eusebius claim an equally ancient origin for Israelite faith, or does he view it as a subsequent development? In incorporating his pagan sources he never clarifies this.

[58] Just as the euhemeristic writers view the worship of terrestrial beings as a degeneration from the originally simple veneration of celestial bodies, early Jewish sources view the worship of celestial bodies (and subsequent idolatries) as a degeneration from the originally pure worship of the single God. See above, chap. 4, n. 53. We have seen that early Rabbinic polemics against idolatry often state that the idols (or false gods) were "latecomers." See above, chap. 4, nn. 32, 50, 56. For references to other extra-Rabbinic Jewish polemics against idolatry see G. F. Moore, *Judaism in the First Centuries of the Christian Era* (3 vols.; Cambridge, Mass.: Harvard University Press, 1927–40) 1.362–63.

as having been righteous, and only subsequently have degenerated:

> For seven generations these people continued to believe in God as Lord of the universe and in everything to take virtue for their guide; then, in course of time, they abandoned the customs of their fathers for a life of depravity. They no longer rendered to God His due honours, nor took account of justice towards men, but displayed by their actions a zeal for vice twofold greater than they had formerly shown for virtue, and thereby drew upon themselves the enmity of God.[59]

While Josephus does not speak specifically of "idolatry," he clearly states that God was initially worshipped, and only subsequently did mankind abandon His worship.[60]

Finally, in the Pseudo-Clementine *Recognitions* we find similar descriptions of the origins of idolatry: "But in the process of time [after the Flood] the worship of God and righteousness were corrupted by the unbelieving and the wicked . . . Moreover, perverse and erratic religions were introduced. . . ."[61] And elsewhere, the author traces the origins of idolatry to the teachings of the fallen angels, identifies Ham as the first magician, and concludes:

> For whereas at first, men worshipping a righteous and all-seeing God, neither dared sin nor do injury to their neighbors, being persuaded that God sees the actions and movements of every one; when religious worship was directed to lifeless images, concerning which they are certain that they were incapable of hearing, or sight, or motion, they began to sin licentiously, and to go forward to every crime, because they had no fear of suffering anything at the hands of those whom they worshipped as gods.[62]

Thus, idolatry is portrayed as one of the earliest sins, leading to the others, yet as a perversion of the originally true worship of God.

The above selection of passages helps us to put the Rabbinic interpretation of the Generation of Enosh in perspective.[63] The rabbis were not unique in their tracing of the origins of idolatry (i.e., false worship) to the earliest generations of mankind. Like others rooted in the biblical tradition, they viewed idolatry as coming *later* than monotheism, being

59 *Ant.* 1.3.1 § 72. I have treated this passage in greater detail above, chap. 1, n. 73.

60 This is similar to *Tg. Onqelos'* interpretation that with Enosh's generation divine worship ceased, which I have argued is equivalent to saying that idolatry (alien-worship) began. See above, n. 25.

61 4.13 (*ANF* 8.137).

62 4.31 (*ANF* 8.141). We have seen that in *3 Enoch* 5.7–9 (*Seper hekalot*) the fallen angels also play a role in the first idolatry. See above, chap. 4, n. 168. Similarly, in *1 Enoch* 7:1 the fallen angels teach mankind the arts of magic. For the origins of idolatry associated with the worship of dead heroes, see *Homilies* 9.5; *Recognitions* 4.30. Cf. Wis 14:15–16.

63 For other references, see L. Ginzberg, *Legends*, 5.150–51.

a corruption of man's original recognition of one God.[64] Similarly, their basic understanding of idolatry was not unique: they viewed its root in the misguided application of God's name and attributes to created phenomena. Thus, our discussion of Rabbinic motivation must focus not so much on the Rabbinic description of earliest idolatry (minimal and common as it is), but on the unique Rabbinic association of idolatry's origins with Gen 4:26 and description of the consequent punishments received by the Generation of Enosh.

2. Contradiction with the Sinaitic Theophany

A number of scholars have suggested that the motivation for the Rabbinic interpretation of Gen 4:26 lies in the contradiction between that verse and Exod 3:15 and 6:3, which are said to credit Moses with being the first to learn God's name, YHWH. According to this view, how could Enosh have been the first to "call upon the name of the Lord" if that name was not revealed until the theophany at Sinai?[65] Such a suggestion, however, is without the slightest support from the Rabbinic sources themselves. The Rabbinic exegesis of these passages does not reflect any awareness of such a "contradiction." In fact, the targumic and midrashic traditions connected with Gen 4:26b *assume* the knowledge of the name of YHWH by Enosh's contemporaries. How else could they have applied it to their "false gods"?[66] Even *Targum Onqelos*, in stating that men ceased to pray in the name of the Lord, assumes that it was already commonly known and used in worship.

The reason no contradiction is seen between Gen 4:26b and Exod 3:15 and 6:3 is that Rabbinic traditions do not necessarily interpret the Exodus passages to suggest the revelation of a *new* divine name. This is especially apparent in the Rabbinic exegesis of Exod 6:3, which stresses that to Moses alone God for the first time revealed the secret *meaning* of his name YHWH, in which sense He was then acting to redeem Israel:

64 But cf. above, n. 57.

65 J. Bowker, *The Targums and Rabbinic Literature* (Cambridge: University Press, 1969) 140–41; idem, "Haggadah in the Targum Onqelos," *JSS* 12 (1967) 59; R. Le Déaut, "Un Phénomène spontané de l'herméneutique Juive ancienne: Le Targumisme," *Bib.* 52 (1971) 517; A. Klijn, *Seth in Jewish, Christian, and Gnostic Literature* (NovTSup 46; Leiden: E. J. Brill, 1977) 5; S. Sandmel, "Gen. 4:26b," *HUCA* 32 (1961) 19. A. Shinan ("The Form and Content of the Aggadah in the 'Palestinian' Targumim on the Pentateuch and its Place Within Rabbinic Literature," [Hebrew] [Ph.D. diss., Hebrew University, 1977] 210 n. 98) accepts this explanation for the midrashim, but not for the targumim.

66 All of the "Palestinian" targumim state that Enosh's contemporaries applied "the name of the Memra of the Lord" to their idols and use a form of the tetragram in their translations. Similarly, the earliest midrashim interpret "to call on the name of the Lord" to mean that they called false gods by God's name. As we have noted (chap. 4, n. 43), the midrashim make little distinction between *'ĕlōhîm* and *YHWH* in their treatment of Gen 4:26b.

> "I appeared to Abraham, Isaac, and Jacob as El Shadday, but I did not make Myself known to them by my name YHWH": I did not divulge to them its interpretation, but to you I revealed it.[67]

While the patriarchs knew and used the name YHWH, they did not know its revelatory content. They did not know that this name denotes God's attribute as fulfiller of promises; his attribute of mercy. The patriarchs knew that God had as one of his names YHWH, but they did not yet truly know *Him* as YHWH. Thus, the theophany is viewed as the revelation not of a new name, but of a new understanding of a familiar name. For the first time, God makes *himself* known as YHWH. Through His fulfillment of His promise to the patriarchs, God now acts as YHWH, and no longer as El Shaddai.[68] Thus, Enosh (and the patriarchs)

[67] *Lōʾ pirsamtî lāhem ʾim mĕpôrāš hûʾ, ûlĕkâ gālîtî ʾôtô. Tanḥ. B. Waʾeraʾ* 5 (p. 21). Also in *YS Waʾeraʾ* 176 (ed. Salonika) 7b, which has *lōʾ pāraštî*. Literally, our text translates, "I did not make known to them if it is interpreted," which is awkward. M. Kasher (*TS* 9.5 n. 23) changes the text to read, *lōʾ pirsamtî lāhem šēm hammĕpôrāš* ("I did not make known to them the Distinctive Name [the Tetragram]"). While his emendation simplifies the passage, the evidence that he adduces is not convincing. Rather, it seems to me that the sense of our passage is like that of *MhG* ad Exod 6:3 (ed. Margulies) 95: "The Patriarchs had no need for the Distinctive Name to be interpreted for them, but the prophets [including Moses] had the name interpreted for them, for the people of their generation were in such need. This can be proven from the case of Moses our teacher, as it is said, 'I appeared to Abraham, Isaac, and Jacob as El Shadday, but I did not make Myself known to them by My name YHWH'! I was not revealed (*niglêtî*) to them as to You." This interpretation is based on the passive voice (*niphʿal*) of the verb *nôdaʿtî* ("I was known") in Exod 6:3. Rashi comments, "'I did not make known (*hôdaʿtî*)' is not written here, but 'I was not known.' I was not recognized by them by my attribute of Veracity (*ʾămittût*), for which I am called YHWH: He who may be trusted to fulfill his word." For similar interpretations, see *Midraš śekel ṭob* (ed. Buber) 32; *LT* (ed. Buber) 30–31; *Midraš ḥadas ʿal hattora* (in Kasher, *TS* 9.5 n. 24); RaMBaN ad Exod 6:3 (ed. Chavel) 302–5; RaŠBaM ad Exod 6:3 (ed. Rosin) 87. While *Tg. Onqelos*, *Tg. Neofiti*, the Vg., LXX, and *Peshiṭta* all translate as if Scripture read *hôdaʿtî*, *Tg. Ps.-Jonathan*, the Cairo Geniza fragments (Ctg D), and the *Samaritan Tg.* all translate passively, reflecting the MT *nôdaʿtî*.

[68] This interpretation agrees with what some scholars have claimed to be the correct understanding of this biblical passage. M. Greenberg (*Understanding Exodus* [New York: Behrman House, 1969] 130–34) and U. Cassuto (*Peruš ʿal seper šemot* [Jerusalem: Magnes, 1953] 50–51) argue convincingly for this interpretation. They cite Ezek 20:5, 9, the earliest interpretation of the Sinaitic theophany, in support of retaining the passive reading of *nodaʿtî*. Greenberg argues that the second half of Exod 6:3 does not suggest the revelation of a new divine name, but is only parenthetical. He paraphrases, "I appeared to the patriarchs as El Shadday (not making myself known to them by my name YHWH) and indeed established" etc. According to Greenberg, the stress is not on revelation, but on self-identification and continuity. This is the same God who spoke to the patriarchs as El Shadday. He will now fulfill the promises made to them. Greenberg states, "All of verse 3 is designed as an assertion of continuity . . . ; thus the change in divine names is not only unexplicated, but is not even stated for its own sake." For a similar, but more qualified view, see B. S. Childs, *The Book of Exodus: A Critical, Theological Commentary* (Philadelphia: Westminster, 1974) 112–16, 119–20. C. Westermann (*Genesis*, fasc. I/6 [BKAT;

could worship God as YHWH long before the special significance of that name was revealed to Moses. There appears, therefore, not to be the slightest hint that the rabbis were bothered by pre-Sinaitic familiarity with the tetragram, whether in the patriarchal or antediluvian eras.[69] Therefore, this explanation of the Rabbinic interpretation of Gen 4:26 proves unsatisfactory when weighed against the Rabbinic sources themselves, and we must turn our attention elsewhere.

3. Gen 4:26 and its Biblical Context

Perhaps we can learn something about the Rabbinic motivation by looking at how the Rabbinic sources treat the scriptural context of our verse. We will first look at relevant Rabbinic interpretations of Genesis 4 (Cain and his descendants), then at Rabbinic views of Genesis 5–6, and finally at the Rabbinic attitude toward the larger context of pre-Israelite history (Genesis 1–11).

Before doing so, however, we should note that while modern biblical critics are in essential agreement on their understanding of Gen 4:26, they are divided (and perplexed) precisely on the issue of this verse's relation to its context.[70] While Gen 4:17–24 is understood to contain a

---

Neukirchen-Vluyn: Neukirchener Verlag, 1966–78] 460–61) argues that within J there is no contradiction between Gen 4:26 and Exod 3:15 and 6:3, since Gen 4:26 simply announces the beginnings of divine worship, rather than the invocation of God's name YHWH in particular.

Some biblical scholars have been bothered by another possible contradiction within the biblical text: How could divine worship have begun with Enosh's birth if Cain and Abel are already said to have offered sacrifices to God (Gen 4:3–4)? Cassuto (above, n. 39) suggests that after Abel's murder Adam and his family ceased worshipping God, recommencing once Enosh was born when they were relieved of their grief. This is clearly forced.

69 If, indeed, the rabbis were bothered by a contradiction between Gen 4:26 and Exod 6:3, they would also have had trouble with Abraham's familiarity with the tetragram, for he too "called upon the name of the Lord" (Gen 12:8; 13:4; 21:33; 26:25), and was told by God, "I am the Lord (YHWH) who brought you out from Ur of the Chaldeans" (Gen 15:7). However, nowhere do the rabbis deny that Abraham and the other patriarchs knew of the tetragram.

70 All agree that this verse announces the beginning of divine worship. Some suggest that the passive *hûḥal* refers to mankind in general, while others take it to refer to Enosh in particular. While most take the expression "to call upon the name of the Lord" to denote divine worship in general, some place greater emphasis on "the name of the Lord" and suggest what was new was the use of God's name YHWH in that worship, i.e., the explicit calling on God by that name. Others suggest that since examples of private worship are previously evidenced in the Bible (Cain and Abel's sacrifices "to the Lord," Gen 4:3–4), Gen 4:26 must announce the beginnings of *public* worship. See commentaries referred to above, chap. 1, n. 3. For additional bibliography, see Westermann, *Genesis*, 457–58. I have found particularly helpful J. M. Miller, "The Descendants of Cain: Notes on Genesis 4," ZAW 86 (1974) 164–73; and R. R. Wilson, *Genealogy and History in the Biblical World* (New Haven, Conn.: Yale University Press, 1977) 138–66.

Cainite genealogy (J) extending from Cain through Lamech's sons (seven generations), Genesis 5 is seen to contain a Sethite genealogy (P), tracing mankind's descent through Adam's third son Seth until Noah (ten generations). The two genealogies are of different sorts. The first is concerned with describing the achievements and eventual disgrace of the Cainite line, telling us something of what they did and said. It is not a linear genealogy, for after Lamech it branches out to include his three sons and one daughter, with whom the genealogy ends. The second genealogy, by contrast, is entirely linear, supplying only genealogical information (names and years, except in the cases of Enoch and Noah: 5:22, 24, 29), its purpose being to trace the uninterrupted transmission of the divine image from Adam through a select line of descendants, culminating with Noah.[71] What then is the function of Gen 4:25–26, found between these two genealogies?

It is usually argued that there were once two J genealogies, one tracing Cain's descendants, the other, Seth's, at least as far as the Flood.[72] Gen 4:25–26 (Seth and Enosh) and 5:29 (Noah) are viewed as fragments from this J Sethite genealogy. While most of this genealogy was replaced by the P Sethite genealogy of Genesis 5, with its emphasis on the direct and uninterrupted descent from Adam through Seth to Noah, the fragments describing the births of Seth, Enosh, and Noah alone were retained and woven into the narrative.[73] However, the question remains: why weren't the descriptions of Seth's and Enosh's births woven into Genesis 5 in their proper places (after Gen 5:2) as was that of Noah (5:29)? Why does Gen 4:25–26 come where it does after the Cainite genealogy, causing an obvious discontinuity with Gen 5:1? The answer often given is that Gen 4:25–26 was lifted from its original context (a J Sethite genealogy) and inserted between the Cainite genealogy of Gen 4:17–24 and the Sethite list of Genesis 5 in order to provide a transition. For since Genesis 5 skips Cain and his progeny and Abel entirely, suggesting that Seth was Adam's firstborn son, the "reader," having already learned of these omitted figures, would surely notice their absence. Therefore, Gen 4:25–26 is inserted, with the phrase "another offspring in

71 Wilson (*Genealogy and History*, 166) argues from anthropological evidence that seemingly contradictory genealogies are sometimes used in order to fulfill different functions.

72 While it is usually assumed that the original J Sethite genealogy contained the same ten names as that of Genesis 5, of this we cannot be certain. It is usually noted that the Cainite and Sethite genealogies contain similar or identical names: Cain=Kenan, Enoch=Enoch, Irad=Jared, Mehujael=Mahalalel, Methushael=Methuselah, Lamech= Lamech, and perhaps Adam=Enosh. Some conclude from this that one list is dependent on the other, some that both are dependent on a third original list, and some that the two lists were intentionally designed to mirror one another.

73 This reconstruction is from Miller, "The Descendants of Cain," 164.

place of Abel" suggesting that Seth had replaced Abel as Adam's heir (and the transmitter of the divine seed and/or image). The inclusion of Gen 4:26, with its association of the beginnings of divine worship with the Sethites, would indicate not only that Seth replaced Abel, but that the whole *righteous* Sethite line, delineated in Genesis 5, is to be viewed as supplanting the *wicked* Cainite line of Gen 4:17–24.[74]

Although there is merit to this explanation, it is not universally accepted, and alternatives have been proposed.[75] What is important for us to note is that Gen 4:25–26 does not fit into its context smoothly and *requires explanation*. The reader, whether ancient or modern, is inevitably struck by the unevenness of this part of the narrative, which describes Cain's descendants through seven generations, then reverts back to Seth, who is a replacement for Cain, continues with Enosh, and then recapitulates, starting anew with Adam. We will recall that it is precisely a notice of this discontinuity which initiates the discussion of Gen 4:26 in *Gen. Rab.* 23:6–7: "[Why does Scripture enumerate] Adam, Seth, Enosh, and is then silent?" and which is commented upon as well by non-Rabbinic exegetes.[76] Thus, the difficulty of understanding Gen 4:26 in its scriptural context is not uniquely Rabbinic, being shared by other exegetes throughout the history of that verse's interpretation. However, for the rabbis this problem had some distinctive aspects, which can be recognized by looking at their treatment of that scriptural context.

I will begin the investigation of the Rabbinic understanding of the biblical context of Gen 4:26 by looking at their attitudes toward the

74 Ibid., 165, with references to those who hold this position.

75 Ibid., 166–67. See also J. Skinner, *A Critical and Exegetical Commentary on Genesis*, 99. Miller argues that Gen 4:17–18 and 4:25–26 are fragments of an original, common genealogy that is preserved in P. In this original list Seth and Enosh would have preceded Cain (Kenan of Gen 5:9–14). However, once the story of Cain's murder of Abel and the Song of Lamech were integrated into the Cainite genealogy, the notices of Seth and Enosh were removed and transposed to their present place so as to disassociate these two and the beginnings of divine worship from Cain and his progeny. Wilson argues that there may have originally been two parallel genealogical lists, one Cainite and one Sethite, which were intended to mirror each other somewhat. The former he compares to the seven Mesopotamian apkallus (culture heroes, see below, n. 81), the latter to the ten Mesopotamian antediluvian kings, the names of which resemble one another. J may have intended to contrast the sinfulness of the Cainite line with the righteousness of the Sethite line. However, once the biblical redactor adopted P's version of the Sethite line, stressing the linear transmission of the divine image (through Seth), the J Sethite genealogy was attenuated. The notice of Noah's birth was integrated into chapter 5, while 4:25–26 was left in place for the sake of contrast and transition, and also because of its important notice of the beginnings of divine worship. Thus, one view sees Gen 4:25–26 as having been transposed to its present place either from an independent Sethite genealogy or from before Gen 4:17 in an originally common genealogy, while another view understands Gen 4:25–26 to be original in its present place, its continuation having been attenuated.

76 See above, chap. 4, nn. 64, 68.

preceding verses (Gen 4:17–24). Genesis 4 has generally been viewed by biblical scholars as an account of humanity's civilized and spiritual "firsts." Just as Gen 4:17–22 attributes the beginnings of civilized tools, arts, and institutions to Cain's descendants, Gen 4:26 attributes a new spiritual institution to Seth's line.[77] Thus, to the very beginnings of human history are traced the beginnings not only of some of the necessities of civilized life, but also the beginnings of divine worship. Yet, one can just as easily understand this description of the civilized firsts within the context of a *negative* estimate of human civilization, especially in light of the preceding account of the first murder (fratricide at that) and the concluding Song of Lamech (4:23–24), which speaks of blood revenge.[78] This larger context in which we find the "culture heroes" may be viewed as depicting the progressive degeneration of human culture, typified by man's manipulation of nature and ever increasing sin. If so, Genesis 4 would juxtapose man's civilized achievements (soon to be destroyed in the Flood) against his escalating moral depravity, which unfolds more fully in chapter 6.

The Rabbinic treatment of the culture heroes of Genesis 4 clearly accords with the negative estimation. These innovators are regarded in Rabbinic traditions as having used their new tools for violent, sexually perverse, and idolatrous purposes. We are told that Cain built a city for vain and selfish reasons, Jabal openly provoked God's anger (a play, *miqneh/mĕqanneh*) through idolatry, that Jubal played his music in idolatrous temples, that Tubal-Cain fashioned his metal instruments for murder (i.e., he refined [*tbl*] or improved upon Cain's sin), and that his sister Naamah made idolatrous music and because of her beauty (*nʿm*) enticed the angels to go astray after her (an allusion to Gen 6:1ff). Thus, Cain and his descendants are viewed as a line of evildoers, their "civilized achievements" being interpreted to their discredit and to the detriment of humanity.[79]

77 E.g., Dillmann, *Genesis*, 1.209.

78 Skinner, *A Critical and Exegetical Commentary on Genesis*, 115; Wilson, *Genealogy and History*, 155. See also P. D. Hanson, "Rebellion in Heaven, Azazel, and Euhemeristic Heroes in 1 Enoch 6–11," *JBL* 96 (1977) 231.

79 *Gen. Rab.* 23.1–3 (ed. Theodor-Albeck) 221–24; *MhG* ad Gen 4:17–22 (ed. Margulies) 125–26; *YS Bereʾšit* 47 (ed. Salonika) 16a; *YS Wayeḥi* 161 from *Midraš ʾabkir* (ed. Salonika) 64c; *p. Yebam.* 6.5 (7c); *Tanḥ. B. Ḥuqqat* supp. 1 (p. 131); *MA* ad Gen 4:17–22 (ed. Buber) 21–22; *Midraš ʿaśeret haddibberot* (in Jellinek, *BhM* 1.79–80); *Menorat Ha-Maor* (ed. Enelow) 1.125–26; *PRE* 22 (ed. Warsaw) 51a with Luria's n. 16; *ShY* (ed. Goldschmidt) 8; *Jeraḥmeel* 24.1–8 (trans. Gaster) 50–51; *LT* ad Gen 4:17–18 (ed. Buber) 3; Rashi ad Gen 4:19–22 (ed. Berliner) 11; RaMBaN ad Gen 4:22 (ed. Chavel) 1.45–46; *Zohar* 1.19b, 37a, 55a; *Zohar ḥadas Bereʾšit* 19d; *Frg. Tg.*, *Tg. Ps.-J.*, *Tg. Neof.* ad Gen 4:21–22. See L. Ginzberg, *Legends*, 1.115–18; 5.144–48. These sources, however, are not entirely consistent with regard to the Cainites. For instance, Naamah, said by some to be the seducer of angels and the mother of shades, is thought by others to be the wife of

Significantly, such interpretation of the Cainite "culture heroes" is not distinctively Rabbinic, but can be found in Philo, Josephus, Pseudo-Philo's *Biblical Antiquities*, and in the Church Fathers.[80] This suggests that Gen 4:17–24 was commonly (though not universally) understood in such a negative fashion. Are such negative interpretations of the Cainite culture heroes simply determined by the biblical context (since they are descendants of Cain the murderer, they must be evil), or may they reflect a negative estimation of such civilized activities in general? It seems to me that both factors are at work.

While in its original context the description of these early benefactors of human civilization may have been intended to instill veneration,[81] as we find them in Genesis 4 they seem to be integrated into an account of humanity's early moral decline, led by Cain and his progeny. Thus, a negative estimation of the Cainite culture heroes appears to be implicit in the biblical author's arrangement of his source materials, and is made unmistakably explicit in postbiblical interpretations. However, in some postbiblical sources the account of these sinful innovations is so embellished as to suggest that these kinds of inventions were themselves viewed negatively, as a corruption of the intended, natural, created order.

Noah, known for her good deeds. See *Gen. Rab.* 23.3 (ed. Theodor-Albeck) 224 and Theodor's note ad loc.

80 Philo, *Post.* 83, 98, 99, 112, 116–20 (LCL 2.372–75, 382–85, 390–93, 394–97); Josephus, *Ant.* 1.2.1 § 53; 1.2.2 §§ 60–66 (LCL 4.24–25, 30–31); Ps. Philo *Ant. Bib.* 2.8–10 (ed. Kisch) 114; Augustine, *De civ. Dei* 15.17, 20–21; Ephraem, *De Ieiunio* 2.2; *The Cave of Treasures* (trans. Budge) 87–89; *The Book of Adam and Eve* 2.20 (trans. Malan) 133–34.

81 For instance, it has been suggested that the culture heroes of Gen 4:17–24 are analogous to the apkallus of Mesopotamian tradition. The apkallus are said to have been seven antediluvian semidivine sages, linked in some traditions to antediluvian kings and cities, who were responsible for revealing heavenly secrets of civilization to Sumer. See E. Reiner, "The Etiological Myth of the Seven Sages," *Orientalia* 30 (1961) 1–11; W. G. Lambert, "Ancestors, Authors, and Canonicity," *JCS* 11 (1957) 1–14, 112; J. J. Finkelstein, "The Antediluvian Kings: A University of California Tablet," *JCS* 17 (1963) 39–51, especially p. 50 n. 4; W. W. Hallo, "Antediluvian Cities," *JCS* 23 (1960) 57–67; Wilson, *Genealogy and History*, 149–51. For a Greek version of this myth as transmitted by Berossus see Jacoby, *FGrH* Nr. 680 (3C.369–77). As mentioned above (n. 54), euhemeristic writers attribute the invention of beneficial tools and institutions to earliest human heroes who after their deaths are deified. See the sources cited there, especially the Sanchuniathon tradition as introduced and presented by Philo of Byblos. According to that account, the descendants of Genos (the second man, perhaps equivalent to Cain [Gifford, 4.42]) are credited with discovering fire, reed huts, clothing, navigation, hunting and fishing, iron work, building crafts, salt, herbal healing, music, writing, and the building of the first city, Byblos. For bibliography on classical heurematology (inquiry into the inventors of the basics of civilization) see H. A. Fischel, *Rabbinic Literature and Greco-Roman Philosophy* (SPB 21; Leiden: E. J. Brill, 1973) 140 n. 18. For positive culture heroes in Jewish tradition and their Greco-Roman analogues, see below, nn. 88–97.

For example, Josephus says of Cain:

> He put an end to that simplicity in which man lived before the invention of weights and measures. The guileless and generous existence which they had enjoyed in ignorance of these things he converted into a life of craftiness. He was the first to fix boundaries and build a city.[82]

Surely, the Bible says nothing about Cain having instituted weights and measures, or boundaries.[83] Yet these are here added to the biblical list of cultural firsts, clearly implying that they are viewed negatively in their own right.

Similarly, in *1 Enoch* 7–8 the fallen angels (the *bĕnê 'ĕlōhîm* of Gen 6:2, 4) are said to have taught mankind such corrupting arts as sorcery and astrology, but also the properties of stones and plants, meteorology, and metallurgy. The fact that such arts, undoubtedly thought by others as being of benefit to mankind, are traced back to these corrupting

[82] *Ant.* 1.2.2 § 61 (LCL 4.28–29). Josephus is probably the source for a similar statement by G. Syncellus in his *Chronographia* (ed. W. Dindorf) 16. For a discussion of Josephus' view of early human decline and its relation to Hellenistic thought see L. H. Feldman, "Hellenizations in Josephus' Portrayal of Man's Decline," in *Religions in Antiquity in Memory of Erwin Goodenough* (ed. J. Neusner; Leiden: E. J. Brill, 1968) 336–53. In *Ant.* 1.2.1 §§ 53–54 (LCL 4.24–27), Josephus states that Cain, who "was the first to think of ploughing the soil," had his offering rejected by God, who "is honoured by things that grow spontaneously and in accordance with natural laws, and not by the products forced from nature by the ingenuity of grasping men." On this see S. Rappaport, *Agada und Exegese bei Flavius Josephus* (Frankfurt a. M.: J. Kauffmann, 1930) 83–84. Note that *Gen. Rab.* 22.3 (ed. Theodor-Albeck) 206 speaks critically of Cain's enthusiasm for (working?) the soil.

[83] Perhaps these are simply associated with urban culture, and hence with Cain the city builder. On boundaries as a sign of degeneration see Ovid, *Metamorphoses* 1.135–36. For a negative assessment of the first city, built by Cain (Gen 4:17), see *Gen. Rab.* 23.1 (ed. Theodor-Albeck) 221–22; Philo, *Post.* 49–51; *Conf.* 122. Ps.-Philo, *Ant. Bib.* 2.3 (ed. Kisch) 113 states that Cain built seven cities, and *Tg. Neof. m.* Gen 4:17 translates "cities." The building of cities, like the fixing of boundaries, is viewed, it seems, as a symptom of human greed. This negative view of cities may be derived from Scripture itself, since all cities in the early chapters of Genesis have negative associations, as with the next city built, Babel (Gen 11:4). Nimrod, whose name is said to mean "he who caused the whole world to revolt against God," is also interpreted in postbiblical sources as a city builder. See *Tg. Ps.-J.* Gen 10:8–11; *b. Pesaḥ.* 94b; and L. Ginzberg, *Legends*, 5.198–99, for further references. Ginzberg (*Legends*, 5.144–45 n. 41) suggests that "weights and measures" is an interpretation of Cain's name: קין = קנה ("measuring rod"). Perhaps these interpretations are also related to his name meaning "acquisition" (Gen 4:1), Cain being thought to have devised the means for greedy acquisition, e.g., of land.

However, other traditions view these very same firsts positively: Artapanus (*Praep. ev.* 9.23 [Jacoby, *FGrH* Nr. 725, F 2]) says that Joseph introduced weights, measures, and boundaries into Egypt, for which he was greatly beloved. Diodorus (5.75) credits Hermes with having invented weights and measures. Philo of Byblos (*Praep. ev.* 1.10.19) credits Kronos with having built the first city, Byblos. The Sumerian king lists associate each king with the founding of a city. See above, n. 81.

angels implies that these activities were viewed as less than desirable in their own right. In the account of *1 Enoch* the disastrous effects of these teachings is unmistakable. According to *1 Enoch* 9:6, they are the source of "all unrighteousness on earth."[84]

Such postbiblical interpretations, shared by the rabbis, reflect not only a sensitivity to scriptural nuances, but a philosophical current of their day: cultural primitivism, defined by one scholar as "the discontent of the civilized with civilization."[85] This perspective views the rise of urban culture and human inventiveness as both a symptom and cause of moral degeneration. In several Greek and Latin writers we find the originators of cities, boundaries, metal mining and working, navigation, jewelry, and agricultural implements criticized for introducing unnatural contrivances that only encourage greed, hubris, and violence, turning man away from a life of natural harmony with fellow man, nature and the gods.[86]

Before proceeding, I should stress that my intention is not to characterize postbiblical exegetes, Rabbinic and non-Rabbinic, as "primitivists." A. O. Lovejoy rightly points out that the term *primitivism* is a relative

[84] On the relation of negative culture heroes to the Enochic materials see P. Hanson, "Rebellion in Heaven, Azazel, and Euhemeristic Heroes," *JBL* 96 (1977) 195–233; G. Nickelsburg, "Apocalyptic and Myth in 1 Enoch 6–11," *JBL* 96 (1977) 383–405. Note *Ep. Arist.* 135, which states that idolatry began as the worship of images and inventors.

[85] A. O. Lovejoy and G. Boas, *Primitivism and Related Ideas in Antiquity*, vol. 1 of *A Documentary History of Primitivism and Related Ideas* (Baltimore: Johns Hopkins University Press, 1935) 7. This work contains the most complete treatment of classical primitivism, including lengthy citations of the relevant sources in Greek and Latin with English translations. The volume also includes a pertinent supplemental essay by W. F. Albright entitled, "Primitivism in Ancient Western Asia (Mesopotamia and Israel)," 421–32. I have also found helpful L. Edelstein, *The Idea of Progress in Classical Antiquity* (Baltimore: Johns Hopkins University Press, 1967). Edelstein prefers the term "cultural pessimism," which he argues had firm roots in classical Greek thought (especially among Cynics), and remained widespread in Hellenistic times. See especially pp. 7, 60–62, 138–39.

[86] See especially the passages from Hesiod, Aratus, Ovid, and Seneca quoted and discussed by Lovejoy (pp. 25–31, 34–36, 43–49, 263–86). The myth of Prometheus represents a mixed view of the introduction of civilized arts. In many ways he is the archetypical culture hero, through whose cunning fire, the source of all crafts, is brought from heaven to earth. As the tale appears in Hesiod (*Works and Days* 42–105; *Theogony* 507–616), fire is viewed positively as a necessary human need, which the gods deny to mankind. Prometheus' attempt to steal fire, therefore, is viewed positively, even though there ensue dire consequences for mankind (Pandora's box). In Aeschylus' version (*Prometheus Bound* 505) *all* arts are traced back to Prometheus, who *alone* suffers punishment from the jealous gods. Philo (*Mos.* 2.219–20) similarly views fire as the source of all arts. While the Prometheus tale in its earliest forms is antiprimitivistic, in some classical sources it is interpreted in a primitivistic manner with the degrading of Prometheus: Diogenes in Dio Chrysostom, *Orationes* 6.25–26, 28–30. The Prometheus legend may have influenced the primitivistic myth of the fallen angels as told in *1 Enoch* 6–11. See references above, n. 84.

one, usually in need of modification.[87] It does not represent a coherent school of philosophy, but rather a general attitude that was held to varying degrees by classical writers. For instance, Lovejoy describes Stoic primitivism as being more "relaxed" than that of the Cynics. The Stoics felt it possible to "prefer" certain civilized amenities without valuing them. They did not necessarily advocate a return to the moral and intellectual innocence of "natural man" since they viewed the moral philosophy of the Stoic masters as having contributed to the improvement of man's lot. In attributing the origins of evil in the world to man himself, they simply drew a connection between man's ever increasing sinfulness and the "unnatural" innovations that he has introduced into the world.[88]

Rabbinic primitivism seems similarly to be somewhat "relaxed" or selective, as does that of other postbiblical Jewish exegetes.[89] For instance, as critical as Josephus is of the inventions of Cain and his descendants, we have seen that he credits Seth's descendants with discovering astronomical phenomena.[90] Similarly: *Jub.* 4:17–19 credits Enoch with the discovery of writing and the astrological reckoning of time.[91] According to *Jub.* 11:23–24, Abraham greatly benefited Chaldean agriculture by inventing a seed planter.[92] Eupolemus says of Moses that he was the first wise man, the first to teach the Jews letters, from whom such knowledge was passed to the Phoenicians and Greeks, and the first

[87] See especially Lovejoy, *Primitivism*, 7–11, noting his distinction between "hard" and "soft" primitivism.

[88] On Stoic primitivism, see ibid., 260–86, focusing on the teachings of Seneca. On Cynic primitivism, see ibid., 117–52, especially the citations from Diogenes.

[89] Fischel (*Rabbinic Literature and Greco-Roman Philosophy*, 53–54) similarly associates Rabbinic attitudes with a Stoic mixed view of primitivism.

[90] *Ant.* 1.2.3 § 69 discussed above, chap. 1, n. 72. We have also noted the attribution of early wisdom to Seth in the Byzantine Christian chronographers (Ps.-Malalas, Michael Glycas, George Cedrenus) and in *Suidae Lexicon*, discussed above, chap. 3, nn. 131, 134. See Ginzberg, *Legends*, 5.149–59 n. 53.

[91] *APOT* 2.18. According to this tradition, Enoch (like the Sethites in Josephus) uses these skills to foresee the future, and writes his wisdom down in a book or on a stone so it can be preserved and transmitted to future generations. In *Jub.* 8:2–4, a postdiluvian Kainam discovers such hidden, secret writings, but in that source these are attributed to the Watchers and thought to be evil. Cf. the negative interpretation of the origins of astrological divination in Ps.-Philo, *Ant. Bib.* 4.16 (ed. Kisch) 122. Thus, the early discoveries of writing and astrological knowledge are often recounted within the context of tracing the origins of esoteric, apocalyptic wisdom, although in some instances the discovery of astrological knowledge is given a negative interpretation as a source of evil.

The discovery of writing or letters is similarly attributed to early culture heroes, particularly Hermes, by euhemeristic writers: Philo of Byblos in *Praep. ev.* 1.9.24; 1.10.14 (Tautos = Hermes); Diodorus 1.16.1–2 (perhaps from Hecataeus) 5.74.1; 5.75. See below, n. 93. On the discovery of the alphabet see Attridge and Oden, *Philo of Biblos*, 72–73 n. 8. For a negative view of the invention of writing (by a fallen angel), see *1 Enoch* 69:9–11.

[92] On agricultural innovations, see above, n. 82, below, n. 97.

to give laws to the Jews.[93] Pseudo-Eupolemus, while crediting Abraham with having invented astronomy, which he in turn taught the Phoenicians and Egyptians, traces this discovery ultimately back to Enoch.[94] Likewise, Rabbinic sources, while critical of the innovations of Cain and his descendants, state that Adam taught "all the arts" (*kol 'ûmāniyyôt*),[95] and that he discovered fire and the mule,[96] while Noah is credited with having invented the plough, by which man's life was made easier.[97] However, except for these, I know of no other early culture heroes in Rabbinic literature.[98] Thus, the rabbis appear to have been selective in

93 *Praep. ev.* 9.26.1; Jacoby *FGrH* Nr. 723, F 1 (3C.672); Clement of Alexandria, *Stromata* 1.23 (153.4). Moses seems to be modeled after Hermes. See above, n. 91. See B.Z. Wacholder, *Eupolemus: A Study of Judaeo-Greek Literature* (Monographs of the Hebrew Union College 3; Cincinnati, N.Y., L.A., Jerusalem: HUC-JIR, 1974) 71–96. For Artapanus on Moses as an inventor identified with Hermes, see *Praep. ev.* 9.27; Jacoby, *FGrH* Nr. 726, F 3 (3C.682–86). On the first lawgivers, including Moses, see Diodorus 1.94.2 (perhaps from Hecataeus).

94 *Praep. ev.* 9.17; Jacoby, *FGrH* Nr. 724, F 1 (3C.678–79); according to Alexander Polyhistor (ca. 80 B.C.E.). Similarly, Artapanus, in *Praep. ev.* 9.18.1; Jacoby, *FGrH* Nr. 726, F 1 (3C.680–81); and anonymous (Pseudo-Eupolemus?) in *Praep. ev.* 9.18.2; Jacoby, *FGrH* Nr. 724, F 2 (3C.679–80).

95 *Gen. Rab.* 24.7 (ed. Theodor-Albeck) 236 in the name of Rav (d. 247), interpreting Isa 44:11 (*wĕḥārāšîm hēmmâ mē'ādām*) to mean that craftsmen trace back to Adam. Rav continues, "Even the ruling [of the parchment] of the book [the Pentateuch] Adam taught." See W. Bacher, *Die Agada der Babylonischen Amoräer* (Strassburg: Karl J. Trübner, 1878) 13–14. On this and the following three notes see Fischel, *Rabbinic Literature*, 51–65.

96 *b. Pesaḥ.* 54a in a *barayta'* attributed to R. Jose (ca. 140). According to this passage, God thought to create these two things before the seventh day of Creation, but instead gave Adam godlike understanding (*dê'â*, Munich MS *bînâ*) with which he rubbed two stones together to make the first fire, and mated two (heterogeneous) animals to make the first mule. However, as a consequence of eating the forbidden fruit, Adam lost his godlike wisdom. On Adam's inventing of fire, see also *PR* 23 (ed. Friedmann) 118b; *Gen. Rab.* 12.6; 82.14 (ed. Theodor-Albeck) 103, 996; *p. Ber.* 8.5 (11b); *MPs.* 92.4 (ed. Buber) 405. See Ginzberg, *Legends*, 5.118 n. 110; 5.113 n. 104. Ginzberg suggests the influence of the Prometheus legend. See also W. Bacher, *Die Agada der Tannaiten* (2 vols.; Strassburg: Karl J. Trübner, 1184–90) 2.178 n. 2.

97 *Tanḥ. Bere'šit* 11; *MA* ad Gen 5:28–29 (ed. Buber) 23; *MhG* ad Gen 5:29 (ed. Margulies) 132–33; Rashi and RaDaQ ad Gen 5:29. See also *Midraš 'abkir* as cited in *YS Bere'šit* 42 (ed. Salonika) 14c. These sources interpret "this one will provide us relief (*yĕnaḥămēnû*, a play on Noah's name) from . . . the toils of our hands" (Gen 5:29) to mean that before Noah men cultivated the land with their bare hands, but Noah invented for them the plough, scythe, and spade. However, according to another view, (*Gen. Rab.* 25.2 and parallels), with Noah the ox and furrow yielded to the will of the ploughman, whereas previously they had resisted. These traditions about Noah are similar to Greek traditions concerning Triptolemus, the inventor of the plough and first planter of corn: Virgil, *Georgics* 1.19; Ovid, *Metamorphoses* 5.642–62; Philo, *Praem.* 8. For negative views of Noah's horticulture, see above, n. 8; below, n. 107.

98 According to *PRE* 8 (ed. Warsaw) 18a–b, God revealed to Adam the calendrical cycles and their intercalation, and Adam in turn passed these secrets on to Enoch, Noah,

their application of primitivistic notions to biblical personages: it is Cain and his progeny who are viewed as having introduced evil into the world through their inventions.

Once introduced, however, how widely did such behavior spread? Did it typify only the Cainites, the more spiritually minded Sethites remaining untainted (as we found in extra-Rabbinic Jewish and Christian accounts), or did it quickly envelop humanity as a whole? While the Bible does not chronologically correlate the Cainite and Sethite genealogies, in a number of Rabbinic sources it is assumed that Cain's descendants (described in Gen 4:17–24) were active in Enosh's time, their activity lasting until the Flood in Noah's time.[99] Thus, if Gen 4:26 were viewed by the rabbis against the background of the preceding description of the Cainites, it would have appeared strange as an announcement of the beginning of divine worship, especially if the verb *hûḥal* was understood to refer not to Enosh alone, nor to his family, but to humanity in general (translating, "humanity began").[100] Unlike Adam's eating of the forbidden fruit and Cain's murder of Abel, the Cainites of Genesis 4 are significant not so much for their sins as *individuals* but for the tools that they give to human society as a whole. They initiate lifestyles and preoccupations that, presumably, are adopted by their contemporaries.

---

etc. According to *MA* ad Gen 5:24 (ed. Buber) 23, Enoch learned these from the angels. This is similar to extra-Rabbinic traditions discussed above (n. 90). Here, Adam and Enoch are not so much discoverers as scribes and transmitters. Note that according to *m. 'Abot* 5:6 such civilized tools as the alphabet, writing tools, and tongs for metalworking are said to have been created by *God* at twilight of the first Sabbath eve.

99 E.g., *YS Bere'šit* 47 (ed. Salonika) 16a, in which the Cainites of Gen 4:17–24 are cited as examples of the sinfulness of the Generation of Enosh. On this passage see above, chap. 4, n. 158. We have seen that Naamah is connected with the fall of the angels, who in turn are associated with the Generation of Enosh. See above, n. 79 and chap. 4, n. 168. Thus, Rashi in commenting on *b. Yoma* 67b says that the angels fell "in the days of Naamah," while on *b. Nid.* 61a and Num 13:33 he says that they fell "in the days of the Generation of Enosh." Similarly, in commenting on Gen 6:2–4, Rashi interprets "in those days" to mean, "in the days of Enosh and the descendants of Cain." Because of the longevity of the antediluvians, their lifetimes overlap considerably. Thus, according to the genealogical figures given in MT Genesis 5, Enosh's lifetime overlaps with that of *every* other antediluvian. If it is assumed that Cain's descendants lived equally long lives, then Lamech would have been born around the same time as Jared, and his sons around the same time as Enoch, all during the period of the so-called Generation of Enosh, their activities lasting almost until the Flood. The term "Generaton of Enosh" is used by the rabbis to refer to a historical age and not to a genealogical line, as "descendants of Seth" or "descendants of Cain." Thus, the activities of the descendants of Cain described in Gen 4:17–19 would have occurred during the Generation of Enosh.

100 Most modern scholars and translators take *hûḥal* to refer to humanity in general, although some suggest that divine worship began with Enosh. See GKC 144 k, where *hûḥal* is given as an example of the use of the passive to express an indefinite personal subject.

Therefore, it is easy for Enosh to be viewed as living in a sinful *age* and for Gen 4:26b to describe the sinful activity of his contemporaries.[101]

Let us look now at the Rabbinic interpretation of what follows Gen 4:26 in Scripture. Genesis 5 elicits little Rabbinic interpretation. As we have seen, Gen 5:1 ("this is the book of the generations of Adam/man") is interpreted to mean that after Enosh's birth *human* history really begins, since Adam, Seth, and Enosh were still godlike.[102] Of Kenan, Mahalalel, and Jared very little is said, both in Scripture and in midrash.[103] Enoch is denied immortality,[104] Methusalah praised for his righteousness,[105] Lamech praised for his prophetic naming of Noah,[106] while Noah himself receives mixed treatment.[107] These antediluvian

101 It may be asked: if the rabbis were not alone in their negative estimation of the culture heroes of Gen 4:17–24, why do they alone interpret Gen 4:26 negatively? We must remember that most of the non-Rabbinic exegetes we have examined (Josephus, Philo, Samaritan and Christian exegetes) begin with a biblical version that renders *hûḥal* in the third person *singular* active, presumably referring to Enosh. Thus, it would not have occurred to them to take Gen 4:26 as a statement concerning mankind in general. It may still be argued that the rabbis could have solved their difficulty more easily by similarly taking Gen 4:26b to refer to Enosh alone. Therefore, our point is not that the Rabbinic interpretation of what precedes Gen 4:26 determines their interpretation of that verse, but that it is one of several influencing factors. Whether the rabbis *initially* understood *hûḥal* to refer to mankind in general because such was their understanding of the Hebrew syntax and this understanding helped shape their interpretation, or whether they desired for exegetical reasons for this phrase to refer not to Enosh but to his contemporaries is beyond our ability to determine.

102 *Gen. Rab.* 24.6 (ed. Theodor-Albeck) 235. See above, chap. 4, n. 71.

103 For interpretations of these names, see *AgBer.* (ed. Buber) intro, 37. On Kenan, see above, chap. 4, n. 65. On Jared, see above, n. 40. On the righteousness of Jared, Methuselah and Enoch, see *Zohar* 1.56a.

104 *Gen. Rab.* 25.1 (ed. Theodor-Albeck) 238–39, where Rabbinic views concerning Enoch appear to reflect a polemical response to sectarians (of whatever brand) who venerated Enoch. What place the hekhalot literature, with its veneration of Enoch, had in this debate is unclear.

105 See Ginzberg, *Legends*, 5.166 n. 64; and below, n. 116.

106 See sources cited above, n. 97.

107 Note especially the following interpretations: "'But Noah found favor before God' (Gen 6:8). . . by the merit of his descendants." *Gen. Rab.* 29.4 (ed. Theodor-Albeck) 269–70. "'Noah was a righteous man in his generation' (Gen 6:9). . . In his generation he was a righteous, but had he lived in Moses' generation or Samuel's generation he would not have been [considered] righteous." *Gen. Rab.* 30.9 (p. 275). "'Noah, a man [tiller] of the soil' (Gen 9:20): There were three who were greedy for land but derived no benefit from it, and these are Cain, Noah, and Uzziah." *Gen. Rab.* 36.3 (p. 337), and Theodor's note ad loc. Similarly, *Gen. Rab.* 30.10 (p. 276) and *Tanḥuma B. Lek leka* 26 (p. 81) contrast Noah and Abraham. Such criticism and qualified praise of Noah contrasts sharply with his positive treatment in Christian and pre-Rabbinic Jewish sources. See J. P. Lewis, *A Study of the Interpretation of Noah and the Flood in Jewish and Christian Literature* (Leiden: E. J. Brill, 1968) 133–35, 151, on Moses' limited righteousness in Rabbinic sources; J. C. VanderKam, "The Righteousness of Noah," in *Ideal Figures in Ancient Judaism: Profiles and Paradigms* (ed. J. J. Collins & G. W. E. Nickelsburg; SBLSCS 12; Chico:

figures, on the whole, receive significantly less attention in Rabbinic exegesis than in certain non-Rabbinic Jewish, Christian, and Samaritan writings.[108]

Some Rabbinic interpretations, cognizant that Genesis 5 interrupts the flow of the pre-Flood narrative, recast that narrative in a way that weaves together Gen 4:26 and 6:1ff., suggesting that they describe closely related, successive, even contemporaneous events.[109] Rabbinic sources often speak of the Generation of Enosh in conjunction with the Generation of the Flood, linking the two as a historical progression. The rebelliousness of the first leads to that of the second. The Generation of the Flood failed to learn from the punishment of the Generation of Enosh.[110] The events associated with these two generations sometimes appear identical. For instance, the rebellion of the fallen angels (the *bĕnê 'ĕlōhîm* of Gen 6:2, 4), usually associated with the Flood generation, is in some traditions connected with the Generation of Enosh, who learn from these angels magical secrets.[111] Thus, it would appear that the generations of Enosh and the Flood represent two stages in what is essentially viewed as one sequence of events. In *Gen. Rab.* 26.7 the expression "and even afterwards" (Gen 6:4) is interpreted to mean that the rebellion of the Flood generation had its roots in that of the Generation of Enosh.[112]

Most significant is the fact that the generations of Enosh and of the Flood (as well as that of the Tower of Babel) have in common not only their sinful, rebellious behaviors, but their punishment with flooding, albeit of different sorts. The flood in Enosh's time, being of a smaller scale than that in Noah's, seems to represent a warning to mankind. The biblical flood is such an absolute decree against "all flesh" (Gen 6:13, 17; 7:4, 21–23) that the Rabbinic sense of divine justice demands both justification for and warning of such a wholesale destruction. The Bible itself does not specify the nature of the sin that occasioned such retribution,

Scholars Press, 1980) 13–32, covering only the pre-Rabbinic Jewish sources; R. Stichel, *Die Namen Noes, seines Bruders und seiner Frau* (Göttingen: Vandenhoeck & Ruprecht, 1979).

108 Besides Enosh (see above, chaps. 1, 2 and 3), Seth, Enoch, and Noah receive particular attention.

109 Note, for instance, *ShY Bere'šit* (ed. Goldschmidt) 7: "And Seth called his son Enosh, meaning that at that time men began (*hēḥēllû*) to increase on earth (Gen 6:1) and to cause their souls and hearts grief, rebelling against God." Here we have a clear conflation of Gen 4:26 and 6:1. This may have been facilitated by the use of the same verb *hēḥēl* in both verses. Enosh's naming seems to be explained by reference to the events of Gen 6:1–4.

110 *Tanḥ. B. Noaḥ* 24 (p. 52) and parallels (see above, chap. 4, n. 124); *Gen. Rab.* 38.5 (see above, chap. 4, nn. 128–29).

111 See above, chap. 4, n. 168.

112 See above, chap. 4, n. 126. Note as well *Zohar* 1.56a in which it is said that magical arts were passed from the Generation of Enosh to the Generation of the Flood.

stating only that the earth had become corrupt and full of violence through man's wickedness (Gen 6:5, 11–13). Certainly, God should not be accused, as is Enlil in the Gilgamesh Epic, of being capricious in His judgment.[113]

While it has been suggested that Gen 6:1–4 was incorporated by the biblical redactor in order to furnish further justification for God's actions,[114] this enigmatic passage creates as many problems as it solves. For if the "sons of God" are understood to be angelic figures who corrupt the "daughters of men," producing the Giants (*nĕpilîm*) who further corrupt mankind, then it is these "sons of God" who should be held responsible for the ensuing human wickedness and not man. This undoubtedly was part of the motivation for "demythologizing" these figures, thereby understanding Gen 6:1–4 to refer to the *self*-corruption of mankind (e.g., the degeneration resulting from the mixing of the Sethite and Cainite lines).[115] If through mankind's own activities *all* men had become evil, then complete destruction would have been justified.

However, for the rabbis, such justification was not sufficient. Even if God had had adequate reason to destroy mankind, he should have forewarned them of their impending doom, giving them an opportunity to avert destruction through repentance.[116] The prior punishment of the

113 Tablet 11, lines 118–26, 167, 177–85. Ea says (11.179–80), "How, O how couldst thou without reflection bring on (this) deluge? On the sinner lay his sin; on the transgressor lay his transgression!" A. Heidel, *The Gilgamesh Epic and Old Testament Parallels* (Chicago: University of Chicago Press, 1949) 88. Thus, the rashness of Enlil's judgment lies in part in his failure to distinguish the righteous from the sinner, punishing the two as one (cf. Gen 18:23). Wherein lay the humans' misdeeds is not specified in the Gilgamesh Epic, which simply states (11.14), "(Now) their heart prompted the great gods (to) bring a deluge." See Heidel, 224–27. Similarly, in *Sefer Hekhalot* (*3 Enoch*) 4.4, God removes Enoch so as to bear witness to the justice of His destruction of all the world, lest the inhabitants of the world say: "The Merciful One is cruel. What sins had all the multitudes committed?"

114 For instance, E. Kraeling, "The Significance and Origin of Gen 6:1–4," *JNES* 6 (1947) 193–208.

115 Such naturalization of the "sons of God" is common to both Rabbinic and patristic sources. See above, chap. 3, n. 54. The Rabbinic sources are particularly interested in providing the details of human sinfulness prior to the Flood. See Lewis, *A Study of the Interpretation of Noah and the Flood*, 127–29.

116 It is a common Rabbinic legal principle to insist that Scripture provides a warning (*'azhārâ*) before imposing a punishment (*'ôneš*) for capital crimes. See, for example, *b. Yoma* 81a; *Sifra 'Emor pereq* 14.7–9. Several Rabbinic sources stress that God gave ample (even repeated) warning before bringing the Flood. The "hundred and twenty years" of Gen 6:3 and the "seven days" of 7:4, 10 are interpreted to be periods of grace granted by God in the hope that the people would repent and avert destruction: *t. Soṭa* 10.3–5 (ed. Lieberman) 214–15; *b. Sanh.* 108b; *p. Mo'ed Qaṭ.* 3.5 (82c); *Gen. Rab.* 3.6; 27.4; 32.7 (ed. Theodor-Albeck) 22, 259, 293; *Num. Rab.* 14.6; *ARNA* 32 (ed. Schechter) 92–93; *Tanḥ. B. Noaḥ* 4 (p. 30); *Tanḥ. B. Šemini* 1 (p. 21); *MhG* ad Gen 6:13 (ed. Margulies) 155; *MPs.* 26.7 (ed. Buber) 220; *AgBer.* (ed. Buber) intro., 38; *LT* ad Gen 6:3; 7:4 (ed. Buber) 33, 41; *ShY Noaḥ* (ed. Goldschmidt) 16; *SER* 31 (ed. Friedmann) 163; *YS Bere'šit* 47 (ed.

Generation of Enosh with a smaller-scale flood would have provided advance notice of a more serious and widespread calamity sure to follow if the people's ways went unchanged. Since, as we are told, the people failed to learn from the flood in Enosh's time and continued their sinful activities, God was justified in bringing the biblical Flood, inasmuch as his earlier, more lenient chastisement was unheeded. By Noah's time, mankind had become so corrupt that he alone was found to be righteous and deserving of being saved. Thus, the Rabbinic tradition of the Generation of Enosh provides background history for the Flood story. Mankind having been warned, and God having been continuously provoked, the Flood could no longer seem unfair.[117]

We have argued that the rabbis in positing widespread human sinfulness and divine retribution already in Enosh's time are responding *in part* to a problem in the biblical account of the Flood: was such sudden and complete destruction justified? However, should it be assumed that the rabbis simply fabricated the occurrence of an earlier flood? The biblical text contains nothing to suggest such a flood prior to Noah's time. Nor is such a flood evidenced in any other corpus of scriptural exegesis, whether Jewish or non-Jewish. Similarly, Mesopotamian traditions, generally thought to reflect the origins of the biblical Flood story, speak of only *one* ancient flood.[118] Interestingly, the only parallels to the Rabbinic notion of a *series* of ancient floods are found in classical Greek and Latin writings, which may have been available, at least indirectly, to Palestinian Sages.[119] For instance, Plato speaks of recurring floods, each

Salonika) 16a; *Zohar* 1.56b; *Tg. Onq.*, *Tg. Ps.-J.*, *Frg. Tg.*, and *Tg. Neof.* Gen 6:3; Cf. Philo, *Qu. in Gen.* 2.13. In several of the above sources God waits until the righteous Methuselah has died and has been mourned before bringing the destruction. This is based on the fact that according to the biblical genealogy Methuselah, the last of the antediluvians, died in the year of the Flood.

117 Such a retelling of the story of the Flood bears striking resemblance to what we find in the Babylonian Atraḫasis Epic. In that version of the story of the deluge, Enlil sends a *series* of severe plagues (approximately ten) as punishments for mankind's tumultuous gatherings. But these plagues prove of no avail and Enlil finally orders the deluge to destroy mankind. Heidel (*The Gilgamesh Epic*, 225–26) suggests that the Atraḫasis Epic may represent a response to the Gilgamesh Epic, especially to Ea's criticism of Enlil. See above, n. 113. The Rabbinic retelling of the Flood story may represent, at least in part, a similar process of interpretation, developing motifs already present in the biblical text. While the biblical author/redactor has adopted an ancient Near Eastern flood narrative to suit his conception of a just and omnipotent God, the rabbis have carried this concern even further, providing additional evidence for the justice of God's act.

118 The Atraḫasis Epic speaks of previous plagues, but of only one flood.

119 There is no need to argue for the *possible* familiarity of the rabbis with such Greco-Roman literary and philosophical traditions. The works of S. Lieberman, E. Bickerman, and H. Fischel, among others, have supplied us with ample data to support such a supposition. We do not attempt here to demonstrate any direct dependence, but only that the rabbis may have adopted a popular and readily accessible Greco-Roman tradition to their own exegetical needs.

of which wipes out civilization, leaving some remnant that must then begin anew. In particular, he says that the best known flood, that of Deucalion (the Greek Noah), was neither the first nor last such flood.[120] Still closer (chronologically and geographically) to the rabbis, we find such a tradition cited by Origen, who quotes Celsus as saying that "there have been many conflagrations from all eternity and many floods, and that more recent than all others is the flood in the time of Deucalion and the conflagration in the time of Phaethon."[121] This belief in recurring floods, popular especially among Stoic philosophers, *may* have been adapted by the rabbis in their efforts to depict prepatriarchal history as a series of human rebellions and divine retributions. Not once but three times did God cause flooding as a punishment of mankind: once in the Generation of Enosh, once in the time of Noah, and once in the Generation of the Separation.[122] Thus while one impetus for the Rabbinic tradition of a flood in Enosh's time may derive from the problematic biblical Flood narrative itself, the specific shape of that tradition may reveal the influence of Greek and Latin accounts of recurring floods both before and after the most famous flood of all.

Finally, let us look at how the Rabbinic interpretation of the Generation of Enosh fits into the overall Rabbinic depiction of prepatriarchal times (Genesis 1–11). As we have seen, from amoraic times on the rabbis discuss the Generation of Enosh as one of *several* rebellious generations, each of which continues in the sinful footsteps of its predecessors, failing to learn from previous divine acts of retribution.[123] This notion of the progressive degeneration of the generations (*qilqûl haddôrôt*) can be

120 *Timaeus* 22 C-E, 23 A-B; *Leges* 3.677 A-B. For similar ideas in other classical sources see: Lucretius, *De Rerum natura* 5.324–50; Cicero, *De Natura Deorum* 2.45.118; Macrobius, *Commentari in somnium Scipio* 2.10; Seneca, *Quaestiones naturales* 3.28.7; 29.1–3. In the last mentioned source (27.1–2) Seneca asks whether the final deluge will result from the rising of the outer sea, from unceasing rains, or from subterranean springs which will burst forth. He concludes that the final deluge will come from all three sources. We have seen that Rabbinic sources also speak of these types of floods. Note as well Seneca's statement (28.5) that the sea is level with the land and only has to rise a little to inundate it, very similar to R. Abbahu's statement (*Gen. Rab.* 23.7) that the ocean is higher than the world. See above, chap. 4, nn. 105–7. On the equation of Deucalion and Noah, see Philo, *Praem.* 23.

121 *Contra Celsum* 1.19 (trans. Chadwick) 20. Similarly in 4.11, Origen attributes to Celsus the view that alternating occurrences of floods and configurations are determined by the recurring alignment of stars. See also Augustine, *De civ. Dei* 12.10; Theophilus of Antioch, *Ad Autolycum* 3.18–19.

122 On the flood during the Generation of the Separation, see above, chap. 4, n. 109.

123 While tannaitic sources contain lists of rebellious generations, the Generation of Enosh is not yet included. See above, chap. 4, nn. 59, 60. In the amoraic sources, however, the Generation of Enosh is usually mentioned in conjunction with one or more of the other rebellious generations, usually the Generation of the Flood and the Generation of the Separation, and occasionally the Sodomites.

traced back to tannaitic sources, as evidenced in *m. 'Abot* 5:2, which states that the ten generations from Adam to Noah as well as the ten from Noah to Abraham were *all* caught up in a downward spiral of moral depravity:

> There were ten generations from Adam to Noah, to show how great was [God's] longsuffering, for all the generations provoked Him continually until he brought upon them the waters of the Flood. There were ten generations from Noah to Abraham, to show how great was [God's] longsuffering, for all the generations provoked Him continually until Abraham our father came and received the reward of them all.[124]

Such a statement must be seen as more than simply justifying the Flood, or glorifying Abraham (both of which are intended, no doubt), but as revealing a historiographic perspective: all of pre-Israelite mankind is viewed as sinful (with some very few exceptions).[125]

The Bible nowhere explicitly divides early history into "generations." The fact that biblical genealogy counts ten generations from Adam to Noah and again from Noah to Abraham is certainly not accidental, most likely intending to attribute special significance to Noah and Abraham within the scheme of sacred history. However, the Bible in recounting the events that transpire in the first eleven chapters of Genesis does not do so in terms of specific "generations."[126] The Rabbinic retelling reshapes the

[124] *ARNA* 32 (ed. Schechter) 92 states that God did not bring the Flood upon the earlier generations because of the righteous and saintly men in their midst (especially Methuselah). For other sources see above, n. 116. Note that the parallelism of the Mishnah's description of the two spans of ten generations is imperfect. The first ten generations conclude not so much with Noah as with the Flood, while the second ten generations end not with another devastation but with Abraham. Thus, Abraham breaks a process of decline which could not be stopped even by the Flood. For other categorical condemnations of *all* the early generations see *SER* 16, 29 (31) (ed. Friedmann) 80–81, 162; *SEZ* 10 (ed. Friedmann) 190; *Lev. Rab.* 23.3 (above, chap. 4, n. 124).

[125] I use the terms historiography and historiographic in their broadest senses. It is commonly remarked that Rabbinic literature shows no interests in the recording of history (or of biography for that matter), therefore being antihistorical, anachronistic, and nonhistoriographic. For bibliography on this point see S. D. Fraade, "Sifre Deuteronomy 26 (ad Deut 3:23): How Conscious the Composition," *HUCA* 54 (1983) 124 n. 6. However, in retelling the sacred history of Israel (i.e., in interpreting Scripture), Rabbinic literature frequently expresses understandings of a collective Israelite past. Although the forms of such expression may not be recognizable from the canons of western, secular history writing, they nonetheless reflect historiography (or historiosophy if you will). For similar arguments, but with respect to another ancient civilization, see J. J. Finkelstein, "Mesopotamian Historiography," *Proceedings of the American Philosophical Society*, 107 (1963) 461–72. Note as well I. Heinemann's discussion of Rabbinic *aggada* as "creative historiography." *Darke ha'aggada*, 15–95.

[126] The only uses of the word *generation* (*dôr*) in the early chapters of Genesis are with respect to Noah: "Noah was a righteous man; he was blameless in his generation" (Gen 6:9). "You alone have I found righteous before Me in this generation" (Gen 7:1). In both cases the LXX translates *dôr* with *genea* ("age or generation"). Thus, while the expression

biblical pre-Israelite history around the central theme of "generations," all of which were wicked. While the Bible tells of the sinful behavior of individuals and groups of people, the rabbis speak of a succession of sinful generations. While the Bible traces the general moral decline of mankind, the rabbis describe this as the "degeneration of the generations." Thus, for them, the degeneration is not sporadic but persistent.

This same sort of attitude is expressed in the tradition of the departure and ascent of the Shekinah (divine presence) in ten stages, from Adam until the time of Abraham. As humanity became progressively more sinful, the Shekinah became progressively more distant, until finally with Abraham the process was reversed. Such pre-Israelite righteous individuals as Seth, Enosh (for some), Enoch, Methuselah, and Noah stand out against the prevailing degeneracy of their contemporaries, providing the basis for future regeneration through the uninterrupted transmission of the "divine image" or "messianic seed." They are clearly a select few, the exceptions to the historiographic rule.[127] The rabbis in retelling the scriptural story of Genesis 1–11 as a series of progressively degenerating generations disclose what for them is the pattern underlying the otherwise disjointed series of pre-Israelite episodes. By making explicit what they perceive as Scripture's underlying pattern, they reveal what to their minds is its true meaning and message. Thus, while the Rabbinic interpretation of Gen 4:26 seems to be without explicit scriptural basis, it conforms excellently with what the rabbis perceive to be the historiographic pattern of Genesis 1–11, the context in which Gen 4:26 is found.

While the Rabbinic view of prepatriarchal history is informed in part by Scripture, it bears strikingly close similarities with a well evidenced historiographic and philosophical motif in classical literature: chronological primitivism, which depicts the progressive degeneration of mankind from an originally idyllic, even semidivine, state, usually referred to as the Golden Age (*chryseon genos*).[128] In such descriptions

---

"Generation of the Flood" is never used in the Bible, one can easily see how it may have been derived from these two verses. The same cannot be said for the terms "Generation of the Separation" and "Generation of Enosh."

127 Unlike the Israelite patriarchs, however, they are unable to arrest or reverse the withdrawal of the Shekinah. As we have seen, extra-Rabbinic Jewish and Christian sources hold these figures in greater veneration, not just as moral models but as salvific agents. While Christian traditions view these as the heads of the righteous descendants of Seth, Rabbinic traditions view them from the beginning as individuals apart from their contemporaries. For a late, eloquent expression of this see Jehuda Halevi, *Kuzari* 1.47, 95.

128 While chronological primitivism is often linked to cultural primitivism (discussed above), the two should not simply be equated since they are frequently attested separately. Again, the most thorough treatment is A. O. Lovejoy and G. Boas, *Primitivism and Related Ideas in Antiquity* (see above, n. 85), especially chapter 2 (pp. 23–102), which is devoted to chronological primitivism.

of mankind's decline, history is often divided into "ages" or "generations" (*genos*, *genea*), anywhere from two to five.[129] The earliest classical authority to so schematize human history is Hesiod (ca. 700 BCE), but scholars generally assume that he was not its originator, its roots perhaps being oriental.[130] Hesiod divides history into five ages (although the original scheme may have contained only four[131]), and describes how in each successive age man experiences increasing hardship and mortality, degenerating both physically and morally. Four of the five ages are associated with metals and are presented in a descending scale of value: gold, silver, bronze, and iron.[132]

Hesiod's scheme was adopted with some revision by later Cynics and Stoics. These later versions placed greater stress on the genealogical connection of the ages, the progression of *moral* decline, and the role of civilized inventions in destroying the original harmonious state between mankind, nature, and the gods. Generally, these accounts idealize the early pastoral stages in human history, are anti-urban, and often advocate vegetarianism.[133]

129 Besides Lovejoy see K. F. Smith, "Ages of the World (Greek and Roman)," in *Encyclopedia of Religion and Ethics*, vol. 1 (ed. J. Hastings; New York, 1951) 192–200; A. Momigliano, "Time in Ancient Historiography," *Quarto contributo alla storia degli studi classici del mondo antico* (Rome: Edizioni di storia e letteratura, 1969) 13–41; idem, "The Origins of Universal History," in *The Poet and the Historian: Essays in Literary and Historical Biblical Criticism*, ed. Richard Elliott Friedman (Harvard Semitic Studies 26; Chico: Scholars Press, 1983) 134–35.

130 *Works and Days* 109–201, discussed by Lovejoy, 25–31. For a more recent treatment see M. L. West's notes to his critical edition: Hesiod, *Works and Days* (Oxford: Clarendon, 1978) 172–204, especially 172–77. West argues for Mesopotamia as a likely source of origin for the legend of the ages (p. 174). Similarly, Momigliano, "Time in Ancient Historiography," 24.

131 Hesiod's Age of Heroes (the fourth) seems to have been inserted into an original scheme of four metallic ages. See West, 174.

132 There is some disagreement as to how clearly Hesiod depicts the process of decline from one age to the next. See West, 173, who argues for a clear scheme of progressive decline. Cf. Lovejoy, 29; G. Nagy, *The Best of the Achaeans: Concepts of the Hero in Archaic Greek Poetry* (Baltimore: Johns Hopkins University Press, 1979) 151–72. The connection with cultural primitivism may be implied in Hesiod's account, but is not explicitly stated. Is each age thought to have been typified by the use of the metal for which it is named? Hesiod tells us that the people of the Bronze Age lived in bronze houses and wore bronze armor, but says nothing like this for the other ages.

133 Nagy (*The Best of the Achaeans*, xii) states, "The Greek version of the Fall is not from innocence into sin but from primeval harmony into conflict." Thus, Philo (*Spec. Leg.* 2.159–60) speaks of the first *two* generations of humanity as having lived in harmony with nature, using the earth's gifts in an unperverted (unprocessed) state. Subsequently, the introduction of yeast and other ways of transforming natural food changed this frugal way of life. The opposite view is expressed by Diodorus (1.8.5–9), who says that earliest humanity led wretched lives in conflict with nature, ignorant of making food for themselves, until gradually they discovered the tools and skills necessary for improving their lives.

The most significant reworking of Hesiod's scheme is that found in Ovid's *Metamorphoses*, for Ovid is the first to combine the "myth of the ages" with the tradition of the Deluge.[134] The Deluge in Ovid's account follows the Iron Age, the most degenerate of all, after which a new human race is begun by the survivors Deucalion and Pyrrha. According to A. O. Lovejoy, "The Ovidian story of the ages was probably more potent than any other in its historic influence; the echoes of it in later literature are innumerable."[135]

The classical "myth of the ages," especially as reformulated by Ovid, bears striking similarities with early Jewish interpretations of antediluvian and pre-Israelite history. As we have seen, the rabbis focus on the series of "generations" that mark man's progressive decline after the original "golden age." Interestingly, the Greek word *genea* (or *genos*) used by Hesiod and other Greek writers to describe the "ages" of mankind is used by the LXX to translate the Hebrew *dôr* ("generation"), suggesting a lexical equivalence, both words referring to a historical age as well as to a genealogical generation. We have seen that in several Rabbinic texts, humanity's moral decline begins not with Adam's or Cain's sins, but with the Generation of Enosh.[136] Adam and Cain sin as individuals, but humanity as a whole begins its sinful behavior in Enosh's time, the third generation. We have also noted that the rabbis extend the duration of the original idyllic age past Adam's sin and expulsion from Eden so as to include the first two or three generations of mankind in general. Those human hardships that would most naturally be associated with Adam's punishment are instead delayed until Enosh's time.[137] Thus, the initial "golden age" is slightly lengthened, and is followed by three "ages" of decline: that of Enosh, the Flood, and the Separation—four ages in all, comprising twenty genealogical generations.

Both Jewish and Greco-Roman sources refer to the discovery of metallurgy as a source of human degeneration, especially with regard to the origins of weaponry and warfare. Hesiod's third generation is that of bronze, a generation marked by violence and destruction, since they used their skills as bronze smiths for the manufacture of weapons.[138]

[134] *Metamorphoses* 1.89–162, see Lovejoy, 43–49. For an earlier reworking of the Hesiodic myth see Aratus (ca. 315–240 B.C.E.), *Phaenomena* 96–140. Aratus was influenced by Zeno, the founder of Stoicism. His version of the myth of the ages has a consistently moral tone, and his cultural primitivism is unmistakable. See Lovejoy, 34–36.

[135] Ibid., 49.

[136] *Gen. Rab.* 5.1; 23.6; *Lev. Rab.* 11.7; *Exod. Rab.* 15.7; *Tanḥ. Wayyera'* 18; *PR* 40; *PR* Supp. 1; *3 Enoch* 5.3–6; all discussed in chap. 4.

[137] Until Enosh's time men lived free from suffering. See *Gen. Rab.* 23.6; and *3 Enoch* 5.3–6. See above, chap. 4, nn. 74, 80, 92.

[138] *Works and Days* 142–55. According to Aeschylus (*Prometheus Bound* 500), Prometheus discovered not only fire, but also bronze, iron, silver, and gold. The association of fire with metal working is an obvious one. On Prometheus see above, n. 85.

Ovid's "Age of Iron" is similarly typified by violence, plunder, and exploitation of nature since weapons of war and tools for boring into the earth were made from this metal.[139] In *1 Enoch* 8:1 the chief angel Azazel reveals metallurgy to mankind, teaching them to make swords, knives, shields, and breastplates. Similarly, Rabbinic and non-Rabbinic sources alike interpret the iron and bronze work of Tubal-Cain (Gen 4:22) to be violence related.[140]

Another interesting parallel is that according to Aratus and Ovid, accompanying mankind's progressive moral decline the goddess Justice (Atraea) gradually withdrew from man's midst. Lovejoy summarizes:

> It is the increasing wickedness of man that brings on his present misery, and the gradual withdrawal of the goddess is a symbol for the gradual growth of injustice. In the Golden Age all men were just "by nature":—she sat amidst them. In the Silver Age she spoke only occasionally and became, so to say, retributive justice. In the Bronze Age she no longer dwelt among men.[141]

This is very similar to the Rabbinic description of the withdrawal of the Shekinah, progressing in stages that correspond to man's increasing decadence.[142]

Other similarities are the emphasis on disharmony between man and animals that accompanies man's decline, his shortened life span and degenerated state after death, the introduction of surveying that divided the land as man's common property, the introduction of unnatural methods of agriculture and animal husbandry, the end of man's "natural" diet, and the introduction of musical instruments.[143] From these parallels and others that could be cited, I do not intend to demonstrate a direct dependence of post-biblical Jewish exegesis on particular Greco-Roman sources but simply to show that the philosophical milieu in which the rabbis lived produced some strikingly similar accounts of mankind's earliest history. The rabbis, like several Greco-Roman historians and

139 *Metamorphoses* 1.125–50.

140 *Gen. Rab.* 23.3; Philo, *Post.* 116, Ps.-Philo, *Ant. Bib.* 2.9; Josephus, *Ant.* 1.2.2 § 64; all cited above, nn. 79–80. On iron representing the sword, see Dan 2:40; *MekRS* ad Exod 20:22 (ed. Melamed-Epstein) 157; *Mek. Baḥodeš* 11 (ed. Lauterbach) 2.290. According to *1 Enoch* 52:7–9, such metals and their unnatural uses will be useless and destroyed when the Messiah comes. Endzeit wird Urzeit.

141 *Primitivism*, 36.

142 *Gen. Rab.* 19.7 and parallels. See above, chap., 4, n. 121. Note also *Bere'šit Rabbati* (ed. Albeck) 41, in which God considers abandoning man's midst. See above, chap. 4, n. 171.

143 For primitive vegetarianism see Plato, *Leges* 6.782 C-E, and above, n. 133. On man's original harmony with the animals see Empedocles, Fragm. 130. Aratus and Ovid are critical of the introduction of the plough (cf. above, nn. 82, 97), while Ovid is critical of the surveyor (cf. above, nn. 82–3) and states that the Golden Age was free of trumpets and horns.

philosophers, wished to show that man's sinful behavior was not original to his nature, but rather the consequence of a subsequent process of steady decline. Once again we see that while the rabbis take their cues from Scripture, the specific ways in which they reshape Scripture's story reveal the subtle yet significant influences of Greco-Roman thought.

However, in comparing the Rabbinic scheme of the degeneration of the generations with the Greco-Roman myth of the ages, especially as it came to be expressed by Ovid, we note a very significant difference. Ovid places the Deluge at the *end* of the process of decline, following the "Iron Age." With this cataclysmic destruction, humanity is totally destroyed, except for one couple from whom mankind begins anew. The assumption, according to the Stoic theory of cycles of history, is that this pattern repeats itself. Regenerated humanity rediscovers the arts of civilization and once again begins the process of descent until this civilization too is destroyed by another flood or conflagration.[144] By contrast, in the Rabbinic interpretation of the pre-Israelite period, the Flood marks not the end of the descent, but its midpoint.[145] In the Rabbinic view, each "age" (or rebellious generation) is marked by a great destruction, with mankind's decline continuing through the Generation of the Separation. This spiral of degeneration is only arrested with the appearance of Abraham.[146] While in Greco-Roman sources the model of chronological primitivism is applied continuously or cyclically throughout human history, the rabbis seem to apply it only to the first twenty generations (Genesis 1–11). After that, following the Bible, their focus shifts to the history of Israel. It is hard to say what the Rabbinic attitude towards universal history is after Abraham, since that ceases to be their interest. With Abraham, history for the rabbis as for the Bible becomes the history of the covenant and its fulfillment. Thus, the rabbis seem to have been influenced by chronological primitivism primarily in their retelling

144 See sources cited above, nn. 120–21.

145 It is possible that in an earlier version of the biblical Flood story a more cyclical view of history was expressed, with Noah being a second Adam. Note that Noah is said to have been the first to till the soil and plant a vineyard (Gen 9:20). Was he the first ever to do so, or was he simply responsible for reinstituting horticulture after the Flood? See *Gen. Rab.* 36.3 (above, n. 8). Several Greco-Roman sources speak of culture heroes arising after each flood to begin civilization anew. See sources cited above, n. 120. As we have seen (above, nn. 8, 97, 107), Rabbinic sources reveal a mixed view of the consequences of Noah's innovations.

146 Abraham is said to have lived during the Generation of the Separation, the third rebellious generation. See *Sifre Zuṭa* ad Num 27:1 (ed. Horovitz) 316. The following sources all suggest that with Abraham the human decline was arrested: *m. 'Abot* 5:2; *ARNA* 33 (ed. Schechter) 93–94; *Gen. Rab.* 2.3; 19.7; 39.5 (ed. Theodor-Albeck) 15–16, 176, 367–68; *Exod. Rab.* 15.7; *Tanḥ. Wayyera'* 18; *Bere'šit Rabbati* (ed. Albeck) 41. On the relation of Abraham to the preceding wicked generations, see L. Ginzberg, *Legends*, 1.185—86; 5.207–8.

of universal, pre-Israelite history.

For the rabbis, early history is divided not so much by the Flood as by the advent of the Israelite patriarchs. The universal history of Genesis 1–11 sets the stage for God's pact with Abraham and his descendants. In several of the sources that we have examined, the rebellious activities of the earliest generations is contrasted with the righteous deeds of these patriarchs, beginning with Abraham.[147] The biblical context of Gen 4:26 is understood as follows: The Creation story demonstrates God's sovereignty as the Lord of all. His creation, including man, is good. But shortly thereafter man begins to go astray, perverting his originally harmonious relationship with fellow man, nature, and God. Humanity's moral and physical decay is in part associated with the origins of urban life and civilized activities, especially as represented by Cain and his descendants. God confronts a series of rebellious generations, to whom can be traced the origins of human sinfulness, especially the cardinal sins of idolatry, bloodshed, and sexual licentiousness.[148] Each such generation is punished, but to no avail. The situation looks hopeless until Abraham appears, with whom God establishes a covenant to establish his seed as a righteous and holy people. It is universal history that establishes the need for such a covenant, and it is through the fulfillment of this covenant that the downward drift of universal history is arrested and reversed. Eventually, universal history is to be redeemed through the fulfillment of Israelite history.[149]

If seen within this wider Rabbinic understanding of Genesis 1–11, the Rabbinic interpretation of Gen 4:26 seems less arbitrary. The rabbis' principal interest is not in glorifying the prepatriarchal biblical figures, whose significance they downplay. Those, such as Noah, who are explicitly honored by Scripture cannot be ignored. But in the case of Enosh, Scripture is ambiguous, and the rabbis choose to take Gen 4:26b to refer not to him but to his contemporaries in general, for their main concern is in tracing pre-Israelite humanity's decline. For the rabbis, once Gen 4:26b is taken to refer to humanity in general, it cannot be understood to announce

147 See sources in previous note.

148 The MaHaRZU in his commentary to *Gen. Rab.* 23:7 (Vilna) 53b connects the Generation of Enosh with idolatry (*'ăbôdâ zārâ*) (Gen 4:26), the Generation of the Flood with sexual licentiousness (*gillûy 'ărāyôt*) (Gen 6:1–4), and the Generation of the Separation with bloodshed (*šĕpîkût dāmîm*), because of its association with Nimrod, the "man of might" (Gen 10:8). Cf. *Gen. Rab.* 31.6 (ed. Theodor-Albeck) 280, which connects all three sins with the word *ḥāmās* (Gen 6:11–13); and *Jub.* 7:21, which gives the three cardinal sins as the causes of the Flood. Note that in *Gen. Rab.* 41.7 (p. 394) and parallels all three sins are connected with the Sodomites.

149 This view of the underlying meaning of Genesis 1–11 is not very different in its general outlines from that recognized by modern biblical interpreters. See most recently B. S. Childs, *Introduction to the Old Testament as Scripture* (Philadelphia: Fortress, 1979) 154–55.

the beginnings of divine worship, for this would contradict the biblical context as they understand it. By "reading between the lines," the rabbis discover this verse to have an altogether different, less obvious meaning, yet one that for them better fits the biblical context: in Enosh's time men began to worship false gods. Their solution not only eliminates a perceived contradiction but also serves to reinforce the central meaning that they understand to underlie Scripture's account of early universal history: a pattern of successive generations each of whose sins contribute to the progressive human decline.

Once Gen 4:26 is taken to refer to the worship of false gods, it is to Abraham that the true worship of God (publicly calling on the name of the Lord, that is, prayer) can be traced.[150] According to early Jewish tradition, Abraham, although raised in an idolatrous environment, recognized (*hikkir*) God as the Creator and converted others to this belief, initiating a religous revolution.[151]

Thus, the rabbis' recasting of the biblical narrative, including their radical interpretation of Gen 4:26, accomplishes two interrelated transformations: (a) It smoothes over some of the abruptness of humanity's descent until the age of the patriarchs. Man's "fall" does not occur with one event, or person, or generation, but over a period of several generations. It is not abrupt, but gradual. Human sinfulness is not traced to the wrongdoings of isolated individuals, nor to the sudden interference of fallen divine beings and their demonic offspring, but to the steady decline of human culture as a whole. In this way, the Generation of Enosh fills the gap between Adam and the Flood, providing an important link in the chain of steadily degenerating generations. Humanity's decline becomes one of stages, and is therefore more easily reconciled with the "goodness" of man's creation, while God's response cannot be said to be rash or of undue measure. The stage is now fully set for the unfolding of Israelite/Jewish history. (b) By no longer associating the

150 It is Abraham with whom the phrase "to call upon the name of the Lord" is most frequently associated in the Bible (Gen 12:8; 13:4; 21:33; 26:25). On the Rabbinic understanding of "calling on the name of the Lord" as an expression of prayer see above, chap. 4, n. 14.

151 In some Rabbinic sources Abraham is said to have encouraged others to pray (reading *yiqrāʾ* as *yaqrîʾ*), thereby making of them converts. See *b. Soṭa* 10a; *Gen. Rab.* 39.16 (ed. Theodor-Albeck) 381 with Theodor's note ad loc; and other parallels. Thus, while Cain and Abel offered sacrifices to God, and Noah built an altar on which to make such offerings, Abraham is the first to institute *public* worship. Note that in a Geniza fragment attributed to Saadia Gaon (L. Ginzberg, *Geniza Studies*, vol. 1 [New York: Jewish Theological Seminary, 1928] 15), it is explicitly stated that Abraham was the first "in his days" to recognize his creator and to pray, citing Gen 12:8 as the prooftext. See Ginzberg's note 2. Note how similar this is to Josephus' statement (*Ant.* 1.7.1 §§ 154–57 [LCL 4.76–79]) that Abraham "was the *first* boldly to declare that God the creator of the universe is one . . . to whom alone it is right to render homage and thanksgiving."

beginnings of divine worship with Enosh or his contemporaries, Rabbinic exegesis further highlights Abraham as the one who reversed a cataclysmic pattern of universal history, (re)introducing the recognition of God the Creator as alone worthy of being called God and of being worshipped.

4. Polemical Motivations

In light of the pronounced differences between Rabbinic and non-Rabbinic exegesis, it is natural to ask whether the Rabbinic interpretation of Gen 4:26 reflects a polemical response to the non-Rabbinic veneration of Enosh. However, when we look carefully at the Rabbinic sources we find no explicit indications of such a polemic.[152] Nor do the Rabbinic sources ever suggest that the rabbis were aware of interpretations of Gen 4:26 other than their own. Furthermore, had the rabbis been motivated by a desire to refute the veneration of Enosh, we would expect to find in their commentaries recurring criticism of him, as we find of Noah and Enoch.[153] Rather, sometimes the Rabbinic sources extol Enosh (at least by implication), occasionally they include him in their condemnation of his generation, but most often they simply ignore him.[154] Thus, it seems unlikely that the Rabbinic interpretations are motivated by a desire to deny the veneration of Enosh found in Samaritan, Christian, and pre-Rabbinic Jewish sources.

More likely is the possibility that the rabbis wished to undercut Christian exegetical efforts at finding in the righteous Sethite antediluvians a prefiguration of their own eschatological election as "sons of God." As we saw in chapter 3, Enosh and Gen 4:26 were regularly interpreted by Church Fathers to this end. Here, however, we face chronological difficulties. We have seen that this Christian exegesis does not emerge until the early fourth century, both in western and eastern Fathers. As we have also seen, the Rabbinic interpretation of Gen 4:26 first appears unattributed in the *Mekilta* and *Sifre Deuteronomy*, collections that are generally thought to have been edited in the mid-third century, although such datings rest on slender evidence.[155] While the Rabbinic interpretation is already taken for granted in these earliest occurrences, I have argued that it is still Rabbinic in its origins. However, it is impossible to know more exactly where to place those origins

[152] Contrast *Gen. Rab.* 28.1, where the question of Enoch's mortality is discussed within the clearly polemical context of replies to "sectarians" (*mînîm*).

[153] See above, nn. 103–6.

[154] The only early Rabbinic source to criticize Enosh explicitly is *b. Šabb.* 118b according to the Munich MS (see above, chap. 4, n. 136). For a few later sources that implicate Enosh in the sin of his contemporaries see ibid., n. 137.

[155] For an early third century *terminus ad quem* for the traditions contained in the *Mekilta*, *Sifre Deuteronomy* and the Palestinian targumim see above, chap. 4, n. 206.

in the first three or four centuries C.E. Hence the difficulty of correlating the emergence of a distinctively Rabbinic interpretation with the distinctively Christian one that does not appear until the four century. Either the Rabbinic exegesis predates the Christian one, and therefore is not initially motivated by it, or our so-called tannaitic midrashim contain traditions that are significantly later than is generally assumed. Given these considerations, it is difficult to posit with any certainty a polemic against Christian exegesis of Gen 4:26 as a principal motivation for the Rabbinic exegesis. However, given our uncertain knowledge about the provenance of the so-called tannaitic midrashim, such a possibility cannot be ruled out.[156]

Despite our inability to find underlying the Rabbinic exegesis of Gen 4:26 a direct polemic against Christian exegesis of the same verse, it is possible to view the two exegeses within a broader polemical context: each community sought in its interpretation of pre-Israelite heroes and history scriptural support for its claim to be the divinely elected vehicle of covenant, revelation, and messianic hope. To this we will return in our final conclusions.

C. Conclusions

Our analysis of the Rabbinic interpretation of Gen 4:26 has led us to conclude that the rabbis were not motivated in their radical interpretation by any difficulty with the specific words of this verse. They seem to have understood them easily. What does seem to have caused them trouble was the aggregate meaning of these words, "then was begun (men began) to call on the name of the Lord," within the larger scriptural context as they wished to understand it.

We have explored a number of *interrelated* motivations, all of which could be present from our earliest sources, becoming more obvious as the initial tradition of interpretation develops in time:[157]

(a) The desire to trace the origins of idolatry, defined as the worship

[156] In general, there is increasing evidence for the interaction of Jewish and Christian exegeses, certainly in Palestine but also in Mesopotamia, especially in the third and fourth centuries. See for instance, N. R. M. deLange, *Origen and the Jews: Studies in the Jewish-Christian Relations in Third Century Palestine* (Cambridge: Cambridge University Press, 1976).

[157] While we have not attempted to trace a history of Rabbinic motivation, it is clear that all of these concerns can be found already in our earliest (tannaitic) Rabbinic sources. While the Rabbinic exegesis is more fully spelled out in amoraic sources, the basic themes are already evidenced earlier. For example, already in tannaitic sources we find both the motif of the chronological decline of *all* prepatriarchal generations and the association of Enosh's contemporaries with "idolatry." Only in amoraic sources, however, are the two integrated, the Generation of Enosh being regularly cited as an important link in the degeneration of the generations.

of false gods and considered one of the cardinal sins, back to antediluvian times, to an early stage in humanity's spiritual degeneration.

(b) The desire to portray pre-Israelite, universal history as a sequence of generations, each of which is progressively more alienated from God and from the rest of creation, and each of which is justly punished, but to no avail in abating the decline and cycle of cataclysms.

(c) The desire to set the stage for the arrival of the Israelite patriarchs, beginning with Abraham, who in contrast to the degeneracy that precedes them reestablish the recognition and proper worship of the one true God, and begin a redemptive, covenantal chain of which the rabbis understand themselves to be the latest links.

We have seen at a number of points that: (a) The rabbis in recasting Scripture's narrative are sensitive to real difficulties in that narrative, particularly the awkward way in which Gen 4:26 resides in its scriptural context and the theological issues raised by the abruptness of the biblical Flood story. (b) The Rabbinic reworking of the story of human origins is significantly influenced by motifs found in Greco-Roman philosophical and historiographical sources. Yet neither the scriptural stimuli nor the adapted literary, philosophical, and historiographic conventions, while being very important to our understanding of *how* the rabbis effected their interpretation, provides the Rabbinic motivation, in part since both of these were equally available to (and are evidenced in) non-Rabbinic exegetes, Jewish and non-Jewish.

Rather, what makes the Rabbinic interpretation unique, and here placing it in comparative perspective has highlighted its contours, is the desire to portray Israelite heroes and history in *sharpest* contrast to their universal, pre-Israelite predecessors, now denied the eschatological, paradigmatic meaning that is regularly attributed to them by non-Rabbinic, especially Christian, exegetes.

Chapter Six
FINAL CONCLUSIONS

Having examined a diversity of interpretative traditions relating to Enosh and his generation, let us venture some final thoughts of a comparative nature.[1] How are we to account for the wide range of interpretations that we have encountered, some of which are diametrically opposed to others?

The interpretations we have examined can be reduced essentially to two varieties: (a) those that understand Gen 4:26 as a *positive* statement concerning Enosh the individual (all non-Rabbinic traditions), and (b) those that view this verse as a *negative* statement about Enosh's contemporaries (Rabbinic traditions alone).

The first interpretation is clearly the more widespread, being evidenced in several groups, from earliest through modern exegesis.

We have seen that in early extra-Rabbinic Jewish, Samaritan, and Christian exegesis Enosh is regularly included as a link in the chain of ancient righteous ancestors, through whom was transmitted the divine image and/or messianic seed. In this regard, the interpretation of Enosh is not very different from that of other pre-Israelite righteous figures. These communities wished to trace their own descent back to the first man through an unbroken line of righteous ancestors, bypassing other less savory biblical figures, who were instead identified as the progenitors of the "other nations," and as the originators of worldly evil. By so doing, these groups were establishing their pedigrees in sacred history.[2] The earliest ancestors in such lists of righteous ancestors, naturally, were particularly venerated as ideal figures, and any scriptural comment that could be construed as praise of these figures was fully exploited.

In an age of apocalyptic expectations, the antediluvian heroes were especially significant within such chains of righteous ancestors, since living during or in close proximity to the "golden age" of history and having been spared the destruction of the Flood, they were thought to

[1] For summaries of the various traditions of interpretation, see the concluding sections of the preceding chapters.

[2] This use of genealogy is especially apparent in the Samaritan chronologies, in part because of the Samaritan need to prove the legitimacy of their priesthood. Similarly, the NT contains two genealogies for Jesus, one going back to Abraham (Matt 1:1–17), and another going back to Adam (Luke 3:23–38).

have special claims to righteousness and esoteric knowledge.[3] Some believed that these figures would play an important role in the approaching redemption since the coming age was imagined as mirroring the prehistoric times in which they were thought to have lived. These righteous ancestors would either themselves return to help usher in the new age or serve as prototypes for new redeemer figures soon to appear. Since Scripture says so little about these earliest humans except for the long lives they enjoyed, and whatever else it says is often enigmatic, they attained a certain mystique, an almost superhuman quality, which further served the apocalyptic interests of some exegetes.[4]

Within this context, Enosh often receives special attention. Because of his name, meaning "man," he is thought to represent both mankind in general and quintessential, ideal man. Because he was the first to call on the name of the Lord, he is viewed as a model of undaunted faith. Because of his hope (deriving from the LXX), he exemplifies the divine trust and/or messianic expectation of the faithful. Different exegetes place varying degrees of emphasis on one or more of these aspects. Thus, Philo, perhaps under Platonic influence,[5] focuses on Enosh as the "hoper," representing the first step in spiritual perfection, which is more fully achieved with the subsequent patriarchs. Marqah and subsequent Samaritan exegetes stress Enosh as the "caller," and view him as a prefiguration of Moses, who in turn prefigures the *taheb* redeemer figure.[6] Early Christian writers similarly, but more emphatically, view Enosh allegorically as representing ideal man fully in God's image, and soon come to view him typologically as foreshadowing Jesus and the Christian faithful because of his "calling on the name of the Lord," since this expression is associated in the New Testament with Christian faith in Jesus.[7]

Enosh's significance is most pronounced in the writings of certain Church Fathers, who, beginning in the mid-fourth century, interpret Gen 4:26b to mean that Enosh was the first, on account of his righteousness, to *be called* "God" and "son of God," prefiguring Jesus, who was similarly called. They view him as standing at the head of the righteous Sethite branch of humanity, who (a) initially remain apart from the evil descendants of Cain, (b) following Enosh, prophetically place their hope

[3] Seth, Enoch, Methuselah, and Noah are often the subjects of such traditions, as are the postdiluvians Melchizedek and Job.

[4] On the eschatological interests of exegetes of antediluvian heroes see J. C. VanderKam, "The Righteousness of Noah," in *Ideal Figures in Ancient Judaism: Profiles and Paradigms* (ed. J. J. Collins and G. W. E. Nickelsburg; SBLSCS 12; Chico, CA: Scholars Press, 1980) 13–32, esp. 25–27.

[5] See above, chap. 1, n. 66.

[6] See our discussion on *Memar Marqah* 2.6 and 2.12 in chap. 2.

[7] See above, chap. 2, n. 28.

(i.e., trust) in the Lord Jesus, and (c) like Enosh, bear the name "sons of God." Enosh and his descendants, then, bear witness to Jesus before his incarnation,[8] serve as models of steadfast faith for later Christians, and typologically prefigure and genealogically antecede the Christian Church as "sons of God."[9] Thus, the Christian interpretations express a sectarian concern not only for grounding the Church's origin in Scripture, but also for tracing it back typologically, as well as genealogically, to the earliest period of human history (or prehistory), thereby strengthening its universal, messianic claims.

We have seen that in three important ways this distinctively Christian exegesis has roots in Jewish antecedents: (a) the inclusion of Enosh in a select chain of righteous ancestors (apocrypha and pseudepigrapha, as well as Samaritan exegesis), (b) the allegorization of Enosh as ideal and first true man (Philo), (c) the depiction of antediluvian humanity as comprising two opposing "camps," the descendants of Seth and those of Cain (*1 Enoch* and Josephus). However, the particular way in which these antecedent traditions are combined and linked to the words of Gen 4:26 draws upon a stock motif in the Greco-Roman world: the belief that extraordinary humans are so marked by bearing divine epithets and being considered sons of God.

Rabbinic exegesis, which views Gen 4:26 as a negative statement about the idolatrous Generation of Enosh, when viewed within the larger context of Rabbinic interpretation of pre-Istraelite history, likewise reveals exegetical concerns of a sectarian nature. The de-emphasis of Enosh and other pre-Israelite righteous, the tracing of the origins of idolatry to the Generation of Enosh, as of the other cardinal sins to pre-Israelite society, and the depiction of the steady, unabated degeneration of the pre-Israelite generations (often depicted as *beginning* with the radical sin and punishment of Enosh's generation) highlight the redemptive role of *Abraham* and his descendants down to the rabbis and their followers. For the rabbis, it is against the background of progressive, universal human decline that the beginnings of Israelite history, and therefore the origins of the Jewish people, must be viewed.

Enosh the individual is of little concern to the rabbis, their interest lying rather in what Scripture is thought to say of prepatriarchal humanity in general. They would not deny that the Jewish people traces its genealogy ultimately back to Adam through Enosh and Seth, but, then again, so could all peoples. What distinguishes the Jews, from the Rabbinic perspective, is the covenant initiated by God with Abraham, who alone in a sinful age turned to the pure worship of the one God. It is

[8] See Origen, *Commentary to Romans* 8.3, discussed above, chap. 3, nn. 27–29.

[9] See especially our treatment of Eusebius of Emesa, John Chrysostom, Cyril of Alexandria, Ps.-Malalas, Ephraem, and Isho'dad of Merv in chapter 3.

through the fulfillment of this distinctive covenant, as formally contracted with the whole Jewish people at Sinai, that the "golden age" will be regained, and even surpassed. The Rabbinic interpretation implies that had it not been for this covenant, human history would have continued its steady decline, with little hope for redemption. Pre-Israelite, universal history prepares for and necessitates Israelite history, the advent of which now appears to change history's course radically. The prepatriarchal righteous can hardly compare with such Israelite figures as Abraham, Jacob, or Moses, to whom the rabbis trace the "chain of tradition" of which they consider themselves the sole guardians.[10]

Once again, although not as decidedly as for Christian exegesis, antecedents to aspects of Rabbinic exegesis can be found in pre-Rabbinic Jewish sources: (a) Philo's view of Enosh and the other pre-Israelite righteous as being inferior and preparatory to their Israelite successors, (b) Josephus' depiction of a widespread moral and spiritual decline several generations before the Flood.[11] Still, there is little in pre-Rabbinic Jewish exegesis of Gen 4:26 that prepares us for the radical use to which the rabbis put that verse. However, if vertical roots are hard to find, some important lateral ones have become apparent, as Rabbinic exegesis of Gen 4:26 is nourished by contemporary motifs in Greco-Roman historiography of earliest times: cultural and chronological primitivism linked to stories of recurring cataclysms.

I have repeatedly stressed that the potential for diverse interpretations of Gen 4:26 must be recognized in the biblical text itself, particularly in the problematic relationship of that verse to its scriptural context. Does Genesis 4–6 contrast the righteous Sethites with the sinful Cainites or does it stress the moral decline of humanity as a whole? Christian and some pre-Rabbinic Jewish exegetes suggest the former, while Rabbinic midrash points to the latter. (The biblical text is suggestive of both.) Related to this question is the ambiguity of Gen 4:26b itself: does it describe the actions of Enosh the individual or of his contemporaries? Again, Christian, Samaritan, and pre-Rabbinic Jewish interpretations generally presuppose the former, while Rabbinic exegesis the latter. Obviously, the way they answer one question affects their answer to the other. While the early versions of the Bible may have narrowed these choices for the exegetes who used them, these versions themselves contain new problems and ambiguities that provided further stimuli or pegs for subsequent interpretation.[12] To

[10] By contrast, extra-Rabbinic exegetes (Jewish, Christian, and Samaritan) speak of a *continuous* chain of piety and revelation extending from the antediluvian righteous down (through their own communities) to the Messiah.

[11] It is interesting that despite the sharp contrast between Rabbinic and patristic exegeses, Philo and Josephus foreshadow somewhat both.

[12] We have repeatedly seen how difficult it is to determine when the versions reflect a variant Vorlage, when a "pseudo-variant," and when actual exegesis. For instance, does

recognize such a continuum between Hebrew Scripture, its versions, and subsequent exegesis, however, is not to presume that postbiblical exegesis (particularly in its diversity) is simply an ahistorical extension of the biblical text (and its authority).

While both early Christian and Rabbinic exegeses of Enosh and his contemporaries need to be understood in relation to difficulties within the scriptural text versions they employed and to the antecedent traditions of interpretation that they inherited, neither can be understood simply as the logical unfolding of the exegetical potentialities of those received texts and traditions. Rather, each group exegetically responded to and employed these received texts and traditions in order to define itself as the divinely elected vehicle and guardian of revelation and redemptive hope. In the second through fourth centuries, in particular, this meant for Jews and Christians defining themselves over against the other. Both groups turned to Scripture's depiction of earliest human history to establish their paramountcy in sacred history.

The Christian Fathers, employing allegory and typology, treated pre-Israelite and antediluvian history as a *paradigm*, claiming that the Church's election and travail was like that of the righteous Sethite "sons of God," at whose head stood Enosh, true man, and the first "son of God." Such righteous figures as Enosh, preceding the Flood and the "failed" covenant of the law, provided a Scriptural foreshadowing and grounding for the contested claims of the Church that they alone, apart from those who had not accepted Jesus, were "sons of God" awaiting final redemption.

The rabbis, employing what might be called "etiological exegesis," treated pre-Israelite history as a *foil*, tracing the origins of humanity's sorry state to the pre-Israelite generations. Such universal righteous figures as Seth, Enosh, Enoch, and Noah were denied *significant* redemptive and revelatory functions since their righteous deeds were unable to prevent the disastrous sins and punishments of their contemporaries.[13] For the rabbis, sacred, redemptive history began with Abraham and the covenant of law contracted with his descendants, but only after universal

the LXX translation "he hoped" reflect a true variant, a careless misvocalization, or an attempt already to qualify Enosh's importance (he *only* hoped) or to accentuate it (he placed his *hope* in God). In any case, this translation created new problems and opportunites for its interpreters. Similarly, we have noted (chap. 4, nn. 70–76, 114) that the interpretation of Enosh and antediluvian history, and therefore the origins of these exegetical problems and opportunities, may extend back into the biblical text itself, as reflected in the way the redactor(s) combined and juxtaposed the materials of Genesis 4–6.

[13] This is not to deny that these figures are sometimes praised (although often in a qualified manner) in Rabbinic sources; rather, it is to argue that their significance in the recasting of sacred history is considerably diminished. The elevation of Enoch/Metatron in the Hekhalot and related literature is a notable exception. See S. D. Fraade, "Enoch," *Encyclopedia of Religion*, forthcoming.

history had, despite *several* divine attempts to tame it, run amok. It was the steadfast adherence to that covenant, and to the rabbis as the interpreters of its terms, which would guarantee the redemption of Israel, and ultimately of universal history.

BIBLIOGRAPHY

PRIMARY SOURCES AND TRANSLATIONS

Hebrew Bible and Versions:

The Bible in Aramaic. Ed. Alexander Sperber. 4 vols. Leiden: E. J. Brill, 1959–73.

Biblia Hebraica Stuttgartensia. Ed. K. Elliger and W. Rudolph et al. Stuttgart: Deutsche Bibelstiftung, 1976–77.

Biblia Sacra: *Iuxta vulgatam versionem*. Ed. Robert Weber. 2 vols. Stuttgart: Württembergische Bibelanstalt

Biblorum Sacrorum latinae versiones antiquae. Ed. Petri Sabatier. Vol. 1. Paris, 1751. Reprint. Munich, 1976.

The Fragment Targums of the Pentateuch According to their Extant Sources. Ed. Michael L. Klein. 2 vols. AnBib 76. Rome: Biblical Institute, 1980.

Das Fragmententhargum. Ed. Moses Ginsburger. Berlin, 1897–98.

Hagiographa Chaldaice. Ed. Paul Lagarde. Leipzig: Teubner, 1873.

Hattargum haššomroni. Vol. 1: Genesis, Exodus. Ed. Abraham Tal. Texts and Studies in the Hebrew Language and Related Subjects, no. 4. Tel-Aviv: University of Tel-Aviv, 1980.

Der Hebräische Pentateuch der Samaritaner. Ed. August von Gail. Giessen: A. Töpelmann, 1914–18.

Kahle, Paul. *Masoreten des Westens II*. Beiträge zur Wissenschaft vom Alten und Neuen Testament. Series 3, vol. 14. Stuttgart, 1930.

Miqra'ot gedolot 'im 32 perušim. 10 vols. New York: Pardes, 1951.

Neophyti I. Ed. A. Diez Macho. 6 vols. Madrid and Barcelona: Consejo Superior de Investigaciones Cientificas, 1968–79.

The New English Bible With the Apocrypha. New York: Oxford University, 1971.

The Old Testament in Greek. Ed. Alan England Brooke and Norman McLean. 3 vols. Cambridge: Cambridge University Press, 1906–40.

Origenis Hexaplorum. Ed. F. Field. 2 vols. Oxford: Clarendon, 1875.

The Palestinian Targum to the Pentateuch: *Codex Vatican*. Facsimile Edition. Jerusalem: Makor, 1970.

Pentateuchus Samaritanus. Ed. H. Petermann and C. Vollers. Berlin: W. Moeser, 1872–91.

Pentateuchus Syriace. Ed. G. E. Barnes. London: Societas Bibliophilorum Britannicam et Externam, 1914.

Pentateuco Hebreo-Samaritano, Genesis: Edición critica sobre la base de manuscritos inéditos. Ed. Luis-Fernando Giron Blanc. Madrid: Consejo Superior de Investigaciones Cientificas, 1976.

The Prophets: Nevi'im. A New Translation of The Holy Scriptures According to the Masoretic Text. Philadelphia: The Jewish Publication Society of America, 1978.

Pseudo-Jonathan: Targum Jonathan ben Uziel on the Pentateuch. Ed. David Rieder. Jerusalem, 1974.

Die Samaritanische Pentateuch-Version des Genesis. Ed. H. Heidenheim. Leipzig: O. Schulze, 1884.

Das Samaritanische Targum zum Pentateuch. Ed. Adolf Brüll. Frankfurt a. M.: W. Erras, 1875.

Septuaginta: id est Vetus Testamentum Graece iuxta LXX interpretes. Ed. Alfred Rahlfs. 2 vols. Stuttgart: Württembergische Bibelanstalt, 1935. Reprint. 1962.

Septuaginta Vetus Testamentum Graecum. Ed. J. W. Wevers. Vol. 1. Göttingen: Vandenhoeck and Ruprecht, 1974.

Targum Onqelos. Ed. A. Berliner. 2 vols. Berlin: Gorzelanczyk, 1884.

The Torah: The Five Books of Moses. A New Translation of the Holy Scriptures According to the Masoretic Text. Philadelphia: Jewish Publication Society of America, 1962.

Vetus Latina: Die Reste der altlateinischen Bible. Vol. 2: Genesis. Ed. Bonifatius Fischer. Frieburg: Herder, 1951.

Vetus Testamentum Syriace: iuxta simplicem syrorum versionem. The Peshiṭta Institute, Leiden. Part 1, fascicle 1. Leiden: E. J. Brill, 1977.

Apocrypha and Pseudepigrapha:

Apocrypha and Pseudepigrapha of the Old Testament. Ed. R. H. Charles. 2 vols. Oxford: Clarendon, 1913.

The Ben Sira Scroll from Masada. Ed. Yigael Yadin. Jerusalem: Israel Exploration Society, 1965.

The Book of Ben Sira: Text, Concordance and an Analysis of the Vocabulary. The Historical Dictionary of the Hebrew Language. Jerusalem: The Academy of the Hebrew Language and the Shrine of the Book, 1973.

The Book of Jubilees. Trans. and ed. R. H. Charles. London: A. and C. Black, 1902.

The Book of the Secrets of Enoch. Ed. R. H. Charles. Trans. W. R. Morfill. Oxford: Clarendon, 1896.
Codex pseudepigraphus Veteris Testamenti. Ed. J. A. Fabricius and Johann Albert. 2 vols. Hamburg: T. C. Felginer, 1722–23.
Ecclesiasticus or The Wisdom of Jesus Son of Sirach. Trans. John G. Snaith. Cambridge: Cambridge University Press, 1974.
L'Ecclésiastique; ou, la sagesse de Jésus, fils de Sira. Texte original hébreu. Ed. and trans. Israel Lévi. 2 vols. in 1. Paris: E. Leroux, 1889–1901.
The Ethiopic Version of the Hebrew Book of Jubilees. Ed. R. H. Charles. Oxford: Clarendon, 1899.
Fragmenta pseudepigraphum quae supersunt graeca. Ed. Albert-Marie Denis. Pseudepigrapha Veteris Testamenti graece, vol. 3. Leiden: E. J. Brill, 1970.
Le Livre des secrets d'Hénoch: texte slave et traduction française. Ed. and trans. A. Vaillant. Textes publiés par l'Institut d'Études Slaves, no. 4. Paris: Institut d'Études Slaves, 1952.
Sapientia Jesu Filii Sirach. Ed. Joseph Ziegler. Septuaginta Vetus Testamentum Graecum. Vol. 12, pt. 2. Göttingen: Vandenhoeck und Ruprecht, 1965.
Seper Ben Sira' Haššalem. Ed. M. H. Segal. 2nd ed. Jerusalem: Bialik Institute, 1972.
The Testaments of the Twelve Patriarchs: A Critical Edition of the Greek Text. Ed. M. De Jonge. Pseudepigrapha Vetus Testamenti Graece 1.2. Leiden: E. J. Brill, 1978.
Die Weisheit des Jesus Sirach: Hebräisch und Deutsch . . . mit einem hebräischer Glossar. Ed. Rudolf Smend. Berlin: G. Reimer, 1906.
The Wisdom of Ben Sira: Portions of the Book of Ecclesiasticus from Hebrew Manuscripts in the Cairo Geniza. Ed. Solomon Schechter. Cambridge: Cambridge University Press, 1899.

Dead Sea Scrolls:

Baillet, Maurice. "Un Recueil Liturgique de Qumran Grotte 4: 'Les Paroles des Luminaires.'" *RB* 68 (1961) 195–250, pls. 24–28.
The Books of Enoch: Aramaic Fragments of Qumran Cave 4. Ed. J. T. Milik. Oxford: Clarendon, 1976.
The Dead Sea Scriptures in English Translation. Trans. Theodore H. Gaster. Garden City, New York: Doubleday, 1964.
The Dead Sea Scrolls in English. Trans. Geza Vermes. Rev. ed. Baltimore: Penquin Books, 1968.
The Dead Sea Scrolls of St. Mark's Monastery. Ed. Millar Burrows. Vol. 1. New Haven: American Schools of Oriental Research, 1950.

The Genesis Apocryphon of Qumran Cave 1: A Commentary. Ed. and trans. Joseph Fitzmyer. 2nd rev. ed. Biblica et Orientalia, no. 18a. Rome: Biblical Institute Press, 1966.

A Genesis Apocryphon: A Scroll from the Wilderness of Judaea. Ed. Naḥman Avigad and Yigael Yadin. Jerusalem: Magnes, 1956.

Milik, J. T., "A propos de 11QJub." *Bib.* 54 (1973) 77–78.

Qumran Cave 4. Ed. John M. Allegro. Discoveries in the Judaean Desert of Jordan, vol. 5. Oxford: Clarendon, 1968.

Woude, A. S. van der. "Fragmente des Buches Jubiläen aus Qumran Höhle XI (11QJub)." *Tradition und Glaube: Das frühe Christentum in seiner Umwelt: Festgabe für Karl Georg Kuhn zum 65. Geburtstag*, ed. G. Jeremias et al., 140–46. Göttingen: Vendenhoeck & Ruprecht, 1971.

Philo, Josephus, and Pseudo-Philo:

The Biblical Antiquities of Philo. Trans. M. R. James. London SPCK, 1917. Reprint with prolegomenon by Louis H. Feldman. New York: Ktav, 1971.

Josephus with an English Translation. Ed. and trans. H. St. J. Thackeray and Ralph Marcus. LCL. 9 vols. London: W. Heinemann, 1926–65.

Philo with an English Translation. Ed. and trans. F. H. Colson, R. Marcus, and G. H. Whitaker. LCL. 10 vols. and 2 supp. vols. Cambridge: Harvard University, 1929–62.

Philonis Alexandrini: Opera quae supersunt. Ed. Leopold Cohn and Paul Wendland. 7 vols. in 8. Berlin: G. Reimer, 1896–1930.

Pseudo-Philon, Les Antiquites Bibliques. Ed. Daniel J. Harrington. Trans. Jacques Cazeaus. With a commentary by Charles Perrot and Pierre-Maurice Bogaert. SC 229, 230. Paris: Les éditions du Cerf, 1976.

Pseudo-Philo's Liber Antiquitatem Biblicarum. Ed. Guido Kisch. Publications in Mediaeval Studies, no. 10. Notre Dame, Ind.: University of Notre Dame, 1949.

Rabbinic Sources:

Aboth de Rabbi Nathan. Ed. Solomon Schechter. Vienna, 1889. Reprint. New York: Feldheim, 1967.

Agadath Bereschith: Midraschische Auslegungen zum ersten Buche Mosis. Ed. Salomon Buber. Cracow: J. Fischer, 1902.

Bet ha-Midrasch. Ed. Adolph Jellinek. 6 vols. Leipzig, 1853–57. Third ed. Reprint (6 vols. in 2). Jerusalem: Wahrmann, 1967.

The Chronicles of Jeraḥmeel. Trans. M. Gaster. London, 1899. Reprinted with a prolegomenon by Haim Schwartzbaum. New York: KTAV, 1971.

The Fathers According to Rabbi Nathan. Trans. Judah Goldin. Yale Judaica Series, vol. 10. New Haven: Yale University Press, 1955.

The Fathers According to Rabbi Nathan, Version B. Trans. Anthony J. Saldarini. SJLA 11. Leiden: E. J. Brill, 1975.

Lekach-Tob (Pesikta sutarta) ein agadischer commentar . . . von Rabbi Tobia ben Eliezer. Ed. Salomon Buber. 5 vols. in 2. Wilna: Romm, 1880–84. Reprint. Jerusalem, 1960.

Maḥzor layyamim hannora'im. Ed. Daniel Goldschmidt. 2 vols. Jerusalem: Koren, 1970.

Masseket Semaḥot. Ed. M. Higger. New York: Bloch, 1931.

Massekhet Soferim. Ed. M. Higger. New York: Debe Rabanan, 1937.

Megillat Ta'anit. Ed. H. Lichtenstein, "Die Fastenrolle, eine Untersuchung zur jüdisch-hellenistischen Geschichte." *HUCA* 8–9 (1931–32) 257–351.

Mechilta de-Rabbi Ismael, der älteste halachische und hagadische Midrasch zu Exodus. Ed. Meier Friedmann. Vienna, 1870. Reprint. Jerusalem, 1967–68.

Mechilta D'Rabbi Ismael. Ed. H. Horovitz and I. Rabin. Frankfurt a. M.: J. Kaufmann, 1928.

Mechiltha: Ein tannaitischer Midrash zu Exodus. Trans. J. Winter and A. Wünsche. Leipzig: J. C. Hinrichs, 1909.

Mekhilta d'Rabbi Ishmael with Amendations [sic] *of the Gaon of Vilna and the Commentary Birkath Haneziv.* Jerusalem, 1970.

Mekhilta D'Rabbi Šim'on b. Jochai. Ed. J. N. Epstein and E. Z. Melamed. Jerusalem: Mekize Nirdamim, 1955.

Mekilta de-Rabbi Ishmael. Ed. and trans. Jacob Lauterbach. 3 vols. Philadelphia: Jewish Publication Society, 1933–35.

Menorat Ha-Maor of R. Israel ibn Al-Nahawa. Ed. H. G. Enelow. 4 vols. New York: Bloch, 1929–32.

Midraš 'aggada 'al ḥamišša ḥummeše tora. Ed. Salomon Buber. Vienna, 1894. Reprint. Jerusalem, 1961.

Midraš Berešit Rabbati ex Libro R. Mosis Haddaršan. Ed. Ch. Albeck. Jerusalem: Mekize Nirdamim, 1940. Reprint. Jerusalem: Mossad Harav Kook, 1967.

Midraš ḥameš megillot. Facsimile of 1519 printing. Berlin, 1926.

Midraš rabba 'al ḥamišša ḥummeše tora weḥameš megillot. Wilna: Romm: 1884–87. Reprint. Jerusalem, 1960–61.

Midraš sekel ṭob 'al seper bere'šit ušemot. Ed. Salomon Buber. Berlin, 1900. Reprint. Tel Aviv, 1963–64.

Midraš tanḥuma ʿal ḥamišša ḥummeše tora. Jerusalem: Lewin-Epstein, 1974.

Midrasch Echa Rabbati: *Sammlung agadischer Auslegungen der Klagelieder*. Wilna: Romm, 1899. Reprint. Tel Aviv, 1963–64.

Midrasch Suta: *Haggadische Abhandlungen über Schir ha-Schirim, Ruth, Echah und Koheleth nebts Jalkut zum Buche Echah*. Berlin: Mekize Nirdamim, 1894. Reprint. Wilna: Romm, 1925.

Midrasch Tanchuma: *Ein agadischer Commentar zum Pentateuch von Rabbi Tanchuma ben Rabbi Abba*. Wilna: Romm, 1885. Reprint (in 2 vols.). Israel, n.d.

Midrasch tannaïm zum Deuteronomium. Ed. D. Hoffmann. 2 vols. Berlin: H. Itzkowski, 1908–9.

Midrasch Tehillim (*Schocher Tob*): *Sammlung agadischer Abhandlungen über die 150 Psalmen*. Wilna: Romm, 1891. Reprint. Jerusalem, 1965–66.

Midrash Bereshit Rabba. Ed. J. Theodor and Ch. Albeck. 3 vols. Berlin. Reprint with corrections. Jerusalem: Wahrmann, 1965.

Midrash Debarim Rabbah. Ed. Saul Liebermann. Third ed. Jerusalem: Wahrmann, 1974.

Midrash Haggadol on the Pentateuch: *Genesis*. Ed. M. Margulies. Jerusalem: Mossad Harav Kook, 1947. Reprint. 1967.

Midrash Haggadol on the Pentateuch: *Exodus*. Ed. M. Margulies. Jerusalem: Mossad Harav Kook, 1966.

Midrash Haggadol on the Pentateuch: *Leviticus*. Ed. Adin Steinzaltz. Jerusalem: Mossad Harav Kook, 1975.

Midrash Haggadol on the Pentateuch: *Deuteronomy*. Ed. Shlomo Fisch. Jerusalem: Mossad Harav Kook, 1972.

Midrash Rabbah: *Genesis*. Trans. H. Freedman. 2 vols. London: Soncino, 1939.

Midrash Wayyikra Rabbah. Ed. M. Margulies. 5 vols. Jerusalem, 1953–60. Reprint (5 vols. in 3). Jerusalem: Wahrmann, 1972.

Mischnacodex Kaufmann. Facsimile edition. Ed. G. Beer. 2 vols. Haag, 1929. Reprint. Jerusalem: Makor, 1967–68.

The Mishnah of R. Eliezer; *or the Midrash of Thirty-Two Hermeneutical Rules*. Ed. H. G. Enelow. New York: Bloch, 1933–34.

The Munich Mekilta. Early Hebrew Manuscripts in Facsimile, vol. 7. Ed. Judah Goldin. Copenhagen: Rosenkilde and Bagger, 1980.

Ozar Midrashim. Ed. J. D. Eisenstein. 2 vols. New York, 1915.

The Passover Haggadah. Ed. E. D. Goldschmidt. Reprint. Jerusalem: Bialik Institute, 1977.

Pesikta de Rav Kahana. Ed. B. Mandelbaum. 2 vols. New York: Jewish Theological Seminary of America, 1962.

Pěsiḳta dě-Rab̲ Kahăna. Trans. William Braude and Israel Kapstein. Philadelphia: Jewish Publication Society, 1975.

Pesikta Rabbati, Midrasch für den Fest-cyclus und die ausgezeichneten Sabbathe. Ed. M. Friedmann. Vienna, 1880.

Pirqe Rabbi 'Eli'ezer . . . 'im be'ur haRaDaL. Warsaw, 1852.

Piyyute Yose ben Yose. Ed. Aharon Mirsky. Jerusalem: Bialik Institute, 1977.

Seder Eliyahu Rabba und Seder Eliahu Zuṭa (Tanna de'be Eliahu). Ed. M. Friedmann. Vienna, 1902.

Seper hayyašar. Ed. E. Goldschmidt. Berlin: B. Harz, 1923.

Seper hazzohar 'al ḥamišša ḥummeše tora. 3 vols. Jerusalem: Mossad Harav Kook, 1964.

Siddur R. Saadja Gaon. Ed. I. Davidson; S. Assaf; and B. I. Joel. Jerusalem: Meqiṣe nirdamim, 1963.

Sifra: Codex Vatican 66. Ed. Louis Finkelstein. New York: Jewish Theological Seminary of America, 1956.

Siphre d'be Rab. Fasciculus primus: Siphre ad Numeros adjecto Siphre zutta. Ed. H. S. Horovitz. Corpus Tannaiticum 3:3:1. Leipzig, 1917. Reprint. Jerusalem: Wahrmann, 1966.

Siphre d'be Rab. Fasciculus alter: Siphre ad Deuteronomium. Ed. Louis Finkelstein. Corpus Tannaiticum 3:3:2. Berlin, 1939. Reprint. New York: Jewish Theological Seminary of America, 1969.

Sipra' debe rab hu' seper torat kohanim. Ed. I. H. Weiss. Vienna: J. Schlossberg, 1962.

Sipra' 'im peruš rabbenu Hillel. Ed. S. Koleditzky. 2 vols. Jerusalem, 1960–61.

Sipre debe Rab. Ed. Meir Friedmann. Vienna, 1864.

Šišša sidre mišna. Ed. Ch. Albeck. 6 vols. Jerusalem: Bialik Institute and Tel Aviv: Dvir, 1952–56.

Talmud babli. 20 vols. Wilna: Romm, 1886. Reprint. Jerusalem, Sifre Qodesh, n.d.

Talmud yerušalmi. Venice: Bomberg, 1923–24. Reprint. n.d.

Talmud yerušalmi 'o talmud hamma'arab . . . usebibo perušim, ḥiqre halakot, girsa'ot wenusḥa'ot šonot. 7 vols. Vilna: Romm, 1922. Reprint. New York: M.P. Press, 1976.

Torath Cohanim (Sifra) Codex Vatican 31. Facsimile ed. Jerusalem: Makor, 1972.

The Tosefta. Ed. S. Lieberman. Vols. 1–4. New York: Jewish Theological Seminary of America, 1955–73.

Tosephta Based on the Erfurt and Vienna Codices. Ed. M. S. Zuckermandel. With a supplement by Saul Liebermann. Jerusalem: Wahrmann, 1970.

3 Enoch; or, the Hebrew Book of Enoch. Ed. and trans. Hugo Odeberg. Cambridge, 1928. Reprint with prolegomenon by J. C. Greenfield. New York: Ktav, 1973.

Yalquṭ hammakiri ʿal yišaʿyahu. Ed. J. Spira. Berlin: I. Itzkowski, 1923. Reprint. Jerusalem, 1963–64.

Yalquṭ hammakiri ʿal sipre ʿamos ʿobadya yona mika naḥum weḥabaqquq. Ed. A. W. Greenup. London, 1910.

Yalquṭ hammakiri ʿal sipre yoʾel ṣepanya ḥaggay umalʾaki. Ed. A. W. Greenup. London, 1913.

Yalquṭ reʾubeni. 2 vols. Warsaw, 1883–84. Reprint. Jerusalem, 1962.

Yalquṭ šimʿoni ʿal hattora. 7 vols. Salonika, 1521–27. Facsimile ed. Jerusalem, 1967–68.

Yalquṭ šimʿoni ʿal hattora. Based on the Oxford MS Vol. 1. Jerusalem: Mossad Harav Kook, 1973.

Zohar ḥadaš ʿal ḥamišša ḥummeše tora. Ed. P. Margulies. Jerusalem: Mossad Harav Kook, 1952.

Post-Talmudic Rabbinic Commentators and Philosophers:

Abraham ibn Ezra. *Peruše hattora*. Ed. A. Vizer. 3 vols. Jerusalem: Mossad Harav Kook, 1976.

David Qimḥi. *Kimhi's Allegorical Commentary on Genesis*. Appendix I in *The Commentary of David Kimhi on Isaiah*. Ed. Louis Finkelstein. New York: Columbia University, 1926.

__________. *Perus RaDaQ ʿal hattora, seper bereʾšit*. Ed. A. Ginzburg. Pressburg, 1842. Reprint. Jerusalem, 1967–68.

Judah Löw ben Bezalel. *Seper gur ʾaryeh*. Prague, 1578. Reprint. Bene Berak, 1972.

Levi ben Gerson. *Peruš ʿal hattora derek beʾur*. Venice, 1547.

Menaḥem Zioni ben Meir. *Seper ṣiyyoni*. Lemberg, 1882. Reprint. Jerusalem, 1964.

Merkebet hammišneh, beʾur raḥab ʿal hammekiltaʾ derabbi yišmaʿel. Lvov, 1895. Reprint. Jerusalem: Oṣar happosekim, 1965.

Moses ben Maimom (Maimonides). *Mishneh Torah*. Ed. M. Hyamson. 2 vols. New York: Bloch, 1937–42.

Moses ben Naḥman. *Peruše hattora*. Ed. Ch. Chavel. 2 vols. Rev. ed. Jerusalem: Mossad Harav Kook, 1976.

Nissim ben Reuben Gerondi. *Commentary on the Bible*. Ed. Leon Feldman. Jerusalem: Shalem Institute, 1968.

ʾOṣar mepareše hattora. 2 vols. Warsaw, 1862. Reprint. New York: A. Friedman, n.d.

Saadia Gaon. *Peruše rabbenu Saʿadya Gaʾon ʿal hattora*. Ed. Joseph Kafiḥ. Jerusalem: Mossad Harav Kook, 1963.

_________. *Version arabe du Pentateuque de R. Saadia ben Iosef al-Fayyoumi*. Ed. J. Derenbourg. Paris: E. Leroux, 1893.

Samuel b. Meir (RaŠBaM). *Peruš hattora*. Ed. D. Rosen. Breslau, 1881. Reprint. New York: Om, 1949.

Solomon Yitzḥaki. *Raši ʿal hattora*. Ed. A. Berliner. 2nd ed. Frankfurt a. M.: Y. Kaufmann, 1905.

Yaʾar. In *Seder ḥamišša ḥummeše tora, ʾorim gedolim*. Vilna, 1912.

Yehuda Halevi. *The Kosari*. Trans. and annotated by Yuhuda Even Shmuel. Tel Aviv: Dvir, 1972.

New Testament:

Novum Testamentum Graece, cum apparatu critico curavit. Ed. Erwin Nestle and Kurt Aland. 26th rev. ed. Stuttgart: Deutsche Bibelstiftung, 1979.

Post-New Testament Christian Sources:

The Ante-Nicene Fathers. Ed. Alexander Roberts and James Donaldson. Revised by A. Cleveland Coxe. 10 vols. New York: Charles Scribner's Sons, 1890–99.

Aphraates, *Demonstrations*. In *Patrologia Syriaca*. Ed. R. Graffin. 2 vols. Paris: Ediderunt firmin-didot et socii, 1894–1907.

Augustine. *The City of God Against the Pagans*. Ed. and trans. Philip Levine. LCL. 7 vols. Cambridge: Harvard University, 1966.

_________. *De civitate Dei*. Ed. Emanuel Hoffmann. Vol. 2. CSEL 40, pt. 2. Leipzig: G. Freytag, 1900.

Bar Hebraeus. *Chronography*. Ed. and trans. E. A. Wallis Budge. 2 vols. Oxford: Oxford University, 1932.

The Book of Adam and Eve. Trans. S. C. Malan. London: Williams and Norgate, 1882.

The Book of the Cave of Treasures. Trans. E. A. Wallis Budge. London: Religious Tract Society, 1927.

Das christliche Adambuch des Morgenlandes. Trans. A. Dillmann. Göttingen: Dieterichsche Buchhandlung, 1853.

Chronicon Anonymum ad Annum Christi 1234. Ed. With Latin trans. J. B. Chabot. CSCO 81, 109. Louvain, 1952, 1953.

Chronicon paschale. Ed. L. Dindorf. CSHB. Vol. 1. Bonn: E. Weber, 1832.

Clement of Alexandria. *Excerpta ex Theodoto*. Ed. Otto Stählin. GCS, vol. 17. Leipzig: J. C. Hinrichs, 1909.

_________. *The Excerpta ex Theodoto of Clement of Alexandria*. Ed. and trans. Robert Casey. London: Christophers, 1934.

_________. *Extraits de Théodote*. Ed. and trans. Francois Sagnard. SC 23. Paris: Éditions du Cerf, 1948. Reprint. 1970.

Cyril of Alexandria. *In sancti patris nostri Cyrilli archiepiscopi Alexandrini in d. Joannis evangelium*. Ed. Philip Eduard Pusey. 3 vols. Oxford, 1892. Reprint. Brussels: Impression Anastaltique Culture et Civilisation, 1965.

Didascalia et Constitutiones Apostolorum. Ed. F. X. Funk. 2 vols. in 1. Paderhorn, 1905.

Didyme L'Aveugle. *Sur la Genèse*. Ed. and trans. Pierre Nautin. SC 233, 244. Paris: Les Éditions du Cerf, 1976–78.

The Early Christian Fathers on Genesis. Ed. Abraham Levene. London: Taylor's Foreign Press, 1951.

Ephraem Syrus. *Des heiligen Ephraem des Syrers Hymnen Contra Haereses. Ed. E. Beck. CSCO 169, 170.* Louvain, 1957.

__________. *Des heiligen Ephraem des Syrers Hymnen de Ieiunio*. Ed. E. Beck. CSCO 246, 247. Louvain, 1964.

__________. *Des heiligen Ephraem des Syrers Hymnen de Nativitate* (*Epiphania*). Ed. E. Beck. CSCO 186, 187. Louvain, 1959.

__________. *Des heiligen Ephraem des Syrers Hymnen de Paradiso und Contra Julianum*. Ed. E. Beck. CSCO 174, 175. Louvain, 1957.

__________. *Sancti Ephraem Syri in Genesim et in Exodum commentarii*. Ed. R.-M. Tonneau. CSCO 152, 153. Louvain, 1955.

Ephrem de Nisibe. *Hymnes sur le Paradis*. Trans. René Lavenant. SC 139. Paris: Les Éditions du Cerf, 1968.

Epiphanius. *Ancoratus und Panarion*. GCS 31. Leipzig, 1922.

The Ethiopic Didascalia. Trans. J. M. Harden. SPCK. London: Macmillan, 1970.

Eusèbe de Césarée. *La Preparation Evangelique*. *Book 7*. Ed. Eduard des Places. Intro., trans., and notes by Guy Schroeder. SC 215. Paris: Les Éditions du Cerf, 1975.

Eusebii Pamphili. *Evangelicae Praeparationis*. Ed. and trans. E. H. Gifford. 4 vols. in 5. Oxford: E Typographeo Academico, 1903.

Eusebius Pamphili. *Die Praeparatio evangelica*. Ed. Karl Mras. GCS 43. Berlin, 1954.

George Cedrenus. *Historiarum Campendium*. Ed. Bekker. CSHB. Vol. 1. Bonn: E. Weber, 1838.

George Syncellus. *Chronographia*. Ed. W. Dindorf. CSHB. Bonn: E. Weber, 1829.

Hippolytus of Rome. *The Treatise on the Apostolic Traditions*. Ed. G. Dix. London: SPCK, 1937.

Ibn aṭ-Ṭaiyib. *Commentaire sur la Genèse*. Ed. and trans. J. C. J. Sanders. CSCO 274, 275. Louvain, 1967.

Isho bar Nun. *The Selected Questions of Ishō bar Nun on the Pentateuch.* Ed. Ernest G. Clarke. Leiden: E. J. Brill, 1962.

Isho'dad of Merv. *Commentaire d'Išo'dad de Merv sur l'Ancien Testament. I. Genèse.* Ed. J.-M. Vosté and C. van den Eynde. CSCO 126, 156. Louvain, 1950–55.

Jerome. *S. Hieronymi Presbyteri Opera.* Part 1: *Opera Exegetica.* CChr. Series Latin 72. Tournhout: Typographi brepols editores pontificii, 1959.

__________. *S. Hieronymi Presbyteri Opera.* Part 2: *Opera Homilectica.* CChr. Series Latin 78. Tournhout: Typographi brepols editores pontificci, 1958.

Joannis Malalae. *Chronographia.* Ed. L. Dindorf. CSHB. Bonn: E. Weber, 1831.

John Zonoras. *Annalium.* Ed. Pindar. CSHB. Vol. 1. Bonn: E. Weber, 1846.

Leo Grammaticus. *Chronographia.* Ed. Bekker. CSHB. Bonn: E. Weber, 1842.

Luther, Martin. *Works.* Ed. Jaroslav Pelikan. Vol. 1: *Lectures on Genesis.* Trans. George V. Schick. Saint Louis: Concordia, 1958.

Methodius of Olympus. *Convivium decem Virginum.* Ed. G. N. Bonwetsch. GCS 27. Leipzig: J. C. Hinrichs, 1917.

Michael Glycas. *Annalium.* Ed. Bekker. CSHB. Bonn: E. Weber, 1836.

Michael the Syrian. *Chronicle.* Ed. and trans. J. B. Chabot. 4 vols. Paris, 1899–1924.

Origen. *Contra Celsum.* Trans. Henry Chadwick. Cambridge: Cambridge University, 1965.

Patrologiae cursus completus. Series Latina. Ed. J. Migne. 221 vols. Paris, 1844–64.

Patrologiae cursus completus. Series Graeca. Ed. J. Migne. 161 vols. Paris, 1857–66.

Die Pseudo-Klementinen. Ed. Bernard Rehm. GCS, vol. 51. Berlin: Akademie Verlag, 1965.

Reliquiae sacrae. Ed. Martin Routh. 5 vols. 2nd ed. Oxford: E Typographeo Academico, 1846.

Die Schatzhöhle. Ed. and trans. Carl Bezold. 2 vols. in 1. Leipzig: J. C. Hinrichs, 1883–88.

Theodorus bar Koni. *Liber Scholiorum.* Ed. Addai Scher. CSCO 55. Louvain, 1954.

Tertullian. *Quinti Septimi Florentis Tertulliani Opera.* CSEL 47. Leipzig: G. Freytag, 1906.

__________. *Tertulliani Opera.* Part 2: *Opera Montanistica.* CChr. Series Latin 2. Tournhout: Typographi brepols editores pontificii, 1954.

Samaritan Sources:

The Asatir: *The Samaritan Book of the "Secrets of Moses"; Together with the Pitron or Commentary and the Samaritan Story of the Death of Moses*. Ed. and trans. Moses Gaster. Oriental Translation Fund. London: The Royal Asiatic Society, 1927.

Bibliotheca samaritana: *Texte aus Samaria und Studien zum Samaritanismus*. Ed. Moritz Heidenheim. 3 vols. Leipzig: 1884–96. Reprint (3 vols. in 1). Amsterdam: Philo Press, 1971.

Memar Marqah: *The Teaching of Marqah*. Ed. and trans. John Macdonald. 2 vols. BZAW, n. 84. Berlin: A. Töpelmann, 1963.

The Samaritan Liturgy. Ed. A. E. Cowley. 2 vols. Oxford: Clarendon, 1909.

Seper 'Asaṭir. Trans. and commented upon by Z. Ben Ḥayyim. In *Tarbiz* 14 (1942–43) 104–25, 174–90.

Mandaean Sources:

The Canonical Prayerbook of the Mandaeans. Trans. E. S. Drower. Leiden: E. J. Brill, 1959.

Ginzā: *der Schatz oder das grosse Buch der Mandäer*. Trans. Mark Lidzbarski. Quellen der Religionsgeschichte, no. 13. Göttingen: Vandenhoeck & Ruprecht, 1925.

Haran Gawaita. Ed. and trans. E. S. Drower. Vatican: Bibliotheca Apostolica Vaticans, 1953.

Mandäische Liturgen. Ed. M. Lidzbarski. Berlin: Weidmansche Buchhandlung, 1920.

The Thousand and Twelve Questions. Ed. and trans. E. S. Drower. Berlin: Akademie Verlag, 1960.

Muslim Sources:

al-Mas'ūdī. *Les Prairies d'Or*. Ed. and trans. C. Barbier de Meynard and Payet de Courteille. Collection d'ouvrages orientaux publiée par la Societé Asiatique, vol. 1. Paris: A L'Imprimerie Impériale, 1861.

al-Tabari. *Annales ques scripsit Abu Djafar Mohammed ibn Djarir al-Tabari*. Ed. M. J. de Goeje. 13 vols. Leiden: E. J. Brill, 1879–98.

Greco-Roman Sources:

Aeschylus, with an English Translation. Ed. and trans. Herbert Weir Smyth. LCL 2 vols. London: W. Heinemann, 1930.

Aratus, with an English Translation. Ed. and trans. G. R. Mair. LCL. London: W. Heinemann, 1921.

Cicero. *De Natura Deorum, Academica*. Ed. and trans. H. Rackham. LCL. London: W. Heinemann, 1933.

Dio Chrysostom, with an English Translation. Ed. and trans. J. W. Cohoon and H. Lamar Crosby. LCL. 5 vols. London: W. Heinemann, 1932–51.

Die Fragmente der griechischen Historiker. Ed. Felix Jacoby. 3 parts. Berlin: Wiedmannsche Buchhandlung, and Leiden: E. J. Brill, 1923–58.

Herodotus, with an English Translation. Ed. and trans. A. D. Godley. LCL. 4 vols. London: W. Heinemann, 1921–31.

Hesiod. *Works and Days*. Ed. with a commentary by M. L. West. Oxford: Clarendon, 1978.

———. *Theogony*. Ed. with a commentary by M. L. West. Oxford: Clarendon, 1966.

Homer. *The Iliad, with an English Translation*. Ed. and trans. A. T. Murray. LCL. 2 vols. Cambridge, Mass.: Harvard University, 1929–65.

———. *The Odyssey, with an English Translation*. Ed. and trans. A. T. Murray. LCL. 2 vols. London: W. Heinemann, 1930–31.

Julian. *The Works of Emperor Julian, with an English Translation*. Ed. and trans. Wilmer Cave Wright. LCL. 3 vols. London: W. Heinemann, 1913–23.

Lucretius. *De rerum natura, with an English Translation*. Ed. and trans. W. H. D. Rouse. LCL. London: W. Heinemann, 1937.

Macrobius. *Commentary on the Dream of Scipio*. Trans., intro., and notes by William Harris Staht. New York: Columbia University, 1952.

Ovid. *Metamorphoses, with an English Translation*. Ed. and trans. Frank Justus Miller. LCL. 2 vols. Cambridge, Mass.: Harvard University, 1976–77.

Philo of Byblos. *The Phoenician History: Introduction, Critical Text, Translations, Notes*. Ed. Harold W. Attridge and Robert A. Oden Jr. CBQMS 9. Washington, DC: Catholic Biblical Association of America, 1981.

Plato, with an English Translation. Ed. and trans. H. N. Fowler, W. R. M. Lamb, R. G. Bury. LCL. 10 vols. London: W. Heinemann, 1921–62.

Seneca. *Naturales quaestiones . . . with an English Translation*. Ed. and trans. Thomas H. Corcoran. LCL. 2 vols. Cambridge, Mass.: Harvard University, 1971–72.

Virgil, with an English Translation. Ed. and trans. H. Rushton Fairclough. LCL. Rev. ed. 2 vols. Cambridge, Mass.: Harvard University, 1937.

SECONDARY SOURCES

Abelson, Joshua. *The Immanence of God in Rabbinical Literature.* London: Macmillan, 1912.

Aberbach, Moses, and Grossfeld, Bernard. *Targum Onkelos to Genesis: A Critical Analysis Together with an English Translation of the Text.* New York: KTAV, 1982.

Adler, Nathan. *Netina Lagger.* In *Seder ḥamišša ḥummeše tora, 'orim gedolim.* Wilna, 1912.

Adler, William. "Notes to the Text of George Syncellus and Pseudo-Malalas." Distributed with "Materials Relating to Seth in an Anonymous Chronographer (Pseudo-Malalas) and in the Chronography of George Syncellus" at the Joint Pseudepigrapha/Nag Hammadi Special Session of the Society of Biblical Literature annual meeting, San Francisco, 1977. Mimeographed. Philadelphia: University of Pennsylvania, 1977.

Albright, William F. "Primitivism in Ancient Western Asia (Mesopotamia and Israel)." In *Primitivism and Related Ideas in Antiquity*, ed. Arthur Lovejoy and George Boas, 431–32. Baltimore: Johns Hopkins University, 1935.

Alexander, P. S. "The Historical Setting of the Hebrew Book of Enoch." *JJS* 28 (1977) 156–80.

__________. "The Targumim and Early Exegesis of 'Sons of God' in Genesis 6." *JJS* 23 (1972) 60–71.

Altaner, Berthold. *Patrology.* Trans. H. C. Graef. New York: Herder and Herder, 1960.

Bacher, Wilhelm. *Die Agada der Babylonischen Amoraër.* Strassburg: Karl J. Trübner, 1878.

__________. *Die Agada der palästinensischen Amoräer.* 3 vols. Strassburg, 1892–99. Reprint. Hildesheim: Georg Olms, 1965.

__________. *Die Agada der Tannaiten.* 2 vols. Strassburg: Karl J. Tübner, 1884–90.

Bamberger, Bernard. *Fallen Angels.* Philadelphia: Jewish Publication Society of American, 1952.

Baumgarten, Albert I. *The Phoenician History of Philo of Byblos: A Commentary.* Etudes préliminaires aux religions orientales dans l'empire Romain. Leiden: E. J. Brill, 1981.

Baumstark, Anton. *Geschichte der syrischen Literatur.* Bonn: A. Marcus and E. Weber, 1922.

Belkin, S. "The Interpretation of Names of Philo." Hebrew. *Ḥoreb* 12 (1956–57) 3–61.

Ben Ḥayyim, Zeev. *The Literary and Oral Tradition of Hebrew and Aramaic Amongst the Samaritans*. Hebrew. 4 vols. Jerusalem: The Bialik Institute, 1957–67.

———. Review of *Memar Marqah*, ed. and trans. J. Macdonald. *BO* 23 (1966) 185–91.

Ben Yehuda, Eliezer. *A Complete Dictionary of Ancient and Modern Hebrew*. Hebrew. Vol. 10. Jerusalem, 1944.

Berkowitz, Ben Zion. *'Abne ṣiyyon*. Wilna: Romm, 1877.

———. *Leḥem weśimla*. Wilna: Romm, 1850.

———. *'Oteḥ 'or*. Wilna: Romm, 1843.

Berliner, Abraham. *Die Massorah zum Targum Onkelos*. Leipzig: J. C. Hinrichs, 1877.

Bickerman, Elias. *Four Strange Books of the Bible*. New York: Schocken, 1967.

———. "The Septuagint as a Translation." In *Studies in Jewish and Christian History*. Vol. 1, 167–200. Leiden: E. J. Brill, 1976. Originally appeared in *PAAJR* 28 (1959).

Bousset, Wilhelm. *Hauptprobleme der Gnosis*. Göttingen: Vandenhoeck and Ruprecht, 1907.

———. "Eine jüdische Gebetssammlung in siebenten Buch der apostolischen Konstitutionen." In *Nachrichten vor der königlichen Gesellschaft der Wissenschaften zu Göttingen, Philologisch-Historische Klasse*, 1915, 435–89. Berlin, 1916.

———. *Kyrios Christos*. Trans. John E. Steely. Nashville: Abingdon, 1970.

Bowker, John. *The Targums and Rabbinic Literature*. Cambridge: Cambridge University Press, 1969.

Bowman, John. "The Exegesis of the Pentateuch Among the Samaritans and Among the Rabbis." In *Oudtestamentische Studiën*, vol. 8, ed. P. A. H. De Boer, 220–62. Leiden: E. J. Brill, 1950.

Brandt, Wilhelm. "Mandaeans." In *Encyclopedia of Religion and Ethics*, ed. James Hastings. Vol. 8, 380a–393a. New York: Charles Scribner's Sons, 1916.

———. *Die mandäische Religion: ihre Entwicklung und geschichtliche Bedeutung*. Leipzig: J. C. Hinrichs, 1889.

Brown, Francis; Driver, S. R.; and Briggs, C. A. *A Hebrew and English Lexicon of the Old Testament*. Oxford: Clarendon, 1907. Reprint. 1972.

Bultmann, Rudolf. "Die Bedeutung der neuerschlossenen mandäischen und manichäischen Quellen für das Verständnis des Johannesevangeliums." *ZNW* 24 (1925) 199–246.

Burkitt, F. C. *Church and Gnosis*. Cambridge: Cambridge University Press, 1932.

Byrne, Brendan. *"Sons of God"-"Seed of Abraham": A Study of the Idea of the Sonship of God of All Christians in Paul Against the Jewish Background*. AnBib 83. Rome: Biblical Institute, 1979.

Cassuto, Umberto. *A Commentary on the Book of Genesis: From Adam to Noah*. Jerusalem: Magnes, 1961.

__________. *Peruš 'al seper šemot*. Jerusalem: Magnes, 1953.

Charaz, Moshe. *Lešon ḥayyim*. Jerusalem, 1970.

Charlesworth, James, H. *The Pseudepigrapha and Modern Re-Research*. Septuagint and Cognate Studies, no. 7. Missoula, Montana: Scholars Press, 1976.

Childs, Brevard S. *The Book of Exodus: A Critical, Theological Commentary*. Philadelphia: Westminster, 1974.

__________. *Introduction to the Old Testament as Scripture*. Philadelphia: Fortress, 1979.

Coggins, R. J. *Samaritans and Jews*. Atlanta: John Knox, 1975.

Colpe, Carsten. "*ho huios tou anthrōpou*." In *TDNT* 8 (1972) 401–4.

__________. *Die religionsgeschichtliche Schule: Darstellung und Kritik ihres Bildes vom gnostischen Erlösermythus*. Göttingen: Vandenhoeck and Ruprecht, 1961.

Dahl, Nils A., and Segal, Alan P. "Philo and the Rabbis on the Names of God." *JSJ* 9 (1978) 1–28.

Dalman, Gustaf H. *Aramäisch-neuhebräisches Handwörtebuch zu Targum, Talmud und Midrasch*. Frankfurt a. M.: J. Kauffman, 1922.

__________. *Grammatik des jüdisch-palästinischen Aramäisch nach dem Idiomen das palästinischen Talmud, des Onkelostargum und Prophetentargum und der jerusalemischen Targume*. Leipzig: J. C. Hinrichs, 1905.

Daremberg, C. V., and Saglio, E., eds. *Dictionaire des antiquités greques et romaines*. 5 vols. in 9. Paris: Hachette, 1877–1919.

Davidson, Israel. *Thesaurus of Mediaeval Hebrew Poetry*. 4 vols. New York, 1924–33. Reprinted with intro. by J. Schirmann. New York, KTAV, 1970.

DeLange, N. R. M. *Origen and the Jews: Studies in Jewish-Christian Relations in Third Century Palestine*. Cambridge: Cambridge University Press, 1976.

Delitzsch, F. *Neuer Commentar über die Genesis*. Leipzig: Dörffling und Franke, 1887.

Dillmann, A. *Genesis Critically and Exegetically Expounded*. Trans. W. Stevenson. 2 vols. Edinburgh: T. & T. Clark, 1897.

Dillon, John. *The Middle Platonists: A Study of Platonism, 80 B.C. to A.D. 220*. London: Duckworth, 1977.

Dimant, Devorah. "'The Fallen Angels' in the Dead Sea Scrolls and in the Apocryphal and Pseudepigraphic Books Related to Them." Ph.D. dissertation, Hebrew University, 1974.
Drower, E. S. "Mandaean Polemic." *BSOAS* 25 (1962) 338–48.
———. *The Mandaeans of Iraq and Iran: Their Cults, Customs, Legends and Folklore*. Oxford: Clarendon, 1937.
———. *The Secret Adam: A Study of Nasoraean Gnosis*. Oxford: Clarendon, 1960.
Drower, E. S., and Macuch, R. *A Mandaic Dictionary*. Oxford: Clarendon, 1963.
Edelstein, L. *The Idea of Progress in Classical Antiquity*. Baltimore: Johns Hopkins University, 1967.
Elbogen, Ismar. *Hattepilla beyiśra'el behitpatteḥutah hahisṭorit*. Tel Aviv: Dvir, 1972.
———. *Studien zur Geschichte des jüdischen Gottesdienstes*. Berlin: Mayer & Müller, 1907.
Encyclopedia Judaica. 16 vols. Jerusalem: Keter, 1972.
Etheridge, J. W. *The Targums on Onqelos and Jonathan ben Uzziel on the Pentateuch*. London, 1862. Reprint. New York: KTAV, 1968.
Faur, Jose. "The Biblical Idea of Idolatry." *JQR* 69 (1978) 1–15.
———. "Idolatry." In *Encyclopedia Judaica* 8.1227–37.
Feldman, Louis H. "Hellenizations in Josephus' Portrayal of Man's Decline." In *Religions in Antiquity: Essays in Memory of Erwin Ramsdell Goodenough*, ed. Jacob Neusner, 336–53. Leiden: E. J. Brill, 1968.
Finkelstein, J. J. "The Antediluvian Kings: A University of California Tablet." *JCS* 17 (1963) 39–51.
———. "Mesopotamiam Historiography." *Proceedings of the American Philosophical Society* 107 (1963) 461–72.
Fischel, Henry A. *Rabbinic Literature and Greco-Roman Philosophy*. SPB 21. Leiden: E. J. Brill, 1973.
Fishman-Duker, R. "Remembering the Elephants: 3 Macc. 5–6 in Byzantine Chronicles." *Byzantion* 48 (1978) 51–63.
———. "The Second Temple Period in Byzantine Chronicles." *Byzantion* 47 (1977) 126–56.
Fitzmyer, Joseph. *A Wandering Aramaean: Collected Aramaic Essays*. SBL Monograph Series, no. 25. Missoula, Montana: Scholars Press, 1979.
Flusser, David. "Palea Historica: An Unknown Source of Biblical Legends." *Scripta Hierosolymitana* 22 (1971) 48–79.
Foerster, Werner. "*kurios*—In the New Testament." *TDNT* 3 (1965) 1086–95.
Fraade, Steven D. "Enoch." *Encyclopedia of Religion*, forthcoming.

__________. "Enosh and His Generation: Scriptural Translation and Interpretation in Late Antiquity." Ph.D. Dissertation, University of Pennsylvania, 1980. Available from University Microfilms, Ann Arbor, Michigan.

__________. "Sifre Deuteronomy 26 (ad Deut 3:23): How conscious the Composition?" *HUCA* 54 (1983), 245–301.

Franxman, Thomas W. *Genesis and the "Jewish Antiquities" of Flavius Josephus*. BibOr 35. Rome: Biblical Institute, 1979.

Gaster, Theodore H. "Samaritans." *Interpreter's Dictionary of the Bible*, ed. Arthur Buttrick, vol. 4, 190–97. New York: Abingdon, 1962.

Gelzer, Heinrich. *Sextus Julius Africanus und die byzantinische Chronographie*. 2 vols. in 1. Leipzig, 1885–98.

Gesenius' Hebrew Grammar. Ed. E. Kautzsch and A. E. Cowley. 2nd rev. ed. Oxford: Clarendon, 1910.

Ginzberg, Louis. "Clementina or Pseudo-Clementin Literature." *Jewish Encyclopedia*, vol. 14 (1903), 114b.

__________. *Genizah Studies*. 3 vols. New York: Jewish Theological Seminary, 1928.

__________. *Legends of the Jews*. 7 vols. Philadelphia: Jewish Publication Society of America, 1913–38.

__________. *Eine unbekannte jüdische Sekte*. Vol. 1. New York: Im Selbstverlage des Verfassers, 1922.

Gluck, Theodore. "The Arabic Legend of Seth, the Father of Mankind." Ph.D. dissertation, Yale University, 1968.

Goldberg, Arnold M. *Untersuchungen über die Vorstellung von der Schekhinah in der frühen rabbinischen Literatur: Talmud und Midrasch*. Studia Judaica, vol. 5. Berlin: Walter de Gruyter, 1969.

Goldin, Judah. "Not by Means of an Angel and Not by Means of a Messenger." In *Religions in Antiquity: Essays in Memory of Erwin Ramsdell Goodenough*, ed. Jacob Neusner, 412–24. Studies in the History of Religion, no. 14. Leiden: E. J. Brill, 1968.

__________. *The Song at the Sea*. New Haven: Yale University, 1971.

Goodenough, Erwin. *By Light, Light: The Mystic Gospel of Hellenistic Judaism*. New Haven: Yale University, 1935.

Gray, G. *The Book of Isaiah*. ICC. 2 vols. New York: Charles Scribner's Sons, 1912.

Greenberg, Moshe. *Understanding Exodus*. New York: Behrman House, 1969.

———. "The Use of the Ancient Versions for Interpreting the Hebrew Text: A Sampling from Ezekiel 2:1–3:11." In *Congress Volume, Göttingen, 1977*. International Organization for the Study of the Old Testament. VTSup. 29, 131–48. Leiden: E. J. Brill, 1978.

Greer, Rowan. *The Captain of Our Salvation: A Study in the Patristic Exegesis of Hebrews*. BGBE. Tübingen: J. C. B. Mohr, 1973.

Gribomont, Jean. "Latin Versions." In *The Interpreter's Dictionary of the Bible*, Supplementary Volume, general editor Keith Crim, 527–32. Nashville: Abingdon, 1976.

Grünbaum, Max. *Neue Beiträge zur semitischen Sagenkunde*. Leiden: E. J. Brill, 1893.

Gruenwald, Ithamar. "Yannai and Hekhaloth Literature." Hebrew. *Tarbiz* 36 (1967) 257–77.

Gunkel, Hermann. *Genesis*, Göttingen: Vandenhoeck and Ruprecht, 1901.

Hahn, Ferdinand. *The Titles of Jesus in Christology: Their History in Early Christianity*. Trans. Harold Knight and George Ogg. New York: World, 1969.

Hallo, William W. "Antediluvian Cities." *JCS* 23 (1960) 57–67.

Hanson, Paul D. "Rebellion in Heaven, Azazel, and Euchemeristic Heroes in 1 Enoch 6–11." *JBL* 96 (1977) 195–233.

Harnack, Adolph. *History of Dogma*. Trans. Neil Buchanan. Vol. 4. Boston: Little, Brown, and Co., 1893.

Harper, W. *A Critical and Exegetical Commentary on Amos and Hosea*. ICC. New York: Charles Scribner's Sons, 1905.

Hatch, E. and Redpath, H. *A Concordance to the Septuagint*. 2 vols. and supplement. Oxford: Clarendon, 1897–1902.

Heidel, Alexander. *The Gilgamesh Epic and Old Testament Parallels*. Chicago: University of Chicago, 1949.

Heinemann, Isaac. *Darke ha'aggada*. Jerusalem, 1954.

Heinemann, Joseph. *'Aggadot wetoledotehen* [Aggadah and its Development]. Jerusalem: Keter, 1974.

Hengel, Martin. *Judaism and Hellenism: Studies in their Encounter in Palestine During the Early Hellenistic Period*. 2 vols. Trans. John Bowden. Philadelphia: Fortress, 1974.

Henning, Walter. "Ein manichäisches Henochbuch." *SPAW* Phil.-Hist. Klasse, 1934: 27–35.

Henrichs, A. and Koenen, L. "Ein griechischer Mani-Codex." *Zeitschrift für Papyrologie und Epigraphik* 5 (1970) 97–216; 19 (1975) 1–85.

Holladay, Carl H. *Theios Aner in Hellenistic Judaism: A Critique of the Use of this Category in New Testament Christology*. SBL Dissertation Series, no. 40. Missoula, Montana: Scholars Press, 1977.

Hyman, Aaron. *Seper tora hakketuba wehammesura ʿal tora nebiʾim uketubim*. 3 vols. 1936–39. Reprint. Tel Aviv: Dvir, 1964.

———. *Toledot tannaʾim weʾamoraʾim*. 3 vols. Jerusalem, 1964.

Ibn Manẓūr. *Lisān al-ʿArab*. 20 vols. in 10. Bulaq, 1883–91.

Jansma, T. "Investigations into the Early Syrian Fathers on Genesis: An Approach to the Exegesis of the Nestorian Church to the Comparison of Nestorian and Jewish Exegesis." *OTS* 12. *Studies on the Book of Genesis*, ed. P. A. H. De Boer, 69–181. Leiden: Brill, 1958.

———. Review of A. Levine, *The Early Syrian Fathers on Genesis*. *BO* 10 (1953) 48–49.

Jastrow, Marcus. *A Dictionary of the Talmud Babli and Jerushalmi, and the Midrashic Literature*. 2 vols. New York: Choreb, 1926.

Kasher, Menachem. *Humaš tora šelema*. 27 vols. (and continuing). New York: American Biblical Encyclopedia Society, 1927–79.

Kasowski, Chaim. *Concordance to Targum Onkelos*. 5 vols. in 1. Jerusalem, 1933–45.

Kaufmann, Yehezkel. "The Biblical Age." In *Great Ages and Ideas of the Jewish People*, ed. Leo Schwarz, 1–92. New York: Random House, 1956.

———. *The Religion of Israel*. Trans. and abr. Moshe Greenberg. Chicago: University of Chicago, 1960.

Keel, C. F. and Delitzsch, F. *Biblical Commentary on the Old Testament*. Trans. J. Martin. Edinburgh: T. & T. Clark, 1878.

Kerrigan, Alexander. *St. Cyril of Alexandria: Interpreter of the Old Testament*. Rome: Pontifical Biblical Institute, 1952.

Klein, Michael. "Converse Translation: A Targumic Technique." *Bib*. 57 (1976) 515–37.

Klijn, A. F. J. *Seth in Jewish, Christian, and Gnostic Literature*. NovTSup. 46. Leiden: E. J. Brill, 1977.

Komlosh, Yehuda. *The Bible in the Light of the Aramaic Translations*. Hebrew. Tel Aviv: Dvir, 1973.

Kraeling, Carl. *Anthropos and Son of Man: A Study in the Religious Syncretism of the Hellenistic Orient*. New York: Columbia University, 1927.

———. "The Episode of the Roman Standards at Jerusalem." *HTR* 35 (1942) 263–89.

Kraeling, Emil. "The Significance and Origen of Gen. 6:1–4." *JNES* 6 (1947) 193–208.

Krauss, Samuel. *Griechische und lateinische Lehnwörter im Talmud, Midrasch und Targum*. 2 vols. Berlin, 1898–99. Reprint. Hildesheim: Georg Olms, 1964.

Kronholm, Tryggve. *Motifs from Genesis 1–11 in the Genuine Hymns of Ephrem the Syrian, With Particular Reference to the Influence of Jewish Exegetical Tradition*. Lund: CWK Gleerup, 1978.

Kutscher, Eduard Y. *The Language and Linguistic Background of the Isaiah Scroll*. Hebrew. Jerusalem: Magnes. 1959.

Lambert, W. G. "Ancestors, Authors, and Canonicity." *JCS* 11 (1957) 1–14, 112.

Lane, Edward William. *An Arabic-English Lexicon*. 8 vols. London and Edinburgh: Williams and Norgate, 1863–93.

Lauterbach, Jacob. "Peshaṭ." *Jewish Encyclopedia*, 9.653.

Le Déaut, R. "The Current State of Targumic Studies." *Biblical Theology Bulletin* 4 (1974) 3–32.

———. "Un phénomène spontané de l'herméneutique juive ancienne: le 'targumisme'." *Bib.* 52 (1971) 505–25.

Levey, Samson H. "The Targum to Ezekiel." *HUCA* 46 (1975) 139–58.

Levy, Jacob. *Chaldäisches Wörterbuch über die Targumim und einen grossen Theil des rabbinischen Schriftthums*. 2 vols. Leipzig: Baumgartner, 1867–68.

———. *Wörterbuch über die Talmudim und Midraschim*. 4 vols. Revised by L. Goldschmidt. Berlin: B. Harz, 1924.

Lewis, Charlton T., and Short, Charles. *A New Latin Dictionary*. Oxford: Clarendon, 1884.

Lewis, Jack P. *A Study on the Interpretation of Noah and the Flood in Jewish and Christian Literature*. Leiden: E. J. Brill, 1968.

Liddell, Henry George, and Scott, Robert. *A Greek-English Lexicon*. Revised by Henry Stuart Jones. With a Supplement. Oxford: Clarendon, 1968.

Lidzbarski, Mark. "Uthra and Malakha." In *Orientalische Studien Theodor Nöldeke zum siebzigsten Geburtstag gewidmet*. Giessen: A. Töpelmann, 1906.

Lieberman, Saul. *Greek in Jewish Palestine*. New York: Jewish Theological Seminary of America, 1942.

———. *Hellenism in Jewish Palestine*. New York: Jewish Theological Seminary of America, 1962.

———. *Tosefta ki-Fshutah*. 8 vols. New York: Jewish Theological Seminary of America, 1955–73.

Loewe, Raphael. "The 'Plain' Meaning of Scripture in Early Jewish Exegesis." In *Papers of the Institute of Jewish Studies, London*, ed. J. G. Weiss, vol. 1, 140–85. Jerusalem: Magnes, 1964.

Lokkegaard, F. "Some Comments on the Sanchuniaton Tradition." *Studia Theologica* 8 (1954) 51–76.

Lovejoy, Arthur O., and Boas, George. *Primitivism and Related Ideas in Antiquity*. Vol. 1 of *A Documentary History of Primitivism and Related Ideas*. Baltimore: Johns Hopkins, 1935.

Lowenstein, Marcus (Mordecai). *Nepeš hagger*. Pietrokov, 1906.

Lowy, S. *The Principles of Samaritan Bible Exegesis*. SPB 28. Leiden: E. J. Brill, 1977.

Luzzatto, S. D. *'Oheb ger* (*Philoxenos*). Cracow: Y. Fischer, 1895.

S. D. Luzzatto's Commentary to the Pentateuch. Ed. P. Schlesinger. Tel Aviv: Dvir, 1965.

Macdonald, John. *The Theology of the Samaritans*. London: SCM Press, 1964.

MacRae, George. "The Coptic Gnostic Apocalypse of Adam." *The Heythrop Journal* 6 (1965) 27–35.

Macuch, Rudolf. *Handbook of Classical and Modern Mandaic*. Berlin: Walter de Gruyter, 1965.

Mandelkern, S. *Veteris testamenti concordantiae*. 9th ed. Jerusalem: Schocken, 1971.

Marmorstein, Arthur. "The Imitation of God in the Haggadah." In *Studies in Jewish Theology*, ed. J. Rabbinowitz and M. S. Lew, 106–21. London: Oxford University, 1950.

__________. *The Old Rabbinic Doctrine of God*. Vol. 1. London: Oxford University Press, 1927.

McNamara, Martin. "Targums." *IDBSup*. (1976), 856–61. Nashville: Abingdon, 1976.

Meeks, Wayne. *The Prophet-King: Moses Traditions and the Johannine Christology*. NovTSup. 14. Leiden: E. J. Brill, 1967.

Melamed, E. *Millon 'arammi 'ivri letargum 'onqelos*. Jerusalem: *Yešibat sa'are raḥamim*, 1971.

__________. In *Leshonenu* 20 (1956) 110–11.

Milik, J. T. "A propos de 11QJub." *Bib*. 54 (1973) 77–78.

Miller, J. Maxwell. "The Descendants of Cain: Notes on Genesis 4." ZAW 86 (1974) 164–73.

Miller, M. P. "Targum, Midrash, and the Use of the Old Testament in the New Testament." *JSJ* 2 (1971) 29–82.

Momigliano, Arnaldo. "Time in Ancient Historiography." In *Quarto contributo alla storia degli studi classici del mondo antico*, 13–41. Rome: Edizioni di storia e letteratura, 1969.

__________. "The Origins of Universal History." In *The Poet and the Historian: Essays in Literary and Historical Biblical Criticism*, ed. Richard Elliott Friedman, 133–54. Harvard Semitic Studies 26. Chico: Scholars Press, 1983.

Montgomery, James Alan. *The Samaritans: The Earliest Jewish Sect: Their History, Theology and Literature*. Philadelphia: John C. Winston, 1907.
Moore, George Foot. *Judaism in the First Centuries of the Christian Era*. 3 vols. Cambridge: Harvard University. 1927–40.
Murray, Robert. *Symbols of Church and Kingdom: A Study in Early Syriac Tradition*. Cambridge: Cambridge University Press, 1975.
Nagy, Gregory. *The Best of the Achaeans: Concepts of the Hero in Archaic Greek Poetry*. Baltimore: Johns Hopkins, 1970.
Naor, Menaḥem. "The Sethites and the Cainites (Kenites)." Hebrew. *Beth Mikra* 53 (1973) 198–204.
Nathan b. Yehiel, *Aruch Completum*. Ed. A. Kohut. 1890. Reprint. Jerusalem, 1970.
Naverre, O. "Oceanus." In Daremberg and Saglio, *Dictionnaire des antiquites greques et romaines*. Vol. 4.1, 143–44.
Neusner, Jacob. *The Rabbinic Traditions About the Pharisees Before 70*. Vol. 3. Leiden: E. J. Brill, 1971.
Nickelsburg, George. "Apocalyptic and Myth in 1 Enoch 6–11." *JBL* 96 (1977) 383–405.
Nikiprowetzky, Valentin. *Le Commentaire de l'écriture chez Philon d'Alexandrie*. ALGHJ 11. Leiden: E. J. Brill, 1977.
Nilsson, Martin P. *Geschichte des griechischen Religion*. 2 vols. 2nd ed. Munich: Beck, 1961.
Ohana, Moshe. "Agneau pascal et circoncision." *VT* 23 (1973) 385–99.
Orlinsky, Harry. *Notes on the New Translation of the Torah*. Philadelphia: Jewish Publication Society, 1970.
Oxford Classical Dictionary. N. G. L. Hammond and H. H. Scullard, eds. 2nd ed. Oxford: Clarendon, 1970.
The Oxford Dictionary of the Christian Church. Ed. F. L. Cross and E. A. Livingstone. 2nd ed. London: Oxford University Press, 1974.
Oxford Latin Dictionary. Fasc. 4. Oxford: Clarendon, 1973.
Pallis, Svend Aage. *Mandaean Studies*. Trans. E. H. Pallis. London: Oxford University, 1926.
Paulys Real-encyclopädie der classischen Altertumswissenschaft. Rev. G. Wissower. 24 vols. in 43. Stuttgart: J. B. Metzler, 1894–1963.
Pelikan, Jaroslav. *The Christian Tradition: A History of the Development of Doctrine*. Vol. 1. Chicago: University of Chicago, 1971.
Petermann, J. H. *Brevis Linguae Samaritanae*. Paris and London: H. Reuther, 1873.

Peters, Norbert. *Das Buch Jesus Sirach oder Ecclesiasticus*. Munich: Aschendorff, 1913.

Pummer, R. "The Present State of Samaritan Studies." *JSS* 22 (1977) 43–45.

Purvis, James D. "Samaritan Pentateuch." *IDBSup*. 772–75.

Quasten, Johannes. *Patrology*. 3 vols. Utrecht-Antwerp: Spectrum, 1964–66.

Quinn, Esther Casier. *The Quest of Seth for the Oil of Life*. Chicago: University of Chicago, 1952.

Rabbinovicz, R. *Seper diqduqe soperim: Variae Lectiones in Mischnam et in Talmud Babylonicum*. 16 vols. Munich, 1867–97. Reprint. (16 vols. in 2) New York: M. P. Press, 1967.

Rabbinowitz, Ḥayyim. *Da'at soperim*. New York: Feldheim, 1953.

Rappaport, Salomo. *Agada und Exegese bei Flavius Josephus*. Frankfurt a. M.: J. Kauffmann, 1930.

Raymundi Martini, *Pugio fidei adversus mauros et judaeos*. Leipzig, 1687.

Reinach, A. J. "Signa Militaria." In Daremberg and Saglio, *Dictionaire des antiquites greques et romaines*, vol. 4.2, 1307–25.

Reiner, Erica. "The Etiological Myth of the Seven Sages." *Orientalia* 30 (1961) 1–11.

Reitzenstein, Richard. *Hellenistic Mystery-Religions: Their Basic Ideas and Significance*. Trans. John E. Steely. Pittsburgh: Pickwick, 1978.

———. *Das mandäische Buch des Herrn der Grösse und die Evangelienüberlieferung*. Heidelberg: C. Winter, 1919.

Rönsch, Hermann. *Das Buch der Jubiläen; oder, die kleine Genesis*. Leipzig: Fues, 1874.

Roth, Cecil. "Ecclesiasticus in the Synagogue Service." *JBL* 71 (1952) 171–78.

Rudolph, Kurt. *Die Mandäer*. 2 vols. Göttingen: Vandenhoeck and Ruprecht, 1960–61.

Sandmel, Samuel. "Genesis 4:26b." *HUCA* 32 (1961) 19–29.

Santos, E. C. dos. *An Expanded Hebrew Index for the Hatch-Redpath Concordance to the Septuagint*. Jerusalem: Dugith Publishers, Baptist House, n.d.

Schäfer, Peter. "Der Götzendienst des Enosch: Zur Bildung und Entwicklung aggadischer Traditionen im nachbiblischen Judenthum." In *Studien zur Geschichte und Theologie des Rabbinischen Judenthums*, 134–52. AGJU 15. Leiden: E. J. Brill, 1978.

———. *Rivaltät zwischen Engeln und Menschen: Untersuchungen zur rabbinischen Engelvorstellung*. Studia Judaica 8. Berlin: Walter de Gruyter, 1975.

Schechter, Solomon. *Aspects of Rabbinic Theology*. New York: Macmillan, 1909.
Schefftel, Baruch. *Be'ure 'onqelos*. Munich: T. Ackermann, 1899.
Scher, A. "Notice sur les manuscripts syrique conservés dans la bibliothèque du patriarchat chaldéen de Mossoul." *Revue des Bibliotheques 17* (1907) 227–29.
Scholem, Gershom. *Jewish Gnosticism, Merkabah Mysticism, and Talmudic Tradition*. 2nd ed. New York: Jewish Theological Seminary, 1965.
__________. *Kabbalah*. New York: Quadrangle, 1974.
__________. *Major Trends in Jewish Mysticism*. New York: Schocken, 1954.
__________. *On the Kabbalah and its Symbolism*. Trans. R. Manheim. New York: Schocken, 1965.
Schürer, Emil. *The History of the Jewish People in the Age of Jesus Christ*. Rev. and ed. Geza Vermes and Fergus Millar. Vol. 1. Edinburgh: T. & T. Clark, 1973.
Schweizer, Eduard. "*huios*—New Testament." *TDNT* 8 (1972) 363–92.
Seeligmann, I. L. *The Septuagint Version of Isaiah: A Discussion of its Problems*. Leiden: E. J. Brill, 1948.
Segal, Moseh H. *A Grammar of Mishnaic Hebrew*. Oxford: Clarendon, 1927.
__________. *Diqduq lešon hammišna*. Tel Aviv: Dvir, 1936.
Shinan, Avigdor. "The Form and Content of the Aggadah in the 'Palestinian' Targumim on the Pentateuch and its Place within Rabbinic Literature." Hebrew. Ph.D. dissertation, Hebrew University, 1978.
Siegfried, Carl Gustav. *Philo von Alexandra als Ausleger des Alten Testaments, an sich selbst und nach seinem geschichtlichen einfluss betrachtet*. Jena: H. Dufft, 1875.
Skinner, J. *A Critical and Exegetical Commentary on Genesis*. ICC. New York: Charles Scribner's Sons, 1910.
Smallwood, E. Mary. *The Jews Under Roman Rule from Pompey to Diocletian*. Leiden: E. J. Brill, 1976.
Smend, Rudolf. *Griechische-Syrisch-Hebräisches Index zur Weisheit des Jesus Sirach*. Berlin: Georg Reimer, 1907.
Smith, K. F. "Ages of the World (Greek and Roman)." *Encyclopedia of Religion and Ethics*, ed. James Hastings, vol. 1, 192–200. New York, 1951.
Smith, J. Payne. *A Compendious Syriac Dictionary*. Oxford: Clarendon, 1903.
Smith, Morton. "The Image of God." *Bulletin of the John Rylands Library 40 (1958) 473–512.*

———. "On the Shape of God and the Humanity of Gentiles." In *Religions in Antiquity: Essays in Memory of E. R. Goodenough*, ed. J. Neusner, 315–26. Leiden: E. J. Brill, 1968.

Smith, William, and Wace, Henry, eds. *A Dictionary of Christian Biography, Literature, Sects and Doctrines*. 4 vols. London: John Murray, 1877–87.

Sokoloff, Michael. "The Geniza Fragments of Genesis Rabba and MS Vat. Ebr. 60 of Genesis Rabba." Ph.D. dissertation, Hebrew University, 1971.

Sparks, H. F. D. "Jerome as Biblical Scholar." *In Cambridge History of the Bible*, ed. P. R. Ackroyd and C. F. Evans, vol. 1, 510–40. Cambridge: Cambridge University Press, 1970.

Speiser, E. *Genesis*. AB. New York: Doubleday, 1964.

Spurrell, G. *Notes on the Hebrew Text of the Book of Genesis*. Oxford: Clarendon, 1887.

Stichel, Rainer. *Die Namen Moes, seines Bruders und seiner Frau*. Abhandlungen der Akademie der Wissenschaften in Göttingen 112. Göttingen: Vandenhoeck and Ruprecht, 1979.

Stinespring, W. F. "The Active Infinitive with Passive Meaning in Biblical Aramaic." *JBL* 81 (1962) 391–94.

Strack, Hermann. *Introduction to the Talmud and Midrash*. Philadelphia: Jewish Publication Society, 1931.

Stroumsa, Gedaliahu Guy. "Another Seed: Studies in Sethian Gnosticism." Ph.D. dissertation, Harvard University, 1978.

Suidae Lexicon. Ed. Ada Adler. Pt. 4. Leipzig: B. G. Teubner, 1935.

Swete, Henry. *An Introduction to the Old Testament in Greek*. Cambridge: Cambridge University Press, 1900.

Tal, Abraham. "The Samaritan Targum to the Pentateuch: Its Distinctive Characteristics and Its Metamorphosis." *JSS* 21 (1976) 26–38.

Thompson, John C. *The Samaritans: Their Testimony to the Religion of Israel*. Edinburgh: Oliver and Boyd, 1919.

Tov, Emanuel. "On 'Pseudo-Variants' Reflected in the Septuagint." *JSS* 20 (1975) 165–77.

———. *The Text-Critical Use of the Septuagint in Biblical Research*. Jerusalem Biblical Studies 3. Jerusalem: Simor, 1981.

Tov, Emanuel, and Kraft, Robert A. "Septuagint." *IDBSup.*, 802–15.

Urbach, E. A. "The Laws of Idolatry in the Light of Historical and Archaeological Facts in the Third Century." *Eretz-Israel* 5 (1958) 189–205 (Heb. sec.).

———. *The Sages: Their Concepts and Beliefs*. Trans. Israel Abrahams. Jerusalem: Magnes, 1975.

———. "The Traditions About Merkabah Mysticism in the Tannaitic Period." Hebrew. In *Studies in Mysticism and Religion Presented to Gershom Scholem*. Jerusalem: Magnes, 1967.

VanderKam, James C. "The Righteousness of Noah." In *Ideal Figures in Ancient Judaism: Profiles and Paradigms*, ed. John J. Collins and George W. E. Nickelsburg, 13–32. SBLSCS 12. Chico: Scholars Press, 1980.

———. *Textual and Historical Studies in the Book of Jubilees*. Harvard Semitic Monographs, no. 14. Missoula, Montana: Scholars Press, 1977.

Van Rompay, Lucas. "A Hitherto Unknown Nestorian Commentary on Genesis and Exodus 1–9, 32 in the Syriac Manuscript (Olim) Dijarbekr 32." OLP 5, 53–78. Louvain, 1974.

Vermes, Geza. "Bible and Midrash: Early Old Testament Exegesis." In *Cambridge History of the Bible*, ed. P. R. Ackroyd and C. F. Evans, vol. 1, 199–231. Cambridge: Cambridge University Press, 1970.

———. *Post Biblical Jewish Studies*. SJLA 8. Leiden: E. J. Brill, 1975.

———. "The Present State of the 'Son of Man' Debate." *JJS* 29 (1978) 123–34.

———. *Scripture and Tradition in Judaism*. SPB 4. Leiden: E. J. Brill, 1973.

Vööbus, Arthur. "Syriac Versions." *IDBSup*., 527–32.

Weiss, Isaac Hirsch. *Dor dor wedorešayw*. Vols. 1–3. Wilna: Zawadski, 1911.

West, M. L., ed. *Hesiod: Works and Days*. Oxford: Clarendon, 1978.

Westermann, Claus. *Genesis*. Fasc. 1/6. BKAT. Neukirchen-Vluyn: Neukirchener Verlag, 1966–78.

———. *Isaiah 40–66: A Commentary*. Trans. David Stalker. Philadelphia: Westminster, 1969.

Wickham, L. R. "The Sons of God and the Daughters of Man." In *Language and Meaning: Studies in Hebrew Language and Biblical Exegesis*. OTS 19, 135–47. Leiden: E. J. Brill, 1974.

Wilson, Robert R. *Genealogy and History in the Biblical World*. Yale Near Eastern Researches, no. 7. New Haven: Yale University, 1977.

Winter, Michael M. *A Concordance to the Peshiṭta Version of Ben Sira*. Leiden: E. J. Brill, 1976.

Wolfson, Harry A. *Philo: Foundations of Religious Philosophy in Judaism, Christianity, and Islam*. 2 vols. Cambridge: Harvard University Press, 1968.

Woude, A. S. van der. "Fragments des Buches Jubiläen aus Qumran Höhle XI (11QJub.)." In *Tradition und Glaube: Das frühe Christentum in seiner Umwelt*, ed. G. Jeremias et. al., 140–46. Göttingen: Vandenhoeck and Ruprecht, 1971.

Wright, William, *A Short History of Syriac Literature*. London: Adam and Charles Black, 1894.

Yumauchi, Edwin M. *Mandaic Incantation Texts*. New Haven: American Oriental Society, 1967.

———. "The Present State of Mandaean Studies." *JNES* 23 (1966) 88–96.

York, A. D. "The Dating of the Targumic Literature." *JSJ* 5 (1974) 49–62.

Zunz, Leopold. *Hadderašot beyiśra'el*. Trans. of *Die Gottesdienstlichen Vorträge der Juden* (1892). Ed. Ch. Albeck. Jerusalem: The Bialik Institute, 1974.

INDEX OF PRIMARY SOURCES

Hebrew Bible

Genesis

1–11	26n, 202, 216–25
1:2	148
1:3	148
1:7	145n
1:9	151, 152n
1:26–27	13, 61n, 133n
1:26	139, 139n
1:28	139, 139n
2:4–3:24	11
2:4	20n, 157
2:8	34n
2:11–14	61
2:11	61
2:17	159
2:23	190
3:9–24	140, 140n
3:14–19	135
3:17–19	165n
3:17	159
3:20	113n, 190
4–6	232, 233n
4–5	16, 27, 72, 76, 79, 105
4	25n, 202–11
4:1–24	22, 25n
4:1–2	7n
4:1	78n, 190, 207n
4:3–4	53, 202nn
4:8	196
4:17–24	25, 134n, 162, 202–6, 211, 211n, 212n
4:17–22	7n, 205, 205n
4:17–19	211n
4:17–18	204n
4:17	77n, 78, 78n, 204n, 207n
4:18	142n
4:19–22	205n
4:20	162
4:21	162
4:22	221
4:23–24	205
4:23	78
4:25–5:8	95n
4:25	7n, 13, 27, 67n, 76n, 95n, 98n, 190
4:25–26	134n, 203, 204, 204n
4:26	passim
5–6	202, 212–16
5	25n, 79, 95, 97, 132n, 133n, 134, 134n, 153n, 190n, 202–6, 211n
5:1	20, 20n, 21, 22, 22n, 32, 32n, 37, 71–72, 133, 133n, 134n, 203, 212
5:2	203
5:3	61n, 99, 99n, 133n, 141
5:4	134n
5:6–11	95n
5:6	168
5:9–14	95n, 132n, 204n
5:11	99n
5:18–24	95n
5:18	16
5:21–27	95n
5:22–24	7n, 99n
5:22	203
5:24	12n, 13, 203
5:25–30	95n
5:29	7n, 9n, 190, 190n, 203, 210n
6–8	25n
6	205

6:1–4	166n, 205, 213, 213n, 214, 214n, 223n
6:1	114n, 142, 170n, 181, 213n
6:2–4	63n, 66, 68, 80, 80n, 82n, 83, 83nn, 84n, 85, 88, 90n, 94nn, 105, 105n, 106, 127n
6:2	27n, 63, 64, 65, 66n, 67, 68, 68n, 70, 72, 73, 74, 75, 79, 82, 83, 84n, 86, 94n, 101n, 103, 124, 196, 207, 213
6:3	214n
6:4	27n, 65, 102n, 150, 165n, 207, 213
6:5	214
6:8	212n
6:9	20n, 212n, 217n
6:11–13	214, 223n
6:13	213, 214n
6:17	213
6:24	27
7:1	217n
7:4	213, 214n
7:10	214n
7:11	148, 158
7:21–23	213
9:2	136
9:6	133n
9:20	8n, 143n, 182n, 212n, 222n
9:26	13
10:8	6n, 8, 9, 142, 181, 223n
10:25	169n, 191, 192n
11:1	150
11:4	197n, 207n
11:5	114n
11:6	142, 143, 185n
11:8	117n, 146n
11:9	160
12:1–25:10	26n
12:8	7n, 35nn, 103n, 114nn, 115n, 202n, 224nn
12:10–20	35n
13:4	7n, 35, 35n, 36n, 114n, 115n, 202n, 224n
15:1	35
15:7	202n
16:4	29n
18:4	7n
18:11	117n
18:23	214n
18:29	157
21:1	157, 159
21:33	7n, 34n, 114n, 115n, 202n, 224n
25:11–36:43	26n
26:25	7n, 202n, 222n
30:21	190n
33:20	174n
37:1–50:26	26n
41:49	117n
44:12	143n
48:16	10n, 37n
50:24–25	12n

Exodus

3:14	35
3:15	32n, 35, 200
4:22	65n, 72, 72n
6:3	35, 35n, 36, 36n, 200, 201nn, 202n
7:1	89, 90n
12:3	32n
13:19	12n
14:23	37
15:1	34, 34n, 130, 130n, 159, 159n
15:2	34n
18:11	122nn
20:3	120, 123, 179n
20:22	221n
21:30	7n
22:19	122nn
22:27(28)	73, 74, 89, 90n
31:14	153n
32:1	122n
32:4	128, 196n
32:11	182n, 187n
32:23	122n
33:19	116n
34:5	116n
34:6	31

Leviticus

11:38 7n
19:12 135
20:12 162
21:14 117n
24:15–16 73
26:6 137
26:22 136n

Numbers

9:13 117n
27:1 222n
30:3 118n, 170n, 182n, 188, 188n

Deuteronomy

3:23 111n
3:24 182n
4:19 198
5:7 120, 123, 179n
23:33 117n
28:10 10n, 37n
32:18 137

Joshua

21:9 7n

Judges

13:5 182n

1 Samuel

4:21 191
14:35 8n
25:7 14n

1 Kings

12:28 128
18:24 10, 11, 122n
22:19 164

2 Kings

5:11 11
14:20 7n
17:24–26 136, 141

Isaiah

1:2 72, 72n
1:12 31
8:1 153n, 189n
10:33 162
13:12 14n
24:6 136, 136n
26:1 7n, 29n
26:10 7n
29:15 148
33:8 154
37:19 120
41:2 148
41:25 10n
43:7 65n
44:11 210n
44:17 128
49:24 7n
56:2 153, 154
63:19 10n, 37n

Jeremiah

2:3 137, 137n
5:22 127n
10:11 73, 122nn
15:18 168, 170, 189n
17:5 77
17:9 189n
30:12 169n
51:9 150, 170n

Ezekiel

2:1–3:11 6n
14:15 137n
14:21 137n
20:5 201n
20:9 201n
22:26 117n
29:5 137n
32:4 137n
33:27 137n
38:8 14n
47:8 146

Hosea

2:1 72n
8:10 117n, 118n

Joel

3:5 (2:32) 31, 54, 54n, 70n, 75n

Amos

5:8 121, 123n, 124, 126n, 129n, 144, 145, 145n, 146n,

	150, 152n, 158n, 159, 160, 161n
9:6	121, 123n, 144, 145, 146n, 152n, 159, 160, 161n

Micah

1:9	189n

Habakkuk

1:16	142n

Zechariah

14:10	162

Psalms

1:1	148n
8:5	14n, 157, 158n, 164, 191n
16:9	140n
29:10	149
33:7–8	152n
40:5(4)	78, 78n, 79n
46:9	168
50(49):1	73–75
52:10(8)	78
77:11	182n, 183nn, 187n
82(81):6	37n, 72, 72n, 73, 74n, 81n
86:8	122n
97:11	152
99(98):6	54–55
103:15	191n
104:9	127n
144:3	14n
148:6	127n

Proverbs

24:17	31
27:22	150

Job

1:6	72n
2:1	72n
9:9	158
14:19	172n, 189n
21:14	150, 167, 167n
22:16	158
22:17	158
25:6	14n
26:10	127n
28:36	127n
36:25	14n
38:7	72n
38:10–11	127n
38:11	144, 147
38:15	152

Oohelet (Ecclesiastes)

2:23	148n

Esther

3:2	141n

Daniel

2:40	221n
3:25	72n
6	138n

1 Chronicles

1:1–4	13n
1:1	22n
6:50	7n

2 Chronicles

25:28	7n

Ancient Versions

Septuagint

Gen 4:26	5–11, 20, 20n, 28, 29, 48, 49, 59n, 62–107 passim
Gen 5:1	20, 50n, 32, 32n, 78
Gen 5:24	22n
Gen 6:2–4	80, 81n, 82n, 83, 84nn, 84, 84n, 85, 88, 90n, 105, 105n, 106
Gen 6:2	66n, 83, 84n, 86
Gen 6:4	66n
Gen 6:9	217n
Gen 7:1	217n
Gen 9:20	8n
Gen 10:8	8n
Gen 12:8	64n
Gen 18:4	7n
Exod 6:3	35n, 201n
Exod 21:30	7n

Exod 22:27 73n, 74n
Exod 33:19 10, 116n
Exod 34:5 10, 116n
Lev 11:38 7n
Lev 24:15 73n, 74n
Num 31:49 14n
1 Sam 14:35 8n
1 Sam 25:7 14n
2 Sam 7:10 82n
1 Kgs 18:24 10, 11
2 Kgs 14:14 82n
Isa 17:11 15
Isa 24:6 136n
Isa 26:1 7n
Isa 26:10 7n
Isa 41:25 10n, 31n, 37n, 64n
Isa 43:1 10
Isa 45:3 10
Jer 10:4 73n
Jer 11:15 9
Jer 17:9 15
Jer 17:16 15
Ezek 32:14 9
Ezek 38:8 14n
Mic 3:4 9
Zeph 3:9 10
Mal 3:16 9
Ps 39:5 78n
Ps 49:1 73:75
Ps 82(81):6 73n, 81n
Job 1:6 72n
Job 2:1 72n
Job 11:15 9
Job 38:7 72n

Aquila

Gen 4:26 5n, 6, 8, 11, 49, 75, 81n, 86, 87n, 93n, 106n, 113n
Gen 6:2 82, 89n

Symmachus

Gen 4:26 5n, 6, 8, 11, 49
Gen 6:2 66n, 74n, 82, 82n, 83n, 89, 102
Ps 80:19 10n, 31n, 64n

"Hebraios"

Gen 4:26 5, 6, 11, 63

Old Latin

Gen 4:26 11n, 48, 49, 61, 76, 79
Ps 40:4 78n

Vulgate

Gen 4:26 49
Gen 18:4 7n
Exod 6:3 35n, 201n
Exod 21:30 7n
Lev 11:38 7n

Samaritan Pentateuch

Gen 4:26 6, 29, 30
Gen 16:4 29n
Gen 18:4 29n
Gen 27:42 29n
Exod 6:3 35n
Exod 15:1 34n
Lev 11:38 29n

Samaritan Targum

Gen 4:26 6, 29, 30, 31
Gen 6:2 66n, 74n
Gen 6:4 74n
Gen 13:4 35n
Gen 48:6 30n
Exod 6:3 35, 35n, 201n
Exod 15:1 34, 34n

Peshiṭta

Gen 4:26 6, 91–92, 93, 93n, 95, 99, 100, 100n, 101, 102, 102n, 104n, 107n, 113n
Gen 18:4 7n
Exod 6:3 35n, 201n
Exod 21:30 7n
Exod 22:27 73n
Lev 11:38 7n
1 Kgs 18:24 11
Ps 40:4 78n, 79n

Targum Onqelos

Gen 3:20 113n
Gen 4:26 114n, 116–19, 123, 123n, 131n, 169n, 170, 170n, 174n, 186, 187, 188, 193, 193n, 194, 199n, 200

Gen 6:1	114n
Gen 6:2	66n, 74n
Gen 6:3	215n
Gen 6:4	74n
Gen 11:5	114n
Gen 11:8	117n
Gen 18:4	7n
Gen 18:11	117n
Gen 22:14	103n, 115n
Gen 33:20	103n, 115n
Gen 41:49	117n
Exod 6:3	35n, 201n
Exod 18:11	122n
Exod 21:30	7n
Exod 22:27	74n
Exod 33:19	116n
Exod 34:5	116n
Lev 21:14	117n
Num 9:13	117n
Num 30:3	118nn, 170, 188
Deut 23:23	117n
Deut 31:18	149n
Deut 32:17	122n

Targum Pseudo-Jonathan

Gen 3:20	113n
Gen 4:21–22	205n
Gen 4:26	112, 113, 115n, 115, 124, 126, 131n
Gen 5:24	34n
Gen 6:1	114n
Gen 6:2	66n
Gen 6:3	215n
Gen 10:8–11	207n
Gen 11:5	114n
Exod 6:3	35n, 201n
Exod 34:5	10n

Fragmentary Targum (Yerushalmi)

Gen 4:21–22	205n
Gen 4:26	112, 113, 114, 114n, 115, 115n, 124, 126, 128
Gen 5:24	34n
Gen 6:1	114n
Gen 6:2	66n
Gen 6:3	215n
Gen 12:8	115n
Gen 13:4	115n
Gen 21:33	115n
Gen 22:14	115n

Targum Neofiti

Gen 4:21–22	205n
Gen 4:26	112 , 113, 113n, 114n, 115, 115n, 124, 126
Gen 5:24	34n
Gen 6:1	114n
Gen 6:2	66n
Gen 6:3	215n
Gen 12:8	103n, 115n
Gen 13:4	115n
Gen 18:4	7n
Gen 21:33	103n, 115n
Gen 22:14	103n, 115n
Exod 6:3	35n, 201n
Exod 34:5	10n

Targum Neofiti marginal gloss

Gen 4:17	207n
Gen 4:26	113, 113n, 114, 115, 126, 128
Gen 6:2	66n
Gen 12:8	115n
Gen 13:4	115n
Gen 21:33	115n
Gen 26:25	115n
Gen 33:20	115n

Cairo Geniza Tg. Fragments

Gen 4:26	112n
Exod 6:3	35n, 201n

Targum of the Prophets

1 Kgs 18:24	10
Isa 24:6	136n
Isa 26:1	7n
Isa 26:10	7n
Isa 41:25	10n
Jer 10:11	74n, 122n
Ezek 22:26	117n
Hab 1:16	142n

Targum of the Writings

Ps 29:10	149n
Ps 50:1	73n
Ps 82:6	74n

Apocrypha and Pseudepigrapha

2 (Syriac) Apocalypse of Baruch

56.6	165n

3 (Greek) Apocalypse of Baruch

2.3	135n
2.7	135n
3.3	135n

Apocalypse of Moses

5	165n
10–12	138n

Ben Sira

7.17	189n
36.17	11n
39.30(31)	14n, 160n
44.16	13, 13n, 22n
44.17	13n
45.14	15n
47.18	11n
49.14–16	12–16, 168
49.15	14n
49.16	50n, 173, 173n
50.1	14n, 160n

1 Enoch

6–11	65, 166n, 208n
6.6	191n
7–8	207
7.1	199n
8.1	221
9	67n
9.6	208
19.2	135n
52.7–9	221n
69.9–11	209n
83.6–9	17n
85–86	27n
86	66n

2 (Slavonic) Enoch

33.10–11	18–19
33.10	17n
35.2	18n
Appendix	26n

2 (Hebrew) Enoch (= Seper Hekalot)

3.5	165n
4.3	166n
4.4	214n
5.3–13	163–66
5.3–6	149n, 152n, 186, 220n
5.7–9	199n
5.10	155n, 158n, 189n

Epistle of Aristeas

135	208n

Jubilees

2.4	145n
4	27n
4.11ff	134n
4.12	6, 16–17, 49
4.13	18
4.15	17n, 191
4.16–17	16
4.17–18	209
4.17	16
5.1–9	166n
7.21	223n
8.2–4	209n
10.18	191
11.23–24	209
13.16	114n
19.23–25	17–18

1 Maccabees

2.51–61	28n

Sibylline Oracles

3.793	138n

Testament of Benjamin

5.2	138n

Testament of Issachar

7.7	138n

Testament of Joseph

20.2	12n

Testament of Judah

19.2	128n

Testament of Levi

2.7	145n
18.12	138n

Testament of Naphtali

8.4	138n

Vita Adae et Evae

30–31	165n
37–39	138n

Wisdom of Solomon

11.15–18 137
13.1–9 128n, 197n
14.12 196n, 198
14.13–14 198
14.15–16 199n
14.16–21 142n
14.24 196n
18.13 72n

Dead Sea Scrolls

Genesis Apocryphon

2 65n
2.5 34n
19.7 114n
21.2 114n
21.3–4 36n

Hodayot

11.10 189n
17.15 13n

Isaiah Scroll—Copy a

Isa 24:6 136n
Isa 26:1 7n
Isa 26:10 7n
Isa 41:25 10n
Isa 49:24 7n

Pesher Habakkuk

6.3–5 142n

Manual of Discipline

4.23 13n

Damascus Document

3.17 189n
3.20 13n
15.1 123n

Other Scrolls

4QDibHam 3.4–6 65n
4QEn[a] 1.3 191n
4QEn[f] 1 27n
4Q*180–181* 65n, 166n
4QpsDanA (= 4Q *246*) 64n, 65n
11QJub M3 16

Philo

Abr.

4–5 19n
7–15 21
7–8 21n, 191n
7 21n, 23
8–9 8n, 11n
9 22, 66n
10 21n
11 22
12–13 22n, 42n
15–16 22n
17–18 22n
31 20n
33 21n
47 23n, 24n
48 23n

Conf.

122 207n

Dec.

61 128n

Fug.

63 69n

Gig.

6–15 66n
65–66 142n

Leg. All.

1.19–20 20n
1.31–42 76n

Legat.

134 142n
138 142n
148 142n
188 142n
207–8 142n
346 142n

De Mutatione Nominum

23n

Post.

40–48 27n
40–41 25n
40 54

42 67n
44–45 25n
49–51 78n, 207n
73–74 25n
83 206n
98 206n
99 206n
112 206n
116–20 206n
116 221n
172–74 67n

Praem.

8 210n
10–14 21nn
10–11 21n
15 138
23 216n

Qu. In Gen.

1.74 137n
1.80 20n, 22n
1.81 25n
1.92 66n
2.13 215n

Quod. Det.

138–140 8n, 20, 20n, 21, 23, 133n, 191n

Sob.

52–58 25n
55 59n, 69n
65 24n, 25n

Spec. Leg.

2.159–160 219n
4.188 69n

De Vita Mosis

2.219–20 208n

Pseudo-Philo

Biblical Antiquities

2.3 207n
2.8–10 206n
2.9 221n
4.16 209n
7.5 135n

Josephus

Ant.

1.2.1 (52–53) 78n
1.2.1 (53–54) 207n
1.2.1 (53) 206n
1.2.1 (59) 137n
1.2.2 (60–66) 206n
1.2.2 (61) 207n
1.2.2 (64) 221n
1.2.3 (67–71) 25, 89
1.2.3 (68–69) 25n
1.2.3 (69–71) 86n
1.2.3 (69) 209n
1.2.3 (70–71) 19n
1.3.1 (72) 26, 177n, 199
1.3.2 (79) 25n
1.3.4 (83) 25n
1.4.2 (113–14) 143n
1.7.1 (154–57) 224n
18.3.1 (55–59) 142n
18.8.2–9 (261–309) 142n

Ap.

2.6 (66–78) 142n

B.J.

2.9.2–3 (169–74) 142n
2.10.1–4 (184–98) 142n

Rabbinic Sources

Mishnah

Pesaḥ. 1.5 136n
Pesaḥ. 2.1 136n, 180n
Peshạ. 9.5 180n
Soṭa 1.9 12n
B. Meṣ 4.2 130n
Sanh. 7.6 128
Sanh. 10.3 130
'Abot 3.14 133n
'Abot 4.4 189n
'Abot 5.2 131n, 150n, 217, 222n
'Abot 5.6 211n
'Abot 5.9 137n

Tosefta

Ber. 3.6(8) 187n
Ber. 5.1 138n
Soṭa 3.6–12 130n
Soṭa 10.3–6 214n
B. Qam. 7.6 140n
Sanh. 10.23 128
Sanh. 13.6–12 130, 130n

Megillat Ta'anit

3 Kislev 142n

Palestinian Talmud

Ber. 8.5(11b) 210n
Ber. 9.1(12a) 73n
Ber. 9.1(13b) 31n
Šeqal. 6.3(50a) 144n, 146, 147n
Meg. 1.9(71d) 123n
Mo'ed Qat. 3.5(82c) 214n
Yebam. 6.5(7c) 205n

Babylonian Talmud

Ber. 7b 168n
Ber. 30b 182n
Ber. 31a 187n
Ber. 32a 118n, 182n, 183n, 187n
Ber. 33a 138n
Sabb. 33a 137n
Sabb. 118b 153–54, 154n, 158n, 182n, 189n, 225n
Sabb. 151b 139
'Erub. 18b 134n
'Erub. 22b 144n
'Erub. 53a 143n
Pesaḥ. 21a 136n, 180n
Pesaḥ. 54a 210n
Pesaḥ. 94b 143n, 207n
Pesaḥ. 96b 180n
Yoma 57a 141n
Yoma 81a 214n
Sukk. 52b 154n
Ta'an. 9b 144n
Meg. 18a 174n
Ḥag. 10a 182n
Ḥag 12a 135n, 152n
Ḥag 13a 143n
Ketub. 59b 141n
Soṭa 9b–10a 118n, 182n
Soṭa 10a 114n, 224n
Soṭa 13a–b 12n
Qidd. 13a 145n
Qidd. 30a 33n
Qidd. 57a–58a 135n
B. Meṣ. 59b 147n
B. Bat. 75b 31n, 174n
Sanh. 25a 58n
Sanh. 38b 135n, 138n
Sanh. 108a 145n
Sanh. 108b 214n
Sanh. 109a 135n, 197n
Šebu. 35a–b 123n
'Abod. Z. 4a 182n
'Abod. Z. 5a 74n
Zebaḥ. 113b 145n

Minor Tractates

ARNA 1 139n
ARNA 29 137n
ARNA 32 131n, 149n, 214n, 217n
ARNA 33 222n
ARNA 34 123n
ARNA 36 130n
ARNA 37 133n
ARNB 1 33n
ARNB 7 164n
ARNB 14 138n
ARNB 36 131n
ARNB 38 123n, 127n
ARNB 42 135, 138, 139
Derek Ereṣ Zuṭa 140n
Sop. 4.1 123n

Tannaitic Midrashim

Mekilta

Bešallaḥ 1 12n
Bešallaḥ 3 114n
Širta' 1 130n
Širta' 2 130
Širta' 8 142n
Baḥodeš 6 74n, 120–29, 144, 166n, 172n, 179n
Baḥodeš 9 149n
Baḥodeš 11 140n, 221n
Kaspa' 4 123n, 197n

Mekilta of R. Simeon

Exod 14:10	114n
Exod 20:22	140n
Exod 15:1	130nn
Exod 15:11	142n
Exod 20:3	122–23, 122n, 123n
Exod 20:22	221n

Sifra

Lev 19:4	122n, 126
Lev 19:12	135, 136, 137–38
Lev 20:3	140n
Lev 23:27	214n
Lev 26:6	137–38, 182n
Lev 26:14	129n

Sifre Num

111	196n
134	118n, 182n

Sifre Zuta

Num 27:1	222n

Sifre Deut

1	169n
2	132n
26	111n
27	118n, 182n
31	11n
34	33n
43	119n, 120n, 121n, 125n, 126, 126n, 127n, 130n, 144, 179n
47	127n
49	31, 69n, 70n, 174n
50	138n
54	119n, 196n
84	166n
87	119n
94	81n
148	149n
306	74n, 133n
310	130n
311	130n
318	122n, 130n, 141n
319	137, 153n, 182n
324	130n

Midraš Tanna'im

Deut 3:24	182n
Deut 5:7	120n, 121n
Deut 32:17	9n, 120n, 121n, 122n, 123n, 125n, 127n, 179n

Amoraic and Postamoraic Midrashic Collections

'Aggadat Bere'šit (ed. Buber)

Intro. p. 37	17n, 170n, 189nn, 191n, 212n
Intro. p. 38	214n
Intro. p. 38–39	66n, 166n
8, p. 20	151n, 152n
15, p. 32	138n

Bere'šit Rabbati (ed. Albeck)

p. 27.7–10	166n
pp. 29–31	166n
p. 31	168–69, 189nn
pp.31–32	153n
p. 37	157n
p. 41	167–68, 221n, 222n
p. 50	131n
p. 56	168–69

Canticles Rabba

2.2	149n
5.1	149n, 153n

Deuteronomy Rabba

2.8	118n, 182n
10.2	152n

Esther Rabba

Proem 11	152n

Exodus Rabba

1.33	169n
15.7	158–59, 167n, 220n, 222n
15.26	148n
23.4	34n, 130n, 159n
32.1	74n
32.4	118n
32.7	74n

35.1 152n
43.1–5 182n, 187n
43.1 183n

Feast of Leviathan

BhM, 6.150 153n

Genesis Rabba

2.3 148, 168n, 222n
3.6 152n, 214n
5.1 151–52, 220n
5.3 144n, 145n
5.6 152n
8.4 157n
8.12 139n
11.2 152n
12.6 135n, 152n, 210n
12.7 134n
13.10 144n
14.3 133n
19.7 148–49, 166n, 168n, 221n, 222n
19.8 135
20.11 134n
22.3 207n
22.11 137n
23.1–3 205n
23.1 207n
23.2 142n
23.3 162n, 206n, 221n
23.5 67n
23.6–7 204
23.6 131–42, 153n, 163, 164, 165n, 166n, 175, 182, 182nn, 186nn, 220n
23.7 120n, 125n, 126n, 129n, 133n, 142–47, 161n, 174n, 181, 216n
24.6 22n, 131n, 133n, 134n, 142n, 212n
24.7 210n
25.1 54n, 132n, 212n
25.2 138n, 146n, 210n
26.1 148n
26.4 142n
26.5 66n
26.7 142n, 150, 213
27.2 148n
27.3 181n
27.4 214n
28.1 225
28.2 151n
29.4 212n
30.9 54n, 212n
30.10 212n
31.6 223n
32.7 214n
32.11 145n
34.12 138n
36.3 182n, 212n, 222n
36.6 143n
37.7 169n, 192n
38.2 150n
38.4 150n
38.5 150, 170n, 213n
38.8 197n
38.10 146n, 160n
39.5 150n, 222n
39.16 114n, 224n
41.7 223n
42.3 148n, 152n
64.7 125nn
65.9 165n
72.6 190n
79.8 174n
82.14 210n
94.8 169n

Jeraḥmeel

23.6–7 153n, 166n
23.7 141n
24.1–8 205n
24.7 19n
24.9 185n
24.10–12 94n
24.10 66n
24.11 26n
25 166n
25.1 165n
26.16 19n
30.5 135n

Lamentations Rabba

Proem 24 154, 158n, 189n
1 142n
1.2 118n, 183n, 187n
1.16 151n

Leqaḥ Ṭob

Gen 4:17–18 205n
Gen 4:26 142n
Gen 6:3 214n
Gen 6:4 150n
Gen 7:4 214n
Gen 9:20 143n
Gen 12:8 114n
Exod 6:3 201n
Lev 19:12 136n

Leviticus Rabba

4.1 74n
9.9 133n
11.3 74n
11.7 152, 220n
18.3 74n
22.3 164n
23.3 149–50, 167n, 217n

Manorat Ha-Maor (ed. Enelow)

1.125–26 205n
4.299 151n

Midraš Abkir

165n

Midraš 'Aggada

Gen 4:17–22 205n
Gen 4:26 170, 183, 188, 188n, 189n
Gen 5:18 191n
Gen 5:24 211n
Gen 5:28–29 210n
Gen 6:1 170n, 183n
Gen 9:2 138n, 139n
Gen 11:8 135n

Midraš Ḥadaš 'al Hattora

BhM, 1.63 144n
BhM, 1.79–80 205n
TS 9.5n.24 201n

Midraš Haggadol

Gen intro. 180n
Gen 1:26 139nn
Gen 3:17 139n
Gen 4:17–22 205n
Gen 4:26 9n, 120n, 121n, 123n, 153n, 169, 183, 184n, 189nn
Gen 5:29 210n
Gen 6:4 139n
Gen 6:5 148n, 166n
Gen 6:13 214n
Gen 30:21 190n
Exod 6:3 201n
Exod 40:34 135n, 149n
Lev 19:12 136n
Deut 3:24 118n
Deut 32:7 9n, 123n

Midraš Tehillim

1.12 148n
1.13 135n
2.2 150n
9.16 58n, 190n
26.7 214n
27.1 152n
29.2 149n
50.1 73n, 123n
77.3 183n, 187n
88.2 120n, 125n, 129n, 144n
92.4 210n

Mishnah Rabbi Eliezer (ed. Enelow)

1.78 151n

Numbers Rabba

5.4 135n
9.24 130n
13.2 135n, 149n
13.5 152n
14.6 214n
14.12 98n
19.29 154n

Pereq 'adam hari'šon (in *Ozar Midrashim*)

1.9–11 135n

Pesiqta deRab Kahana

1.1 135n, 148n
5.3 135n
13.11–12 192
17.2 118n, 182n, 183n

Pesiqta Rabbati

5 148n, 152n
15 135n
23 152n, 210n
40 156–57, 168n, 220n
42 159–60
46 152n
supp. 1 144n, 145n, 146n, 160–61, 170, 188n, 220

Pirqe Rabbi Eliezer

3 145n
6 145n
7 165n
8 210n
14 135n, 139n
22 66n, 67n, 133n, 176n, 205n

Qohelet Rabba

1.4 127n
2.21–23 148n
3.14 152n

Qohelet Zuṭa

2.8 148n

Ruth Rabba

Proem 7 152n

Seder Eliahu Rabba

16 153n, 217n
29(31) 131n, 217n
31 214n

Seder Eliahu Zuṭa

10 217n
21 152n

Seder Olam Rabba

1 192n
4 127n

Sekel Tob

Exod 6:3 201n

Seper Hayyašar (ed. Goldschmidt)

Bere'šit, p. 7 167n, 213n
Bere'šit, p. 8 205n
Noaḥ, p. 16 214n
Noaḥ, p. 31 135n

Seper Hekalot—see Apocrypha and Pseudepigrapha, *3 Enoch*

Tanḥuma

Bere'šit 6 135n
Bere'šit 11 210n
Bere'šit 12 166n
Noaḥ 3 152n, 180n
Noaḥ 13 143n
Noaḥ 18 120n, 125n, 129n, 135n, 150n, 172n
Wayyera' 18 157–58, 168n, 189n, 220n, 222n
Bešallaḥ 9 114n
Bešallaḥ 10 130n
Bešallaḥ 12 130n
Yitro 16 120n, 121nn, 129n
Ki Tiśśa' 17 157n
Pequde 6 149n
Šemini 9 152n
Ḥuqqat 23 154n

Tanḥuma, ed. Buber

Bere'šit 18 135n
Bere'šit 29 53n
Noaḥ 4 214n
Noaḥ 20 143n
Noaḥ 24 120n, 125n, 150, 150n, 213n
Lek leka 26 212n
Wayyera' 10 157n, 168n
Wayyera' 24 148n
Wa'era' 5 201
Bešallaḥ 12 34n, 130n, 159, 162n
Yitro 1 182n
Šemini 1 214n
Bemidbar 32 166n
Naśo' 24 148n
Ḥuqqat 39 53n
Ḥuqqat 53 154n
Ḥuqqat supp. 1 205n
Wa'etḥannan supp. 1 182n

Yalquṭ Hammakiri

Isa 56:2 153n
Joel 3.5 31n
Amos 5.8 120n, 144n, 150n, 158n, 159n

Yalquṭ Re'ubeni

Gen 4:26 149n, 155n, 163n, 169n, 186n
Lev 2:13 147n

Yalquṭ Šim'oni

Bere'šit 4 148n
Bere'šit 7 151n
Bere'šit 27 135n, 148n
Bere'šit 39 120n, 131n, 132n
Bere'šit 40 142n, 144n
Bere'šit 42 210n
Bere'šit 44 165n, 166n
Bere'šit 47 131n, 135n, 150n, 161–63, 182n, 204n, 211n, 214n
Wayeḥi 161 205n
Wa'era' 176 201n
Yitro 286 120n, 121n, 125n
Ki Tiśśa' 392 182n
Oedošim 605 136nn
Wa'etḥannan 815 118n, 182n
'Eqeb 866 120n, 125n
Isa 485 153n
Jer 335 150n
Ezek 367 54n
Amos 543 144n, 145, 146n
Micaah 522 154n
Ps 614 148n
Ps 732 148n
Ps 816 183n
Ps 848 151n
Job 924 144n, 146n, 152n
Qoh 968 148n
Chr 1072 131n, 132n

Zohar

1.19b 205n
1.37a 66n, 205n
1.55a 66n, 205n
1.56a 153n, 212n, 213n
1.56b 215n
2.113b 146n
2.192b 153n, 189n

Zohar Ḥadaš

Bere'šit 19d 205n

Post-Talmudic Rabbinic Commentators and Philosophers

Abraham ibn Ezra, *Commentary*

Gen 1:6 145n
Gen 4:26 169n, 184, 184n, 185, 186, 186n, 193
Gen 6:2 66n
Gen 9:20 182n
Exod 20:3 122n
Exod 33:19 10n
Exod 34:5 10n
Amos 5:8 145n

David Luria (RaDaL), *Commentary*

Gen. R. 23.6 162n
Exod. R. 15.7 158n
PRE 3 145n
PRE 7 165n
PRE 22 66n, 205n

David Qimḥi (RaDaQ), *Commentary*

Gen 4:26 116n, 125n, 128n, 133n, 169n, 184, 184nn, 192n, 194
Gen 5:29 210n
Mic 5:4 154n

Elijah Gaon of Wilna, *Emendations*

Mek. Baḥodeš 6 126n

Elijah Mizraḥi, *Commentary*

Gen 4:26 184n, 185n

Isaac Abravanel, *Commentary*

Gen 4:26 184n

Issachar Berman b. Naphtali, *Mattenot Kehunna*

Gen. R. 23.6 137n 141
Gen. R. 23.7 126n
Gen. R. 38.5 151n

Judah Halevi, *Kuzari*
- 1.47 218n
- 1.95 66n, 133n, 218n
- 2.14 66n

Judah Löw b. Bezelel (MaHaRaL) of Prague, *Gur 'Aryeh*
- Gen 4:26 194n

Levi b. Gerson (Gersonides, RaLBaG), *Commentary*
- Gen 4:26 128n, 184n, 192n, 194n

Moses b. Maimon (Maimonides, RaMBaM), *Mishnah Torah*
- *Hilkot 'Abod. Zar.*
- 1.1 128n, 153n
- 1.3 153n
- 2.1 128n
- 3.4 128n

Moses b. Naḥman (Naḥmanides, RaMBaN), *Commentary*
- Gen 4:22 205n
- Gen 6:4 66n, 132n, 165n, 169n, 186n
- Exod 6:3 201n

Moses David Treves Ashkenazy, *Merkebet hammišneh*
- fol. 89b 122n

Nissim Gerondi (RaN), *Commentary*
- Gen 4:26 128n, 193n, 194n

Obadiah Sforno, *Commentary*
- Gen 4:26 194n

Rashi (Solomon Yitzhaki), *Commentary*
- Gen 4:19–22 205n
- Gen 4:21 162n
- Gen 4:26 126n, 185, 185n, 192n, 194n
- Gen 5:29 210n
- Gen 6:2–4 211n
- Gen 6:4 150n, 165n
- Gen 9:20 143n
- Gen 11:6 185n
- Exod 6:3 201n
- Lev 19:4 122n
- Num 13:33 165n, 211n
- *b. Ber.* 31a 187n
- *b. Šabb.* 118b 153n
- *b. Yoma* 67b 211n
- *b. Soṭa* 9b–10a 118n
- *b. Nid.* 61a 165n, 211n

Pseudo-Rashi, *Commentary*
- *Gen. R.* 8.12 139n
- *Gen. R.* 23.3 161n
- *Gen. R.* 23.6 137n
- *Gen. R.* 24.6 134n
- *Gen. R.* 25.2 146n
- *Gen. R.* 38.5 151n
- *Gen. R.* 49.9 157n

Saadia Gaon, *Arabic Translation*
- Gen 4:26 169n, 184

Saddia Gaon, *Commentary* (of questionable attribution)
- Gen 4:26 170n, 184n, 188n
- Gen 12:8 114n

Saadia Gaon (?), Geniza Fragment
- 224n

Samuel b. Meir (raŠBaM), *Commentary*
- Gen 4:26 194n
- Exod 6:3 201n

Samuel Edels (MaHaRSa'), *Ḥidduše 'aggadot*
- *b. Šabb.* 118b 153n

Samuel Jaffe Ashkenazi, *Yepeh 'anap*
- *Lam. R.* Proem 24 154n

Solomon Yitzhaki—see Rashi

Zeeb Wolf b. Israel Issar Einhorn (MaHaRZU), *Commentary*
- *Gen. R.* 8.12 139n
- *Gen. R.* 23.6 133n, 14nn
- *Gen. R.* 23.7 126n, 146n, 147n, 223n
- *Gen. R.* 32.11 145n

Gen. R. 38.5 151n
Exod. R. 15.7 158n

Zvi Hirsch Chajes, *Commentary*

b. Soṭa 9b–10a 118n

New Testament

Matthew

1:1–17 229n
5:9 81n
5:45 81n
11:5 43
16:18 158n
22:30 72

Mark

12:25 72

Luke

3:23–28 67n, 229n
3:38 49
6:35 81n
7:22 43
8:2 41n
10:6 82n
20:35–36 76
20:35 72
20:36 81n

John

1:12 81n
10:34 81n

Acts

9:14 54n
9:21 54n
15:19–21 51
22:16 54n

Romans

3:23 53, 54
5:12–14 53, 54
5:12 54
8:14–17 94n
8:14 81n
8:15 81n
8:16 81n
8:22–23 94n
8:23 81n
8:24–25 77
10:12–14 54n
10:12 54
10:13 77
10:14 55
11:5 77

1 Corinthians

1:2 54n, 55
8:5 73, 74n, 120n

2 Corinthians

4:4 99n

Galatians

3:26 81n
4:4–7 94n
4:5 81n

Philippians

3:19 63n
3:20 63n

Colossians

1:15 99n

2 Timothy

2:22 54n

Hebrews

2:11–13 81n, 94n
11:1–31 49n
11:4–7 95n
11:8–16 78n
12:23 50, 104n

Post New Testament Christian Sources

Ambrose, *De Isaac*

1 48n
1.2 61–62

Ambrose, *De Paradiso*

1.3.19–23 48n, 61, 191n

Anastasius Sinaita, *Questions*

25 80n

Anastasius Sinaita, *Viae Dux*

86n, 90n

Aphraates, *Demonstrations*
13.5 91n
13.6 91n
18.9 91n
23.21–24,31 91n

Apostolic Constitutions
2.55.1 50
6.12.13 50, 51
7.38.2 50, 51
7.39.3 50, 51
8.5.3 50
8.12.4 50

Augustine, *De Civitate Die*
12.10 216n
15.17–18 76–78, 94n, 191n
15.17 206n
15.18 48n
15.20–21 206n
15.21 48n, 78–80, 94n, 133n
15.22–23 79n, 81n, 82n
15.23 102n

Bar Hebraeus, *Chronograaphy* (ed. Budge)
2.2a–b (trans. 1.3) 100n

Book of Adam and Eve
1.1 145n
2.11 96n, 165n
2.12 96n
2.17–20 97n
2.17 191n
2.20 96n, 206n

Book of the Bee
ch. 18 19n

Cave of Treasures (trans. Budge)
p. 74 96
pp. 74–75 165n
p. 77 96
p. 78 19n
p. 84 191n
pp. 87–89 206n

Chronicon Anonymum ad Annum Christi 1234
96n

Chrysostom, see John Chrysostom

Clement of Alexandria, *Excerpta ex Theodoto*
54.3 62n–63n

Pseudo-Clement, *Homilies*
4.12–13 65n
9.5 199n

Pseudo-Clement, *Recognitions*
1.29 26n, 65n
4.12.1 62n
4.13 199
4.26 65n
4.30 199
4.31 199

Cyril of Alexandria, *Contra Julianum*
9 82–83

Cyril of Alexandria, *Glaphyra*
2 80–82, 94n

Cyril of Alexandria, *Responsiones ad Tiberium diaconum Sociosque*
83n

Didymus the Blind, *On Genesis*
Gen 4:26 68–70, 191n
Gen 7:1 68n

Ephraem Syrus, *Commentary to Genesis*
Gen 4:26 91–92, 93n
Gen 6:2 93n, 165n

Ephraem Syrus, *Hymnen Contra Haeresis*
5:12 95n
19.1 93n

Ephraem Syrus *Hymnen de Ieiunio*
2.2 94n, 206n

Ephraem Syrus *Hymnen de Nativitate*

1.48 94–95

Ephraem Syrus, *Hymnen de Paradiso*

1.11 94n

Epiphanius, *Panarion (Haereses)*

39.3–5 67n

Eusebius of Caesaria, *Praeparatio evangelica*

1.9–10 197–98
1.9 190n, 197n, 198nn, 209n
1.10 19n, 197n, 207n, 209n
2.2 197n
7 58n
7.7 59
7.8 8n, 11n, 57–60, 191n
9.17 210n
9.18 210n
9.23 207n
9.26 210n
9.27 210n
11 58n
11.6 57n, 190n

Eusebius of Emesa, *Commentary on Genesis*

Gen 4:26 63–68

George Cedrenus, *Historiarum compendium*

86n, 87nn, 90n

George Syncellus, *Chronographia* (ed. W. Dindorf)

pp. 16–28 86n
pp. 16–17 86n
p. 16 207n
pp. 17–18 87, 87n
p. 17 8
pp. 34–35 67n, 86n

Gregory of Nazianzus *The Theological Orations*

2.18 52n

Ibn at-Taiyib *Commentaire sur la Genese*

100n, 101n

Isho bar Nun, *Selected Questions*

fol. 9v,9–13 98n, 99n, 100n

Isho'dad of Merv, *Commentary on Genesis*

Gen 4:26 98–104, 191n
Gen 5:3 99, 99n
Gen 5:22–24 99n
Gen 6:2 102–3
Gen 6:4 102n
Gen 12:8 103n

Jerome, *Adversus Jovianum*

1.17 62nn

Jerome, *Commentary on Galatians*

1 48n
1.3 48n, 62n

Jerome, *Homilies*

45 ad Ps 132 80n

Jerome, *Liber interpretationis hebraicorum nominum*

s.v. Enosh 58n, 190n
s.v. Seth 76n

Jerome, *Quaestiones Hebraicae in Genesim*

Gen 4:26 48n, 49, 58n, 62n, 191n
Gen 6:2 80n

John Chrysostom, *Expositio in Psalmum*

49:1 73–75, 86n, 93n, 102n, 120n

John Chrysostom, *Homolies in Genesis*

20.4 70–72, 133n, 191n
22.2–3 72–73

John Zonoras, *Analium*

1.4 87n

Julius Africanus, *Chronicles*
66–68, 94n

Leo Grammaticus, *Chronographia*
87n

Luther, *Lectures on Genesis*
Gen 4:26 54n

Pseudo-Malalas *Chronographia*
88, 88n, 89n, 90n

Michael Glycas, *Annalium*
87n, 90n

Michael the Syrian, *Chronicle*
96n, 100n

Origen, *Commentary on Romans*
5:1 53–54, 55, 105n
8:3 8n, 54–56, 105n, 231n

Origen, *Contra Celsum*
1.19 216
4.11 216n

Origen, *Hexapla*
1.20 5n, 63n

Pamphilus, *Apologia pro Origen*
52n, 53n

Paschal Chronicle (ed. L. Dindorf)
p. 38 85–86, 93n

Procopius of Gaza, *Commentary on Genesis*
Gen 4:26 63n

Theodoret of Cyrus, *Quaestiones in Genesim*
47 80n, 81n

Theodorus bar Koni, *Liber scholiorum*
98n, 99n, 101n

Theophilus of Antioch, *Ad Autolycum*
3.18–19 216n

Samaritan Sources

Asatir
2.2 190n

Memar Marqah
1.2 31n, 32nn, 133n
1.9 31n, 32nn, 33n, 45n, 133n
2.4 38n
2.6–7 86n
2.6 30n, 31n, 33–34, 130n, 159n, 230n
2.7 159n
2.8 31n, 32n, 33n, 35n, 86n, 159n
2.9 34n
2.10 31n, 33n
2.12 31n, 34–37, 41n, 230n
3.2 31n, 32n, 45n
5.3 30
6.2 31n, 32n, 33n, 42n, 133n

Samaritan Liturgy (ed. Cowley)
1.42 32n
1.54.28 30nn

Mandaean Sources

Haran Gawaita (trans. Drower)
pp. 5–10 42n
p. 8 42n
p. 21 42n

Qulasta (trans. Drower)
p. 22 41n
p. 58 41n
p. 87 41n
p. 91 41n
p. 104 41nn
p. 108 41n
p. 155 41n
p. 172 41n
p. 260 41n
p. 296 41n

Right Ginza (trans. Lidzbarski)
1 (29.32–30.14) 43n
2.1 (47.40–48.14) 43n

10 (243.30) 39n
11 (251.12) 39n
12.1 (269.9) 39n
12.1 (270.8) 39n
13 (286.19) 41n
15.11 (341.20–27) 41n
15.11 (341.28–33) 43n

1012 Questions (trans. Drower)
p. 293 41n

Muslim Sources

al-Tabari *Annales* (ed. Goeje)
1.1123 164n

Greco-Roman Sources

Aeschylus, *Prometheus Bound*
500 220n
505 208n

Aratus, *Phaenomena*
96–140 220n

Cicero, *De Natura Deorum*
2.45.118 216n

Diodorus, *Bibliotheka*
1.8 219n
1.11–13 197n
1.16 209n
5.75 207n
6.1 197n

Diogenes, cited in Dio Chrysostom *Orationes*
6.25–26 208n
6.25–30 208n

Empedocles, Fragm. 130
221n

Herodotus, *History*
2.21 144n
4.36 144n

Hesiod, *Theogony*
507–16 208n
786 145n

Hesiod, *Works and Days*
42–105 208n
109–201 219n
142–55 220n

Homer, *Odyssey*
21.303 132n

Julian, *Against the Galileans*
82n

Lucretius, *De Rerum natura*
5.324–350 216n

Macrobius, *Commentarri in somnium Scipio*
2.10 216n

Ovid, *Metamorphoses*
1.125–50 221n
1.89–162 220
1.235–36 207n
5.642–62 210n

Plato, *Cratylas*
397C 197n

Plato, *Leges*
3.677A–B 216n
6.782C–E 221n

Plato, *Theatus*
176B 69n

Plato, *Timaeus*
22C–E 216n
23A–B 216n
24E–25D 146n

Seneca, *Quaestiones naturales*
3 27.1–2 216n
3 28.5 216n
3 28.7 216n
3 29.1–3 216n

Tacitus, *Hist.*

5.9	142n

Virgil, *Georgics*

1.19	210n

Ancient Near Eastern Sources

Gilgamesh Epic

11.14	214n
11.118–26	214n
11.167	214n
11.177–85	214n

Atrahasis Epic

	177n, 215nn

GENERAL INDEX

Aaron: 54, 55
Abba bar Kahana: 148, 151
Abba Kohen Bardela: 132, 133, 134, 134n, 141n
Abbahu: 144, 145nn, 216n
Abel: 22n, 27n, 32nn, 39, 44, 45n, 49n, 50, 53, 61, 68, 68n, 76n, 77, 95nn, 98, 98n, 134n, 202nn, 203, 204, 204n, 211, 224n
Abelson, J.: 149n
Aberbach, M.: 117n
Abimelech: 118n, 125n
Abraham: 7n, 17, 21, 23, 23n, 24n, 25, 28n, 33n, 35, 35nn, 36, 36n, 48n, 49, 49n, 51, 53, 55, 58, 60, 78n, 103n, 114nn, 148, 149, 150n, 157, 157n, 160, 167, 177, 201, 201n, 202n, 209, 210, 212n, 217, 217n, 218, 222, 222n, 223, 224, 224nn, 225, 227, 229n, 231, 232, 233
Abraham ben Jacob: 38n
Abraham Ibn Ezra: 10n, 66n, 122n, 145n, 169n, 182n, 184, 184n, 185, 186, 193, 194n
Acco: 144, 146, 147, 147n, 160, 161
Adah: 76
Adakas: 39
Adam: 12, 12n, 13, 13n, 14, 14n, 17, 18, 20n, 22n, 25, 27n, 32nn, 33n, 44, 49, 53, 53nn, 54n, 56, 57, 57n, 58n, 61n, 67n, 69n, 76, 78, 87, 91n, 95, 95n, 96n, 98, 106, 131n, 132n, 133, 133n, 134, 134nn, 135, 138, 138n, 139n, 140, 140n, 148, 150, 150n, 152, 153n, 154n, 155, 159, 160n, 163, 165n, 167n, 173, 174, 175, 176n, 202n, 203, 203n, 204, 210, 210nn, 211n, 212, 217, 218, 220, 222n, 224, 229, 231
Adam's sin ("fall"): 50, 53n, 56, 61, 95n, 99n, 135, 138n, 148, 152, 155, 159, 163, 165, 165n, 167n, 174, 175, 176n, 211, 220
Adam Qadmaia: 39
Adam Kasia: 39, 41n, 44
Adam Pagria: 39, 44
Adler, Nathan: 117n, 118n
Adler, William: 86n, 88n
Aeschylus: 208n
agricultural innovations: 143n, 182n, 206n, 207n, 208, 209n, 210, 210n, 211n, 219n, 221, 221n, 222n
Aḥa: 126n, 143, 144, 174n
Albeck, Ch.: 111n, 167nn
Albright, W. F.: 208n
Alexander, P. S.: 66n, 163n
Alexander, Polyhistor: 210n
Altaner, Berthold: 48n
Ambrose: 48n, 52, 61–62, 69, 76n, 100, 104, 105, 191n
amoraic interpretations: 111, 111n, 113, 129n, 130, 131–56, 173, 175, 180n, 181, 182, 183, 188, 192, 193, 216, 216n, 226n

Amram: 149
Amram Darah: 32n
Anastasius Sinaita: 76n, 80n, 86n, 90n
angels,
Ariukh: 18
Azazel: 165n, 205n, 208n, 221
Azza: 165n
Azza'el: 164, 165n, 166n
Azzi'el: 165n
Pariukh: 18
Shemḥazay: 165n, 166nn
Uzza: 164, 165, 165n
angels, fallen: 18n, 65, 65nn, 66n, 67n, 72, 83n, 165n, 166n, 199, 199n, 208, 208n, 209n, 211n, 213, 224
angels of God: 26, 27, 27n, 40, 50, 63n, 65n, 66, 66nn, 79n, 82, 82n, 85, 86, 88, 90n, 94n, 102, 106, 109, 127n, 134n, 154, 164, 167, 168, 205n, 211n
angels opposed to man's creation: 157, 158n, 166, 166n
Anosh: 39
antediluvian kings, Mesopotamian: 204n, 206n
Anuša: 37, 38n
Anush Uthra: 38–44
apes, man's resemblance to: 132, 135n, 139, 140
apkallus: 204n, 206n
Aphraates: 91n
apocalyptic: 13n, 44, 45n, 65n, 107n, 209n, 229, 230
Apostolic Constitutions: 50–52, 104nn
Aquila: 5, 6, 8, 17, 49, 59n, 62n, 64n, 75, 81n, 82, 83n, 86, 87n, 89n, 93n, 106n, 113n
Aratus: 208n, 220, 221, 221n
Aristotle: 21n
Ark: 145n
Artapanus: 207n, 210nn
astrological/astronomical knowledge: 25, 66, 89, 90n, 154n, 166n, 207, 209, 209n, 210
Atlantis: 146n
Atrahasis Epic: 177n, 215nn
Attridge, H. W.: 197n, 209n
Augustine: 48n, 71n, 75–80, 81n, 82n, 94n, 96n, 100, 102n, 104, 104n, 105, 107, 133n, 191n, 206n, 216n
Azariah: 150

Baal: 10
Babylon: 150, 151, 151n
Bacher, Wilhelm: 147n, 210nn
Baillet, M.: 65n
Bamberger, Bernard: 65nn, 66n, 67n
baptism: 39n, 40
Barbary Coast: 144, 147, 147n
Baumgarten, A. I.: 197n
Baumstark, Anton: 91n, 97n
beasts, God's punishing agents: 136, 136n, 137, 137n, 138, 139, 141, 164n, 182n
beasts, man's resemblance to: 21, 21n, 57, 59, 132, 133, 133n, 135, 139, 139n, 140, 182n
beasts, man's vulnerability to: 132, 135, 136, 136n, 137, 137n, 138, 139, 140, 141, 164, 182n, 186, 221n

beasts, the righteous unharmed by: 137n, 138, 138n, 139
Ben-Ḥayyim, Z.: 29n, 30n, 31n, 32nn, 33n, 35n, 190n
Ben Yehudah, Eliezer: 12n, 125n, 169n
Berakiel: 17n
Berkowitz, Ben Zion: 116n, 118n, 187n
Berliner, A.: 116n, 185n
Berossus: 87, 206n
Bezold, Carl: 96nn
Bickerman, Elias: 8n, 141n, 215n
Boas, G.: 208n, 218n
book of nature: 22n
Bousset, Wilhelm: 43n, 52n, 81n
Bowker, John: 118n, 200n
Bowman, John: 31n, 34n, 36n
Brandt, Wilhelm: 38n, 43n
Braude, William: 183n
Brüll, A.: 35n
Buber, Salomon: 170n
Budge, E. A. W.: 96nn, 100n
Bultmann, Rudolf: 43nn
Burkitt, F. C.: 43n
burning bush: 32n
Byrne, Brendon: 64n, 65n, 94n
Byzantine Chronographers: 85–90, 95, 95n, 104n, 105, 106n, 173n, 209n

Cain: 20, 22n, 26, 27n, 53, 61n, 71, 72, 73, 74n, 77n, 78, 78n, 79, 84, 96, 98, 98nn, 100, 101n, 133n, 134n, 137n, 148, 152, 155, 174, 176nn, 202, 202nn, 203, 203n, 204, 204n, 205, 206, 206n, 207, 207n, 209, 210, 211, 212n, 220n, 223, 224n
Cain, descendants of: 18, 22, 25, 25nn, 26, 27, 27n, 61n, 63, 65, 66, 66n, 67, 71, 72, 75, 76, 78, 83, 84, 85, 86, 86n, 89, 90n, 91, 91n, 92, 94n, 96, 96n, 97, 97n, 98, 98n, 100, 101n, 103, 106, 107, 134, 134nn, 162, 165n, 176, 176nn, 191n, 202, 203, 204, 204n, 205, 205n, 206, 209, 210, 211, 211n, 214, 223, 230, 231, 232
Calabria: 144, 147
Caleb: 32n, 33, 50, 51
cardinal sins: 223n, 227, 231
Cassuto, U.: 6n, 191n, 201n
Cave of Treasures: 95–97, 165n, 191n
Celsus: 216, 216n
centaurs: 132, 132n, 133, 135, 139, 162n
Chajes, Zvi: 118n
Charaz, Moshe: 185n
Charles, R. H.: 12n, 16n, 17n
Charlesworth, James: 19n, 96n, 163n
Childs, Brevard, 201n, 223n
Christian interpretations: 1, 14n, 24, 25, 25n, 27n, 28, 30, 37n, 40n, 42n, 44, 45n, 47–107, 122n, 134n, 156, 165n, 173, 176, 187n, 190n, 211, 212nn, 213, 218n, 225, 226, 226n, 227, 229, 230, 232, 232n, 233
christological debates: 81, 84, 84n, 85, 85n, 107n
chronological primitivism: 218, 218n, 222, 226n, 232
Church Fathers, scriptural interpretation of: 2, 5, 47n, 49–85, 94n, 103, 109, 173n, 176, 206, 214n, 225, 230, 233
cities, negative view of: 25, 78n, 79, 190n, 207n, 208, 219, 223

civilized culture and tools: 67n, 89, 90, 90n, 205, 206, 206n, 207, 207n, 208, 208n, 209, 209nn, 210, 210n, 211n, 219n, 220, 221, 221n, 222n
Clark, Ernest: 100n, 102n
Clement of Alexandria: 62n, 210n
Coggins, R. J.: 42n
Colpe, C.: 114n
covenant: 222, 223, 232, 233, 234
Cowley, A. E.: 32n, 38n
creation: 34n, 49, 50, 88n, 127n, 138, 147, 151, 155, 156, 157, 161, 171
cultural primitivism: 208, 208n, 209, 218n, 219n, 220n, 232
culture heroes: 204n, 205, 206, 206n, 208nn, 209n, 210, 222n
Cynics: 208n, 209, 209n, 219
Cyril of Alexandria: 80–85, 86n, 89n, 94n, 105, 106, 231n
Cyrus: 10n

Dahl, Nils: 59n
Dalman, G.: 113n, 117n
Daniel: 28n, 187n
Daniel, Book of: 42n
David: 49, 51
David Luria: 66n, 165n, 205n
David Qimḥi: 116n, 125n, 128n, 133n, 169n, 184, 192n, 194
Davidson, Israel: 171n, 172n
Dead Sea Scrolls: 4, 7n, 12n, 13n, 16, 27n, 28n, 34n, 36n, 64n, 65nn, 107n, 114n, 123n, 136n, 166n, 189n, 191n
Dead Sea sectarians: *see* Essenes
deLange, N. R. M.: 54n, 56n, 64n, 226n
Delitzsch, F.: 6n, 184n, 191n
demons: 22n, 66n, 132n, 134n, 137, 137n, 138n, 140, 141, 141n, 182n, 224
Deucalion: 216, 216n, 220
Didymus: 59n, 68–70, 73n, 92, 100, 104, 105, 191n
Dillmann, A.: 6n, 17, 96nn, 97n, 117n, 184n, 205n
Dillon, John: 69n
Dimant, Devorah: 65n
Dinah: 190n
Dindorf, L.: 88n
Dio Chrysostom: 208n
Diodorus: 197n, 207n, 209n, 219n
Diogenes: 208n, 209n
divine image/likeness: 61, 61n, 68, 69, 69nn, 70, 76n, 95n, 99n, 105, 106, 132, 133, 133nn, 134nn, 135, 135n, 139, 139n, 140, 140n, 141, 141n, 153n, 182n, 203, 204, 218, 229, 230
divine man: 106n
divine names, used interchangeably: 123, 200n
divine names, false gods called by: 73, 73n, 74n, 110, 114, 120, 120n, 121, 122, 122nn, 123, 124, 128, 129, 132, 142, 143, 150, 154, 158, 159, 160, 162, 169, 171, 171n, 172, 173, 174, 174n, 177, 180, 185, 192, 200n
divine names, interpretations of: 59, 59n, 69, 69n, 73n, 74, 74n, 101, 149n, 157n, 200, 201
divine name, profaning of: 117n, 135, 136, 137n, 139, 169, 170, 170n, 183, 184n
divine name, revelation of: 34–37, 200, 201

divine names, humans called by: 10n, 30, 30n, 37, 37n, 63–68, 70, 73, 74, 75, 79n, 80, 80n, 81, 81nn, 83n, 84, 87n, 89, 89n, 90nn, 92, 93, 102, 103, 106n, 121, 121n, 126n, 127n, 129n, 134n, 142, 142n, 174, 174n, 185, 185n, 231
Dix, G.: 52
double translation: 59n, 114, 114n, 115n
Drower, E. S.: 38n, 39n, 40nn, 41nn, 42nn, 44n
dualism, body/soul: 61–62

Ea: 214n, 215n
Eber: 192n
Edelstein, L.: 208n
Egyptians: 35n, 37, 130, 149, 151n, 210
Eisenstein, J. D.: 161n
El Shaddai: 36, 201, 201nn
Elbogen, J.: 171nn, 172n
Eleazar (Rabbi): 144, 147, 147n
Eleazar ben Azariah: 138n
Eleazar ben Jose: 147n
Eleazar ben Menaḥem: 144, 145, 145n
Eleazar (ben Pedath): 144
Eliezer ben Jose Hagelili: 180n
Eliezer (ben Hyrcanus): 144n, 147n
Elijah: 51
Elijah Gaon of Wilna: 126n
Elijah Mizraḥi: 184n, 185n, 194n
ellipsis,
  mishnaic: 180n
  scriptural: 114, 175, 179–80, 192n
Enlil: 214, 214n, 215n
Enoch: 4n, 12, 12n, 13n, 16, 17, 17n, 18, 19, 22, 22n, 23, 23n, 27n, 32nn, 33n, 39n, 44, 45n, 49n, 50, 51, 53, 58, 60, 61, 62, 62n, 89, 89n, 90n, 94, 95nn, 97, 99, 99n, 107n, 153n, 154n, 166n, 203, 203n, 209, 209n, 210, 211nn, 212, 212nn, 214n, 218, 225, 230n, 233, 233n
Enoch, the son of Cain: 78
Enosh, called by God's name: 11, 37, 63, 64, 64n, 65n, 67, 68, 68n, 69, 70, 73, 74, 75, 80, 81n, 82, 83, 83nn, 84, 87, 87nn, 88, 92, 93, 99, 103, 105, 105n, 106, 106n, 230
Enosh, confusion with Enoch: 12n, 32n, 39n, 62, 62n, 89n, 99, 99n
Enosh, criticized in rabbinic sources: 5, 58n, 129, 149n, 153, 153n, 164, 169, 173, 188, 189n, 225, 225n, 229
Enosh, head of (new) human race: 21, 22n, 23, 32, 32n, 33n, 37, 41n, 42, 42n, 63, 71, 83n, 90n, 133, 134, 155, 156, 164, 165n, 188
Enosh, historically flawed: 23, 24, 53, 54, 56, 61, 71n, 100n
Enosh, godlike: 30, 61, 63, 69, 69n, 70, 76n, 80, 81n, 82, 83, 85, 90n, 105, 106, 106n, 173
Enosh, foreshadows Christian faithful (the Church): 47, 55, 60, 63, 75, 77, 78, 79, 81n, 84, 106, 230, 231, 233
Enosh, foreshadows Jesus: 47, 55, 60, 63, 70, 79, 81, 88, 106, 230, 231
Enosh, the hoper: 8, 8n, 11, 19, 20, 21, 23, 24, 28, 32n, 47, 48n, 54, 55, 56, 58, 59, 60, 61, 62, 67, 68, 69, 70, 71n, 72, 75, 76, 77, 79, 80, 99, 100, 100n, 102, 104, 105, 106, 107, 172n, 230
Enosh, the true (ideal) man: 8n, 19, 20, 21, 21n, 22, 23, 24, 47, 56, 57, 59, 60, 61, 62, 68, 69, 70, 71n, 76n, 87, 88, 104, 105, 105n, 106, 107, 134, 188–92, 230, 231, 233

Enosh, positively treated in rabbinic sources: 5, 11, 110n, 134, 154n, 173, 187n, 225, 229
Enosh, the proclaimer: 32, 32n, 33n, 34, 36, 37, 230
Enosh's name interpreted: 20, 21, 21n, 22, 24, 32, 32n, 33, 37, 41, 41n, 42, 44, 57n–58n, 59, 61, 68, 69, 70, 71, 76, 77, 79, 80, 87, 98, 98nn, 99, 105, 137n, 153, 154, 155, 156, 168, 169, 175, 186, 186n, 187, 187n, 188–92, 213n, 230
Ephraem Syrus: 87, 92–95, 96, 96n, 97n, 99, 103, 104, 105, 106, 107n, 165n, 231n
Epstein, J. N.: 132n
Essenes: 45n
Esther: 51, 51n
Etheridge, J. W.: 118n
Euhemerus: 197n
Eupolemus: 209
Eusebius of Caesaria: 8n, 11n, 52, 56–60, 62, 62n, 63n, 69, 70, 71n, 79, 100, 100n, 104, 105, 190n, 191n, 197–98, 197n, 198n
Eusebius of Emesa: 63–68, 75, 81, 81n, 83, 84, 85, 85n, 87n, 90, 92, 101nn, 105, 231n
Eve: 134n, 135, 140, 152, 155, 163, 165n, 174
evil, origins of: 65, 66, 67n, 75, 176, 196–200, 209, 209n, 214, 223, 233
Eynde, C. van den: 101n

Fabricius, J. A.: 81n
false gods, worship of: 110, 110n, 112, 114, 119, 126, 127, 128, 140, 142, 143, 147, 150, 153, 155, 158, 159, 169, 170, 171, 171n, 172, 172n, 174, 175, 177, 180, 187, 224, 227
Faur, Jose: 110n, 128n
Feldman, Louis: 25n, 142n, 207n
Finkelstein, J. J.: 206n, 217n
Finkelstein, Louis: 121n, 125n, 137n
Fischel, Henry: 206n, 209n, 210n, 215n
Fishman-Duker, R.: 90n
Fitzmyer, Joseph: 34n, 54n, 64nn, 107n
flies: 164, 164n, 165n
Flood: 18, 19n, 25n, 26, 26n, 27, 27n, 34n, 50, 57, 62n, 67, 75, 78, 87, 90, 91, 91n, 98, 105, 106, 128, 129n, 134n, 145n, 146, 149, 158, 161, 171, 175, 199, 203, 205, 211, 211n, 213, 214n, 215, 215n, 217, 217n, 222, 222n, 223, 224, 227, 229, 232, 233
flood in Enosh's time: 121, 124, 125, 126, 126n, 127, 127nn, 128, 128n, 129, 129n, 134n, 144, 145, 146, 146n, 147, 147n, 151, 155, 158, 159, 160, 161, 162n, 169, 172, 172n, 173, 174, 177, 213, 215
floods, different types of: 145n, 146, 146n, 147, 158, 161n, 216, 216n, 222
floods, recurring: 215, 216, 222
Flusser, David: 90n
Foerster, Werner: 54n
four, number: 22, 42n, 55, 61, 72n, 143, 219, 219n, 220
Fraade, S. D.: 4n, 12n, 31n, 32n, 38n, 42n, 43n, 48n, 50n, 53n, 84n, 94n, 111n, 117nn, 118nn, 187n, 188n, 217n, 233n
Franxman, T. W.: 25n, 26nn, 27n
Frazer, J. G.: 146n
Freedman, H.: 131n, 139n
Friedmann, M.: 124n, 137n, 156n
Funk, F. X.: 50n

Gaster, Moses: 45n, 66n
Gaster, Theodore: 13n, 31n, 166n, 185n
Gelzer, Heinrich: 63n, 68n, 87n, 88n, 90n
genealogy: 19, 26, 33, 39, 49, 63, 66, 71, 73, 73n, 76, 77, 79, 83n, 84, 91n, 93, 97, 133, 134, 134n, 162, 176, 182n, 203, 203nn, 204n, 211n, 215n, 217, 220, 229, 231
Generation of the Flood: 113, 130, 138n, 142, 143, 148, 148n, 149, 150, 151n, 152, 156, 157, 157n, 158, 160, 161, 165n, 166nn, 167nn, 181, 213, 213n, 216, 216n, 218n, 220, 223n
Generation of the Separation (Tower of Babel): 113, 130, 130n, 135, 143, 146, 146n, 148n, 149, 149n, 150, 151nn, 152nn, 156, 157, 157n, 160, 161, 161n, 167n, 169n, 181, 191, 197, 197n, 207n, 213, 216, 216nn, 218n, 220, 222, 222n, 223n
Generation of the Wilderness: 130
Geniza Fragment: 35n, 112n, 201n, 224n
Genos: 206n
George Cedrenus: 86n, 87nn, 90n, 209n
George Hamartolus: 88n
George Syncellus: 8, 67n, 68n, 86–88, 105n, 207n
Gerizim, Mt.: 33n
Gesenius, W.: 9n, 211n
gezera šawa: 143, 181, 181n
giants: 26, 27n, 64, 66, 82n, 87, 89, 102n, 165n, 166n, 214
Gifford, E. H.: 57n–58n
Gilgamesh Epic: 214, 214n, 215n
Ginsburger, Moses: 112n
Ginzberg, Louis: 17n, 18, 18nn, 19n, 25n, 26n, 53n, 65n, 67n, 81n, 114n, 120n, 134n, 135nn, 138nn, 142n, 143n, 145nn, 152n, 153n, 160n, 165n, 166n, 189n, 199n, 205n, 207n, 209n, 210n, 212n, 222n, 224n
Gluck, Theodore: 26n, 67n
gnostic writings: 4, 25n, 38n, 45n, 67n, 83n, 90n
godlike humans: 22n, 44, 64, 75, 83n, 85, 86n, 100, 105, 106, 106n, 133, 133n, 134, 140, 140n, 174n, 176, 210n, 212
Goldberg, Arnold: 149n
golden age: 218, 220, 221, 221n, 229, 232
Golden Calf: 146n, 196n
Goldin, Judah: 120n, 130n
Goodenough, Erwin: 21n, 52n
Gray, G.: 136n
Greenberg, Moshe: 6n, 201n
Greer, Rowan A.: 56n, 85n
Gregory of Nazianzus: 52n
Gribomont, Jean: 49n
Grossfeld, B.: 117n
Gruenwald, Ithamar: 163n
Grunbaum, Max: 58n
Gunkel, H.: 6n

Hacohen, S.: 149n
Hahn, Ferdinand: 54n, 64n
Hallo, William W.: 206n
Ham: 199
Hammeliṣ: 30n, 35n
Ḥanina: 144, 147n, 156
Ḥanina ben Dosa: 138n

Ḥanina ben Hama: 156n
Hanson, Paul D.: 205n, 208n
Hebraios version: 5n, 6, 11, 63, 64n, 87n
Hecataeus of Abdera: 197n, 209n
Heidel, Alexander: 214n, 215n
Heidenheim, Moritz: 30n, 31n, 32n, 34nn, 35nn, 36n, 38n
height, man's shortened after Creation: 135, 162, 163, 175
Heinemann, Isaac: 181n, 189n, 196n, 217n
Heinemann, Joseph: 145n
Hengel, Martin: 13n
Henning, Walter: 45n
Henrichs, A.: 45n
Hermes: 209n, 210n
hero worship: 19, 24, 199n
Herodotus: 144n
Hesiod: 145n, 208n, 219, 219nn, 220, 220n
Hexapla: 5n, 11n, 49n, 63n, 64n
Hibil: 39, 40, 41, 41nn, 42n
Hippolytus of Rome: 52
historiography: 217, 217n, 218, 227
Ḥiyya bar Abba: 153
Holladay, Carl: 106n
Homer: 21, 132n
hope, attribute of: 19, 20, 22, 23, 24, 28, 56, 59, 62, 69, 75, 76, 77, 79, 100n, 104, 105, 172n, 189n, 233n
Horovitz, H. S.: 120n, 121n, 124, 124n
Horowitz, C. M.: 165n
ḥullin: 132n, 136n, 137n, 143n, 185, 185n
Huna: 144
Hyman, Aaron: 111n, 132n

Ibn at-Taiyib: 98n, 100n, 101nn
Ibn Manzur: 169n
Ichabod: 191
ideal man: 21, 21n, 23, 24
idolatry: 109n, 110, 110n, 112, 114n, 116, 124, 125n, 126, 126n, 127, 128, 128n, 129, 129n, 131, 135, 137n, 141, 141n, 143, 143n, 149, 149n, 153, 153n, 154, 155, 155n, 156, 160, 160n, 161, 162, 162n, 163, 165, 165n, 166, 167, 168, 169, 170, 172nn, 173, 181, 185n, 186n, 194, 198, 200, 205, 223n, 226n
idolatry, origins of: 109, 109n, 110, 110n, 114, 129, 129n, 154, 164, 169, 174, 196, 196n, 197, 198, 198n, 199, 199n, 208nn, 226, 231
image of God: *see* divine image
images, bowing to, worship of: 127n, 132, 141, 142, 160, 161, 161n, 162, 166n, 167, 167n, 185n, 199
imperial cult: 142n, 161n, 174n
indefinite subject in Hebrew: 7, 7n, 75, 75n, 86, 92, 93n, 113, 113n
inventions: *see* civilized culture and tools
Irad: 142n, 203n
Isaac: 21, 23, 24n, 32n, 33n, 49n, 58, 60, 125n, 149, 157, 167, 201, 201n
Isaac Abravanel: 184n
Isaac (ben Pinḥas): 132, 132n, 141, 142, 161n
Isho bar Nun: 98n, 99n, 100n, 102n
Isho'dad of Merv: 80n, 97–104, 105, 105n, 107n, 191n, 231n

Jabal: 162, 205
Jacob: 17, 21, 23, 32n, 33n, 49n, 58, 60, 148, 149, 157, 165n, 167, 201, 201n, 232
Jacob of Kefar Hanan: 139
Jacoby, Felix: 197n, 206n, 210nn
Jaffa: 144, 146, 147, 147n, 160, 161, 161n
Jannai: 132n
Jansma, T.: 97n, 98n
Jared: 16, 18, 97, 189n, 191, 191n, 203n, 211n, 212, 212n
Jastrow, M.: 98n, 100n, 113n, 117n, 125nn, 169nn, 187n
Jellinek, A.: 144n, 153n, 163n, 166n
Jeremiah, name interpreted: 192
Jerome: 47n, 48nn, 49, 49n, 58n, 62n, 68n, 71n, 76n, 80n, 104n, 105n, 114n, 174n, 177n, 190n, 191n
Jerusalem: 42, 43, 43n, 44, 142, 154
Jesus: 42, 43, 44, 44n, 45, 47, 47n, 49, 50, 51, 53n, 54, 54n, 55, 56, 60, 64, 64n, 66, 67, 77, 77n, 78, 79, 81, 83n, 85, 88, 91n, 94, 94n, 95, 95n, 99n, 104n, 105, 105n, 107, 107n, 229n, 230, 231
Job: 50, 51, 58, 59n, 230n
Joḥanan: 138n, 153, 154
Joḥanan ben Zakkai: 143n
John Chrysostom: 70–75, 81n, 83, 83n, 85, 86n, 93nn, 101n, 102n, 105, 120n, 133n, 191n, 231n
John Malalas: 83, 88n
John the Baptist: 42, 42n, 43n, 50
John Zonoras: 87n
Jordan: 40, 40n, 45n
Jose (ben Halafta): 121, 122, 123n, 210n
Jose ben Ḥanina: 147n
Jose ben Jose: 171–72, 171n
Joseph: 12, 12n, 13, 14, 32n, 33n, 49n, 58, 59n, 207n
Josephus: 25–27, 86n, 87, 90, 90nn, 91, 105, 137n, 142n, 177n, 198–99, 206, 207, 207n, 209, 212n, 224n, 231, 232, 232n
Joshua: 33, 50, 51
Joshua ben Karḥa: 127n
Jubal: 19n, 205
Jubilees, Book of: 6, 16–18, 27n, 28n, 29, 47n, 49, 114n, 127n, 134n, 145n, 166n, 191, 209, 209n, 223n
Judah (bar El'ai): 137, 148, 150
Judah Löw ben Bezalel: 194n
Judah the Patriarch (Rabbi): 120n, 127, 127n, 150
Judah bar Simon: 148, 152
Judan: 144
Judas Maccabeus: 51, 51n
Judges: 51
Judith: 51, 51n
Julian the Apostate: 82n
Julius Africanus: 63n, 66, 66n, 67, 67n, 68n, 84, 87, 87n, 88, 88nn, 94n
justice: 22n, 26, 221

Kafiḥ, Joseph: 169n
Kainam: 209n
Kasher, M.: 125n, 126n, 142n, 201, 201n
Kasowski, Chaim: 117n

Kaufmann, Yehezkel: 196n, 197n
Kenan (Kainan): 18, 94, 95n, 97, 132n, 134nn, 153n, 162n, 203n, 204n, 212, 212n
Keel, C. F.: 191n
Kerrigan, Alexander: 83n
Kings: 51
Klein, Michael: 112n, 119n
Klijn, A. F. J.: 4n, 6n, 12n, 25n, 67n, 117n, 137n, 200n
Koenen, L.: 45n
Kohath: 149
Komlosh, Yehuda: 112n, 117n, 118nn, 188n
Korah, company of: 130
Kraeling, Carl: 42n, 43n
Kraeling, Emil: 214n
Krauss, Samuel: 167n
Kronholm, Tryggve: 92n, 95, 95nn
Kronos: 207n
Kutscher, Eduard: 7n

Lambert, W. G.: 206n
Lamech (Cainite): 27n, 71, 77, 96, 203, 203n, 211n
Lamech (Sethite): 27n, 94, 95n, 97, 142n, 203n, 212
Lamech, Song of: 204n, 205
Lane, E.: 169n
Lauterbach, Jacob: 120n, 121n, 124, 124n, 127n, 175n
Le Deaut, R.: 112n, 200n
Leo Grammaticus: 87n
Levene, Abraham: 97n, 98nn, 99nn, 101n
Levi: 149, 171
Levi (Rabbi): 151
Lévi, Israel: 12nn, 15n
Levine, L. I.: 154n
Levy, Jacob: 113n, 117n, 169n, 187n
Lewis, J. P.: 212n, 214n
literal interpretation: 175, 185, 188, 193, 193n, 194
Lidzbarski, Mark: 39n, 40n, 41n, 43n
Lieberman, Saul: 31n, 110n, 129n, 166n, 187n, 215n
light of Creation: 152, 152n
Loewe, Raphael: 175n
Lot: 50
Lovejoy, Arthur: 208, 208nn, 209n, 218n, 219nn, 220, 220n, 221
Lowenstein, M.: 117n
Lowy, S.: 33n
Luther: 54n
Luzzatto, S. D.: 66n, 118n, 185n, 194n

Macdonald, John: 31n, 33nn, 34n, 35nn, 37, 38nn
Macuch, Rudolf: 41n
magic: 36, 66, 153n, 164, 165, 166n, 199, 199n, 207, 213, 213n
Mahalalel: 17, 17n, 18, 97, 153n, 203n, 212
Maimonides: 128n, 153n
Malaleel: 18
Malan, S. C.: 96nn, 97n
Maleleil: 19

Manda-d-Hiia: 39n, 40, 41n, 42n, 44
Mandaean traditions: 3n, 38–45, 76n, 155n
Manichaean writings: 45n
Margulies, M.: 152n, 180n
Marmorstein, Arthur: 59n, 69n
Mary Magdalene: 41n
Masada: 12, 13n
Masoretic Text (MT): 1n, 5, 6, 7n, 8, 8n, 9, 9n, 10, 10n, 11, 16, 20n, 29, 29nn, 30, 30n, 32nn, 34, 34n, 35nn, 36, 49, 79n, 113n, 117, 117n, 127, 139, 148n, 201n, 211n
McNamara, M.: 112n
"measure for measure": 124, 129, 129n, 136, 137n, 172
Mediterranean Sea: 145, 146, 146n, 147, 147n, 175
Meeks, Wayne: 38n, 43n
Mehujael: 142n, 203n
Melamed, E.: 101n, 118n
Melchizedek: 19, 33, 50, 51, 58, 59n, 107n, 230n
Memar Marqah: 30n, 31–37, 41, 42n, 71n, 86n, 133n, 230
Menaḥem Ziyyoni b. Meir: 163n
Meshullam b. Kolonymus: 172, 172n
metals, discovery and early use of: 205, 211n, 219, 219nn, 220, 220n, 221, 221n
Metatron: 44, 233n
Methodius of Olympus: 49–50, 51n, 104nn
Methuselah: 17, 25, 26n, 27n, 33, 50, 53, 54n, 94, 95n, 97, 153n, 203n, 212, 212n, 215n, 217n, 218, 230n
Methusael: 142n, 203n
Michael: 18
Michael Glycas: 87n, 90n, 209n
Michael the Syrian: 96n, 100n
Milik, J. T.: 16nn, 166n
Miller, J. Maxwell, 202n, 203n, 204n
Miller, M. P.: 112n
Miriai: 41n
Mirsky, Aharon: 171nn, 173n
Momigliano, A.: 219nn
Montgomery, J.: 37, 38n
Moore, George Foot: 69n, 198n
Mordecai: 51, 51n, 141
Moses, 10n, 12n, 20, 21n, 22, 24, 25, 30, 30n, 31, 32n, 33, 33n, 34, 34nn, 35, 36, 37, 38n, 47, 49n, 50n, 51, 53, 55, 57, 58, 59, 59n, 60, 66n, 85, 86n, 89, 130n, 149, 159, 183n, 200, 201n, 209, 210n, 212n, 230, 232
Moses b. Naḥman (Naḥmanides): 66n, 132n, 165n, 169n, 186n
Moses Haddaršan: 167n, 170n
mountains and hills, origin: 135, 162
Murray, Robert: 94n

Naamah: 205, 205n, 211n
Nag Hammadi texts: 4, 45n
Nagy, G.: 219nn
name plays: 14, 20, 22, 27n, 32n, 40, 40n, 41, 42, 44, 57n, 58n, 59, 61, 69, 71, 76, 77, 79, 97, 98, 98nn, 105n, 132n, 142, 153, 153n, 154, 155, 166n, 167n, 168, 169n, 170n, 186, 186n, 187n, 188–92, 207n
Nathan b. Yehiel: 125n, 132n

Nautin, P.: 68n, 69nn
Naverre, O.: 145n
Nehemiah: 13
Nehemiah (Rabbi): 137
Nehemiah, son of Samuel bar Nahman: 150
Nestorians: 44n, 85, 97
Neusner, Jacob: 111n
Nickelsburg, George: 208n
Nikiprowetsky, V.: 20n, 59n
Nilsson, M. P.: 197n
Nimrod: 9n, 38n, 142, 142n, 143, 143n, 207n, 223n
Nisan, first ten days of: 32n
Noah: 4n, 9n, 13, 13n, 17, 21n, 22, 23, 25, 27n, 32nn, 34n, 45n, 49, 49n, 50, 51, 53, 54n, 58, 60, 61, 83, 94, 95n, 97, 107n, 131n, 133, 134n, 138nn, 143n, 145n, 148n, 153n, 154n, 182n, 203, 204n, 206n, 210, 210n, 211, 211n, 212, 212n, 213, 213n, 215, 216, 216n, 217, 217nn, 218, 222n, 223, 224n, 225, 230, 233
Noam, Enosh's sister and wife: 18

oaths, vain: 136, 191n
Oceanos: 144, 144n, 145, 145n, 147n
Odeberg, Hugo: 163n, 166n
Oden, R. A., Jr.: 197n, 209n
Ohana, M.: 119n
Old Latin version: 11n, 48, 48n, 49, 61, 62, 62n, 75, 76, 79, 80, 104, 107n
Origen: 5, 8n, 11n, 52–56, 60, 61, 62n, 68n, 69n, 77nn, 104, 104n, 105nn, 216, 231n
Orlinsky, H.: 8n
Ovid: 208n, 210n, 220, 221, 221n, 222

Palestinian targumim: 112–16, 123, 124, 128, 162, 172n, 174, 174n, 179, 180, 181, 200nn, 205n, 225n
Pallis, Svend: 38n, 39n, 45n
Pamphylus: 52n, 53n
Paschal Chronicle: 85–86, 93n
paschal lamb: 32n
Paul: 14n, 48n, 50, 53, 54, 55, 74n, 77n, 176n
Peleg: 169n, 191, 192n
Pelikan, Jaroslav: 54n, 84n
pešat, plain meaning: 116, 143, 175, 175n, 184, 184nn, 188, 193, 194
Peshitta: 6, 16, 91–92, 93, 93n, 95, 99, 100, 100n, 101, 102, 102n, 104n, 107n, 113n, 201n
Petermann, H.: 39n
Petermann, J. H.: 30nn, 33nn, 34n
Peters, Norbert: 13n, 15n
Phaethon: 216
Philo: 5, 8, 11n, 19–25, 27, 28, 28n, 32, 32nn, 41, 41n, 42nn, 44n, 47nn, 50n, 51, 51n, 54, 54n, 56, 58, 59, 59n, 60, 60n, 61, 62n, 66n, 69, 69nn, 70, 71nn, 76n, 78n, 79, 100n, 104, 105, 105n, 107, 133, 133n, 134, 142n, 168, 191n, 197n, 206, 207n, 208n, 210n, 212n, 215n, 216n, 219n, 230, 231, 232, 232n
Philo of Byblos: 90n, 190n, 197n, 206n, 207n, 209n
Phinehas: 33, 50, 51
plant: 40n, 50, 76n
Plato: 21n, 24, 28n, 69n, 146n, 197n, 215–16, 230
polemics: 196, 198, 198n, 212n, 225–26

Pontius Pilate: 43, 44
Porphyry: 197n
prayer: 40, 41, 44, 59n, 96, 97, 114, 114n, 115n, 116, 116n, 117n, 118, 125n, 169n, 170n, 180, 184, 184nn, 187n, 188, 188n, 193, 194, 194n, 224, 224nn
prepatriarchal history, rabbinic view of: 218, 220, 222–25, 226, 227, 229–34
primal (primeval) man: 43
primitivism: *see* chronological primitivism and cultural primitivism
Procopius of Gaza: 63n
profanation (*see also* divine name, profaning of): 117, 117n, 118, 118n, 143n, 153, 154, 169, 169nn, 170, 170n, 181, 182, 182n, 183, 184, 185
Prometheus: 208n, 210n, 220n
Pseudepigrapha: 4, 107n
Pseudo-Clementine literature: 26n, 62n, 65n, 199
Pseudo-Eupolemus: 210, 210n
Pseudo-Malalas: 86n, 88–90, 90n, 95n, 104n, 106n, 209n, 231n
Pseudo-Philo: 25n, 28n, 135n, 206n, 207n, 209n
"pseudo-variants": 11, 232n
Pummer, R.: 29n, 30n
Purvis, James: 29n
Pyrrha: 220

Quasten, Johannes: 48n, 68n, 70n, 73n, 80n, 82n, 84n
Quinn, Esther C.: 26n

Rabbah bar Ulla: 136n
Rabbenu Hillel: 136
rabbinic traditions, dating of: 3n, 25, 111, 131, 158n, 161n, 163n, 169n, 170n, 171n, 174n, 177n, 183, 188n, 225n
rabbinic view of Enosh: 2, 12, 58n
Rabbinovicz, R.: 153n
Rabbinowitz, Hayyim: 186n
Rabbinowitz, L. I.: 110n
Rabin, Ch.: 7n, 9n
Rahab: 49n
Rami bar Abba: 139
Rav: 210n
Rappaport, S.: 26n, 207n
Rashi: 118n, 122n, 143n, 153n, 165n, 166n, 170n, 180n, 184n, 185, 185n, 192n, 194n, 201n, 205n, 210n, 211n
Raymundi Martini: 166n
rebellion: 129n, 139, 142, 142n, 143, 143n, 151, 159, 160, 161, 167, 172, 172n, 173, 174, 177, 181, 205n, 208n, 213, 223
rebellious generations: 130, 138, 146, 147, 148, 149, 150, 151, 152, 156, 158, 160, 160n, 161, 167n, 168, 171, 173, 176, 181, 213, 216, 216n, 217, 220, 222, 222n, 223
rebellious generations, did not learn from their predecessors: 150, 151n, 161, 174, 213, 215, 216, 223, 227
Red Sea: *see* Sea of Reeds
Reiner, Erica: 206n
Reitzenstein, R.: 43nn
repentance: 22, 22n
Reu: 191
reward: 13n, 21n, 33n, 36, 51, 52, 165n, 217

righteous biblical ancestors: 12, 15, 17, 19, 24, 27, 28n, 31, 31n, 32, 32n, 37, 44, 45, 47, 47n, 48, 49–62, 84, 85, 91, 95n, 104, 104n, 106, 107, 134, 148, 156, 173, 176, 177, 225, 229, 230, 231
Ronsch, H.: 17n
Roth, Cecil: 173n
Routh, Martin: 67n
Rudolph, Kurt: 38n, 43n
Rufinus: 8n, 52n, 68n

Saadia Gaon: 114n, 169n, 170n, 171n, 186, 188, 224n
Sabbath: 34n, 51, 152, 153n, 156n, 211n
Sabbath, profaning of: 117n, 135n, 153
Sabbath, observing of: 153, 154
Sabrisho bar Paulus: 97n
Samaritan exegesis: 1, 25, 29, 134n, 225, 229, 229n, 230, 231, 232, 232n
Samaritan Pentateuch: 6, 29, 29nn, 30, 30n, 31, 34n, 35nn, 36, 92, 92n
Samaritan Targum: 6, 29, 30, 30nn, 31, 34, 35nn, 37, 57n, 92, 92n, 201n
Samaritan traditions: 12, 29–38, 42n, 45n, 47, 47n, 49n, 53, 60n, 104, 155n, 156, 187n, 190n, 212n, 213, 225
Samaritans: 42n, 45n, 52, 60n
Samuel: 51, 55, 212n
Samuel b. Naḥman: 150
Sanchuniathon: 197n, 206n
Sandmel, S.: 6n, 117n, 200n
Sarah: 157, 158, 159
Schafer, P.: 9n, 14n, 18n, 27n, 127n, 134n, 158n, 166n
Schechter, Solomon: 12n, 13n, 69n, 142n
Schefftel, Baruch: 116n, 118n, 187n
Scher, Addai: 97n, 99nn
Scholem, Gershom: 159n, 163n, 166n
Schroeder, Guy: 57n, 58n, 59n
Schürer, Emil: 111n
Schwarzbaum, H.: 166nn
Schweizer, Eduard: 64n
Sea of Reeds: 33n, 34n, 35n, 159, 159n, 161, 162n
Seeligman, I. L.: 10n
Segal, Alan: 59n
Segal, Moshe: 7n, 12n, 13n, 15n, 121n
Seneca: 208n, 209n, 216n
Septuagint: 5–11, 17, 29, 20, 23, 24, 29, 30, 34n, 37n, 48, 49, 55, 56, 59n, 62, 62n, 63, 64n, 65n, 66n, 69nn, 70, 72n, 72n, 74n, 75, 79, 82n, 91, 92, 93, 93n, 99, 100n, 101, 101n, 102, 102n, 104, 105, 106, 106n, 107n, 113, 113n, 116n, 122n, 136n, 183n, 201n, 217n, 220, 230, 233n
Seth: 1, 4, 7, 8, 9, 11, 12, 13, 14, 15, 17, 18, 19, 19n, 22n, 25, 25n, 26, 26n, 27, 30, 32n, 33, 39, 40n, 44, 44n, 49, 50, 50n, 51, 54n, 60n, 61n, 70, 71, 72, 73, 74n, 76, 77, 80n, 81n, 82, 84, 85, 86, 86nn, 87n, 88, 89, 89n, 90, 90n, 91n, 92, 93, 94, 95, 95n, 96, 97, 98, 98n, 100, 101, 101n, 102nn, 104, 104n, 106, 107, 107nn, 113, 121, 131, 132, 133n, 134nn, 138n, 139n, 140n, 153n, 162, 173, 176n, 190, 190n, 192, 203, 204, 204n, 209n, 212, 213nn, 218, 230n, 231, 233

Seth, descendants of: 18, 25, 25n, 26, 26n, 27, 27n, 49, 63, 63n, 65, 66, 66n, 67, 67n, 68, 70, 71, 72, 73, 75, 76, 78, 79, 79n, 82, 82n, 84, 85, 76, 86n, 87, 88, 89, 89n, 90, 90nn, 91, 91nn, 92, 93, 93n, 94, 94nn, 95, 96n, 97, 97n, 100, 102, 103, 104, 105, 105n, 106, 107, 132, 132n, 133, 134, 165n, 176, 177n, 191n, 198, 203, 204, 205, 209, 209n, 211, 211n, 214, 218n, 225, 230, 231, 232, 233
seven, number: 17, 18, 18n, 19, 21n, 22n, 26, 26n, 33, 33n, 59n, 94, 120, 130, 130n, 149, 153n, 154n, 177n, 199, 203, 204, 204n, 206n, 207n, 210n, 214n
seven pillars: 18, 18n
seven shepherds: 18, 18n, 153n, 154n
Shekinah: 152n, 163, 164, 165n
Shekinah, removal of: 148, 149, 149nn, 153n, 164, 165, 166n, 168, 174, 218, 218n, 221
Shem: 12, 13, 14, 15, 17, 24n, 25, 25n, 33, 44n, 50, 50n, 173
Shinan, Avigdor: 114n, 117n, 200n
Shitil: 39, 40, 40n, 41, 41nn, 42n
sickness, human: 58n, 98n, 137n, 164, 165n, 170, 170n, 186–87, 189, 189n, 190
Siegfried, C.: 22n
Simeon (bar Joḥai): 137
Simlai: 73n
Simon (ben Pazzi): 142, 143
Simon, High Priest: 13
Sinaitic theophany: 74n, 200–202, 201n
Sisera: 151n
Skinner, J.: 6n, 117n, 184n, 191n, 204n, 205n
Smallwood, E. Mary: 142n
Smend, R.: 12n, 14n, 15, 15n
Smith, K. F.: 219n
Smith, J. Payne: 98n, 100n
Smith, Morton: 69n, 133n, 139n, 142n
Snaith, John: 22n
Sodomites: 50, 130, 149, 151n, 157, 157n, 160, 216n, 223n
Solomon: 138n
Son of God: 63, 64, 64n, 65, 65nn, 67, 68, 70, 72n, 75, 79, 81, 81nn, 82n, 84, 85, 94, 105, 106, 107, 107n, 230, 233
son of man: 43n, 72, 87, 88, 88n, 107n, 114n
Song of the Sea: 33n, 34, 34n, 35n, 37, 86n, 130n, 159, 159n
sons of God: 63, 63n, 64, 64n, 65, 65nn, 66, 66nn, 67, 68, 70, 72, 73, 74, 75, 76, 79n, 80, 81n, 82, 82n, 83, 84nn, 84, 84n, 85, 86, 88, 89, 90n, 93n, 94, 94nn, 95, 96, 96n, 97, 100, 101, 101n, 102, 103, 104, 105, 105n, 106, 107, 124, 142, 165n, 166n, 174, 214, 214n, 225, 231, 233
Sparks, H. F. D.: 49n
Speiser, E.: 190n
Sperber, A.: 116, 116n, 117n, 187n
spies: 130, 130n
Spurrell, G.: 6n, 117n
stars, worship of: 109n, 125n, 164, 164, 184n, 197, 197n
Stichel, R.: 213n
Stinespring, W. F.: 93n
Stoics: 209, 209nn, 216, 219, 220n, 222
Strack, Hermann: 111n, 180n
Stroumsa, Gedaliahu Guy: 67n
suffering, origins of: 140, 164, 165n

Suidae Lexicon: 90n, 209n
Sumer: 206n, 207n
Swete, Henry: 62n
Syro-Hexapla: 11n
Symmachus: 5n, 6, 8, 10n, 11, 49, 62n, 64n, 66n, 82, 82n, 83n, 89, 102

Tacitus: 142n
Tal, Abraham: 30nn, 35, 35n
Tanhuma: 157n
tannaitic interpretations: 111, 111n, 113, 119–31, 142, 155, 172n, 174, 175, 177, 181, 182, 183, 188, 192, 193, 216n, 217, 226, 226n
Targum Neofiti: 10n
Targum Onqelos: 35n, 103n, 113n, 116–19, 122n, 123, 123n, 149n, 169n, 170, 170n, 174n, 186, 187, 187n, 188, 193, 194, 199n, 200, 200n, 201n, 215n
Targum Pseudo-Jonathan: 10n, 34n, 35n, 112, 113, 113n, 115, 126, 131n, 162, 201n, 205n, 207n, 215n
targumim: 6, 9n, 34n, 35, 35n, 59n, 66n, 75n, 93n, 97n, 102n, 103n, 111, 112–19, 122n, 123, 124, 128, 136n, 162, 170, 172n, 174, 174n, 175n, 182, 186, 191, 200, 200n, 201n, 225n
ten, number: 22n, 26n, 32nn, 33, 33n, 49n, 53n, 58, 59n, 60, 130, 131n, 153n, 203, 203n, 204n, 215n, 217, 217n, 218
ten tribes: 130
tetragram: 11n, 334–37, 123, 149n, 157n, 200, 200n, 201n, 202, 202n
Tharasidam: 19
Theodor, J.: 114n, 131n, 133n, 134n, 137n, 139n, 143n, 144n, 147n, 151n, 152n, 160n, 161n, 162n, 212n, 224n
Theodore of Mopsuestia: 97n
Theodoret of Cyrus: 64n, 80n, 81n, 83n, 85, 87n, 106n
theophoric names: 126n, 127n, 166n
thirteen, number: 33, 54n, 154n
Thompson, J. E. H.: 37, 38n
three, number: 21n, 22n, 23, 39, 40, 40n, 41, 44, 45n, 60, 61, 73n, 94, 100n, 133, 140n, 143, 143n, 148n, 150, 162, 163, 171n, 172, 172n, 173, 181, 203, 212n, 216, 216n, 220, 222n, 223n
Titus: 164n,
Tov, Emanuel: 6n, 8n, 11n
Tower of Babel: *see* Generation of the Separation
translations,
    ancient: 5–28, 122n
    modern: 1n, 8n, 10n
Triptolemus: 210n
Tubal-Cain: 162, 205, 221
Tur-Sinai (Torczyner), N. H.: 57n
twelve, number: 33

Urbach, E.: 69n, 110n, 142n, 163n
Uthra: 39, 39n, 40, 40n, 41, 42, 44, 45n
Uzziah: 212n

VanderKam, James: 16, 16nn, 212n, 230n
Van Rompay, Lucas: 97n
vegetarianism, primitive: 219, 221n
verb conflation, hope/begin: 8, 8n, 56n, 62, 62n

Vermes, Geza: 2n, 13n, 65n, 111n, 114n
Virgil, 210n
Vizer, A.: 186n
Vorlage: 6, 11, 16, 29, 44, 92, 232n
Vulgate: 7n, 13n, 35n, 49, 74n, 201n

Wacholder, B. Z.: 210n
watchers, 86, 87, 96n, 209n
waters of creation: 127n, 145n, 151, 152, 152n, 158, 159, 160, 161, 172, 175
weakness, human: 58n, 71n, 98n, 136n, 137n, 164, 164n, 169, 169n, 183n, 186–87, 189, 189n, 190
Weiss, Isaac Hirsch: 111n, 135n
West, M. L.: 219nn
Westermann, Claus: 10n, 201n, 202n
Wickham, L. R.: 84n
Wilson, Robert R.: 202n, 203n, 205n, 206n
Winter, Michael M.: 15n
Wolfson, Harry: 19n, 20n, 21n, 24n, 69n
word plays: 54n, 57nn, 98, 98n, 99n, 105n, 115, 117nn, 118nn, 136, 136nn, 137, 137n, 139n, 142, 144, 147, 151, 152n, 154, 160n, 162n, 164, 168, 170, 175n, 181–88, 205
Woude, A. S. van der: 16n
Wright, William: 91n

Ya'ar: 118n, 188n
Yadin, Y.: 13n
Yahia-Yuhana: 42
Yamauchi, E. M.: 38n, 39nn

Zeno: 220n
Zillah: 76
Zosimus: 87
Zunz, Leopold: 111n